THE ART OF ROGER WINTER

The Art of Roger Winter: Fire and Ice
is made possible by the generous support
of Elise and Burk Murchison

Publication was also assisted by a gift from
Kirk Hopper

Number Twenty-Two
Sara and John Lindsey Series
in the Arts and Humanities

THE ART OF ROGER WINTER

FIRE AND ICE

SUSIE KALIL

TEXAS A&M UNIVERSITY PRESS : COLLEGE STATION

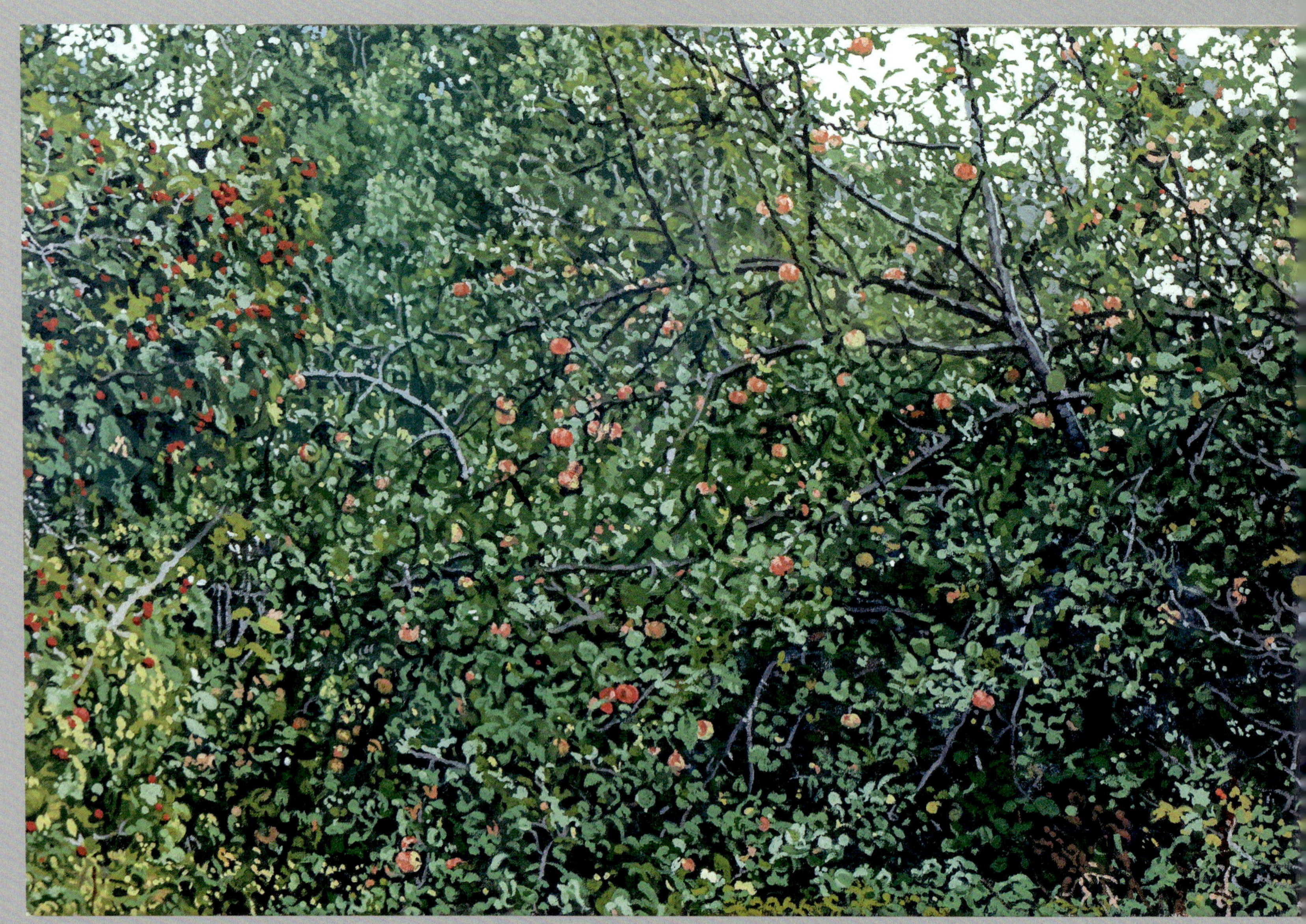

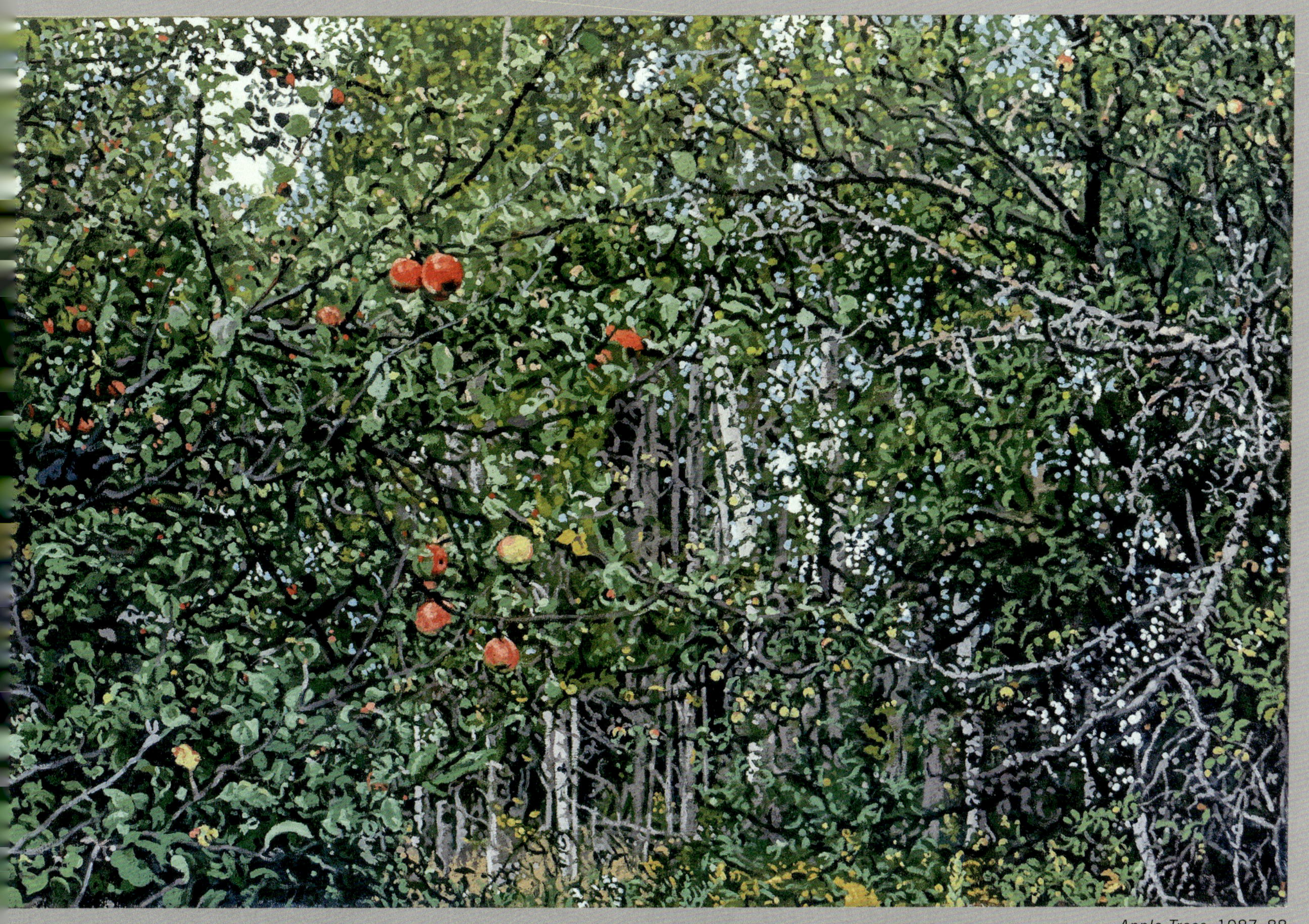

Apple Trees, 1987–88

oil on linen | 36" × 84" | Collection of the Roger Horchow Family | Photography by Joshua Nefsky

First edition

This paper meets the requirements
of ANSI/NISO Z39.48-1992 (Permanence of Paper).
Binding materials have been chosen for durability.
Manufactured in Canada at Friesens
♾

Unless otherwise indicated, all archival photographs are from the collection of Roger Winter.

Library of Congress Cataloging-in-Publication Data

Names: Kalil, Susie, 1952– author.
Title: The art of Roger Winter: fire and ice / Susie Kalil.
Other titles: Sara and John Lindsey series in the arts and humanities; no. 22.
Description: First edition. | College Station: Texas A&M University Press, 2020. | Series: Sara and John Lindsey series in the arts and humanities; number 22 | Includes index. | Description based on print version record and CIP data provided by publisher; resource not viewed.
Identifiers: LCCN 2019040144 (print) | LCCN 2019040145 (ebook) | ISBN 9781623498641 (ebook) | ISBN 9781623498634 (cloth) | Subjects: LCSH: Winter, Roger, 1934– | Painters—Texas—Biography. | LCGFT: Biographies.
Classification: LCC ND237.W773 (ebook) | LCC ND237.W773 K35 2020 (print) | DDC 759.13 [B] —dc23
LC record available at https://catalog.loc.gov/vwebv/search?searchCode=LCCN&searchArg=2019040144&searchType=1&permalink=y
LC record available at https://catalog.loc.gov/vwebv/search?searchCode=LCCN&searchArg=2019040145&searchType=1&permalink=y

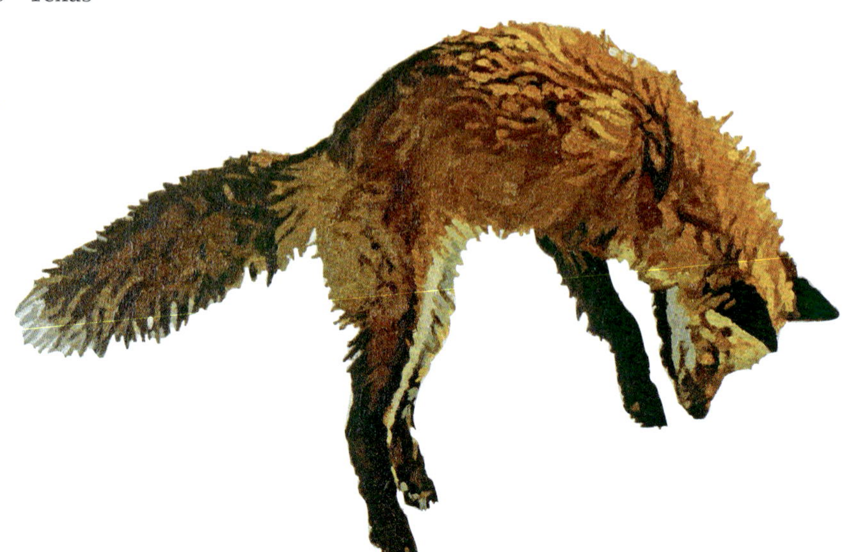

Jumping Fox (detail), 1993
oil on linen | 13" × 18" | Private collection, Dallas

CONTENTS

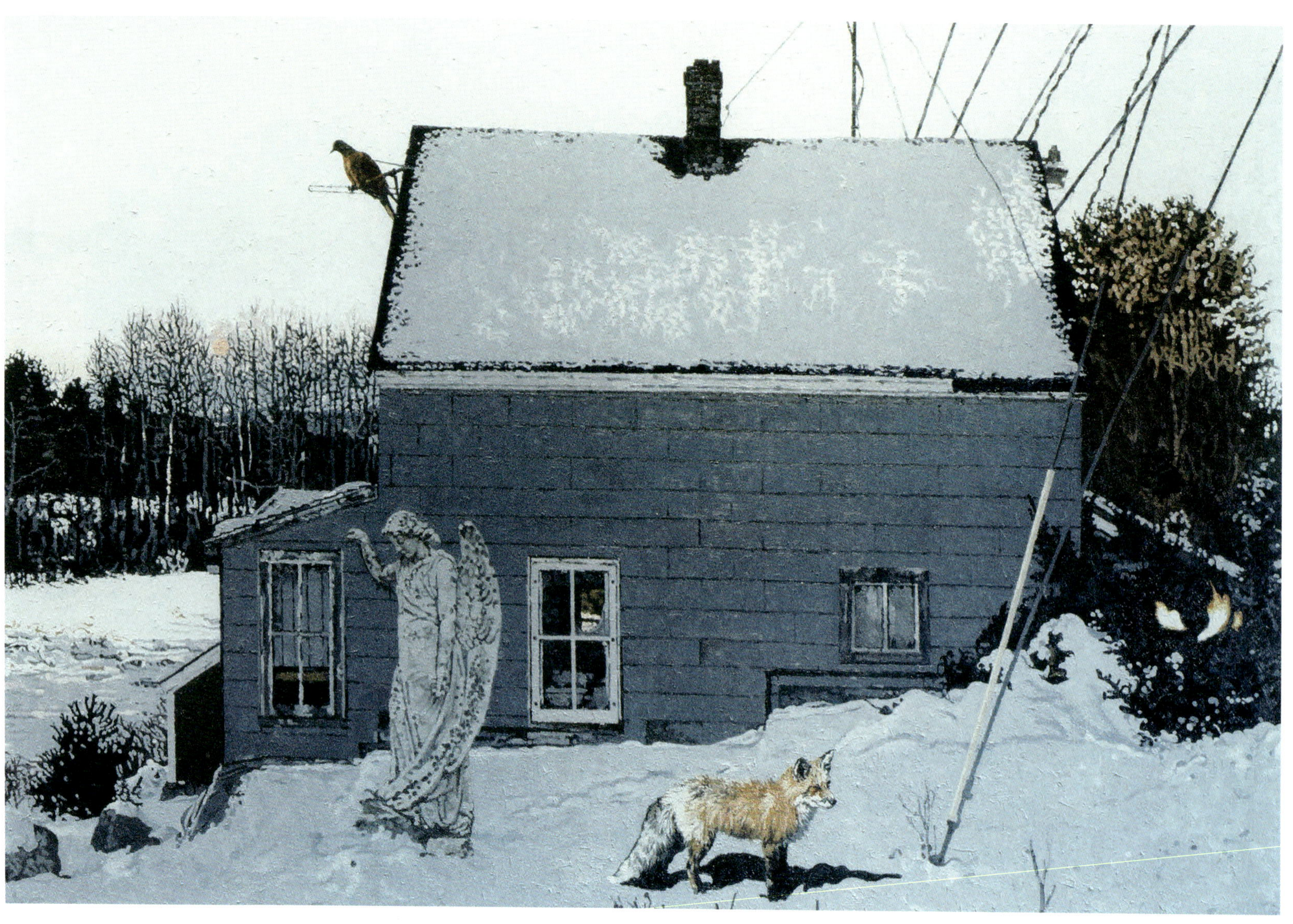

Winter Solstice, 1990

oil on linen | 56" × 78" | Albritton Family Collection, Dallas | Photography by Fernando Rojas

FOREWORD

There is little to be added to this enlightening and well-written account of Roger Winter's life and his journey to becoming an artist of regard. It is clear he has done a lot of living and made a whole lot of art worth looking at. The text insinuates his tenacity and passion as an artist and his heartfelt concern for justice in the world, his integrity as a human being. These qualities inform all his opinions and his work, and just might make him a role model these days.

While this book indicates that Winter looks at the world with a raised eyebrow (so much so it really should be permanently pinched by now), it refrains from expounding on his high-spirited humor, which he wields with deft delight. This informs all of his observations and has perhaps guided him through the sheer irreconcilable confoundedness of human experience. It is a privilege to know Winter, even better than reading about him, but you will enjoy that too. Most importantly, make sure you see his art. The world will look different afterward, better even, and that might just surprise Winter.

Jennifer R. Gross
Founding Director, Hauser & Wirth Institute

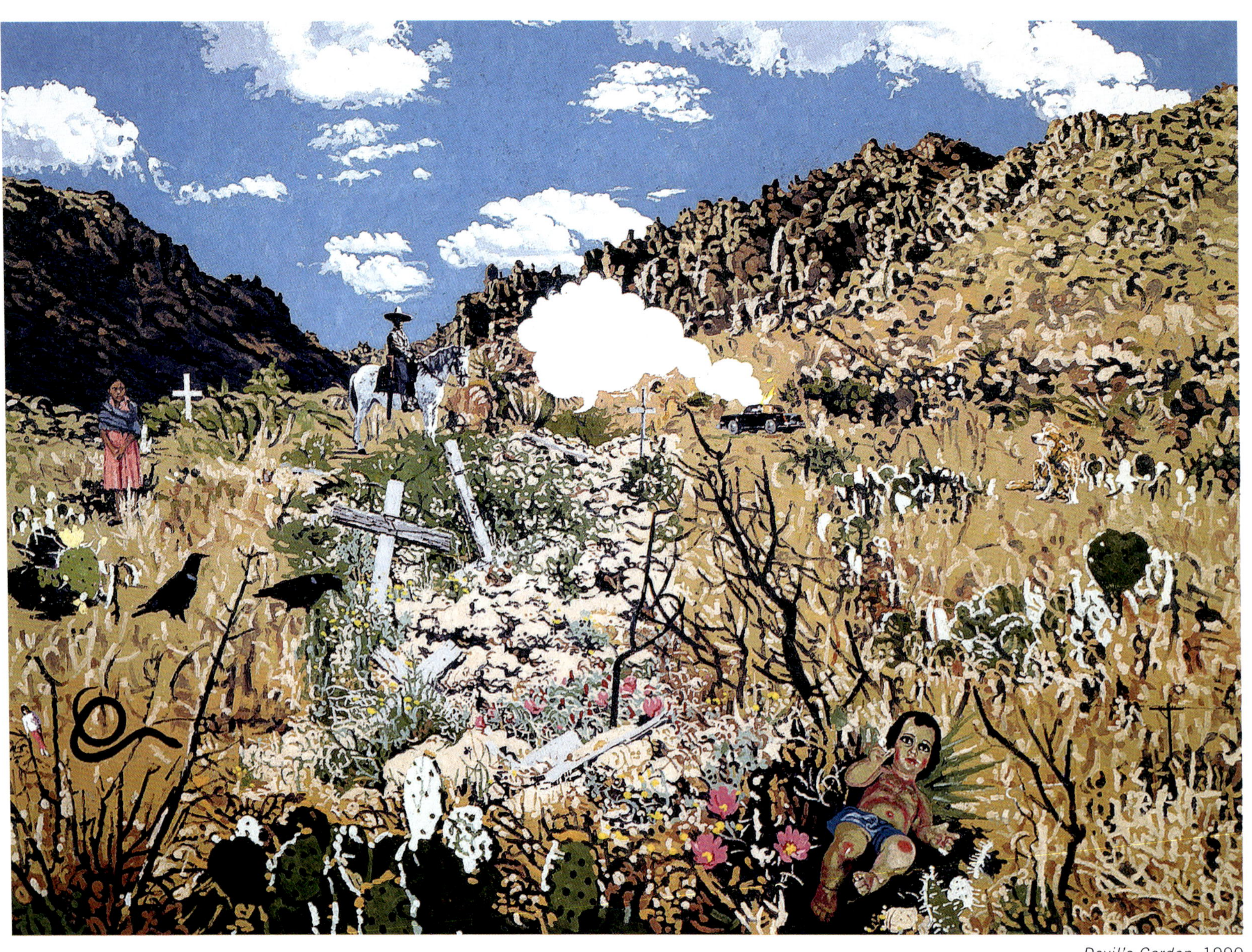

Devil's Garden, 1990

oil on linen | 62" × 86" | Collection of the El Paso Museum of Art, gift of the artist

ACKNOWLEDGMENTS

It has been a privilege and rare opportunity to plumb deeply into the life and art of Roger Winter.

This book has been several years in the making, and over that period we have benefited from the support of many individuals. First and foremost, we must acknowledge Winter's art dealer, Kirk Hopper, who has been central to the success of this publication. He has been at the forefront of every stage of the project. Over countless meetings and many visits to institutions, in addition to the homes of collectors, Kirk has offered his insights and gallery files, both of which have been invaluable. His generosity, support, and friendship, as well as the assistance of his gallery director, Giovanni Valderas, have made our task especially rewarding.

The book came together through the combined outstanding efforts of the Texas A&M University Press team, which helped shape the book, implement changes, and ensure its successful completion. Thom Lemmons, senior editor, provided encouragement, skillful guidance, and a determined grasp of the possibilities of this book. Throughout the publication process, Thom was a wonderful ally and constantly motivated us to move forward. Our gratitude is extended to Shannon Davies, Edward Campbell '39 press director; Linda Salitros, assistant to the director and rights manager; Jay Dew, editor in chief; Katie Duelm, managing editor; Patricia Clabaugh, associate editor; Mary Ann Jacob, design and production manager; Gayla Christiansen, marketing manager; and Christine Brown, publicity and advertising manager. We would also like to thank Ashley Moore, who edited the manuscript with care and sensitivity, and Helen Wheeler, production editor.

A project of this scale requires the participation of many, and we are indebted to the individuals who have played key roles over the years of its research and development. We are deeply grateful to the funders for the support of this publication. Without them, this undertaking would not have been possible.

Elise and Burk Murchison's major contribution stems from their absolute belief in Roger Winter and the art of this region. Lead funding was also provided by the Chatham Hill Foundation, which served as an early and strong advocate. Their vital support enriched this project from the beginning.

We are grateful to the benevolence of each visionary donor:

Elise and Burk Murchison
Chatham Hill Foundation
Charlie Adams
John Alexander
Jan Lee and David Bates
Steven Borick
Dr. Mavis Anne Bryant
President and Mrs. George W. Bush
John Carpenter
Judge B. Michael Chitty and Elise Chitty
Mary and Walter Crain
Jennifer Crohn
Kaleta Doolin and Alan Govenar
Tim Hanley
Roger Horchow
Sally Horchow
Erica Huang
Melissa Miller
Molly E. Moore

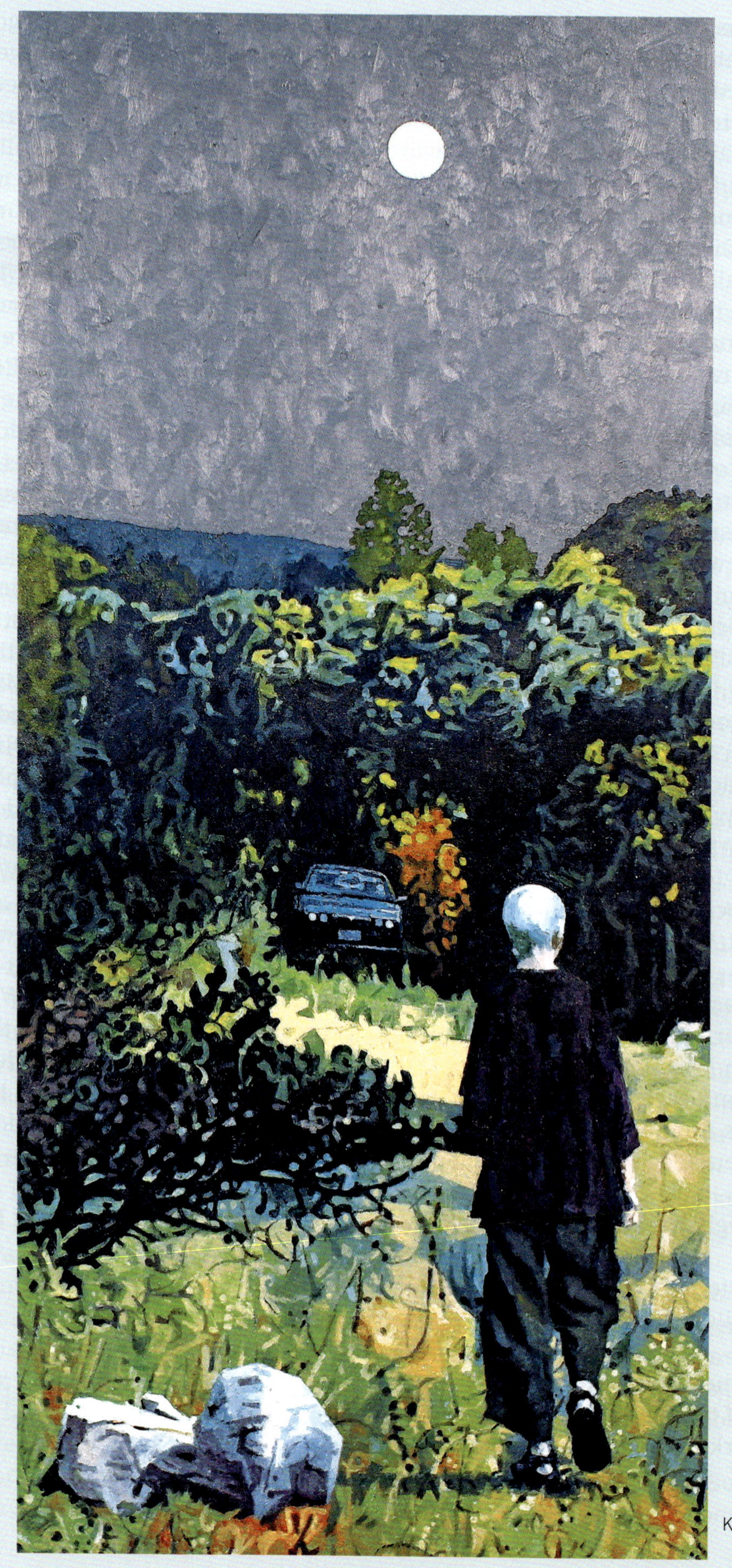

Hunter's Moon, 2010
oil on linen | 56" × 24"
Courtesy of the artist and
Kirk Hopper Fine Art, Dallas
Photography by G. Valderas

INTRODUCTION

Why is it that some people become artists and others don't? And if a person is an artist, what makes him the particular artist he has become?

Roger Winter has painted prolifically and innovatively for over sixty years, following his own path through the gap between abstraction and representation. Intensely observant, the Texas-born, New York City–based artist has spent a lifetime making images that matter out of subjects often overlooked. Painters like Winter are seasoned, skillful navigators of the intersections between the personal and the generalized, the heartfelt and the crafty, the everyday and the idealized. He can string his details into garlands of metaphors. Yet much of the time, with true observation and patient work, he records reality in all its strangeness. He paints cows grazing on some godforsaken piece of Texas flatland. He paints branchy scrub, a mucky ditch, train tracks, and a highway. He paints an old, rusted car because he likes it parked there among the weeds. He paints foxes in midair, leaping above snowdrifts in Maine. He paints mannequins in a shop window, the lights inside it and the reflections of passersby, and the graffiti along the street. He looks up and paints the vastness of Manhattan skyscrapers, old Coney Island buildings, the Hudson River, a burning New Mexico desert, or the luminous Iceland sky. Winter shows how our in-between spaces slip past. He slows art down, letting the eye catch on the paint. However ugly or lost the area around a vacant lot or concrete overpass may be, Winter addresses them with unflinching attention and respect.

He has always culled his subjects from his immediate surroundings. Winter's art acquaints us with his parents, his siblings, his dogs, his wife and sons, the houses he has lived in, and the landscapes he knows and loves. Life astounds him.

It strikes me that art for Winter was the beginning of a journey of his own, a way of igniting responses and provoking thought, but always approached with a kind of innocent curiosity. It is his freedom as an artist that I admire. At eighty-five, he has both backbone and playfulness, illuminating his subjects in unexpected and often disconcerting ways that feel grounded in experience, yet alert to the complexities of all kinds of art making. The question he seems to ask again and again and with startling force throughout his career is how to feel, how we *do* feel, not only in spite of pain but also because of it—how emotional or physical collision with people and places is in fact the only way to wake up and become fully alive.

The hardships he endured growing up in Denison, Texas, during the Depression are not simply romantic fodder for his paintings. His commitment to embodying a sage persona, toughened by circumstances, is at the core of his artistic identity and has much to do with why his paintings often convey a red-blooded vitality. Those in the Winter family—eight children in a four-room house without plumbing or electricity—like everyone else who lived on the wrong side of the Katy tracks, barely scraped by. It was a world in which nothing was fixed—and that included comforting notions of home, material success, and individual identity.

I asked him questions during an interview session in his New York City studio that were ultimately unanswerable, such as, Where does your art come from? How do we separate the version of you that we've come to know through your work from the real one, and how do we determine whether the life reveals the art or the art the life? Winter pulled out a guitar from its case and began to sing "Love Lifted Me," a hymn of extraordinary poetic powers that he learned as a small child. Winter's voice was an aged quaver, sounding like the smoothly polished stone of accrued wisdom. The words that followed were modest in bearing, but in a way that telegraphed heart and despair:

> I was sinking deep in sin, far from the peaceful shore;
> Very deeply stained within, sinking to rise no more.
> But the Master of the sea heard my despairing cry;
> From the waters lifted me, now safe am I.
> Love lifted me, love lifted me.
> When nothing else could help, love lifted me.
> Love lifted me, love lifted me.
> When nothing else could help,
> Love lifted me.

As it happened, the soundtrack in Winter's head was always switched on. Gospel music fed him when he was despondent as well as ecstatic, functioning as a means to call down the spirits and prick the senses. Winter has always been obsessed with time, memory, and the fleeting moments of joy snatched from a grim existence, even if that beauty is discernible only in the imagination. All it took to be transported from hell to a spiritual retreat was the sound of a hymn that seemed to emanate from heaven and conjured a poignant yearning.

For Winter, such songs lived in the air—despite a hardscrabble life, his mother sang to him about love, death, and rising up like a soul set free. He sang the hymns at the evangelical, holy roller church down the road and heard them daily from a loudspeaker attached to its roof. For Winter, hymns served as admissions of faults, as well as a means to find redemption even in those. They helped assuage his deepest fears—that evil lies around every corner, that ordinary life can be ripped apart at any moment by some random, unforeseen event.

But it was how Winter sang on that particular afternoon in this studio that clenched it: struggle, loss, joy—with all of himself out of life, even as his aching fingers strummed the chords. The combination of emotional registers conveyed how in touch he had been with shame and resilience and life lived on the margins of society. He was singing about the enormous capacity for love, the weighty responsibility of it, the loneliness of it. His drifting voice connected in a visceral way that wasn't really explainable but expressed an affection for question over closure, for open air and wide skies. "Love lifted me" is a revealing metaphor for an artist who has seemed to stand alone his entire career. At that moment, I encountered a childlike Winter who played with a kind of desperation, listening in a state of urgency with a need to hear the old hymn and, through hearing it, feel a sense of a shared world. I came away with a clear understanding of Winter as a die-hard romantic whose reflection on the passage of time conveys a bittersweet awareness of the fragility of beauty, which, for him, is synonymous with sentiment. What we regard as the present is also the past. Life is what we remember, although all of us will eventually be forgotten. And yet, there is that gospel music in the air from a faraway place. For over a half century, Winter has taken in the full breadth of human experience, managing to find new ways, through story and image, to transport the listener and viewer elsewhere and put them deep inside a song.

This seems fitting for a man who creates art that is, among other things, about the fragments we try to piece together to tell our stories. Winter's paintings, drawings, collages, and sculptures are about the search for meaning in our lives—the stories we tell others and especially the stories we tell ourselves. What's important is the story and how Winter turns every walk down memory lane into surprise-filled turns through a labyrinth, taking us right and left and then down apparent roadblocks before guiding us home. His art excels when a balance is achieved between an extroverted, pleasing style and an introverted rumination on moral and spiritual ideas that are at the core of what he has to say, even if they may sometimes be hard to decipher.

His work is varied—maybe overvaried, but it does offer up a cohesive world view. Looking at his paintings evokes a time when we placed a premium on families, friendships savored, and nature and its splendors. His pure landscapes are sustained, moving reflections on the human life cycle at a time when people were more in tune with the earth. Out of these fragments emerges a complicated story, one of continual rebirth, constant seeking, revised identities, and profound wonder as his art pushes toward graver, more spiritual ideas, the stakes rising with each change of locale. Significantly, the contradictions of an artist are usually what make him or her most interesting, and with Winter, the paradoxes abound. His development has been nothing if not eclectic. At different points over the decades, his work has been inflected by Cubism, Surrealism, Magic Realism, Pop, Constructivism, Primitivism, Realism, Precisionism, Hard Edge, and other idioms, all of which he combines and recombines in all sorts of ways. Surveying his life and art, we may wonder, then, who is Roger Winter? What is the glue that holds together a body of work that seems at times to be contradictory and disjunctive? Throughout his staggeringly productive career, Winter has never adhered to a signature style. All of his work is circuitous, making manifest a sense of place and direct experience—Texas, England, Maine, New York, New Mexico, Iceland—but also a sharpened sense of interior worlds, richly layered and nuanced. Over the decades, he has gone various directions with skill—it's not a question of inconsistency but rather one of openness and growth. He is an artist who has never been afraid of change or pushing the limits. There is a recognizable tension in his paintings between the priority of structure and the boisterous claims of the world, a tension as old as realism itself.

For Winter, art has been a way to sort through the crosscurrents of his life—race, class, family—as well as integrate all the pieces of himself into something whole. At the core of his landscapes and portraits is a spiritual search that plumbs the depths of the human condition. Through storytelling, he weaves tales together into a tapestry that is complex, beautiful, and flawed—a deliberate strategy meant to convey the chaos of life, distortions of memory, and the bright threads of meaning that can be extracted, with imagination and will, from the mess. Winter moves effortlessly between the serious and the comic, the existential and the merely personal. In doing so, he has pursued a legacy of endurance and an understanding of the magic powers of storytelling to provide both solace and transcendence. For Winter, stories serve to unify and engage, rather than divide or marginalize. Like a writer or musician, Winter developed an ability to be in the moment while standing apart as an observer, a novelist's eye and singer's ear for detail, and a precise but elastic voice capable of moving easily between the lyrical, the vernacular, and the profound. He has been sustained by an adventuresome emphasis on materials and an athletic approach to process that builds on the notion of specificity. For Winter, however, specificity has evolved into a highly charged compression of feeling, surface fact, and optical experience. At the same time, his work and his world are rendered with a disciplined intensity that is guided by intuition and personal need. The intensity we feel in his paintings is the tenderly ordered projection of human emotion. We sense this in the brick-and-mortar brushwork of a carefully rendered surface, in the near-seismographic touch of pencil to paper.

Indeed, the pleasure of looking at Winter's art is immediate, but it is not a fleeting experience. The paintings demand time to fully absorb what they have to offer, as we respond to the beauty and complexity of the world through the artist's eyes. His work often shimmers with light that both unifies the surface and defines form in a complex, intriguing way. The paintings convey a joy and appreciation of Winter's surrounding environment, which he intensifies and imbues with life-affirming energy. To that end, he keeps each aspect of presentation, each successive decision, firmly in hand. Emotion and intellect—like point and counterpoint—amplify and inform each other, establishing a continued dialogue in his work. Throughout, an innate sense of connection among people, places, nature, society, and self animates his thinking and approach as an artist. His attention to the micro- and macroscopic aspects of the world and his intuitive sense of their relationships, his rejection of barriers and boundaries, and his commitment to a wide range of sources have generated an original body of work that continues to evolve. Winter's art exemplifies a wonderful fusion of art history, childlike vision, fine craftsmanship, and aesthetic integrity.

Significantly, his extraordinary, beautiful paintings of the mundane and unobtrusive pay close attention to subjects seen on the quick, in a glimpse. Yet all of the landscapes and portraits are rendered as if by virtue of a stare that never seems to end. Winter captures the spirit of diverse locales and environments, from the arid plains of West Texas to the congested intersections of New York City. But to say that he is a detached realist is to miss all the ways he merges precise observation with structural rigor and painterly sensuality. Winter's meticulous attention to the appearance of things and their capacity for mysterious drama yields lyric passages that evoke feelings of transcendence.

There is always a deep sense of quiet in a Winter painting, of breath both held and released. His art is balanced between abstraction and realism, not because he moves from one to the other but because he has found a space between the two. The representational elements of his paintings act not only as signifiers of the outside world but also as pretexts for the physical act of painting and as templates for viewing. They demand a scanning, allover read. But by keeping the images close to the surface, he maintains the flatness of the picture plane while allowing us the pleasures of a modernist flip-flop between a material surface and illusory depth. Yet to experience one of his paintings is to feel simultaneously the sudden reality of a specific place and the slow passing of time.

Winter has always been an artist of tenacity, deeply conscious of the tradition he works in and the homages to other art that it entails—Cycladic sculpture, Egyptian Fayum portraits, Roman frescoes, Netherlandish miniatures, and the paintings of Pieter Bruegel the Elder, Johannes Vermeer, Nicolas Poussin, Jean-Baptiste-Camille Corot, and Edouard Vuillard, as well as those of the twentieth-century artists who form the core of an American spirit: Edward Hopper, Stuart Davis, and Romare Bearden. Closer to home, Winter often cites the preeminent Texas artist Tom Lea for helping him "see" a place and make the Southwest visible by painting it into existence. Winter comprehends the nature of art at its most fundamental as a mutating, vibrant, and evolving force. To many viewers, however, his landscapes and portraits represent the reembrace of bygone values sorely missed in painting today. Their fine qualities of light, surface, form, and space blow fresh air into the lungs of an audience seeking the wholeness of a unitary visual expression. Still, the successful bodies of work that Winter has produced during his career do not so much "develop" from the previous ones as loop back and branch out, so each body of work clears a new visual space adjacent to the previous one. Accordingly, Winter's earlier works may be taken as clearing a visible field for later landscapes. Throughout, he celebrates the everyday miracles that only paint can achieve, miracles that come from attention to and engagement with the materials at hand. All in all, his finely tuned paintings, animated by contrasting forces of palette and structure, seem alternately spare and generous. It's as if radiant energy has been collected between the tufted and skittering staccato dabs of paint. Nature is visible here, albeit in hiding. It is simultaneously close and distant, encompassing and eluding. The philosophical questions that emerge from his compositions deal with the mystery and enigma of our identity and existence, our desire for the infinite.

Winter is among the very few who have consistently pushed boundaries in an ongoing quest for self-discovery. It is impossible to account for the past half century without including him in the picture. He is the vital link between generations of Texas artists—his mentors and teachers during his time at the University of Texas, Austin, between 1952 and 1956 included Robert McDonald Graham, Constance Forsyth, Loren Mozley, Everett Spruce, and William Lester. As an esteemed faculty member of Southern Methodist University from 1963 to 1989, Winter taught nationally recognized artists such as John Alexander, David Bates, Robert Yarber, Tracy Harris, Gail Norfleet, Lilian Garcia-Roig, and Brian Cobble, among others. Over the decades, Winter's work has been regularly shown in prominent galleries across the country, as well as in major solo exhibitions organized by the Baxter Gallery, Maine College of Art (Portland, Maine), and the Meadows Museum, Southern Methodist University (Dallas). He has taught painting and drawing at the National Academy of Design, New York City, and served as visiting artist at the Vermont Studio Center (Johnson), the University of Pennsylvania (Philadelphia), and Washington University (Saint Louis). He received a National Endowment for the Arts Fellowship Award in Painting and was honored with the Legend Award for Contribution to the Visual Arts in Texas. Significantly, Winter authored four editions of the definitive publication *On Drawing*, which is widely used in university art departments.

Nevertheless, Winter remains just on the edge of the radar and is not nearly as well known as he ought to be. His importance as a teacher, mentor, and inspiration is well documented. What are less known, particularly outside Dallas, are his innovations and accomplishments as an artist. In this regard, Winter is less famous than some of his students. Is it because he refused to assimilate and work in a widely accepted, mainstream style? Is it because he shifted between abstraction and figuration? In many respects, he became an artist other artists would build on until, generations later, his achievements became part of a larger American heritage.

One of the naively held opinions in art is the notion that an artist's standing is fixed. No matter how well one knows the work of an artist, there are always fresh questions, new angles and combinations to be examined, new mysteries to be explored.

The art world has always laid claim to its share of mavericks, including those who pose as such. Genuine originals, however—people who follow their own lights, make their own rules, and create their own frames of reference—are rare in this context, as in any other. Winter's career stands out for its willful resistance to the evolutionary logic or consistency so beloved by art critics and museum curators. He has never sought the avenues that measure success by sales, publicity, or branding. Rather, Winter's enterprise is one of digressions, of lateral shifts, of traveling opposite paths simultaneously. Moreover, for a long time, museums and galleries didn't know how to deal with him. The standard procedure was to isolate a slice of work that had some visual or thematic coherence, but Winter resisted categorization, art world expectations, and almost any kind of authority. His story is of an artist doing his own thing, come hell or high water. It helps to think of him as a kind of philosopher-carpenter with an inborn, almost mystical love of paint as paint. He wants us to understand its sensuousness while also grasping that paintings are essentially "built" from scores of decisions and details. Accordingly, Winter's path does not move in a simple arc but rather meanders between his interior life and his life in the world, connecting dreams, reflections, and memories.

It is a complex story of how art is made by one person of protean energy over the stretch of time. At the core of Winter's art is the passage of time—the way places and events can mean different things at different stages in a person's life. Time—the ways it can accelerate through years, freeze in moments, and defy measurement altogether—is his chief preoccupation, his major theme and raw material. His story is also a guide to living as a creative individual. In contrast to those requirements that dictate that the artist develop a signature style and stay with it, choose a single medium and stay with it, get into the market easily and stay there, Winter advocates change: lose the artist the world thinks you are, and you'll begin to find your true self. Art history wants wrap-ups, final accounts. But in Winter's case there are no stops. Rather than pursuing a typical, linear development from point A to point B and onward, Winter has spent his career proving that there are an infinite number of ways to meet painting's basic requirements.

This monograph gives Winter a deeper consideration as a necessary figure in American art. *The Art of Roger Winter: Fire and Ice* is the first major publication to examine his art in a critical context—its prodigious breadth and great wingspan. It presents Winter as a complicated, relentlessly rethinking experimenter, an artist who combines brain and hand in ways that artists still have everything to learn from, precisely because he is so difficult to categorize and fully absorb. He redefines the possibilities of portraiture and landscape, bringing to both genres an intimacy, urban swagger, and psychological vulnerability with equal authority and self-knowledge. A main theme to emerge is a profound understanding of human loneliness. Just beneath the confident paint handling and luminous hues are the insecurities of an isolated boy growing up by the railroad tracks in Denison, Texas—poor conditions that have given his art depth and dimension. The book provides a gripping account of Winter's artistic roots, deftly mapping early influences and the discovery of his own voice—unguarded, openhearted, profuse. The title of this monograph brings to mind Robert Frost's famous poem, which hints at the equally destructive powers of love and hate, ending in an abrupt reversal of competing energies. Winter also seeks to hold such forces in dialectical tension—a push-pull of potential opposites. He puts essential truths before us—the brevity and immensity of life. Winter's realism butts up against his romanticism even as the existentialist in him has searched for ways to coexist with the artist. His work is half fire, half ice.

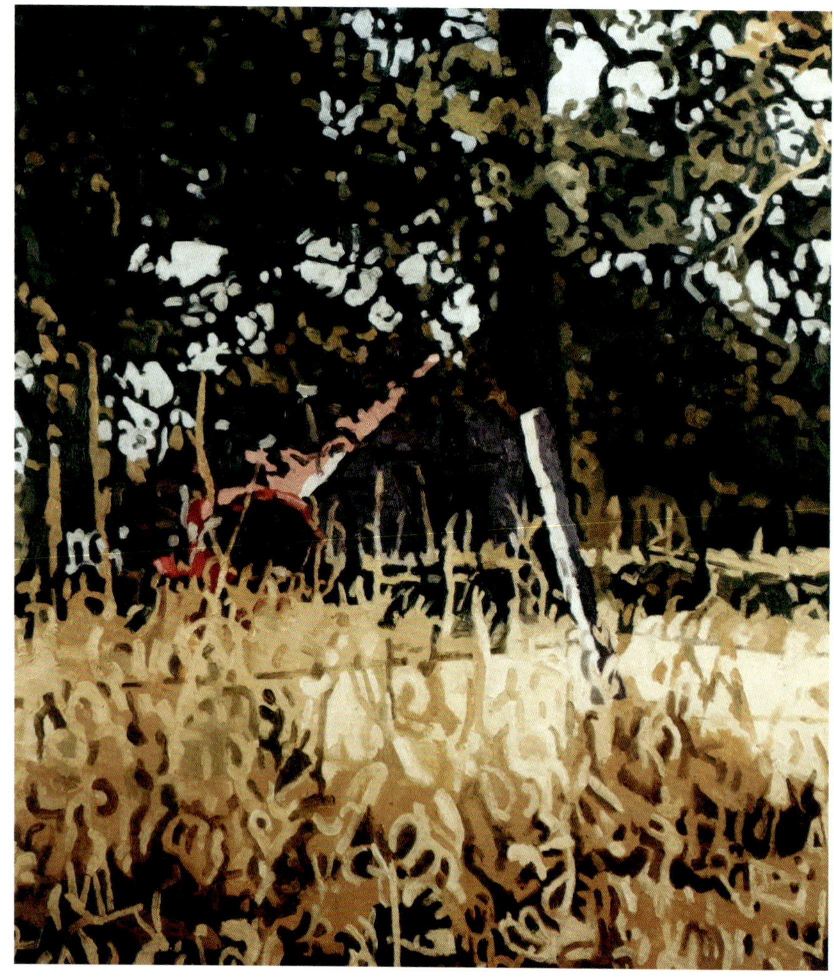

Hopkins County Field (detail), 1979

oil on linen | 60" × 72" | Collection of Gary W. Knoble and Robert A. Black | Photography by Dean Batchelder

CHAPTER 1

EARLY YEARS: BETWEEN THE CROSS AND THE SILVER SLIPPER

WHEN WE LOOK BACK ON OUR LIVES, trying to figure out how we wound up where we are and who we are, there is a tendency to focus on events that, in retrospect, are weighted with course-determining significance. From the beginning, family was Winter's central focus. It is by them, by his home, by his music and art—by all he has loved most—that he was formed. There is always a story within a story. In fact, stories are like onions: peel one layer off and another appears beneath it. Storytelling matters desperately to Winter. It is a means of grappling with personal isolation and loneliness, a tool for connecting the dots of his family's life and making sense of the past. His recollections are spiked with scrappy wildness and plain talk about life, death, things left undone, things left behind, the urgency and the mundane nature of it all, which is both undercut and underscored by issues of race and class. Winter's sense of emotional homelessness in a segregated railroad town was at once a burden and a motivation—a source of personal pain and of deep philosophical insight. He invites us into an intimate place that's messy and chaotic and hard to shake. Winter goes at things freestyle. His anecdotes have snap—the crazy-making detritus of daily living; what touches him and why. Winter's family is not a static unit. It is in continual flux, dissolving and reassembling, its natural state one of midwreckage. For Winter, art became a way to define himself and tease apart all the tangled threads that go into the making of an identity. What emerges is a powerful portrait of the artist as a young man: conflicted, rebellious, self-conscious, and deeply thoughtful, a seeker after an understanding of his own place in the world.

Roger Lee Winter was born on August 17, 1934—the youngest of five boys and three girls in a white frame house on a red dirt road that ran parallel to the Kansas–Missouri–Texas (Katy) railroad tracks on the outskirts of Denison, Texas. His parents were itinerants who homesteaded, farmed, or labored in Arkoma, Oklahoma; near Fort Smith, Arkansas; and in Greenville, Texas, before settling in Denison near the Oklahoma border.

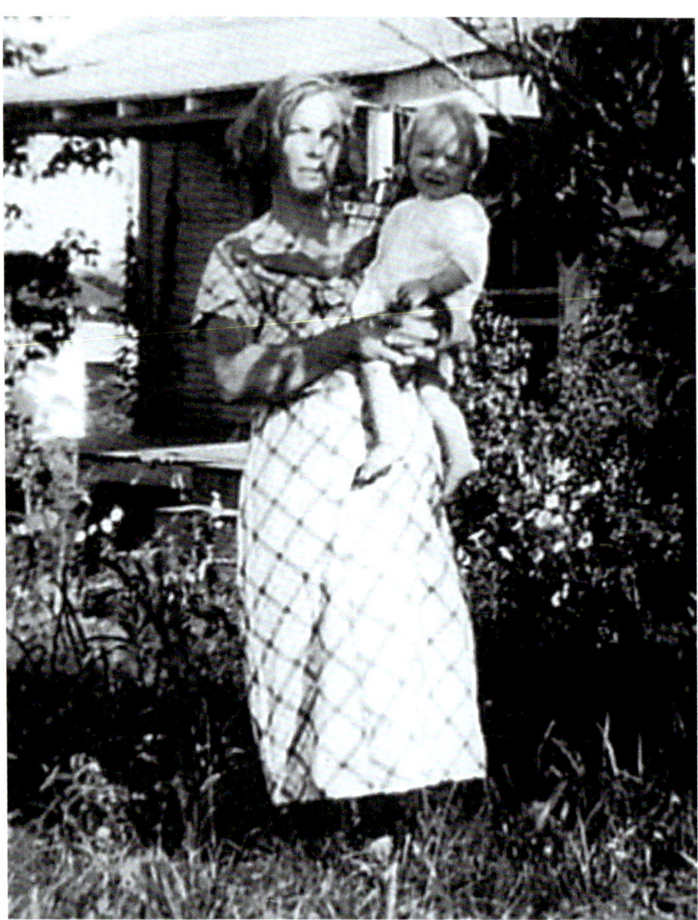

Roger's mother holding him, 1935

Winter's father, Gordon Fillmore Winter, was born in 1889 in Lebanon, Tennessee. Winter's paternal grandfather, William Buchanan Winter, worked as a blacksmith and played the fiddle with a group of country musicians. According to Winter, he was a rough man with a drinking problem and was killed in his fifties when a small rock went through his derby hat and into his head at a blasting site in Sulphur, Oklahoma. The derby became an object of great fascination for Winter through his early childhood.

Winter's mother, Etta Mae Kennemer, was born in 1895 in Como, Texas. Her father, John Aseph Kennemer, had moved with his parents from Kennemer Cove, Alabama, to Hopkins County, Texas, to grow cotton. Winter remembers them as religious and poorly educated farmers who had odd names—Alamo, Possum, Ioma, Goo Baby—and weird habits—praying constantly, going to the bathroom in the barn, using corn cobs instead of toilet paper, dipping snuff. Winter's father was a laborer in a Denison creosote plant that preserved crossties and utility posts for the Katy Railroad. His mother cooked, washed, raised chickens and cows, and worked the garden with very little help or money. Their water came from a well dug and walled by his father. It was the only source of water for drinking, cooking, and bathing. Winter recalls, "We had no indoor plumbing. A two-hole outhouse stood at the back of our acre of land, and we—all ten of us—bathed in washtubs that hung when not in use on the sides of our four-room house. The house had two rooms when my parents bought it, and my father built two shed-roof rooms onto the back. Sleeping was difficult—always more than one person to a bed. The walls were water stained and the wallpaper was torn. We had no electricity or gas. All our fires for cooking and heating came

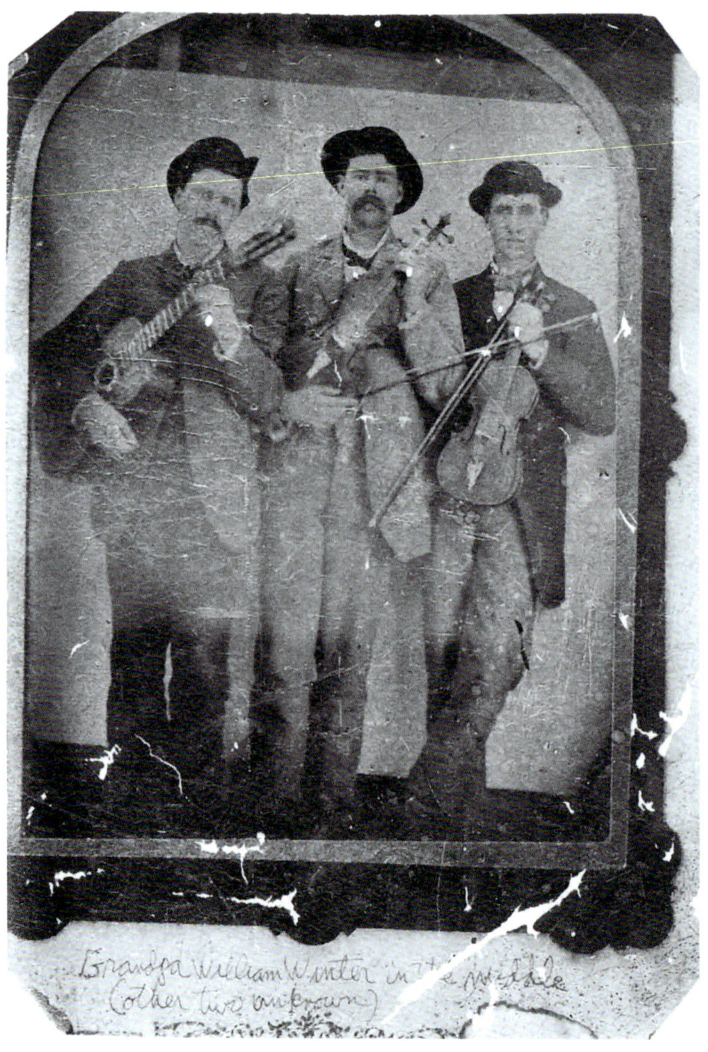

Grandpa William Winter (*center*) with musicians

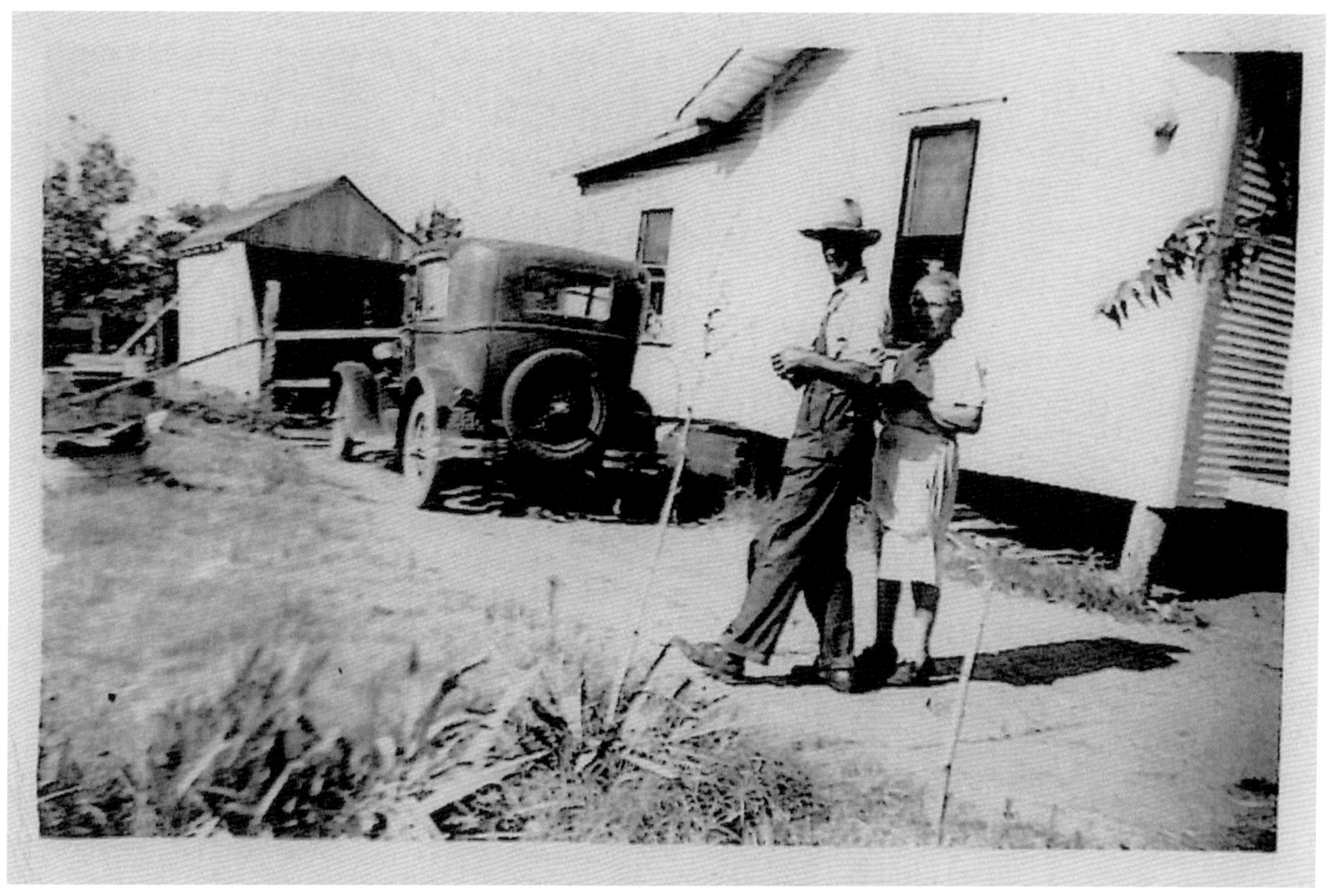

"Ann," Model A Ford, with Roger's father and mother

from wood salvaged at the creosote plant. Our light was from kerosene lamps."[1]

Winter's father was very dark skinned, which caused him great embarrassment as a teenager. According to Winter, he changed jobs frequently and wore old overalls, a dreamer who never made much money. "He was perhaps afraid of the world and taking chances," says Winter.

> Yet he was a brilliant man and terribly independent. In those days, the wood was loaded on the railroad cars by hand. He learned to carry a crosstie, which is very heavy, on his shoulder. He had to be very strong to work at the wood-preserving plant. The men liked him because he would tell funny stories. Although he didn't get past the ninth grade, he was an avid reader—anything from Milton to Zane Grey. I think they represented the adventures he never had. He carried what my mother called a Pink Card. My father was a Socialist, and he would speak to the labor people. We're talking about a different time—the Depression years, a time when America needed some help from its government. I remember this so well—he stood at the opening of a boxcar door in front of a large group of workers. He said, "Jesus Christ was a Socialist and look what he did—he had twelve disciples and they shared everything equally. So he was a proponent of Socialism." A man in the crowd shouted, "Just a goddamn minute; now, I've heard him called everything in the world but never a goddamn Socialist." As a little kid I thought it was really funny, but it probably scared my father. He told the truth but people didn't want to hear it. He was very political in the farm labor

area. So from childhood on, I've always stood up for things I thought were right.

Among the few visitors to the Winter household was Mrs. Dorman, a religious fanatic and midwife who helped deliver Winter. "She and my mother would always pray together," says Winter.

Perhaps she was the first to hold me. I remember something they liked to say: "Lord, I ain't ashamed to come to Thee." Mrs. Dorman had spent time in a mental institute in Terrell, Texas. Her husband, a kind man, built a white wood-frame church for her on the Bells Highway. Two signs stood outside: PREPARE TO MEET THY GOD and A HOUSE OF PRAYER FOR ALL PEOPLE. It was called a "holiness" or "holy roller" church, but it was the only church I ever knew until well into my teens. We sang many of the hymns I still know from a small songbook called *The Inspired Evangel*—among the songs were "I'll Fly Away," "Jesus Hold My Hand," "Love Lifted Me," and "The Old Rugged Cross." When it comes to song lyrics, I have always been a quick study. I learned the words and melodies in preschool years. The church had no underpinning and we could sometimes hear dogs howling under the floor. There was a singing on Wednesday night that my brother Luther liked to attend with his friend Jack Dorman, one of the sons. Luther would sing the hymns around the house. So did my mother and sisters. When electricity came to our neck of the woods, Mrs. Dorman got a loudspeaker put on top of the church. She'd play scratchy old 78 rpm hymns at odd hours. And in between songs, she would whoop and moan prayers that traveled far and wide over our impoverished section of Denison.

It is likely that Winter heard those hymns on the first day of life, along with the sounds of steam

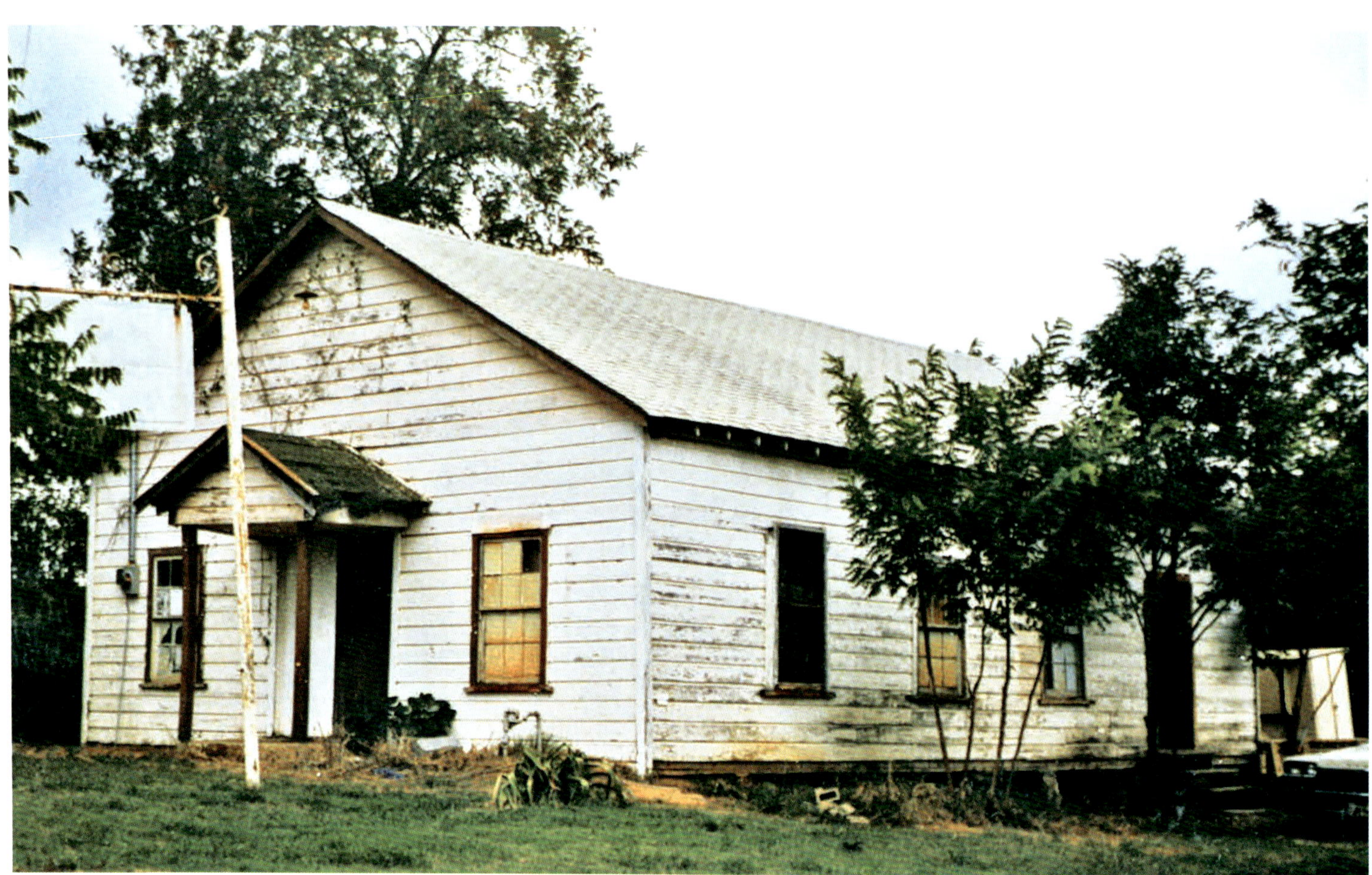

Mrs. Dorman's church

steam engine trains passing by and the hillbilly songs from his father's old windup Victrola. Winter remembers,

> My father played a five-string banjo and sang old-time songs—"Soldier's Joy," "The Twelfth of January," "Jesse James"—until he lost his thumb and a finger of his right hand at work. He could also do a double-shuffle dance he had learned from black men in Tennessee. I loved to watch him dance, but it seemed to bother my mother for unknown reasons. I think she wanted him to be more ascetic and fear the Lord. Other than my father's singing and banjo playing, the collection of 78 rpm records—Vernon Dalhart, Carson Robison, Fiddling Doc Roberts, Jimmie Rodgers—was the only entertainment we had. I was born into country music. The great country music singer/songwriter Buck Owens grew up on a farm within ten miles of where we lived. He said country music was about commonplace things "like the dirt under your fingernails." Yes, like train whistles and biscuits sopped in gravy. My knowledge of country musicians widened when we were able to have a radio. I learned about Bob Wills and his Texas Playboys, Ernest Tubb, Roy Acuff, the Light Crust Dough Boys, Patsy Montana, the Carter Family and the Chuck Wagon Gang. Due west of us, on Highway 69, a honkytonk called The Silver Slipper sprang up in our view and earshot. Next door was the Rainbow Inn and alongside lived the Huff family, Denison's most notorious bootleggers. Their son, Leon Huff, became a successful country musician known as the Texas Songbird. He sang and played rhythm guitar, first for Governor Lee "Pappy" O'Daniel's band and later for Bob Wills, who was a frequent guest at The Silver Slipper. I have fond memories of lying awake on summer nights and listening to the sounds of Texas Swing bands and country singers drift through our open window.[2]

When he was a small child, Winter asked for and received a ukulele at Christmas. "It was easy to tune, and I learned G, C, and D chords from the book that came with it," recalls Winter. "This allowed me to play and sing many of the songs I knew by heart. My mom would get these country women to come in to help her do the quilting on the frames. The frames hung from the ceiling, but would get rolled up at night so you wouldn't bump your head on them. One afternoon I got my ukulele and crawled underneath the frames while the women were quilting. Just so no one would get suspicious of what I was up to, I played the ukulele and sang 'Back in the Saddle Again.' One of the women said, 'Lord listen to that! Does somebody have a radio turned on?' Forgive me: I was six years old, not even in school yet! It was just a private place for me to hide in a very crowded house."

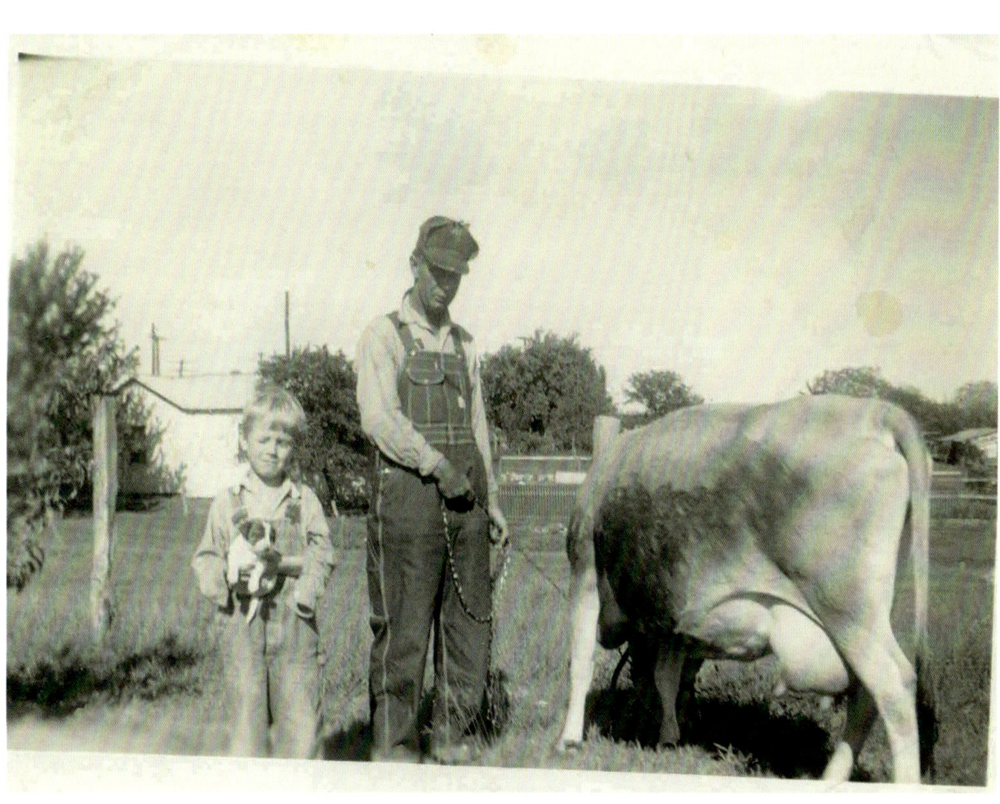

Roger's father, Roger holding Clip, and Tiskit the cow, 1941

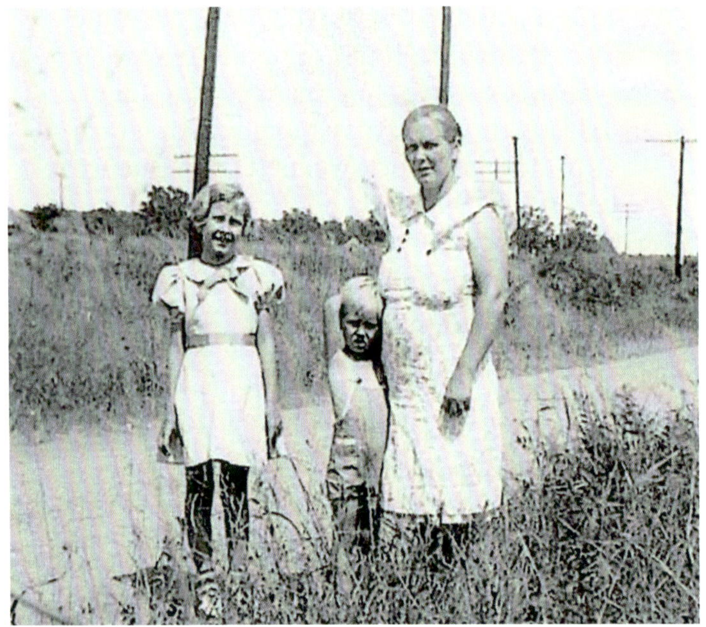
Ada, Roger, and their mother, 1939

There is a self-deprecating wink to spinning the scene, even as it comes from an artist who cuts through the pretensions right to the bone. By Winter's account, however, he didn't laugh, play, or carry on like other children.

> When my mom found out she was pregnant with me, my sisters told me she lay in bed and cried all day. But after I was born, she loved me too much. As a two-year-old, I had dust pneumonia. Everyone thought I would die. I remember my oldest brother, Ed, probably twenty-one years of age at the time, sitting by my bedside and crying. The sister next to me in age, Ada Mae, told me that I was taken to a hospital in Dallas. My mother was afraid of no one; she was afraid of no animal. Somehow a bull got into the pasture with our cow and she literally grabbed the bull by its horns and drove it away. But she overprotected me to a serious fault. Whatever the cause, I had a barren social life as a child. I was never allowed to go anywhere by myself, play sports, or join in school activities. I think she developed some neuroses from hopelessness. It must have been hell to clothe and feed ten people—killing chickens, chopping wood, and firing up the stove with it over one hundred degrees outside. If my father was a few minutes late from his job, she'd scream, "Oh, Daddy's dead! He's been killed!"

Although Winter's mother often displayed great physical courage, she was terrified of storms. As a young girl in Como, she claimed to have been picked up by a cyclone and blown away into a nearby field. "While my mother hung clothes on the lines to dry, she would also keep an eye on the clouds and say, 'Well it's going around.' And then she'd shout, 'It's coming back!'" Anytime the faintest thunder rumbled in the distance, she would force the entire family down in the storm cellar. "I was usually awakened during the night and there was nothing to sleep on in the storm cellar," says Winter, "except grain doors, which were three-by-six-foot laminated pieces of wood maybe two inches thick. It was punishment just to be down there."

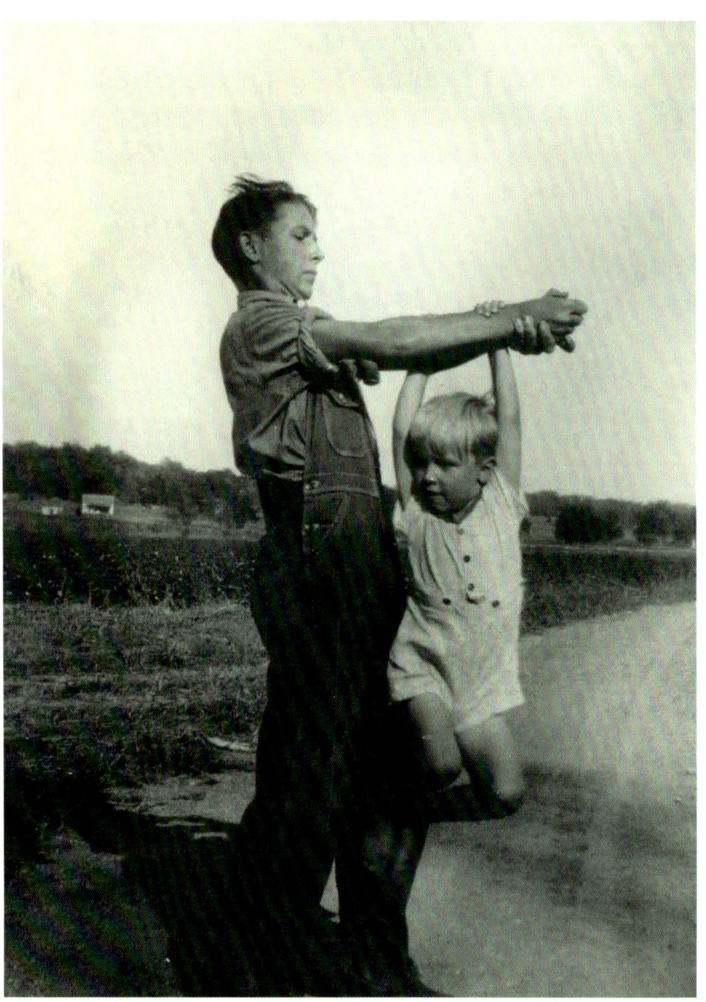
Harry and Roger (hanging from Harry's arm)

“My mother would wail, ‘Good Lordy, mercy!’ ‘God is going to punish us. Oh, Lord, we’re all gonna die!’ It was like a den of madness.”

Throughout his childhood and teenage years, Winter had to witness terrible altercations between his mother and siblings. He remembers one brother hurling the lid of a slop jar (chamber pot) at another’s head, opening up a bloody gash that required stitches. He remembers his mother turning on the gas stove behind a locked door after a violent tussle with an older sister. Winter will never forget wrestling his mother to the floor as she threatened to harm herself with a razor. “You had to make your own life,” Winter says. “Especially with such emotional things going on. There were lots of fights and arguments in my family that I never wanted to be a part of.”

The poverty of the Depression also made hunting and gathering necessary as a means to supplement the family’s diet. Winter recalls foraging in the expansive woods along the Katy tracks as if they were their own, even though the land was on private property. “The male members of the family hunted for rabbits, squirrels, possum, quails, doves, field larks, yellowhammer. And in Clear Creek, Iron Ore Creek and Choctaw Creek, we fished for bream, catfish, drum, crawfish and perch. In the fall, we would gather ‘tow sacks’ full of pecans and black walnuts. In the spring, we gathered pokeweed, which was considered to be a tonic to ward off illnesses. Camphor leaves would cure scratches and bites and toothaches almost instantly. My father knew how to bud and graft trees. This was in addition to our large garden, our cows and chickens, and my parents’ ability to grow, harvest, can, pickle, churn, butcher, parch and so on.”[3]

It is important to note that Winter’s was the only white family living among African American households at the edges of Denison. “Those were the days of racism,” Winter recalls.

> And yet, I knew as a child what people felt about each other. I knew my parents really liked our African American neighbors. They were the most frequent visitors to our house. Sometimes they would come over just for company. My mother would trade milk for a variety of greens or whatever they grew. I remember an older, heavy woman, Laura, and her sister Charity. Her husband, Alec Nash, had a favorite fishing hole down the Katy tracks, just twenty feet from our house. Laura took in washing, and I’d see her walking down our road with a bundle of clean clothes balanced on her head. Carrie and her sister Bell lived next door. They were survivors of the Galveston flood. One morning my brother David and I brought a bucket of milk to Laura’s house and she asked us to come in and look at something we’ve never seen before. We went inside and Laura showed us how she heated her irons on a bed of red-hot coals. I still remember the house as dark with deep, rich colors—as they called them, “soul colors.” We never told my parents about it. Denison, like most towns in the South

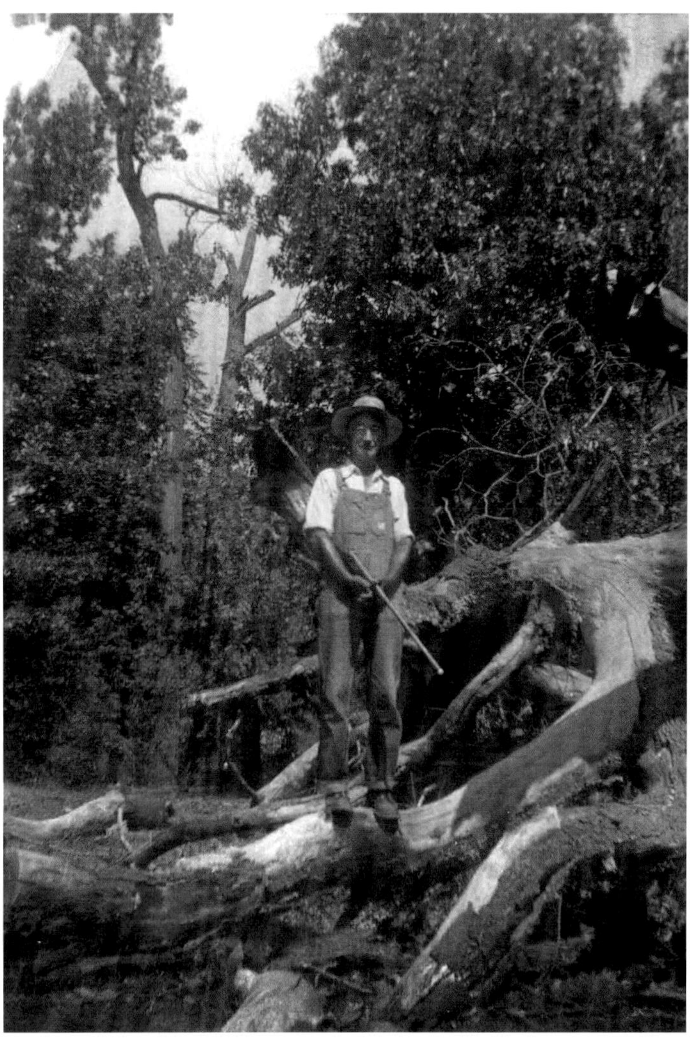

Roger’s father holding a rifle

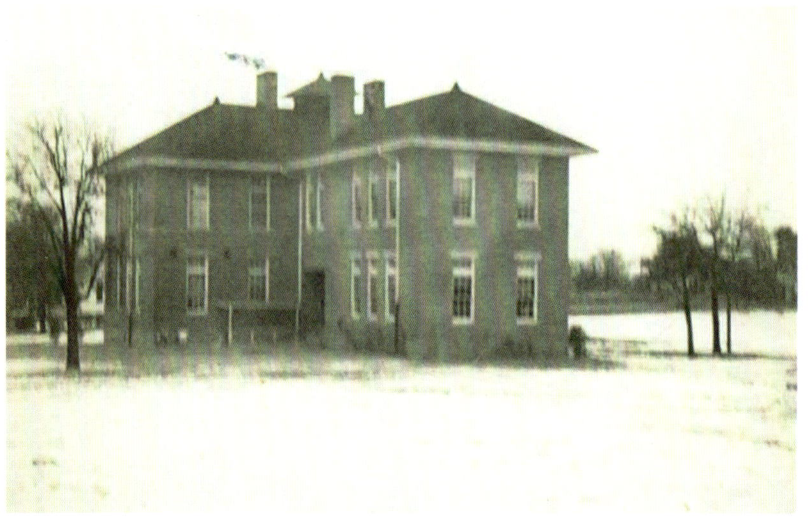
Lamar Grade School

and Southwest of this time, was a deeply segregated place: this included schools, movie theaters, restaurants, water fountains, buses, restrooms, and neighborhoods.

From Winter's perspective, it was also very class conscious. He recalls that most of the children in grade school were from poor parents who had not quite made the transition from nineteenth-century rural to mid-twentieth-century urban life. "Shame is one of the things I struggled with as a child, of being poor," Winter admits. "My parents were so rural looking and lived literally on the wrong side of the tracks. We all felt at home with each other in elementary school. I knew at least three families who lived in lean-to structures in the woods. But in high school the majority of students were from wealthier neighborhoods. None of us could become part of the 'silk stocking row,' as my father called it. I had never learned to dance, to swim, or not to get drunk around girls. I was so out of it, so painfully maladjusted, so secretive about my personal life that I tried to compensate in various ways. One way was to identify with the 'white trash,' many of whom had already been to reform school or prison."

The country music Winter heard through his window at night from the Silver Slipper was like a siren's song, luring him to the roadhouse, the juke joint, the highway. It was the songs that spoke of endless troubles, domestic and universal, and the will to survive them. Winter clearly understood that the birthright of his music was geographical—American, but particularly Texan—and with it came a willingness to move past genre lines and all their connotations of race and class. It was at his fingertips, inviting listeners in spare language that could be both oblique and telling—themes of love and faith, despair and exultation, solitude and connection. A photograph shows a teenaged Winter posing with a guitar on his knee, slicked-back hair, a sneering grin, and a pack of cigarettes rolled up in the sleeve of his white T-shirt. He is the spitting image of a young James Dean, conveying the defiant strut of a have-not finally having his say. Winter had plenty stored up.

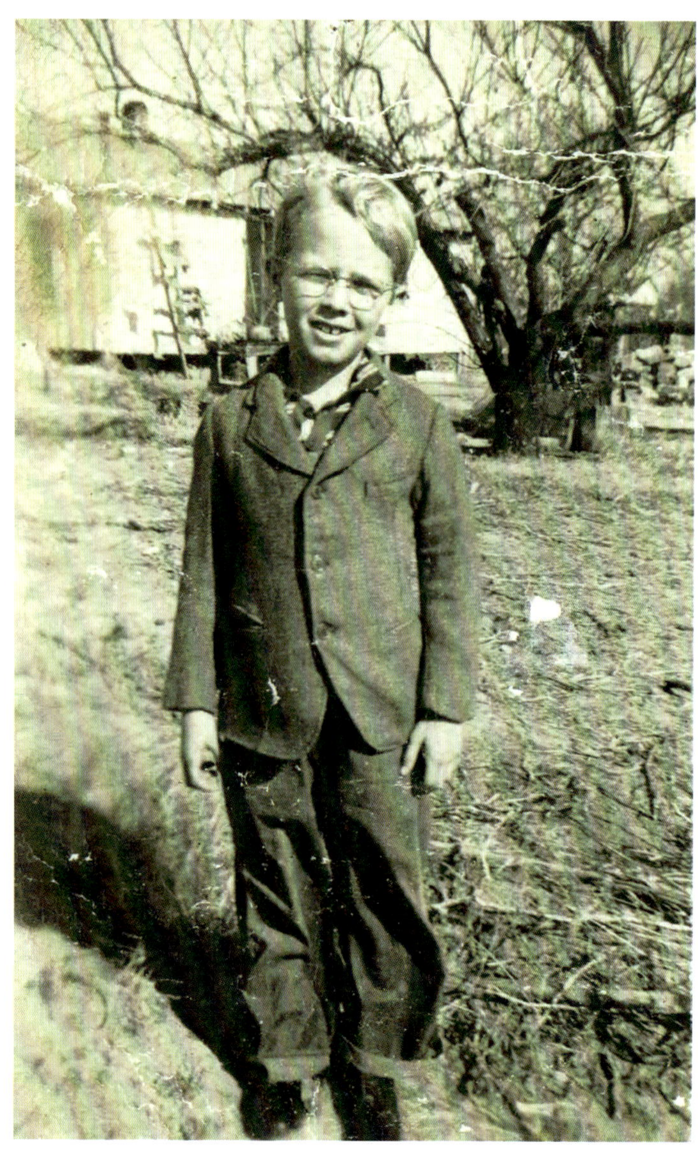
Roger, 1943

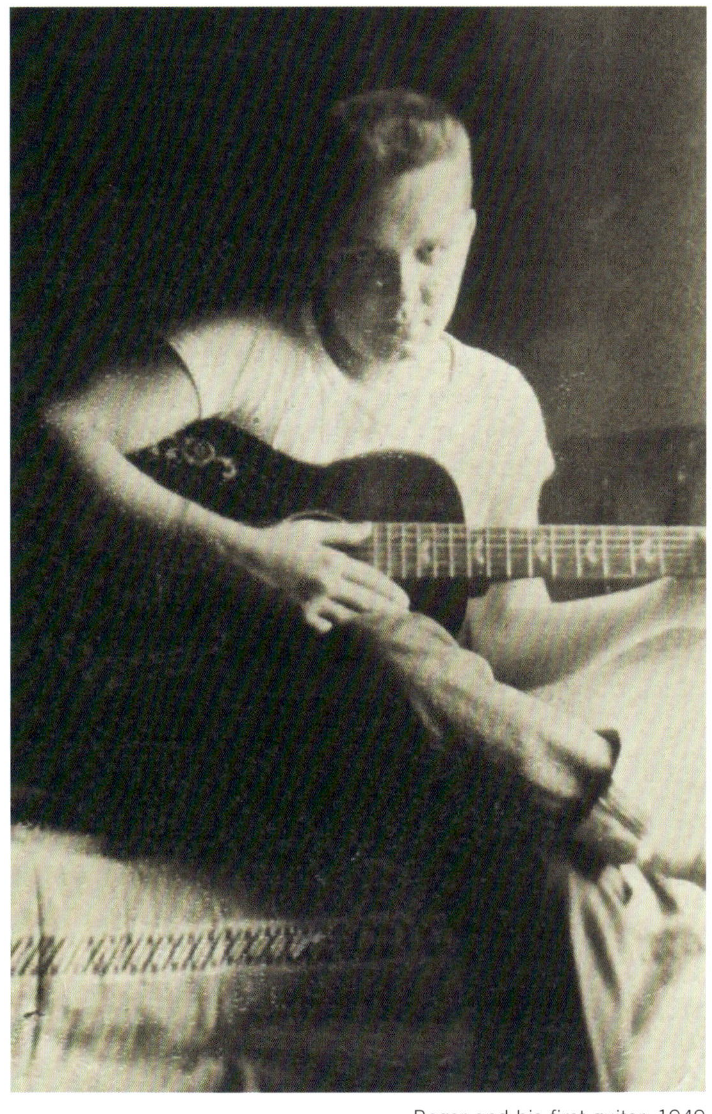

Roger and his first guitar, 1949

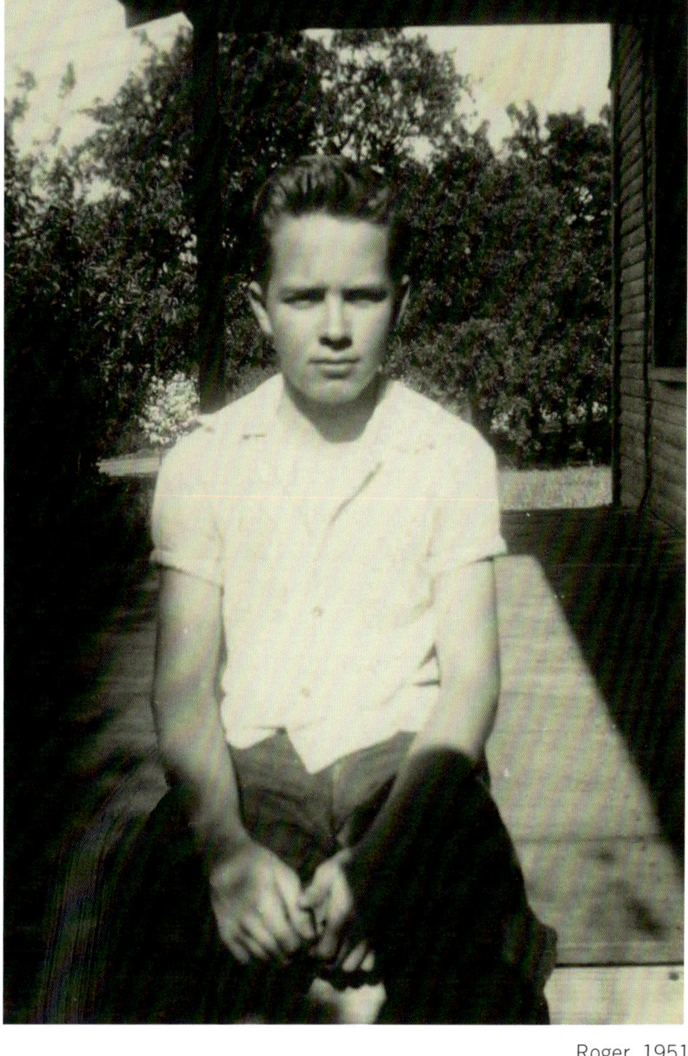

Roger, 1951

I sold garden seeds and made enough money to buy a used guitar for seven dollars and fifty cents from the Syd Maples Pawn Shop. I taught myself how to play. From a warped neck it had string action half an inch high in places, but I learned to chord it and accompany myself singing country songs and hymns. I was introduced to the greatest country singer when some kid got up in the high school auditorium and sang Hank Williams's "Lovesick Blues." Wow! The honesty and directness of Williams's voice, the simple beauty of his songs—most of them about love gone wrong. They were like nothing I'd ever heard before. I wanted to be a country singer. For me, country music had a wail that wanted to find its own and communicate with something far away. I started writing songs and would sing them to my father every few minutes. He said I turned out songs faster than Irving Berlin. But he discouraged my becoming a country musician because it would be an awful life spent traveling all night on the road to honky-tonks and other low places.

That last detail is telling. As willing as he was to feel the heat of a gutbucket swing, Winter was never much of a laid-back wanderer. He could play the showman or the clown, but inside the scrawny misfit burned a restless soul motivated by deep impulses and deep appetites to serve something larger than himself. Although Winter suffered from ridicule throughout high school, he was determined to be an exemplary student. His scholastic efforts came to fruition when he was named salutatorian at the end of senior year. Still, peace of mind was as elusive as the scattering quail. "I remember clearly the day one of the most popular and wealthy boys came over to sit with me in study hall so I could help him with an algebra problem. Out of nowhere, he said, 'You're just not college material, are you?' I asked him what he meant, and he said, 'Your parents are poor, and none of your brothers or sisters ever went to college.' Nothing changed when I was named salutatorian of my graduating class and awarded a scholarship to various private Texas colleges. Clara Tarpley, a social studies teacher, made a point in saying to the class I was enrolled in, 'I think this should be taken away from Roger and given to some other student who would use it.'"

Winter, however, had a personal trait that helped him survive such biting comments. Although he did well in school, he also possessed an inexplicable desire to look at and make pictures.

> My first love was of snapshots of relatives: parents, siblings, grandparents, aunts and uncles, cousins—and of acquaintances of relatives I would never know. The backgrounds of the snapshots had houses, dogs, trees, fences, railroad tracks, dirt roads—anything that happened to be there. My mother had two shoeboxes full of these, which went back to the late 19th century: One box from my mother's side of the family, and the other that my Grandma Winter had left in an old trunk that contained her clothes and other personal items. I constantly asked my mother to bring out the two boxes. I looked at them as often and for as long as I was allowed. This was always a private activity not to be shared with siblings and especially not with the outside world. I would ask so many questions about the people in each photo. How tall were they, what color were their eyes? Did they own horses? What kind of hair oil does this uncle use? I think I was the only one among my siblings who knew the surnames of the various branches of our relatives.[4]

He began to draw faces—his mother and father, his brothers and sisters. Winter was fascinated with family histories and memories. He savored the tintypes and anything that could be drawn or painted. "Drawing from the snapshots was something I started at a very early age, perhaps prememory," says Winter. "I learned to draw faces years before I heard the words 'art' and 'artist.' My mother would save the gray pasteboard dividers from shredded wheat boxes for me to draw on or sometimes I would use notebook paper, and a number two Ticonderoga pencil. I don't know of any other family members who drew or painted. It's almost as if I was a savant. I loved to draw to replicate

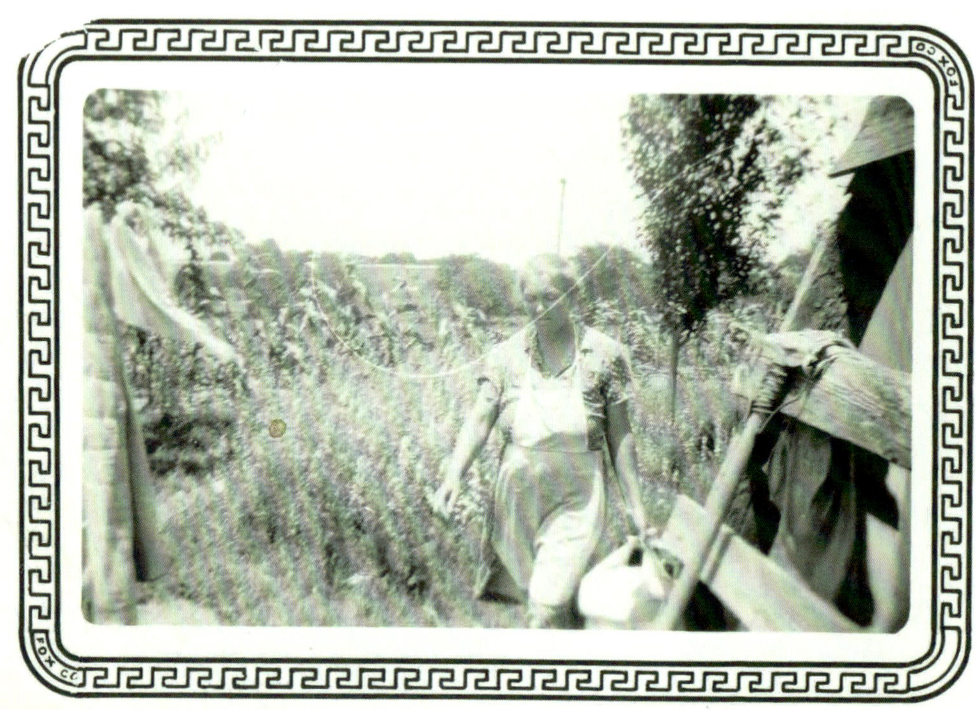

Roger's mother bringing important papers from the storm cellar

something. The box of photographs gave me a chance to daydream."

Winter's parents also owned an oversize family Bible with large, exotic illustrations, such as of Joseph's coat of many colors and David and Goliath, that he often copied. "It seems I was born with an ability to measure relative sizes, values, and angles. I could measure the light and dark; I knew the relationship of the nose and the mouth. I wasn't taught these things; I was born with them. Drawing had a certain magic for me. I decided I needed a friend, so I drew this boy on a piece of shredded wheat pasteboard. I made him look like someone who I would get along with. I thought—if I hide it and go look tomorrow, it will be a real boy. I took it to an unknown part of our property with a shack-like barn and hid it—when I went back the same drawing was there. The boy became the drawing, but also like a real boy to me."

Although Winter had never seen actual works of art, he was able to pore over magazines such as *Collier's* and *Saturday Evening Post*. "Someone would leave them with us and I could linger over them," Winter recalls. "I knew of Norman Rockwell, but don't think I saw much of his work. There was a whole crew of illustrators and looking at them would be like chewing each bite of food a hundred times. I wanted to see every part of it and think, How did they do that and could I do it? That's the reason why art has never really seemed a commercial enterprise to me. It's a calling. I didn't choose art; it chose me."

At some point early on, Winter realized that the same ability to measure faces "could be applied to arranging objects into an order—where and how something was placed to create linear rhythm, organizing things in deep space without losing the sense of a two dimensional image."[5] These arrangements included furniture, garden divisions, even tag labels that he would cut from inside the collars of clothes. "I collected labels out of people's clothes when I was a child," explains Winter. "The backs of them were colorful abstractions, though I didn't know that word at the time. I just liked the beautiful patterns. The front would have a little picture or letters, but the back was all loose threads. I had to cut them on the sly. It didn't help me get along with my siblings when they found out I cut labels out of their clothes. My older sister, Joyce, smoked Chesterfields, and she'd leave the packages around the house. I'd steal a big kitchen match and a cigarette, then crawl underneath the house, which was held up by two-by-four floor joists on the top of bois d'arc wood. I pinned up all my tags with stickpins. At nine or ten years, I was like Nelson Rockefeller, admiring my collection and smoking cigarettes. Thank God I didn't set the house on fire! It was foolish of me to smoke under a wooden house, but it made me feel like I had more power as a kid."

Winter's sisters didn't share the same neurotic concerns as his mother and never criticized him. Joyce, in fact, was fifteen when Winter was born and dropped out of high school to take care of

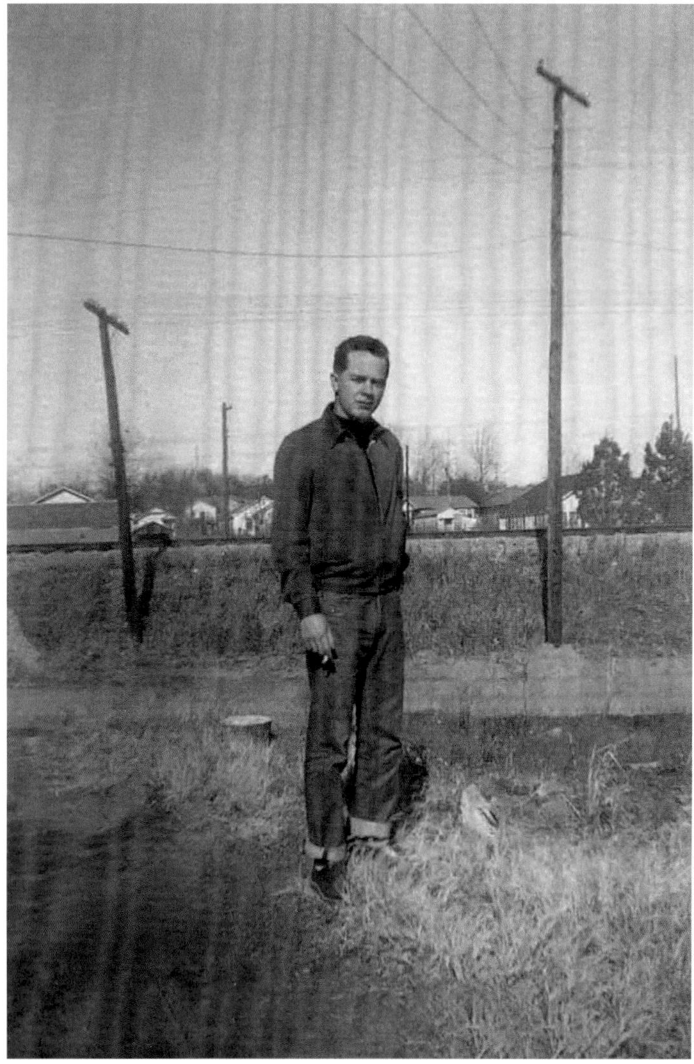

Roger standing in front of the railroad track between two telephone poles, 1953

him. It was a choice that haunted him for years. "Did my birth rob her of the education that she so deserved?" Winter wrote upon her death in 2003. "She had the dreamy spirit of an artist, and I'm sure she could have accomplished something professionally with a little early guidance. But I've also looked at it from another perspective. I give this beautiful and imaginative girl credit for my life in art. How lucky I am to have this pre-memory tutelage from someone who hates conventions as I do! Who saw life as something to be spent, not saved for a rainy day!"[6]

Winter's brothers, however, regarded him as a "sissy" and "one step away from a ballet dancer." Still, his mother and father offered encouragement, even though they knew very little about art. "One Christmas I wanted a box of oil paints that I'd seen in a Sears Roebuck catalog. It came with a bottle of linseed oil, turpentine, and a few brushes," Winter says. "My oldest brother made a special trip to our house to tell my parents they shouldn't get it for me. I remember this going down. My father said, 'He's our son and we'll get him what we want to.' And they did buy those paints for me. As it turns out, that brother became my biggest fan and was really supportive in later years." In school, the teachers and students appreciated Winter's skillful drawings from snapshots even as he isolated himself from normal participation in classroom activities. "I learned to camouflage the insecurity by making humorous remarks and pretending I wasn't serious," explains Winter. Still, the disability, constraints, and lack of freedom he endured throughout his young life hit a boiling point during his senior year.

"We had a fox terrier dog named Ricky. He wasn't well behaved and my parents kept him chained. Now and then, Ricky would break loose. You could see him a half mile away just running, looking, sniffing at everything. He would come back home, but once he was free, he wanted to make good use of that freedom. One night I came in around three in the morning—I was seventeen or so. I know now the suffering my parents experienced as they wondered where I was. My dad was awake in bed and said, 'I'd like to know what someone would be doing at this time in the morning.' I replied, 'I'm like Ricky. I've broken my chain and I have no control over myself.' He said, 'You don't know how it hurts us for you to say that.' And I said, 'Well the truth is supposed to hurt.' Now that I think about it, I know how mean that was—but I had broken free."

Winter was a young man with a deep sense of place whose vision of that place was too keen and roving for him to remain in its limits. For him, freedom was learned from walking the ground under his feet and studying the horizon that was just out of reach. It was a sense of freedom nurtured by a mix of indolence, reverie, inspiration, and a determined resistance against hopelessness. The highway, of course, symbolized that independence, as did the boxcars that seemingly stretched to infinity. "Our house was one of the first that the trains passed as they emerged from the woods," recalls Winter.

> Hoboes, would hop off the trains and ask us for food in exchange for doing chores. Sometimes they drew pictures on mailbox posts in our area to let other men know about a vicious dog, an officer of the law, or what generosities might be expected from a household. So I knew from an early age that you could ride a train. A freight train often couldn't make it all the way up the hill and would stop for a minute. One day, I climbed up one of those ladders on the boxcar and rode it up to an overpass about a quarter mile away. It started chugging faster, so I jumped off. The next stop would have been somewhere outside of Denison and my parents would have worried about me. T. S. Eliot said something in this direction: after we have done all our explorations over so many years, we finally return to where we started, but then we understand it. The endless line of the railroad was such a major part of my life for the first 17 years. I walked to school on the railroad tracks; I watched freight trains and passenger trains pass by. It's really the story of my life. During the Christmas season, the Texas Special would move by our house and all the dining cars had Christmas trees with blue lights on them. Those blue lights and the people

dressed in nice clothes sitting at tables with clean white tablecloths gave me an inkling of something larger out there. I don't know if I had more ambition than my brothers and sisters, but I probably had less fear of taking chances. I've heard the Hillbilly Appalachian expression "The only way up is out." That's the thinking that caused me to hitchhike from Denison to Austin in July of 1952. I'm glad I did, although my insecurities came with me.[7]

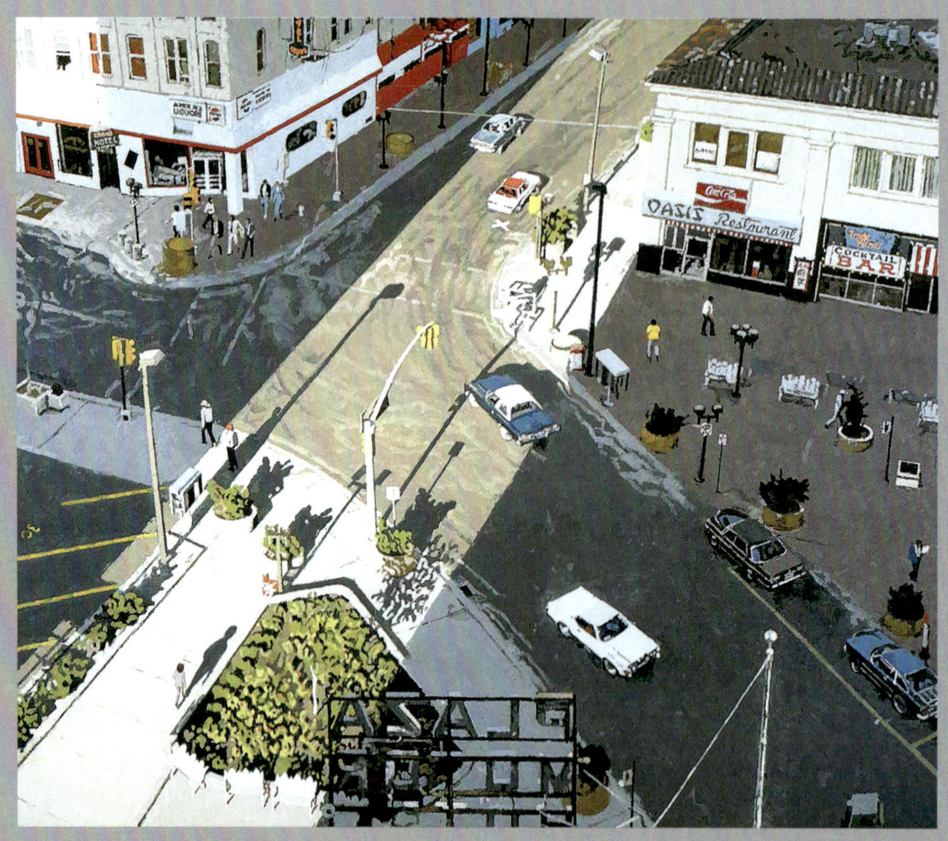

El Paso, 1983

oil on canvas | 62" × 74" (1 m 57.48 cm × 1 m 87.96 cm) |

Dallas Museum of Art, gift of Mr. and Mrs. S. Roger Horchow | 1990.184

CHAPTER 2

THE EDUCATION OF AN ARTIST, PART I

DURING WINTER'S EARLY YEARS HE grappled, or at least came to terms, with the pull between freedom and roots, as well as the hard-to-erase dissonances of family life. Along with composite portraits of the 1951 high school graduates, the *Denison Press* newspaper featured a large formal photograph of Winter on its front page. Boldface captions identified the young man with a serious demeanor as an "Honor Student" and "Salutatorian."[1] Significantly, an article in the *Denison Herald* also recognized Winter for his work on the school yearbook and his achievements as a budding young artist: "Roger has taken art for three years and has been a member of the Annual Staff for two years as assistant art editor from 1950–1951. He really can do portraits, gets four dollars for 'em too: His portrait of Sonny Wilkinson was a state winner at the Sangers show in Dallas recently."[2] Even with such public accolades, however, Winter felt separated from the community. "Because I was poor and from a lower class, you start out a step behind," Winter recalls. "You're always a little step behind."

Although Winter was restless to "find himself" and pursue uncharted territory, he chose to stay in Denison the following year and work for Donald L. Mayes, the city's leading architect. It was a decision that would change the course of his life. "Being an honor student had an accidental perk I couldn't have imagined," Winter says. "As salutatorian, I was invited to a Rotary Club luncheon and afterwards, a man introduced himself as Donald Mayes. He was an architect and needed someone with drawing skills to work for him. Since I had no plans for college, I was excited about the job. I became his draftsman. I drew the final plans for buildings and houses, made presentation drawings in two-vanishing-point perspective, and had blueprints made for each set of plans. There was one small house that Mayes let me design. I knew all his design motifs and I knew specifications, floors, walls, and roofs." For Winter, a shy, young man who was not considered "college material" by his teachers or peers, Mayes's mentoring provided the confidence needed to attend the University of Texas at Austin. "The Rotary Club loaned me five hundred dollars," recalls Winter. "Tuition was cheap and I knew how to live cheap. I hitchhiked to Austin. At Mayes's urging I pledged a fraternity and became an architecture major. I owe much of what has happened in my life to Donald Mayes. He paved the way for my leaving home."

Winter, however, never fulfilled Mayes's hope of becoming an architect. "Everything went to hell that first semester," says Winter. "I was socially trying to catch up after all those years of being an overprotected poor boy from the Katy tracks, so I was wild. I mean wild—failed two classes, got kicked out of the first room I rented, depledged the fraternity in anger. I was psychologically wounded but discovered a resilience I never knew I had."

Winter landed a job as draftsman for the Texas Legislative Council in the capitol building. One day, by chance, he went along with a friend to the art building. "It was in an old army barracks salvaged from the Second World War," according to Winter. "There was art up on the walls from the students. There was a place for drawings, a place for paintings, for graphic design and ceramics. There were real artists—they weren't dead and buried in Europe five hundred years ago—and it was the most wonderful discovery. It was an epiphany moment in my young life and I've never looked back."

It is important to note that other than visits to his grandparents' cotton farm near Como, Winter had never been more than one hundred miles away from home. However, his lack of money and social skills didn't seem to matter in the art department. His fellow art students and the impressive faculty—Robert McDonald Graham, Loren Mozley, William Lester, Everett Spruce, and Constance Forsyth—became Winter's first community beyond a bleak and depressing family life. "I could draw and paint and I was a quick study in art history," he recalls. "At least my teachers saw something worthwhile in me. No doubt, the teachers had worked with many other poor Texas kids who were smart enough to turn it all around."

Winter also became aware of the art department's formal process of working from life. His teachers regarded drawing or painting from photographs as "a sin, a crime, a disgrace of the most ignorant and tasteless kind." Yet Winter quickly found out that he could "draw from life better than ninety-nine percent of the other art students." Right out of the gate, he signed up for Boyer Gonzales's basic design class and Constance Forsyth's life drawing course. Forsyth, the first female faculty member hired by the University of Texas art department, produced paintings, drawings, and prints distinguished by a silvery, fluid, often abstract style. "I learned something the first day of Forsyth's class," Winter recalls. "I'd not drawn from life before, and I was smearing charcoal and picking out highlights with an eraser. An older student told me that 'they don't like that kind of drawing here. Look at the drawings pinned up on the walls in the hall.' I looked and looked. I saw that filling the page with the figure and using the charcoal directly was a preferred approach."

According to Winter, Forsyth had students make quick drawings to see the overall movement of the model. "In a typical three-hour class, we'd do a twenty-five-minute session of quick one-minute drawings. We'd have a short break and then maybe some five-minute drawings. By the time the morning was over, you would have done a lot of work and each one different from the others." Winter discovered Kimon Nicolaides's book *The Natural Way to Draw* and studied new concepts of gesture, contour, and weight. Winter later wrote about the impact of Forsyth's instruction in an essay for an exhibition of her work at Valley House Gallery in Dallas. "In that first drawing class, Forsyth steered me away from the superficial art ideas I arrived with and into more fertile visual ground. She taught me to ignore the surface and to look for form. 'Work on the form,' she would say, 'and let the surface take care of itself.' Often she worked on my drawings, never to give it her identity, but to redirect a line or to help me clarify a composition. She always provided nude models, and if a model didn't show we drew portraits of each other. Drawing the human form was not presented as a method of copying nature. Rather, we learned to see relationship through the study of the figure. And through the figure we learned to compose the page, to work with materials, and to stay honest."[3]

Winter recalls taking several classes from Forsyth, who was head of the printmaking department. "She seemed to care about me and guided me toward the best I could offer. She was always kind and forthcoming. She never lost her smiling patience with any of us. Her father had been a painter and she had studied at the Pennsylvania Academy of Fine Arts. She was a small woman, a chain smoker, and very strong. She lifted the heaviest lithograph stone as if it were a feather." Forsyth and senior faculty members were the first artists that Winter had ever encountered. They became surrogate parents to the aspiring artist. "They were so mature, world-wise and had studios," says Winter. "They had clear ideas about what to teach and how to teach it. Each studio class met for nine hours a week. Hard work was the key to survival. Coming to class late was not tolerated. I remember Everett Spruce telling a student, 'If you can't paint eight hours a day, then you should find something you can do eight hours a day.' I realized then that I wanted to be both an educator and an artist."

Winter studied the paintings of great artists in books at the university art library. There, he discovered the French Post-Impressionist master Edouard Vuillard, who used unnatural color, boldly exaggerated shapes, and distorted space to emphasize that his paintings were expressions of feelings and imagination. Winter became inspired by the artist's approach to everyday reality, appreciating his ability to paint events from the life of his family and friends in a highly personal way. "It was love at first sight," recalls Winter. "Here were paintings that, for the first time, understood the feelings of intimacy—although I didn't know that word at the time—I'd felt with almost everything. Intimate colors are close in value. Intimate edges overlap or don't quite reach, a silent closeness." Winter also studied the work of seventeenth-century Dutch painter Johannes Vermeer. "He gave a mystery to the commonplace, painting each square inch with the same care as any other square inch. That thoroughness appealed to me, and I saw it as somewhat of a rebellion toward the 'hot spots' of some paintings—even Rembrandts."

Just as Winter seemed to be making headway in the art department, however, tragedy struck the family at the end of his first year in Austin. Winter's brother David, a petty officer in the US Naval Air Force, was killed in a plane accident off an aircraft carrier near Hawaii.

> We had been inseparable growing up—we slept in the same bed, went to the outdoor toilet together, got drunk together. What an introduction to death. I was eighteen. He had turned twenty-one. I was lost. After his funeral, my sister Joyce asked if I would like to come live with her made-with-spare-parts family in Philadelphia. I got a job quickly as a draftsman for a commercial kitchen equipment factory, which was two streetcar rides from my sister's row house in "Brewery Town." His death set me back eight months. It could have been for good. I returned to Denison with the intention of joining the army. But my brother Ed got to the recruiting sergeant before I did and told him to talk me out of it and encourage me to go back to UT. What a wonderful brotherly act! I returned to Austin, reentered the art department, and got a job with the Calcasieu Lumber Company. From this point on, I was a top student. I stayed enrolled continuously until I graduated in the summer of 1956 with honors.

Winter looked forward to seeing the paintings of Constance Forsyth, Loren Mozley, Robert McDonald Graham, William Lester, and Everett Spruce in the faculty exhibitions. He would spend hours analyzing the work, comparing the soft brushstrokes of Forsyth and Graham or the angular structures in paintings by Mozley, Lester, and Spruce. The vital roles of Winter's teachers at the University of Texas and their subsequent impact on his development as an artist cannot be overstated. Their steadfast encouragement, patience, and support enabled Winter to follow an individualized path of stylistic growth and change. As it happens, Winter was front and center to a core group of the Southwest's leading artist-educators. Graham had studied with Thomas Hart Benton at the Kansas City Art Institute. His early paintings often emulated the American Scene artist's sinewy figures amid landscapes of cadenced contours and vigorous, earthy hues. Mozley's impressions of painting and its processes and his attitude toward the representation of nature were formed during his many years in Taos, New

Mexico, and through close friendship with such luminaries as Georgia O'Keeffe, Andrew Dasburg, Victor Higgins, Ward Lockwood, and John Marin. His dialogue with the works of Paul Cézanne and the Cubist painters turned into a lifelong commitment. Marked by painterly exuberance and physicality, Mozley's carefully honed and faceted structures cohered as lush vignettes of specific Austin sites. During the 1930s and early 1940s, Lester and Spruce were integral to a group of young Dallas painters, including Jerry Bywaters, Alexandre Hogue, Otis Dozier, and others who advocated their own brand of regionalism that drew inspiration mainly from the Texas landscape.[4] Lester focused on the abstract qualities of nature in orchestrated compositions of jagged lines, rich colors, and balanced, geometric forms. Spruce, however, viewed nature as a source of mystery and a vehicle for his display of expressionistic brushstrokes, striking planar contrasts, and precise tactile transitions. Both developed highly personal iconographies that included old houses and rugged terrain—rock, trees, and birds—as well as people at work. Their observations of the Texas landscape, sharpened and experienced, identified its varying moods and topographic structures.

Significantly, all of these artist-educators had broken through the limitations of provincialism and attained national recognition. For Winter, their presence at the University of Texas represented a dynamic period of intellectual and creative ferment. "They showed me that teaching *was* a very serious vocation," Winter says. "You didn't mess around with it. You were helping someone grow and transform the way one thought about things. I did get to the point where I saw them as perhaps too much related to one place and to each other—a sort of Cubism. But that was OK. It didn't worry me; it didn't make me love them less. If a student never surpasses the teacher, then art is not moving forward."

More important, the art professors taught Winter about structure. "I learned how a painting holds together two-dimensionally. Everything had to be in the right place—how to locate space in relation to the canvas or page, and in relation to the edge. How does the figure relate to top and bottom, left and right sides? Is it a dynamic use of that space? When you choose a piece of paper, you've already started a drawing, because you've put certain limitations on it. You've given it a certain room to fit in. You have to use that two-dimensional plane. They taught me that every mark you make must relate to those four sides."

About his first painting teacher, Robert McDonald Graham, Winter recalls,

> After studying with Thomas Hart Benton, he lived in Paris and, young as he was, had a deep love for painting and teaching. He fraternized with his students by having parties at his house near Lake Austin. At one party, he announced, "All of you know that Roger has a softer touch with a brush than I do." My God, that kept me going for years, whether it was true or false—the fact that he would say it in front of other students was very good teaching in my case. He encouraged me to paint personal subjects. He taught me how to tie things together with shapes. In his house were two of his paintings that influenced me: a small one of a burglar wearing a mask in a dark room and with a small open bag of shiny jewels; and one essentially abstract work that he painted while listening to flamenco music. Another student and I would play guitars and sing at his parties, and Graham would sing along with us. He encouraged me to make a painting of singers playing guitars. I did, but it looked a little too much like a Ben Shahn, and he pointed that out. He continued to critique my paintings even after I was no longer in his class.

By Winter's account, Graham also organized field trips to get students out of the classroom. One Sunday, Graham took Winter and three others to the Marion Koogler McNay Art Museum (now McNay Art Museum), the Spanish Colonial Revival residence in San Antonio that became Texas' first museum of modern art. It was Winter's first experience in an art museum. "The El Greco painting—*Head of Christ* [ca. 1579–1586]—was the first painting from Europe's history I'd ever seen," recalls Winter. "I was struck by its dark colors and intense light and by the reality of the paint on the surface, despite its age. The whole outing was great. While I admired all my teachers, Graham was more idealistic and less concerned about overteaching than the others. When I started teaching, I remembered how important this was to me as a young person eager to learn about art and what I could bring to art."

About Loren Mozley, Winter recalls signing up for his drawing class in sophomore year and developing a close relationship with the artist from that point on.

> I think Constance Forsyth had more sense of the gestures, while Loren Mozley's focused on structure. He could really put together every square inch of a painting in a way that could never be broken. He was a sound teacher and, for me, a father figure in the way he seemed proud of the work I was doing. He always found time to play chess with me. When Mozley suggested I might want to attend his summer classes in Mexico City, I remember the thrill of thinking, "My God! My horizons are expanding." I couldn't afford to go to Mexico City, but what a thrill to be thought capable of that. He was concerned with my economic state, so he sent a portrait commission my way that could have been his. After grading periods, Mozley would always make sure that works of mine were displayed on the hallway walls. Mozley, Forsyth, and Graham were among my role models when I started teaching. I learned through them that teaching was an ancient and noble profession and not to be used simply as a way to support a studio.[5]

Conversely, Winter recalls that William Lester was "always there for a student but seemed to be afraid of overteaching and normally limited his comments to local criticisms." However, Winter adds, "He was all painter, a mature man and easy to be around. He was king of the fractured landscape in Texas art, and he no doubt helped me in putting colors and space division together in a workable way. But he kept his distance as a teacher. Perhaps he lacked the experience with art teachers and institutions that made him comfortable with teaching art. Once I asked him if my painting was too much influenced by his, and he answered that his paintings were hard and crystalline, whereas my work was lyrical through my feeling for light. He used to say that color was hue, value, and intensity. I've always remembered that, and I thank him for it."

Although Winter took only one class with Everett Spruce, he greatly admired the artist-professor throughout his four years at the University of Texas. "He was the real deal as a painter," says Winter.

> But he had a telegraphic way of writing that influenced me more than his painting. Mr. Spruce was grumpy on the surface and never wasted a word. But inside he was generous and thoughtful. Before I left Austin, he said, "You're one of our only favorite students who can paint figures and I hope you follow through with it. The figure is and always has been the strongest symbol in painting. Just think of figures doing something." One day, he told me that he had a red hawk that had been stuffed and would bring it in if I wanted to make a painting of it. I was flattered, and he brought it in the next day—my last painting before I went in the army. No idea what happened to it, but I like to think he kept it. Spruce was the most respected painter in Austin—perhaps in Texas—at the time. And although I didn't know him as well as Mozley, Forsyth, and Graham, I looked up to him and his work. Spruce once told me, "Technique is something you have to teach yourself." I took him at his word.

Significantly, Winter cites *The Painter's Eye*, by Maurice Grosser, as a major influence in expanding his aesthetic viewpoint and stimulating dialogue among fellow undergraduates.[6] Grosser, a painter known for his picturesque landscapes, still lifes, and portraits, was also a writer and art critic. He moved in a circle of avant-garde authors and musicians, working alongside Virgil Thomson and Gertrude Stein on two operas: *Four Saints in Three Acts* (1934) and *The Mother of Us All* (1947). He spent long periods traveling abroad—Morocco, Greece, Spain, North Africa, Brazil—but also in New England, California, and New Mexico, where he developed a close friendship with Georgia O'Keeffe. Grosser often turned to writing to express personal perspectives of the artist at work. *The Painter's Eye*—the first of four volumes covering the themes, principles, and methods from the Renaissance to the 1960s—became Winter's indispensable guide for many years. "At UT's art department, my best friend, John Rhodes, and I loved to talk about painting and we often visited over a beer," explains Winter. "Maurice Grosser's book *The Painter's Eye* was a frequent source of conversation during our final semester. Grosser talked about things that we had never heard about in a painting class. He wrote about paint itself. He wrote about painting from a model in great detail. We found reproductions of some of his paintings and tried to see how they fit his words." Winter has kept his dog-eared 1956 copy of Grosser's book. The starred and underlined passages give us clues as to what Winter was thinking about and learning or absorbing from Grosser's vast experience. He highlighted an especially forthright statement on portraiture: "A portrait may be well or ill and still succeed. But if it does not present a convincing likeness of the sitter, it is not a successful portrait."[7] And this: "Four to eight feet is the portrait distance. At this distance the painter is near enough so that his eyes have no trouble in understanding the sitter's solid forms, yet he is far enough away so that the foreshortening of the forms presents him no real problem. Here, at the normal distance of social intimacy and easy conversation, the sitter's soul begins to appear."[8] Winter also marked Grosser's comments on the introduction of oils and their tremendous upheaval in painting. "In the hands of the Venetians, oil painting turned into something quite different from any other sort of painting that had ever been done before. It lost every tempera characteristic and became a large, free, and easy way of painting, which oil provides today. Venetian pictures were not improvised. They were planned in advance. They began with drawing. These drawings were not exercises in skill. They were the plans made by the painter for his work."[9]

Winter admired Grosser's great knowledge of European painting, his ability to cultivate the high art communities of his time, his curiosity about the world, and the breadth of his intelligence. "Maurice Grosser was my hero," Winter says.

> I loved my teachers, but Grosser was more sophisticated. He wrote about colors and how far you should be from the model when you're painting. He introduced me to vermillion and mars violet, which I still use. He was enamored of an earlier age and aesthetic positions: you mix your own paints, you learn all you can from the great schools of Europe. He knew all that was good and revolutionary about the Venetian painters. He understood which colors were fugitive, the degree of opacity or transparency the various pigments had by their very nature. I think the scope of his writings gave me the possibility of moving around—not just staying in one place or being a one-trick pony. I've never claimed to have learned as much as Grosser knew, but he gave me the authority to work in ways that weren't necessarily popular. He seemed "honest." I went in the army the day after my last class at the University of Texas, and I took Grosser's book with me.

Upon receiving his undergraduate degree, Winter's draft classification changed from 4-A to 1-A. Rather than "hang around" and wait to be drafted or postpone the army to after graduate school, Winter decided to volunteer. "All of us in that group were flown to Fort Bliss, El Paso, for basic training. The draftees and all the cadre seemed

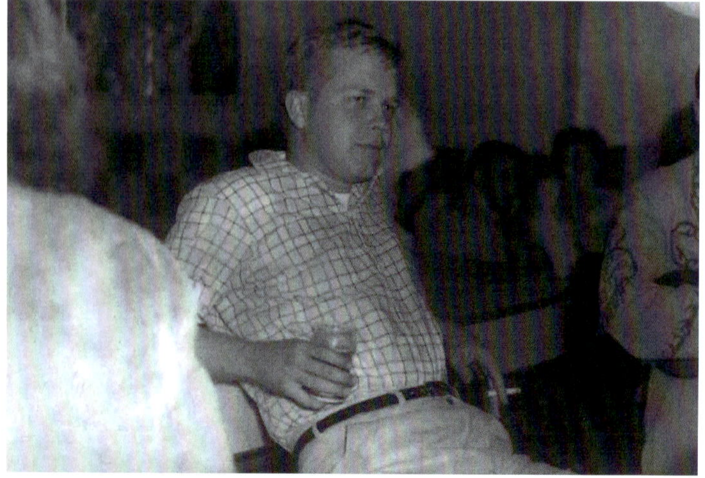

Roger at Fort Bliss in a Juárez bar

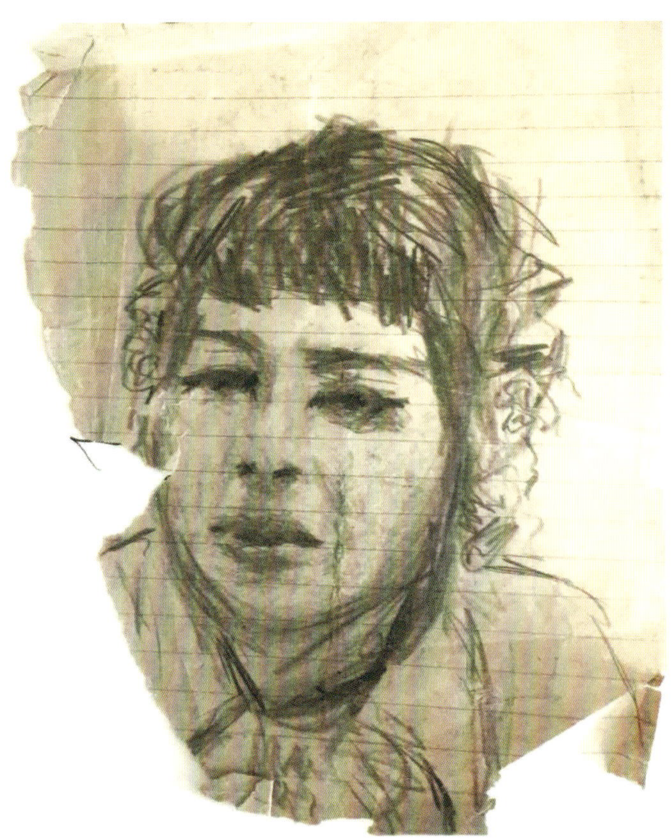

Drawing of a prostitute, 1957

so ignorant and immature to me. It was quite a test to live in a barracks with the trainees and take screamed orders from those in charge. But it would have been far more difficult after graduate school. Although there was no war anywhere in 1956–58, our trainers promised war and taught us to use weapons aggressively. I was never aggressive enough and once had to stand in front of the battery thrusting my bayonet and growling! For me, it was a humiliating experience." According to Winter, the army barracks was no place to pursue painting. At night, Winter and his army buddies often drank beers and listened to mariachi music in the "sin city" bars of Juárez. Since he had a college degree, however, Winter was sent to clerk school, where he learned to type. "I wrote all the letters for the battery commander and first sergeant. I wrote the morning report, the charges on each court-martial, the schedules for KP [kitchen patrol] duty and guard duty. I got so interested in writing that it became a substitute for painting and drawing. I read every book on how to write from the El Paso library."

Perhaps influenced by his father's social consciousness, Winter corresponded with Senator Lyndon Baines Johnson regarding improper training methods used in the reserve forces. In a letter to Johnson dated January 29, 1958, Winter writes, "The significant failings of the program result from a few strange and inexplicable policies created at some remote echelon. An example of the harm of one such policy can be found in our battalion this moment. Eight of our Non-Commissioned officers are walking Private of the Guard every fourth day while two hundred privates receive an eight-week recapitulation of their preceding two months' training. Why isn't this group of reserve privates qualified for guard duty, a necessary and fundamental military detail?"[10]

Winter may have been pushing back against the system, but his missives to Johnson also defied the structure of army protocol. "I complained that the short-term reserves were being coddled, while those of us in the army for a longer period had to do their guard duty, their KP, and all sorts of horrible things," explains Winter. "I got in serious trouble for writing those letters. I was sent to the main Fort Bliss office and put before brigadier generals and colonels. I was nothing—and could have been court-martialed. They had prepared a letter to Senator Johnson for me to sign, which said that everything I told him wasn't true; that the army is right; and I was sorry for writing to him. Well, I've also got a kind of cockiness, so I agreed to sign only if they let me edit it first. I took the letter and very meticulously crossed through every line, then signed my name at the bottom. I returned to my barracks, but was mistreated by the officers running the battalion from then on. I wasn't exactly suicidal, but it was a terrible period in my life. I felt that I'd never get out of this and maybe I just shouldn't go on."

Still, the traumatic experience only bolstered Winter's social and political resolve. He comes off as a courageous individual who does not shy away from hot-button issues. His deep sensitivity and strong opinions would be instrumental as an artist-educator. In universities as well as the mainstream art world, he gained respect for championing the unexpected and the individual as opposed to the predictable and institutional.

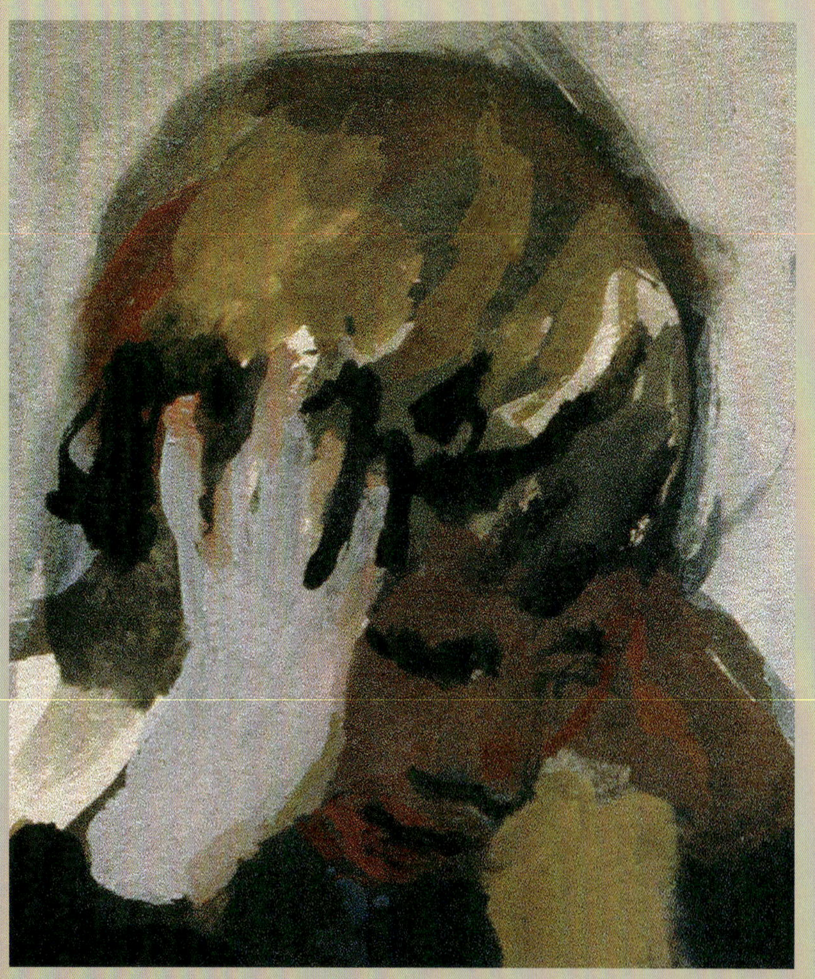

Jeanette (detail), 1960
casein on mat board | 12 1/2" x 9" |
Collection of the artist

CHAPTER 3

THE EDUCATION OF AN ARTIST, PART 2

WHILE STILL IN THE ARMY, Winter sought advice from University of Texas faculty artists William Lester and John Gruen about applying to graduate school. Both suggested the University of Iowa (at the time known as the State University of Iowa), which already held an indisputable track record in arts education. Under the direction of Princeton-trained Lester D. Longman, the innovative program was founded on the "Iowa idea" of combining studio and art history.[1] Moreover, the University of Iowa was one of the first American universities to hire professional artists as professors. Grant Wood, a leading figure in the Regionalist art movement, was on the faculty from 1934 to 1941. Philip Guston, who would become a leading New York School painter, was part of the faculty between 1941 and 1945. Byron Burford, a student under Wood and Guston, was appointed to the faculty in 1947 and would go on to represent the United States in the 1968 Venice Biennale. The University of Iowa was also among the first universities to establish the master's of fine art degree as a standard for graduate study in the arts. In 1940, the sculptor and printmaker Elizabeth Catlett was the "first person, first woman, and first African-American to receive the M.F.A. degree." According to the university, "Owing to the influx of returning veterans on the G.I. Bill, the University of Iowa conferred more graduate arts degrees in the post-war period than any other university."[2] Moreover, for Winter, it seemed to be "an academically sound place to study painting" and "the best place as far as getting a job afterward." He applied, was accepted, and moved to Iowa City in 1958 upon being discharged from the army. However, by the time he had arrived at the university, Longman, Wood, and Guston had left, their studio positions filled by the painters Eugene Ludins, Stuart Edie, and James Lechay and the printmaker Mauricio Lasansky. "The department had become aesthetically conservative," recalls Winter. "And I'm speaking of the faculty as well as the student body. Something residual from Regionalism caused the faculty and older students to think of Texas painters as slick and mannered and superficial. So I started with two strikes against me. In addition, having been out of school for two years, I had an uphill battle trying to survive in this negative zeitgeist." According to Winter, the only acceptable style for Iowa painting students was a "pre-pop painterly realism." Winter recalls that professors advocated "a mixture of formal and figurative work, with closely valued hues. No bright colors or contrasts. Abstract Expressionism, nonobjectivity, or anything that looked like it might be new was taboo in the art department. They really tried to reposition you in the past. Creativity was seemingly held in contempt. There was very little positive criticism. Nobody cared if you came to class or not. Teachers would say terribly mean things to the painters. Something about the teaching at Iowa was the opposite of the University of Texas, which had given me the love of the artist-teacher and a sense of place—how a person or place can become part of what you're doing. Iowa taught me a lot about what was *not* good. I fought with the teachers, especially James Lechay, who always called me 'boy.' I felt that I was once again at the bottom of the barrel."

Winter considered leaving Iowa but was determined to "get back up" and "learn from the negative example." Significantly, it was in his first class with Eugene Ludins that Winter also met the quiet, intelligent young woman with whom he would spend a lifetime. As Winter tells it, Ludins asked a fellow student, Jeanette Ragner, if she would pose for the class for pay, in addition to attending one of his other sections for credit. "I had painted her twice before we ever spoke," Winter says. "I liked everything about her, so one day during her break from posing, I asked her if she would like to go to lunch with me after class. She said yes. That was autumn of 1958. And we have been together ever since. Asking her to lunch was the smartest thing I ever did."

Significantly, Winter credits their meeting with turning his life around. Just two months out of the army, Winter was still accustomed to wearing army-issue fatigue paints and combat boots. "Jeanette helped me shop for new clothes. I loved her advice and followed it. No girl had ever taken this much interest in me, or at least no girl of whom I was so enamored. Although I was five years older than Jeanette, she had more worldly knowledge than I because she had grown up in a large city with important cultural centers that she had frequented throughout her teens."

Ragner was born and raised in Chicago, where her parents had settled upon emigrating from Sweden. During her high school years, she studied at the Art Institute of Chicago and worked with the multimedia visionary artist June Leaf. "Painting was not her interest and she had planned on attending Pratt Institute, but was a bit afraid of striking out on her own in New York City," says Winter. "After visiting the campus, she felt comfortable in Iowa City. At the time, it was a charming town where houses had birthdays. The university had dormitories near the lovely campus on the Iowa River. A footbridge crossed over the river to the art building. But in the art school, Jeanette found teachers who were unable to teach her what she wanted to learn about—the graphic design world and illustration." Nevertheless, Ragner stayed on, encouraging Winter's talents and nurturing his self-confidence. In turn, Jeanette became his muse and model even as she urged him out of his "rough-cut manner."

About their courtship at the University of Iowa, Winter recalls,

> We saw each other every day, and we didn't seem to need other people or a social group in our lives. We became a couple. A graduate student told me that people thought we resembled the boy and girl on the Dutch weather clock. We shared our knowledge of jazz with each other. We played records by Anita O'Day, Sarah Vaughan, Chet Baker, and a half dozen others. We talked about painting and drawing. I discovered Jeanette had her own ideas about art that were not always in sympathy with the faculty and other older students in the Iowa art department. But Jeanette had a fortuitous experience. One evening, a graduate student invited us to dinner at her apartment. When it was time to leave, a violent spring storm arrived and we were stranded. As entertainment, our host took out some children's books by the great English illustrator Kate Greenaway, whom neither of us knew about at the time. Jeanette was so excited by them. I think it was an

> epiphany moment that led her to illustrate and author more than seventy books.

The importance of the crossflow of aesthetic sensibilities between the two artists cannot be overemphasized. From the beginning and throughout their long marriage, Jeanette's fortitude and keen perspective would have an indelible impact on the development of Winter's art. Significantly, he would go on to draw or paint her likeness thousands of times over the next six decades.

During his first year in Iowa, Winter shared an apartment with Frank Sampson, one of Mauricio Lasansky's assistants. Sampson was more mature, at least seven years older than Winter, with a promising career ahead as an artist and teacher. "Toward the end of the spring semester I asked Frank what I needed to learn in my work. He thought that I should 'learn what a line can do.' At the time, my drawing was all soft edges and all light." At the end of the 1959 spring semester, Winter returned to Denison and worked at the Johns-Manville plant, where he taped the joints on sewer pipes with soft putty. He was offered several portrait commissions. All of the subjects were children, mostly girls, and rendered in pastel. More important, he made dozens of line drawings of vegetables, plants, and his mother, nephews, and nieces. Winter also drew Jeannette, who rode the train from Chicago to Denison for a visit. "It was the summer while we were still dating," Winter recalls.

> I picked her up at the train station and she walked over to the water fountain for a drink. She was puzzled by two fountains; one had a sign that said Colored; the other said White. Jeanette had never seen anything like this and asked, "What colors are the water?" I had some explaining to do. After she left, I quit my job to work on portrait commissions. I charged thirty-five dollars each and made enough money to buy a 1953 Chevrolet, which I drove back to Iowa City. I had discovered in Constance Forsyth's printmaking class at UT that I could make up groups of children playing outside. This was a subject that Forsyth and my friends seemed to like, but it was also a compositional grouping that I recovered during that summer break from Iowa. Shapes of clothing and hairstyles and movement helped me relate to the painters of the past, like [Nicolas] Poussin, or even [Francisco] Goya's painting of children being bounced in a blanket. Everything I drew that summer was with a line. I started using line to divide the space or page. When I returned the next semester, I showed all the drawings to Lasansky, who was my printmaking teacher. I learned a lot about things you shouldn't do when I was at Iowa and "too sweet" was one of them. I asked Lasansky if some of my drawings were too sweet or sentimental. He answered, "They're not sweet. They're tender and you can't buy tender at the corner drugstore." Lasansky was so impressed by the drawings that he told me, "An angel was guiding your hand." His comment opened the door for me. Lasansky also taught me that a portrait should look like someone looks all their life—not just a certain age, but how they look at five and at fifty years of age. It's the same essence, a kind of psychological perception which I learned could not be transferred to things—a house, a dog. Drawing became my native tongue. And in a sense, drawing is still what I do. Whether on a piece of paper or canvas, it's concerned with all the aspects of drawing—like placing the periphery of the surface; the relationship of values; the measurement of proportions—and the relation of shape to shape to periphery. I think it's about empathy. You have to become what you're drawing or painting—"feel into" is the term Nicolaides used. The concept of drawing has changed over the years. Now drawing is an idea or a noun. But I learned about it as a verb. I don't think the light ever vanished from my work, but I think it was strengthened that summer from finding out what a line could do.

At the same time, Winter also began to pursue distinctly compelling approaches to the world around him. He discovered "how to let paint happen." Stuart Edie, whom Winter chose as his studio chair for the semester, taught the young artist about the value of color. Winter also recalls the modern art history professor Li showing a slide from Max Ernst's *Une semaine de bonté*, an engraving of a man and woman walking along, with the man's head replaced by that of a lion—thus introducing Winter to a form of surrealist collage that juxtaposed unrelated images. Moreover, he traveled to major museums in the Northeast. The exhibitions, permanent collections, and individual works added important layers to his ongoing development as an artist. He recalls taking the train to Chicago in 1959 to see an exhibition of paintings, drawings, prints, and sculptures of the French Post-Impressionist Paul Gauguin at the Art Institute. "From the Gauguin show, I remember most the impact of a personality that made these works. Seeing so many paintings by one artist—the evocations of mood, the arrangements of form, color, balance, and movement—especially of Gauguin's stature, conveys so much more than a random work here and there. But at that point, I was also amazed at the linear possibilities of painting in his hands." Winter made an additional trip to Chicago, this time piling in a car with four or five grad students to see paintings by Richard Diebenkorn, David Park, and Elmer Bischoff. The three artists from San Francisco came to prominence in the mid-1950s, the heyday of Abstract Expressionism, as practitioners of what came to be called Bay Area figurative painting. At the time, young artists everywhere were concerned about how abstraction and image could be presented simultaneously—how to get the human but also preserve the intensity of nonobjective painting. Diebenkorn, Park, and Bischoff bridged both. Diebenkorn, especially, made line a human abstraction. His still lifes and figures from this period reveal how he began to see objects as possessing lines that organize space into separately differentiated and guarded units. All three painters built solid compositions in which gestural spontaneity and chromatic atmosphere made peace with an architectural sense of order. Their fluent gestures, as well as taut balance of color and line, struck a chord with Winter, who was also aiming for a dramatic intensity that seemed to build within the painting itself. "Like most young painters of the time, the works of the Bay Area artists had enormous impact on me," says Winter. "These painters found a legitimate path beyond action painting, perhaps by going through it to the other side."

By his own admission, however, Winter was still very naive—even after two years at the University of Iowa. "The professors didn't teach about Constructivism or anything much that was recent. I thought I needed to learn more about geometry, which, without my knowing it at the time, would become part of my 'handwriting.' The artist I looked to is Marsden Hartley. I had seen reproductions of his paintings and thought they were put together in a geometric way—more than just a painting from a figure." Winter made a trip to the Cedar Rapids Museum of Art, where he saw Hartley's *Young Sea Dog with Friend Billy* (1942), the final painting in a group of distinctive figure compositions—lobstermen, lumberjacks, hunters, and athletes—that were produced during his late Maine period. Here, Hartley presents an idealized self-portrait, an imposing, saintlike figure with sensuous, piercing blue eyes and a rooster perched on his shoulder. "I was fascinated by that bird," Winter recalls. "I brought up Marsden Hartley to my painting teacher, Stuart Edie. He had lived in New York City before coming to Iowa and said when Marsden Hartley would go to the Metropolitan Museum he was known for walking up the steps in an eloquent manner with a long purple sash trailing behind him. I thought, here is a strong painter who wore foppish clothes. He was very effeminate and proud of it. How different from the way he painted. It opened up my mind in terms of subject matter. I wanted my work to have that solid, chunky quality."

Each graduate student in the Iowa art department was required to write a thesis supervised by an art history professor. Winter's thesis, "Vermeer and the Critics," under the direction of Wallace Tomasini, examined Johannes Vermeer's relation with the art world during his lifetime in the seventeenth century and through modern times. "I compared his sense of arrangement with Japanese ukiyo-e prints that wrapped pottery—and which he may well

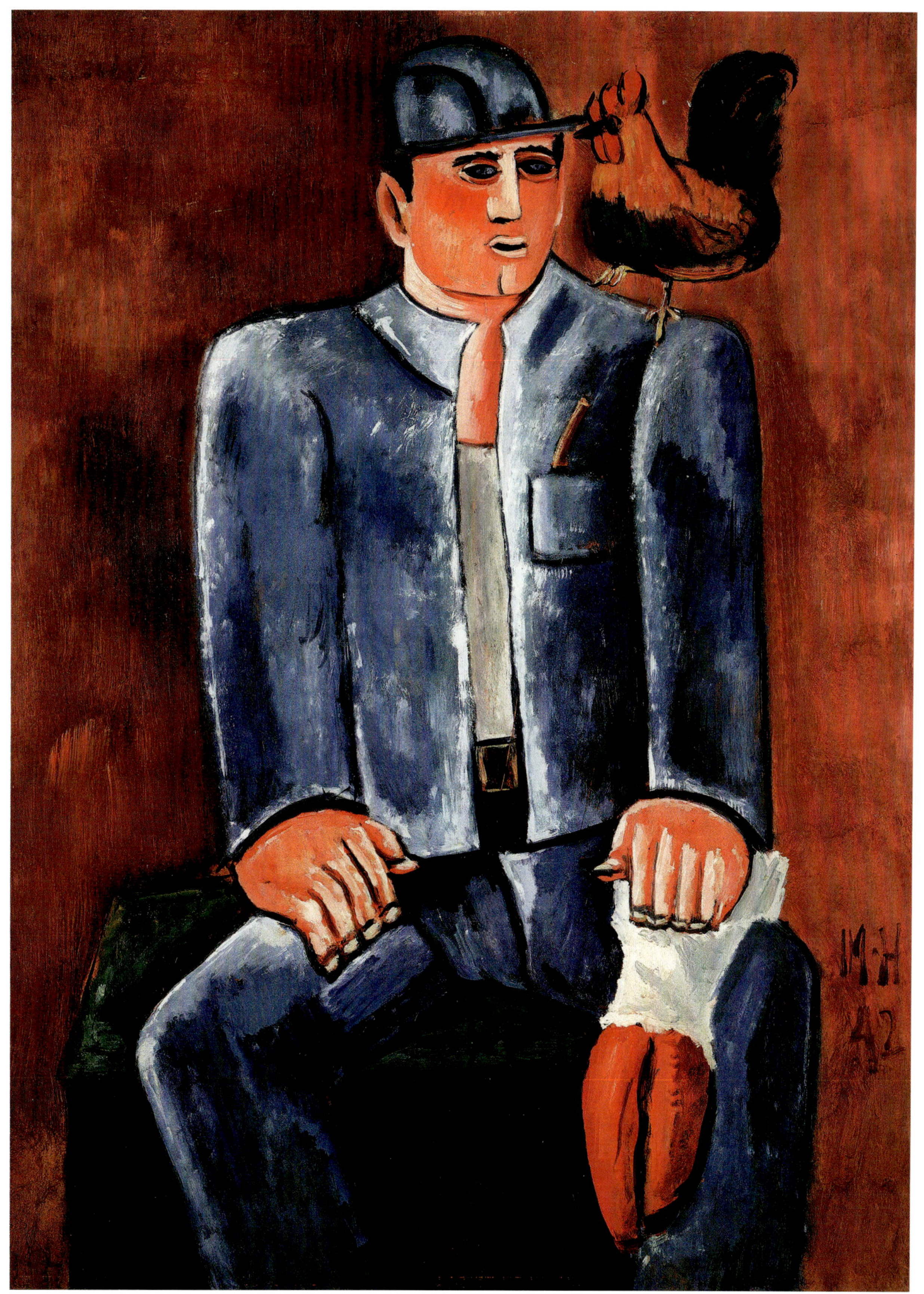

Marsden Hartley, *Young Sea Dog with Friend Billy,* 1942
oil on board | 40" × 30" | Private collection, courtesy of Alexandre Gallery, New York

have seen, since they were exchanged with Delft blue-and-white ceramics. These prints, of course, had great influence on the nineteenth-century French painters in the last half of the century. I also compared him with his fellow countryman, the twentieth-century Dutch artist Piet Mondrian. Both arranged the canvas space in the most beautiful way they could invent, despite the surface differences. Since 1958, I have had Vermeer's *The Milkmaid*, in the form of one poster reproduction or another, in the space where I work. There's a stillness in a Vermeer painting of a moment caught. It has such a wonderful formal rhythm—very close to perfection. The small dots on the blue-and-white jug are repeated in the bread, on her buttons, on her nose, lip, and chin."

Overall, the inroads Winter made during his second year in the graduate program would form his own center of interest and direction for several years. He and Jeanette were married in Chicago in April 1960. "My paintings and drawings of Jeanette, as well as other subjects, were the talk of the school. Some of the professors bought caseins I'd done of Iowa City subjects. Roy Sieber, the renowned African art scholar, even had Jeanette and me over for dinner with his family to show how he had framed the two caseins he bought. I had a painting accepted in the Iowa Annual. What a change it was from the first miserable year in Iowa City! But school, any school, is insular. The real world, like a raptor, was out there waiting for me."

For Winter, electric new currents were "in the air" and they infiltrated and took hold. The avant-garde film *Black Orpheus*, which Winter saw in an Iowa City theater, became an important touchstone for the artist. The mythical love story retold in the modern-day setting of Rio de Janeiro's carnival was rife with exotic costumes and masks, bossa nova music, and frenetic dancing. Its all-black cast and surreal montages—jump cuts that went back and forth in time and between heaven and earth—burrowed deep in Winter's psyche. "I remember so well the scene of Orpheus carrying the dead Eurydice through a landscape, then leaping off a cliff and landing in the embrace of a huge tropical plant. It changed the landscape of my mind. That film was among the earliest seeds of mixing time and places. *Black Orpheus* was such a poetic blend of reality and fantasy of life, death, and rebirth. It helped me look for subjective answers in my painting." Accordingly, a number of Winter's early works convey a sense of constant flux and perpetual motion. His portraits of Jeanette painted during the final semester at Iowa are gestural and layered with loosely transparent slips of paint anchored by a scaffolding of geometric shapes. Another portrait depicts Winter's and Jeanette's reflections in a mirror that, in turn, becomes part of a still life. Here, Winter renders simultaneous and competing notions of space. "It shows the painting on the painting that I'm painting," Winter explains. "It was a very spontaneous, complex work at the time—potentially like the girl on the Morton Salt box who is carrying the same box."

Conversely, *Comedy*, chosen by Stuart Edie as Winter's thesis painting, is among his first ventures into expressive context, with figures and animals either floating or anchored in luminous, ambiguous landscapes. Winter's style was dramatically changing to a "meatier," vigorous, gestural painting characterized by dynamic paths of movement, lush surfaces, and dissonant color. Significantly, *Comedy* exemplifies many of the general features that would mark his approach to painting for the next decade.

Winter was thus ready for a more challenging and stimulating environment. As he approached the completion of his MFA degree, he applied for and received a Max Beckmann Memorial Scholarship from the Brooklyn Museum Art School. "Jeanette and I both wanted to move to New York City, and the scholarship was something to tell her parents. I was tired of schools and the regimentation of the army. In the summer of 1960, we drove to New York City in my '53 Chevrolet. The car was loaded inside and on the roof with all our possessions, and we had no idea where to stay when we got there. Both of us just wanted to be on our own in the world's greatest art center."

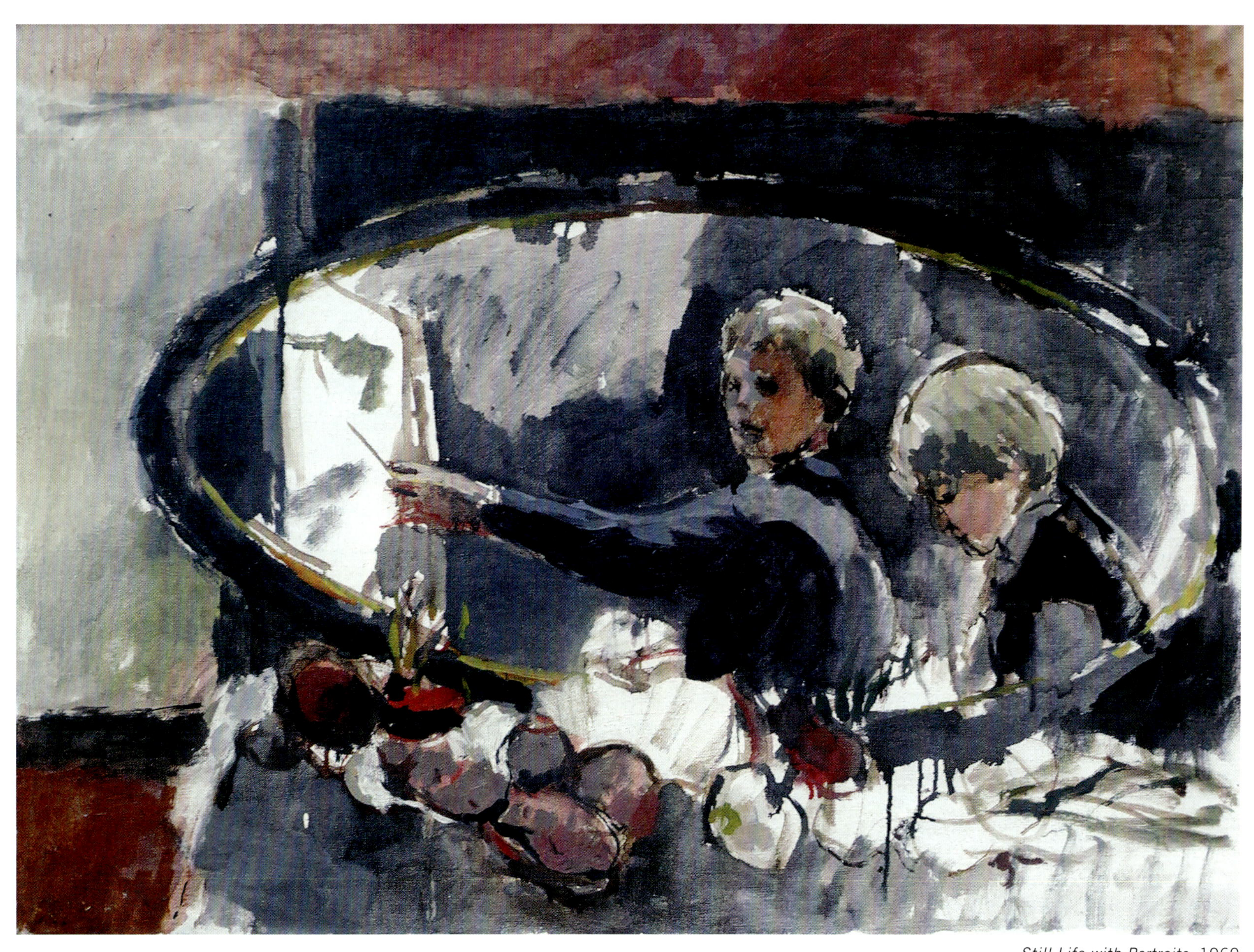

Still Life with Portraits, 1960
oil on canvas | 22" × 30" | Collection of the artist

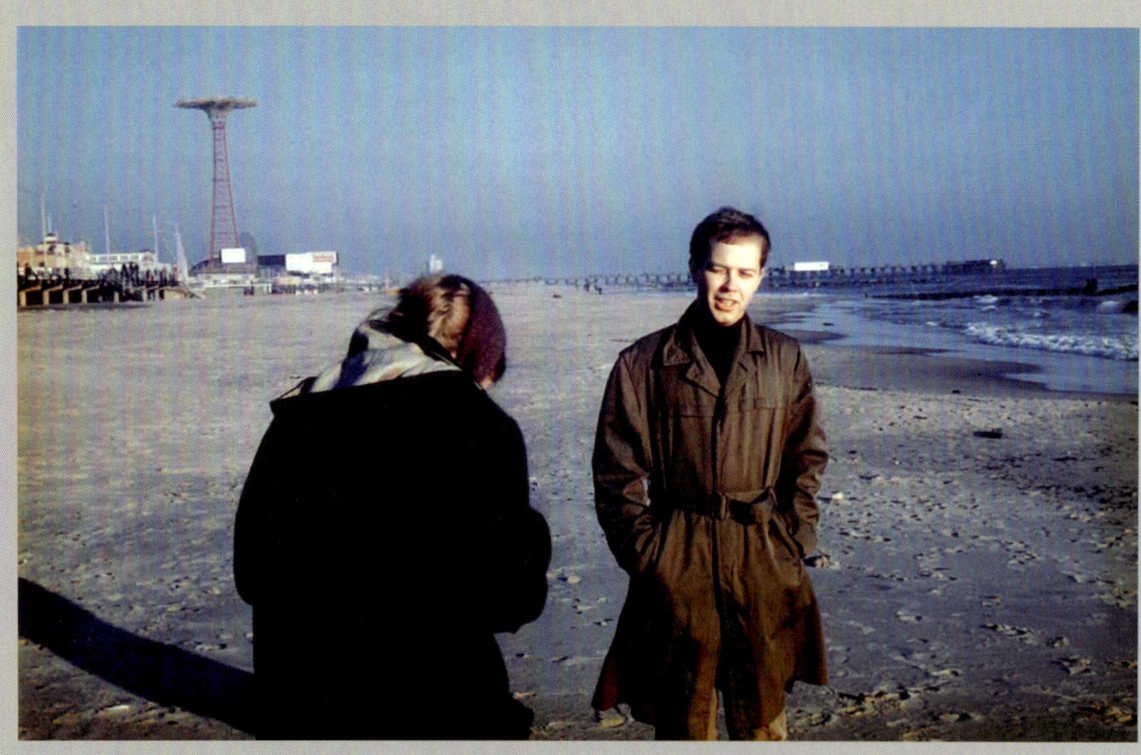

Jeanette Winter taking a photograph of Roger, as photographed by her father, Christmas, Coney Island, 1960
Collection of Roger Winter

CHAPTER 4

1960: CONEY ISLAND

UPON ARRIVAL IN BROOKLYN, Winter asked a service station attendant where they could find a hotel. "The only one he knew was The Saint George where he and his bride had spent their wedding night," Winter recalls. "So we parked the car on a nowhere street and stayed a couple of nights in The Saint George, famous for having a swimming pool on the roof. Miraculously, no one bothered the car."[1] As it happens, Winter's art history professor at the University of Iowa, Wallace Tomasini, mentioned that he and his wife spent a winter in Seagate, a gated community at the southwestern tip of Coney Island. "So we headed out there and rented the second floor of a Victorian house," Winter recalls. "The rent was sixty-five dollars a month during fall, winter, and spring—that was really cheap for New York. We were a few feet from the ocean—climb just over the sea wall and you'd be right on the sand. We couldn't sleep well for the first several nights because the water was so loud!"

Roger and Jeanette spent many weekends and evenings walking down the beach to the boardwalk, which still pulsed with the energy and spirit of Reginald Marsh's ecstatically colored 1930s paintings of Coney Island sideshows. Often, they would meet after work and go to the original Metropolitan Opera in Midtown. "Standing-room tickets were one dollar and fifty cents. We would join the mad rush to the SRO [standing room only] to get a place not behind a post. We were young and fast, and the competition, older Italian couples, usually ended up behind posts. It didn't seem to matter—they knew all the arias and sang along with the cast."

During this period, Winter also became interested in existentialism and the theater of the absurd, particularly the explorations of Jean-Paul Sartre and Albert Camus as to the nature of being, in addition to Samuel Beckett's *Waiting for Godot*, which portrayed life as senseless futility. Roger and Jeanette frequently attended performances at the Circle in the Square Theatre, and even caught the spring 1960 debut of Jean Genet's *The Balcony*. For Winter, the existentialist's indeterminate, chaotic void was at once terrifying and liberating. He responded to the themes of metaphysical alienation and moral enigma shot through with dizzying disorientations that tightroped between fantasy and reality.

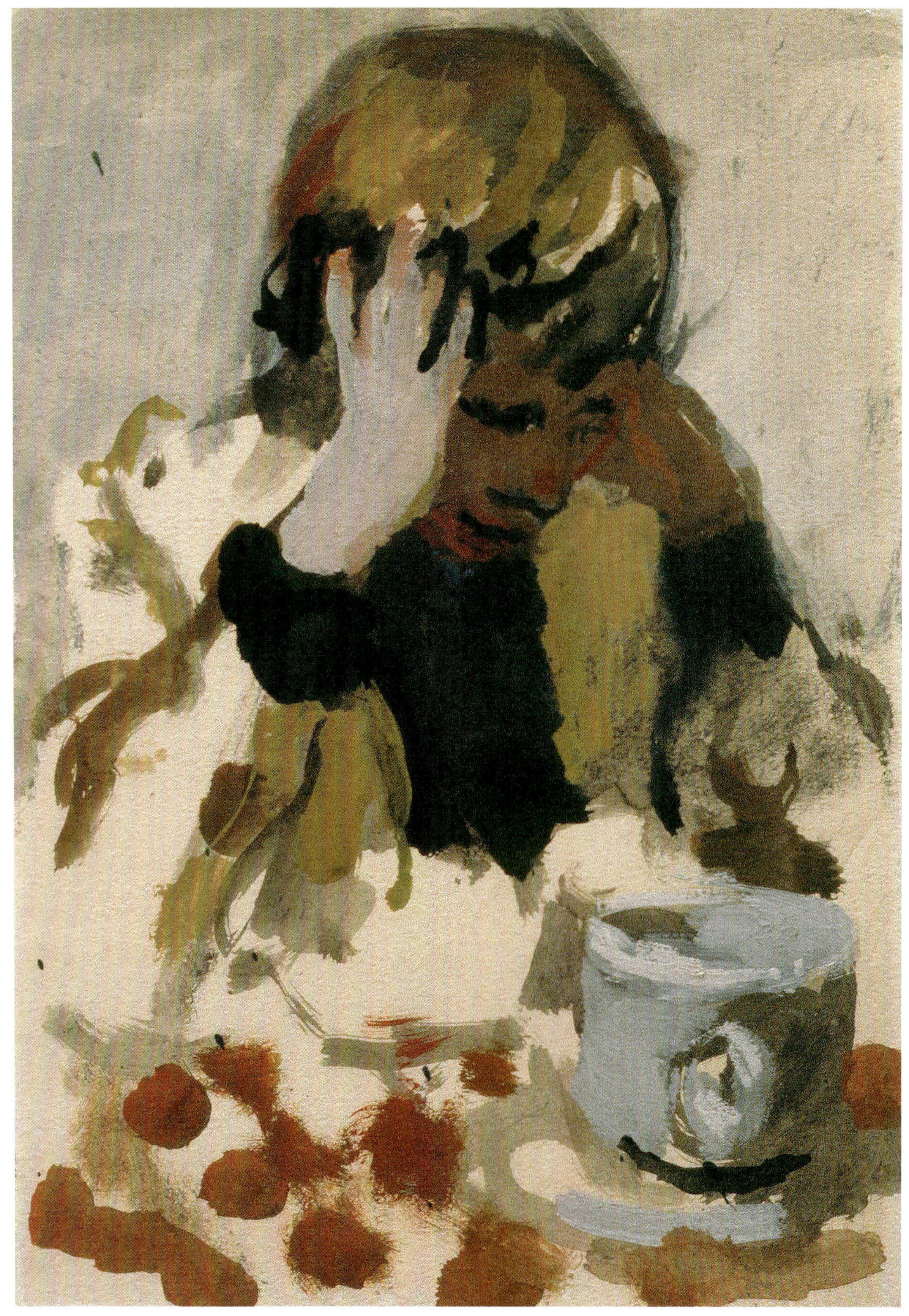

Jeanette, 1960

casein on mat board | 12 1/2" × 9" | Collection of the artist

How could it be otherwise? Winter was still in his twenties, an intense young artist with limited exposure to the important art of the past and present. For him, the year in New York City was a time of rapid creative growth. "I saw my first Vermeer paintings in the flesh," he recalls.

> At the Frick, the Vermeer paintings were such an eye-opener in terms of their small sizes. I think my favorite paintings at the Frick were *The Polish Rider* and Goya's *The Forge*. On weekends, we liked going to the Cloisters. I loved the complexity of the Unicorn Tapestries—stitch by stitch, like the backs of labels in clothing. I loved the colors of medieval paintings: red, green, earthy gold. On every visit to the Metropolitan Museum, I would go and look at [Pieter] Bruegel [the Elder]'s *The Harvesters*—the various gestures of the figures, the arrangement of deep space, the scale relations. I'd seen so few actual paintings in my life, and here they were from every place and time; Roman wall painting, [Diego] Velázquez, [Edouard] Vuillard, [Jean-Baptiste-Camille] Corot, Monet, Matisse, Stuart Davis, Edward Hopper. What a feast for a guy from the wrong side of the tracks in Denison! The totality of the experience, along with seeing so many operas and contemporary theater, began to turn my head from the painterly realism I had done in the second year of graduate school. A new vision started taking root that eventually moved into the art world and out of the insular world of an art school.

The 1950s and early 1960s was an explosive period in American art, a time when New York became the indisputable center of the avant-garde. After 1955, however, a number of New York artists moved away from a driving gestural style toward an art based on clearly defined forms. As the preeminent art historian and critic Irving Sandler notes, "The stylistic common denominator of fifties art was the 'hot,' dirty, painterly look, and of the sixties art, the 'cool' antiseptic, mechanistic look!"[2] Although the period has often been viewed as a parenthesis between Abstract Expressionism, on the one hand, and Pop Art and Minimalism, on the other, many styles and methods surfaced during this in-between era. Some artists developed a suggestive art of memory, rejecting the very notion of expressionism for a cool realism or reductive geometry. Others reinvigorated abstraction by describing landscapes or figures with vigorous brushwork. An equally strong tendency within this younger generation—Jan Müller, Robert Beauchamp, Bob Thompson, Tony Vevers, Grace Hartigan, and Lester Johnson, among others—was to apply some of the gestural, action-oriented style and scale of the Abstract Expressionists to deliberate exploration of biblical, mythological, and classical literary sources. They were not exclusive of each other, but the two together represented what the late 1950s and early 1960s was all about—a stimulating dialogue based on two halves of the same coin.

As curator Judith Stein observes in *The Figurative Fifties: New York Figurative Expressionism*, "The New York School painters who used the figure compositionally and thematically saw no essential difference in rank between abstraction and figuration. Some chose the figure from the start, others slowly gravitated toward it, and still others shifted back and forth between abstraction and representation out of internal necessity."[3]

Although Winter had felt isolated at the University of Iowa, he was not out of step with the cultural zeitgeist. An important touchstone for him during his two years in graduate school was Max Beckmann's *Karneval* (Carnival), which was on continuous display in the Student Center.

Created during the artist's 1942–43 exile in Amsterdam from Berlin, the painting expressed, according to the University of Iowa's description, his "disillusionment with war-torn Europe" by experimenting with "abstracted figural forms" in a triptych format. Significantly, "Beckmann set his masked and costumed figures, some with musical instruments, on a street-like stage reminiscent of an actual Lenten carnival." Pervasive throughout are classic German Expressionist approaches: "abraded forms akin to woodblock prints, radical spatial compositions, and garish color outlined with black. . . . These

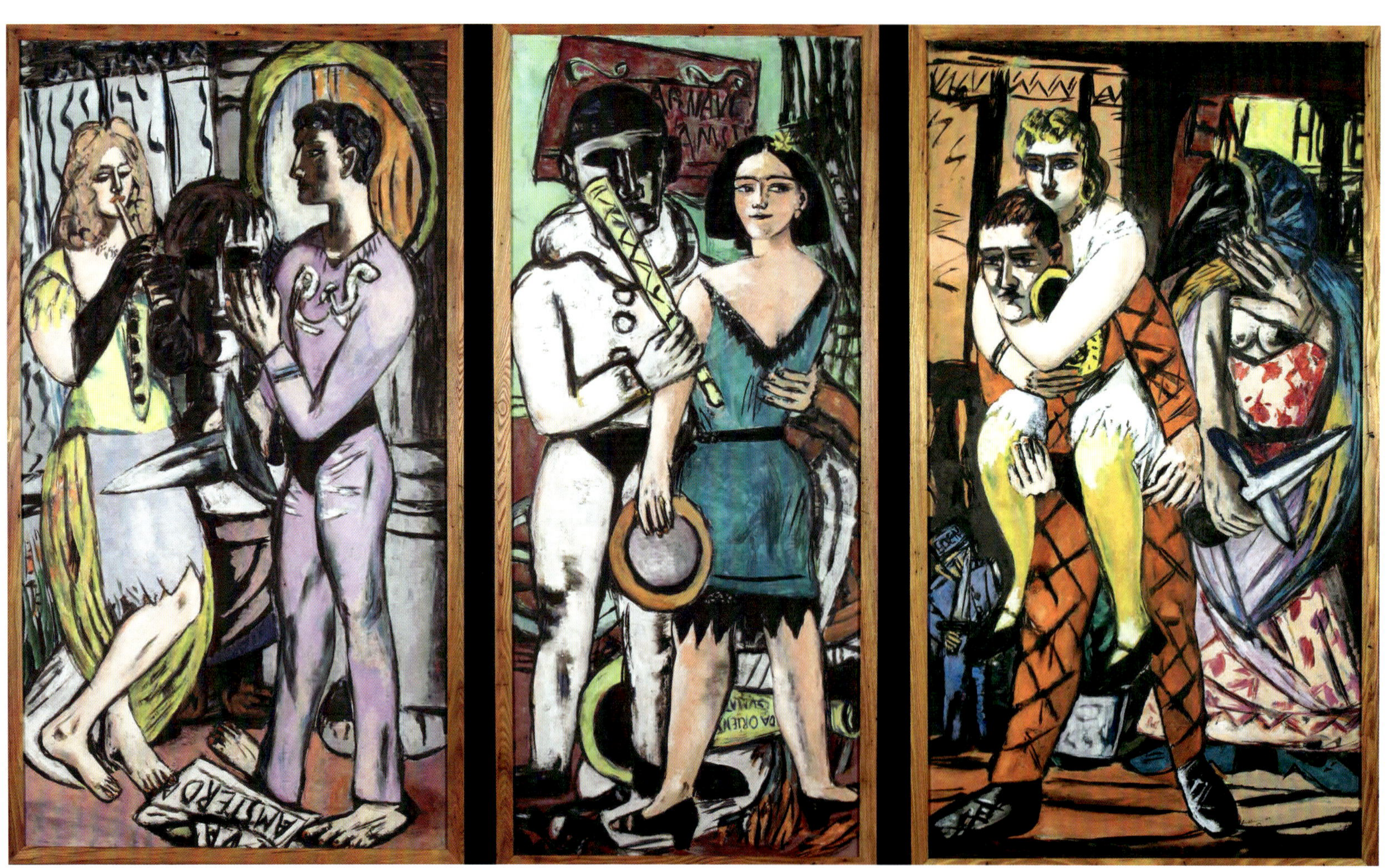

Max Beckmann, *Karneval* (Carnival), 1943

oil on linen canvas | 74 7/8" × 41 3/8", 75" × 33 9/16", 74 15/16" × 41 7/16" (190.5 × 85.25 cm) | Mark Ranney Memorial Fund, Stanley Museum of Art, University of Iowa, 1946.1 |

elements create forces of tension, . . . simultaneous narratives, and compressed vertigo-inducing spaces.[4] "I enjoyed standing in front of it and studying the individual figures but also overall structure—how the three complex panels, each its own, worked together," recalls Winter. While a graduate student, Winter frequently examined Jack Levine's *Study for a Gangster's Funeral* (1953), which was also on view in the Student Center. Levine depicts a crew of thugs in formal attire gathered at the coffin of a slain mob boss. Winter, no doubt, felt a kinship to the realist painter whose satiric tableau often directed sharp commentary at big business, political corruption, racism, and human folly.

During the final semester, Winter became increasingly aware, primarily through slides and reproductions, of paintings that resonated with allegorical overtones by historic and leading modern artists. He was absorbed by the imagery and compositional strategies found in such diverse sources as Nicolas Poussin's *The Adoration of the Golden Calf* (1633–34) and Thomas Eakins's *Baby at Play* (1876). Winter was particularly affected by Philip Guston's *If This Be Not I* (1945), a horizontal frieze featuring nine children assembled among urban detritus—trash can lids, ropes, doors, kitchen pots, and newspapers. The central figure wears a paper bag on his head and a mask over his eyes and nose. The child lying on the ground holds a light bulb in his hand. A little girl, the smallest of the children, wears a crown. Another child holds up a blindfold in front of his face. At the far right and seen from the back, still another changes into an adult's striped shirt or oversize top. In an essay for the *Philip Guston Retrospective* catalog, Michael E. Shapiro refers to *If This Be Not I* as "a richer, more atmospheric and deeply poetic painting. . . . In it an armistice has been declared: the children have ceased fighting and now are reflective, standing amid the rubble."[5]

Significantly, the painting frames the years of World War II, as well as the artist's faculty position at the University of Iowa. "My theory teachers liked to show it as a painting with a meaningful title," Winter explains. "I saw a slide of it at least once a semester. And we were always told that the background was Clinton Street in Iowa City. I'm sure Guston was a great influence at the time. He, too, would allow himself to be lost for the sake of finding a new path. There's a relationship in my painting from that period and the early Guston in that figures seem to be posing for the painter—like old snapshots, or families on Christmas cards. I was also finding that shapes of faces, hair, and clothing of children made an aggregate of shapes that played against more open areas of landscape space."

A turning point of sorts occurred when Roy Sieber, the distinguished scholar of African art, handed Winter a reproduction of a Jan Müller painting shortly before the young artist left the University of Iowa for New York City. A native of Germany, Müller arrived in New York in 1941 at the age of nineteen, studied with Hans Hofmann, and invented complex, mythical paintings in which specters stare at the viewer, thrust into the picture plane at odd angles, or levitate amid a formless universe.

In the brief period between the emergence of his mature style and his death in 1958, Müller had created haunting works in which masklike faces and ghostly white figures were rendered with emotional intensity. His vigorous brushstrokes and jarring compositional rhythms channeled stylistic elements of the German Expressionists, while the freedom of execution, mosaic-like surface design, and heroic scale demonstrated the impact of the Abstract Expressionists. For Winter, the images of figures floating or on horseback, the contests of angels and demons, amounted to an act of great daring that could only have been sustained through deep and hard-won convictions. "I was thirsty for something figurative," says Winter. "His work was so direct and everything was so well placed. A story was implied, but not translatable into words. He generalized objects and let the paint and color arrangements carry the lion's share. The mix came across as emotional. I felt an affinity with this and looked for metaphors for my own work."

All these sources were on Winter's radar as he left Iowa City—artists who went against the grain in ways that reinforced an intuitive desire to broaden his pictorial feelings. By the early 1960s, Winter was pushing his work into new territory even as he maintained an abiding interest in

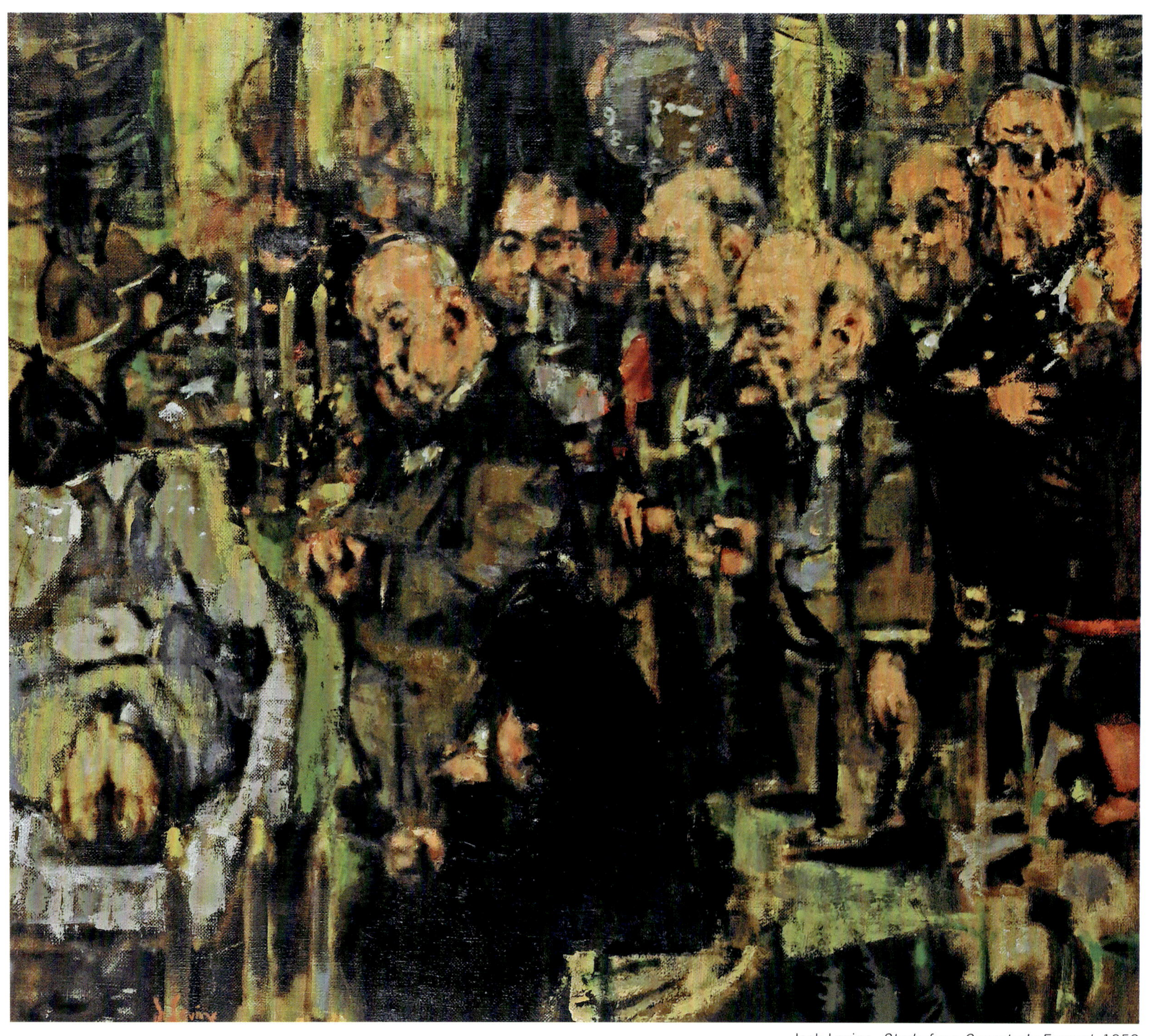

Jack Levine, *Study for a Gangster's Funeral,* 1953
oil on canvas | 44 3/4" × 48" (113.67 × 121.92 cm) | University acquisition, 1953.3 | Stanley Museum of Art, University of Iowa |

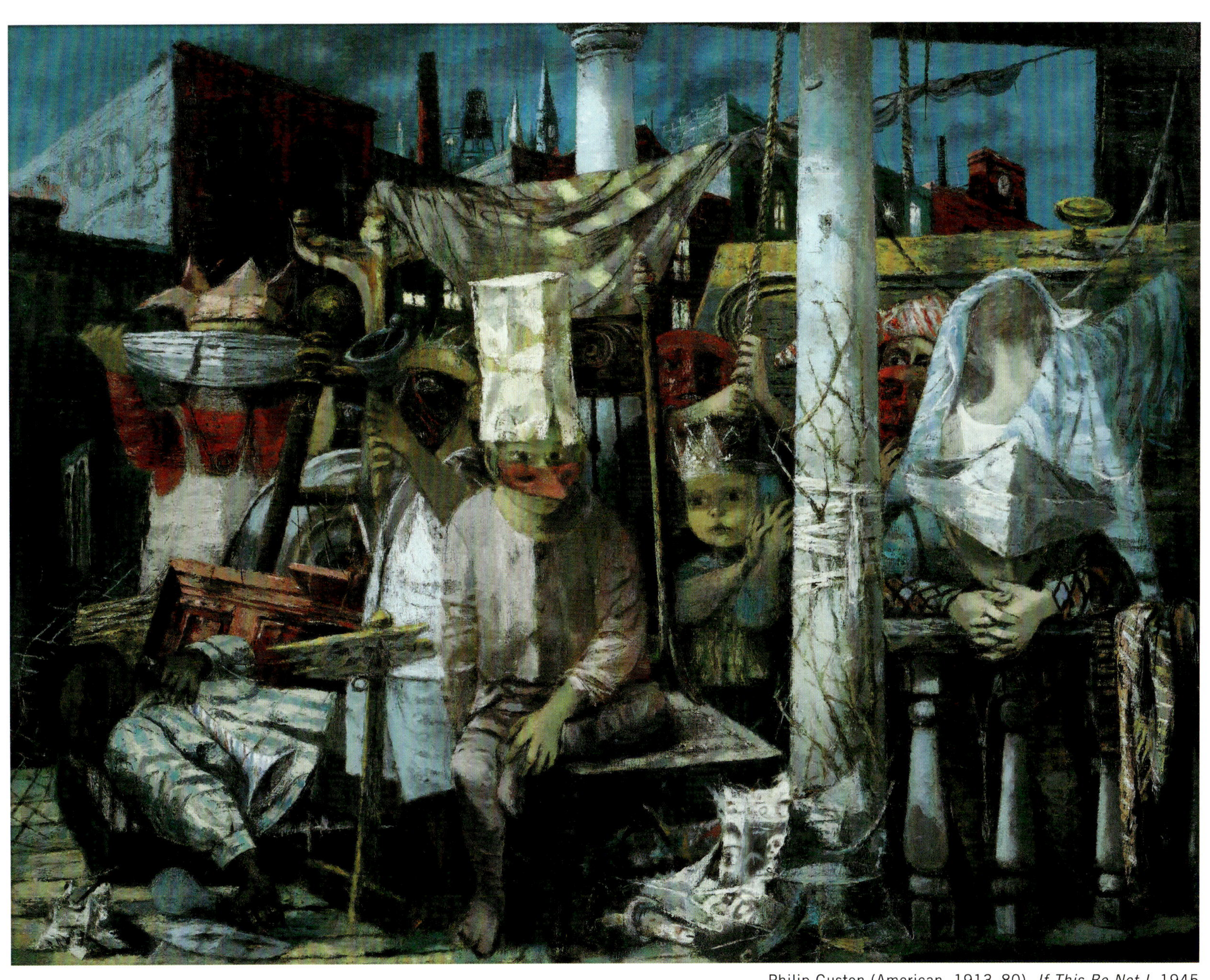

Philip Guston (American, 1913–80), *If This Be Not I,* 1945

oil on canvas | 42 1/4" × 55 1/4" | Mildred Lane Kemper Art Museum, Washington University in Saint Louis | University purchase, Kende Sale Fund, 1945 |

figurative groupings, outdoor settings, expressive color, and autobiographical content. It was a time of exploration, as he shifted back and forth between abstraction and figuration while searching for the most direct way of expressing the substance of his art. In the process, Winter's brushwork became more animated; his forms mutated from voluptuous calm to aggressive agitation. He was learning to trust his instincts, thereby setting himself on the path to developing a genuine voice and solid foundation on which his art could rest.

So when Winter packed up the Chevy in Iowa City, he included the Müller reproduction along with their belongings. New York was a nexus of gravitational shifts that surely appealed to his burgeoning imagination. To that end, Winter sought out Müller's paintings at the Zabriskie Gallery and obtained a catalog of the artist's work. "I loved the way figures and animals were placed in such a graceless, direct manner. I also liked his artless way of applying paint, not at all like Fairfield Porter and his crowd. I saw Jan Müller's work as a path forward for me in painting. I had no wish to imitate his style, but his staged arrangement of figures—reclining, floating, flying in a limited space, and the confrontational poses, had an immense impact on the way I wanted to work."

By Winter's own admission, the gallery shows were less important to him than the permanent collections of the museums. However, he recalls seeing paintings by Guston, as well as Franz Kline, at the galleries and was aware of the current work by Figurative Expressionists Lester Johnson and Grace Hartigan. He was especially drawn to the raw, childlike paintings of French artist Jean Dubuffet and the psychologically charged canvases that explored human isolation by Bay Area artist Nathan Oliveira. "With Dubuffet in mind, I was willing to distort, be silly, and forget about art school dogma. With Oliveira, I became interested in his single silhouetted figures on a beach. I was willing to use paint more vigorously. No one was around to make ethical judgments or tell me what I shouldn't do. I'm certain their works, along with our nightly walks at the water's edge, influenced my paintings. I saw an exhibition of Ellsworth Kelly's work and wasn't sure what I was looking at. Nothing had prepared me for Minimal painting. I also saw a show of works by Alex Katz and Wolf Kahn that I enjoyed, although [I was] not overwhelmed. Wolf's work looked slick to me, although attractive back then. I liked Alex's work but I had no wish to emulate it. I was taught to react against action painting, and so in memory the gallery exhibitions I visited were contemporary figure painting."

Winter, however, was "blown away" by an exhibition of paintings by Tony Vevers at the Padawer Gallery. Born in London, Vevers was evacuated to the United States in 1940 to escape the Blitz during World War II. Like Müller and Bob Thompson, he had studied with Hans Hofmann in New York, later becoming part of a core group of young Provincetown artists who worked in the figurative expressionist mode. At the time, some saw Vevers as following the lead of his great precursor, Milton Avery, who also summered in Provincetown and had spent decades honing landscapes into concentrated vessels of affective color and feeling. Vevers's art differed substantially from Avery's, however. In the younger artist's paintings, the overwhelming content is one of ambiguity, mystery, and the enigma of equivocal forces. Mythic and dreamlike, Vevers's figures and primordial landscapes reverberate with multiple echoes—the joyous, sensual communion with nature and, in some instances, an eerie "dark undertow" roiling beneath a seemingly placid surface. At Padawer Gallery, Winter's encounter with Vevers's painting of silhouetted figures surrounding an enormous whale washed up on a beach was like a shockwave.

The paintings of Müller and Vevers inspired Winter to define the true nature of his artistic concerns. "Tony Vevers's show had such a great impact," Winter recalls. "His sensitivity toward light, edges, choice of subjects, perfect arrangements at both two-dimensional and deep space, a love of the ocean—I identified with all of this. But I've always had a soft touch with the brush, an evolving interest in edges, a sense of placing things in a harmonious scale in relation to the proportions and size of a rectangle, of arranging images and dissolving them into brushstrokes that carry a language of their own." It was clear that what was being sought was a

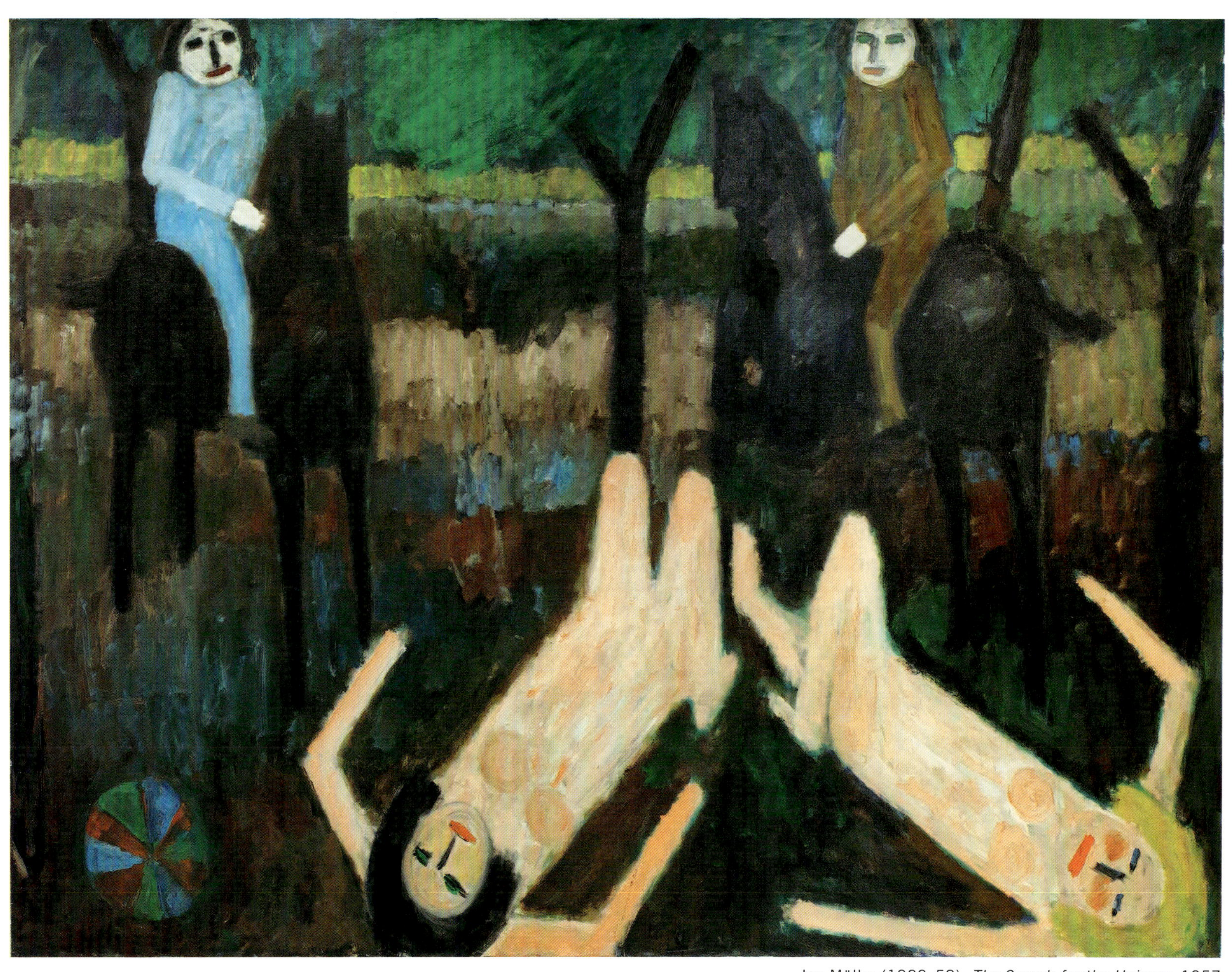

Jan Müller (1922–58), *The Search for the Unicorn,* 1957
oil on canvas | 70 1/8" × 93 3/4" signed | Courtesy of Michael Rosenfeld Gallery, LLC, New York, NY |
In cooperation with Bookstein Projects, New York

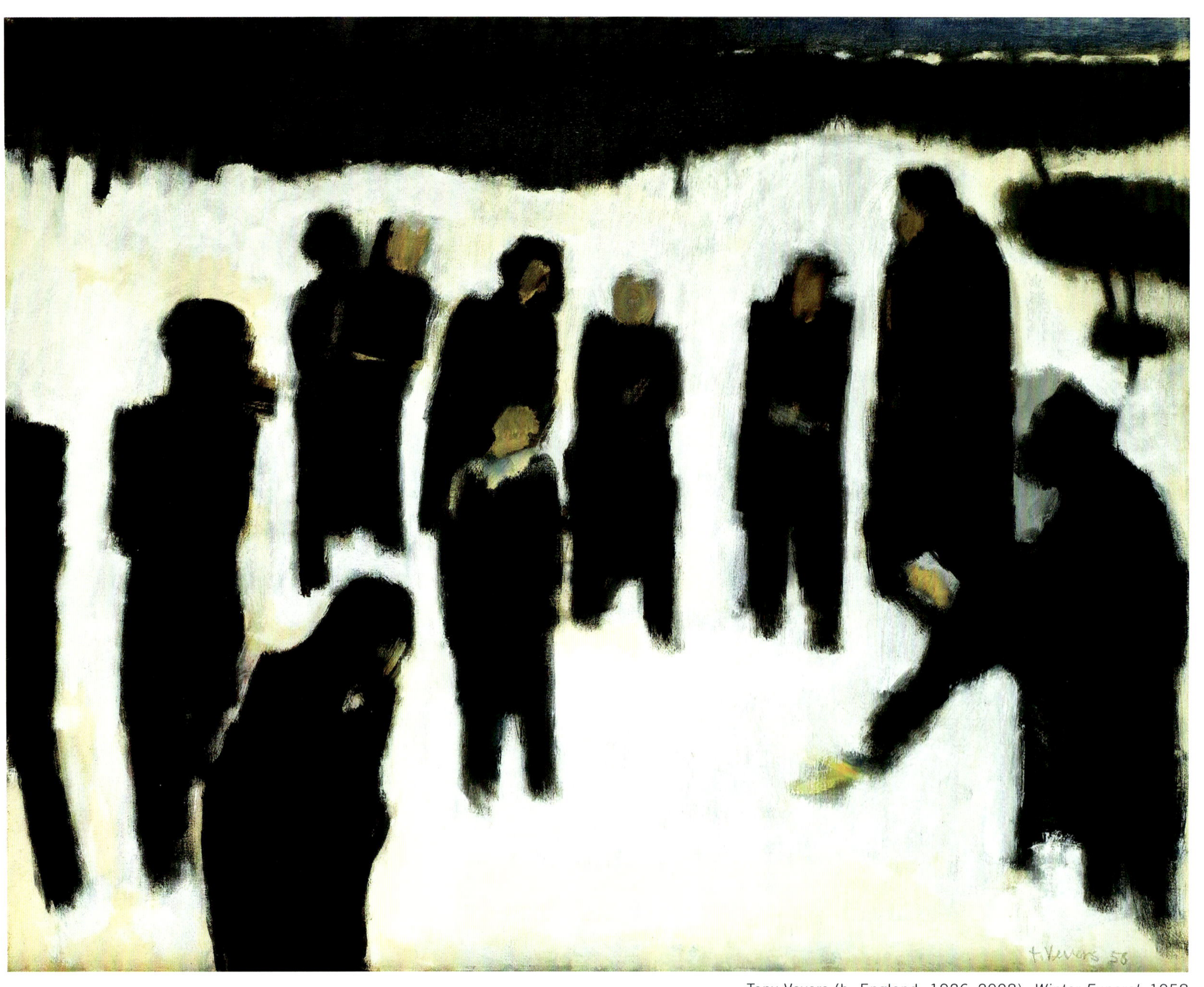

Tony Vevers (b. England, 1926–2008), *Winter Funeral,* 1958

oil on canvas | 28 1/4" × 36 1/8" (71.5 × 91.6 cm) | Hirshhorn Museum and Sculpture Garden, Smithsonian Institution, Washington, DC | Gift of Joseph H. Hirshhorn, 1966 | Photography by Lee Stalsworth way to make recognizable images with surface energy equal to that of the most abstract paintings. Accordingly, the few extant works produced by Winter during his year on Coney Island are impassioned evocations of what would become, in a short time, the focused and powerfully enigmatic paintings that made evident his deepest feelings about life. *Big Blue Fish* and *Family Group* not only prefigure future work but also reveal the stirrings and gropings of a significant artist before he became his mature self. Winter had already learned to zero in precisely on what he wanted to express. In *Big Blue Fish* the ocean is an ineluctable, absorptive force. A group of six figures—apparitions, really—are bound together by some mutual gravitation. They wade through shallow water toward the beached leviathan, which stretches across the low third of the painting. The figures appear to be slipping into an inky void. There is no sun, no spatial context—only shifting sand and the gray abyss of the sea.

Nonetheless, a structural principle is evident in all of Winter's paintings, even in the earliest landscapes. The application of paint hugs the surface; brushstrokes, with which figures or shapes are rendered, are wedded to gesture. Often a painting will be divided into distinct horizontal and vertical components. In *Big Blue Fish*, the spirits are formed by jabbing, vertically oriented strokes arranged in a shifting parade of shafts. The monstrous dead fish is a dark, sweeping mass with scratched and scrawled zigzag lines of teeth, an eye, and fins. Admittedly, Winter was directly influenced by the Vevers image of a washed-up fish. However, his painting also grew out of the haunting night views of the Coney Island beach and weird daytime experiences along the boardwalk.

"At night, it was inevitable to imagine presences on the sand or at the water's edge," Winter says. "I dreamed up the spiritual figures from the sounds and sights of the ocean." Accordingly, his figures are half seen and half conjured, expressed as transitory beings. Yet they are poetically weighted: people move in space but also change in time—they come and go, in and out of the picture plane, in and out of one's life. Everything here, including the burnt-black bone color, bears the poignancy of something remembered. Ordinary, familiar events may suddenly seem menacing.

Winter invests the scene with a primal emotion that amplifies the temporal character of personal relationships and makes death palpable. It's significant that Winter's father had passed away in recent years before the Coney Island period. Moreover, Winter had experienced recurring dreams over the years of his brother David's death by drowning. "I've thought of a story my brother Ed told me after David's body was recovered from the ocean and shipped home," Winter explains. "Ed wanted the funeral director to unseal the coffin so he could see the body. The funeral director refused. He said to Ed, 'You wouldn't be able to recognize him from a nigger.' I never saw his body, and that shameful racist comment still haunts me. The giant fish has been in the human psyche in every culture. From the giant fish that swallowed Jonah to Moby Dick. I don't know if that fish was David, but I've had gruesome thoughts about what might have happened to his body. This painting is all about facing my fears."

Winter was trying to get at the ways we are all haunted by the primal myths that run through our world. Thus *Big Blue Fish* operates on a mythic as well as an immediate level. It insists that some shadowy part of us is part of it, burrowing under our skins and festering. For Winter, the outer world served to jog his memory and trigger the emotions that were the point of making art.

Even as an undergraduate student at the University of Texas, Winter had been absorbed by children—a classic intimist subject—and one of his major themes during the Coney Island period and throughout the decades. In *Family Group*, Winter means to convey a kind of snapshot informality, a quality of sundrenched pleasure as five children standing arm in arm gaze at two women reclining amid a bucolic landscape. Winter depicts a white horse at upper right; a child holds a white dove on the far left. The bird, horse, and dog would become familiar icons in future works. Symbols of fear and freedom, as well as life and death, they are linked to dramas that are both specific and mysterious. Here, Winter's composition crystallizes into a vibrant tapestry of crude brushstrokes, heavy paint, and bold colors. Nevertheless, whatever

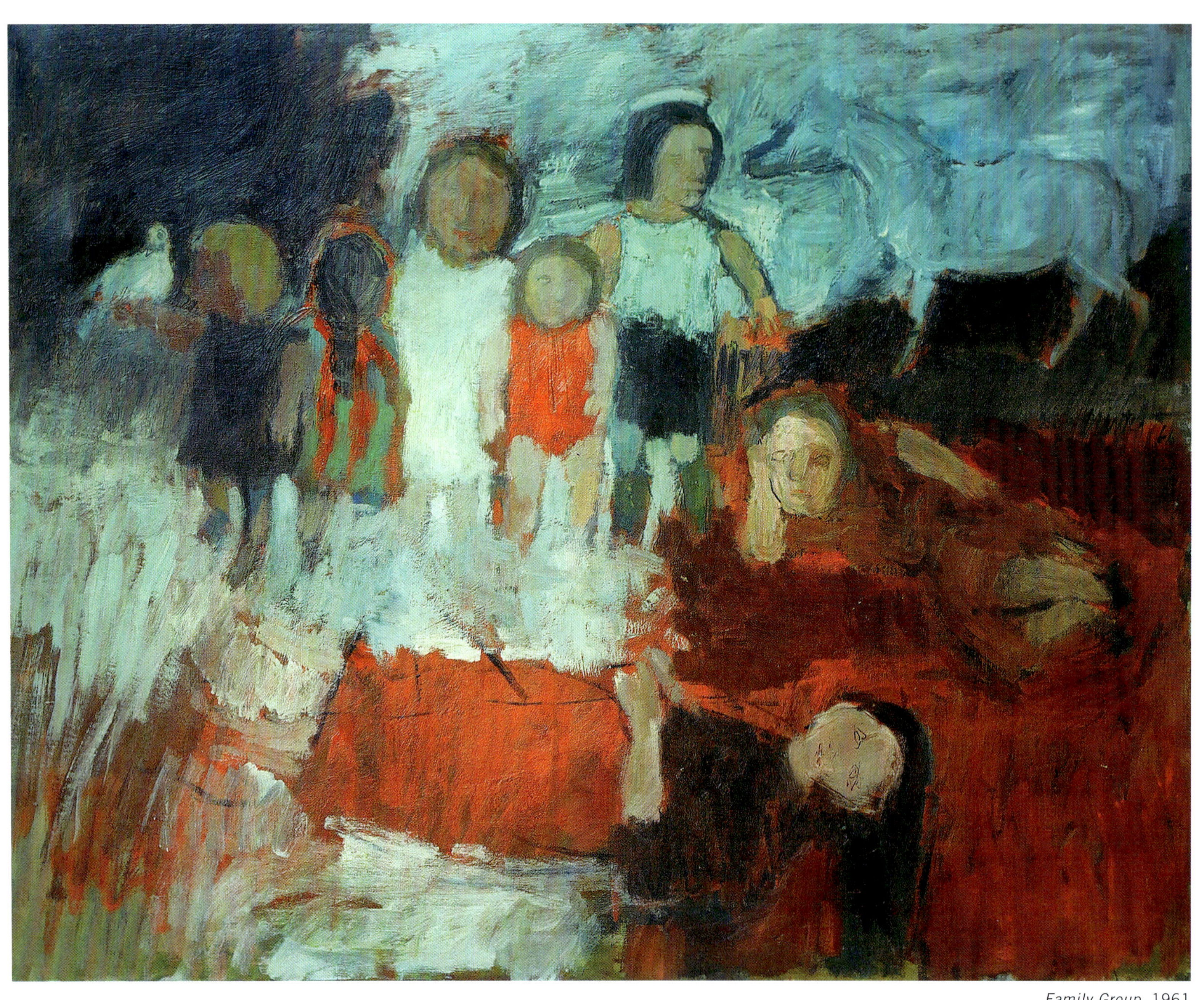

Family Group, 1961

oil on canvas | 40" × 50" | Courtesy of the artist

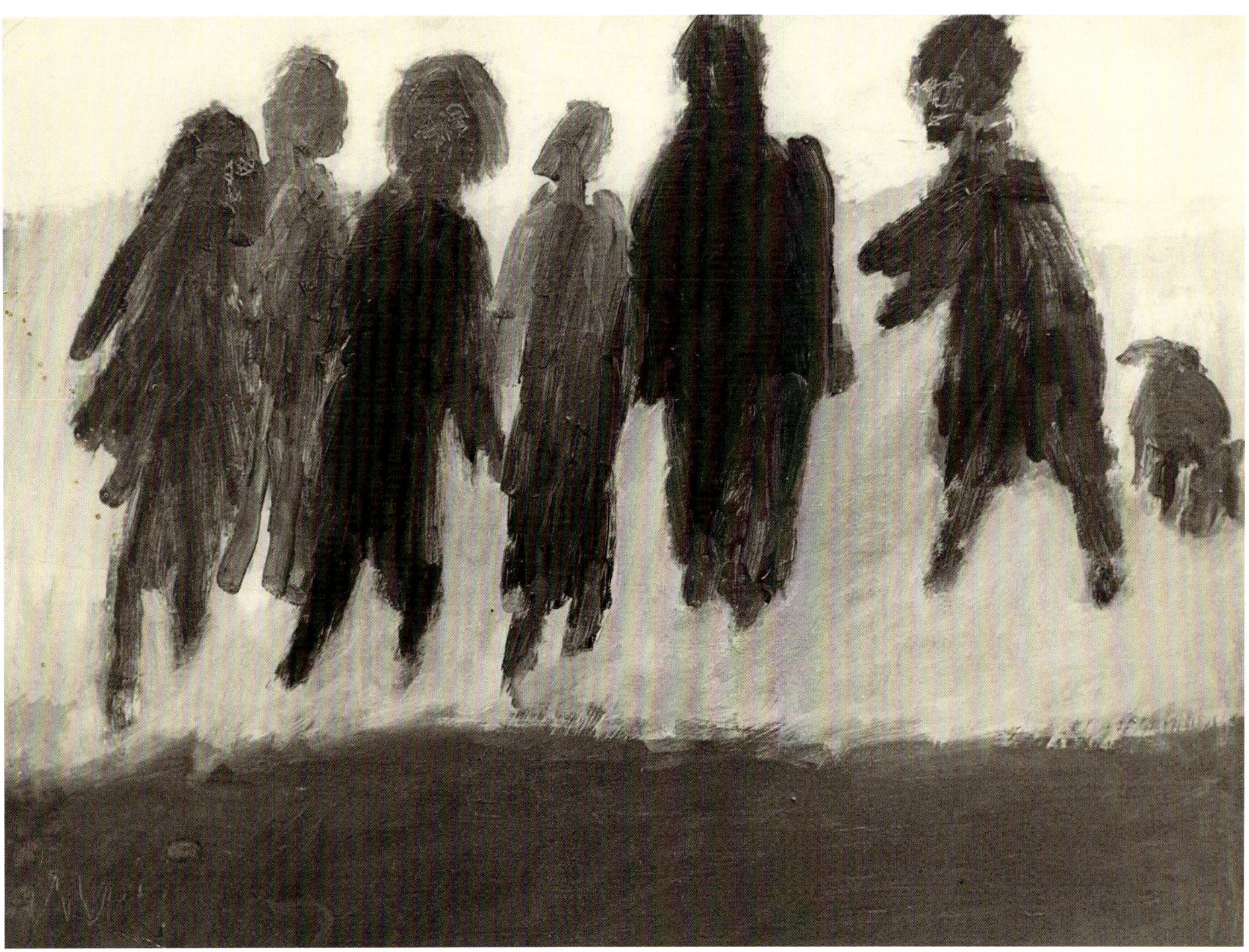

Big Blue Fish, 1960
oil on canvas | 24" × 30" | Courtesy of the artist

enchantment Winter was able to achieve on Coney Island, the paintings *Big Blue Fish*, *Family Group*, and others like them reaffirm that his early years were difficult and often painful. They convey the complexity of his feelings—the troubled inner voice—during this period, but also reflect the deep-seated imperatives of Winter's vision. In Winter's realm, we recognize the distortive power of our own emotions and where anomalous terrors lurk beneath the surface of daily life.

What Winter terms his "blended world" is a highly charged place of constant flux and rich emotional potential. Overall, the 1960–61 period on Coney Island made Winter realize that he had "worked hard for any worthwhileness in life." From that resolve, he "dug into the canvas until those figures and animals finally emerged out of the chaos." Looking for easy answers in art, he learned, was like "giving a cough drop for pneumonia." By the end of his stay on Coney Island, Winter was determined to follow an uncompromising commitment to the dictates of inner need. "For me, worthwhile painting was making a valid figurative work emerge from painted space. I was progressing in my medium—ordering space, mastering brushes, handling edges, finding images in the wake of the formalist 1950s—and hearing a faint voice that I recognized as mine."

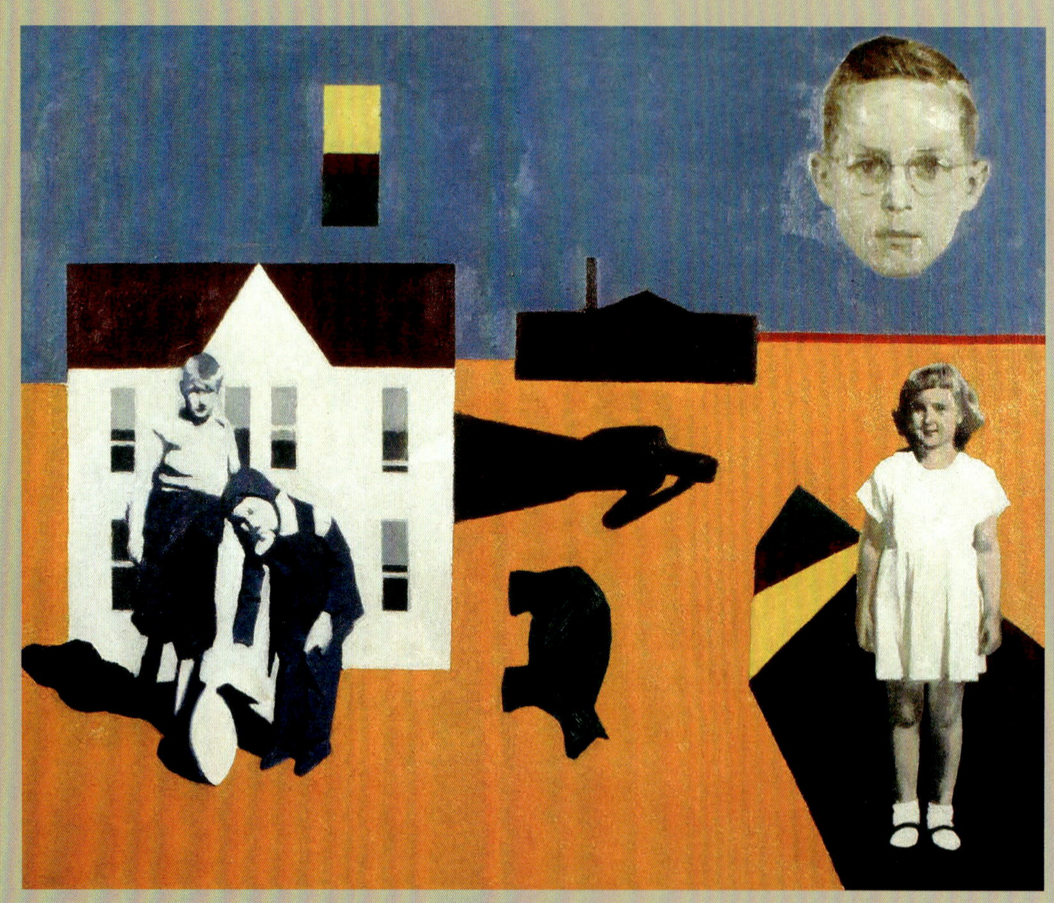

Interurban, 1968
oil on linen | 25″ × 31″ | Collection of Quin Mathews

CHAPTER 5

BACK TO TEXAS

IN THE SPRING OF 1961, the artist Joe Hobbs, a friend from undergraduate studies at the University of Texas, offered Winter an opportunity to teach classes at the Fort Worth Art Center. Hoping the position would be an entrance to the teaching and gallery worlds, Roger and Jeanette loaded up their scant belongings in the 1953 Chevy and moved from Coney Island to Fort Worth. "I'd never faced a group of people before who needed my help, but I took to the job instantly," Winter recalls. "I could see that the students felt my enthusiasm and responded energetically." However, the Winters quickly discovered that Fort Worth was a very conservative town in 1961—"a complete letdown" from the great museums and cultural events they experienced in Manhattan. What's more, Winter and Hobbs were fired just six weeks into the job for criticizing the art writer of the *Fort Worth Star-Telegram* in a harsh letter to the editor. "We knew what we were talking about—Joe held an MFA from the University of Southern California and I from Iowa, plus a year in New York—even if our methods were coarse and ill-advised," says Winter. "Perhaps we were fired for wanting to change too much too quickly." In any case, Winter became despondent over the forfeiture of his first teaching position, as well as gallery connections, because of the bad publicity. He produced only a few works during the Fort Worth period, Pop Art–inspired painted plaster sculptures—a dog and balls, a woman in a bathtub—in addition to the painting *Prufrock* (1961), a response to T. S. Eliot's 1915 poem about an isolated yet sensitive thinker in an uncertain world. Winter's rendering of a balding, middle-aged man with schematic facial characteristics and a sinewy, elongated form cuts a bleak figure. Set against a brushy dark-green background, the emotionally stilted Prufrock wears a heavy black coat and a red tie and holds three red flowers. "I was hooked on T. S. Eliot and 'The Love Song of J. Alfred Prufrock' at the time," Winter explains.

> I grow old . . . I grow old . . .
> I shall wear the bottoms of my trousers rolled.
> Shall I part my hair behind? Do I dare to eat a
>   peach?
> I shall wear white flannel trousers and walk
>   upon the beach.

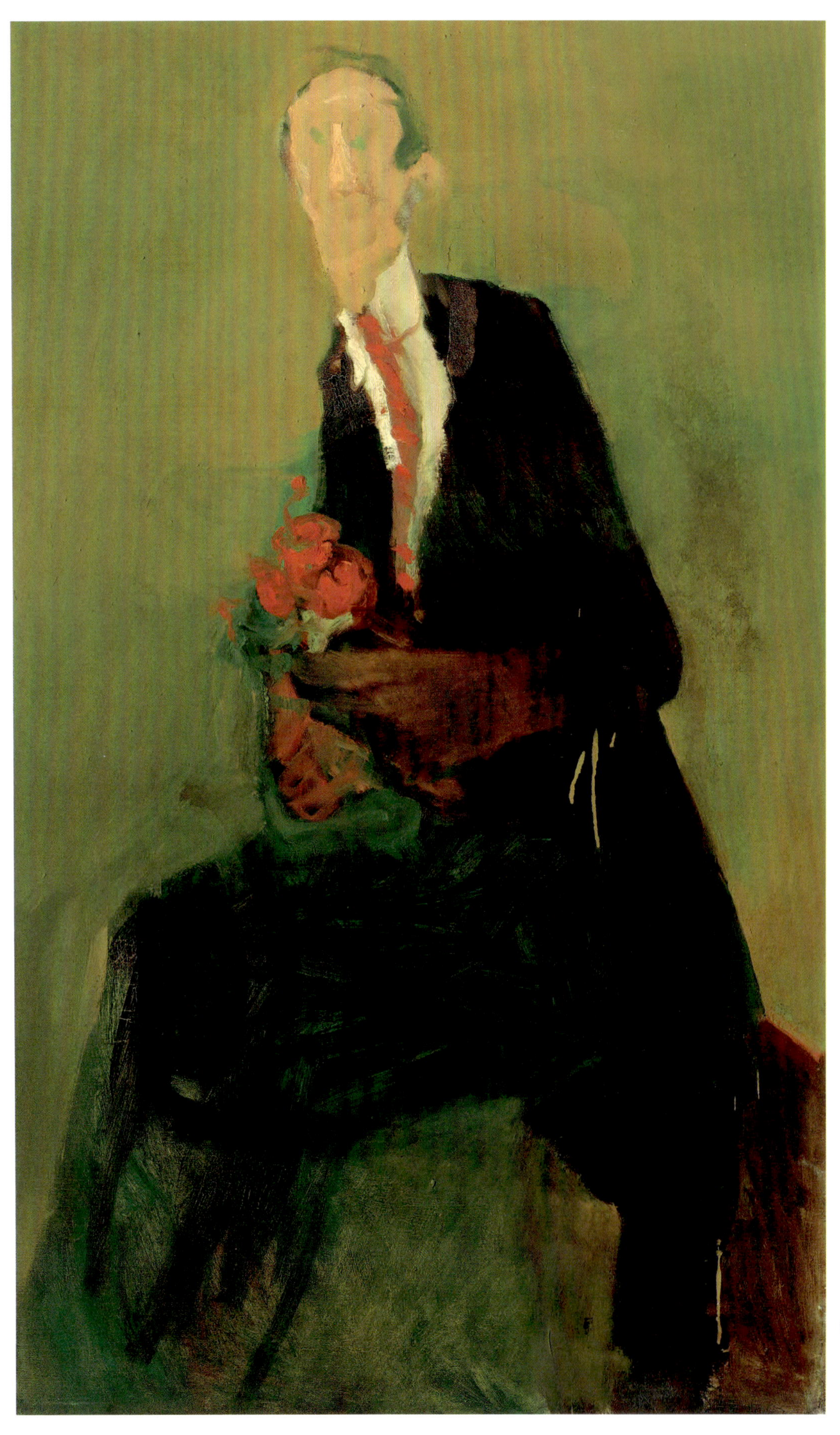

Prufrock, 1961
oil on canvas | 46" × 27" |
Collection of Craig Smyser, Houston | Photography by Thomas DuBrock

I have heard the mermaids singing, each to each.
I do not think that they will sing to me.

"I had recently turned twenty-seven and was really searching. I was without plans or money. Painting time was scarce. My life was at a low ebb, just barely hanging on." For Winter, the painting and plaster pieces represented a struggle to "climb out of the bottom of the barrel, more or less caused by following Joe Hobbs into a brave new world of art as business. Losing the teaching job at the Fort Worth Art Center and being dropped from the Electra Carlin Gallery could hardly be seen as a good start." Nevertheless, *Prufrock* was given the first-place award by Hobson Pittman in the 1961 Fort Worth Annual. Moreover, Hobbs and Winter started a school of their own, the Handley School of Art, in the basement of a YMCA building. While the director was away for the summer, the pair built easels, painting tables, and clay modeling stands and assigned rooms in the two-story brick building for various classes. "We decided to have a grand-opening party," says Winter. "We sent out invitations, made signs announcing the opening and posted them along Lancaster Avenue, and bought cheap wine. The party was a huge success, as if Fort Worth was waiting for this event. We had full classes and everything was going well until the YMCA director came back into town and wanted to know what in the name of god was going on in his building!" As it happened, Hobbs and Winter found a large, white-frame Catholic church that had the holy sacrament removed and could be rented for fifty dollars a month. They built ladders out of the long church benches and strung television antennae wire from the ceiling to install floodlights. The former altar was used as a model stand. Things seemed to be on the upswing. Their original students followed them to the new "school," which received favorable publicity in the newspaper. Classes moved along smoothly. But then Hobbs was offered a teaching job at Arlington State College (now UT Arlington) and Winter was left "holding the bag." He and Jeanette were forced to close the school, move to another area of Fort Worth, and look for other means of income. As a sort of "cleansing" from the Coney Island period, the ensuing conflict with the Fort Worth Art Center, and futile attempts to operate a fledgling art school, Winter wrote a powerful statement of renewed determination: "I have listened to endless manifestos, made the attempt to absorb and to put into practice the discoveries of numberless schools and individuals. If any one of those sensations and perceptions have come through in my work it has surely been by accident. I have fed at the breasts of the past and present until I have but one ground which is virtually untouched by me, one authority which has not known my dependence and that is me. The time is come when I must listen to myself and trust my own eyes to look at my experience in all its nakedness. Common in its nakedness, nevertheless it is what I must pursue."[1]

To that end, Jeanette landed a job at the Fort Worth Public Library and Roger was hired as a studio assistant by sculptor Charles T. Williams, whom he had met through Hobbs. Based in Arlington, Williams had earned great respect and admiration for infusing his art with unusual metaphorical power. His probing attention to materials—metals, wood, stone, and found objects—often grappled with the wellsprings of myth, collective and personal, to fuel the imagination. By turns enigmatic and humorous in their hybrid configurations, Williams's works embraced a wide range of sources: the biomorphic surrealism of Jean Arp; the organically shaped abstract bronze and stone figures of Henry Moore; the ductile irony of the steel tempered by David Smith with a blacksmith's persistence. Added to the mix were elements from American primitive images, as well as animistic totems of African and pre-Columbian art. "Charles always had big commissions going for public work," Winter recalls. "I learned to weld, solder, and make casts for bronze sculptures. He asked me to help with his book of titles for small works. My best one was 'MOMA, You've Been a Dada to Me,' which he used. Charles showed me that art could be silly and fun. It didn't have to be so heavy, but could be playful—the three Ps of art: patience, persistence, and play. Nobody had ever taught me about the play part."

As Katie Robinson Edwards notes in *Midcentury Modern Art in Texas*, Williams's "studio served as an informal locus for avant-garde activity

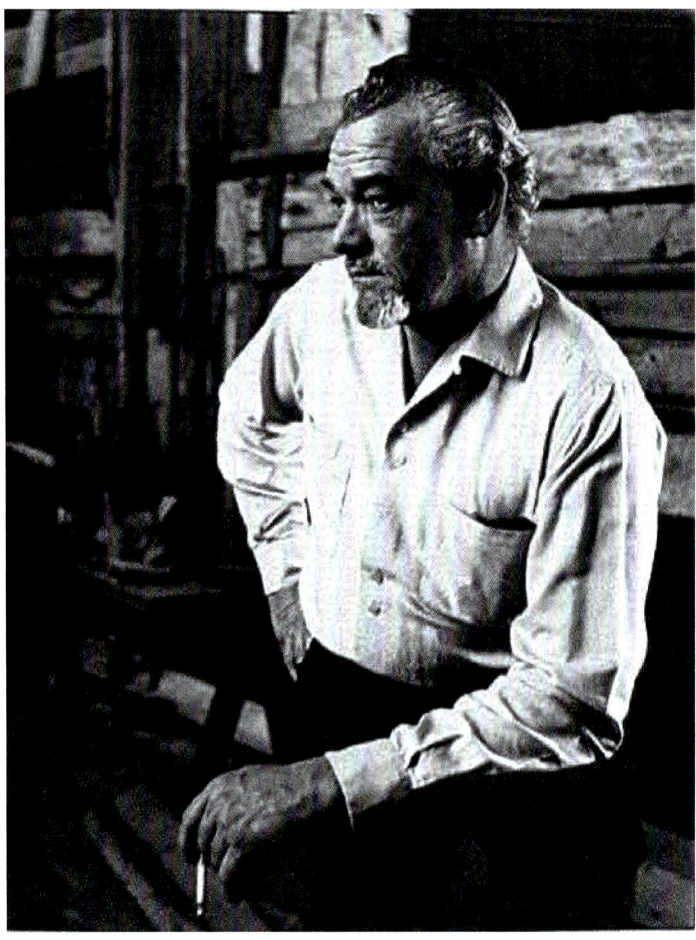

Charles T. Williams, ca. 1965
Arlington, Texas | Collection of Karl B. Williams

in Northeast Texas, attracting artists, critics, and collectors from around the state and the country."[2] For Winter, the sculptor was both "spiritual father" and "social organizer" for a tightly knit group of artists that, though not necessarily an art movement in any formalized manner, was largely centered in the Oak Lawn area of Dallas. "Charles and Anita Williams became our best friends," Winter recalls. "Charles was generous toward Jeanette and me in every way and Charles was not dependent on the Fort Worth establishment at that time. He was well connected with artists and patrons in Houston and Dallas."[3] Williams, in fact, introduced Winter to Houston sculptor Jim Love, who was frequently commuting to Dallas to visit his friend, artist Roy Fridge, while also learning to cast metal at the Arlington Studio. At a Williams dinner party, Jeanette and Roger met Fridge, as well as Norma and David McManaway.

"The McManaways started inviting Jeanette and me to weekend parties at their house on Wellborn Street when they found out I could play the guitar and sing country music—Anita and Charles would ride over with us. We met Peggy Wilson, Paul Harris, Ruth and Hal Pauley, Jett and Herb Rogalla, Janet and Jon Kutner. Peggy Wilson introduced Jeanette's work to a children's book editor at Knopf, a branch of Random House. This led to Jeanette's first illustrated children's book, a Norwegian folk tale. The Oak Lawn crowd seemed to enlarge right away. We each had a sense of irrational imagery and space. The Surrealists and Dadaists were more real to us than the older Texas artists' realism. All of us shared an edgy sense of humor."

Winter and the other Oak Lawn artists were also front and center to the earliest flurries of contemporary art in Texas. The momentum generated by these energetic and progressive individuals was sustained in the early 1960s by outside professionals who descended on the state with the zeal of missionaries. There was a brief period when Douglas MacAgy and his ex-wife Jermayne both served as directors of new Texas museums—he at the Dallas Museum for Contemporary Arts (DMCA) and she at Houston's Contemporary Arts Museum. The two are generally credited with introducing contemporary art to the Texas public, and their operations were a focus for a generation of Texas artists—McManaway, Love, Fridge, and Winter, among others—who worked on and sometimes were included in MacAgy exhibitions.

When Douglas MacAgy was hired in 1958 to head the DMCA, he had already served as curator of the San Francisco Museum of Art and was a former director of the California School of Fine Arts, consultant to the director of the Museum of Modern Art, and director of research at Wildenstein and Company in New York.[4]

In Dallas, MacAgy and his longtime principal assistant, Urban Neininger, sparked critical dialogue among artists and the viewing public about ideas and issues important to contemporary art. They introduced artists to one another, acting as catalysts to develop a community of shared interests and inspirations. The artists, in turn, looked to each other for support, thereby exchanging ideas and opinions. And while their art did not overtly express it, they felt a relationship, a kinship, to the state in which it was accomplished.

The short-lived DMCA, which merged with the Dallas Museum of Fine Arts (DMFA) in 1963, was generally considered to be less a museum and more an "artists' place"—a location to meet, talk, and work with friends in the presence of great art. The camaraderie would later prompt MacAgy to observe that the artists often talked more about pranks and parties than they did about art.[5] About the Oak Lawn coterie of artists, MacAgy writes, "What is refreshing about these artists is that they don't care a hoot about outside judgments along this line. They care about caring, and if others should say that their cares are small and maybe parochial, they'd simply reply that they care hugely about little things. For this reason the over-heated rhetoric of the metropolitan market-place has slight attraction. Their felt destiny is foreign to it. On the other hand, apart from the puffs, they are immensely interested in what other artists are doing."[6] According to Winter, the bohemian group took a vow of "exotic poverty." They were representative of a new breed of artists who, having received scant credibility and economic support for their art, had nothing to lose by being as independent and tough-minded as they wished. More important, each artist had been involved in the development of weighty, irreverent symbolic and mythical imagery, as well as wild experimentation that found expression in specific iconography and manipulated message.

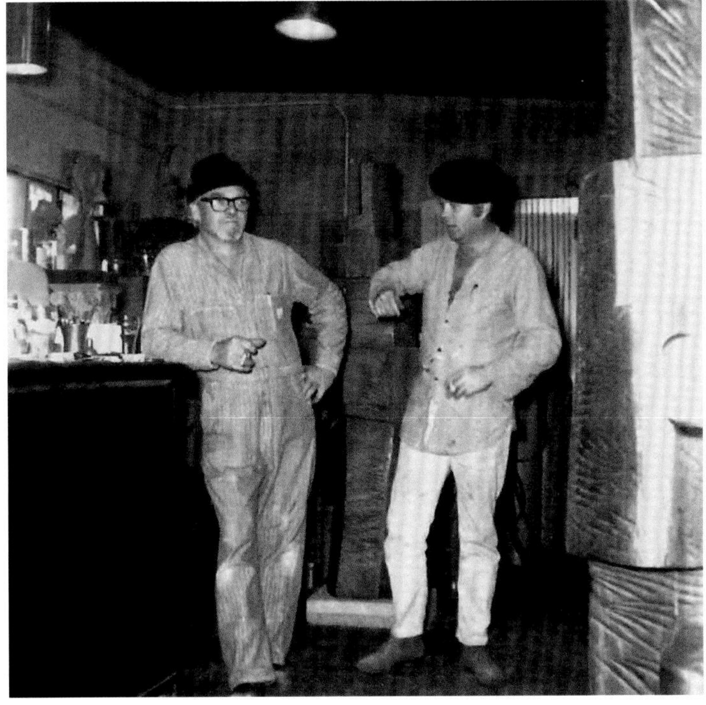

Charles T. Williams *(left)* with Jim Love, 1966
Arlington, Texas | Collection of Karl B. Williams

As in other regions throughout the country where serious art making was taking hold, in the Texas of the 1960s, contemporary art had its beginnings in found-object assemblage and Surrealist-inspired junk sculpture. Indeed, by the time the Museum of Modern Art's *Art of Assemblage* came to Dallas in the early 1960s, some Texas artists were already working with similar ideas. The landmark exhibition included Jim Love's junkyard "put togethers," which mixed Surrealism and a tinge of Pop Art. Artists seeking to combine greater visual complexity and freedom of spirit in their art were encouraged by MacAgy's courageous leadership. He well understood the community's limited exposure and tried to establish a broader grasp of modern and contemporary art through complex, dazzling thematic exhibitions that elicited visual and psychological responses in viewers and artists alike. Work by some of the most important artists of the twentieth century was first presented at the DMCA, yet placed in a comprehensible and historical context. Among the many exhibitions that consisted of wonderful and surprising combinations of works were *Rene Magritte in America*, the first retrospective exhibition of the artist's oeuvre in North America; *The Art That Broke the Looking-Glass*, including works by Paolo Veronese, Picasso, Albrecht Dürer, Joseph Cornell, Kurt Schwitters, and David McManaway; *The Arts of the Circus*, featuring paintings by Picasso, Georges Rouault, Grant Wood, and Walt Kuhn, as well as painted carousel horses by Winter, Fridge, McManaway, and Peggy Wilson. Most important was *1961*, with works by James Rosenquist, Robert Rauschenberg, Robert Motherwell, Joseph Glasco, and Fridge, among others. As part of the landmark exhibition, Claes Oldenburg set up his famous *Store* at the DMCA and stayed for three weeks to improvise and stage *Injun*, the first Happening anywhere on museum commission. Significantly, Fridge designed catalogs for a number of MacAgy's groundbreaking exhibitions and made a film of *Injun* in which several members of the artist group took part.

By spring 1962, however, Winter had grown tired of the Fort Worth–Dallas commute. "I joined Chapman Kelley's gallery, much to the dismay of the group, and Chapman managed to get two classes for me to teach at Julius Schepps Community Center in North Dallas. Douglas MacAgy hired me to join the installation crew at the DMCA. I was coming to Dallas one week a month to install new shows, one day a week to teach at Schepps, and three or four days a week at Charles's studio. And Jeanette was pregnant with our first child, Jonah, so it seemed sensible to be near our friends in the Oak Lawn area."

As Winter tells it, MacAgy and staff welcomed him into the coterie. What's more, their relationships didn't stop after the whistle blew. The Winters socialized with Norma and David McManaway, Jett and Herb Rogalla, Betty and Douglas MacAgy, Jean and Urban Neininger, Roy Fridge, Paul Harris, and Peggy Wilson and her partner, Jane Nightingale, several times a week. "When Jim Love or Charles Williams came to town, David and Norma's house was a gathering place," Winter recalls. "Hal and Ruth lived just across the street, so it was something of a movable feast. We talked about and listened to music, when we weren't making it ourselves. Lightnin' Hopkins, Blind Lemon Jefferson, early jazz musicians like Jelly Roll Morton. We each brought what we could to the conversations. We enjoyed each other's company and formed some prevailing values about art. Not a style, but prevailing principles. We talked about Rauschenberg and Jasper Johns. Through Douglas, at the moment, the Oak Lawn group was tuned in to the cutting edge of the avant-garde in art. Douglas was the sun; we were his satellites—each of us found a new energy and strength that we never forgot."

William B. Jordan, the preeminent art historian and former chair of fine arts at Southern Methodist University, later observed that "there was something special about the vibrations of that time."[7] The tight group of artists who banded together in Oak Lawn living rooms—Fridge, Love, David McManaway, Hal Pauley, Bill Komodore,

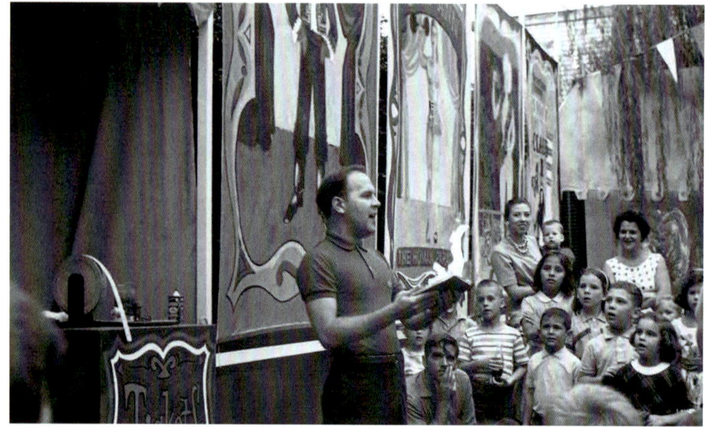

Dallas Theater Center actor Claude Crowe at the party for the Dallas Museum for Contemporary Arts exhibition *The Arts of the Circus*, October 9–November 11, 1962
© Paul Rogers Harris, courtesy of the Dallas Museum of Art Archives, Paul Rogers Harris Papers

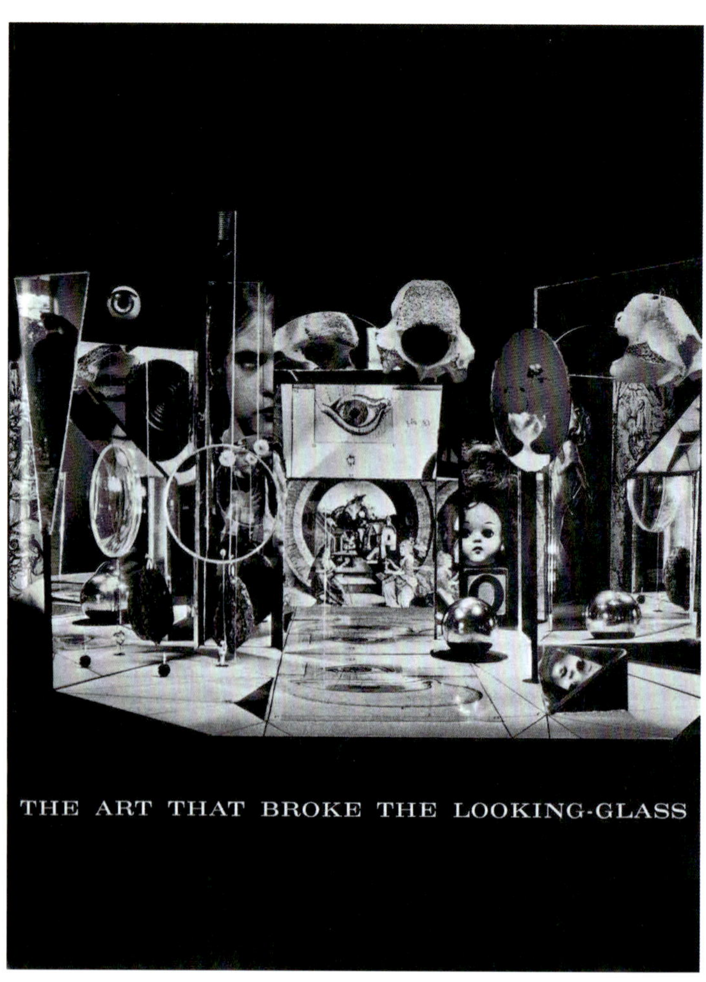

The Art That Broke the Looking-Glass, 1961
Dallas Museum for Contemporary Arts exhibition catalog | Courtesy of the Dallas Museum of Art Archives

Herb Rogalla, Charles Williams, and Winter—not only developed a close association with the DMCA but also embodied "a certain commonality of sensibility—a sensibility which could have been cultivated nowhere but Texas."[8]

An important influence on the group of artists was Paul Baker, founder of the Dallas Theater Center (DTC). Fridge and Love had both studied with Baker at Baylor University. There, Fridge met his future wife, Mary Sue Birkhead, who, after their divorce, married Baker's successor as director of the DTC. Fridge maintained his interest in theater, designing several innovative sets for the Dallas Little Theater, including *Waiting for Godot* and *Don Juan in Hell*, which featured surrealistic, abstract scenery. Significantly, a position at the Alley Theater as set designer took Love from Dallas to Houston, where he was hired by Jermayne MacAgy to install exhibitions. "Jim Love would fly back and forth between Houston and Dallas," Winter recalls. "He thought it was ironic that he flew up to Love Field. Paul Baker was very much an ally of Douglas MacAgy. Through associations, David and Norma McManaway became friends with Mary Sue and patrons of the Theater Center. Jeanette and I saw *Krapp's Last Tape* and *Waiting for Godot* at the DTC while I was with the installation crew at the DMCA. The Happenings and absurd theater, promoted by MacAgy and Baker, added fire to the private inner world that generated our art."

According to Winter, the Oak Lawn group was also stimulated by the nonlinear films of Federico Fellini and Ingmar Bergman, which set the tone for a revival of images in art. "We felt a part of the moment in art, turning away from nonobjectivity and allowing the milieu of the street and cottages of Oak Lawn to be our world and our source," Winter explains. "I think we each felt a love and some nostalgia toward a bypassed world swept away by the exclusive formalism of action painting. Those films were part of the zeitgeist that my works of the early 1960s grew from—the almost circuslike clothing, the interplay of figures, the playful objects, the darkness and light." Indeed, many Surrealist and Dadaist artists of the 1930s had arranged objects in unlikely combinations that challenged rational thought and summoned poetic associations. Although Abstract Expressionism

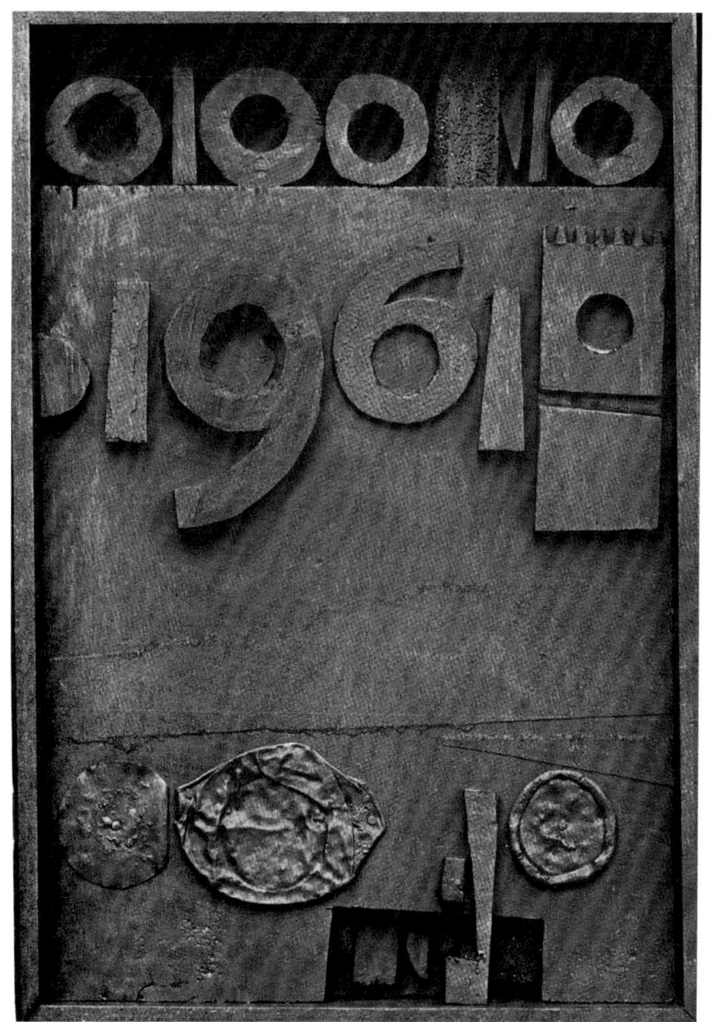

1961
Dallas Museum for Contemporary Arts exhibition catalog | Courtesy of the Dallas Museum of Art Archives

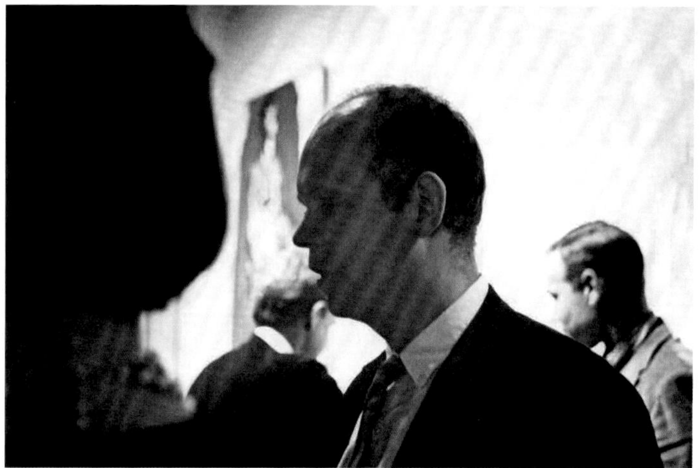

Claes Oldenburg at the opening of the Dallas Museum for Contemporary Arts exhibition 1961, April 3–May 13, 1962
© Paul Rogers Harris, courtesy of the Dallas Museum of Art Archives, Paul Rogers Harris Papers

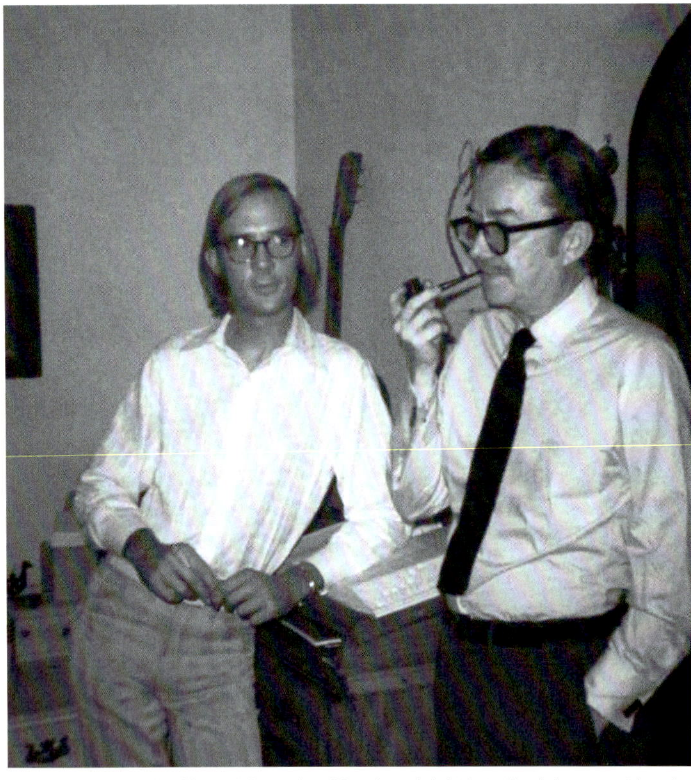

Bill Jordan (*left*) and Douglas MacAgy *(right)* at the idea meeting for the exhibition *One i at a time*, 1970

reached its height as a movement in the 1950s, its emphasis on the act or process of making a work of art was of major consequence for artists who began to produce assemblage.[9] As an additive process, assemblage introduced a wide range of materials and forms. It brought into play a whole new body of work that could not be strictly codified as either painting or sculpture. Rather, assemblage traded on both, expanding on the found or constructed object as it was first recognized by such pioneers of collage, the readymade object, and relief sculpture as Picasso, Marcel Duchamp, and Max Ernst.[10] Celebrated for its unorthodox use of materials, the medium became the basis for the innovative work of a generation of American artists from the postwar period to the early 1960s, including Rauschenberg, Johns, and their circle. For Winter, the found object began to percolate in his work by way of Pop Art in MacAgy's *1961* exhibition and through the works of McManaway, Love, and Fridge.

Love and McManaway, according to MacAgy, got along like cousins. Both showed a fairly sanguine humor and an eye for the discarded. During this formative period, each artist learned to trust his intuition. Putting the right thing next to some piece of junk gave distinction and significance to both the whole and its components. MacAgy writes, "An oil canister, disposable after use, is supposedly junkyard bound. Instead, on the street, it is crushed by a passing truck. By chance, McManaway finds its remains worth picking up. One day, when fiddling with a pale wax mold that he has teased into looking like the face of a bartender with a walrus mustache, he sees the squashed can and its legend, 'Pioneer.' The two go well together and also make a joke. The joke's on me: it's my portrait."[11] At the same time, Love developed an "animal style" out of pipe—humorously bewildered characters who are not quite sure about the world, creatures that emerge from plumbing joints and fixtures with an element of surprise. "Ridiculous pathos in the commonplace is a frequent quality in Love's way of looking at things," writes MacAgy. "The way is affectionate, shy, and a little sad and strangely lonely."[12] Metal caps rose like flowers out of pots; periscopes were formed by fitting an "elbow" to a straight joint of pipe; elegant little handles were attached to pieces in case of a quick and unexpected departure.

Although Fridge spent many years producing commercial films and building theatrical set constructions, his sculpture—like that of Love and McManaway—was made from scavenged parts, some of which he found in Dallas junkyards or collected on trips to the beach of Port Aransas. Similarly, Fridge's work often integrated elements of language, in the form of written or visual puns with influences of primitivism and Surrealism, particularly the totemic sculpture of Constantin Brancusi. The *Hero* series—a satirical response to the post-McCarthy era and conservative atmosphere of Dallas in the early 1960s—combined collaged newspaper headlines and dolls with faces and torsos that could be manipulated with the pull of a toilet chain. Whereas the sculptures playfully mocked society's need for living heroes, they also conveyed a kind of homespun animation reminiscent of Victorian antique toys.

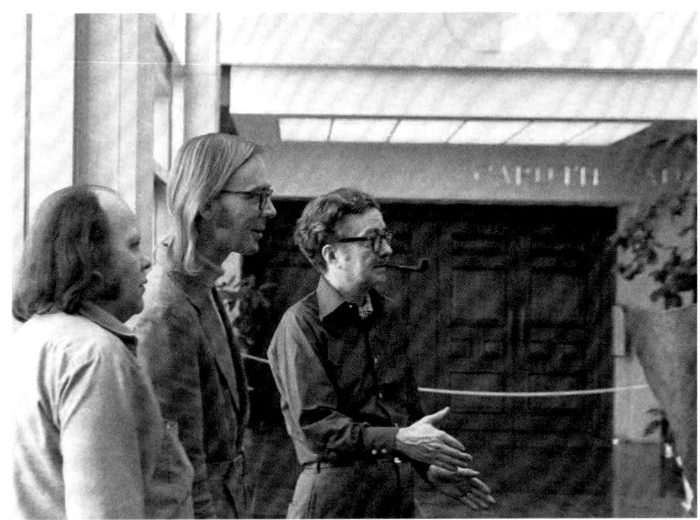

Left to right: Jim Love, Bill Jordan, and Douglas MacAgy at the installation of the exhibition *One i at a time*, 1970
© Paul Rogers Harris, courtesy of the Dallas Museum of Art Archives, Paul Rogers Harris Papers

Significantly, the humor that was central to the trio's work was most effective when finely balanced between pessimism and wit. In McManaway's case, the relationship involved a kind of aesthetic double take in which the amusing preciousness of funky antique baubles deferred to wily, puzzlingly elusive personal messages. His ambitious Jomo boards, fastidiously selected objects arranged like specimens in an obliquely magical narrative, revealed the artist's uncanny ability to use bric-a-brac to invoke character. McManaway slowly produced Jomos for more than three decades; the name comes from a film he saw as a boy in which a black man sells magic charms called jomos. Organized into niches as if they were altarpieces, McManaway's Jomos often contain severed doll heads and doll arms, skulls, bones, old sticks, baby shoes, pull toys, snakes, wooden blocks, old puppets, and stuffed bears with kewpie doll feathers.

Because of the ties between the components and the society that produced them, what we see in found-object art is inevitably tied to what we know, what we think, and what we remember. The beauty of timeworn materials contrasts with queasy textures, Gothic imagery, and the disintegration of form. To that end, an interpretive unease is created by these artists' exposure of hypocrisy on one hand, and, on the other, by their humorous delight in eroticism and in the seamy side of American culture. At the core is the notion of assemblage as an art of reference—an inherently theatrical one at that—and as an art of psychological association that reminds us uncomfortably of our own foibles and anxieties, decay and mortality.

The 1960s were all about freedom but also a time when art movements brought about huge changes. It was the decade in which Winter started to become the painter he would be. The close friendships nurtured with McManaway, Fridge, and Love, as well as their shared aesthetic sensibilities, had a life-changing impact on Winter's art. He explains,

> Jim got much of his material from used metal scrapyards around Houston and Dallas/Fort Worth. David found his material on the street, in dime stores, and at the Goodwill. Roy's work had more to do with whittling, and yet his tub bass was made from a washtub, a broomstick notched on both ends, and a long strand of clothesline. Except for Roy's films, the three of them used objects in 3-D works. I began to use such objects as elements in my paintings, but also in collage and silkscreens. The subjects of many of my snapshots, even in more recent decades, are found objects. We were making art look like things—separating art from life. I think knowing David, Jim, and Roy caused me to move fifty or seventy-five years into time. They helped me catch up and get an idea of things that were going on. It was exciting for me. It was like, goodbye school, goodbye Iowa, goodbye to all that. It's a different world out here and I'm going to be part of it. I learned through David, Jim, and Roy how to make something that didn't fit, that jumped, that didn't belong—that wasn't supposed to be there in a logical way.

At the same time, Winter's close contact with MacAgy and especially Claes Oldenburg had a lasting impact on his art. The two commissioned works by Oldenburg for the exhibition *1961* generated tremendous controversy in the Dallas art community. For *Store*, the artist re-created his

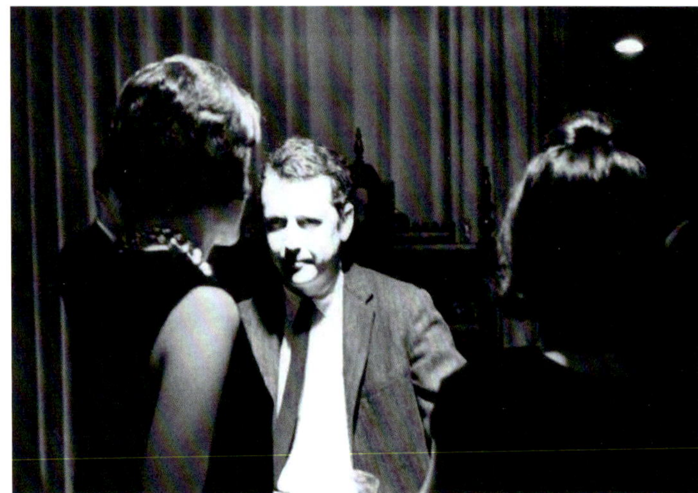

Roy Fridge at the opening of the Dallas Museum for Contemporary Arts exhibition 1961, April 3–May 13, 1962
© Paul Rogers Harris, courtesy of the Dallas Museum of Art Archives, Paul Rogers Harris Papers

New York City "retail space" of expressionistically sculpted consumer goods. Each piece was supported by chicken wire, on which Oldenburg placed strips of muslin soaked in plaster and then painted with enamel. This produced an abstract interior structure with numerous folds and lines. Sometimes the strips of muslin resembled broad brushstrokes. By presenting a living theater of sorts, the object-as-commodity became a symbol of the fantasies, desires, and obsessions inherent in our daily lives.[13] Although Pop Art's rapid takeover of the New York art scene had already begun in the early 1960s, Winter maintains that he was not fully aware of it until the DMCA installation. "I knew more about the figurative Abstract Expressionists," he says.

> Pop Art came with quite a big bang. David, Roy, and I had the job of unpacking all the crates for Oldenburg's *Store*. We would ask, "What's this object?" Then we'd get up on ladders and look at it on the floor and say, "It's a Pepsi lid!" We wouldn't be able to recognize it up close. In his *Store*, Claes had all kinds of food products. One of the local TV stations came over to interview Oldenburg. All of this was in the wake of Abstract Expressionism and nobody could really get it. The interviewer asked, "Mr. Oldenburg, some of us don't understand these things or what you're about. Could you explain this to us?" And Oldenburg said, "Oh yeah, I'd be happy to—that's a banana split and that's a donut and that's a tomato." His wife at the time, Pat, said, "That's not a tomato, it's a candied apple." And all of this was going into Dallas TV news. It was just such a shock. I remember the slice of coconut pie sitting on a chair he borrowed from Norma and David McManaway. And that had such an impact on me, that slice of pie on a chair. Bror Utter, a painter from Fort Worth, was so outraged by the whole thing that he picked up the piece of pie off the chair and took a bite out of it. Immediately, I knew which side I was on. All of a sudden, the grocery store for me was the most exciting place to go!

As previously mentioned, the Pop Art provocateur's other work for *1961* was the first Happening outside of New York City and the first commissioned by a museum. *Injun* was the most notorious event produced by the DMCA. With the help of his wife, Pat; the museum staff; painting students; and other individuals from the art community, Oldenburg took over a vacated squatter's cottage located at the edge of the

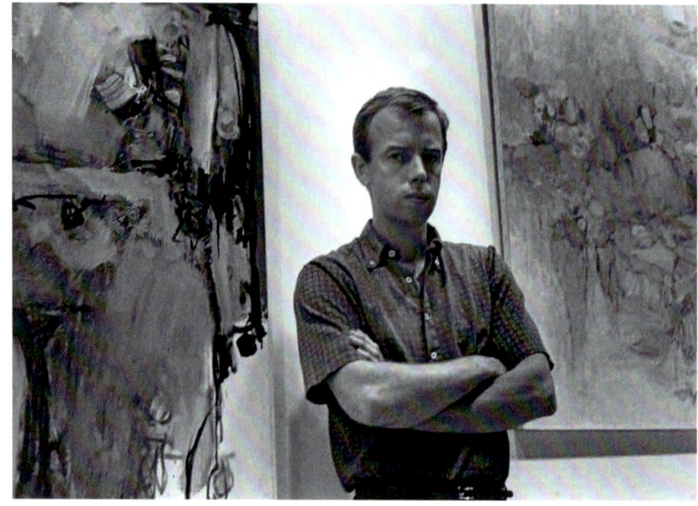

David McManaway at the Dallas Museum for Contemporary Arts exhibition *Three Texas Artists*, May 23–June 10, 1962
© Paul Rogers Harris, courtesy of the Dallas Museum of Art Archives, Paul Rogers Harris Papers

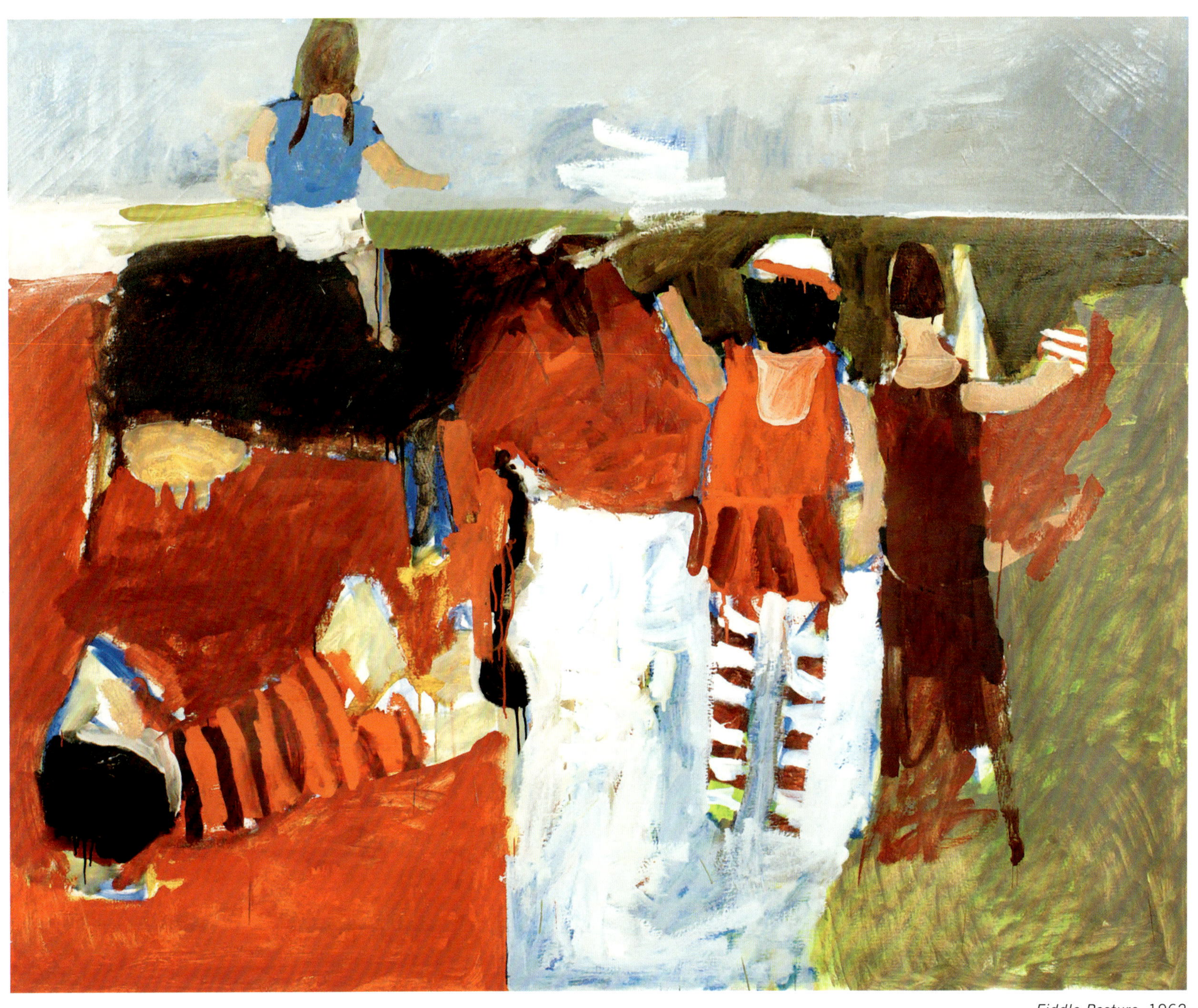

Fiddle Pasture, 1962

oil on canvas | 48 5/8" × 60 11/16" | Fred Jones Jr. Museum of Art, University of Oklahoma, Norman | Museum purchase, 1962

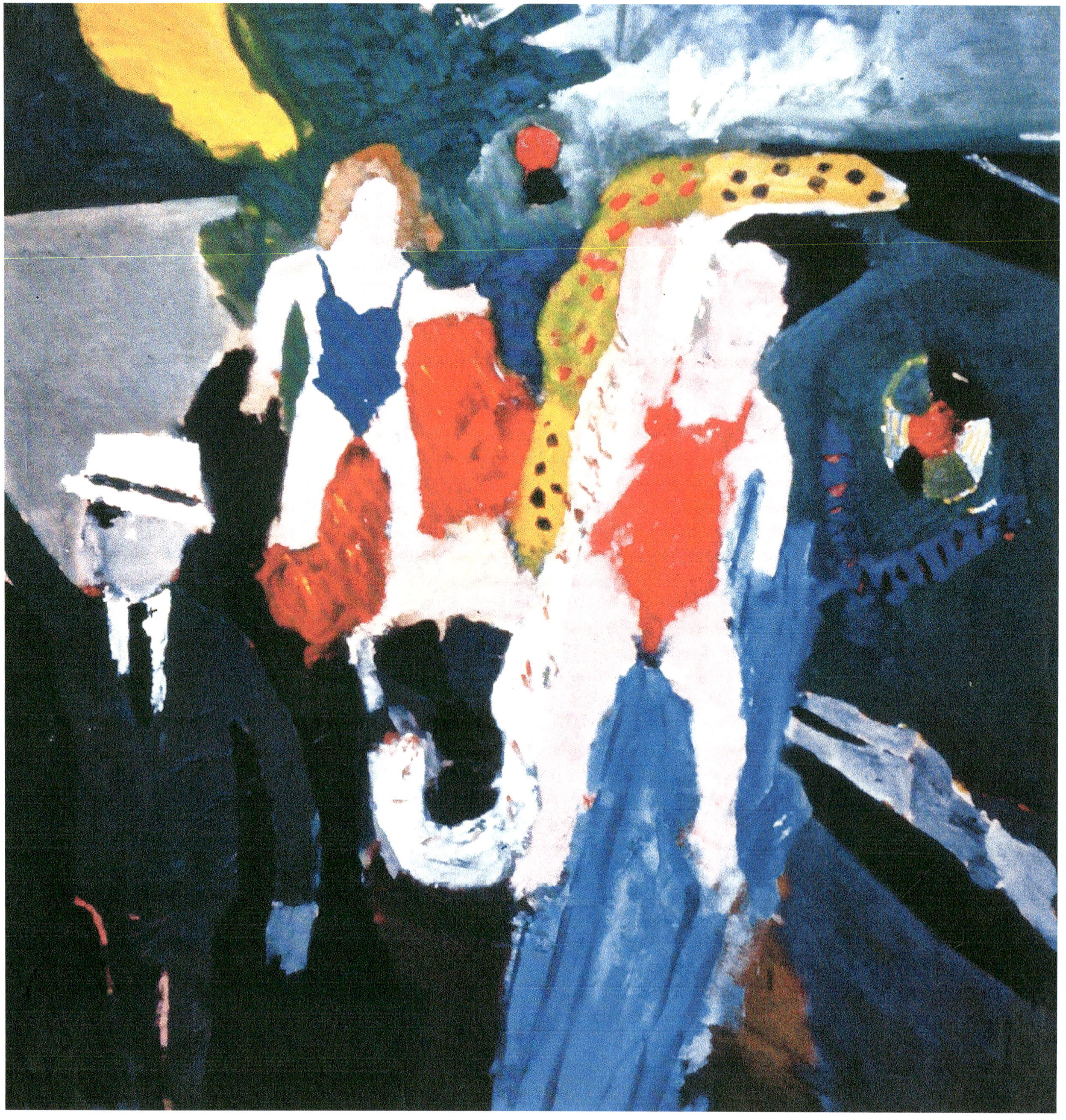

Games, 1963

oil on canvas | 60" × 60" | Courtesy of the artist

museum's property. Years later MacAgy had these reflections: "The site was kept secret. Dressed up as always for any occasion, that night socialite Texas convened in the Museum building. Solemnly the throng was asked to line up and grasp a rope. Lights went out. The line was silently led over rough ground to the obscure shack and its goat house. From this point, the experience was tatterdemalion and pandemonium. Cops came with drawn guns and could be turned away only when local dignitaries with boiled or ruffled shirtfronts were singled out of the crowd."[14] According to Winter, Oldenburg guided viewers through the rooms to the sounds of Native American drums and chants. Joe Hobbs and his students wrestled on the floor while Hal Pauley pretended to play a violin amid piles of newspapers. As Leigh Arnold describes the scene, Oldenburg, dressed in a savage-looking costume of shredded newspaper, danced around and, at the end of the Happening, "dragged his wife's limp body onto the roof of a shed behind the house and chopped a tornado-like object made of papier-mâché."[15] Winter recalls, "Jeanette and I were about the only ones who didn't take part in the Happening because she was seven months pregnant with Jonah. But we were enthusiastic members of the audience. There was a rope that we had to hold on to while moving through the cottage that Claes had transformed into the Happening. Jeanette and I were holding the rope behind a Dallas business couple. The man said, 'The membership at the DMFA is really going to skyrocket tomorrow.' I think Dallas people were just flabbergasted—they couldn't believe this was going on in Dallas. How exciting to know that my friends and I helped usher in the art of that tumultuous decade."

Veteran art dealer Murray Smither, who studied and worked for Chapman Kelley in the early 1960s, also volunteered as a lighting assistant for the DMCA exhibitions. Just twenty years old at the time, he grasped that "something was changing" in the Dallas art world. "MacAgy and the museum were the starting points," Smither recalls. "It was in the air—Jermayne MacAgy and her incredible shows in Houston—but Douglas MacAgy was wonderful in that he got the whole community involved, including the artists by hiring them. McManaway, Love, Fridge, and Komodore and Winter—everybody got involved. Janet Kutner was the museum's secretary before she became art critic for the *Dallas Morning News*. The activity began to create interest in galleries and it was because of the spirit of the Dallas Museum for Contemporary Arts."[16]

The upshot of *1961* and Winter's experiences with Oldenburg were epiphany moments in his life. Art was presented in a most vital and current way that transformed his outlook permanently, while also cutting him free from the pre-pop gestural approach to realism via action painting. "All of this together, along with David's, Jim's, and Roy's works, changed me forever and set my art on a track that was vital and frightening," Winter explains. "But I was fearless." While teaching at the Julius Schepps Community Center, Winter began painting brash figurative works. Dorothy Miller, the esteemed curator for the Museum of Modern Art, awarded the purchase prize to Winter's *Fiddle Pasture* at the Southwest Annual in Oklahoma City. The painting features visceral, drippy brushstrokes and bold color. At upper left, a child rides a cow, whose udder dangles as protruding abstract shapes. A figure in a striped shirt reclines on the ground below them. At right, two figures, one in black leggings and one in striped leggings, stand side by side and hold out instruments. The central area reveals a vertical violin, half-covered by a massive white shape. According to Winter, the painting refers to playing country music at parties with his artist friends: "Roy played a tub, stick, and string fiddle, David a banjo, and I a guitar." As in *Family Group*, the painting is an arrangement of horizontal, vertical, and geometric forms.

Since the DMCA was winding to a close, Winter took a job with Hallmark Electronics delivering diodes and transistors in the Dallas vicinity. He added a class at Schepps Community Center, but that hardly paid the rent. "We were poor as beggars," Winter recalls. "We couldn't afford a telephone, so I'd drive over to David and Norma's house to call our pediatrician, Dr. William Dean, who bartered medical care for paintings—or any other call." However, when Chapman Kelley suggested a solo show for late spring 1963, Winter took a big chance: he quit the

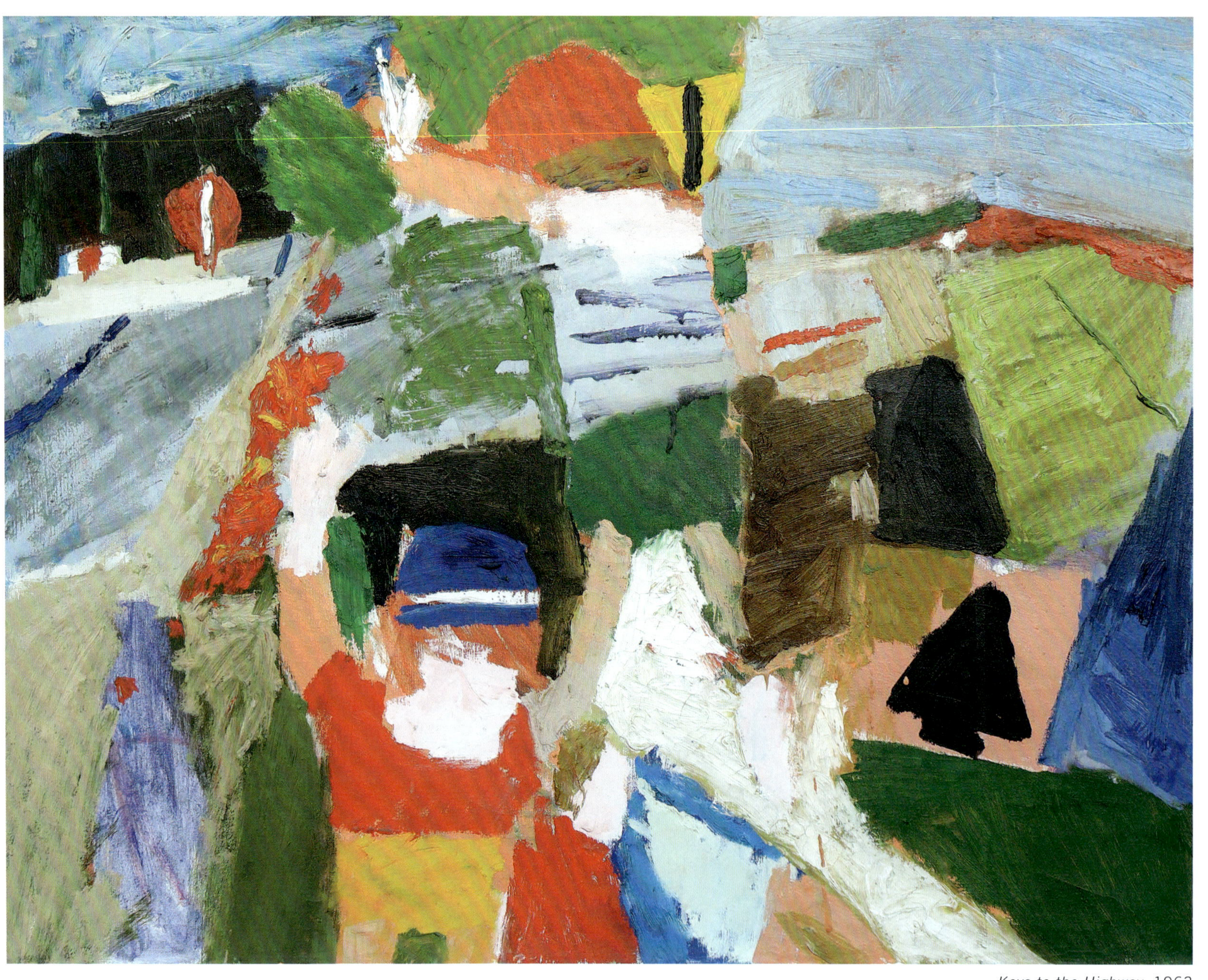

Keys to the Highway, 1963

oil on canvas | 24" × 30" | Collection of Gerri Strauss, Cincinnati, Ohio | Photography by Andrew Tanen delivery job and started painting full time and in between the classes at Schepps. He finished a painting each day. During that same period, Winter and Fridge drove to Houston to see *Pop! Goes the Easel*, curated by Douglas MacAgy for the Contemporary Arts Museum. Featuring work by Andy Warhol, Jim Dine, James Rosenquist, Roy Lichtenstein, Idelle Weber, Tom Wesselmann, and Wayne Thiebaud, among others, the show responded to the "cool" surfaces, mechanical reproduction, and the overtly affirmative embrace of the market and mass consumption. The imagery pointed viewers to what was found on store and kitchen shelves, the magazine stand, in movies, and on television. For Winter it only reaffirmed Pop's aim to be more accessibly human and cerebral at the same time, but also to smirk, slouch, and revel in playing at art.

As it happened, Winter's exhibition at Chapman Kelley—his first solo effort—completely sold out. The works produced at the time were heavy with paint; overall the content reflected an act of the absurd. In *Games*, some of the depicted objects were Pop inspired, but most were based on Jonah's soft baby toys. Two central figures in red and blue swimsuits play with yellow and orange toys; a yellow thought balloon hovers in the distance. The lower left is anchored by a figure in a dark business suit with a white hat and blue hand. In *Keys to the Highway*, Winter flanks the figures alongside a crusader's flag, highway signs, and other symbols. Unlike the more relaxed and harmonious array of *Family Group*, these paintings seemingly juxtaposed figures in dynamic and dissonant relationships. Both, however, give clear evidence of Winter's strong dependence on form and structure, as well as an abstract distribution of color areas all over the surfaces. Reds located spatially and laterally in the central areas of his paintings—as swimsuits, balls, or signs—are balanced by and held to the picture plane by reds of like temperature placed to the side or behind them. There is a tussle in the early works between the substance and the subject of paint that would come to define his art. Right out of the gate, Winter aimed to fuse formal analysis and structure with pure emotional energy.

The early 1960s were a whirlwind of activity for Winter. The show at Chapman Kelley created a buzz in the Dallas art community, prompting Jerry Bywaters, then director of the DMFA, to offer Winter teaching positions at the Museum School and Southern Methodist University's night school in downtown Dallas. "Jerry Bywaters was a generous and good man," says Winter.

> But he was often spoken of as weak because of his giving in to some Dallas followers of the 1950s anticommunist movement. That image of weakness, along with his unwavering support of homegrown artists—Otis Dozier, Everett Spruce, William Lester—was anathema to the Dallas wish of the sixties to be a world city and to live down its guilt for the Kennedy assassination and its international reputation for right-wing political leaning. Realism, regionalism, painting from life—these were dirty words to the would-be avant-garde of the Dallas art world. Both sides were a bit narrow-minded. I had come to see a different world. The Oak Lawn group of artists were funambulists balancing above the fray that continued below. When the DMCA closed and MacAgy moved to Washington, DC, the Oak Lawn artists had to learn to live at room temperature. David started teaching at the DMFA, Roy moved to various South Texas areas and became a hermit—his word. I had to go to Houston to see Jim Love. I suppose that my teaching and showing at Atelier Chapman Kelley was like a betrayal, but it became clear that the path I chose promised survival and growth, as well as an independent voice in the art community. My fearlessness and messianic approach as a teacher was something people were looking for at that time. And I wasn't a self-appointed artist-teacher. I had been through the fires, and I was ready.

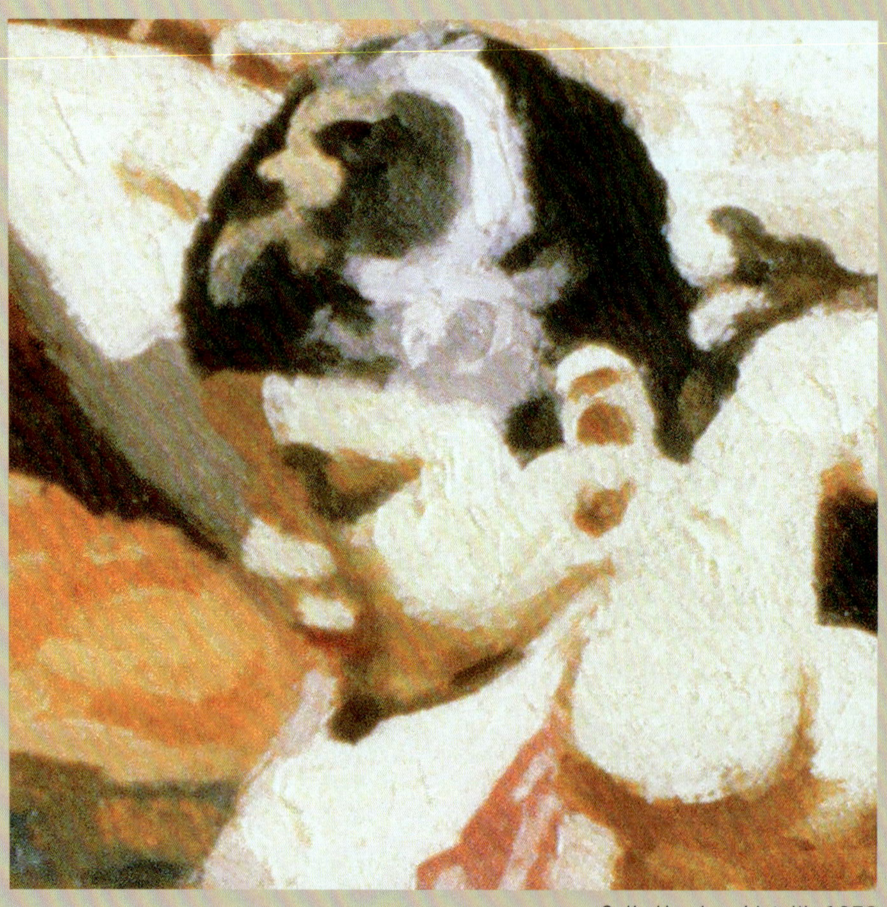

Sally Horchow (detail), 1978

oil on linen | 6" × 8" | Collection of the Roger Horchow Family |

Photography by Kevin Todora

CHAPTER 6

ARTIST-TEACHER

MAYBE IT SEEMS WISTFUL to look back from our more global era, but having a sense of place, registering a sense of belonging, was important for a young artist. Once, perhaps, the contemporary art world was composed of small, more or less local communities of struggling creatives who scraped along by helping one another and relying on the largesse of the occasional wealthy benefactor. For a while now, however, that art world has really been an art industry patronized by financiers and flippers whose chief aesthetic interest is the extra zero on their new asset's price tag. It's no secret that the art market can consume new artists as fast as they emerge. Many become victims of a recent trend fueled by a zeal for newness that places young artists in the spotlight before they are ready, or deserve, to be there. Youthful passion is often mistaken for brilliant work, encouraging many artists to expect midcareer surveys before they hit thirty. For some, art school is just a finishing school, rather than an arena in which to square ideas. Others emerge as hyperprofessionals, institutional guarantors of the New. Indeed, the support system of galleries, collectors, curators, and universities that once made it possible for emerging artists to pursue serious careers is in a state of near collapse. There is simply no longer a structure that nourishes such incremental artistic growth. Often, exhibitions are not events that evolve naturally, presented in rhythm with an artist's development; rather, they are responses to market pressures. Every year, MFA programs mint hordes of professionally trained artists who compete for representation by galleries, which in turn compete for collectors. Is this why students aspire to become artists? To strategize and game-play to an extent that shuts the door on great traditions of thought, technical skill, and invention?

It wasn't so long ago that artists were still viewed as vital change agents, opening our eyes to radical new ways of seeing the world and their possibilities within it. Ideas mattered; social cultural and political issues were at stake. Art had a broader importance. It once stood for the free operation of a thinking mind. The school of art was a site for argument about what contemporary art production might entail, rather than a place to repeat received behavior. This created a process that wasn't comfortable but made the school of art a serious place to get work done, for students and faculty alike.

From the outset, Winter encouraged his students to rethink what becoming an artist might be about, rather than training them to ply their craft, quietly in wait for some personal revelation. What he conferred was the sense of responsibility to their own integrity, even as teacher and students challenged each other and were highly supportive of each other, especially after the students left school and students and teacher convened like members gathering at a family reunion. In many ways, Winter's classes during the early 1960s at the Julius Schepps Community Center, the Dallas Museum of Fine Arts, and Southern Methodist University (SMU) night school represented an ever-receding type of social life among creative people, one in which the friendships built and circles configured seemed more firmly rooted in genuine affection, in affinity, in shared notions of play, than in the prospect of mutual professional advantage. An independent individual who understandably guarded his privacy and artistic integrity carefully, Winter nevertheless became a kind of painting uncle figure and trusted mentor who moved students from acknowledging an innate artistic ability to fully committing to it as a path through life. He comprehended the nature of art at its most fundamental as a mutating, vibrant, and ever-evolving force that contrasted with packaged and predictable presentations. Winter's painting and teaching methods continued to develop over the decades, demonstrating the artist's capacity for constant self-criticism and self-awareness, which was rarely matched by any of his contemporaries. Some of Winter's students have become great artists, others have learned something, and still others have gotten lost or been overlooked in the catacombs. About the role of artist-teacher, Winter writes, "Many current university programs have all but removed the hand from art-making so that the mind can be unfettered by any necessity for skill. . . . So questions occur. . . . Isn't ignoring the time-honored accumulated history of teaching art, hubris in the extreme? The dilemma can only be solved if art teaching establishments, artist/teachers, and art students stay in a constant state of evolution. Each must continually, carefully, assimilate and analyze new knowledge and new insights. In a moment's time, truth can turn into half-truth."[1]

Admittedly, Winter was teaching himself as he was also helping scores of other people—ages fourteen to seventy-five—grow and become younger as they accrued information. He was able to effect change by instilling intellectual curiosity and an abiding faith in one's voice. Winter explains,

> Life changes with teaching. People depended on me to help them grow. The success signs were an intensified interest in their own work and the work of others; a fearlessness toward materials; an improved vocabulary both of visual words and forms; phone calls to me during the week to discuss questions or misgivings; visits to our house to talk about ideas. But I would always say, "When you are no longer around me, don't return to room temperature. Keep your work alive through growth." I *knew* that it worked because it was working for me. Through teaching, I was learning more about color, reviving my interest in drawing and art history. It had a refining impact, because of a need to communicate, to persuade. My commitment to the job was often misread by colleagues who saw teaching as a convenient way to support a studio. To me, it was a very important profession that deserved all I could give. It was as important to me as painting is important. The more I learned and explored, the more I could bring to my students. I would never let it rest in my studio or the classroom.

For the Julius Schepps Community Center, Winter taught painting classes exclusively. Given only small table easels on which to work, he immediately built standing adjustable easels. Moreover, he insisted that the women students stretch their own canvases and work large. At the Dallas Museum of Fine Arts, Winter taught a Saturday morning high school class, as well as an adult painting class in the afternoon and a Wednesday night life drawing class. Among the high school students—Robert Yarber, Carol Hoy,

Charlotte Seifert, Arleigh Stark, Tim Coursey, and other artists—many still visit Winter whenever possible, meet for lunches, and send annual holiday cards. Stephen Mueller was especially close to the Winter family during high school and as an undergraduate at the University of Texas. His correspondence to Winter, in the form of handwritten letters, drawings, and enigmatic collages, related the highs and lows of art school. In Austin, Mueller wrote, "Hail from the land of the semi trailer tractor truck—and the carnival. . . . A girl and myself flew airplanes out of the 23rd floor of the tower (where we weren't supposed to be) at the campus cops. And on some we wrote 'make love not war' . . . and we paint—and we decided that the faculty plan to dispose of us heretics is to conquer by intimidation (grades and all)."[2]

In another, Mueller complained that "the old avant-garde around is really too much for me—I just barely perfect one palate [*sic*] knife technique when one of the old masters around here comes up with another—Old McNulty of the Philadelphia Museum rejected both of my drawings from the drawing show."[3] In still another letter, Mueller excitedly describes an exhibition in Austin with "all the famous artists"—"Richard Lindner, Richard Diebenkorn, Andy Warhol, (Elizabeth Taylor), Rauschenberg (2 good ones), Jim Dine, Gorky, de Kooning, Lee Bontecou. . . . I had never seen a real Larry Rivers before, or a Rauschenberg—Good grief!"[4] In the same missive, however, Mueller is confused about art school teaching methods: "Shawn and myself had a big huge awful war concerning the manner in which art students are trained and the 'freedom' which they are allowed to flaunt—aren't design, anatomy, and landscape elements discipline—or—I'm not sure I understand!"[5] Significantly, the correspondence reaffirms that Winter's friendship with the young artist helped shape the kind of painter he would become. As a mature artist in New York City, Mueller combined a palpable sense of light, dazzling spatial effects, and buoyant mystical shapes in works that presaged current concerns in abstract painting.

According to Winter, the students at Schepps and the Dallas Museum of Fine Arts attended classes to learn—no credit, no grades. In every class, he exposed students, regardless of age, to new approaches that would strengthen their works. "I let them know that painting was a medium through which to learn—about art, about the world, about who they were," Winter says. "That was takeaway enough for me and the students. I had no fear of overteaching or being a friend to my students. Negative criticism doesn't get you very far." At SMU night school, however, Winter was charged with the responsibility of grading his students, some of whom entered his classes with the idea that art was an easy A. "The first day of each class, I would say that I took my work seriously and that I would take their work just as seriously. If anyone didn't like the sound of that, then it would be a smart idea to drop my class while they still could without penalty. One or two would drop."[6] In painting, drawing, and design classes, Winter learned to be inventive and sensitive to each personality in order to break through preconceptions that might hold back a student.

> In my first class at SMU's night school, I projected a slide of a [Amedeo] Modigliani mother and child next to a hokey, academic mother and child and asked students which was the better painting. At first, people laughed at the Modigliani, but a few liked it. I would ask why in either case, and by the end of the class, everyone thought it was the better painting. It was like watching people evolve in visual perception as faulty preconceptions melted away. I, too, had to get beyond some of the dogma of art schools and flavor of the week in my studio. Teaching and painting were twins. My mantra was to move forward in a strengthening way. I never adhered to a lesson plan, but approached the classes through my experiences of looking for solid, lasting work. Art is not about therapy. My classes were never sandboxes. They were structured by specific projects: Push the forces *out* from the center to the four sides of the plane and even beyond. Set up unpredictable still lifes that go up the wall and trail onto the floor. Use bright, clashing colors that force an emotional response. Fill an entire space on cardboard in twenty

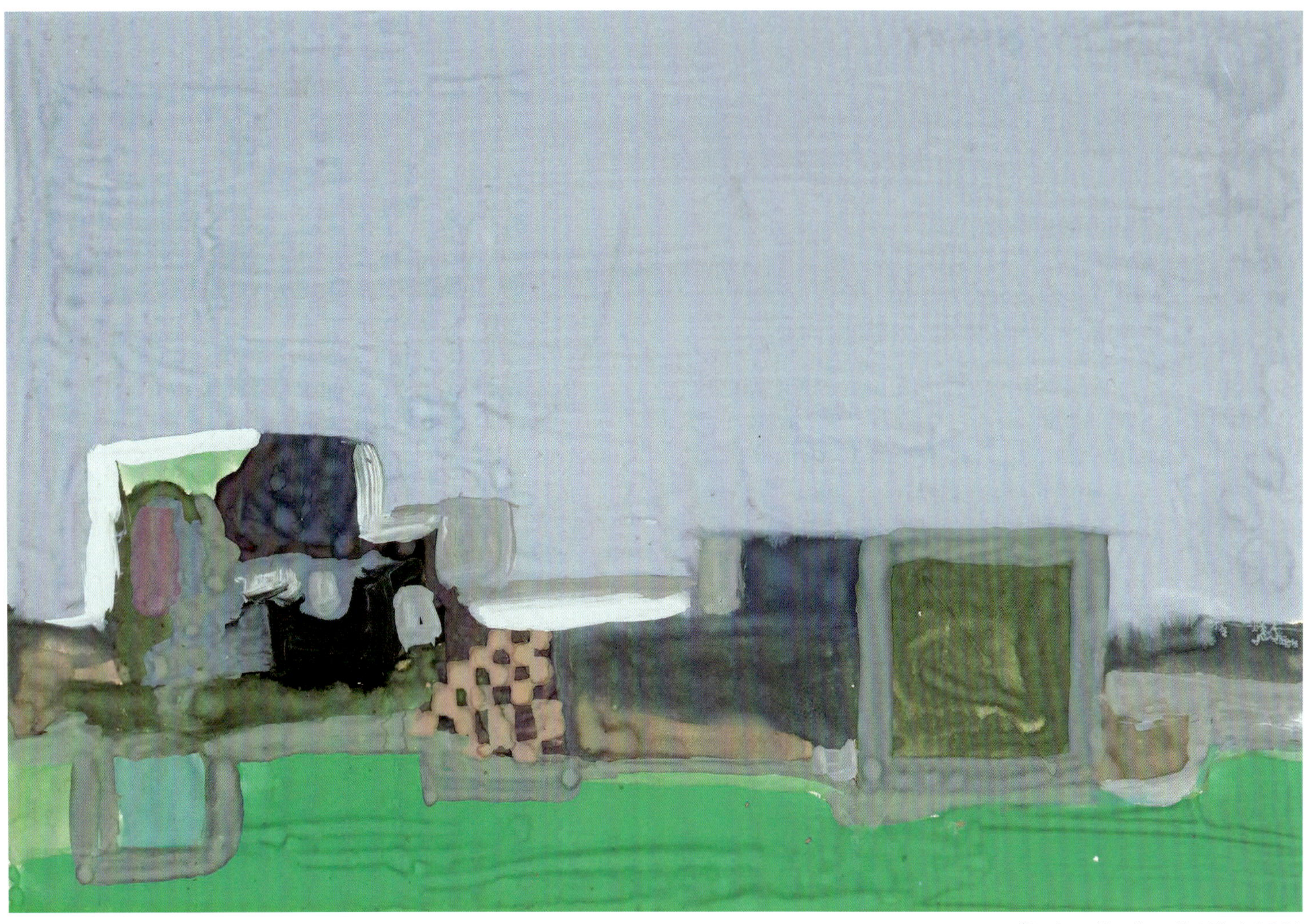

Stephen Mueller, *Untitled*, 1964
tempera on paper | 6 3/4" × 10" | Collection of the artist | © The Estate of Stephen Mueller

> minutes from a model's pose. Build up the square footage that each student has faced—art is not a passive activity. And *always* forte before piano, so softness will have a resolution. The SMU classes met six hours a week, during which I slowly gained a better understanding of art and of human nature.

Indeed, Winter aspired to make the classes worthwhile for students. He hired nude models for the drawing classes, built movable walls for the first-floor lobby so that work from the classes could be on exhibition at all times. Winter also invited students to his home in the Oak Lawn area.

Although Winter had gained confidence as a teacher, he felt insecure about his paintings. By all accounts, his first solo exhibition at Atelier Chapman Kelley was a flat-out success. The paintings were wild and drippy, full of animals and children playing in landscapes mixed with Pop imagery. The exhibition may have signaled the beginning of Winter's professional career, but he was unhappy with where the work had arrived. It was time to challenge his comfort zone and forge new paths. With the closing of the Dallas Museum for Contemporary Arts, Winter began to look increasingly inside himself and at family memories for content. "In the sixties, I wanted to resurrect the early years that I had buried in order to find a route into my life—like cleaning out the attic of all that no longer needs to hide. I started turning memories into medium." To that end, Winter left Chapman Kelley and joined the Haydon Calhoun Galleries. In an effort to clarify and soften his work, Winter stopped painting and made dozens of lightly penciled line drawings of Jeanette, along with pages of surreal ink drawings of dreamy images—people flying, animals with human heads. Significantly, his first painting after the hiatus, *Flying Farmer* (1964), which featured floating figures and illogical imagery in a disjointed space, was awarded the E. M. Dealey Purchase Prize in the Thirty-Fifth Annual Dallas County Painting, Drawing and Sculpture Exhibition at the Dallas Museum of Fine Arts. Here the simplified figures—a young girl with a dove perched in her hand, another child astride a bay horse, a farmer in overalls horizontally set adrift—and resplendent crimson hues reinforce the primordial nature of the event. Do the large birds represent deliverance, oppression, or a preoccupation with the ultimate flight of death? The painting is created with fierce abandon—hotly colored and steeped in personal fantasy. Still, the more consistent and controlled brushwork gives an almost elegiac quality to its unsettling imagery—an archaic time of innocence forever out of reach.

According to Winter, the "flying farmer" is an imaginary portrait of his father, who had died eight years earlier. At far right, the well-dressed seated figure refers to an often-told story by Winter's mother of a Jehovah's Witness woman who had persuaded his father to join the faith and also attempted to take over their large family. "My mother developed a lifetime hatred for that faith, and when they would come to our door, my mother would scream and sweat and grow red in the face before ordering them to leave. They were always women and they were always dressed better than my mother could afford to dress. I think this painting may have been the beginning of my family history themes. My brother's horse Gypsy was pictured in that painting. School and the worldly wisdom of teachers and students my age had made me ashamed of my earlier life and its particulars. I came about recovering it with an excessive approach to paint and canvas, and *Flying Farmer* was facing a few facts." A follow-up painting, *Hopes and Fears* (1964), won an award at the Texas Annual. Winter's familiar icons—a horse, a dog, children, and adult figures—oscillate between a pastoral idyll and tortured dream. The large, muted shapes seemingly float in an equally elusive landscape in which planes continually trade depths with one another as the eye seeks a resting place. The title refers to the lyric, "The hopes and fears of all the years are met in thee tonight," from Phillips Brooks's 1868 carol "O Little Town of Bethlehem." For Winter, the painting represented a kind of purge: things calm down at the center; the colors are dulled; figures and objects decrease in number and close ranks.

Overall, Winter was evolving toward a more refined time in his life and painting. He was plumbing more deeply in the work, using a more sensitive, delicate approach rather than a brash, sloppy application of paint. He was also becoming more astute in how to coexist with the art world. "I was lost in the spring of 1964," Winter recalls. "I was teaching, turning thirty, maybe mellowing a little. I had hopes and fears in constant conflict. I was battling my way into the artist-teacher role that I so wanted. While the images were made up—essentially figures in a landscape—drawing and realistic proportions were making their way back into my work." Winter was ready to explore paint and structure, to step away from the rough, harsh brushstroke, in favor of a gentler and more contained way of working. We can almost hear Winter asking himself the basic questions, What subject matter? What colors? How to compose? The yearning for wholeness, for resolution, that had been at the center of his art and a primary source of his frustration and pain had not diminished. Rather, his ability to give form to an expression of that yearning had increased considerably. Winter was finding his voice, thereby expanding the scope of his art in ways that had been impossible before. His work was becoming more keen and incisive. His subjects began to range across a spectrum of what he had seen, experienced, and imagined to include witty and compassionate studies of animals, places, and things and images of the broadest human and metaphysical significance.

In his desire for more subtle painting, Winter bought some acrylics and cut up cardboard boxes into small rectangles. He made a painting each day for two months. The aim was to explore abstraction until "figures emerged from painted

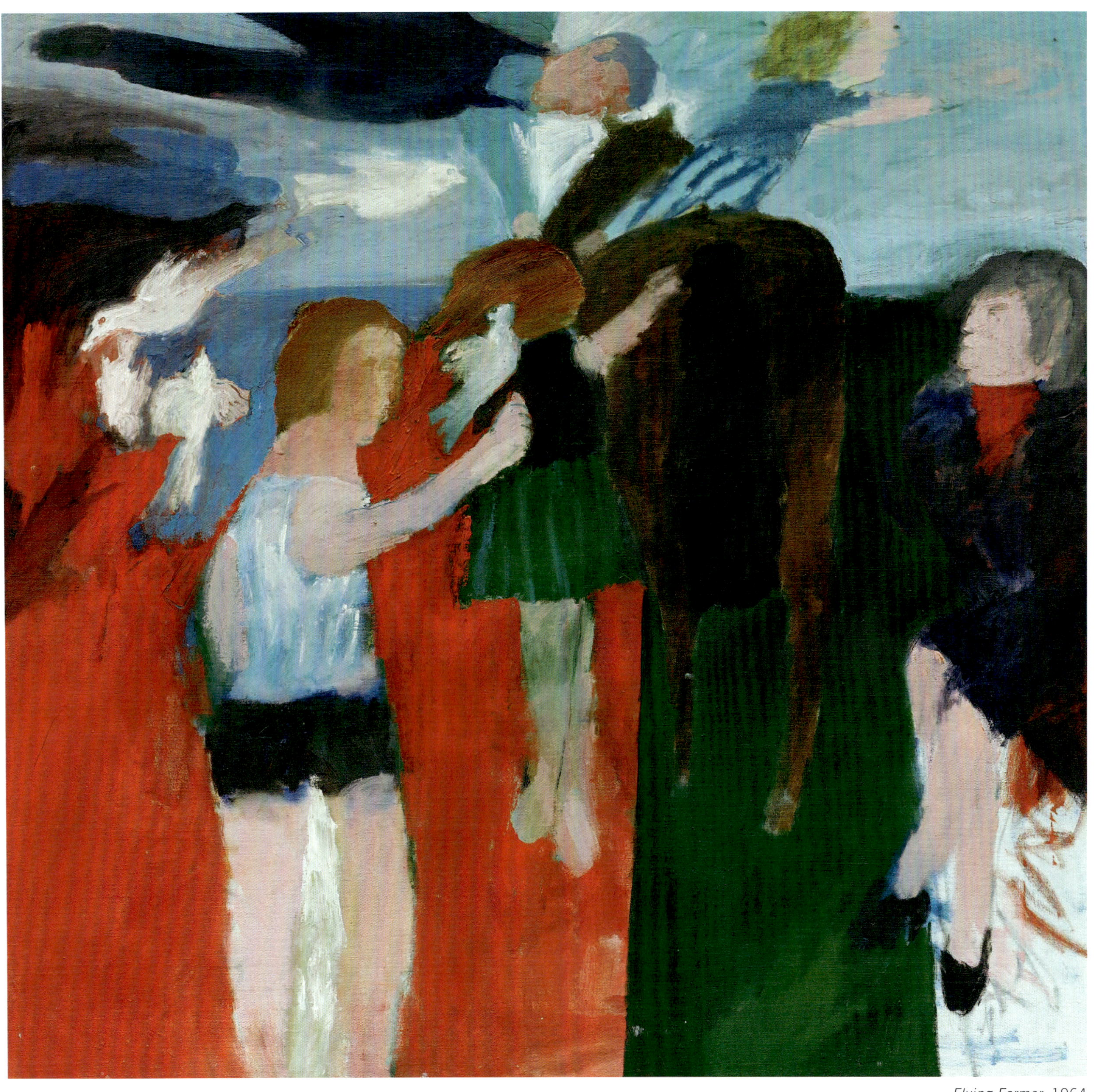

Flying Farmer, 1964

oil on canvas | 47 3/16" × 49 1/4" (119.86 × 125.1 cm) | Dallas Museum of Art, E. M. Dealey Purchase Prize, Thirty-Fifth Annual Dallas County Painting, Drawing and Sculpture Exhibition, 1964 | 1964.30

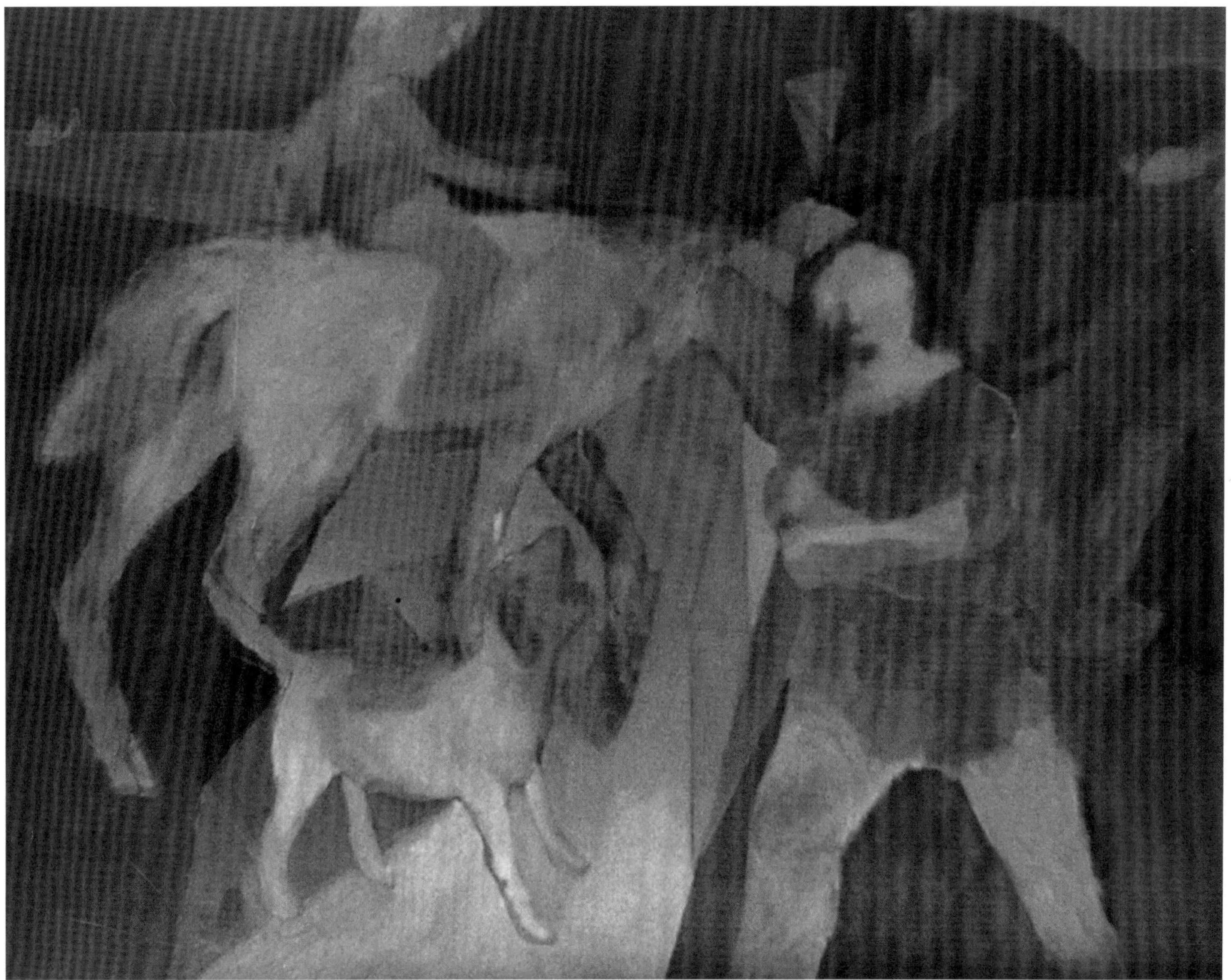

Hopes and Fears, 1964
oil on canvas | 41" × 54" | Courtesy of the artist

space." Winter sat on the floor while painting the multiple layers without regard for keeping whatever was found. Colors would brighten, darken, become white, and change back again to pure hue. Winter would see a possible image, as well as evocative color and light relationships. "I would paint half a day or more just making space with paint and color, avoiding edges or specific shapes, until a landscape or part of a figure or a house would occur and then I would let it predict the final painting rather quickly." Winter repeated the process the next working day with a different size or piece of cardboard, turning the painting in every direction until a slightly recognizable subject appeared. Light and color are paramount forces in these small works. To that end, his palette grew more complex and sophisticated—replete with granite grays, creams, oranges, and a range of blues from deep ultramarine to pale sky. Similarly, his brush became a felt rather than an entirely visual phenomenon. The rambling strokes are almost buttery in their smoothness. A primary concern is the capacity of light to provide plastic unity, wherein light creates a luminous, shimmering atmosphere that effectively dematerializes form. In *Cold Light*, zones of smeared blue push out

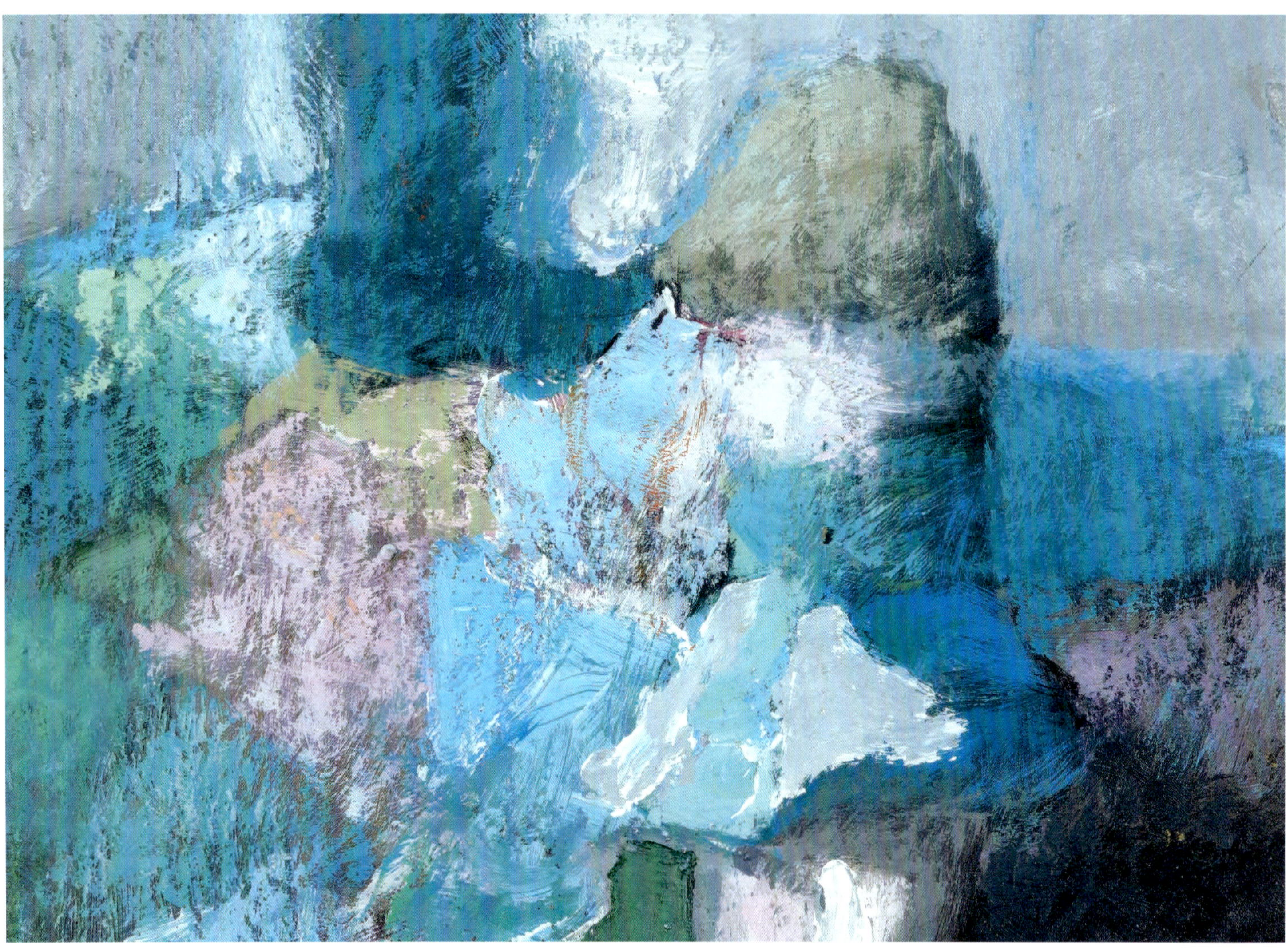

Cold Light, 1965
acrylic on cardboard | 6" × 8 1/2" | Collection of Britti Himelfarb | Photography by Kevin Todora

from the center, destabilizing the composition and giving the brushwork it impinges on a frenetic quality. The painting alternates markedly between warm and cool, evoking heated air and frigid water, the weather's changeability and, by implication, restlessness and uncertainty. In *Boy with Ice Cream Cone*, a figure lingers somewhere within the patchy and feathery layers of pinks, lavenders, and darker tones, but it is tentative and shifting. Color often arrived at through layers of dissonant hues opens up the surface to spatial depths. At its best, his color breathes.

Larger oils grew out of the small drawings and acrylics. Light evolved from the contrasting, close values of color and spatial divisions. Edges became harder; objects were more realistic; subjects were arcane but clearly stated. Mostly, Winter was influenced by his immediate surroundings. As the father of a three-year-old son, eating ice cream cones and riding carousel horses at Dallas Fair Park were personal experiences as much as responses to the Pop Art imagery of Wayne Thiebaud and Claes Oldenburg. In *Carousel* (1965), the boy and girls holding ice cream cones while astride boldly chromatic horses become fulcrums around which complex geometric planes are structured. Forms seem to appear and dissolve, revealing a welter of delicate brushstrokes. Hues are trickier to describe—pearly grays, acidic greens, not reds—alternately juiced up, hushed, velvety, or precious like a jewel box. In *Frozen Mother* (1965), Winter deftly interweaves cake-icing colors—blues, pinks, creams—with the subtlest orchestration of cool tones. The entirety is suffused with a strangely emotionally charged kind of glow that envelops the three figures in an enigmatic psychological drama. According to Winter, the painting refers to Jean Genet's *The Balcony*. A pregnant woman with an ice cream cone occupies the center position; she is flanked by a policeman and Winter himself, who is walking out of the picture plane. In these paintings, as well as *Valentine Comfort* (1965), *Three Figures*, and others, the immediate impact of structure and painterly richness gives way to a more restrained, dramatic intensity that seems to build from within the works themselves. Colors and forms, light and space, literal imagery and abstract shapes enter into a complex dialogue in which formal and expressive qualities, the recognizably familiar and the ambiguous, set up a reverberating chain of associations.

Significantly, all of the works produced between 1963 and 1965, including the small acrylic paintings, were presented in a solo show at Haydon Calhoun Galleries. Writer John Neville, in a review for the *Dallas Morning News*, proclaimed the 1965 exhibition "a solid success for Roger Winter." Neville notes, "Winter's work has a vague, haunting quality that is never clearly defined but is always provocative. His statements are subtle. His canvases are peopled by soft figures seemingly seen through a mist: These figures have an aloofness from each other and are never on really intimate terms with the viewer. You can see them, understand what they are doing and yet, never really 'know them.' . . . They seem to 'come through' the barrier almost as though the artist was in some way closer to them himself. They are, perhaps, a more personal statement."[7]

After 1965, Winter began to develop a coherent and distinctive style, signaling a decisive shift toward a more subjective vision based on memory and imagination, as well as direct observation. Nowhere is this more evident than in *The Dove* (1966), which attempts to reconcile geometry with expressionism, and delicate lyricism with compulsive insistence. He explores the changing relationships between repetition and difference, between part and whole, within a matrix of rigorous structure. Here, for the first time, Winter uses a direct translation of a photograph into paint—a small image of Jonah in a sailor suit from a black-and-white snapshot, painted high in the center. Inasmuch as the Hebrew translation of Jonah is "dove," Winter depicts the bird of peace fluttering to the right of his son's portrait and toward an equestrian statue of Robert E. Lee in the distance. Below, a young girl in a blue sundress strides into lush green parkland with her back turned toward the viewer. A con man wearing a red, white, and blue porkpie hat, a red tie, a navy blazer, and pinstripe trousers sits dead center with arms folded. Half of his face is obscured by shadow, but the right eye—an intense, piercing blue orb—stares unflinchingly at the viewer. To the left, a prim

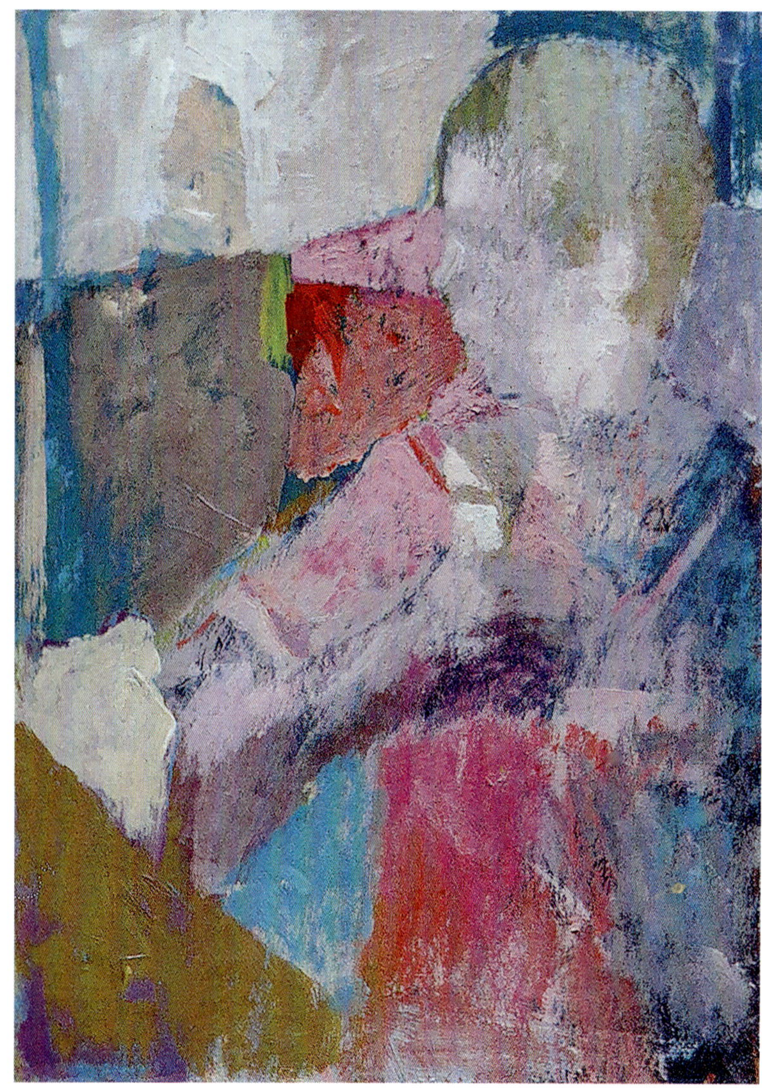

Boy with Ice Cream Cone, 1965
acrylic on cardboard | 13 3/8" × 9 11/16" | Private collection

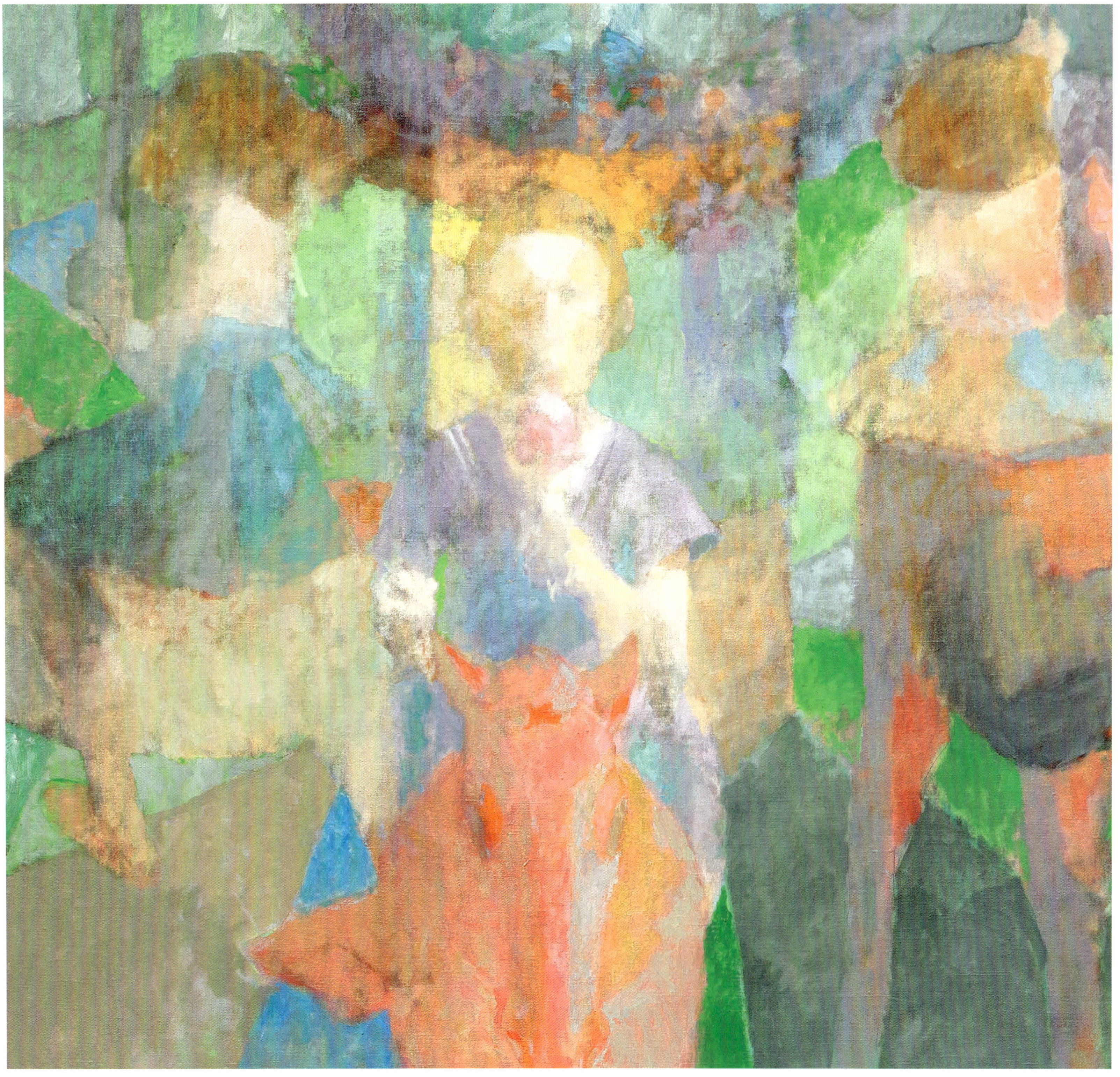

Carousel, 1965
oil on canvas | 52" × 50" | Collection of the Einspruch Family | Photography by Kevin Todora

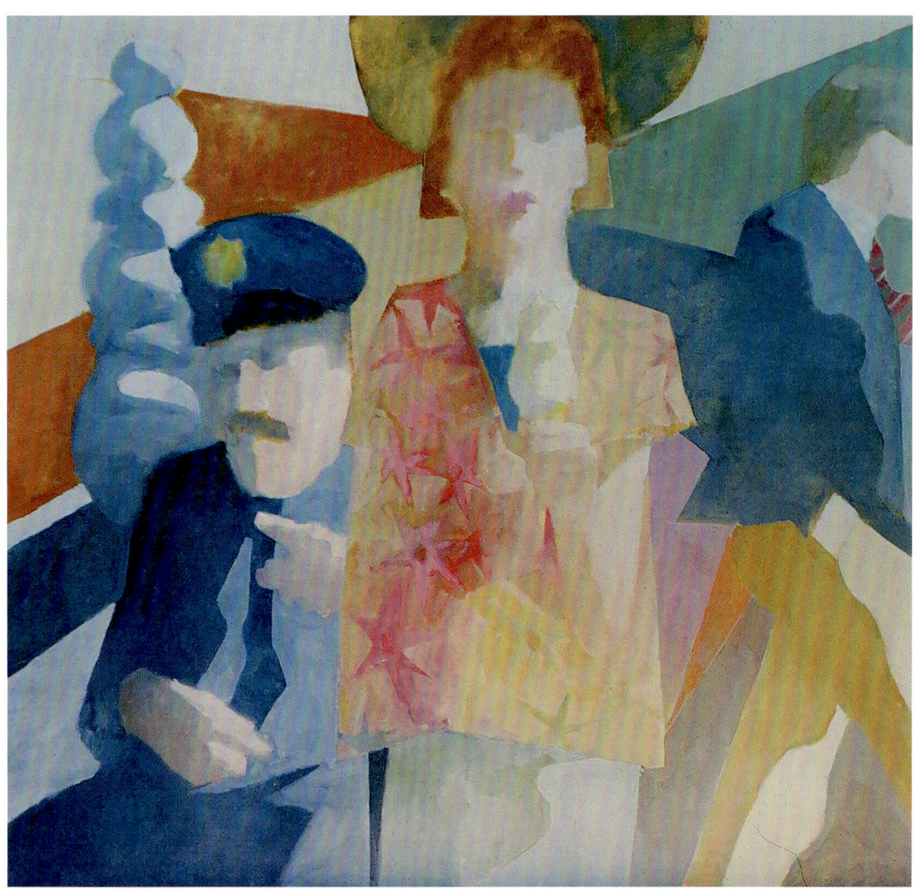

Frozen Mother, 1965
oil on linen | 48" × 48" | Courtesy of the artist

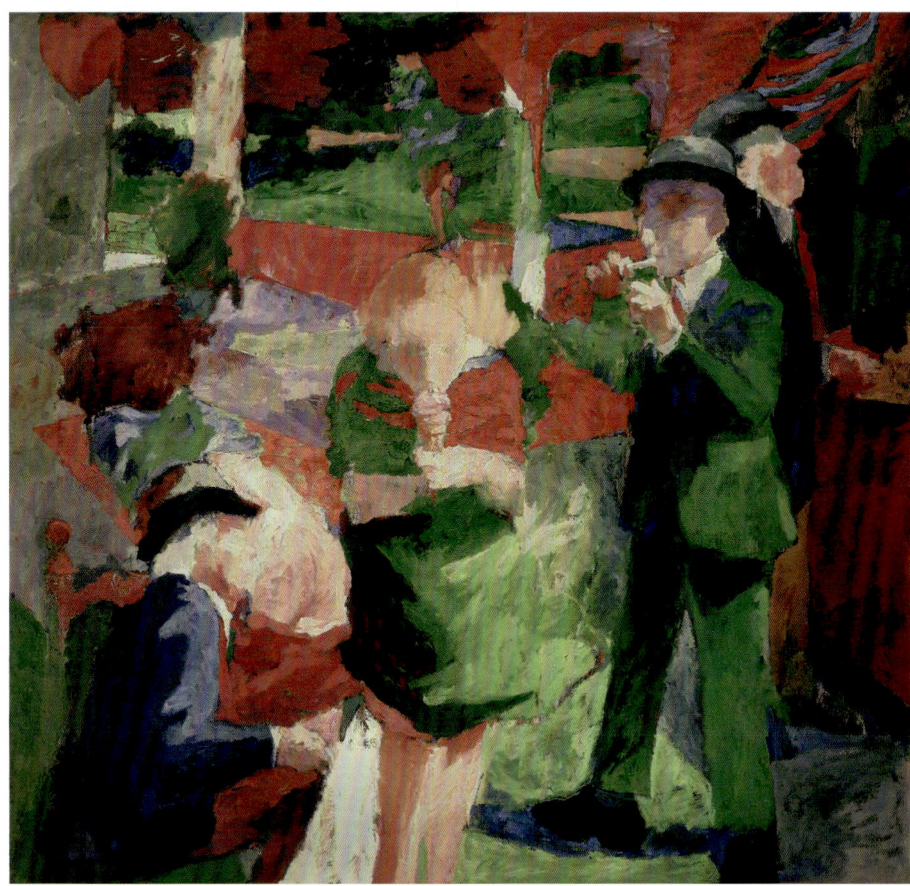

Valentine Comfort, 1965
oil on canvas | 51" × 53" | Private collection, Atlanta | Photography by Digital Arts Studio, Atlanta

Dallas socialite in a ruffled blouse and plumed hat is seated in a fuchsia brocaded chair. She raises a teacup while turning away from the scene, preoccupied by self-importance. Winter comments, "I used my first photo image in this painting. It was scary and very exciting. In the wake of Pop Art, this wasn't new. And it certainly wasn't new to me to draw from photographs. I'd done that from prememory, I was told. I felt in dangerous territory doing this, because working from photographs had been thought of as a major crime during all those student and poststudent years up to that point. But for me, it had a magic that making things up or working from life never had."

Significantly, Winter's frequent use of "pressure points" on the canvas—concentrated, pivotal areas containing the figures and the most intense coloristic activity—begins with *The Dove*. The con man sits at the intersection of at least three vertical planes of color. Jagged, irregular shapes spread across the planar support in a vibrant, patchwork montage. Moreover, the dispersal of patterned roses within the rectangular planes serves as a structuring device that allows Winter to demarcate the spaces between them. The painting is not only strongly rhythmic but also daringly disjunctive in its use of jump cuts and unusual angles.

Shortly after Winter had finished the painting, he "discovered" the work of Romare Bearden, whose 1964 collage of the same title also features a group of figures and a white dove. In Bearden's composition, the dove perches unobtrusively on a ledge above a busy Harlem street scene packed with faces and people. One of the first artists to depict black popular culture from an African American point of view, Bearden created the frenetic rhythms of an ever-changing neighborhood by gluing cut-up photographs, as well as clippings from newspapers and magazines, to a piece of cardboard. The eye travels into the street, from one person to another, from light to darkness, and from pattern to pattern in abstract optical shifts. In Bearden's version, however, the bird of peace watches a white cat prowling the street at lower left, a metaphor for the ongoing struggle to survive amid predators. For Winter, the experience of seeing Bearden's *The Dove* was like an epiphany. He felt an immediate spiritual connection that would persist throughout the coming years. "It was quite a shock," Winter recalls. "Too much to be coincidental. Bearden and I had very similar childhoods. He was African American and I was white trash, living by the railroad tracks. My father's people came from North Carolina. We were haunted by the same ghosts. It's very familial and personal—something *he* knew about and *I* knew about being poor in a rural situation. Bearden wanted to tell the story of his 'people' in the same way that Pieter Breugel told about the lives of sixteenth-century Flemish peasants. But Bearden also told universal stories. That's what I had been doing for a decade without really making the association with any other artist."

Winter's compositions became more fragmented, layered, and disjointed even as a deeper story revealed a self striving for wholeness. The new approach evolved toward paintings of his original family from the old box of childhood snapshots, but now mixed in with imagined details and backgrounds of condensed times and spaces. In many respects, Winter was attempting to resurrect the early years that he had buried in order to find other routes into his own life. A 1966 painting, *Untitled*, features images from a photograph of his brother David and sister Ada standing before the Denison viaduct. Underneath are the Katy freight yards, car shops, and his dog Clip. To the left of this grouping, Winter paints an imagined version of himself in a baby carriage, attended by his mother, who is sitting on a wall. The upshot of combining photo details and invented contexts is a distinctive emotional component. The mood may be comic and sometimes hypnotically disturbing, but more emphatic is the immanent feeling of sadness and isolation. Nostalgia, yearning, loneliness—these intangibles, all having to do with the pathos of disconnection, are what give his art its soul.

Bearden's spatial conjunctions of photomontage, which transformed memories of African American life into statements of mythic proportions, not only influenced Winter's continued blending of photographic images within geometric structure but also reaffirmed the use of his early life and background as a source for art. All of these concerns achieve full expression

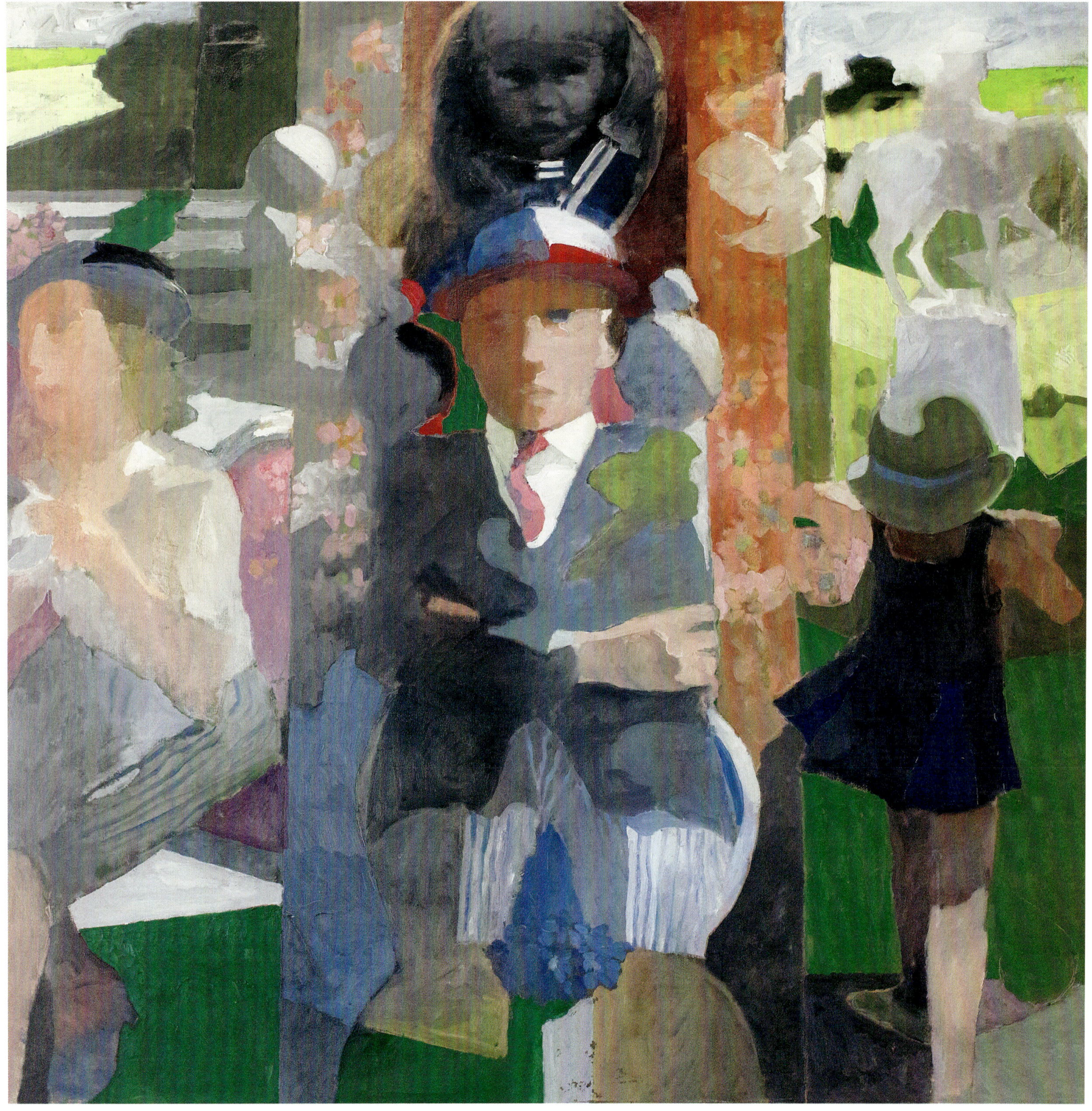

The Dove, 1966

oil on canvas | 54" × 52" | Collection of Pamela and Jere Mitchell, MD | Photography by Allison V. Smith

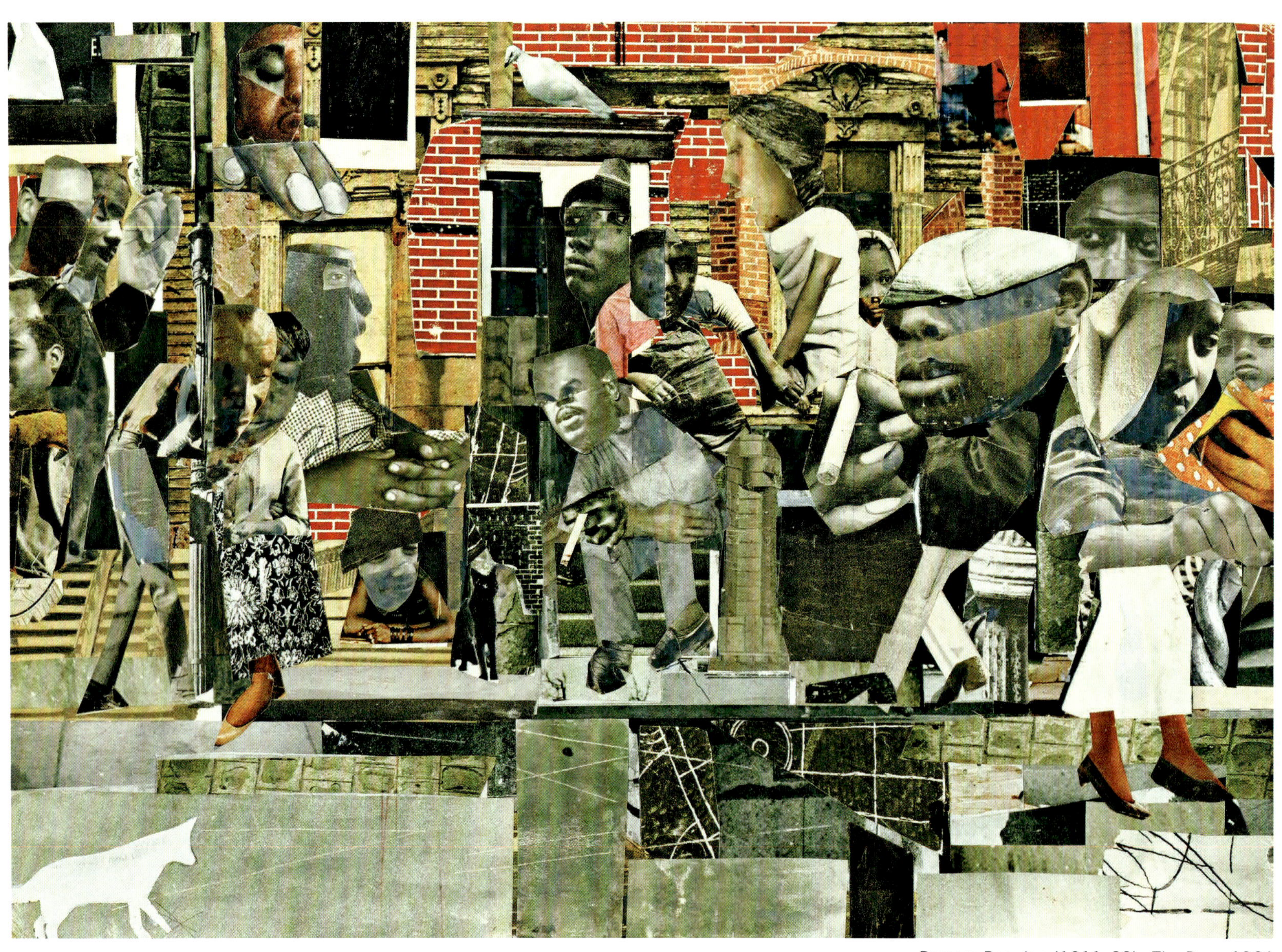

Romare Bearden (1911–88), *The Dove,* 1964

cut-and-pasted printed paper, gouache, pencil, and colored pencil on board | 13 3/8" × 18 3/4" (33.8 × 47.5 cm) | Blanchette Hooker Rockefeller Fund, the Museum of Modern Art | Digital image © The Museum of Modern Art / Licensed by SCALA/ART Resource, NY |

in *The Family* (1966), a landmark canvas with figures of Winter's siblings sunk into or strewn across imagined details of his boyhood home. The entirety is composed, almost mathematically, as interactions of shapes, colors, and directional elements: concrete steps, culverts, and garden decorations; rectangular windows and square architectural features; the round engine head and cow-catcher grill of an approaching steam locomotive. Indeed, *The Family* signifies a major turning point in Winter's development. Whereas fabricated places and figures were treated realistically in previous works, he knew the locale and all of the background objects and individuals in *The Family* intimately. More important, the painting resurrected his childhood talent of drawing the faces of family members from photographs, but without relinquishing disjunctive space and time. Here, the past, the present, and fantasy form a new reality, one restructured to Winter's own narrative specifications. At far left, the massive train barrels around the backside of the old house; alongside is a tightly grouped composite of Winter's siblings—Joyce, Oleta, Harry, Luther, Ada, and David—all clad in white clothes. Winter's oldest brother, Ed, in the extreme foreground, wears a somber business suit and hat, which casts a dark shadow across his face. Winter portrays him holding on to the pole of a carousel horse, painted a fiery orange-red and stylized with tiny ears and demonic almond-shaped eyes. Joyce appears again, at center, as a young mother standing on the steps with her arms around the shoulders of her son Jimmy, who never knew his criminal father and also grew up to be "bad to the bone." At the far right, an enormous black raven flies out of the picture plane toward the viewer. Below, Winter depicts himself as a young boy with his head buried in the crook of his arm. A large conch shell rests on a narrow concrete ledge, anchoring the lower right corner.

Although the vertical pole serves as a solidifying element in the painting, the vignette also allows for metaphorical implications. "My brother Ed became a bank president in our home town," Winter explains. "But I think he could have gone further. He was a little like our father in that he was afraid of life. His mouth was injured at birth—it always went to one side and drooped back. Perhaps his holding the carousel horse meant he was going in circles and not getting anywhere. But a merry-go-round is also the place where you catch the brass ring or even suggests the rotation of the earth, the planets circling the sun." About including himself as a young boy, Winter recalls, "That's me with my head down, crying or dreaming. In reality, I was crying. It's from a snapshot my brother Harry took of me at age seven or eight. He was on leave from the air force and wanted to go hunting. My mother wouldn't allow me to go with him. The seashell always makes me think of sound—like listening to the ocean in a seashell. It may have been fortuitous or memory, since Jeanette and I lived on Coney Island."

Significantly, the large canvas gives a strong sense of Winter's inexhaustible vitality, his brilliant color sense, and his innovative skill at composition. Throughout, he juxtaposes organic, curvilinear elements—the green bushes against the house; the soft, creamy, pink chamber of the conch shell, the mint-green and pale-yellow flowers in the concrete planter—to horizontal, jagged, or parallel lines and planes. While the images of the raven and a young Winter with his head down may evoke the slumbering protagonist and monstrous nightmare of Francisco Goya's etching *The Sleep of Reason Produces Monsters* (1777–79), the tilting planes, empty space, and compressed, almost airless view recall the dreamlike metaphysical paintings of Giorgio de Chirico.

What is most remarkable about *The Family* is that Winter leaves these allusions so dissociated. Things don't always cohere or make sense. They hover mysteriously, as puzzlingly poetic evocations of modern consciousness. Just as the great American realist Edward Hopper captured the loneliness and tragic sadness of isolated figures and empty cityscapes, so does Winter create a kind of portrait of an American community, which unfolds as a meditation on dreams and the disappointments of ordinary people longing for connection but often feeling forsaken.

How does Winter make his fractured family stay together? It's tempting to conclude that families determine who we are, no matter how we

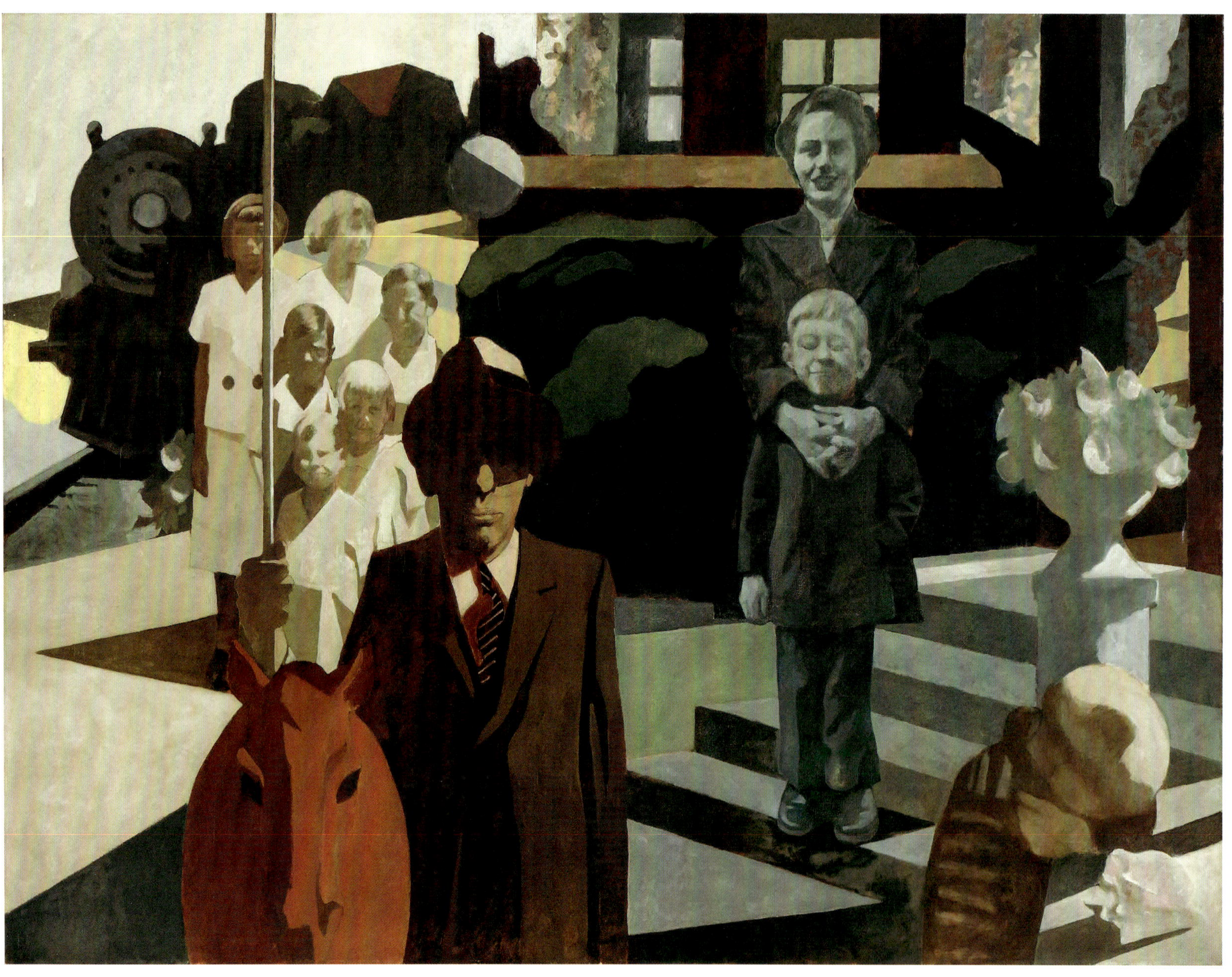

The Family, 1966

oil on linen | 72" × 96" | Collection of John Alexander and Fiona Waterstreet | Photography by Joshua Nefsky try to imagine otherwise. At its core, his painting is about how the sins of one family member affect and jeopardize the whole group. Winter's siblings are isolated from one another. The dynamics get at how families can function as both liabilities and sources of strength, the yawning space between even the closest people. Winter's painting displays a remarkably mature understanding of the delicate emotional balances in families—how feelings can flow back and forth like electricity—and the subtle, irrational vicissitudes of people's psyches. Can a past that has slipped out of reach be reclaimed by nostalgia? Significantly, *The Family* is a painting that shows us how many emotional octaves Winter, just thirty-two years old, could already reach, how seamlessly he could combine the real, the surreal, and the imagined with more wide-angled concerns. Winter was clearly after something big, and certainly his work is unsettled and unsettling. Deep in the painting is the need to be separate and the fear of it, and also, conversely, the need to connect and the fear of it. If *The Family* is suffused with a twilight melancholy, it is also shot through with immense tenderness.

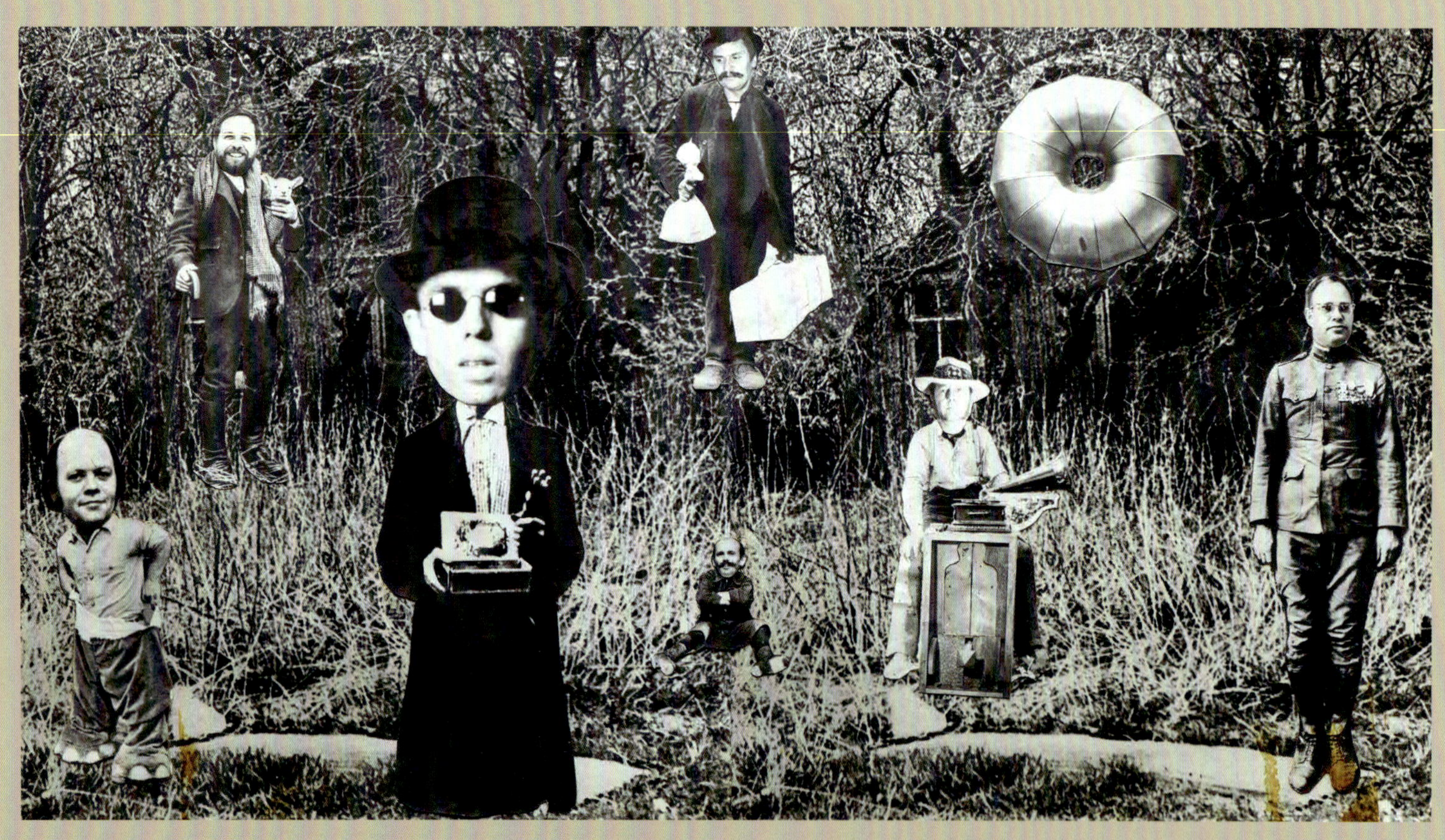

One i at a time, 1971

montage on museum board | 20" × 40" | Courtesy of the Dallas Museum of Art Archives | Photography by Brad Flowers

CHAPTER 7

SOUTHERN METHODIST UNIVERSITY AND BEYOND

IN 1966, WINTER WAS HIRED by Jerry Bywaters, then the art department chair at Southern Methodist University (SMU), to teach drawing classes on the main campus. At the time, the art department was tucked away on the third floor of Dallas Hall and shared space with the theater department. Based on first impressions, however, Winter regarded it as little more than a "playpen" for students. Immediately he sensed that faculty meetings were a waste of valuable studio time and functioned as displays of contentious power struggles. Winter recalls, "A woman who taught ceramics complained often that we had to get rid of Communists who were infiltrating the schools. I remember a long discussion started by Jerry Bywaters about how to find a good Roto Rooter company. Deforrest Judd smoked and cleaned his pipe and never said anything. Barbara Maples told me she thought I would be much taller since I did such large paintings. Barbara also once called me a bastard in a faculty meeting for my well meaning comments about my priorities in teaching drawing."[1]

Clearly, Winter had joined an art department caught in the throes of growing pains. Still, he stuck by his belief that teaching was the most important part of an art school. To that end, Winter taught his students to grow from the inside and toward their own voice by giving them the tools—drawing skills, design skills, a knowledge of art from all times—to guide that voice. Winter strove to train the eyes in order to make them more sensitive; train the hands in order to bring them into command but also make them feel the effect of the form elements—shape, color, space, volume. In many respects, Winter's teaching methods echoed those of Josef Albers, who, in the 1930s, along with a small, shifting group of teachers and students, maintained a productive experiment in learning as life at Black Mountain College, near Asheville, North Carolina. Winter adopted Albers's dictum that education is a mutual service that demands first the self-education of the teacher. As Albers notes, "It is not adequate to call teaching a 'job,' education is a kind of religion based on the belief that making ourselves and others grow—that is making stronger, wiser, better—is one of the highest human tasks."[2]

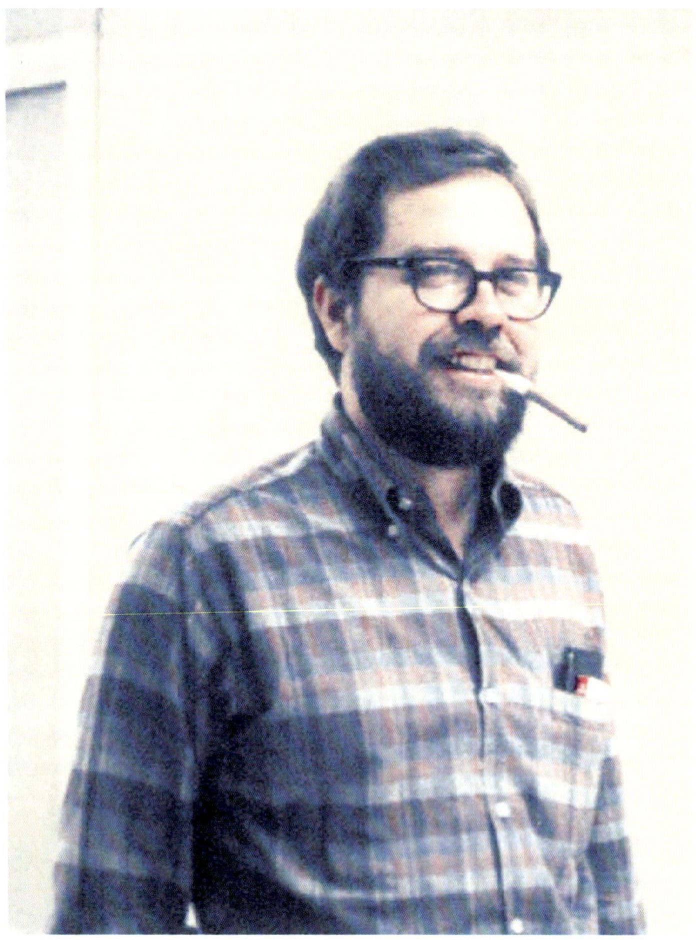

Roger Winter, early 1970s

> Most of the other models were younger, often dance students, or occasionally, especially male models, exhibitionists. Lucette was none of these. A French Italian woman with a husband from Hopkins County, Texas and several children, she had always loved life and people of any rank or stature. She was absolutely dependable, and would hold a pose for 40 minutes if asked to do that. Compared to most of the students at SMU, art or otherwise, Lucette seemed Bohemian, utterly open about any subject, able to let her feelings show. She worked for the students and for me. I mean she WORKED. She seemed to sense anything I wanted to emphasize—the five second pose, the verb, the mood, an emphasis of one or another set of muscles in use—and she made friends with students, staff and faculty. Lucette was a big enough human to be professional without losing her love for the students. I think this made it easier for students to relax and attempt new ideas in their approach to drawing. Her son Rex and our son Jonah became friends enough to spend nights at each other's house. And when I needed a model, she would pose in our home in exchange for drawings.[3]

Like Albers, what Winter was after was education as an end in itself that aimed at "being something instead of getting at something."

From the outset, Winter ignored university pressures and protocol. "I knew that art would not fit snugly into any university, so I went my own way," he says. "Getting degrees was a student's worry. Caring about their growth as artists was my job. I was single-minded." At SMU, Winter was the kind of committed painter who told his students that art is about an individual way of seeing rather than rote reproduction. With this in mind, he hired the uninhibited model Lucette Cumming for his classes, beginning in 1966 and continuing until her retirement some twelve years later. Always willing to accommodate students, Cumming often borrowed hats or garments from the theater's costume storage closet. As Winter recalls, she was unlike any life-class model that had ever worked at SMU.

Among the students in Winter's initial drawing classes were Jan McComas (Bates), David Searcy, Gail Norfleet, Martha Whitman, Alfred Martinez, and many others who were eager to learn. McComas continued in both drawing and painting classes with Winter through the opening of the Mudge Art Building in 1969 and until completion of her BFA. Upon returning to SMU for an MFA, she served as Winter's teaching and studio assistant for two years.

McComas's work during this period—a "charming wildness" that Winter encouraged—was included in the prestigious 1975 Whitney Biennial at the Whitney Museum of American Art, New York. McComas sets the scene:

> When I was a sophomore, the art department consisted of three or four small rooms on the top floor of Dallas Hall, the oldest building on campus—and no air conditioning. The art department rooms were on one side, the

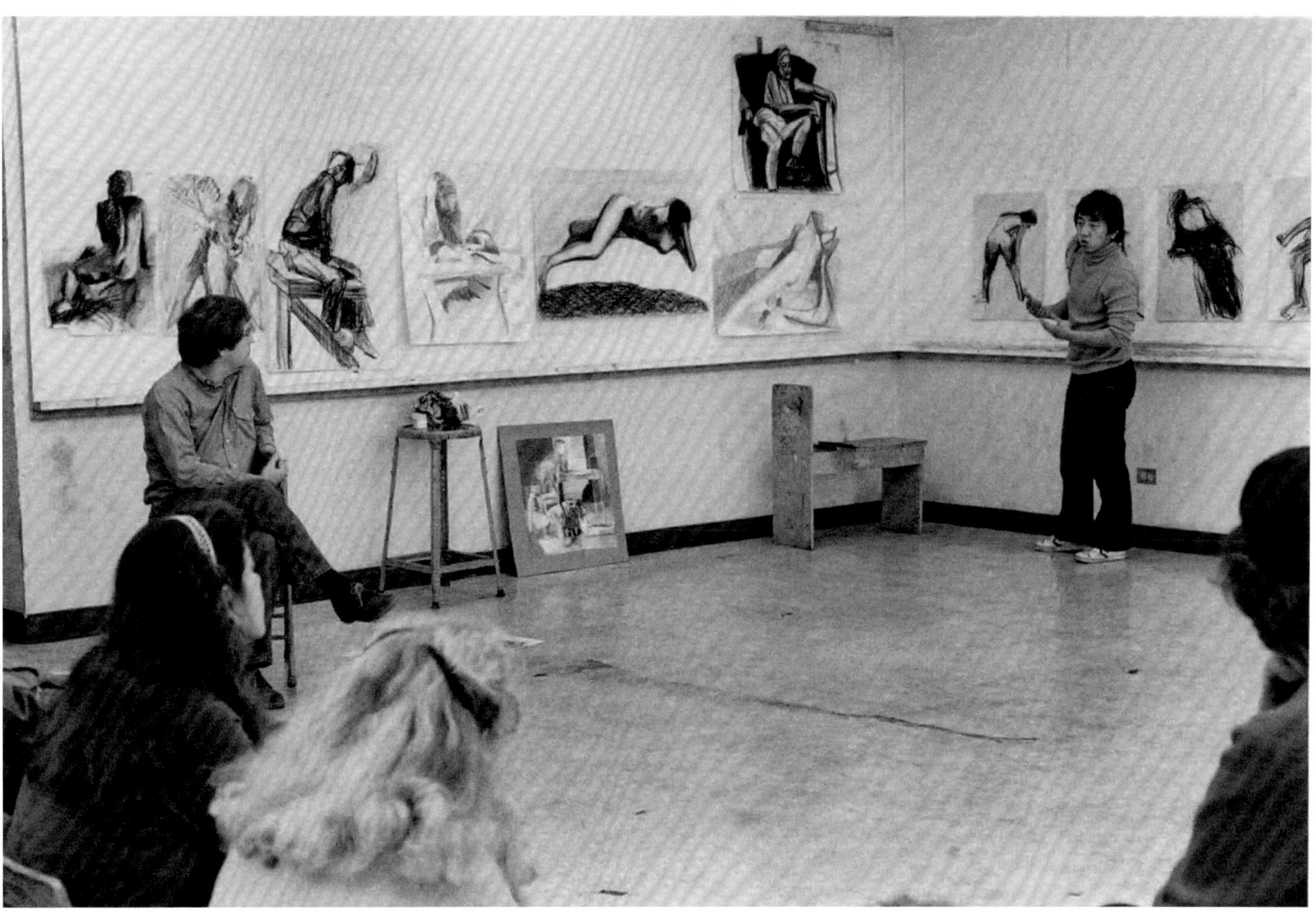

Drawing class, early 1970s

drama department was on the other side. Jerry Bywaters was chair of the art department—there was no graduate school at the time. The rooms had huge windows, and on break we'd sit out on the windowsill just to get fresh air. There was a strict dress code—no jeans or shorts on campus. So I had to put on a raincoat every time I walked out of Dallas Hall. Roger and I had a professional relationship, but he was the first person I connected with. His teaching wasn't about *A*, *B*, *C* in a book—it wasn't about the academic. It was about finding something deeper other than technical ability, the deep impetus to do the work. Roger would pop off and say what was on his mind without consequence—but there was always a distinct aesthetic sense of right and wrong.[4]

Changes occurred when the $20 million Owen Fine Arts Center opened in 1969, providing up-to-date facilities for instruction in a wide spectrum of studio media and in the history of art. Consisting of three main buildings—the Mudge Art Building, the Forbes Music Building, and the Ruth Sharp Collins Drama Building—the complex became home to dance, music, film, and theater performance. The move also connected the art building to the Pollock Gallery, the setting for faculty, student, and important loan exhibitions, as well as the Meadows Museum and its collection of Spanish paintings, drawings, and prints. Significantly, the Mudge Art Building ushered in a kind of golden era at SMU that attracted both stimulating, rule-breaking faculty members and dedicated, hardworking students.

About those heady years, Winter recalls, "There was to be a printmaking department in the Mudge Building and Jerry Bywaters asked if I would help find a printmaking teacher and research equipment that we needed. I contacted Mauricio Lasansky and two of his teaching assistants who were friends of mine and teaching in noted universities. By this time, Bill Jordan had become director of the Meadows and the department chair. Lasansky recommended Larry Scholder, who turned out to be an excellent choice. In our new building, Jordan hired other teachers, including James Surls to work with Bill Verhelst in sculpture, John McElroy to oversee the ceramics department and Dan Wingren to be the senior painting teacher, along with Mary Vernon in art history." In addition to painting and drawing classes, Winter also rebuilt the shoddy studio equipment—easels, taborets, figure model stands, clay modeling stands for drawing classes, metal armature for drawing with clay. What's more, he constructed pinning boards for the rigid plaster hallways and classroom walls to exhibit student works and engage in critiques.

The 1960s were passionate years in the art world, a time when artists cared deeply about their media and about teaching. Winter reminisces, "I once threw a cup of coffee at Bill Jordan—he had made comments that I disagreed with strongly and he refused to hear an argument. But he was always behind me in physical changes to the art building, in getting permission and department payment for the materials needed. And despite the cup of coffee incident, Bill Jordan was a constant lifetime supporter of me and my work, and a faithful friend. He brought glamour and scholarship to the art department. I think he and I both were a large part of its success in the late '60s, the '70s and into the '80s."[5]

For his part, Jordan wrote glowingly of Winter's accomplishments as an artist and teacher in a 1969 report for a potential fellowship at the American Academy in Rome:

> I have had the opportunity to know Roger Winter and to work closely with him during the two years that I have been at SMU. He has been an instructor of painting and drawing for 3 years and in that time, he has proved himself to be an indispensible member of our faculty, which now numbers 17 full-time. I would say his effectiveness as a teacher and his professional promise place him at the top of the list among our studio faculty. . . . Our department recently sponsored a one-man exhibition of paintings and drawings by Mr. Winter, and it was one of the most impressive shows I have seen in some time. His work is personal, probing and bears the strong stamp of intellectual integrity that characterizes him as an individual. I think Mr. Winter is an important young painter and I have confidence that he will gain wide recognition as such. As a teacher, he has attracted a large following and has shown himself to be imaginative, resourceful, hard-working and pleasant. He has carried a heavy teaching load here but has, nevertheless, sustained the initiative to prosper as a growing talent.[6]

In a series of interviews with Leigh Arnold for an oral history of contemporary art in Dallas, Winter observed that the years during which Jordan was director of the Meadows Museum were the most vital and exciting: "I think SMU, of all places, became like a breeding ground for young artists."[7]

For Gail Norfleet, the life drawing classes were the beginning of her development as an artist. "Roger was very respectful of my early marks," she recalls.

> In every drawing he looked for the "good" parts, encouraging and guiding me and the other students to our strengths. Sometimes artists are not very articulate—not so with Roger. He was able to speak about being an artist and I learned what it was to be an artist from him. Roger took teaching seriously, but did it with a lot of humor and interesting stories. I remember that Roger liked to talk about [Edgar] Degas in relation to line. He showed us drawings by Degas that emphasized contour. I understood what Degas saw and the grace of the flowing line. I learned to feel it and follow with my eye in unison with my pencil along the edge of an arm, leg or torso. It felt at home for me to

do this. Roger also said it was as important to leave something to the imagination. What you leave out is important too. My interest in composition was formed by much of what Roger said about shape and contour. How beautiful! And the space around the shape is essential and completes the whole.[8]

In the 2012 film *Roger Winter and the Line*, produced by Quin Mathews, artist Brian Cobble recalls his initial months as a student in Winter's drawing class: "On the first day, we're doing thirty-second and fifteen-second poses, and I've only got one ear half done! He made me dig deeper for skills I didn't know I had." Indeed, if there was an aesthetic at SMU in the early years, it may have been in Winter's effort to bring finely honed skills as a teacher and maker, but also in his grasp of the dream of art as a lived condition: why art is conceived; what it means; what is done with it.

Winter, of course, is a huge part of the SMU story, but still only a part. As word of the art department's outstanding faculty and new facilities spread throughout the state and beyond, talented students arrived. John Alexander, Julian Schnabel, and David Bates—artists with Texas roots whose works would be exhibited and acquired by the most prestigious private and museum collections worldwide—studied or were advised by Winter during various years in the undergraduate and graduate programs. All have endeavored, in different ways, to break boundaries in expressionist paintings that tautly balance inventive power and structural rigor.

Born in Beaumont, Texas, Alexander received his BFA in 1968 from Lamar University before entering the MFA program at SMU. According to Alexander, SMU had a growing reputation and offered a scholarship. Moreover, Dallas provided the "big city" experiences he was looking for. About his initial contact with faculty, Alexander recalls,

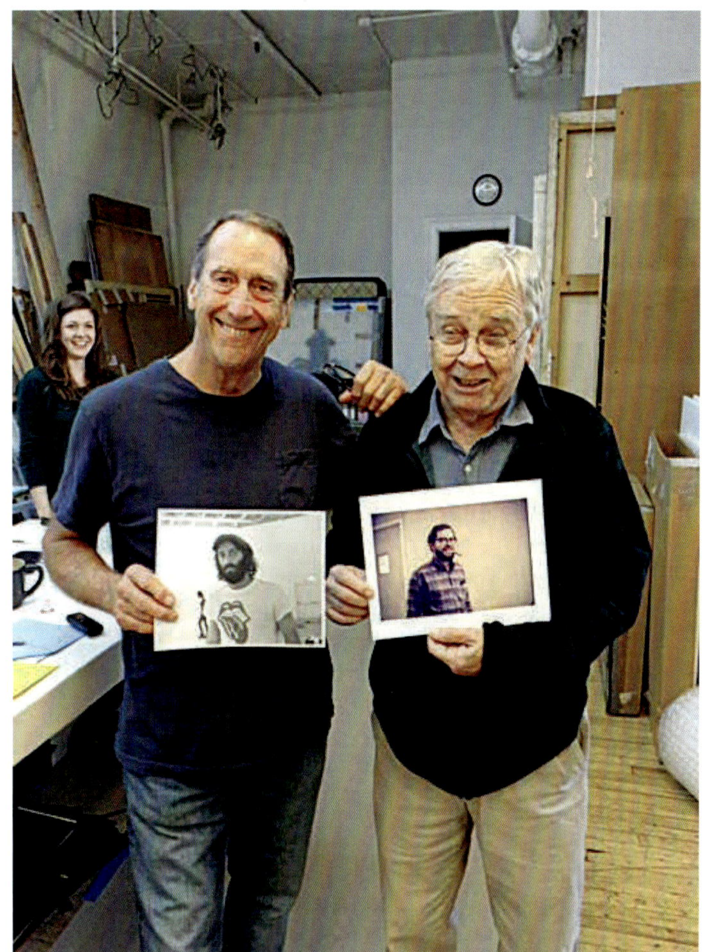

John Alexander (*left*) and Roger (*right*) holding photographs of themselves at Southern Methodist University, early 1970s in John Alexander's studio, New York City, October 2015

> You had to pick a graduate committee—three people with whom you were supposed to meet at least once a month. At the end of the semester, the committee looked at everything you did, evaluated it, gave you a grade, and moved you through the system. I picked Dan Wingren, Roger Winter, and Jerry Bywaters. I got to thinking about that period—Jerry Bywaters was of his generation—very gifted, very bright in his ability to communicate and teach, but also a painter. The next generation comes along—Dan Wingren, an interesting guy, influenced by Texas painters, taught students how to look at life. And then there's Roger, exactly ten years older than me, and he had a great ability to communicate, along with an astounding respect for drawings and paintings. How lucky I was as a young graduate student, twenty-four to twenty-five years old, to pick these three painters. Each influenced the other—Dan Wingren would reference Jerry Bywaters and Roger would reference Dan Wingren. Each brought something to the table.[9]

Toward that end, Winter helped Alexander concentrate on essentials while also establishing his own unmistakable view of the world. "When I got to SMU, it was the beginning of Conceptualism and a whole shift away from painting as an art form," Alexander says.

> All the art magazine articles—over and over—at the time proclaimed, "Painting is dead." But Roger taught me to look at art in a different way—that is, from a spiritual context. There's something magical that you have to find and understand—then you can apply to technical skill. But without both, you end up doing boring academic works. Roger looked at art and talked about art with me in terms of something much more meaningful and deeper. He helped me see a much bigger world. If you have a professor, like Roger, who you observe working and also have a rapport with, then it just stands to reason you're going to absorb it. And I was like a sponge in those days—still am. All through my career, I've been invited to speak at universities and museums. What I've learned is that very few people are gifted enough to give back to the students. With Roger, there was always a connection—his teaching the love of paint, the love of human experience.
>
> If you have an eye, you have the visual ability to see the world around you, whether beautiful things or an old rusty train. Then you have a brain that can cook all that information like a stew or gumbo. If you have the skill sets to execute what these ideas are, then you get close to making something meaningful. That's what Roger did and why he was such an influence on me. I learned how to draw and use my craft—charcoal, pencils, erasers—different ways of applying paint and scraping it down, reapplying and directly painting, and washes and drips. Roger taught me how to see a world in which to fill those canvases. So many people who make it in the art world become completely different people. But Roger, to this very day, is not in any way afraid to honestly lay out who he is, where he came from, and with great integrity. There are several ways to find subject matter. You can drive around, disconnect, escape life. That's the easy way out. But Roger looks inward and confronts his own demons and those closest to him, laying out the emotion in the loneliness of the studio. He's wise and kind, always wanting you to push yourself to do well.[10]

Upon receiving his MFA in 1971, Alexander took a teaching position at the University of Houston. During the same period, Julian Schnabel was just beginning his career as an artist at the university, earning a BFA in 1973. With Alexander's recommendation, Schnabel enrolled in the SMU graduate program on a scholarship. Although he was in Dallas for a brief period—1974–75—Winter served as his faculty committee adviser and spent many hours with the young artist at his downtown studio. According to Winter, Schnabel would drive him to the studio every week or two, where they would discuss poetry and current issues of painting. "Julian was very good natured and generous toward me," Winter recalls.

> He loved poetry, above all, and gave me a book of poems by William Carlos Williams. Julian had a gargantuan belief in himself. He told me that he disliked everything happening in painting and that he was going to change the direction of it. He was using something called Bondo to glue things, like broken dishes, onto a painting surface. I talked to Julian about scale, surface placement, form—matters that I didn't think he had heard much about. He was not at all unreceptive. Drawing was not Julian's forte. When he dropped by my class to draw, I would keep it simple, like filling the page with his drawing or having a range of values. Often, I served as a sounding board for his thoughts. Julian was putting highly contrasting images and objects around one surface. He liked the disjunctive works of the German artist Joseph Beuys at that time. We talked about Beuys's works in relation to contemporary poetry and its disdain for the music and order of older poetry. I remember

> that he responded to my autobiographical paintings in which I collaged space and imagery in an illogical way. Even then Julian, like James Surls and John Alexander, was bigger than life. He was a very energetic talker and I think he understood the art world better than students normally did at that time. He saw that New York City was obviously the place for him to be. I liked him and was sorry to see him leave the program—but he had bigger fish to fry. Julian was born educated.

Admittedly, Winter had a reputation of working his students hard, challenging them to the point that some became afraid to take his classes. Among his many priorities for students, however, were an attachment to materials and an ability to make gestural drawings—placing things on a page, filling the space—as much as understanding drawing as the "probity" of art. Born in Dallas in 1952, David Bates studied at SMU, receiving a BFA in 1975 and an MFA in 1978. As Winter tells it, he advised Bates early on to "paint what he knew." Winter showed him how the Texas regionalist painters—Otis Dozier, in particular, as well as Everett Spruce and William Lester—turned their experience into existence by painting it. "A teacher helps a student find a productive path, a sense of what his voice sounds like," says Winter. "I encouraged students to go outside the page—drawing as a verb instead of a noun. It was a more dynamic way of teaching young artists to draw. It's the verb that makes up aspects of the human figure."

Nowhere was this aim more emphatic than in the life drawing classes. "Roger focused on people who needed certain things," Bates explains. "I was in his drawing classes more than anything else at SMU. Drawing is really the foundation for my paintings and sculptures. He saw that I wasn't doing the figure. I thought he was going to kick me out of class but instead he put me on a bus and told me to draw all day. He knew it would be more to my liking and what I would relate to—not drawing in class, but to life. So I made weird little drawings of people on the bus."[11] Winter recalls the scene: "When David came to my class, he had been trying to draw a certain way. One day, I got the model's money and separated it into bus fare for David. I told him to ride for six hours and draw whatever he saw. Well, David went underneath the Houston Street Bridge and drew the derelicts who lived down there!"

According to Bates, Winter taught him to follow his vision and be true to that vision rather than copy whatever was in New York. "Roger would put people's work on the classroom wall—Brian Cobble's beautiful drawings. I never expected my quirky drawings to be on the wall. He'd stick my stuff up and I'd be so surprised! I look at Roger's work and there are always devices—railroad tracks, fence lines, highways, the Texas space—that keep the viewer at a distance, as if to say, 'Stand back, take a look, but I don't know you.' Roger saw art at a particular time that was so American. Within the lineage of Texas artists, each generation became more successful. A whole society of art started crystallizing. John Alexander and I came along at the right time. Roger handed it off to us."[12]

When Jerry Bywaters decided to retire as an artist, he gave Winter all of his paints and brushes, thereby passing the baton. In turn, Winter fittingly shared Bywaters's precious art materials with his classes at SMU.

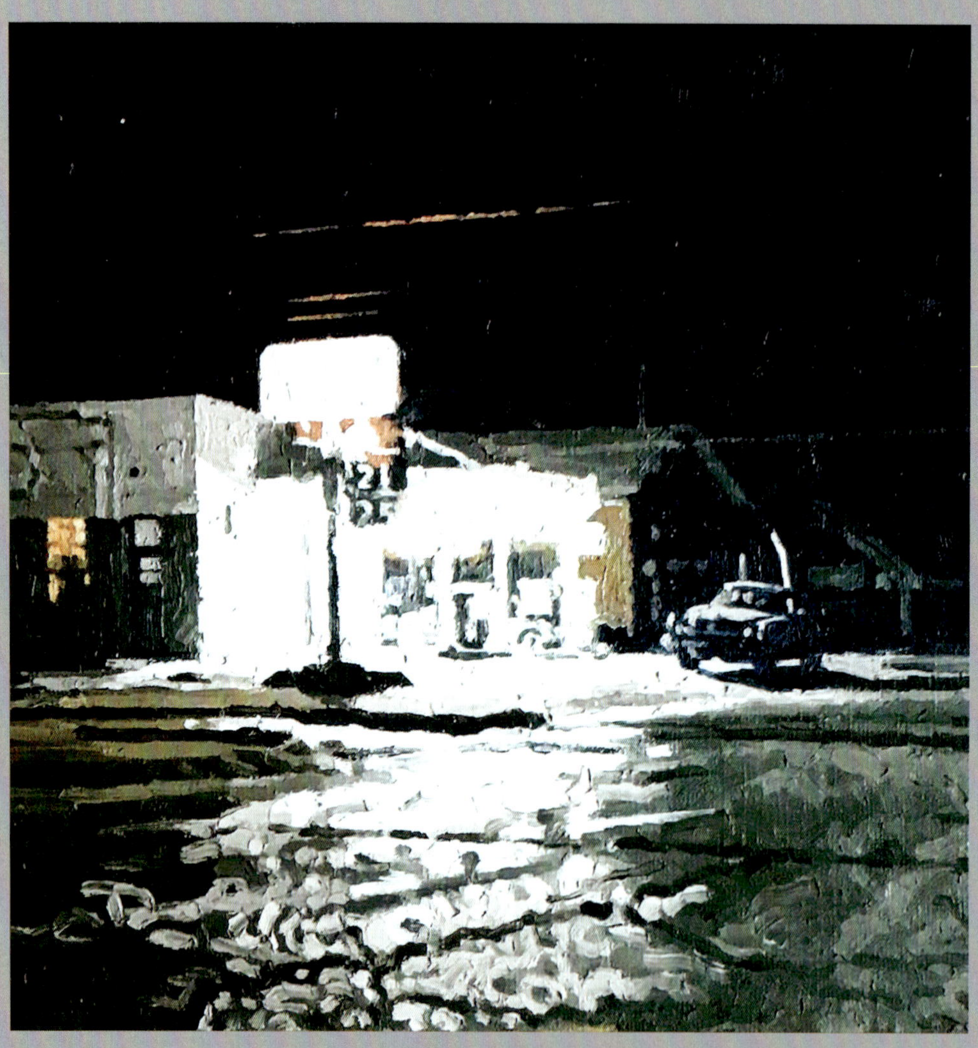

Corner Station (detail), 1983
oil on linen | 14" x 16" |
Collection of Jonah Winter

CHAPTER 8

OUTER WORLD AND INNER REALM

WINTER'S SEARCH FOR MEANING has been a way for the artist to define himself and explain his life experiences. In the process, his power to uncover the pulse of a contingent world has become formidable. It extends from the anxiety and uncertainty of loss, through the everyday wear and tear of family friction, to the reaffirmation of fate's terrible indifference. Winter's search does not proceed along compass course; it wanders and meanders, revealing a core that becomes deeper by living out the messes and gaps. Perhaps most consistently, it is an exploration of how storytelling—the causal narratives we manufacture in our heads—shapes our identities and provides a hedge against the chaos of real life. His works render phenomena that seem impossible to describe: the passage of time, the texture of consciousness. The meaning of his images is perhaps intuitively sensed rather than rationally understood. Flowing associatively, they traverse a strange yet hauntingly familiar terrain that evokes the realm of dreams, memory, and imagination—those subliminal layers of human experience in which the potential for self-discovery resides.

Winter's primary subjects are the physical and mental landscape and the connections between the outer world and inner realm. He sees the world as composed of interacting opposites—light and dark, spiritual and physical, life and death. Throughout the 1960s and early 1970s, Winter's paintings acknowledged the echo of the distant past in the present moment. As the philosopher Gaston Bachelard writes, "Great images have both a history and a prehistory. They are always a blend of memory and legend, with the result that we never experience an image directly. . . . Indeed, every great image has an unfathomable oneiric depth to which the personal past adds special color. . . . Primal images . . . are but so many invitations to start imagining again. They give us back areas of being, houses in which the human being's certainty of being is concentrated, and we have the impression that by living in such images as these, . . . we could start a new life, a life that would be our own, that would belong to us in our very depths."[1] This is what Winter does—he creates reverberative images that reach the very depth of being, resonating in time, flowing on, and ultimately changing. He probes that elusive area in between childhood memories, which over the years assume mythic proportions; the physical present; and the timeless world beyond. Winter's art reaches for the sweep, force, and sense of inevitability of primal myths, but as translated to the mostly poor railroad town where he grew up, as well as the Oak Lawn and university neighborhoods of Dallas, where he lived with his young family. All of the works from this period are riveting in their spatial disjunctions, their varied pursuit of turbulence, and expanding techniques.

As previously discussed, drawing serves as the core foundation of Winter's art. Line carries the message in drawing, the most immediate, least self-censored way of working. More than painting and sculpture, it approximates closely the artist's mind. The lightweight materials—pencil, charcoal, ink on paper—give his efforts a genuine transparency that exposes the very nerve endings of the creative process. The reduced scale, the openness to invention, the close physical contact between hand, marker, and surface often convey a more intimate and ultimately more revealing work. A drawing can be highly controlled and delicate, redolent of personal memory, history, or desire. For Winter, drawing is improvisatory and always in motion, offering an extraordinary range of possibilities. In many respects, drawing is the extension of sight, as logical and instinctive a response to seeing as language is to thought. Accordingly, the images that arise in Winter's drawings hold personal and powerful significance. They are landmarks on a psychic map and, as symbols, become part of a glossary of visual elements that occur frequently in the work. The personality of marks and lines serves to reflect the artist's personality while also involving us in the process of the hand shaping and making visible certain emotions and experiences. Drawing functions as a resource and constant point of reference for Winter to investigate, examine, and reconsider priorities. For him, to draw is to explore. It is an autonomous medium that can reveal a world of untapped images, providing insights into the subconscious—of dream and fantasy, wishes and fears. In the illusory medium of painting, several states can be represented simultaneously; in drawing, however, time itself is the only space, and it is alive, open, vibrating, mutating.

During the late 1960s, Winter made dozens of drawings of his wife, Jeanette, a topic that will be addressed in another chapter. The impact of *The Family* painting, however, with its complicated, ambivalent relationships, had given shape not only to the subjects but also to the manner in which he approached them. *The Rogalla Family* (1967) is a bridge to a way of seeing that became the basis for later paintings. Winter pares the figures—artist Herb Rogalla; his wife, Jett; their son and daughter—to their elegant and essential lines, sometimes as highly detailed renderings or straining toward a kind of plain abstraction. Here is, at heart, a compendium of small moments that chime in unexpected ways, little clips of intimate experience.

Winter's portals to past and future underline everything that's fragile and temporary about the present. "I wanted to convey a sense of another family," Winter explains. "It's when I first started to float the images. Also, I wanted to pay homage to drawing by using inscribed lines. All of the Rogalla family, except daughter Erica, has the line around their heads or hair. A couple of fingernails have polish. Their son Adam wears red shoes—it was all about attending to details. I've given the Rogalla women more definition and presence. They seemed ambitious, where the men were introverted. It's also the first time I used symbols—a large jellybean, a rooster's eye and comb. The floating figures and objects are about overcoming gravity. The dark-green square is a metaphor for the Rogalla house. The patch of blue is like a little fragment of sky showing through invisible buildings. The flame is a form of light, but also something destructive and to be feared." The drawing displays a kind of meditative outspokenness, an artist conversing with himself on what to do next, then making that conversation his subject and style.

To that end, the paintings from the late 1960s follow the slow evolution of the figure from objective to subjective, from life to dreams and back again. *The Wake* (1967) combines modernist idioms—grid painting, collage, geometric abstractions—with a kind of bright Pop public

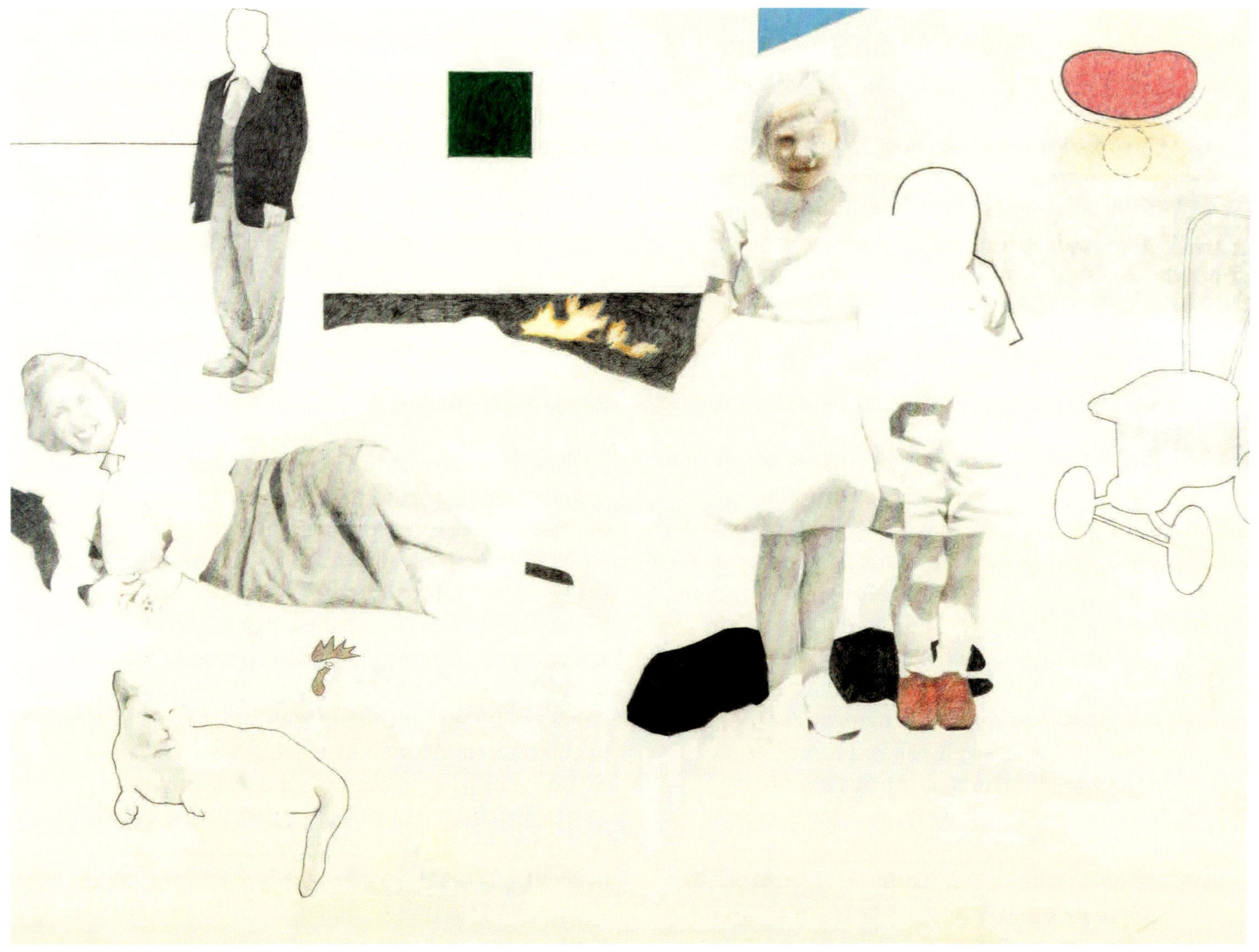

The Rogalla Family, 1967
graphite and colored pencil on paper | 42" × 54" | Collection of Murray Smither | Photography by Kevin Todora

address and a darker, private experience. Here, a nude woman wears a wide-brimmed hat and sits with arms folded and legs crossed in a high-back chair. Directly behind her lurks a figure in a white straw hat. To the lower left is the body of a man stretched out in a coffin. A draped table with a potted plant links two additional figures—a young girl in a blue coat and a tall, bearded man with dark sunglasses and a pinkish-gray trench coat—who stand and face us with stoic expressions. Between them, a white dove seemingly flutters out of the picture plane. To the right of the mysterious man is a schematic map of Texas, with a blue star marking the location of Dallas. There's a wall featuring a pattern of pink roses and, in the distance, a glimpse of limitless blue sky. Both beautiful and repellent, the flowers convey a hunger for life, as well as the fear of failing flesh. The refractions and shadows are quietly hypnotic, so much that as we stand before them, we literally feel ourselves travel through the dreamscape, letting our minds simply drift. A work of this kind that explores motifs of preservation and decay is perhaps not so much a terminal expression of disenchantment as it is a resolute effort to restore some mythic and spiritual aspects of life itself. Here, the lyric and the lurid seemingly reflect each other and conspire. Winter comments, "I was trying to break away from using family images and photographs. The only photo image involved was the nipple of the woman.

I painted Jack Ruby in a coffin—by coincidence, he died a few days after I finished the painting. When Douglas MacAgy left the DMCA [Dallas Museum for Contemporary Arts], many of the Oak Lawn crowd—looking for a new guru—started attending therapy sessions with Dr. Smith, who turned out to be a monster. I think the tall figure in the painting is him. Dallas was still in the shadow of the Kennedy assassination. The collection of images in *The Wake* are like those in twilight sleep: magical, but without any rational roots. I think the painting is about Dallas—a city isolated and theatrical and self-conscious, yet untempered by the feminine spirit at its core."

Indeed, Winter's account of city life is matched only by the painting's tremendous frontal force and stage-like setting, its play of strong and pale colors, its use of fragmented forms and tight composition, which present an impenetrable scene that seems to continue beyond the canvas in all directions. The painting reflects an admiration of Jack Levine's biting social commentaries, as well as of R. B. Kitaj's disorienting erotic tableaux that contemplate philosophical and moral themes. Similarly, Winter's painting functions as a metaphor for our subconscious landscape and acknowledges the possible turbulent activity constantly occurring there. His careful control of the cool, formal construction sharply contrasts with the agitated, potentially volatile content, resulting in an underlying brittle tension.

Can a past that has slipped out of reach be reclaimed by means of nostalgia? In *Sunday Float* (1968) and *Interurban* (1968), Winter illuminates the haunting quicksilver counterpoint of myth, memory, and identity. Both paintings explore the web of recollection and mythologizing that underpins the human longing for vanished worlds, in the dreams of another place and another time. *Sunday Float* features the artist as a boy drifting horizontally in the sky. He is also the blue-and-light-gray young man with the dog in the center. According to Winter, the dog had come to their place in Denison with tin cans tied to its tail. The house, upper right, belonged to the woman who attempted to involve Winter's father with Jehovah's Witnesses. Winter's sister Oleta stands in front of the trees; two nieces are playing lower left. The yellow form is a Piper Cub airplane, which the Winter family would watch take off and land during Sunday visits to nearby Gray Field. Throughout, Winter uses dissonant hues—yellow, white, gray, and blue—to make images jump. Depth is unspecified but not unlimited, kept shallow in part by the bright advancing colors.

Interurban is more spatially ambiguous: the large, disembodied head is Winter as a ten-year-old. He renders Jeanette as a young girl of the same age and references her hometown in the yellow, red, and green shapes in the sky and foreground, all colors of Chicago buses. The factory in the background is a trademark for Utrecht Art Supplies, while the images of the green bear and silhouette of a photographer reaffirm the flat picture plane. Everything seems ready to burst apart or collapse together, as if the painting is made of fragments derived from something larger and unknowable. In both paintings, Winter has gone beyond his concern with continuous change and difference, entering a spatial realm where shifts, ruptures, and irreparable figures are part of the natural flow. Sentiment, sharp and painful as a dart, is one of Winter's most devastating and powerful weapons. He understands the space between people, how we long to move through it. Real life, its dreamy past and the daily, ordinary present, with its deep roots and complex possibilities, is his subject. Time in *Sunday Float* and *Interurban* stretches endlessly in every direction, pulling and threatening and beckoning. In the process, he creates unfamiliar worlds that somehow feel ineffably familiar—the sort of places that we visit as we are falling asleep. And all the places we have ever lived, all the people we have ever been, start to mingle into one eerie, endlessly reflected entity.

Both paintings were produced during a period when Winter was undergoing a difficult struggle to evolve but also to keep his balance. "I was afraid of the photograph," he explains. "It was so sinful and terrible to paint from a photograph, even though it brought back the magic of my childhood. I was afraid that the family paintings were slipping back into a past that I couldn't reenter. But the compositional ideas and the images just were not ready to go away. And they revealed the edge of

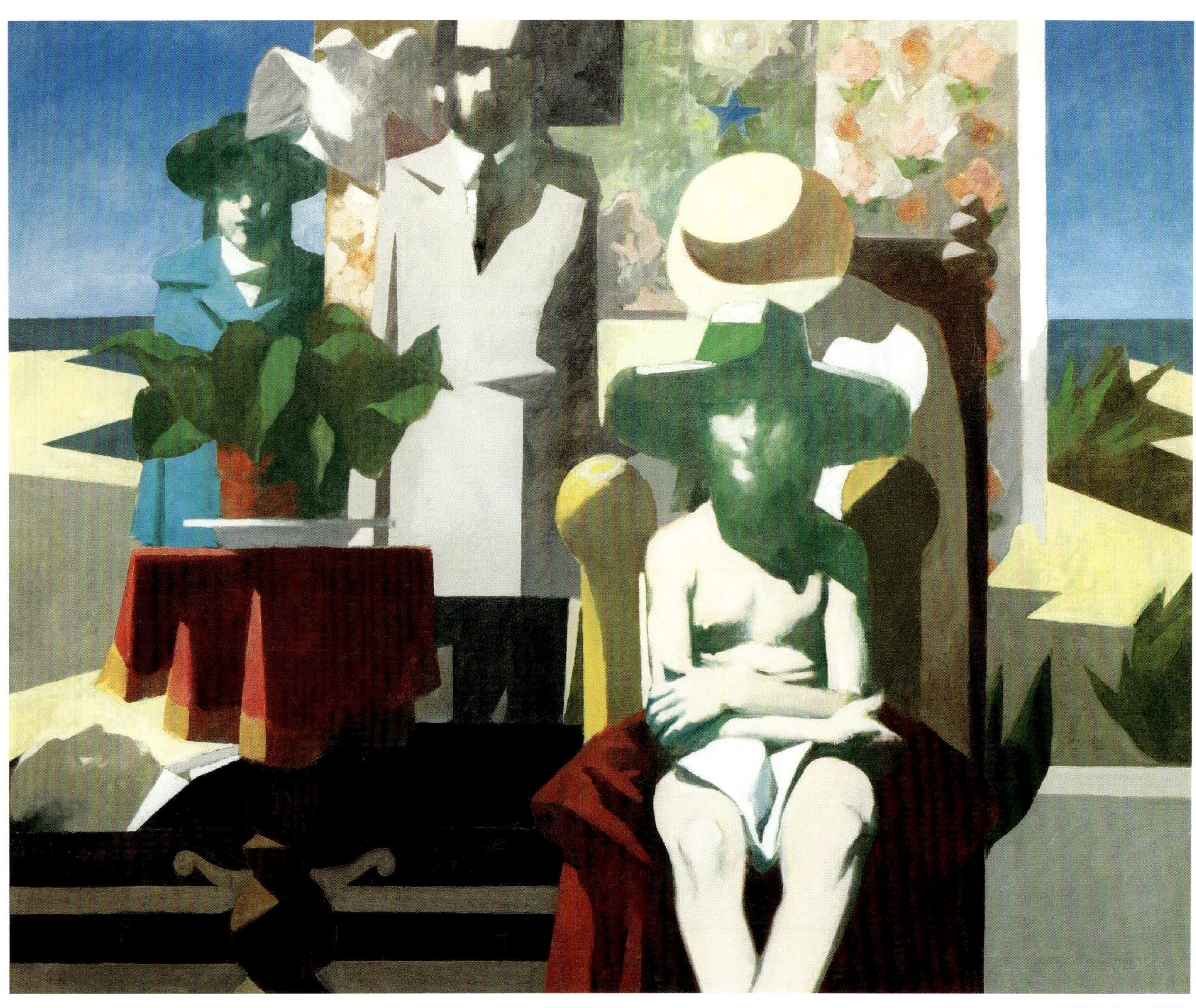

The Wake, 1967
oil on canvas | 48" × 60" | Collection of the Einspruch Family | Photography by Kevin Todora

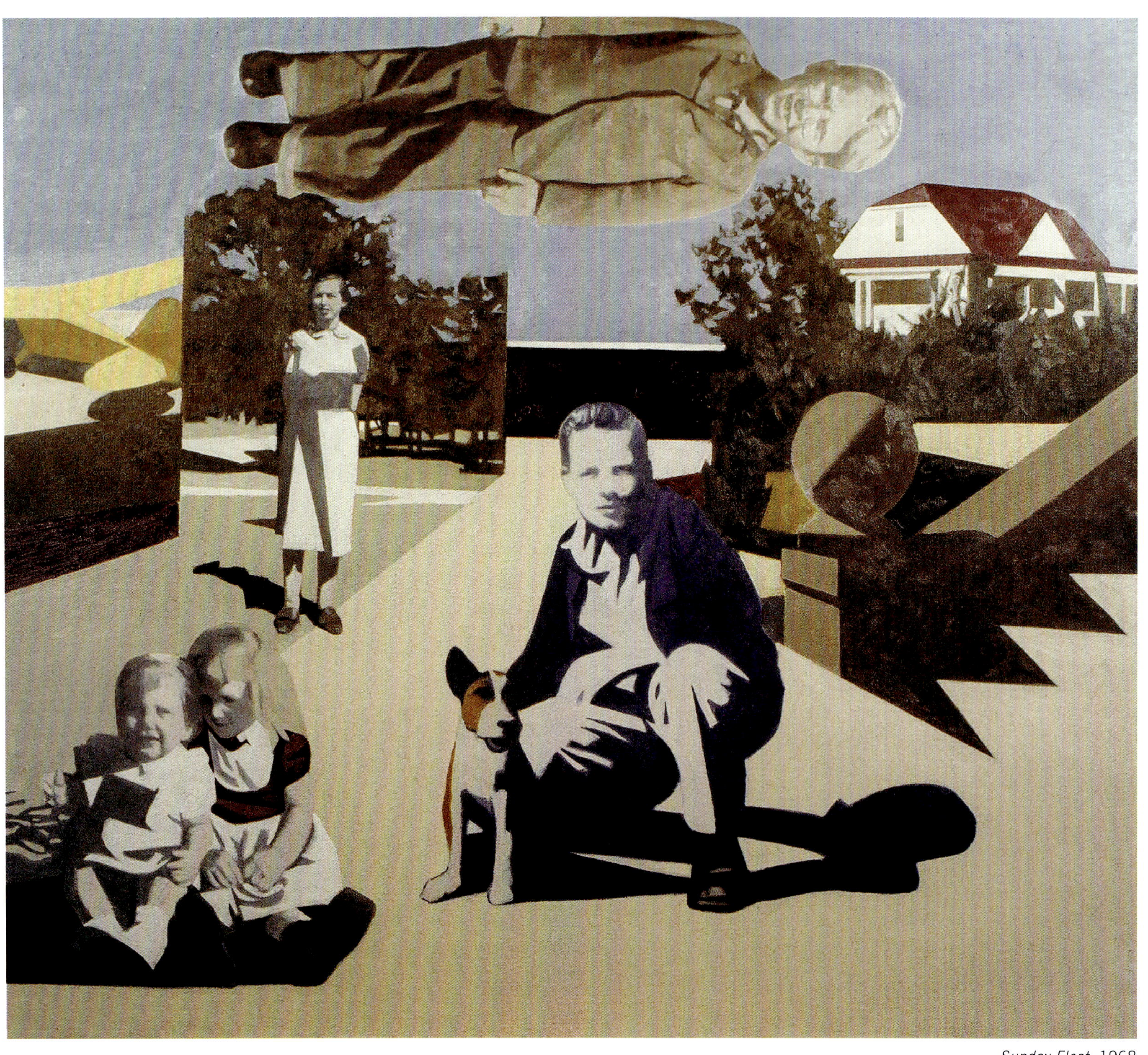

Sunday Float, 1968

oil on linen | 50" × 52" | Collection of Mr. and Mrs. Robert A. Rowland III town background that I refused to hide any longer, or at least until I worked my way through it."[2]

Interurban, especially, slips between stasis and transformation, the familiar and the unrecognizable. The disorienting torque to the work arises out of forces of stability and change flowing through and past each other. The compositional structure is more than just a clever device; it's also a buoyant, dynamic expression of the artist's radiant curiosity. Winter writes, "I was reading something about Giorgio de Chirico and how his work related to the darkness of Edward Hopper's paintings and it occurred to me how Romare Bearden's works relate to both, especially his paintings of North Carolina with the distant trains and their puffs of smoke and a feeling of lonely figures. When I was painting *Interurban*, I was wondering where the orange color in the field was coming from. I looked in my studio closet for something and realized that I'd pinned up a reproduction of a de Chirico painting with that same orange in it. It reminds me of Andre Breton's comment about a painter seeing something through a crack in a door and the sight influences the next few years [of] work. I didn't even need a crack in the door. Things just get in my subconscious without any fanfare."[3]

At the time, Winter aimed to balance his inner world with the outer world—art, teaching, and family, including the birth of their second son, Max, in 1970. To that end, he decided to bring his current family into the paintings. Jeanette and the children became his muse and brushstrokes. Using snapshots as a matrix, *Self-Portrait with Family* (1969) and *Self-Portrait with Family #2* (1970) move back and forth between childhood and maturity in surreal, collage-like compositions. Here, the haunting space of memory converges with the physical reality of the painted surface. Mementos, curios, and old photographs figure prominently, as evidence of past and present actions, as well as symbols of hidden significance. Through these objects and figures, Winter constructs both a family melodrama and relationship story about love and loyalty, secrets and lies, and how the past, never being dead, hovers around waiting to ambush us with deep, almost operatic emotions. Both paintings are about the mutability and the cycle of life, coming of age and coming into oneself; the pain it can put us through; as well as the roots that sustain us and the need for new growth. In *Self-Portrait with Family*, Winter stands with his legs apart, feet firmly planted, and arms at his side. With his head tilted slightly, he looks at us with a quizzical, perhaps confrontational expression. Winter's father-in-law, in dark suit and fedora, arms folded, lurks in the shadows between a tree and the window of a building. At far right, Jeanette sits comfortably, one leg crossed over the other. Her casual demeanor is conveyed by her blue dirndl skirt, white blouse and thong sandals, her pixie haircut and broad smile. Between them are images of Jonah as a toddler and of a young Jeanette in a beret and brown coat standing alongside her mother, who is dressed in gloves and an elegant mint-green suit. For *Self-Portrait with Family #2*, Winter has placed medieval-like signifiers above each individual—a bush, flame, or tree form. Here, Winter stands at far right, his eyes are closed, and his facial expression reveals a deep sadness. One hand is pushed in his trouser pocket; the other grabs the edge of his jacket. An image of Jeanette's mother is perched near Winter's right shoulder; a large, metaphysical cube is suspended above his head. Jonah, blue-eyed and sunny-faced, stands next to his father. At far left, Jeanette stands with legs crossed at the knee, arms folded tightly at her chest. She stares at us with an unnerving confidence. Jeanette's somber father, directly behind her, assumes a similar formidable pose. Significantly, Winter's little black-and-white dog Clip is the central pivot point of the composition. In the distance is a ghostly image of Winter's mother holding the artist as a baby and standing in front of a stark brick building with a single black window.

All of the figures take on affecting, palpable qualities that encourage a reading of every nuance of their appearances for meaning. They—and by extension us—seem to be watching each other like spectators at a play when the lights have just come up in a theater. Winter makes us want to know what has happened, what is happening, and what is going to happen. Winter and family are the main actors in imaginary time, in imaginary space. His means, however, are strictly dependent on the skills of painting—the ability to render form and mood

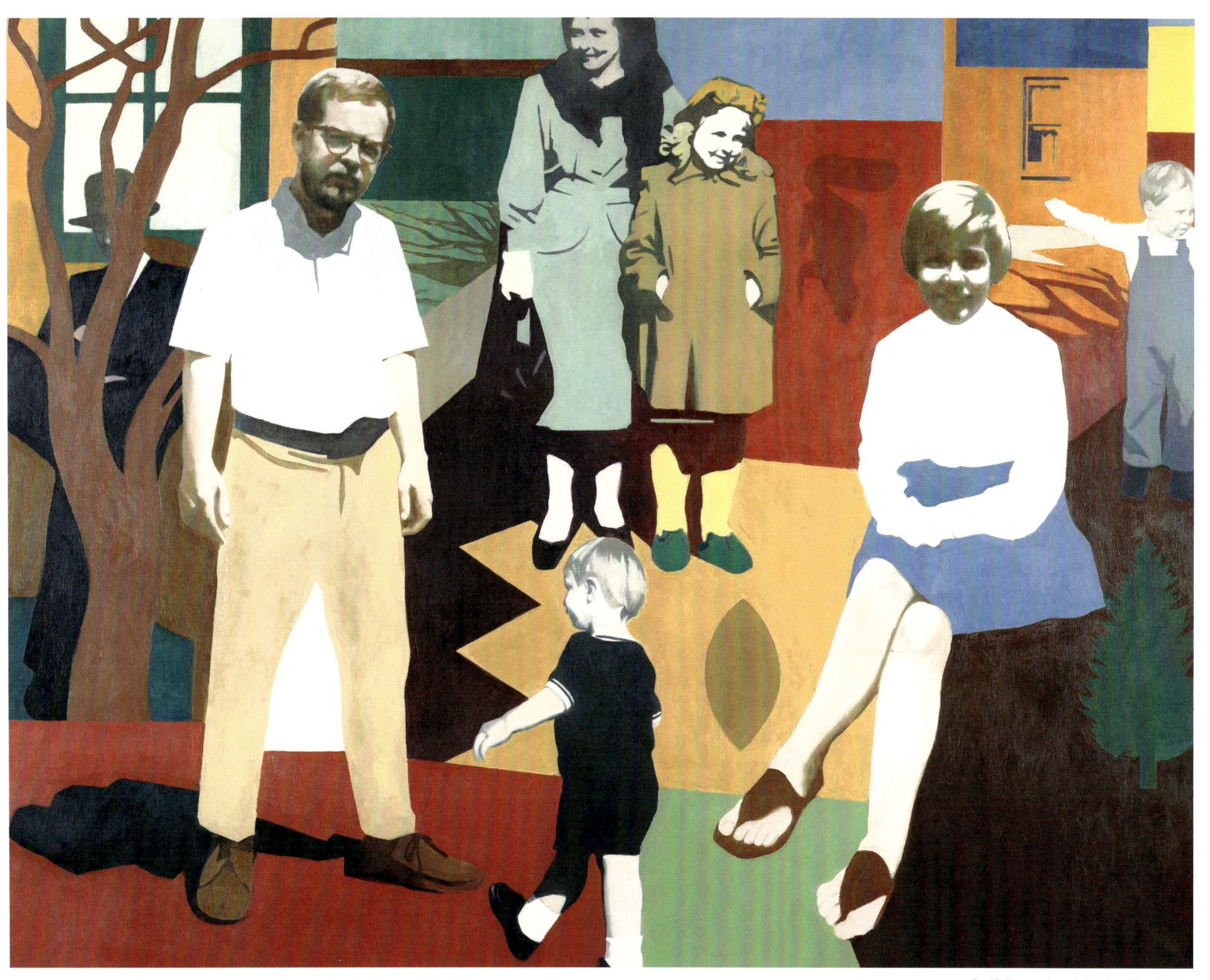

Self-Portrait with Family, 1969

oil on canvas | 62" × 80 13/16" (157.48 × 205.26 cm) | Dallas Museum of Art, gift of Mr. and Mrs. George J. Perutz | 1980.9

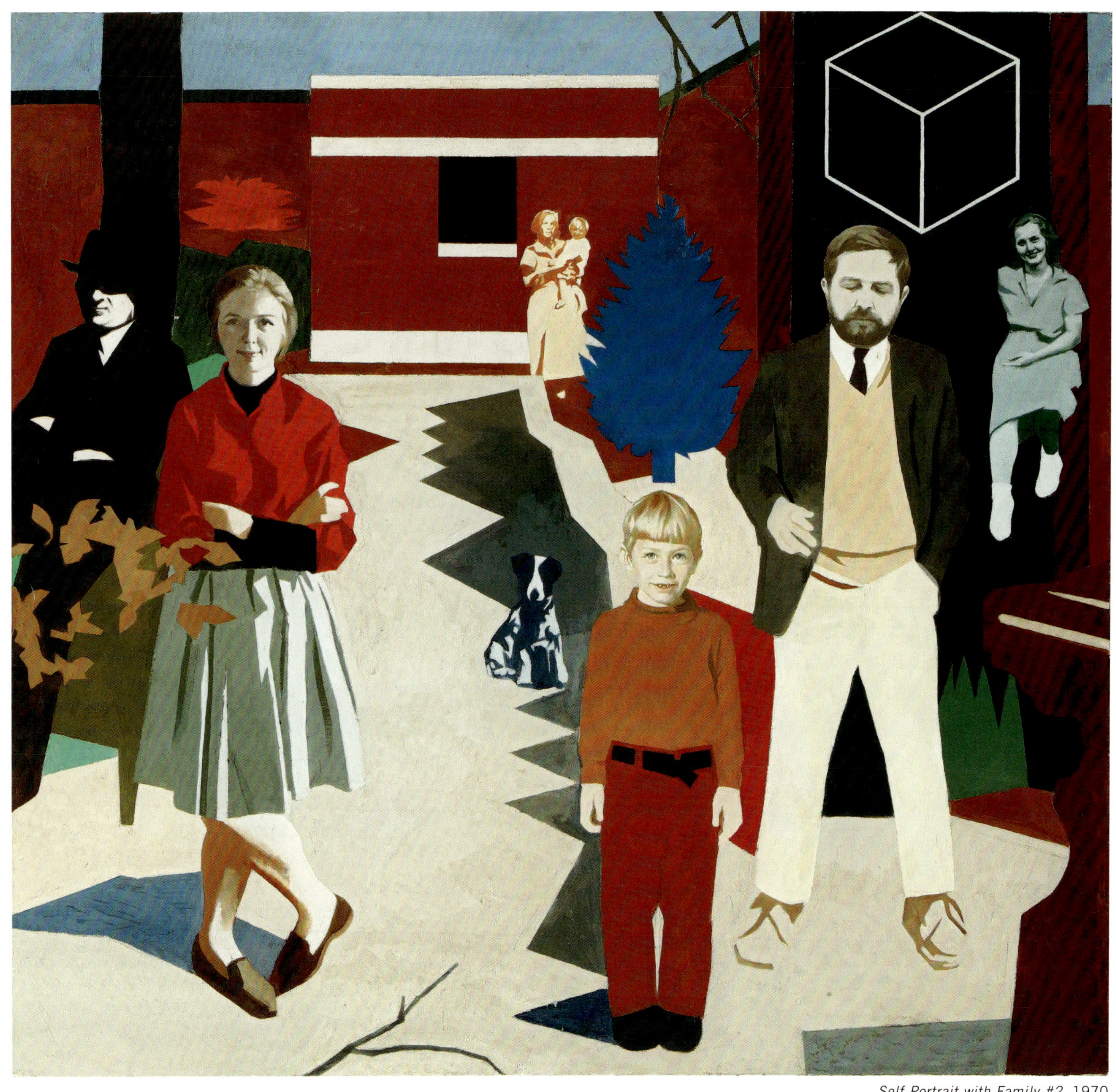

Self-Portrait with Family #2, 1970
oil on canvas | 60" × 64" (152 × 163 cm) | University Art Collection at Meadows Museum, Southern Methodist University, Dallas | Gift of the artist, UAC 2005.01

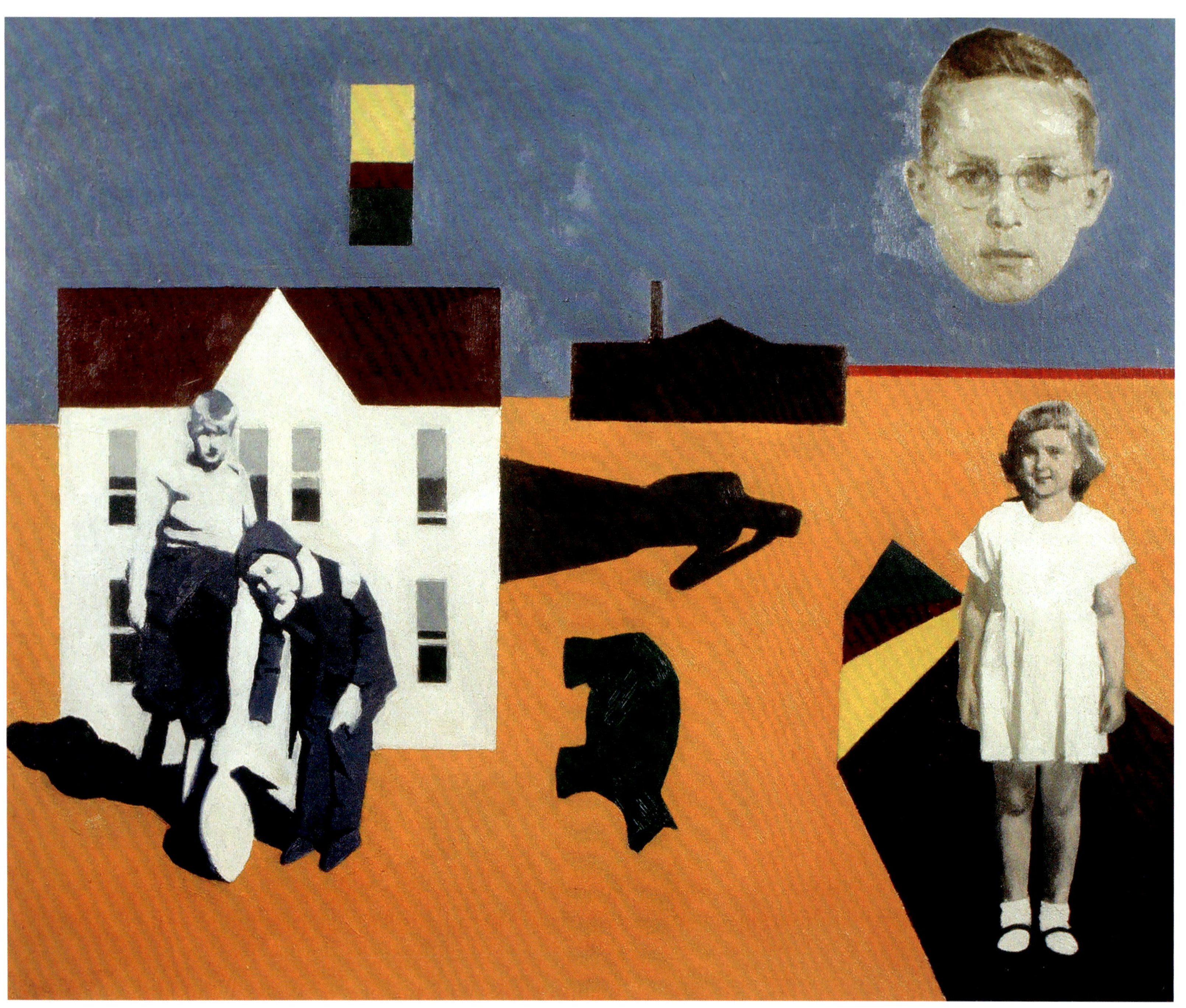

Interurban, 1968

oil on linen | 25" × 31" | Collection of Quin Mathews

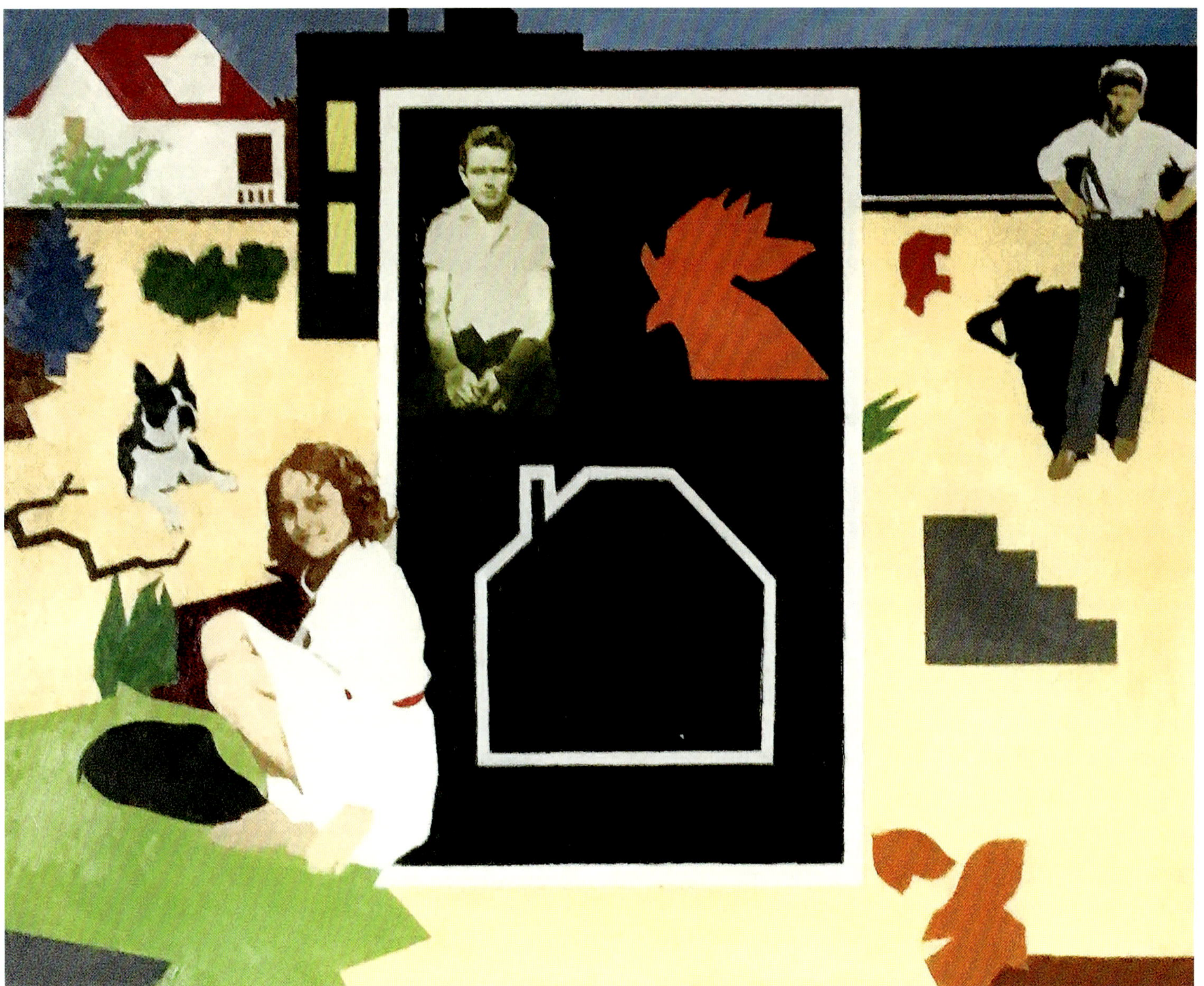

Waiting for a Train, 1973
oil on canvas | 20" × 25" | Collection of Jonah Winter

with dissonant and subtle modulations of color. The graphic aspects startle our photographically informed eyes into believing in Winter's imagery. The specificity of painted, photographic detail produces his complex illusion of reality. Nevertheless, things are presented not as they are in the real world but rather as they are in Winter's imagination.

The jazzy, patchwork structures of both works evoke the flag-bright paintings with crisp planes, musical rhythms, and buttery textures of Stuart Davis, who early on applied an investigation of cubist space to the kaleidoscopic variety of contemporary urban life as experienced in the streets. Indeed, Winter's paintings reveal complex juxtapositions of conflicting perspectives and flat shapes; of abrupt shifts in modes of spatial definition; of large, bold forms and hard edge elements; and of geometric abstraction with realistic figures. As Douglas MacAgy writes, "Roger Winter is intimately concerned with the potency of a time-factor in personal existence. . . .

Winter's schematic patterns are more overt and discontinuous, a device that suits his special way of dramatizing individual subjects by seeming isolation where each still vibes with the others. . . . To convey this relationship in terms of his own graphic rhetoric, Winter thinks of his pictorial setting as being neutral—as being devoid of the spatial reference that connects objects within a continuum which provides everyday linkage. It is without earth's gravity and there is no chance of physical collision. . . . Images can be floated in rightside up, in groups, single, sideways; they may appear as if solid or fading like a tintype."[4]

Creating links between seemingly disparate forms is Winter's gift. It is what gives his painting its eccentricity, its spirit, and its frenetic energy. Both paintings include narratives and memories, whole or partial, as well as capturing what occurs when they are stitched together. Overall, Winter's family members and objects are rendered in silhouette, deep shadow, or dramatic half light, as if caught in a liminal state between worlds. Winter comments, "The building in *Self-Portrait with Family #2* is a version of one that occurred in a childhood dream: my brother, sister, and I, closest in age, would go out at night with a can of 8:00 black coffee. There was a window like this, completely dark, and we would put the can up on the windowsill. Only hands would come out and take the can. We would never see the person. I'd have that dream every few weeks. I think the dream had something to do with me being a dark painter. What shocked me—there's an almost identical scene in Balthus's street painting, *Passage du commerce Saint-Andre* [1952–54]—a figure of a girl in the window that's completely dark on the side of the building. She's standing up or leaning against the window and looked like my sister Ada." During this same period, however, Winter was also striving to get rid of the personal in his work and to venture outside himself. His son Jonah would later write, "It must have been exhausting—mentally and physically. To spend that much time in an interior reality is hard. He abandoned the surrealistic, introspective approach because he *had* to, in order not to lose his mind. And before he abandoned the early approach, he had to do it, regardless of how time-consuming it was. It tied into a profound emotional need; it was tied into *who he was* as a person."[5]

Various events stimulated Winter to abandon the "psychic spelunking" for a more objective, non-ego-based artistic approach. As it happens, he came across a passage by the poet William Carlos Williams about the clarity of ideas based on facts—how ideas "beneath the surface of facts would drown." At the same time, Winter also discovered George Rickey's book *Constructivism: Origins and Evolution*, which helped open pathways for the artist to create geometric-based work that was less personal.[6] According to Winter, the fetishistic family images and the nonlinear arrangement of time and space no longer fit. He explains, "As odd as it may seem, I knew nothing about Constructivism when I read Rickey's book. What I found was that Max Bill and other Swiss artists, [Kazimir] Malevich and Russian artists, as well as Ellsworth Kelly, worked toward ridding their art of personality or personal intentions, quite often letting numbers or games of chance determine results. My own work had grown so very personal and so dependent on intuitive structure that this idea was like a breath of fresh air." To that end, Winter established a few ground rules: "I didn't want to use anything that came directly from me. So I decided to choose a photograph and I will reproduce that photograph in pencil. It will have nothing to do with style. It will be using myself, but without subjectivity or personality." Ironically, Winter chose a photograph of himself as a six-year-old, a subject that couldn't have been more personal. It seemed that no matter what Winter tried, he couldn't get beyond the self and invariably fell back on the known. At some point during this period, he attended an art historian's lecture at Southern Methodist University about Rembrandt's unification of time and space, which seemed to crystallize Winter's own intentions. "I thought that's exactly what I've been trying to do," Winter recalls. "I didn't want to use my personality in terms of style, color, or manipulation of materials. I wanted one instant and I wanted a unified space." But he had no answers. Although Winter was not yet ready to reject the family imagery, the exercises reaffirmed the kind of clarity and unity conferred by a snapshot to an instant of time. "The subjectivity of my work in the '60's, at least on the surface, needed changing and I knew it," he writes. "My evolution took many years of daily search, but the Rickey book on Constructivism and the gridded drawing of myself as a six year old eventually shaped the 1970s and 80's paintings that used snapshot compositions with an expanded language of brushstrokes. I reached a point when my life and family led me to paint the world around me. I wanted my paintings to be entire dinners with many courses—not just visual cocktails."[7]

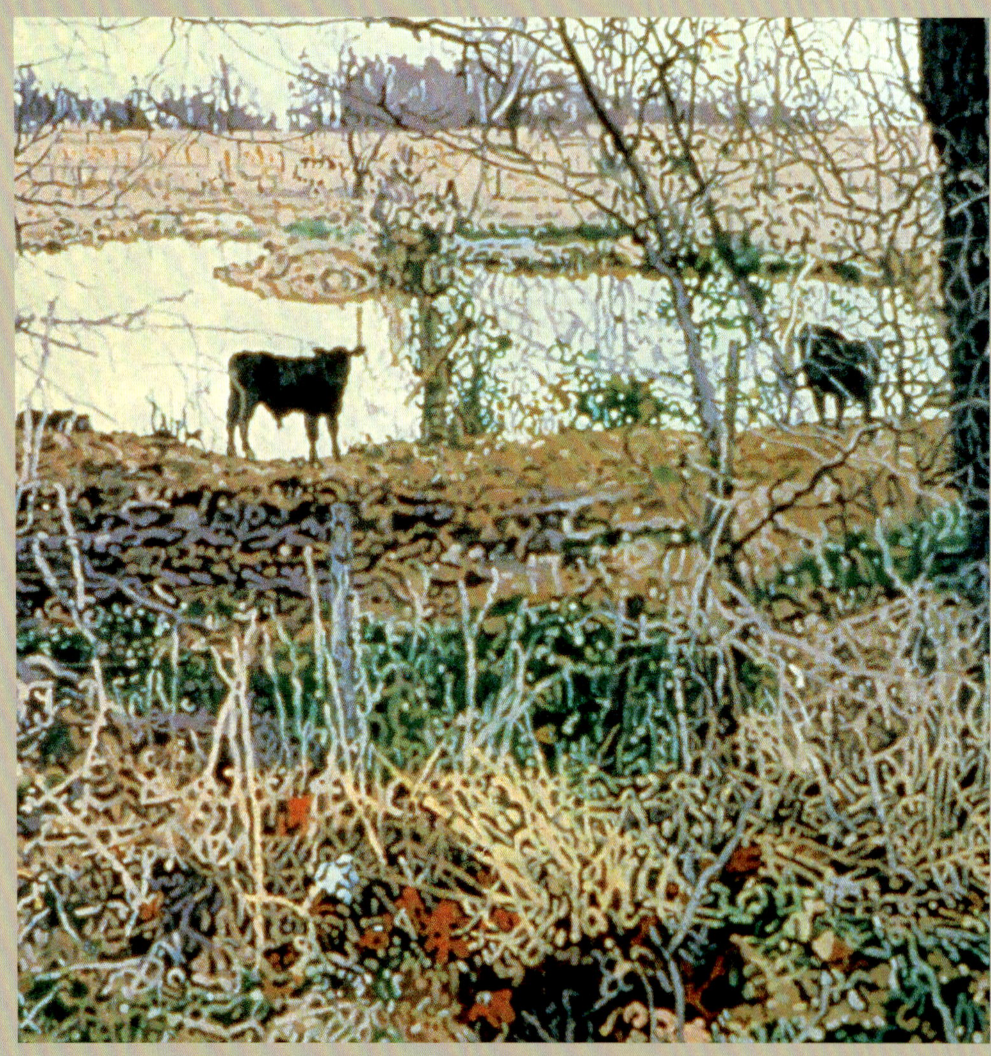

Landscape with Bulls (detail), 1981

oil on linen | 48" x 72" | Cele and John Carpenter Family Collection | Photography by Jason Voinov

CHAPTER 9

THE 1970s: TOWARD A NEW REALISM

PERHAPS THE DALLAS of the 1960s was not yet ready for Douglas MacAgy, who aimed to reveal a "deeper face" of contemporary art through his provocative and imaginative exhibitions. However, nearly a decade after his departure, William B. Jordan, the visionary director of the Meadows Museum and Southern Methodist University (SMU) art department chair, asked MacAgy, then director of exhibitions for the National Endowment for the Arts in Washington, DC, to curate a groundbreaking show that honored the common sensibility of artists whose activities centered on the Dallas Museum for Contemporary Arts. The landmark 1971 exhibition, *One i at a time*, brought together Roy Fridge, Bill Komodore, Jim Love, David McManaway, Hal Pauley, Herb Rogalla, Charles Williams, and Roger Winter in an effort to document the first and only avant-garde of Dallas.

Winter sets the scene:

> MacAgy made at least two visits to Dallas for planning and discussion of the show. On one of his visits, all of us gathered at Janet and Jon Kutner's house. The Kutners had been patrons of the museum. During the buffet dinner, Jim Love was trying to tell me something and I wasn't really listening. I've had a lifelong nervous tic of blinking my eyes. This grew out of the fact that each eye sees differently the colors, angles and shapes of things. Jim threw his dinner napkin at me and said, "GODDAM IT, stop blinking your eyes and listen to me." I answered, "It's not eyes. It's one eye at a time." MacAgy was sitting next to me and suddenly he slapped my knee and said "Roger, you've done it! You've named the show!" He heard the words I said, and he also heard them as "one I at a time"—as in artists at a certain period. The title stuck and became quite a historical show in Dallas from 45 years ago! I'm the only exhibitor still living.[1]

Significantly, James Surls and John Alexander helped install the legendary exhibition. Moreover, Winter produced the photomontage group portrait of the artists used for the cover of the catalog and

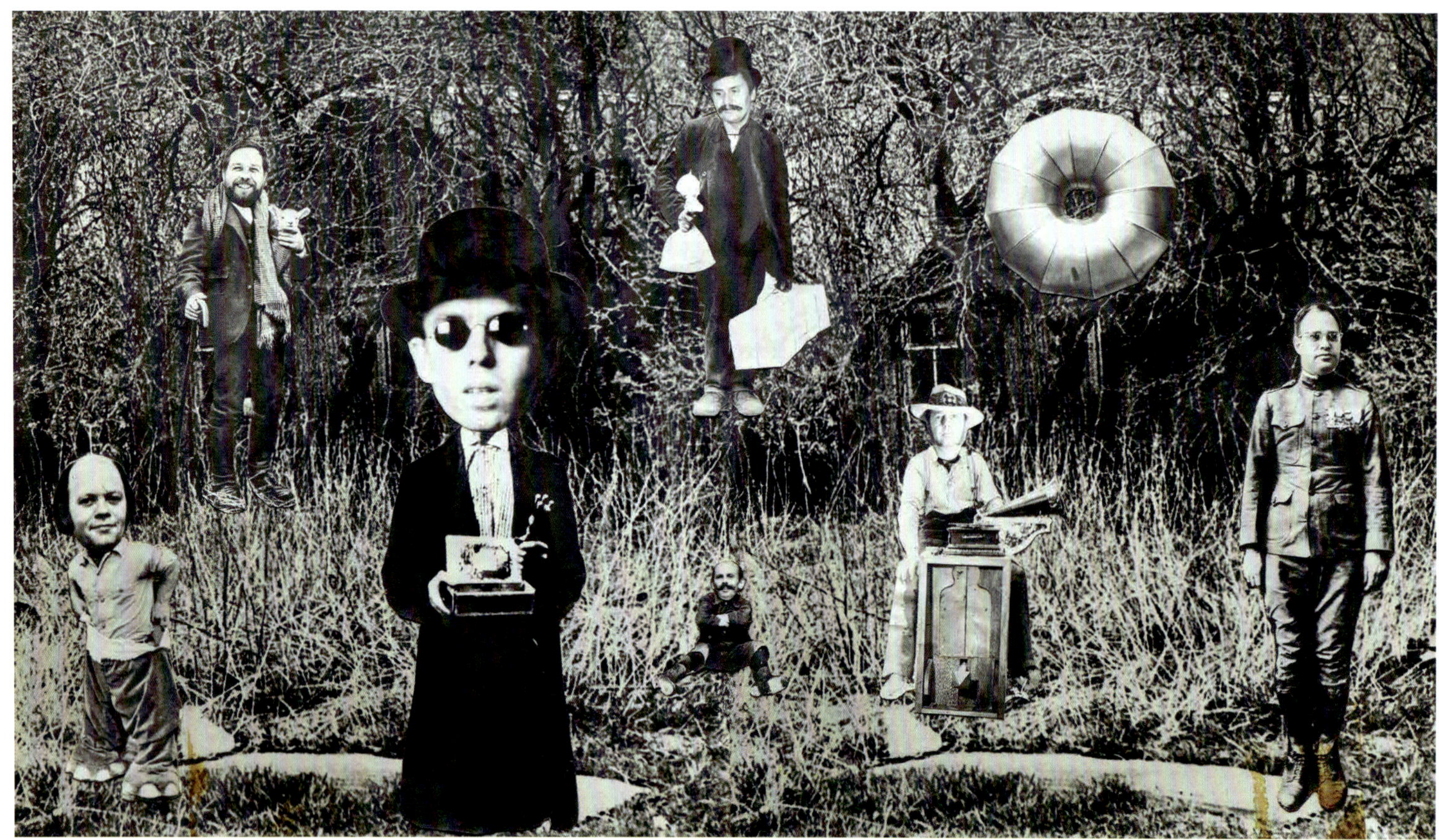

One i at a time, 1971
montage on museum board | 20" × 40" | Courtesy of the Dallas Museum of Art Archives | Photography by Brad Flowers

also printed as a public billboard. It is interesting to note that Buckminster Fuller, the architect, theorist, and inventor, was visiting as a guest of the SMU art department during the run of *One i at a time*. Upon viewing Winter's work, Fuller asked to meet the artist. "He saw something else in my paintings," Winter recalls. "He told me, I can smell newspapers in your work. Your paintings represent the end of an era. That era was the ending of newspapers and the beginning of new media."

For Winter, the exhibition acknowledged an important period in his life when art was presented in dynamic and progressive ways that altered his scope. But the decade that served as Winter's foundation—a time when the art community was relatively small—was totally different from the 1970s. With a decent teaching salary and painting sales, Winter and his family no longer lived in the "exotic poverty" of the Oak Lawn days. While struggling to emerge from subjective autobiographical content in his work toward a more objective outlook, Winter also sought to strike a balance between his newly refined lifestyle and his early role as a painter of tenacity and grit.

Winter's narratives come not from received information but rather from his actual perception of life. Instead of progressing from one event to the next, they drift among all levels of insight—dreams, things we long for, a conscious present, an imagined future, a reality that is beyond us. With this in mind, Winter traveled to small towns in Northeast Texas during the early 1970s with the aim of documenting what he saw. Tape recorder and notebook in hand, with gas money and Polaroid film provided by a small grant from the SMU art department, Winter took to the road in a quest to find out who lived in these isolated places and why. How would these people like it in the city? Are they not ambitious? Are the women more restless than the men? The *Outskirts* project, which developed as a series of silkscreen prints, examined a specific part of the world at a point in time that had deep meaning for the artist. The *Outskirts* fused a sense of loneliness inherent in dead-end Texas towns with incongruous elements and disjointed spatial arrangements. The series was featured in a 1973 exhibition at the Smither Gallery, prompting Janet Kutner, in her role as art critic, to write, "Winter's work, while apparently simplistic and realistic, tends to hit the viewer behind the eyes. Hope, sadness, love, happiness, contentment and frustration all are integral parts of Winter's expression. . . . He has in fact made something extra-ordinary out of the commonplace. Whether paintings on canvas, pencil drawings, collages of photographic and magazine images or the serigraphs made of these combined compositions, Winter's daydream style arrangements of image-pattern carry the common spirit of poignancy and nostalgia even as the newer work takes off into more of an interest in imagery as form for its own sake."[2]

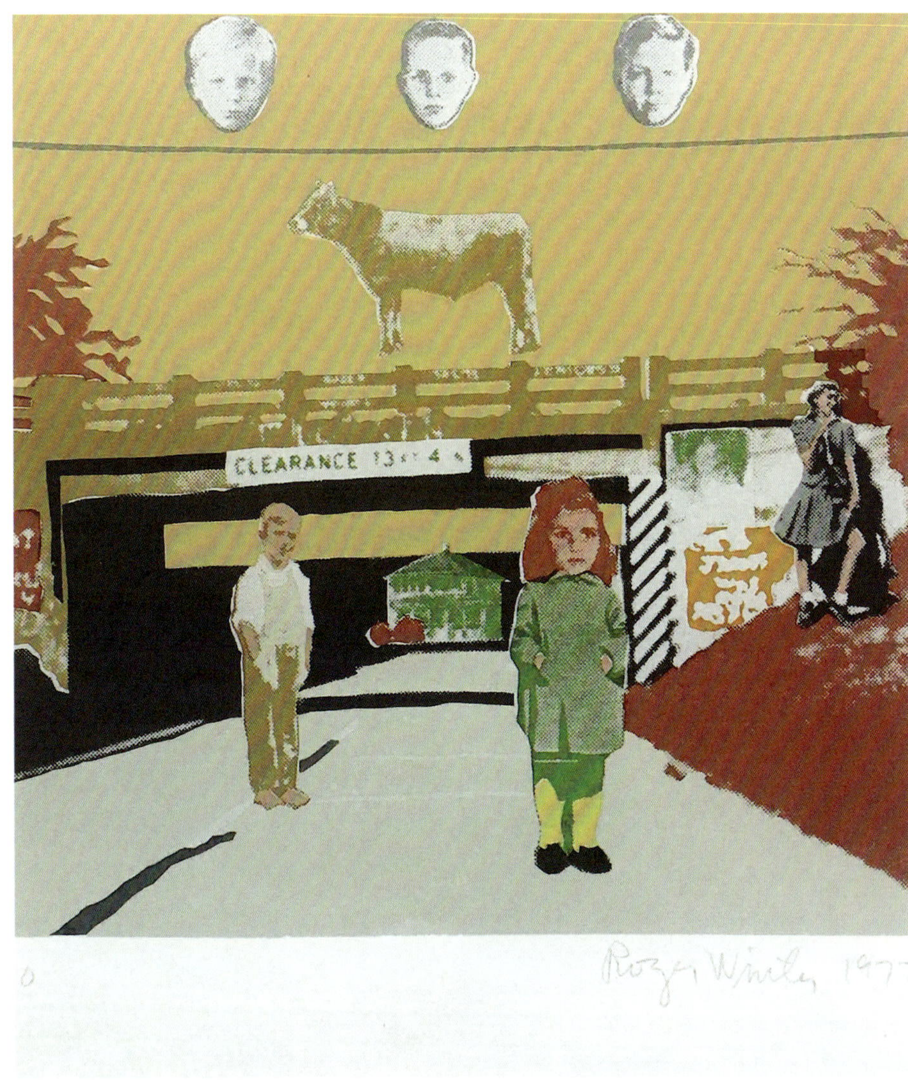

The Outskirts #2: Lost Highway, 1972
silkscreen on paper | 10" × 10" | Collection of Barbara and Mark Ashworth

Admittedly, the *Outskirts* series was intensely autobiographical. The interplay of people, dogs, cows, houses, bridges, and dirt roads still related in tone and style to earlier montages of family imagery. So in the summer of 1973, Winter decided to pull out all the stops—no more photographs, no more geometry, no more paint. He made "reconnaissance" trips on the bus around Dallas and to nearby Snider Plaza, where he observed the local denizens, drawing them from life and by memory. Through crackling, wiry lines and loose calligraphic gestures, Winter captured their expressions, poses, and movements with empathy and keen perception. His vibrant drawings portray the diversity of urban life: an African American man in a baseball cap sits patiently with his hands resting on the top of his cane; an old woman takes cover under her umbrella; a bald man with bulbous nose and paunchy stomach, hands in pockets, teeters on the weight of his heels with the toe of one shoe slightly raised.

"I had Crayolas, colored and regular pencils all over the floor," Winter says. "I would cut out the figures with scissors and pin them upon the wall of my studio. By the end of the summer, the studio was completely covered with people I'd seen. I was after a freedom from structure and care, an emphasis on playing and not taking any of it too seriously. Sometimes I would catch people doing intimate and humorous things. Mostly, I did them because of my fear of people and because of my love of people. I was very shy when I was young and have never really gotten over it. So the *Snider Plaza* drawings served as an emotional connection that I didn't feel with anything else."

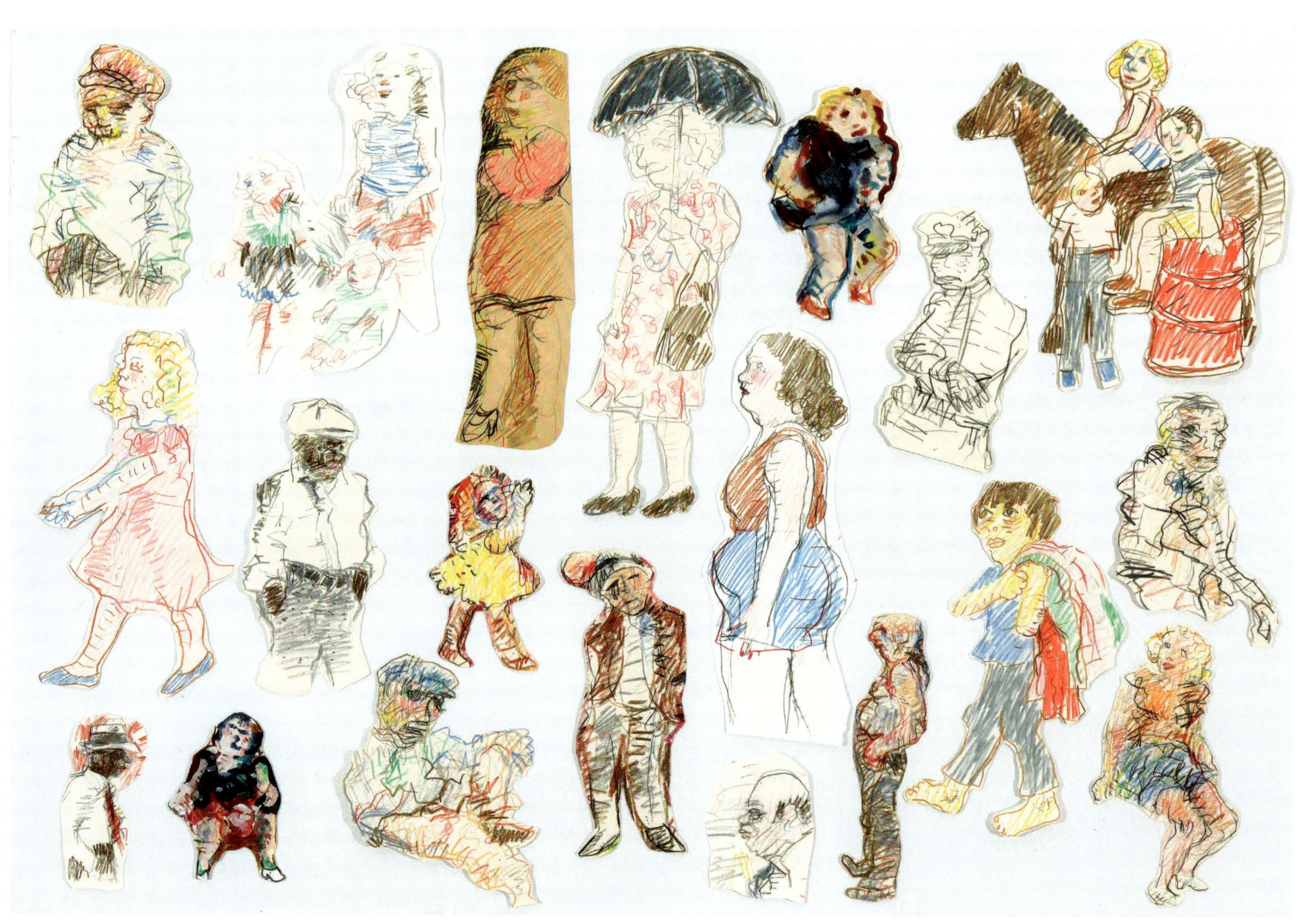

Snider Plaza drawings (composite), 1973

mixed-media cutout drawings | 24" × 36" | overall | Collection of the artist | Photography by Joshua Nefsky

As the art historian Edmund Pillsbury would point out, the *Snider Plaza* drawings prefigure Winter's *Subway* scenes nearly three decades later, in which he observes the multitudes of passengers riding to work or going home on New York's extensive commuter system. About the impact of the *Snider Plaza* sketches on Winter's development, Pillsbury writes, "They also bridge the metaphysical works and the straightforward realist works, which the artist has alternately explored throughout his career. To Roger Winter, drawing is a vital tool to the artist—getting him out of himself, loosening the reins that grip the artist's stylistic and contextual concerns, and facilitating a switch in focus or method. . . . Winter places emphasis on the role of play, of letting go, of not looking over one's shoulder, of being oneself."[3]

At the time, however, Winter worried that he had wasted an entire summer—several months excused from teaching—on scores of little drawings that didn't seem to lead anywhere and had no purpose. "I was completely lost and looking for something that would be an area to explore," he recalls. "I became very depressed—one of two times in my life that I felt slightly suicidal. But as it turns out, one thing leads to another, and the drawings from that summer eventually developed into the paintings of the late seventies and early eighties that had the sort of calligraphic identifiable symbols and images—what I call my 'secondary language.'"

Just as Winter's art was moving in new, uncertain directions, he applied for and received a one-semester sabbatical leave to England in 1974. It was his first trip to the great cities and museums of Europe. Upon landing in London with Jeanette, Jonah, and Max, Winter chronicled his initial impressions:

> Amidst rumors of potential Arab rocket attacks on Heathrow Airport, IRA bombs in department stores, and other public places, strikes, inflation, fuel shortages, extreme enough to darken the city, strikes by the railway people, cold hotels, we arrived in London and immediately found it more pleasant, less frightening and less expensive than New York, Chicago or possibly Dallas.
>
> The weather changes are not so extreme, as for instance, in Texas. Clouds are constantly moving by. London is old and low to the ground. The lowness caught me off guard after America. The streets are more complicated than anything I've known. Everything angles . . . squares and circles (circuses) abound. . . . I feel that despite an urbane air about Londoners that they are in reality isolated. Londoners are like small town people, staring at outsiders. I don't think they mind hardships, and I doubt if even in the best of times they feel a sense of plenty as many Americans do.[4]

The Winter family took up residence in a small cottage in Box Hill, Wiltshire, and almost immediately settled into a cozy domesticity. While Jeanette worked on children's books at the top of the bed, Winter made collages with images cut from English and Scottish magazines on the floor at the foot of the bed. He corresponded with the renowned British Pop artist Peter Blake and, through an introduction by Jim Love, developed a friendship with Hassel Smith, the celebrated Bay Area painter and teacher who worked under Douglas MacAgy at the California School of Fine Arts and alongside Clyfford Still, Elmer Bischoff, and Richard Diebenkorn, among others. Winter describes their first dinner with the Smith family:

> Everybody wrote letters in those days, so Hassel sent a note and arranged a time for us to visit him, his new wife, and son from a previous marriage. I remember so clearly, as if it could be happening now. They made supper for us at their home in Bristol. His son put the bottle of wine on the table, but Hassel didn't think it was visually compatible with the setting and asked him to decant the wine. Hassel had the quality of a California gentleman artist—the way he dressed, conducted himself. He may have been a little more rough-edged, but he still had that look. He told me there was too much one-upmanship with artists in California. He got tired of it and took a teaching job at Bristol

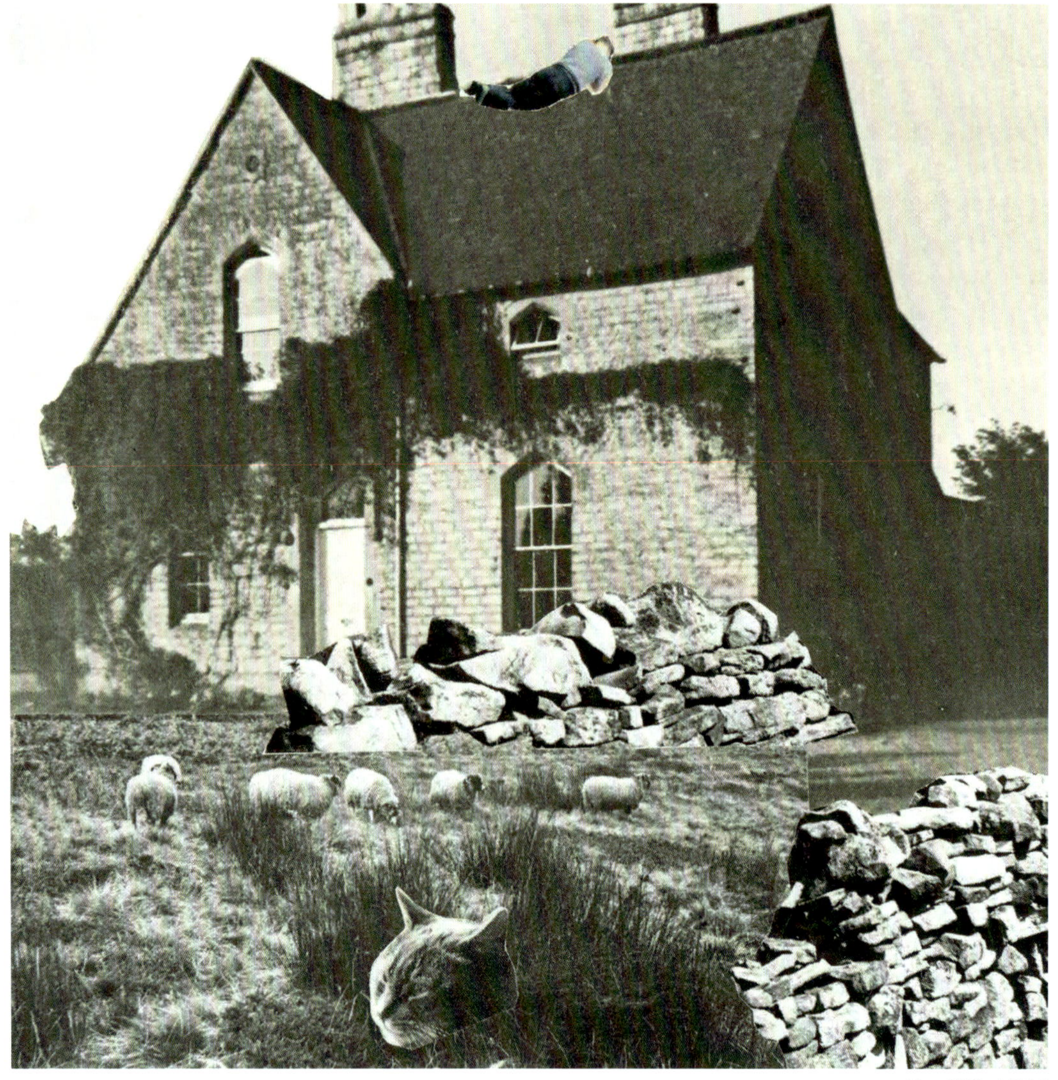

Box Hill, 1974
collage | 6 5/8" × 6 5/8" | Collection of the artist | Photography by Joshua Nefsky

Polytechnic. He used the entire third floor of their house as a studio. Hassel's paintings at the time had a certain influence on my work. He would make shapes with a line in a painterly area that looked like thought balloons with tails on them and circular forms. That really fascinated me. It was a way to make a shape that would break up an area. I started using those thought balloons in my paintings, which later evolved into a moon, and even the shapes and strands of Jeanette's hair.

Although Winter had learned about past painters through the strong art history program at the University of Iowa, he had seen few masterpieces in person. To that end, the Winter family traveled extensively around England, Scotland, and Wales. They visited Paris and Italy—Rome, Naples, Pompeii, Florence—by train and drove through Belgium, Holland, Germany, Denmark, and Sweden. In each country, Winter made detailed notes about the people, food, archaeological sites, and art museums, which, he writes, "changed the landscape of [his] mind for good." He took frequent trips by bus or train from Box Hill to London, where he spent countless hours exploring the National Gallery room by room. His journals are fascinating accounts of the artist's revelation upon standing in front of a masterwork for the first time. About the Piero della Francesca paintings in room 3, the fifteenth century, Winter noted, "*The Nativity*—the head of Mary and those of five angels are the most beautiful I've ever seen. The wonderful animals, the perfect cold look of grey, white, blue. The painting stands four feet high by a little less width. *The Baptism*, a most wonderful light about four feet by six feet. The strange group of angels on the left. The dark landscape to the right—tiny fragments of the city in the middle." In room 7a, Winter noticed that the "huge [Hans] Holbein of *The Ambassadors* is in a square. A most strong and daring composition—a most impressive picture. A rich combination of circles and right angles." On the spot, Winter sketched a diagram of the painting's pivotal areas and geometric structures. In room 19, French eighteenth-century painting, Winter wrote with excitement, "Chardin was such a painter! Such a lover of physical things. But through the physical, attained a feeling of life, not pretentious. So simple."

More than once, Winter rode the bus from Corsham, Wiltshire, to London just to spend time with two Nicolas Poussin masterpieces in the National Gallery: *Adoration of the Golden Calf* (1633–34) and *Landscape with a Man Killed by a Snake* (1648). In room 20, seventeenth-century French painting, he noted, "Poussin, who is always good and a great composer is nevertheless, sometimes obvious in his compositions. The greatest of his paintings here seems to be the *Adoration of the Golden Calf*, which I like very very much. But a good good painter. *Landscape with a Man Killed by a Snake*, is a shocking painting. Man is overcome by nature, but always man is seen as on a more equal basis with the forces of nature, either in his power *vs*. the forces of nature, or in his delight of nature, he is an intoxicated one with nature's forces. [It is] a great example of how the human figure's gestures can serve as directional lines of length, width and depth on a two-dimensional plane."

On another visit to the National Gallery, on February 8, 1974, Winter wandered among fifteenth-century Italian paintings by Sassetta (Stefano di Giovanni), Giovanni di Paolo, and Lorenzo Monaco (Piero di Giovanni). Rather than react to their formal qualities, he seems to have been overwhelmed by their magisterial powers, writing, "What is heaven, but man's dreams? What is earth, but man's perceptions?"

Clearly, Winter's sensitivity to the depth of human pathos grew out of his intense regard for the art of his predecessors. The 1974 sabbatical in England stimulated a period of rapid creative growth. His response to the masterworks at the National Gallery, in particular, was a kind of wonder and exhilaration experienced in the very act of recognition. All of those individual works, as well as his friendship with Hassel Smith, added important layers to Winter's development as an artist, his painterly vocabulary, and his process of exploration. Winter had, in these visits, located the great themes that would concern him for the next thirty years: a sense of place—the essences and cross-fertilization of a day's light, a place's history, a place's sky and earth; the slippery nature of time; the connectedness of past, present, and future; the fluidity of identity; the yearning for metaphysically charged images that not only probe the nature and quality of the spiritual but also give form and expression.

The Roger Winter who returned to Dallas was "a far more seasoned artist just from looking, looking, looking." Although he still produced a few family-oriented paintings, the idea of unifying time and space became a driving force. "It's always sad to turn loose of something that has been important to you," Winter explains. "But one can't get to second base without taking both feet off first base. Photorealism and Painterly Realism were in the air, but neither of these quite fit my needs other than the authority to face the world outside myself." *Landscape with Children and Animals* (1974) signals a transition from the hard-edged montages toward a more exploratory process of structure, gesture, and spatiality. Here, Winter portrays himself as a geeky kid with glasses in the extreme foreground; a blank white thought balloon floats above his right shoulder. The family dog, Polly, at far right sets her sights on the balloon, as does Jeanette, who is rendered as a bare-chested toddler. Their young son, Max, positioned slightly off center, wears a festive hat and holds a white flag in each hand. Oddly enough, Jonah, age twelve, is depicted as the oldest of this family group. He stands to the far left, anchoring the composition, while playing a violin. A cow hovers midair in the distance; to its left is a large frame house with a tiny rat scurrying down the roofline. Winter's aim is to evoke the texture of ordinary life, but in ways that suggest layers of deep meaning. Time and memory function as "sliding doors" and are constantly in motion. The heightened sense of shifting relationships among the family members is also captured by passages of explosive visual energy. The brushwork is painterly, light, and airy. Repeated triangular shapes jostle one another rather than lock together, but with diagonal planes holding them down. The entirety seamlessly fuses impending disorder and resilient structure. Acidic yellows and fluorescent oranges pop up among forest greens and blazing blues. Flamboyant reds bump against deep grays and browns. Dancing between abstraction and allusive narrative, Winter skillfully builds a consciousness-stirring arrangement that conveys the numinous aspects of longing, loss, and expectation.

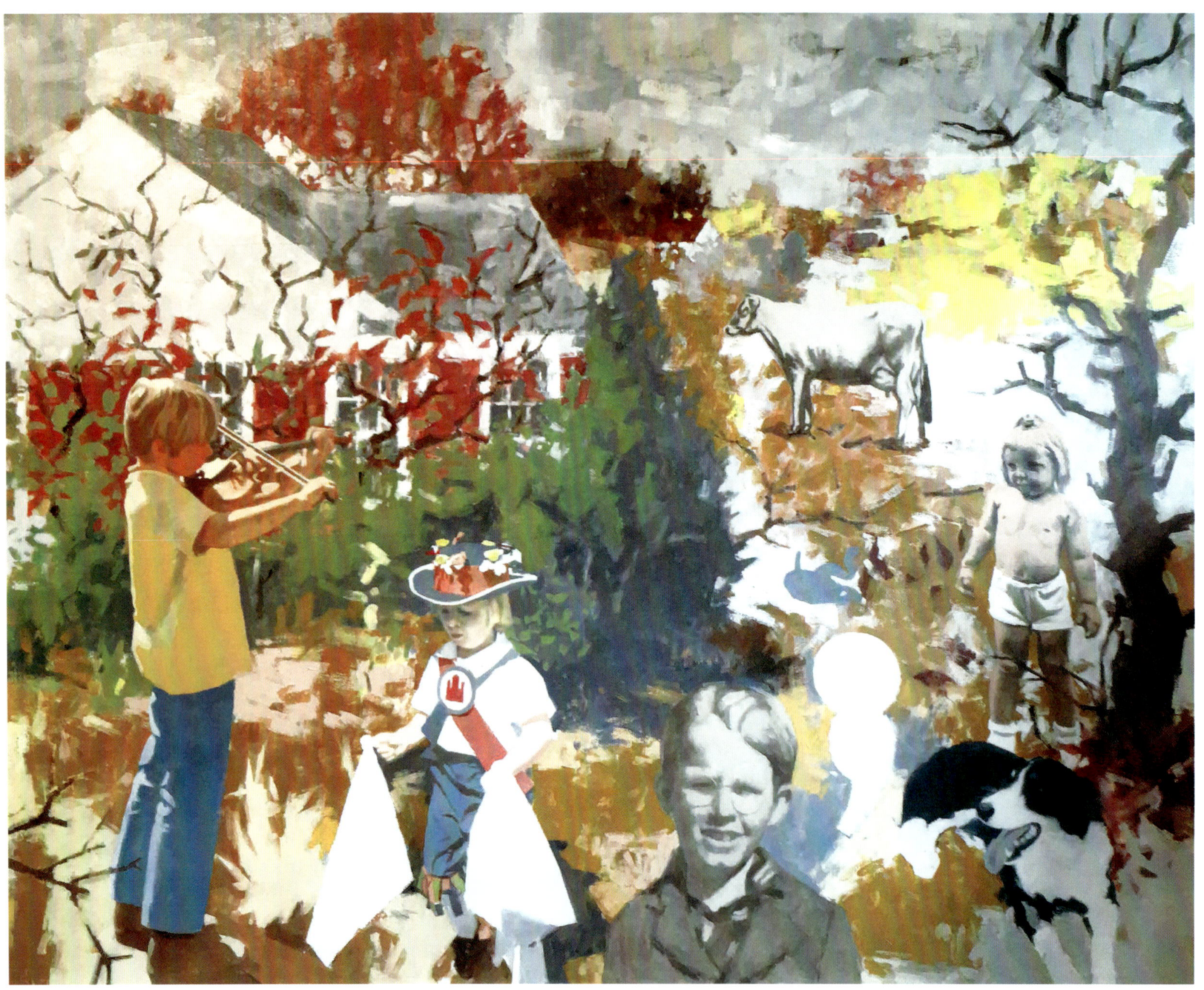

Landscape with Children and Animals, 1974

oil on canvas | 48" × 50" | Collection of the artist

After the years of traveling, reading nonfiction, and becoming immersed in teaching, however, Winter was ready to move into a more current, unified world. "I woke up one morning knowing that a snapshot could be used as the one and only matrix for a painting. I went into my studio and made several quick studies in acrylics based on snapshots I'd taken of urban and rural landscapes with figures. There was no montaging of figures over the snapshot images, no attempt to alter space, no invention of color. The idea excited and scared me, because I knew I was dealing with taboo and turning loose of something in my work that was an established pictorial language. It would take another year for me to try this in oil on canvas. My colleague Dan Wingren had begun using photographs as a matrix for paintings on canvas with a loose brush, so I had a partner in crime. It all seemed so dangerous and thrilling."

According to Winter, the fall of 1975 was his "golden semester." He stopped smoking, started exercising daily, and continued reading nonfiction. He also aspired to be a better instructor. He embraced teaching the SMU art students—Mary McMahon (Crain), Nancy Hanley, Danny Williams, and Don Mangus, among others—with an energy and purpose he had not known before. Most important, Winter started to paint directly from snapshots and with a language of brushstrokes that developed into secondary imagery. He was also following through with atmospheric backgrounds toward a united space and time. At the end of the semester, however, Jonah required emergency surgery and Winter fell back on old habits. *Oak Cliff* (1976) is based on the experience of his son's ordeal at Methodist Dallas Medical Center. From Jonah's room, Winter could look out at the Oak Cliff neighborhood and scan the vast Texas landscape beyond. Using open brushwork, he achieves a compression of time and space in the realistic background. But then he reverts to familiar stylistic tropes—the same autobiographical imagery and collage effects he had been struggling to eliminate. "I started painting at the top and worked my way down," Winter recalls. "It was pure cityscape down to the street. While staying with Jonah, I had seen Jeanette and Max walking toward the hospital one day. I put myself in the corner; Jonah in the foreground; our dog Polly over here at the right. For half of the painting, I broke new ground, but then got to the bottom and had to use these elements to make it work."

Significantly, *Oak Cliff* was the final painting that incorporated Winter's earlier stylistic concerns. While he often worked on several fronts at once, uniting past, present, and fantasy or accumulating an assemblage of small elements to form unexpected wholes, Winter began to structure a more objective vision by turning to the outside world. It took years for him to develop the kind of painting that is razor sharp and completely worked through—an art of truly honest weight. In the process, he examined painting in terms of object, personal expression, visual philosophy, and mirroring—not just of reality but of existence itself. The shifts in his work, from disjointed compositions to a more rational melding of space and time, also paralleled a daily life of reading, traveling, teaching, and building. His brushwork, ranging from fine to spontaneous, almost separates from the image, becoming an abstract or biomorphic form in its own right. Simply put, Winter begins to work the canvas like brick and mortar—piece by piece, stroke by stroke.

A series of cut paper collages led to the new freedom in his paintings. As Paul Rogers Harris astutely observed at the time, "The broad, bold visible strokes that he now employs came as a result of some small funky drawings Winter made of people. . . . This spontaneity comes from using his own hand rather than the more restrained 'perfect' surfaces of collage."[5] *Three Boys* is a taut balance of form and color with each element upholding the integrity of a brushstroke. In some respects, the cut paper shapes hark back to the thread labels Winter would snip from the backs of garments as a young boy. But the piece also poses the challenge of separating a shape physically from its neighbor and making a narrative out of painted, cutout forms.

The upshot of the cut paper pieces was a relaxed, more spontaneous style that abandoned the eerie dislocation of earlier works. Moreover, Winter read books on architecture, earth sciences, and urban design, particularly John A. Kouwenhoven's *The Arts in Modern American Civilization*, a comprehensive study of vernacular

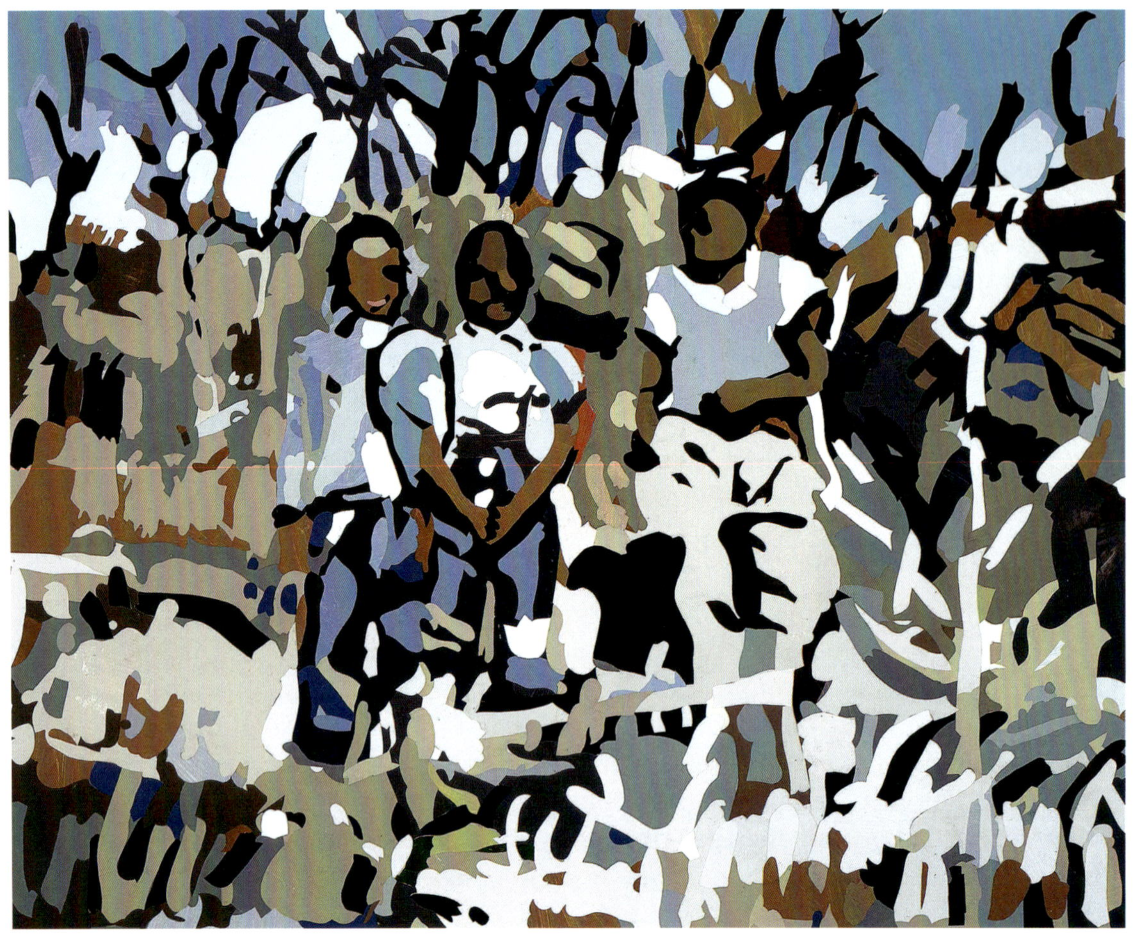

Three Boys, 1977
painted and cut paper | 32" × 34" | Collection of June Francis

hundred-acre cotton farm near Como and his parents were married there in 1911—the painting goes beyond the sentimental to evoke a sense of place. The wild grasses and local color fuse as a kind of abstract naturalism. About the shifts occurring in the late 1970s, Janet Kutner writes, "Winter's art has evolved from paintings of people to pictures of places with people, to the newest works which are pure landscapes. Yet the more objective approach Winter now prefers in no way affects the intensity of the work. His new paintings may be less nostalgic, less overtly poignant. But, they continue to attract the spectator psychologically, in this case urging him toward the discovery of hidden elements—ghosts of animals or people—within their lush and loosely gestural surfaces."[6]

style. He began to paint the University Park neighborhood—a white frame house, a street with melting snow—with great attention to marks and surfaces. As Winter traveled to other places, he made his own box of pictures and turned them into paintings of compelling forms and subjects. On a trip to Mexico, at the Pyramid of the Sun, he captured Jeanette and Max walking away in the distant foreground. Paintings of Lake Michigan and an Illinois highway are more spacious, filled with sky and water and a seemingly limitless expanse of land that plunges us into deep space. In *Kenosha*, Winter depicts his wife and sons walking with their backs to us across a sunlit field toward a street lined with houses and buildings. Jeanette holds Max's hand as Jonah strides slightly out in front, the three figures forming a triangle that reaffirms the painting's solid geometric structure. Although *Hopkins County Field* pays tribute to Winter's relatives—his grandfather owned a one-

Indeed, Winter's "secondary language" abounds with animalistic iconography, with brushstrokes cohering as frog-like and other strange little critters even while retaining their abstract forms. None of these paintings are trapped between the pains of the past or situations of intense isolation. If there is a thematic thread weaving through them, it is the complexity of an artist often probing, picking, and searching with his fingertips, as if seeking beauty and potential grace. Their pleasures derive from the sensations of looking into the lives of Winter's present family and catching a glimpse of not only its particular character but also a particular emotional and social milieu. Overall, the paintings give us a sense of watching a fluent, deeply talented artist extend himself and take risks in his quest to expand an angle of vision that radiates meaning at all levels. At this point, Winter's art has one foot in the modern America of the late 1970s and another in some odd, overgrown places. Perhaps he was struck by what new beauty painting could possess if it opened up to the bumptious real world while also holding on to principles of balance, composition, and touch. In any event, a sea change was occurring in the work, which he approached with a craftsman's care and experienced with a scintillated focus. Winter was developing a hands-on, eyes-on art method that forced him to slow down, look hard, and find the profound in the everyday.

The probity and plentitude of Winter's work gives the impression of an artist in a constant state of creative flux and ferment. However, Winter has always chosen his own path and insisted on keeping his own tempo. The journey has not always been comfortable. At times he has been tormented by self-doubts and has experienced transitional periods when the possibilities seemed exhausted, when he would have to wait for a perplexing and indeterminate span of time before the next step would be instinctively revealed.

At the dawn of the 1970s, just as critics were proclaiming the appearance of a postmodern sensibility with many different styles coexisting—realist, hard-edge, conceptual, video, and performance art—Winter could seem an artist who had lost his way. And it may not be irrelevant that his return to confidence came in the later 1970s, when painterliness was once again fashionable. There is an all-or-nothing drama to Winter's work—emotion and intellect amplifying and informing each other, establish a continuing dialogue. Not only do the paintings of the late 1970s capture an infectious fluidity, they sustain a mature level; in them we see an artist who is firmly in control of his means, his work, and his world, grounded in real experiences, perceived and understood, rendered with a disciplined intensity guided by intuition and personal need. The intensity we see and feel in these paintings is the ordered projection of Winter's toughness, his ability to push things through, yet humanized by the heartbeat of a visual sensibility. In his paintings, each separate part, each stroke or group of strokes, functions with the vigor of muscle and bone and nerve. At this point, Winter has developed great powers of visual analysis; he can hardly look at a scene without breaking it down and resolving it as structure.

Nowhere is this more evident than in *Highlander Band* (1977), which features dozens of teenagers at practice, all of them moving together, in neat rows and with the same distance between them. Significantly, Winter matches their pell-mell urgency, moment for moment, with this brilliantly controlled handling of paint. He uses no shortcuts. He eschews sharply abbreviated forms, high contrasts of tone, and grabby oppositions of color. Rather, the figures, instruments, and landscape elements seep deliberately into our attention. At first glance, they start vaguely—individual silhouettes, a vibration of one form and color against another. Gradually, they develop on the eye so that we begin to grasp their internal relationships.

Winter's brushstrokes have a kind of stinging rococo power—all elaborate flourish and steely accent. The strokes can be curvy and beguiling; the colors convey a 1970s vibe, only with the volume turned up: bright blue-and-red plaid shirts with gleaming white shorts and faded bell-bottom jeans. Here, Winter weaves together many small painterly acts. His art of accretion, however, is based on unity and the idea that the essential experiences are the ones that hit us all at once. "This painting was the most important of my works that unified time and space and brought my work into the present moment of my life," Winter says.

> Our older son, Jonah, was at band practice so often that summer of 1977. He's the clarinetist in the white T-shirt, behind the front-and-center clarinetist in an orange T-shirt, Barbara Hanley. They practiced at the large athletic field bordering Highland Park High School. It was quite a spectacle to see so many teenagers in such disciplined formation, dressed for Texas heat. It had to be the subject for a painting. I painted it with patience and without compromise of time or detail in my newly found approach to painting subjects from my daily life as in reportage. To be free from painting displaced time and space, from my past, from cubistic fragmentation of two- and three-dimensional

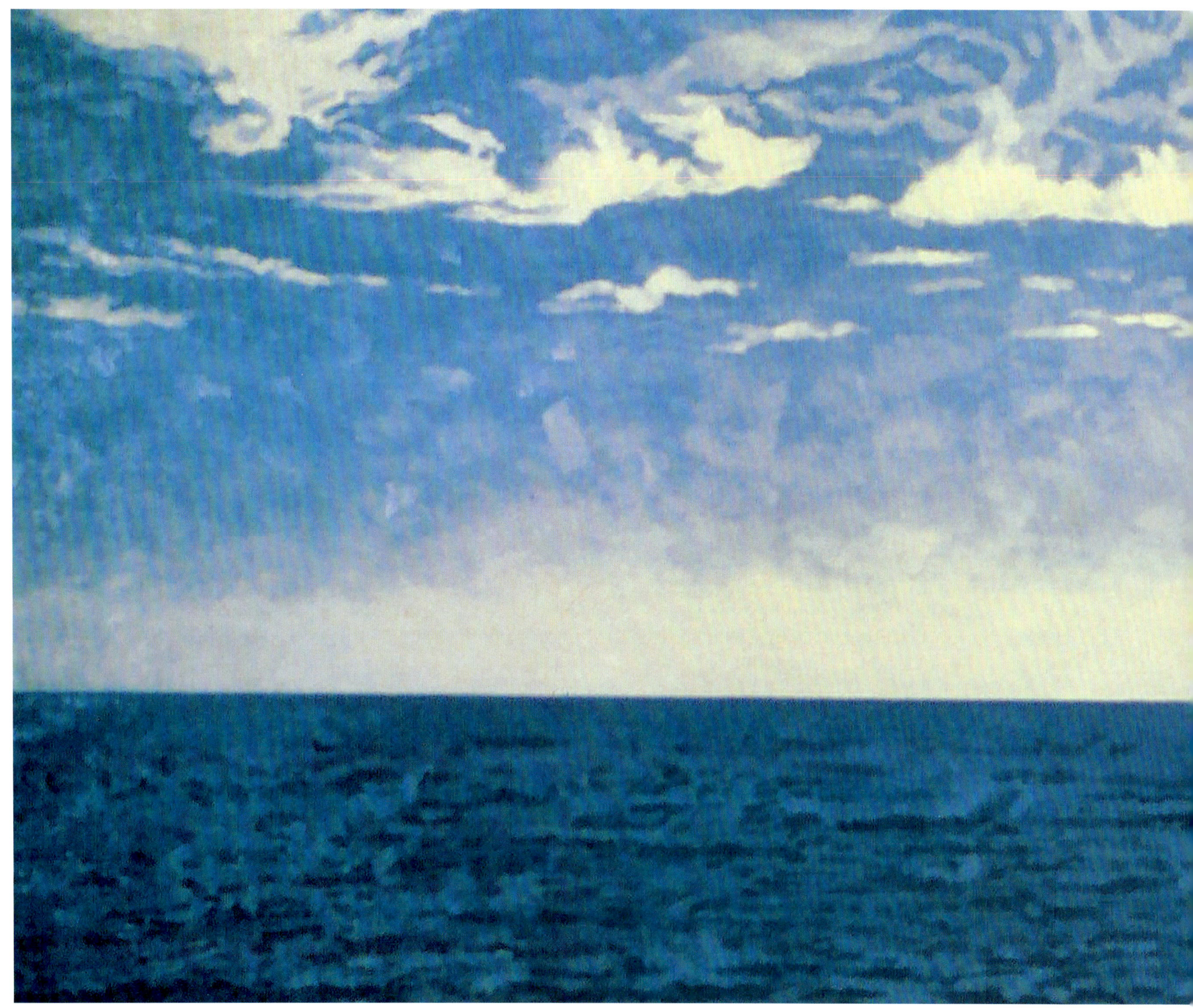

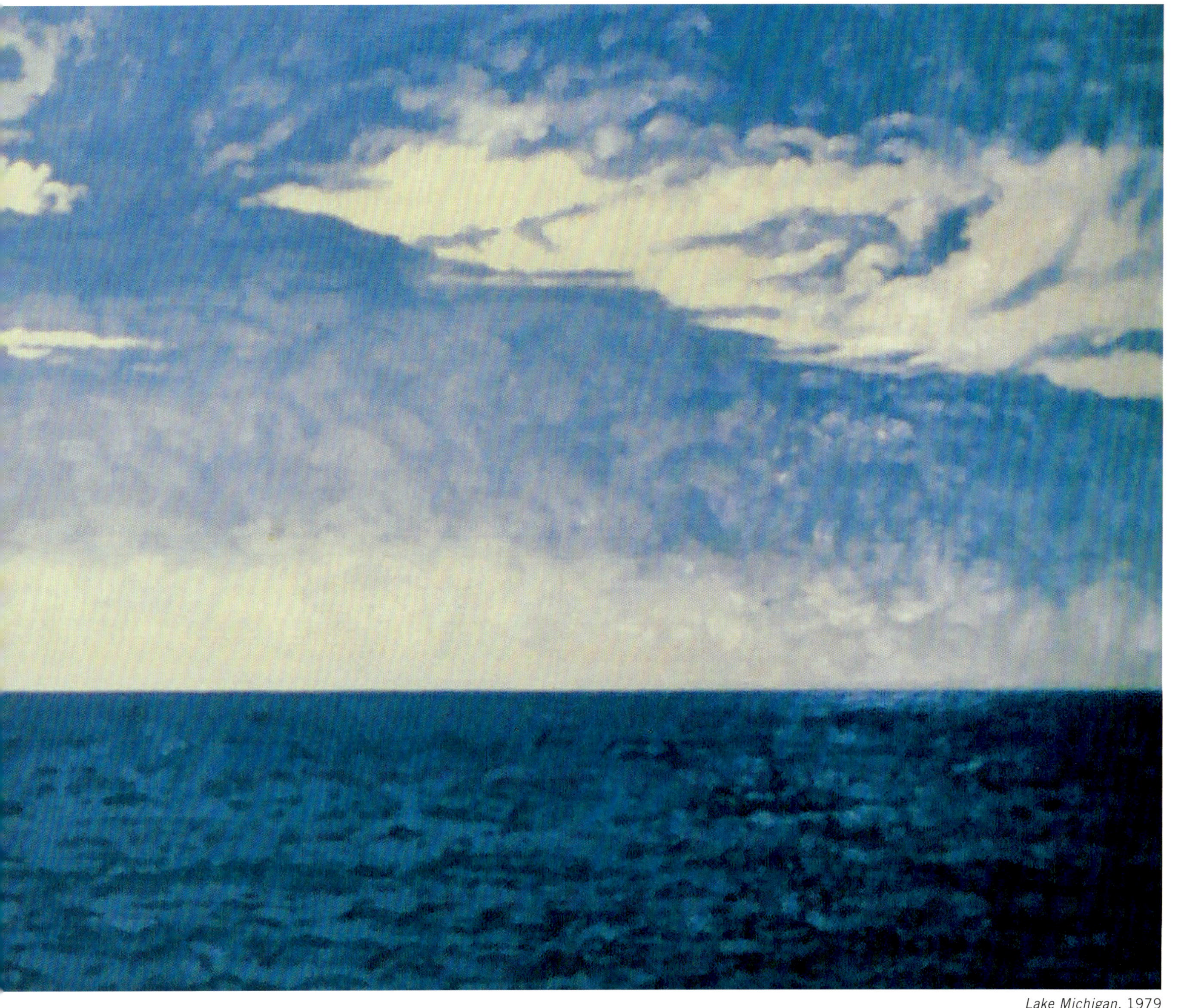

Lake Michigan, 1979
oil on canvas | 48" × 120" | Courtesy of the artist

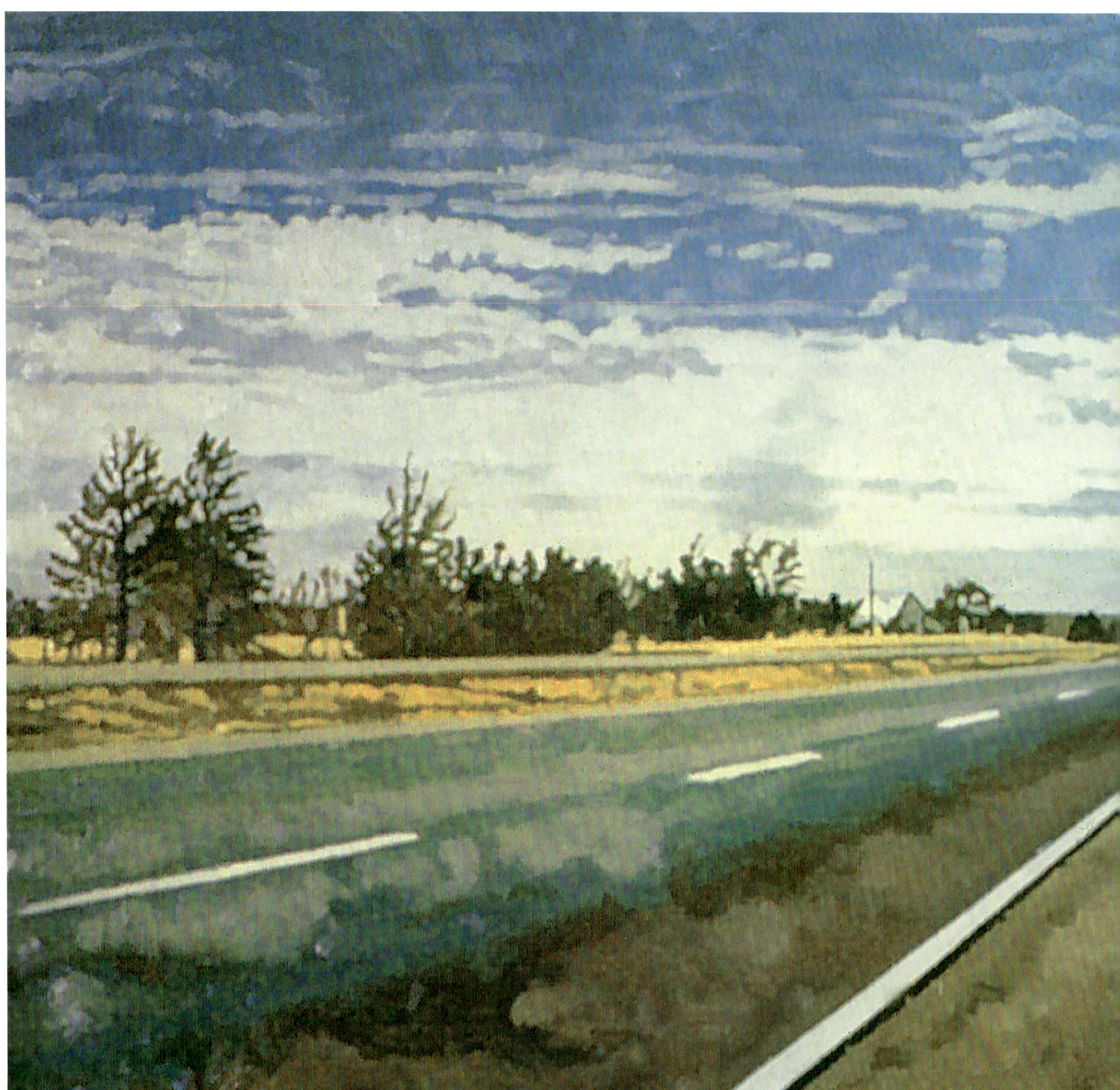

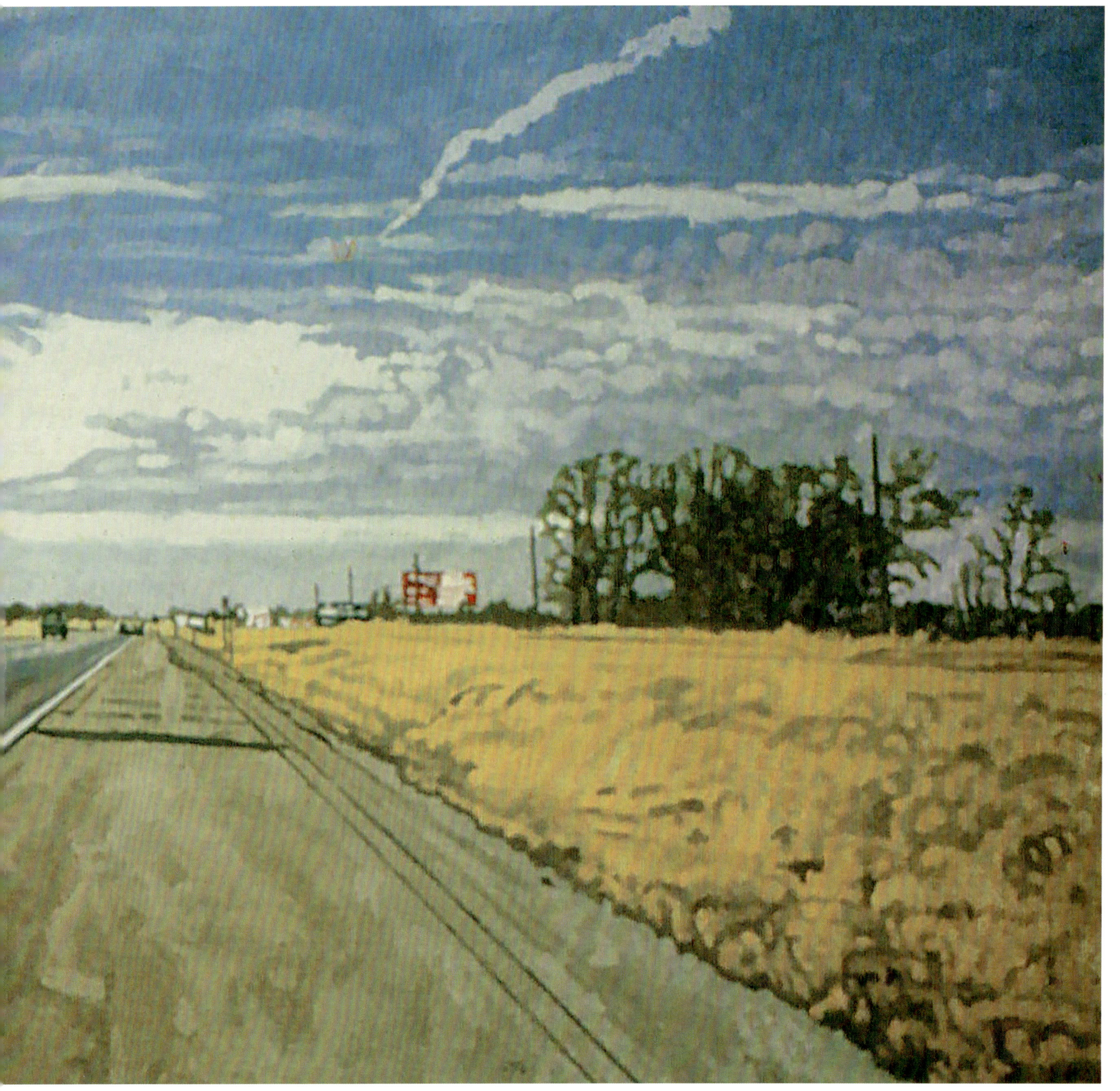

Illinois Highway, 1979
oil on canvas | 60" × 108" | Courtesy of the artist

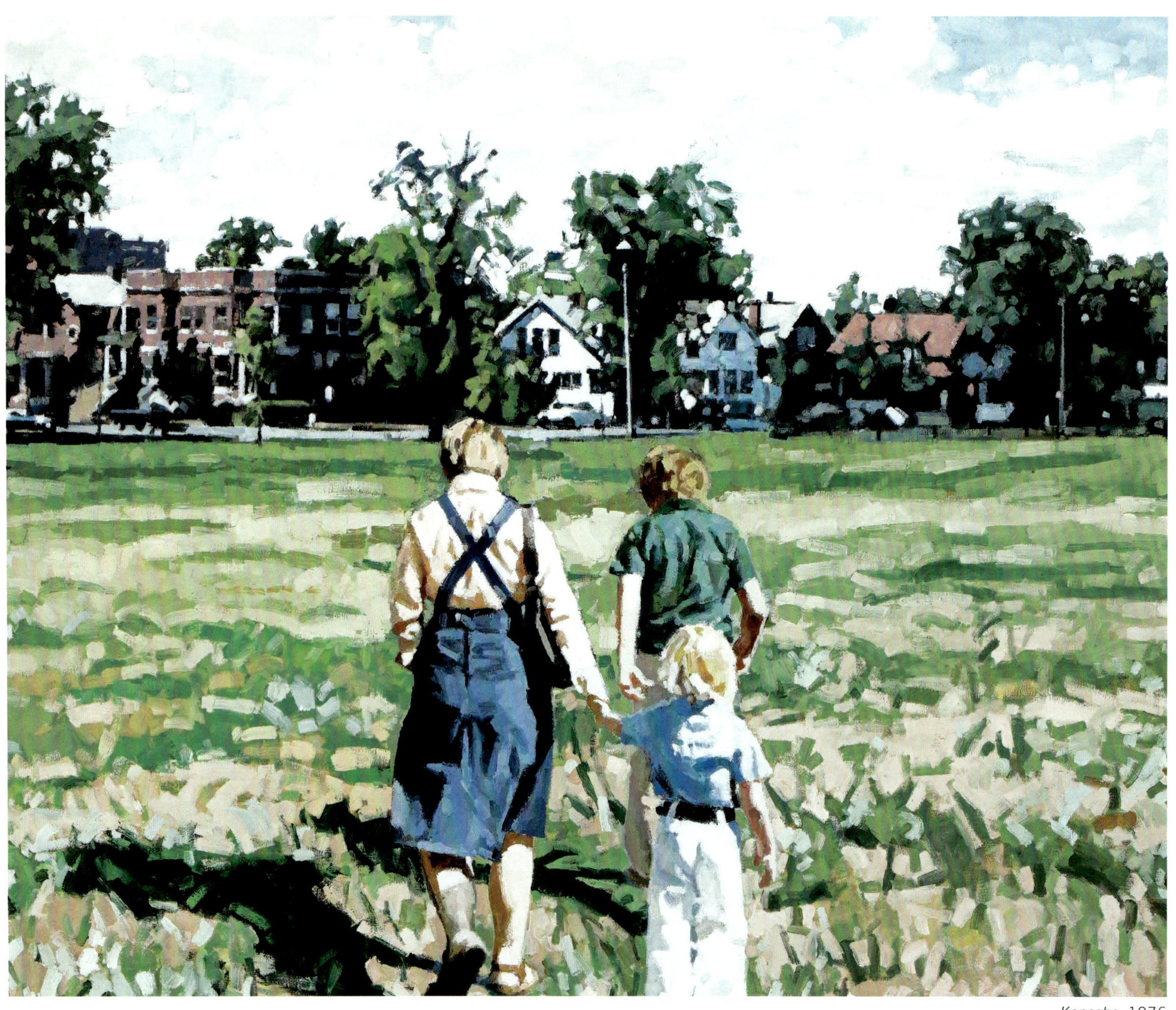

Kenosha, 1976

oil on linen | 63" × 76" | Collection of Mr. and Mrs. William B. Dean Jr., Dallas, Estate of Dr. and Mrs. William B. Dean | Photography by Kevin Todora

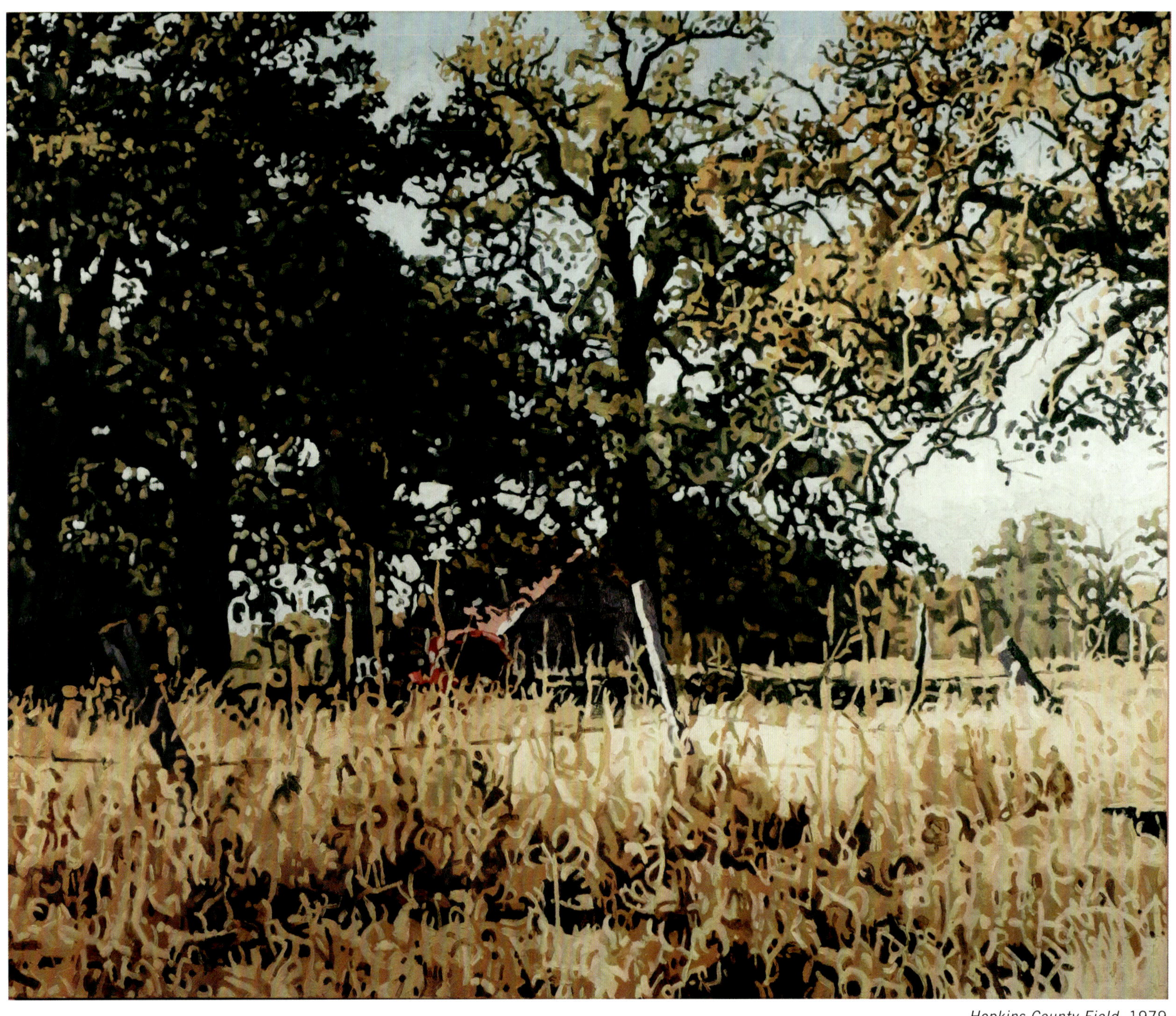

Hopkins County Field, 1979

oil on linen | 60" × 72" | Collection of Gary W. Knoble and Robert A. Black | Photography by Dean Batchelder

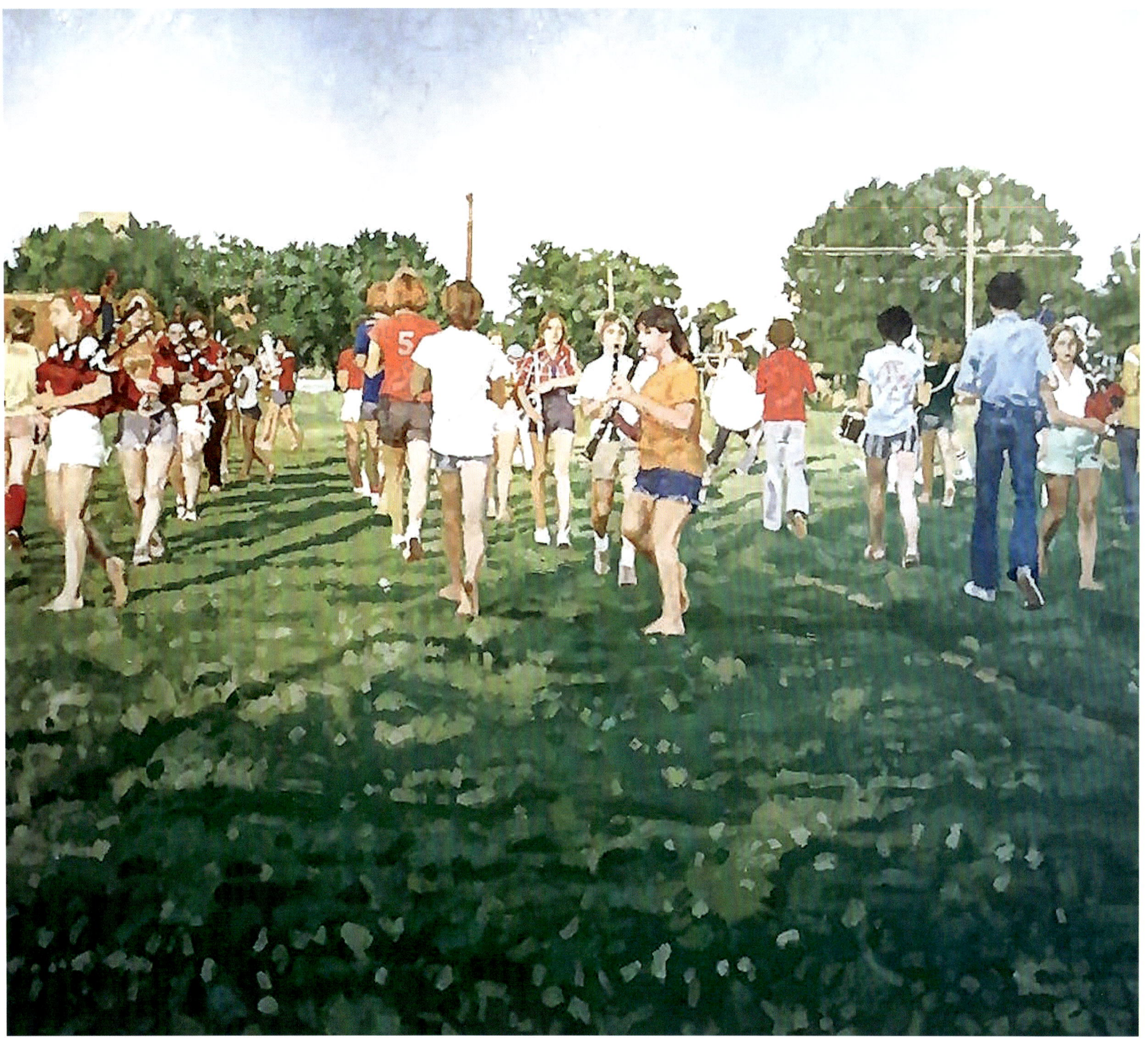

Highlander Band, 1977

oil on linen | 64" × 76" | Collection of Bryant and Nancy Hanley space—all this was so refreshing to me in the late seventies. The content of *Highlander Band* celebrated growth—the band members and mine. You have no idea how many legs there are in a marching band!

The girls and boys walking barefoot in formation toward and away from us, including the bagpipers at far left, fill the entire surface of the painting save for the two trees in the background and the sultry blue sky. Winter's deft orchestration of light, color, form, and action is more than a record of a passing moment; it is a memory lingering in the imagination of a younger, more innocent time. The result is a distinctly American painting firmly rooted in place, poetic, and vibrantly alive.

In this regard, Winter's paintings of the late 1970s serve as soulful distillations of the mood and character of the Dallas environs, allowing us to burrow more deeply into the cultural circumstances in which they emerged. His finest works of the period are distinguished by their carefully nuanced descriptions of time, place, and ambience. Significantly, Winter relies on his familiarity and knowledge of his subjects, interpreting the particulars of individuals or locales with great insight and often uncanny intimacy.

For the *Horchow Sisters* (1978), Winter spent time around the family pool, photographing the Horchow children—Sally, Elizabeth, and Regen—while they swam or relaxed amid the lush gardens in the sweltering Texas heat. The portrait depicts two of the girls at the pool's edge; the third, Sally, is nearly invisible as she swims beneath the splash of water that marks her path. Winter describes the scene:

> I had not done a commissioned portrait in perhaps twenty years when Carolyn Horchow asked me if I would paint something for Roger Horchow's fiftieth birthday. Everyone I knew seemed to know who Roger Horchow was through the Horchow Collection. But I didn't. I visited their house and property in North Dallas, met their three daughters, plus their black lab named Sister, and everyone was in or around the swimming pool. It was a hot summer afternoon, and so quintessentially Dallas: a lovely pool with crape myrtles in bloom and hackberry trees and one evergreen as backdrop—not to mention the fair-weather clouds slowly moving overhead. It was "the good life" but a life with an enormous amount of responsibility. I knew what I wanted to paint: the Horchow sisters with the pool and landscaping as their setting. I told no one what I was going to do, but took dozens of photos. I made another visit and then made dozens more. I put it all together as a collage in my mind, but a collage without disjunctive space. It took a couple of months to paint. And it all looked like one moment.

Such is the essence of the realist enterprise. For Winter, the act of painting negotiates an agreement between what he sees and what he knows—between memory and impulse, between the brush's gestures and the multitude of gestures that constitute the history of painting. The special aura of the *Horchow Sisters* is an intimacy that verges on voyeurism, an intimacy whose sense of place and even social milieu come through quite clearly. But it is the light that is most distinctive: a languid, almost chalky emanation from the putty whites and iridescent blues that seems to bathe and lift the whole image. The painting connects Winter back to John Singer Sargent's portraits, with their flickering impasto, their palpable joy in light and freshness embodied in substance. Like Sargent's intimate renderings of children at various stages of adolescence, Winter's scene conveys a rapport between the girls, even as each figure is captured in a given instant. Daringly composed, beautifully illuminated, its four subjects are revealed with touching and finely differentiated empathy. Significantly, Winter's painting style has a tensile strength that is pulled to the very point where it threatens to break apart. But it never does. Here, the "splash" is the pivotal focus, a moment frozen in time. The palpable deep space, bordered by tranquil foliage and suffused with the stillness of Dallas humidity, seems to be a function of the time essential to our perception of the scene. As we

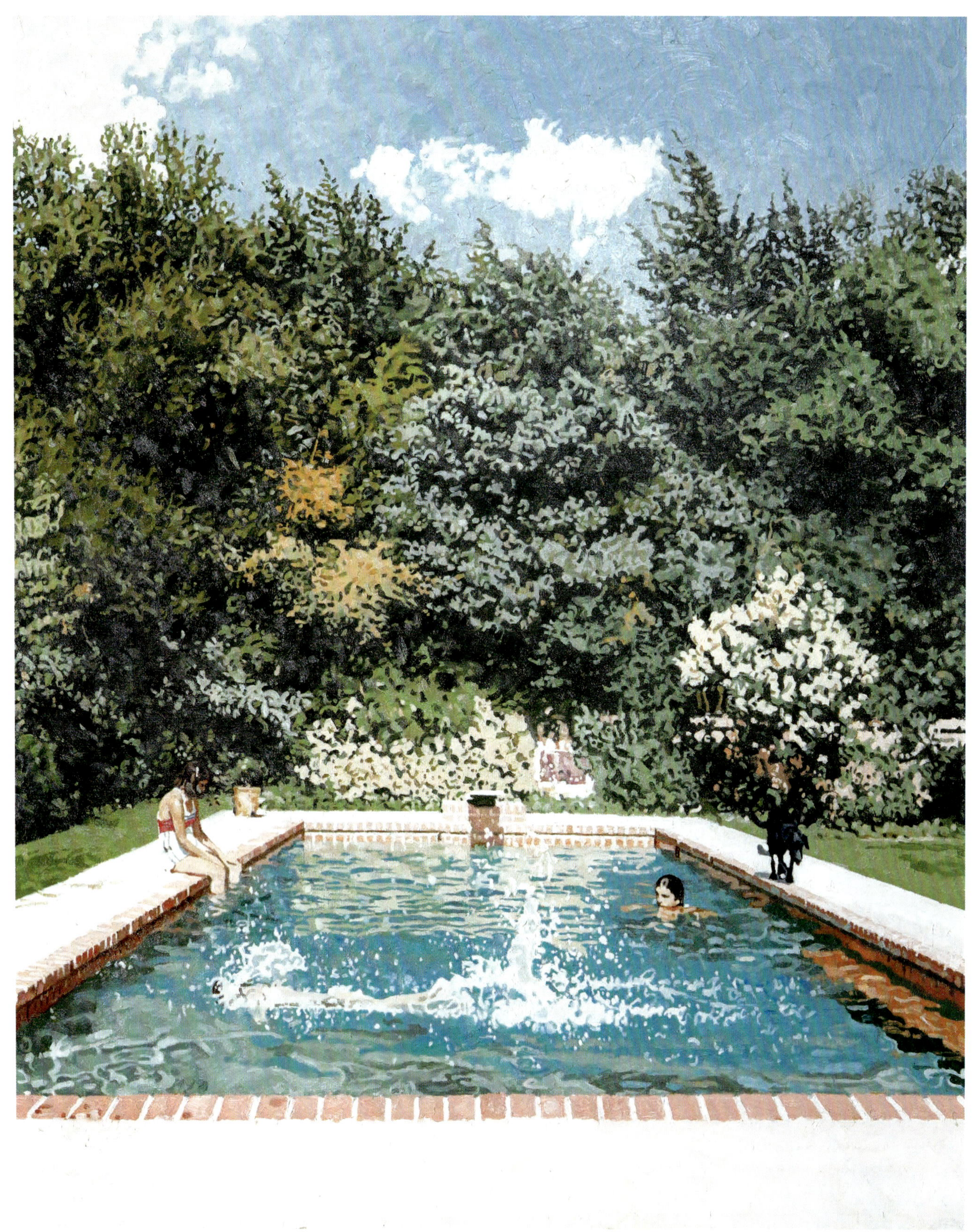

Horchow Sisters 1978

oil on linen | 60" x 52" | Collection of the Roger Horchow Family | Photography by Kevin Todora look, the Horchows' backyard literally unfolds itself. The trees, hedges, clouds, and rippling water begin to dismantle into carefully considered painterly components. The entirety shimmers like a mirage, then dissolves into full abstraction.

According to Winter, the youngest Horchow sister, Sally, was perplexed that her face could not be seen in detail as she swam underwater, which prompted an additional portrait. Winter explains, "She was eight at the time, the same age as our son Max, and she had been very enthusiastic in my visits to show me how she learned the butterfly stroke that summer. And that's how I remembered her. It also allowed me to paint a wave in water and emphasized the instant in time created by the Horchow family on so many levels. I empathized so easily with what Sally felt, and when I was told this I knew what to do: paint the small portrait of Sally sitting on the edge of the pool, her arms raised—no one else. I think it is the most monumental and near-perfect painting I have ever painted, despite its tiny size."

Indeed, Winter depicts the figure in a classical pose with simplified features that are illuminated by bracing half shadow—a likeness but also invested with inner life.

Features become abstract shapes in themselves, composed of layered, delicate color and forthright brushwork. Winter focuses our gaze on wedges of light that rhythmically define Sally's hair, cheek, eye, and forehead, as well as refract her torso and leg amid the undulating motion of water. Winter's is an obdurate way of looking—sharp as the green accuracies of an early summer, the pungent vapors of chlorine in water. Both paintings concentrate on the span of vision—time, the memory of time, the otherworldly radiance of dreams, all caught in paint.

After years of painting in spare bedrooms, Winter decided in 1979 to build a studio in the backyard of their University Park home. Designed by James Pratt of Pratt, Box and Henderson in Dallas, the new studio would allow him to work on a larger scale. In journals kept throughout the construction process, however, Winter admits to qualms about costs and physical labor, which also seem to have triggered nagging concerns about the direction of his art. In the entry for Monday, October 22, 1979, Winter writes, "First voiced doubts about building studio. Told Jeanette that (A) hated to get strapped with such a debt when roof needed replacing, house needed painting, Jonah starting to college, Max might need private school, and (B)—I just couldn't see spending that much on myself . . . felt that this would put me on a treadmill of producing marketable paintings and I couldn't be free or happy again! At this point, I thought of paying off Pratt, postponing studio indefinitely, reroofing and painting house and maybe porch repairs."[7] Not easily deterred, however, Winter followed through and tackled much of the arduous construction process himself—moving trees and setting up chicken-wire fencing, mixing and laying concrete, digging in posts, and piling dirt. At the same time that he persevered with the manual labor, Winter continued to grope for ideas in painting. He writes, "Something seems unhealthy and out of whack—in my methods [painting methods] and habits toward my work."[8] A week later he notes, "I somehow managed to get all the cyclone fence wire cut out of the trees, etc. and I got that back area cleaned up. It really hurt my hands and I think I broke some blood vessels in my right hand. Now I have the posts either to cut off or pull up. . . . I don't think I want to do *anymore* art that I don't enjoy. Life is just too damn short and goes by too fast to torture myself, no matter what money or regional or larger recognition it might bring me. I want something besides boredom and pain."[9] By mid-November, however, Winter seems to have turned a corner: "Cut down other tree and put limbs etc. out front. Called the city for pick-up. Now all that's left is taking down remainder of fence, taking down (or up) fence posts and taking up my brick walk. I think this is a day's work. All clear really, for slab. Wish I could find someone to do it. Damn it. All considered, I have some ideas about my painting."[10]

Even as Winter was physically building the studio, he was mentally setting the terms for the kind of art he would create in the next decade. On a day's reprieve from studio labor, Winter and his son Max drove to Lake Texoma, where they relaxed by picking up fossils and "stoking the fire for wieners." He writes, "It occurred to me that if you face your problems, there are some unforeseen bonuses. I saw the backside of Van Alstyne and thought of it

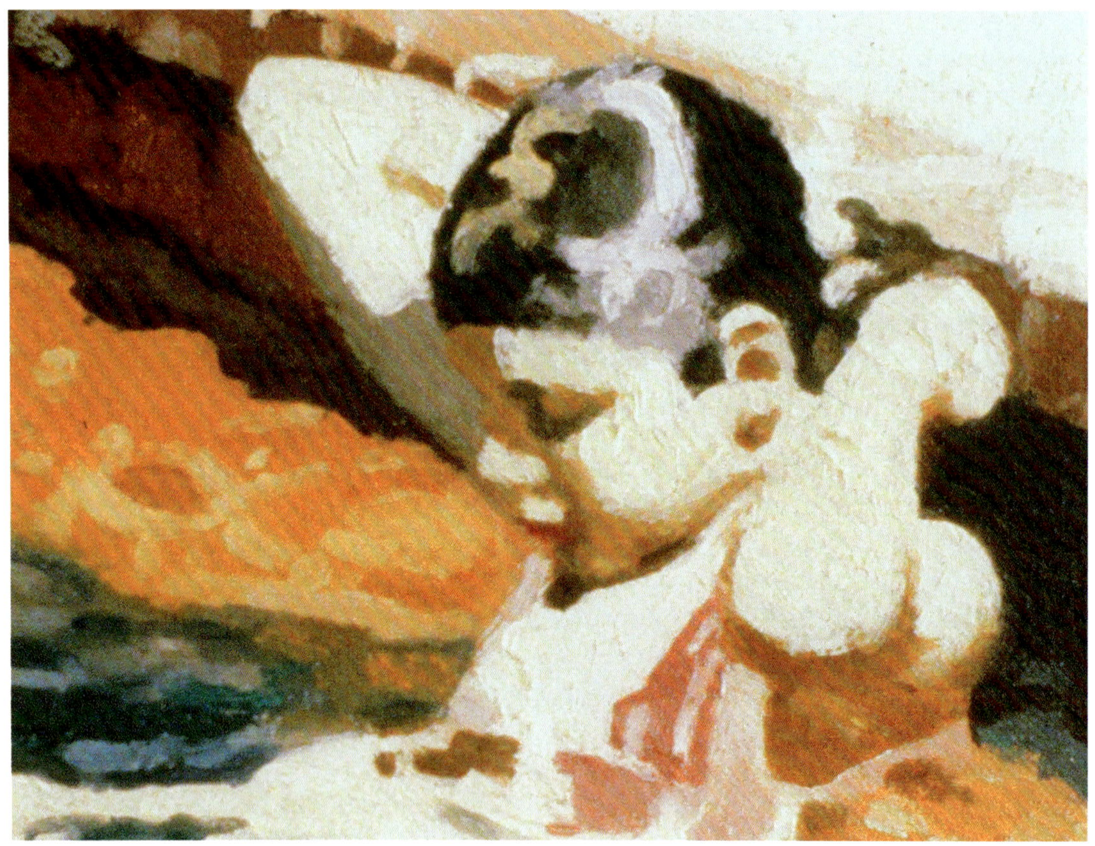

Sally Horchow, 1978
oil on linen | 6" × 8" | Collection of the Roger Horchow Family | Photography by Kevin Todora

as a painting. . . . I see it as a huge work. I think it would have to be to come off at all. I've thought of it as a painting for a long time."[11] As he approached completion of the studio, Winter was nearly awestruck by the scale and, perhaps, the challenges he would encounter in going forward: "Two walls raised—to east and west. Jesus! How high the painting wall is! It scares me, and I can hardly believe it."[12] The new studio not only expanded Winter's repertoire, it also became a well-known meeting place in the 1980s for poetry readings and musical sessions.

About Winter's studio and that heady period, longtime friend and prominent Dallas artist Pamela Nelson observes, "I like to remember gatherings at the Rankin Street studio surrounded by Roger's paintings and friends and surprises. Dallas poets reading, and the dawning that art grows with community. We all seemed to understand that this was a golden time. I hold the image of the very tall Tim Siebles, African American, bringing us to one attention with his poetry. He is now poet laureate of Virginia. There were all ages together. As a young artist, I felt for the first time, a part of a tribe of creators, and people who cared about imagination."[13] Most important, the studio featured a wall of fifteen feet by thirty feet, on which Winter installed a set of pulleys and ropes to raise a large canvas so that the bottom was near eye level. *Street* (1979) and *Tennis Court* (1980), among the first oversize paintings produced in the new studio, pay homage to the landscape tradition through the context of the present time. In the former, Winter lays out nearly ten feet of road and sidewalk as horizontal bands that lead the eye to a background of white frame houses and trees. *Tennis Court* is a dense tangle of trees, vines, and fencing through which we spy a single figure in play. Both are composed of rich surfaces and infinite details that William B. Jordan regarded as "the ineffable lure" of subjects, "like the evocations of a skillful novelist."[14]

Tennis Court, in particular, affirms Winter's theme of paintings based on the life and culture in University Park and Highland Park. He became fascinated by the many layers of the Park Cities—the faculty and student life at SMU; the Highland Park Country Club; the mansions along Turtle Creek, as well as the modest rental cottages north of the SMU campus. Playing tennis, walking for exercise, swimming, and the manicured lawns all became fresh themes for the artist. "I saw them not only as a challenge of complex subject items—the chain-link fence, spontaneous human movement—but also as interesting symbols of the good life, which no longer bothered me as it had in my early years," Winter explains. "By the 1980s Jeanette and I had become social friends with art collectors and company who were of a higher economic class. So that extended my subject matter, without *an ounce* of criticism, beyond the world I'd known as a child. I grew up thinking that wealthy people would sic their dogs on you. My father often referred to the wealthy streets in Denison as 'Silk Stocking Row.' Playing tennis was a symbol of worldly success—of belonging to a world where leisure was part of life."

As his ideas coalesced in the late 1970s and early 1980s and his focus shifted from autobiographical content toward a more objective outlook, Winter endeavored to understand more about moneyed people. "It occurred to me that aspects of our new and more refined lifestyle, like a dinner for six, also followed a form." To that end, Winter began reading John Cheever's novels and short stories, which gave him various insights into the higher social classes. Cheever's searing observations about the conflicts and lifestyles of Westchester and upscale Manhattan dwellers—about swimming pools, puddings after dinner, and money—helped Winter understand the trials and "language" of the entitled that were beginning to infiltrate his daily life.

It is important to understand that Realism, along with its complex subcategories—Painterly Realism, Abstract Realism, Conceptual Realism, Superrealism, and Photorealism—was a pervasive movement throughout the 1970s and early 1980s. As art historian Linda Nochlin writes in her book *Realism*, "Its aim was to give a truthful, objective and impartial representation of the real world based on meticulous observation of contemporary life. . . . As realism evolved, the demand for—and conception of—contemporaneity, became more rigorous."[15] About images that purport to give us the facts, unqualified, upfront, prominent art critic Donald B. Kuspit argued that "the fundamental structuring of reality is left to our interpretation of reality in the name of our desire for it. As Hegel observed, the cow understands the grass not by observing that it is green and resting content with that observation, but by eating it to satisfy hunger." Kuspit continued, "In realist art, the self makes room for itself in the world—as in any other art, but with different means. The realist artist intervenes in and intrudes upon the world more slyly than other artists, yet his presence is as stubborn . . . as the world he depicts and thereby makes his own."[16]

For Robert Bechtle, Richard Estes, and Richard McLean, among others, Photorealism has served as a mode of painting in which they painstakingly translate the look of photographs onto their canvases. For a number of these artists, the initial move to using photographs and depicting the seemingly banal facts of everyday life arose in response to Pop Art's embrace of commercialized subjects. Often, their photo-based painting was an attempt to free themselves from the influences of teachers who were working in more expressive modes of abstraction and figurative art. Winter's paintings from this period have been frequently misread as literal photorealist works despite their active surfaces. Rather than exploit the shine, crispness, and focal variations of the photograph, however, Winter explores its ability to fix and hold an entire field of imagery on a plane.

If anything, Winter shares the disciplined severity of Chuck Close, whose work begins with a gridded photograph of a face that he copies, cell by cell, to a larger scale but with enormous variation in the kinds of marks that he uses to construct the final image. Winter comments on the discrepancy: "Photorealism was a minimal approach to Realism. Painterly Realism was an abstract expressionist approach to Realism. Maybe I have some traits of both, but I don't want to imitate the surface of a photograph, and I never work a painting overall." For Winter, realism includes conscious life and whatever else roils in the unconscious. In the point-blank actuality of representing "the real," he tests the realness of paint, the realness of vision, how the real is or is not distinct from memory.

In his work from the 1980s, Winter's world appears to reach out and envelop us. The strongly felt presence of his paintings is amplified because they acknowledge our own presence. Increasingly, their interwoven layers of human perception are conveyed with singular clarity. Realism is brought to light through its many guises, thereby implying the plural nature of life. In the coming decade, Winter's paintings would set free our preconceptions to encounter a world that is more extraordinary than we ever imagined.

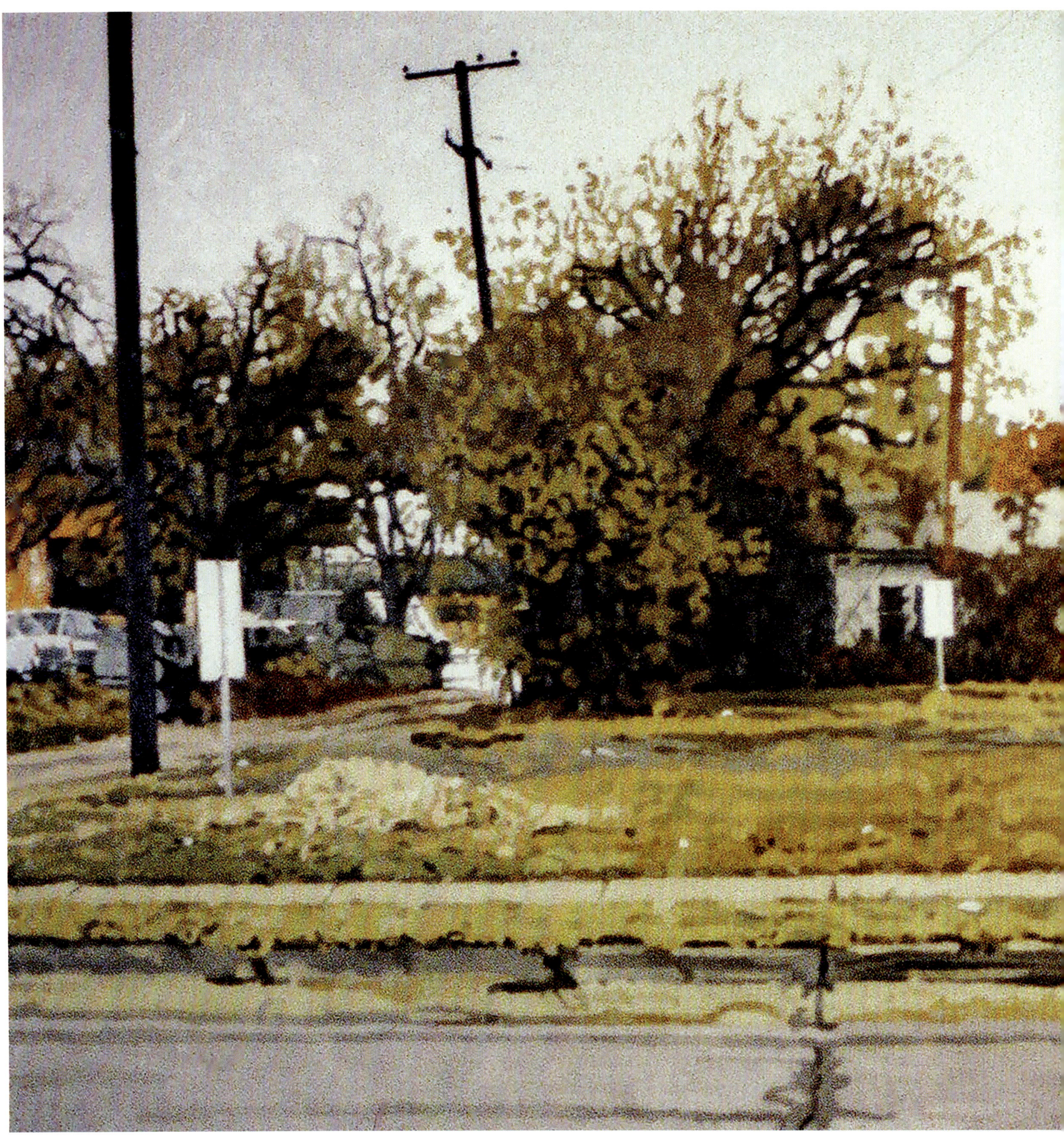

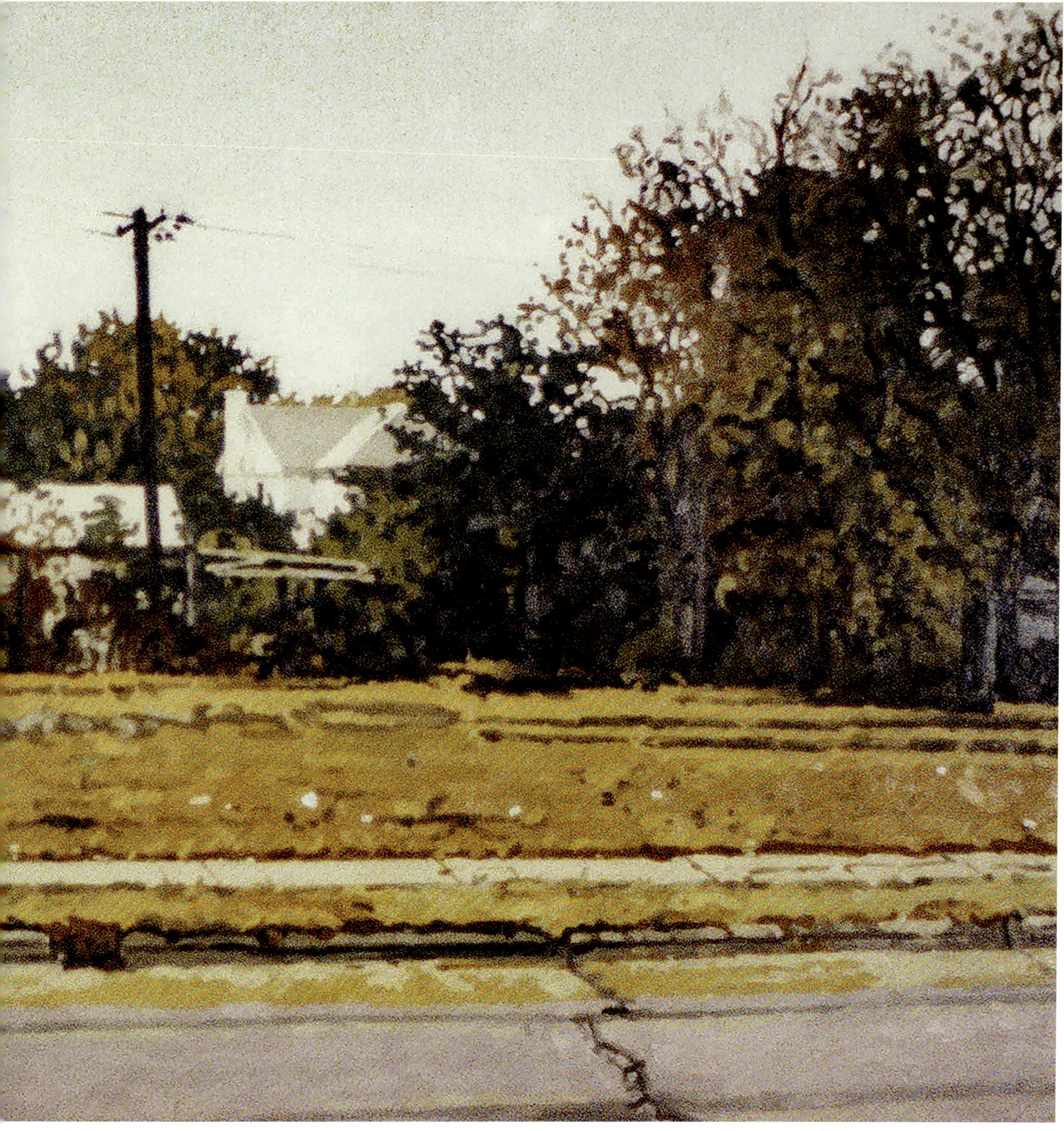

Street, 1979

oil on linen | 48" x 120" | Courtesy of the artist

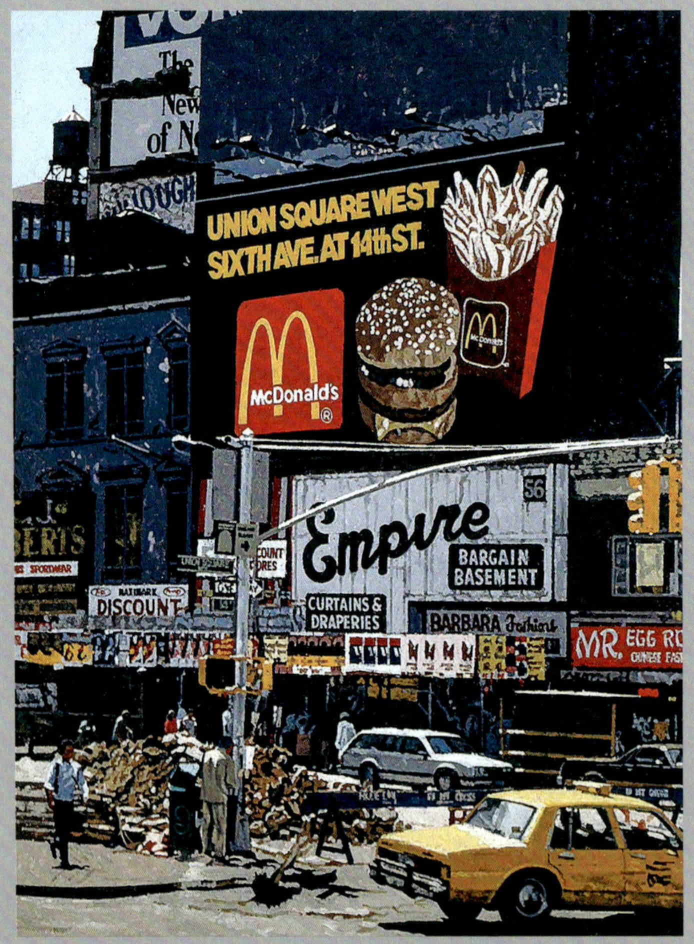

Union Square (detail), 1988

oil on linen | 72" x 120" | Collection of Bryant and Nancy Hanley

CHAPTER 10

THE 1980s: CONNECTING CHANGE

WINTER IS AN ARTIST who continues to grow in stature as his work evolves and changes. Through an ongoing concern with light, color, and gesture, his paintings demonstrate not only formal virtuosity but also a highly personal view of the world. While Winter is a realist to the degree that he employs a great deal of control and attention to depict his landscapes, a closer look reveals an individual sense of touch. Most of his paintings from the 1980s have a thickly worked yet delicate layering of impasto and direct brushstrokes that belie the very illusions they create. As William B. Jordan observes, "Whether they are tiny pictures only a few inches in size or monumental ones of very large dimensions, it is only upon close examination that the viewer becomes aware of the prodigious skill—indeed the artistry—that has transmuted the emphatic physicality of pigment into vibrant illusions of sunlight or rain, of temperature even, of movement, of thought, and of feeling. Capturing the ineffable is not something that painters of our age have been known for, but it is one of the abilities that sets Roger Winter apart from most of his peers."[1]

Indeed, a prevailing notion of landscape painting implies that the artist must apprehend some likeness of a certain geographic locale. To render a sense of place, an artist should have a primitive soil consciousness of his native region. For Winter, the understanding of a place includes but goes beyond the local characteristics of a given topography and becomes a matter of the artist's intuitive grasp not just of the immediate or local but also of the larger, universal implications of what has been discerned in a given "place." Winter's paintings, and our experience of them, are movements of creation, metamorphosis, and evolution. Affirming the individuals, however contingent, they ask that we be accountable to "place," no matter how geographically fluid and discontinuous over time. The issue is one of how we pay attention to things in the world. The emphasis is on associations that cut across mainstream narrative structures. Connections are made between the macroscopic and the microscopic, conveyed in a synthesis of form and color: empty trash cans are lined up in front of a vacant lot on a Dallas street; cows pass along a fence row through an East Texas landscape and brilliant panorama, expanding and contracting in visual patterns. Associations occur across and between images, denying a linear structure and functioning more like a dream remembered. They are like presences, these paintings, superb and deep in thought, and they declare a world of their own.

In the course of the 1980s, Winter became committed to a kind of painting that is intensely active, full of incident both in the handling of the paint and in the nature of the image. Significantly, there is now a strong sense of everyday natural place in the works. As Winter moved into what would be the mature phase of his career, he was able to bring all of his skills into play. He has the courage and intellect to inform his work with what he sees and feels. He is intensely aware of his surroundings and responds with acutely critical objective observations, as well as a highly intuitive sense that sometimes borders on an understanding beyond a mere physical reality. Winter's rural and urban landscapes tap into memories and emotions—about familiar and strange places, and the wonder of that which attracts us for reasons unknown. Nature is present and visible here, but still in hiding; it is simultaneously close and distant, encompassing and evading. Confronting Winter's art, we may seek meaning in a world perceived but unseen, a place of primal recognition and poetic elusiveness. His narratives have no beginning or end; they are also timeless. Still, there is nothing precious about Winter's images, because that preciousness would encourage a reading of the works in terms of nostalgic appeal. If anything, his natural elements are passive-aggressive. Addressing the majesty of the land and its loss, each painting beckons us to take up an idea and follow where our eye and imagination lead us. Feeling is made the issue at stake. The emotional charge of materials, the personal relationship to experience, and the desire to make contact with something real provide the challenge. For Winter, all the senses feed all the feelings that bring a painting to life.

In many respects, Winter's development throughout the decade was as open and fluid as the paintings themselves. It is important to note that the early 1980s were the time of a renewed interest in large-scale expressionist painting. The works of artists such as Anselm Kiefer, Georg Baselitz, and Julian Schnabel lent a validated credence to paintings of determined physicality. Their emotive, subject-driven, and often series-based work helped attune viewers to a sense of referentiality. Though Winter perhaps considered himself a bricklayer rather than a matador, he began to alter the length, direction, and compressed density of his brushstrokes, seeking out new configurations of color and light that could encapsulate the perceptual climate dominating his vision at any given time. Thus, multiple events organize themselves, dissolve, reform, and coalesce within certain imposed boundaries. His strokes, always rigorous, became looser and highly energetic. Sometimes his squiggly marks form themselves into strange beings or hidden imagery. At other times they exist as flurries of energy or as trails of delicate, almost calligraphic streamers of color. The paint is fluid, not dry, and has an edgy tactility. Each varying stroke maintains a purposeful distinctness. Still, the rich paint handling always pulls the eye back to the surface, to the world of artifice, just as the image itself is pulled out of its natural setting. Overall, the paintings are filled with life's ebb and flow—its changing seasons, cows coming and going, junked cars rusting in fields. Winter loves silence and stillness, and the image of sunlight on a wood-frame house. But he is a searcher, and that searching informs his visual style with its restless depictions of moments that might otherwise seem mundane.

In the 1980s, Winter was all over the place, but in a good way. A search for fresh astonishments kept him peripatetic, on productive road trips across Texas to the Mexican border town Nuevo Laredo, or on sojourns to New York and Maine. At every turn, Winter was the vestigial romantic, stopping in space and time to catch views that exerted a peculiar tug on him. Any subject seemed to be fair game. "I just wanted to paint the things that really interested me," Winter says. "I did not want to have a signature subject. The idea was, you pick one thing and you painted it forever. Or you got tired and quit. To me, that meant your mind didn't have enough imagination. But the 1980s was a very generative time—I was coming into

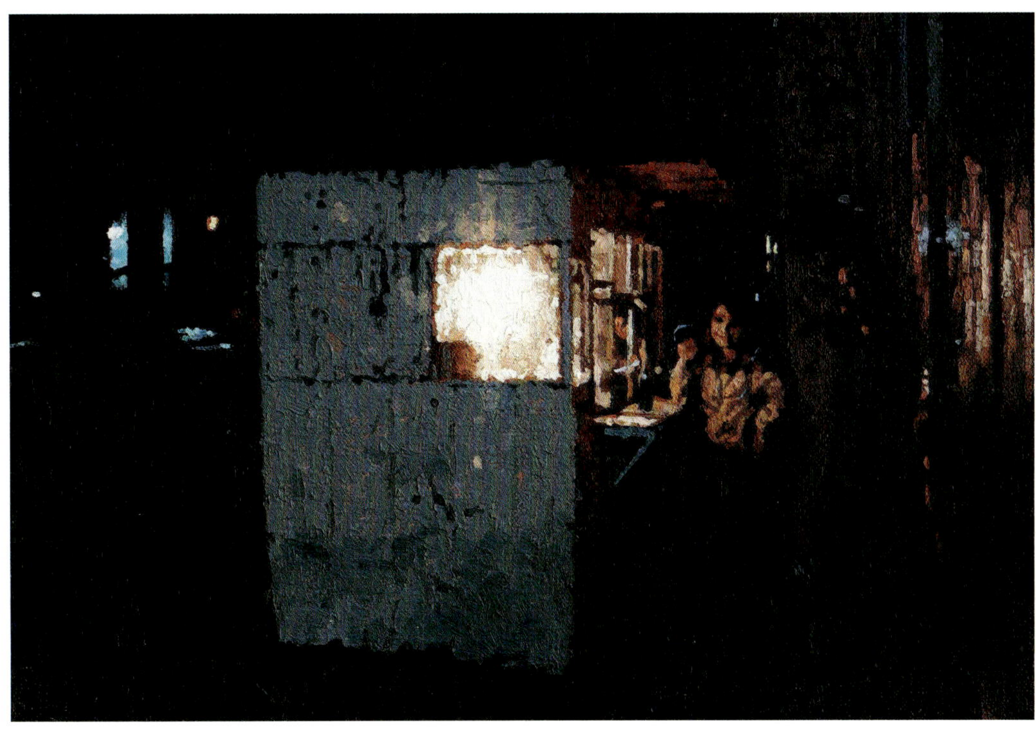

Puestecito, 1987
oil on linen | 10" x 15" | Collection of Susanne Maurer and Eugene Binder | Photography by Bob Anderson

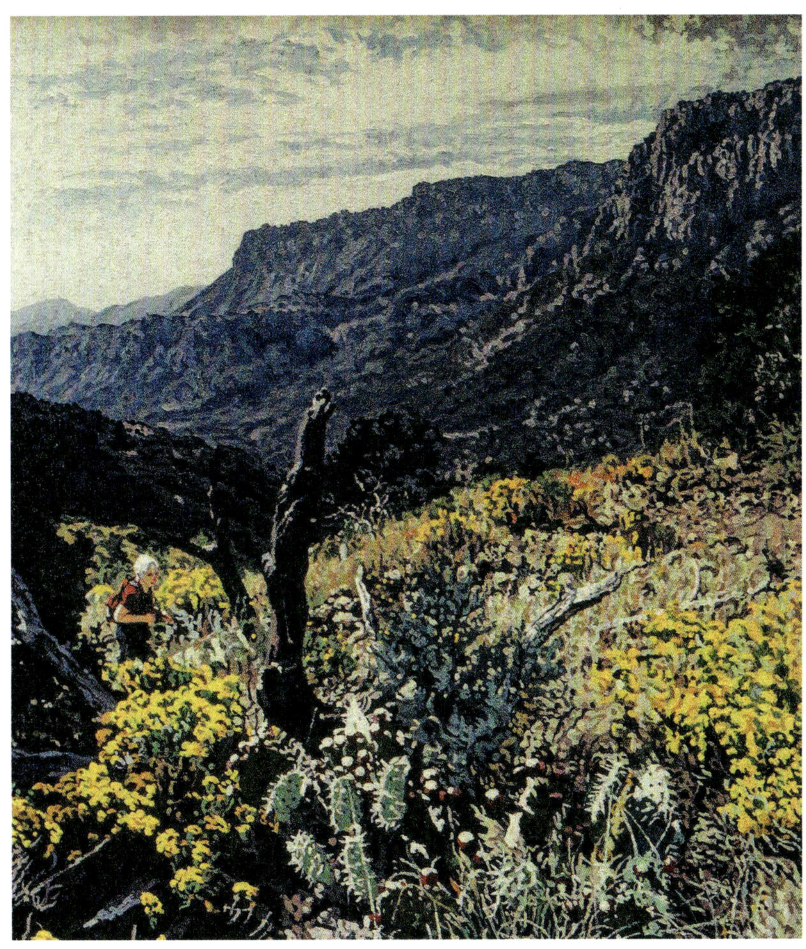

Lost Mine Trail, 1989
oil on linen | 27" x 24" | Collection of Jeanette Winter | Photography by Joshua Nefsky

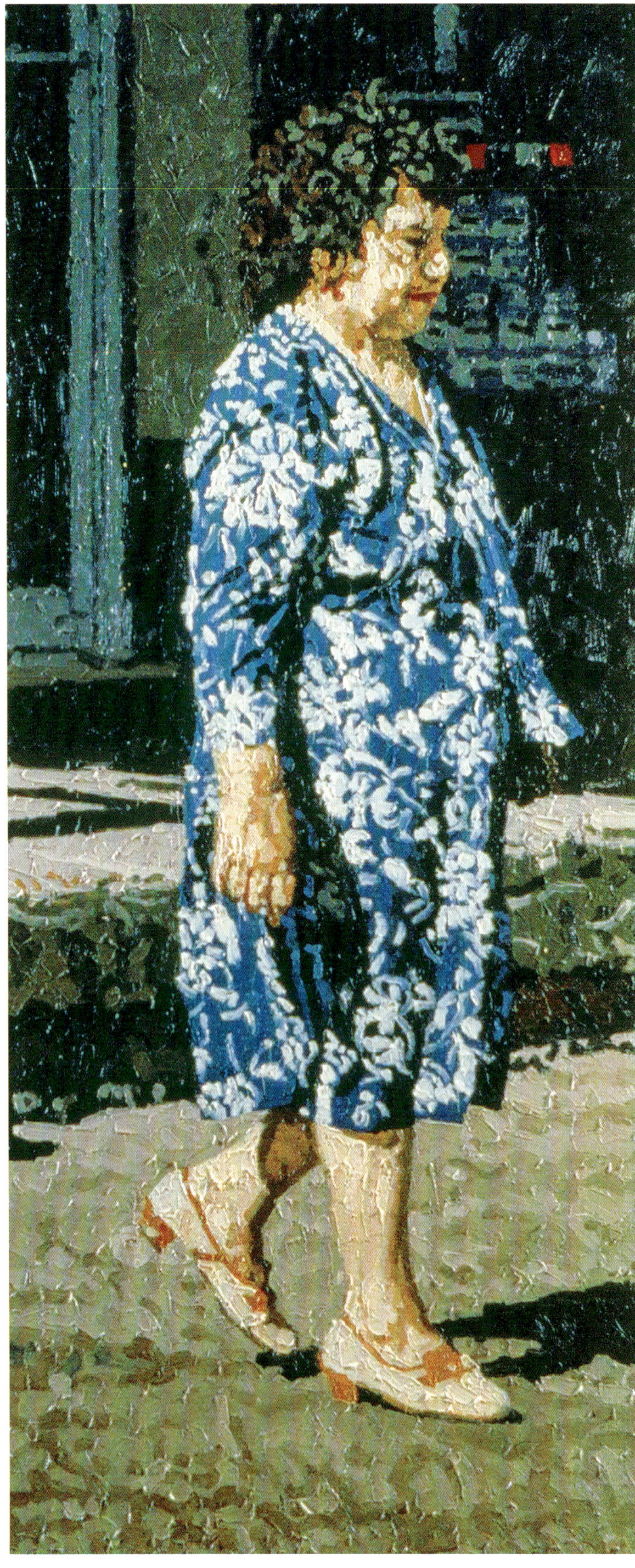

Woman, Nuevo Laredo, 1987
oil on linen | 30" x 18" | Albritton Family Collection, Dallas

my own as a painter, finding my voice and gaining confidence." Throughout, Winter painted scenes that seem more like shards of memory, like those flashes from the past that suddenly materialize in the temporal slipstream. Thus, his paintings of the 1980s became meatier and more and more meaning made itself felt. A tightwire between the emotive and the formal had to be walked. Accordingly, Winter pursued a synthesis of compositional exactness and psychological complexity, a quest for what we can find beneath and within the surface of appearances if we probe intensely enough. To that end, he began to excel at painting marginal, sometimes desolated landscapes—whether rural or urban—with tremendous sympathy, as well as progressively complicated challenges of perspective, composition, and scale. Significantly, his orientation toward commonplace scenes also evokes an air of mystery, coupled with an ill-defined feeling of an uneasy sublime. At a time when realism was still considered beyond the pale, Winter made it a habit to disrupt critical assumptions and predictions. And like most artists of lasting interest, he drew on many sources in his work, which meant that it changed, sometimes dramatically.

"New Realism was all over the place in the eighties," Winter recalls.

> William Bailey, Neil Welliver, and James McGarrell were guests at SMU's [Southern Methodist University's] art department during this time. And I learned a dirty word in the American art scene. Bailey's linear clarity and Welliver's starting in the upper left corner and ending in the lower right corner underscored the way I worked and gave it authority. I became acquainted with Rackstraw Downes's carefully painted realism and his writing about realism. I saw a silkscreen print by Richard Estes where each shape was a cut stencil, and this gave me the idea of realistic renderings in cut paper that in time became realistic renderings in paint with marks made by a brush. But even in flat areas, the brush is always visible. I was most interested in the painters who achieved a balance between formalism and illusion. John

Button achieved this in a very reductive way, as did Louisa Matthiasdottir. Susan Shatter had a good balance of seeing and forming. As Lois Dodd once said, "They stuck to the basics." Realism, Naturalism, Photorealism—all these categories refer to subject matter. My work of the eighties spoke in more than one language. In choosing rural and urban subjects, I think they were both transfixed in my childhood. We loved and spent most of our time in sparsely populated and wooded places. Going to Denison on foot or in a Model A Ford was full of a more challenging adventure. Rural landscapes represent a nostalgic yearning in me. I could go back to the past and stay forever. Urban landscapes represent energy and discovery. I'm always a private person, but never feel isolated in the city. I continue to condense time and space without giving up invention. No change for me is ever sudden. But I've always wanted to appeal to a broad audience of viewers. I was always pleased when the maintenance people at SMU would spend time with my work in eighties faculty shows. I wanted it to be accessible to the community, not just to the art community. In retrospect, I think I was seeing my work as educational—an extension of teaching as educational. Not just a private game for the initiated.

This belief in the revelatory power of painting is characteristic of American artists. While the revelation has nothing to do with realism, it is grounded in private experience, in things seen. Winter's knowledge of and respect for the tradition of landscape painting—Winslow Homer, Ralph Albert Blakelock, and Albert Pinkham Ryder, for example—suggest an affinity of one part of nature for another. Everything interacts; nothing stands in isolation. In his preface to *Leaves of Grass*, Walt Whitman wrote that the genius of America is found in its "common people" rather than in its executives or ambassadors. He found an "unrhymed poetry" in "their manners speech dress friendship—the freshness and candor of their physiognomy, . . . their deathless attachment to freedom—the practical acknowledgement of the citizens of one state by the citizens of all other states."[2] Whitman desired personally to experience all, to feel as broadly as possible and thus identify himself with humankind's vitality. What permeates Whitman's poetry is the sense of expansiveness, a thrusting outward to encompass wider and wider areas, from the rural countryside to the life of the city. It is this expansiveness and reverberating energy that also links Winter's often overlooked areas within the landscape, the parts that mirror the subconscious familiarity of American places. The content of his work, springing from extremely human desires, is rooted in a discovery of what we are and how we fit into the world.

Whatever blew the lid off, the 1980s was the most prolific decade of Winter's career. As he moves through various groups of paintings, we sense the artist's glowing enthusiasm and respect for ugly, lost, or overlooked areas and more forceful ways of representing them. Again and again, he depicts horizontal swaths of space that are at once fluid and fixed, loosened and taut, faraway and nearby. Roads, telephone wires, fences, cows, and old buildings crisscross the land, which is mostly unpeopled. Countless artists have explored the Texas landscape before, of course, but Winter does so with intense subtlety, confronting both the physical and metaphysical character of our in-between places. He emerges as a painter who has actually experienced and looked—looked very hard—at the modern landscape. One of his gifts is for evoking a kind of loneliness that is almost unknown now in the wired world. The care that Winter expends on the slightest gesture and detail is the means by which he gives his vision concrete reality. But while his strokes and utilization of subdued color are tactile and immediate, the realm of his imagination remains elusive.

Winter is a true romantic in his obsession with grand themes that deal with rural symbols and landscapes, in which we can interpret our own emotions and values. If his paintings of the 1980s don't exactly tell stories, however, they do express a deep feeling, and with awe-inspiring vitality. His pictures revolve around narrative situations that provoke speculation without necessarily satisfying it. We are left wondering what has happened, and what is going to happen and to whom, as in an

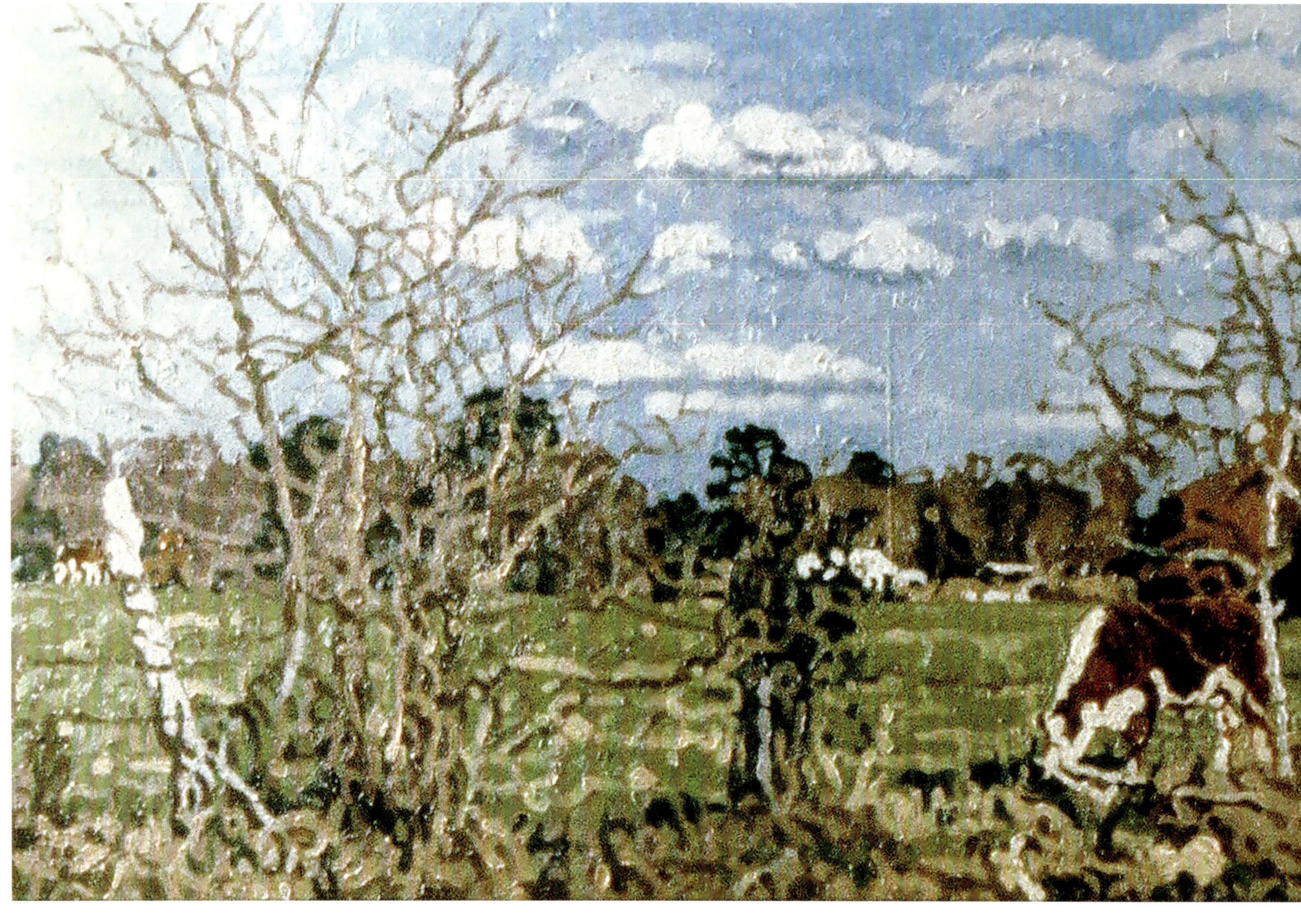

unsolved mystery. To that end, Winter extracts the maximum number of dramatic possibilities with unflinching candor. His dynamic compositions are carefully massed and dramatically lit. Moreover, Winter has acquired a broader range of brushstrokes that now define specific forms in very particular ways. Overall, the dozens of paintings produced during the 1980s show Winter throwing himself whole hog into a union of technique and meaning. If anything, his content was maturing as quickly as his heightened understanding of pictorial space.

We can detect Winter's breakthroughs in paintings of bulls grazing on open ranges in West Texas and lush pastures in East Texas; of an abandoned old Coupe deteriorating in a field of branchy scrub; or of frame houses and bare trees in a car's-eye sweep of Van Alstyne, a town between Denison and Dallas. In the early 1930s, Winter's father picked cotton there and students were allowed out of school to work during the cotton-picking season. The intimacy of Winter's view evokes the matter-of-fact and instructive knowledge that any true native has of the place in which he or she lives. In cinematic terms, Winter goes for the long shot; spatial distance here equals aesthetic distance. When buildings appear, they are usually small in relation to the whole area, far off,

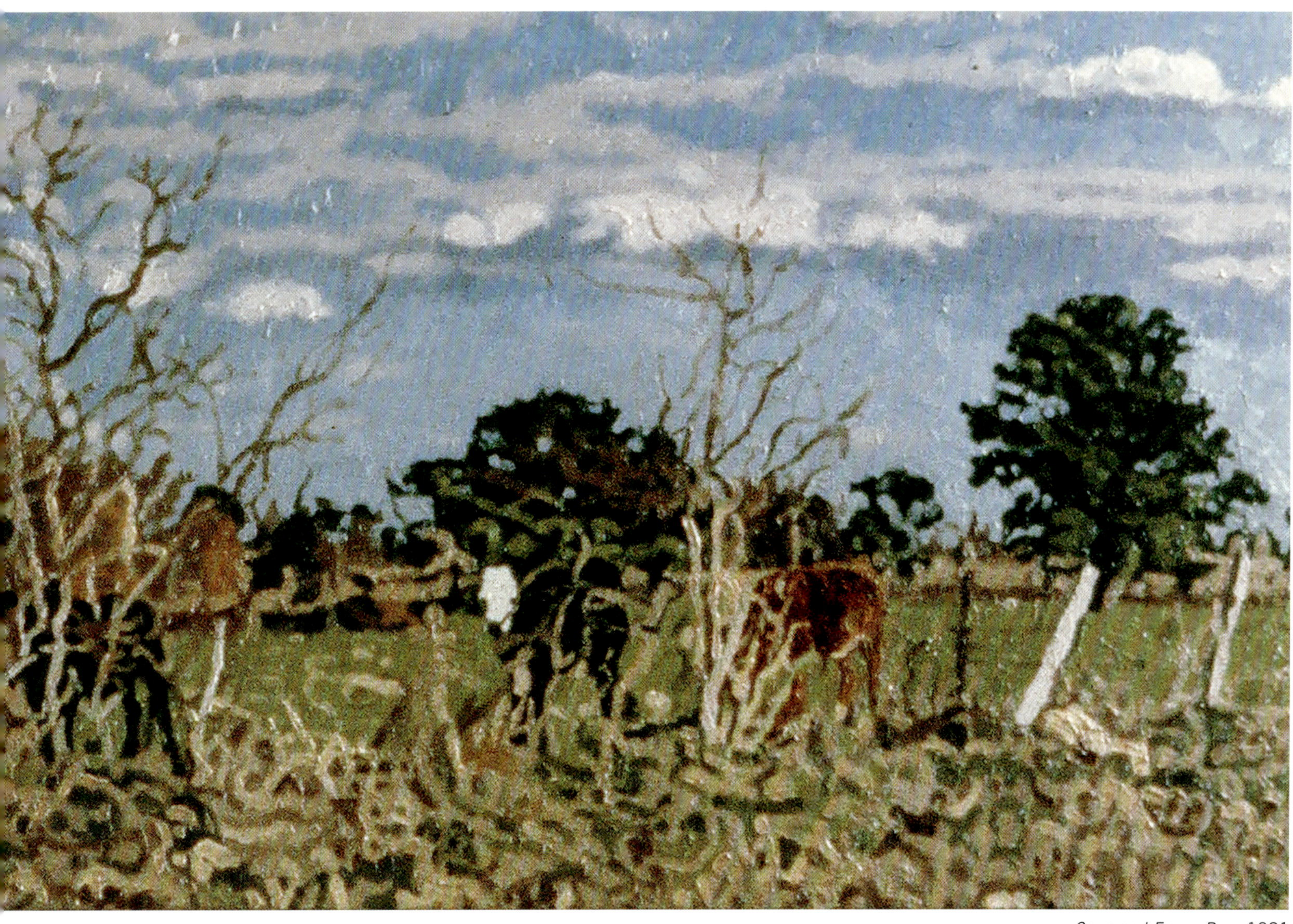

Cows and Fence Row, 1981

oil on linen | 24" × 72" | Collection of Pamela and Jere Mitchell, MD | Photography by Allison V. Smith

or off to one side, masked or obscured by dense foliage. They remain far from the viewer, patiently resisting becoming engulfed by the vastness of the spaces surrounding them. The paintings evoke seventeenth-century Dutch panoramas, but more important, their spaces call up the memories from Winter's childhood. "I knew the shape and attitude of the cow better than any other farm animal," Winter recalls.

> In the eighties, cows were easy to find grazing fields of East Texas because the dairy industry had taken over the former cotton farms. The subject was seen as "down home" and a little hokey in Texas, but I saw the cow as a universal and traditional subject. I made day trips to Hopkins County for the sole purpose of taking snapshots of cows and bulls. Hopkins County had a strong pull on me from childhood memories. My grandfather Kennemer had a cotton farm near Como, and we took family trips there a few times a year, once in the caboose of a freight train on the Katy line. For me, a protected child, those trips were like voyages to Mars. In my adult years in Dallas, Hopkins County was a fairly nearby place where one could see pastoral landscapes: fields

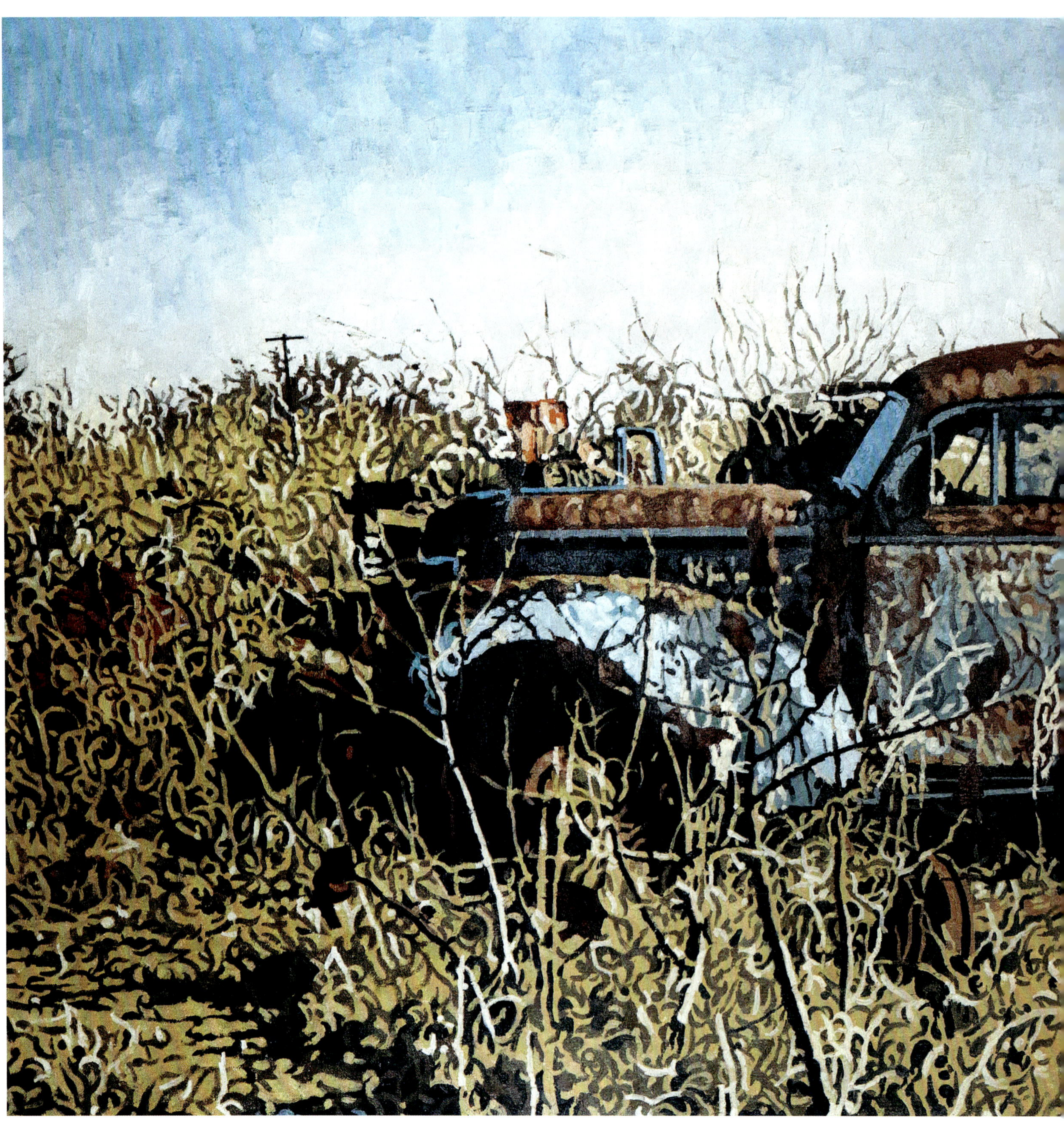

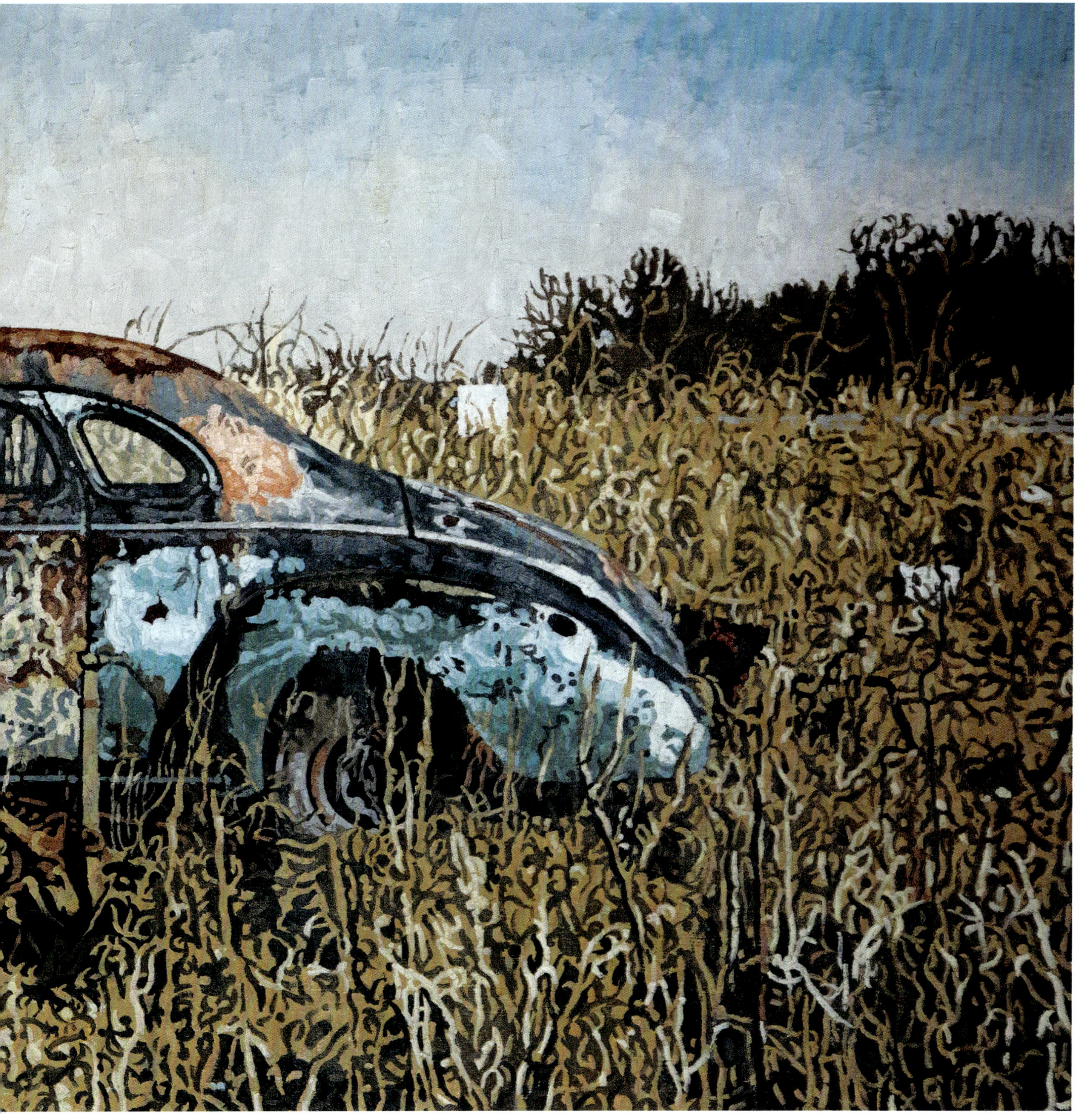

Coupé, 1986

oil on linen | 42" x 84" | Collection of Pamela and Jere Mitchell, MD | Photography by Allison V. Smith

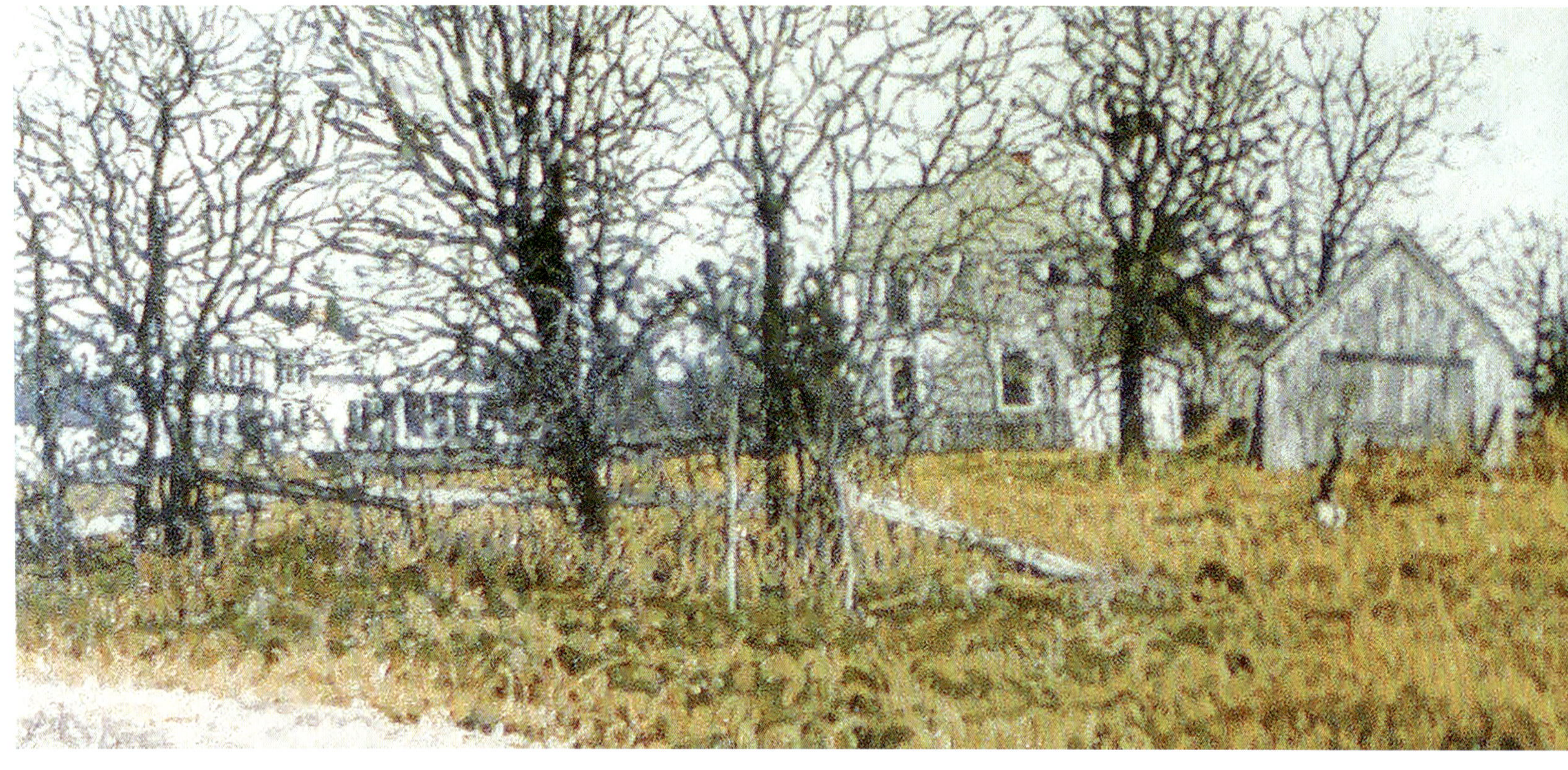

with grasses, trees, cows, and bulls, little or nothing in the way of human-built structures. To me, it was holy ground. It was not so much about Texas as it was about trying to connect with a time and place that was simple and real and transfixed in physical memory.

Indeed, *Landscape with Cows* (1979), *Landscape with Bulls* (1981), and *Cows and Fence Row* (1981) convey close observation of and respect for what Winter sees. Although some of the animals are alert to the presence of the artist—and us—others calmly go about their daily business of grazing, resting, or meandering. In *Cows and Fence Row*, the animation is not life on parade; rather, it is life in procession, moving to a languid rhythm. *Landscape with Cows* and *Landscape with Bulls* have a palette of sunny tans and browns and dark greens. In the latter, black-and-white bulls are settled comfortably around a pond. The animals, trees, and foliage that occupy the pictorial field are integral to it—below it, fused with it, immersed in it. Gnarly clusters of brushstrokes seemingly hover, at once defiantly confrontational and vulnerable. Each dab and contour seems directed toward forming a shape; every color is chosen to establish a relational, tonal light with its neighbor. In all of these landscapes, Winter's activated paint surface can strike us with the force of a sudden squall. Brushstrokes become trails of shimmering tangles and vertical marks, in addition to patterns of dots and scrawls, both speckled and mottled. They quicken the pulse, exuding an emotional intensity that ranges from deep melancholy to painful discordance to a kind of ecstatic jubilation. At the same time, Winter's meticulous attention to the memory or appearance of a place and its capacity for mysterious drama yields lyric passages that evoke feelings of transcendence.

Inasmuch as Winter's painting world is energized, everything around him is also sensate—the trees, the clouds, the water, and of course the animals. In the portrait *Young Bull* (1988), Winter attempts to capture some essence of the animal's muscular grace and inner life. We are made to feel in the expression in the eye, in the tilt of the

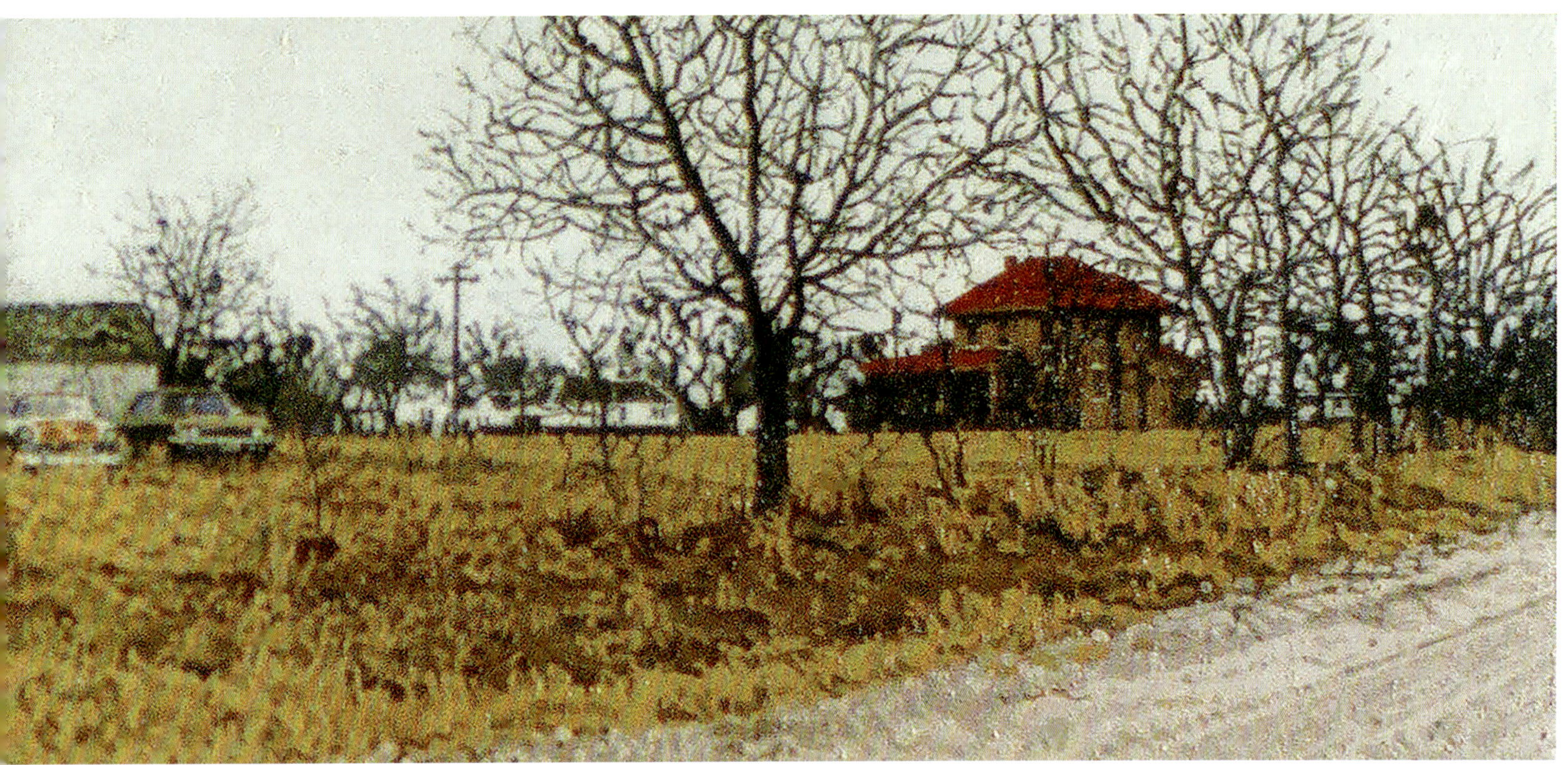

Van Alstyne, 1983
oil on linen | 14" x 72" | Collection of Claude C. Albritton, Dallas

head and its tenuous position behind the barbed wire that holds it within a lushly rendered pasture, a kind of consciousness that cannot be easily reduced to an identifiable emotion or condition. By the same token, Winter's sensitivity to atmospheric conditions results in a breathtaking expanse of space that yields to the eye as far as we wish to penetrate it. *Cows and Water Tank* (1981) evokes West Texas' heroic scale and daunting vastness. Electric wires swerve across a sky punctuated by scudding clouds. We can almost taste the dust on our tongues while contemplating the play of sandy browns in the searing desert air. Winter depicts the cows gathering around the water tank or hovering amid the clotted green scrub. The landscape fairly glints like a mirage, then dissolves into full abstraction. We sense Winter's drive to focus the West Texas experience, compressing or expanding its physical and psychological space, opening up a seemingly infinite scale of blues, creams, and tans and an almost obsessive level of pictorial incident, keeping each aspect of presentation, each successive decision, firmly in hand. The entirety is marked by tuft-like swirls, squiggly strokes, and organic shapes giving impressions of constant, restless movement. Like the landscape, ever in flux yet soothing in its permanence, Winter simulates a tension between change and constancy, those variations of hand and mind that record a moment in time and our awareness of the act of painting itself.

Winter expends enormous effort on his compositions. He deliberates in the placement of each form and how the elements fit. To that end, he slows it down, allowing the eye to catch on the paint. While we may travel along the highway, rushing from here to there, Winter treats mundane places with unflinching attention. For *Fence Row* (1982), he weaves grass and primroses around fence posts and barbed wire. He connects the tubelike pink flowers with diagonal patchy areas of dark gray to evoke soft winds and light-suffused shadows. Here, Winter is generous in the leeway he allows the eye. It is even possible to view the leaning posts as a sort of musical staff. Winter explains, "The overall rhythm of the brushstroke

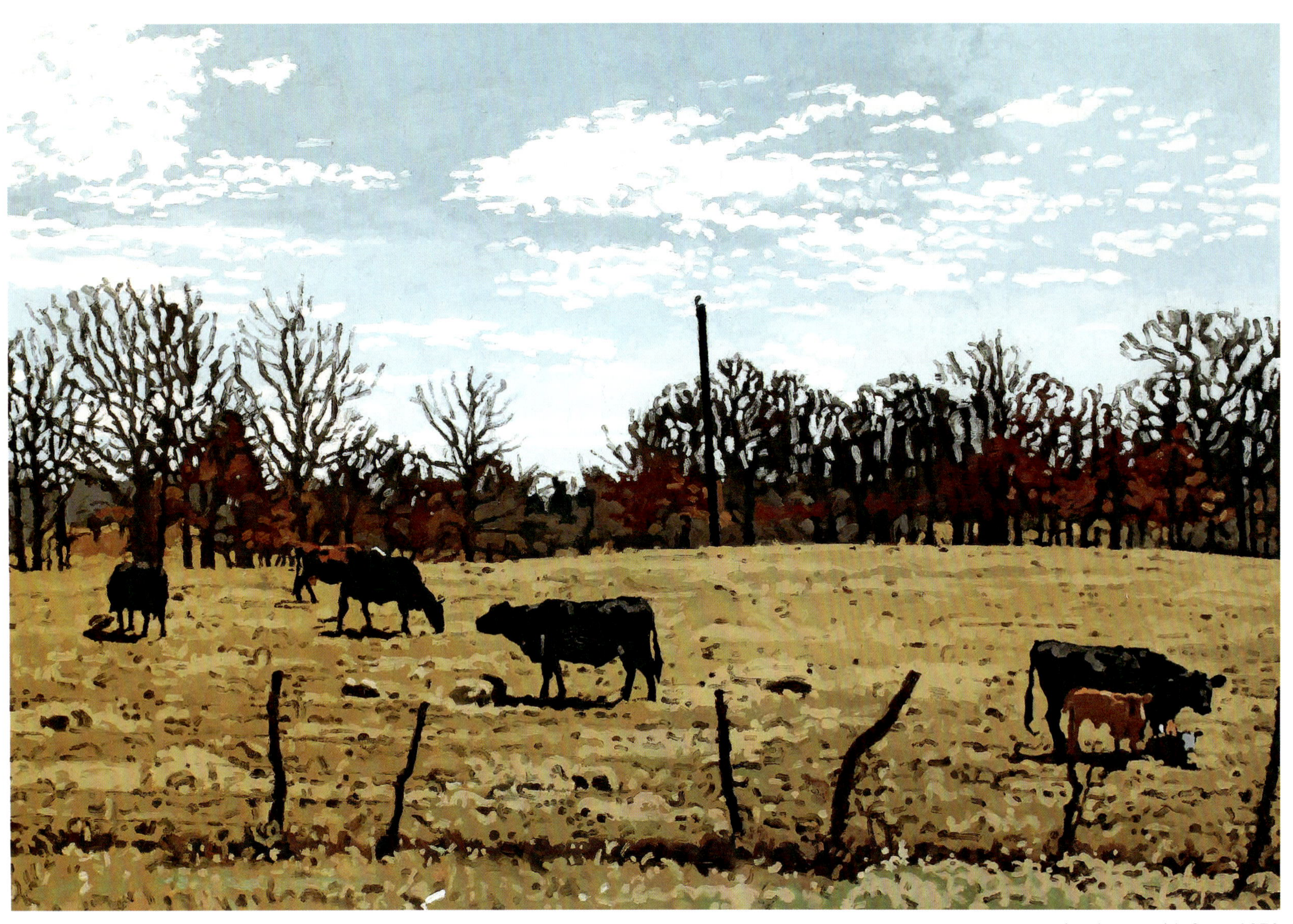

Landscape with Cows, 1979

oil on linen | 42 1/4" × 68 1/4" | The Hunton Andrews Kurth Collection | Photography by David P. Gray

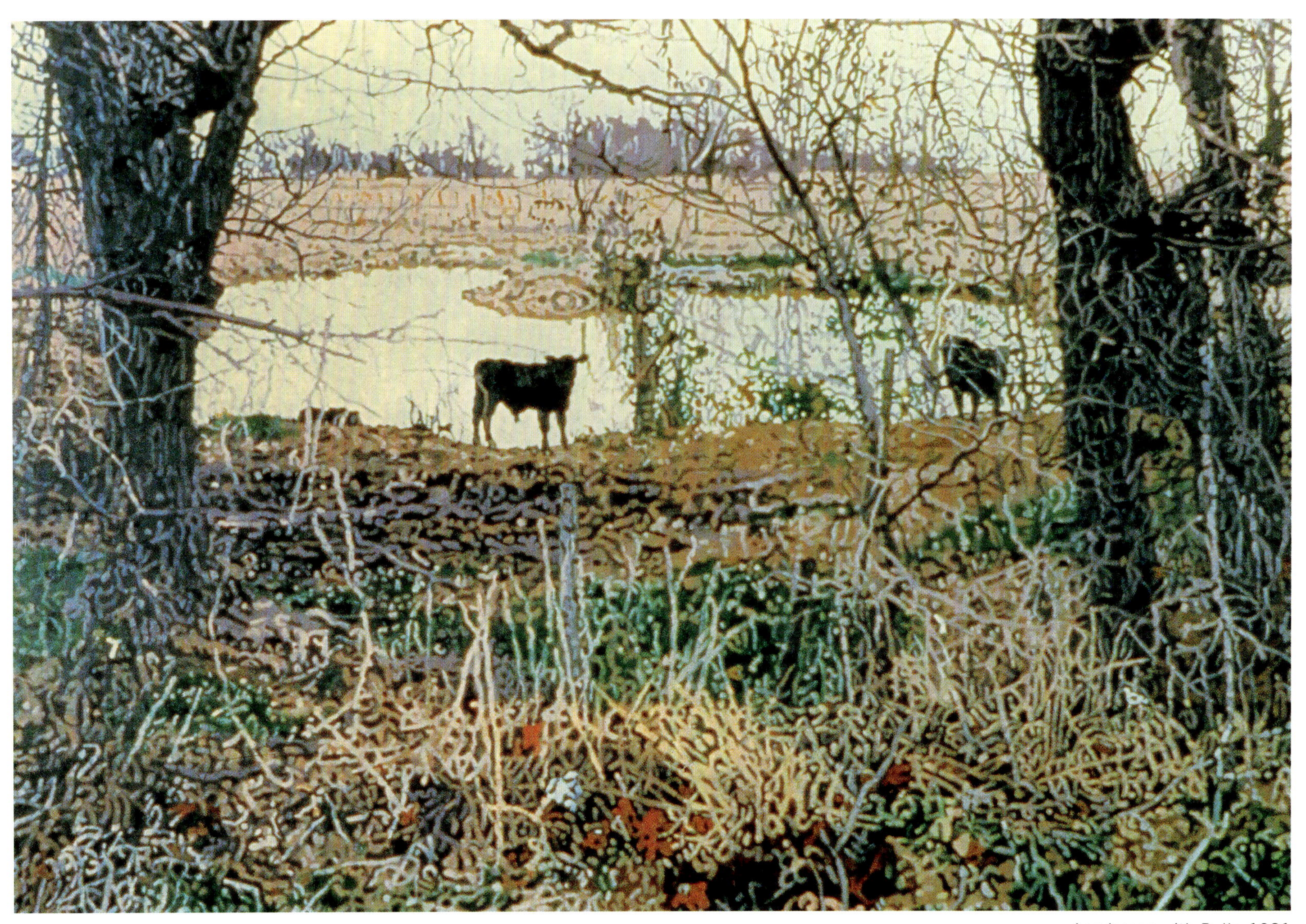

Landscape with Bulls, 1981

oil on linen | 48" × 72" | Cele and John Carpenter Family Collection | Photography by Jason Voinov

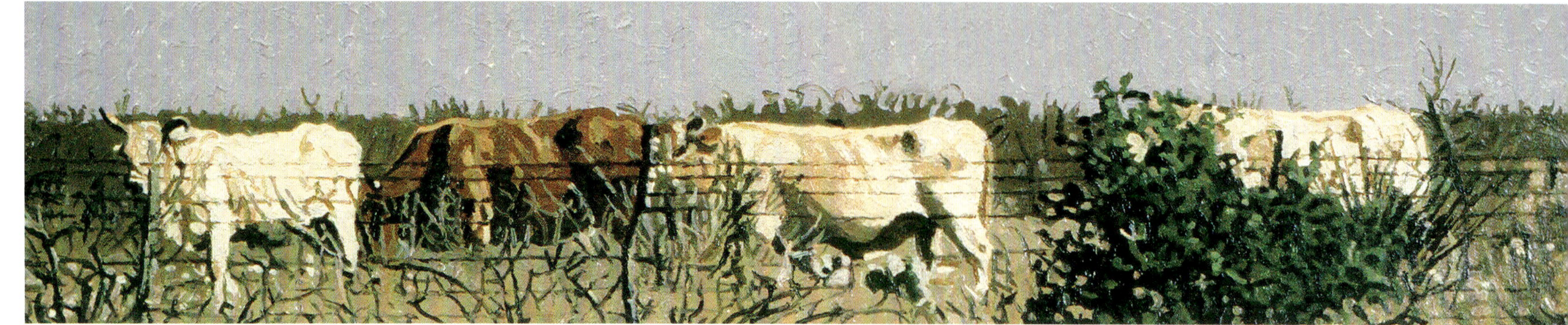

Cows and Fence Row, 1997

oil on museum board | 3" × 15" | Collection of Elise and Burk Murchison, Dallas

is like playing a guitar. A lot of times in a country band, the guitar provides rhythm and structure. So this painting is like keeping four-four or three-four time and staying in the right chord, even while the melody—the landscape in this case—was changing. And you must never let that go. You can't suddenly get faster or slower."

Whatever the symbology, this is Winter in a new key—still deliberating on the canvas, still luxuriating in pigment, stroke, and gesture. He reveals that setting is more than scene, that it is often the armature around which the work revolves. At a time when so much painting could be understood at a glance or by description,

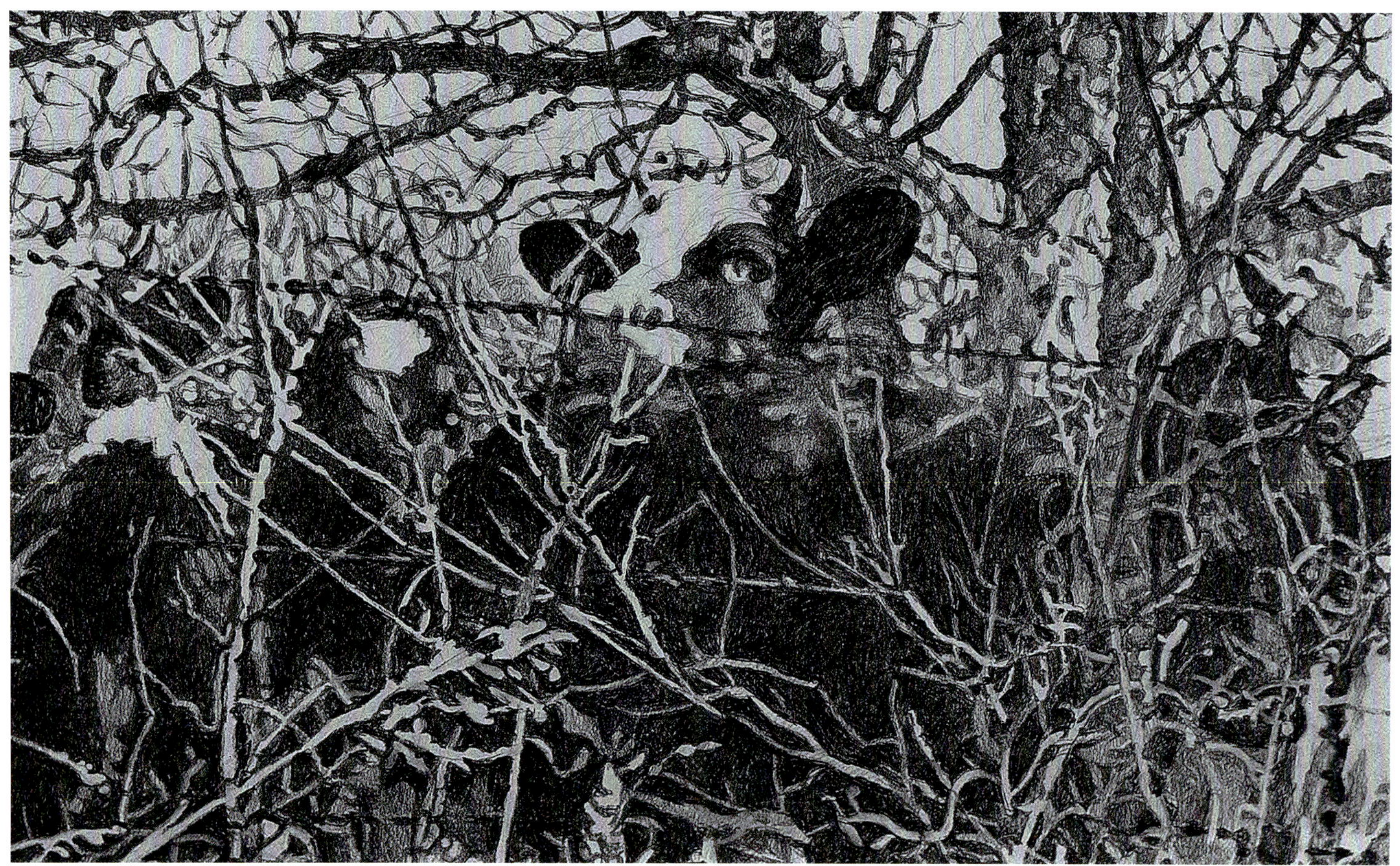

Cows, 1989

pencil on paper | 7 1/2" × 12" | Collection of Mary and Walter Crain

Winter's landscapes were deep ruminations that required looking and figuring out how spaces could be poetry. In 1982, Winter's paintings took another turn. A commission from the Federal Reserve Bank of Dallas for a ten-by-twenty-foot painting of a Texas landscape sent the artist to the farthest regions of the state—from the Hill Country to the Gulf Coast to the Big Bend—in search of the essential scene that would capture one moment and place in time. At the outset, Winter painted five ten-by-twenty-inch studies: a cattle pond in West Texas, a stand of cedar elms in a nature conservancy south of Dallas, an outcropping in the Big Bend, a panorama in the Hill Country, and a wildflower field in South Texas. For the artist's largest undertaking to date, the bank chose a vista from the nearby Greenhills Nature Conservancy (now the Cedar Ridge Nature Preserve)—a big cedar elm surrounded by smaller mesquite and cedar trees in the background with a fair-weather sky. As it happened, however, the project also necessitated a change in the approach from earlier work. "Unlike most painters, I had never painted a pure landscape," Winter says. "I knew I couldn't broad brush à la Fairfield Porter and his 'school.' And I couldn't divide the canvas into large chunks like Richard Diebenkorn. I had painted my way into a different camp. I finally found out that if I gave each tiny detail its own integrity—not just brushstrokes, but as shapes—that, no matter how tedious the painting might be, it would work for me. I had to find a way that I could believe in that abstract subject." In preparation for the Federal Reserve's immense *Silhouetted Trees*, Winter worked out an approach of continuous detail from edge to edge on several canvases. *Sunflowers* (1982), *Chisos Mountains* (1983), *Landscape* (1982), and, later, *Fallen Tree* (1985), among others, evince a crystalline clarity and precision in the rendering of light and form. Devoid of human presence while at the same time soliciting viewer engagement, they embody the romantic view of nature as a space that transcends everyday human concerns even as they invite us to regard ourselves as part of a larger whole.

In many respects, the "pure" landscapes of the early 1980s reveal the effort when two artistic antagonists—abstraction and representation—are brought together head on. In *Fallen Tree*, the canvas brims edge to edge with spindly branches. At first glance, the painting appears as dense brambles of snarling and intersecting lines of paint. Winter works the feisty strokes, breaking and stretching them; he twines the nimble and the staid, the sinewy with the brittle, letting them inch forward, double back, and sweep across the canvas. Layers upon layers result in a depth and luminosity of brown, green, and white pigments that hold the entire surface in stasis, transforming it into a vibrantly transparent membrane. At the same time, Winter makes us aware of the cycles of life and death in nature, of the tree trunk returning to the soil while the wind blows and new life begins. Conversely, the majestic panorama of *Chisos Mountains* evokes our romantic belief in the land as a last guarantor of physical and psychic freedom.

Using the photograph as referent and matrix, Winter developed a distinct spatial range in the pure landscape paintings. His images read as dense, sharp fields from a certain distance; they are barely legible at close range, yet intensely sensuous and physical, making us conscious of their material reality, of the oil on canvas. Discipline and reflection heighten rather than dissipate the intensity of Winter's art. His aim is accurate; the movements of his gestures are varied in their multiplicity, but they are almost always multiples of elegant concision. Their vital grace makes more immediately visible and accessible Winter's vivid orchestration of the energies of color, light, and stroke. At this juncture, his paintings give body to memories of deep visual and emotional sensation cued by his responses to nature.

Landscape (1982) envelops us with its dense foliage and the glinting white light of the Dallas area. Here, Winter paints a scrim of trees and thickets through which the sultry sky and growth of shrubs are glimpsed. Up close, however, Winter's brushstrokes seemingly detach themselves from the picture surface. Linear skeins of white that denote light peel away from their descriptive function, as do the dark green, mint, and yellow dabs that serve as the plush tangles of leaves. Some

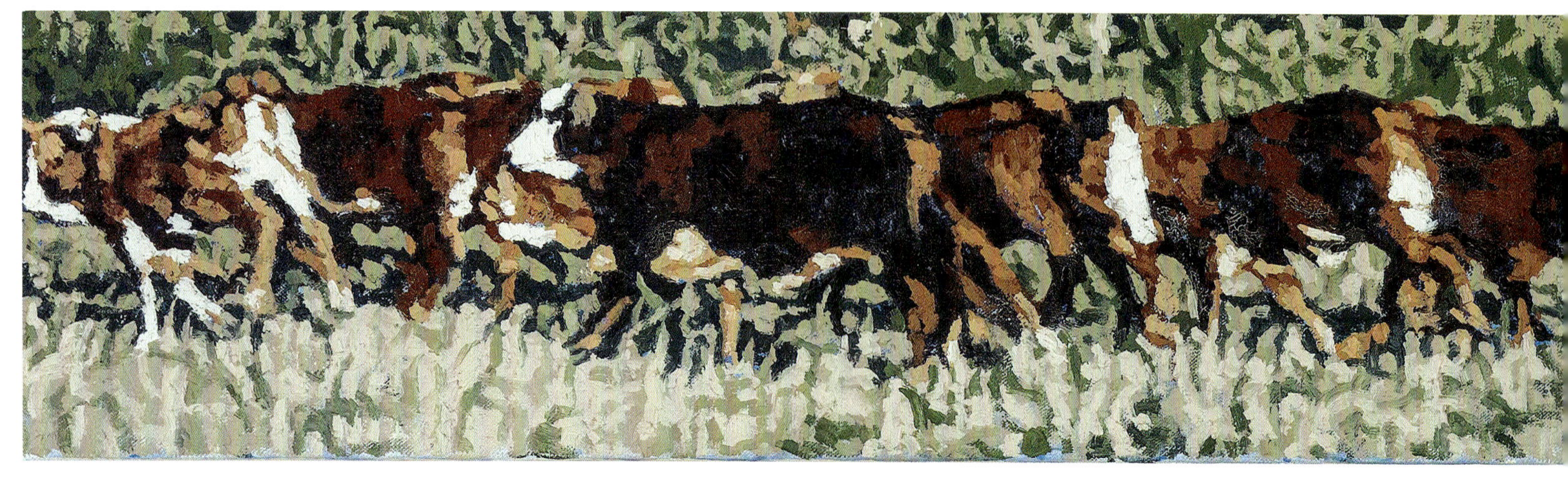

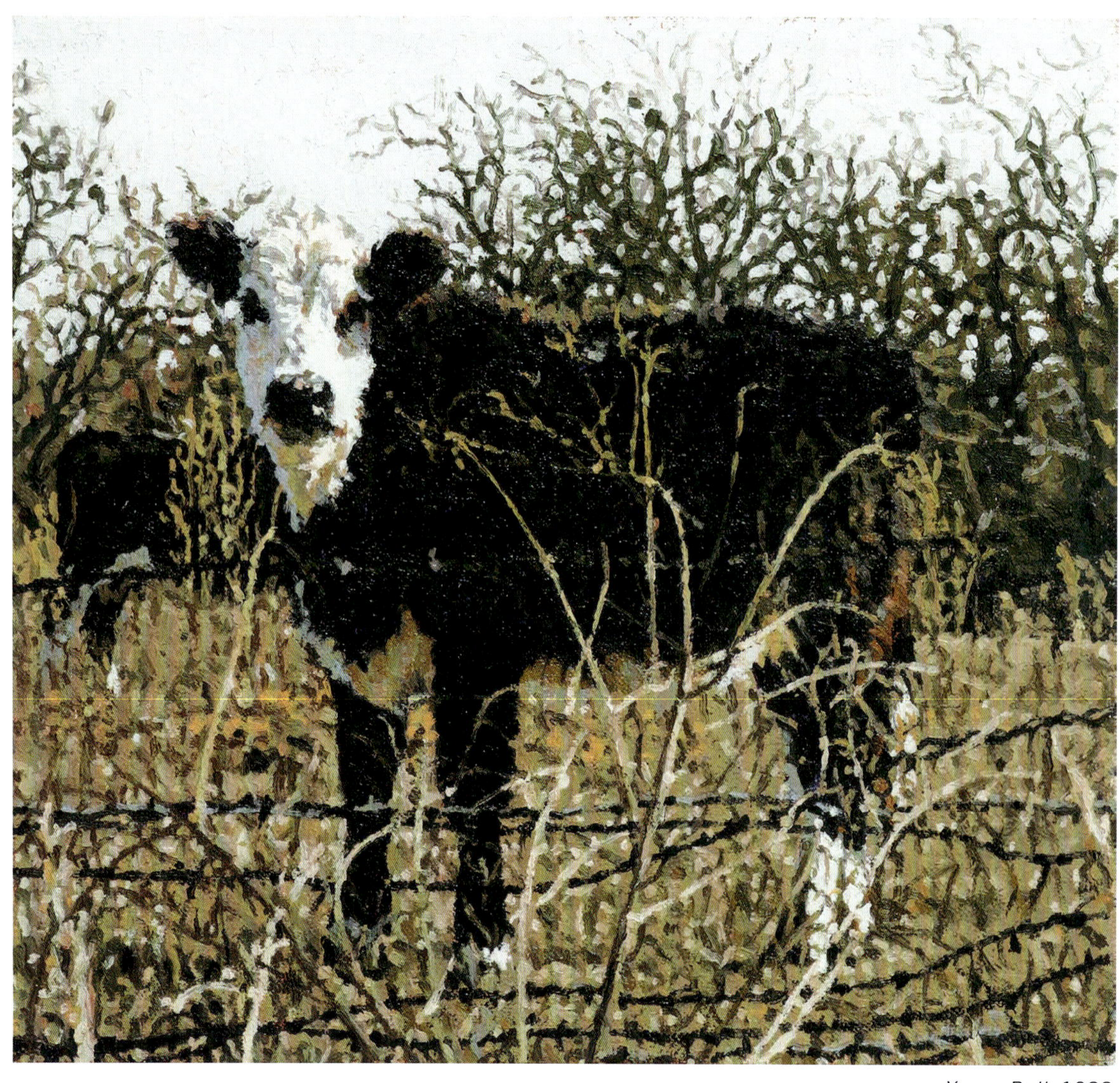

Young Bull, 1988

oil on linen | 12" x 12" | Albritton Family Collection, Dallas |

Photography by Fernando Rojas

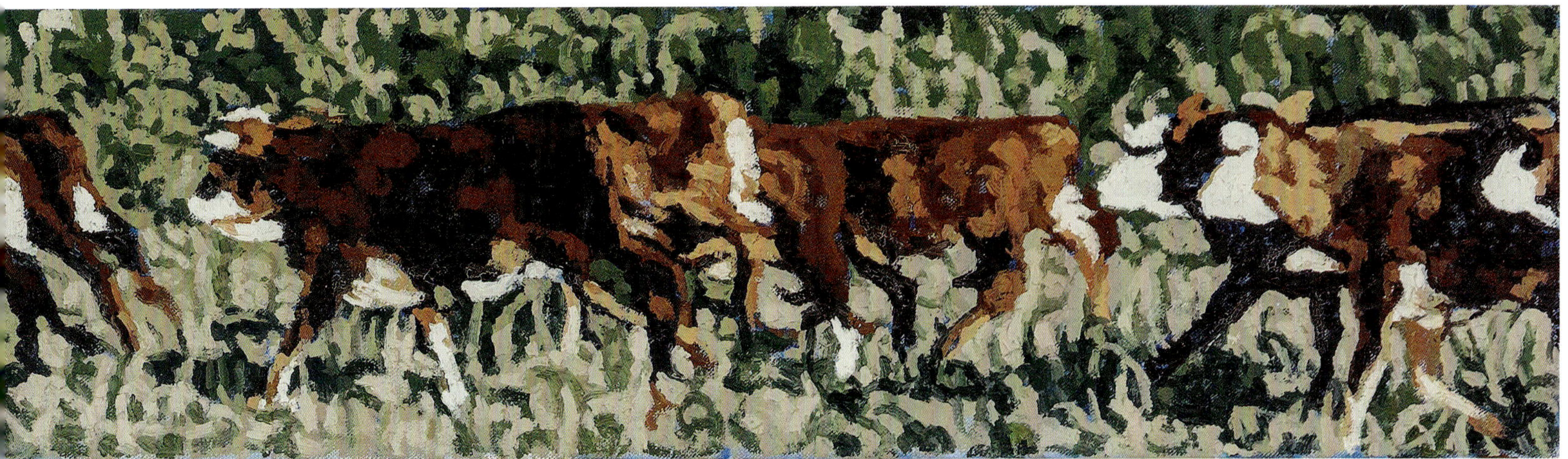

Running Cattle, 1989
oil on linen | 8" × 60" | Collection of the Roger Horchow Family | Photography by Joshua Nefsky

of them seemingly twist at odd angles to the overall flow; others remain as squiggly, gestural shapes on a flattened ground or push forward, defying their role as signifiers of depth. Still, none of this seductive play of the paint robs the work of its realist vigor. The unraveling of these elements is a visual exercise in which they may snap back to being light on the side of a tree trunk or receding depth in the woods at any moment. *Landscape*, in particular, cleared the way for Winter to take on the twenty-foot *Silhouetted Trees* as a mutating, vibrant, and evolving force. Through this pure landscape painting, he had learned to work on at least two levels: constructing a painting in which forms, colors, and brushstrokes establish a set of unique relationships, independent of subject matter, while at the same time capturing and preserving the physical and emotional overtones aroused in him by visual experience.

Admittedly, elms, shrubs, grasses, and fair-weather clouds are subjects with which Winter had been familiar since childhood. In tackling the huge landscape commission, he knew what to emphasize and what to leave out, according to the best of his painting ability at the time. While the logistics of working on such a grand scale had to be resolved, the artist's desire to translate his vision and the emotional experience provided by nature in the Greenhills Nature Conservancy was unrelenting. Not only did he have to wrestle with the much-considered flatness of the canvas as he attempted to create on its surface visual volume and depth, but it was his aim now to create a believable space, a "breathing" space that wholly absorbs the viewer in the spirit of the land. So demanding was the commission that Winter took a leave of absence from SMU to complete it. The enormous scale required hard-to-find eleven-foot canvas plus an accommodating stretcher that was equally difficult to track down. Winter describes the complex preparation:

> I hired a man in Houston to build the 10′ x 20′ stretchers and braces with expansion joints. I ordered raw linen canvas, 4 x 8 yards. Two guys that worked for Delahunty Gallery helped me stretch it on my studio floor. I worked out a system of pulleys to lift it onto the painting wall. A Dallas contractor I know rented the multi-level scaffolding on 2″ x 12″ floor boards—the insurance company wouldn't let scaffolding be rented to amateurs. The 10′ x 20′ canvas had to be primed three coats before painting could begin. With each coat, I started at the top and across and primed downward. Any drips of gesso on the canvas had to be flattened before they dried and made lumps, so I'd come down the ladder after each 20′ span was gessoed. After the priming was finished and dried, I put a thin lean turpentine ultramarine blue wash over the entire surface so that

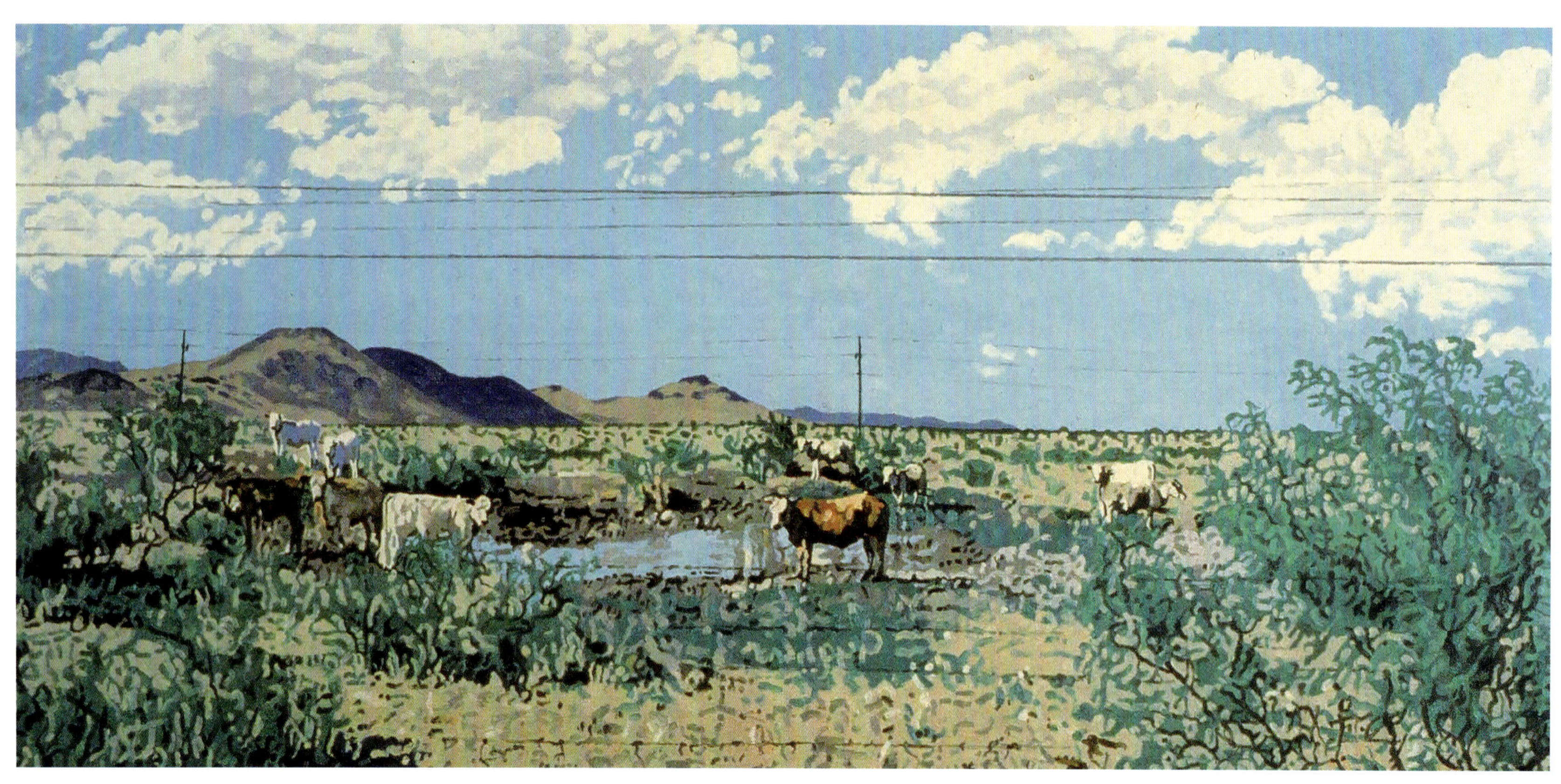

Cows and Water Tank, 1981

oil on linen | 34" x 72" | Courtesy of the artist

my brushwork had touched every inch of canvas before proceeding. This was done with my largest brush. Then I drew a 12" x 12" grid over the entire surface with a darker umber line applied with a smaller brush. This grid matched the proportions of the grids on a photo of the 10" x 20" study and on an enlarged photo of the snapshot the study was derived from. After the roughly done drawing, I made a thin underpainting, using approximate colors of the study, covering the entire surface plane. I started by freely blocking in the darkest areas and working toward the lightest. Some of these early stages might peek through the overpainting, which was done with opaque mixtures of paint. I would premix several of the colors at a time and store them in glass jars in case they were needed in lower levels of the painting. Each brushmark had a purpose: to be descriptive of the area of foliage and sky that I was painting and to be a shape that related in a formal way to each adjacent shape. I worked the painting from top to bottom for practical reasons. I went up and down on the scaffolding platform to back up for a distant view many, many times a day. And then I would need to change the level of the platform to work on each lower area. I was happy to finally get to the point where I could stand on the floor to paint. I had to keep the structure and the meter and the melody going so that it ended up as one painting, rather than a collection of poorly related parts. When the painting was finished, I held a party in my studio to celebrate. It was New Year's Day of 1983. People from the Bank, JoAnn and James Pratt, Carolyn and Roger Horchow, A.C. Green, Laura Carpenter and the Delahunty staff, people from Channel 13 were there, plus various artists I knew. In the Southern Tradition, I cooked pots of black-eyed peas and cornbread. A week later, when time came to move the painting it was discovered that a 10' by 20' painting wouldn't fit through the doors of the Federal Reserve Bank! And so it had to be unstretched and stretchers disassembled in my studio, rolled, then restretched and reassembled at the Bank by the Delahunty Gallery crew.[3]

Silhouetted Trees is riveting to behold. The painting abounds in visual incident, dramatic shifts of space and light, and an unflagging energy. At a distance, the trees, grass, and cloud-filled sky create a dreamlike, idyllic environment. Viewed up close, the seamless illusions break into myriad patches and swirls of browns, greens, and blues; the magic partly is in how the eye and mind flip between seeing the realism and seeing abstraction. Winter's deliberate, ruminative temperament never loses touch with the picture surface; his fluid marks seem to be engaged in reconnaissance. Yet all are delineated by an almost alarming liberation of gesture and directness of stroke. The painting is defined at each point by a tension between delicate lyricism and compulsive insistence. This tension gives Winter's work the altogether unexpected quality of something seen for the first time.

In our frantic, noisy culture, we can easily overlook the inestimable value of things close at hand. Intimacy is not only the emotional closeness between people but also a preference for a more immediate encounter with the things of nature. What does it mean to be part of all forms of life? That there are traces of us in plants and minerals, tenacious traces of what we once were and shall become? Winter's painting investigates the land rather than represents it, reminding us of seasonal change, transformation, and the transience of existence. To that end, he makes us conscious of nature as a metaphor for the internal journey we take in life. In the isolation of their vast setting, the great cedar elm and mesquites demand our attention. They shape the landscapes of our lives and are bound up with our sense of identity. We see them as living organisms that exist in our own environment and rely on the same air, earth, and water for survival.

For Winter, the installation of *Silhouetted Trees* represented a watershed moment that also marked a renewed clarity and sense of achievement. Along with the Federal Reserve Bank commission, the artist was promoted to full professor of painting and drawing at SMU.

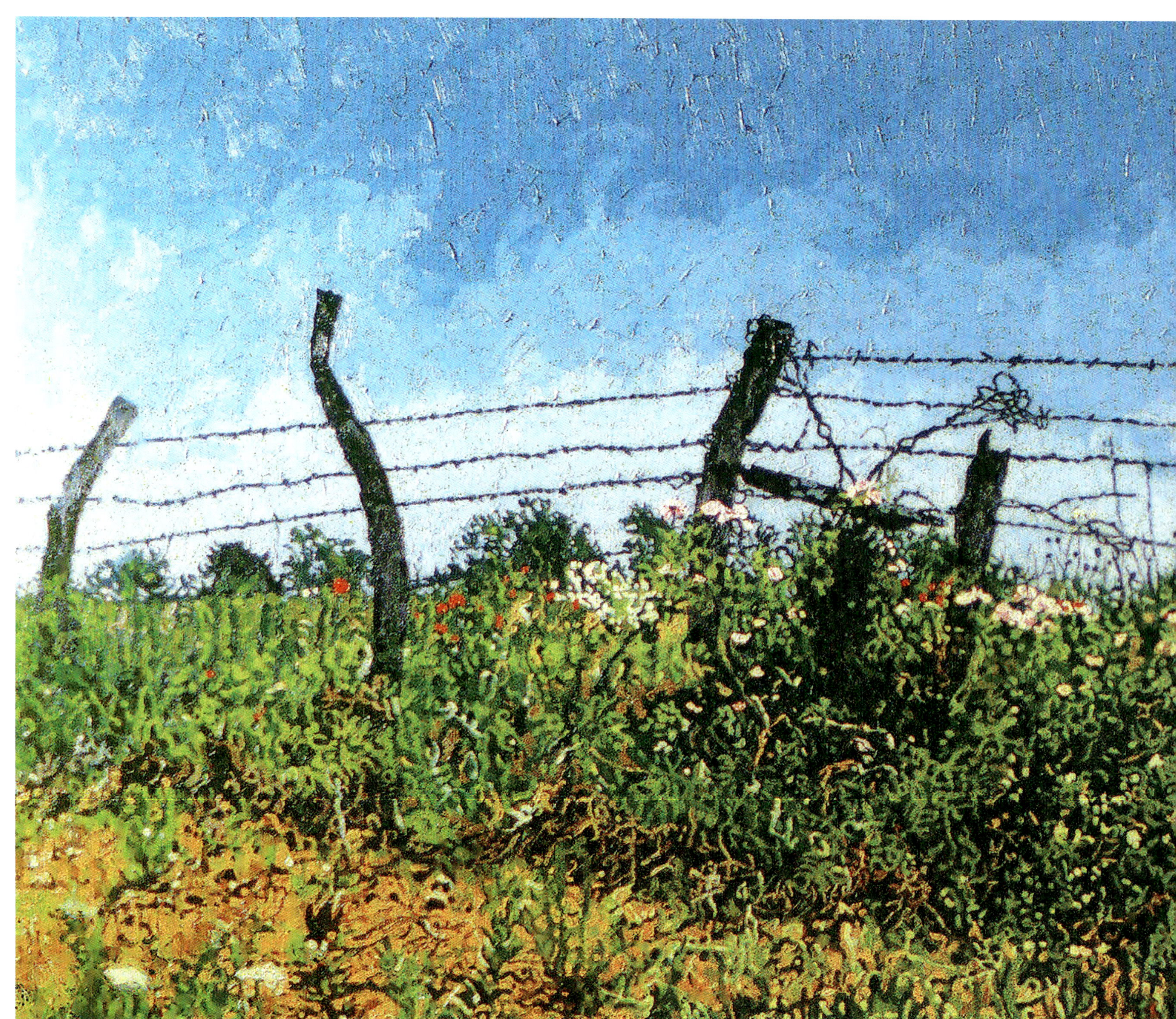

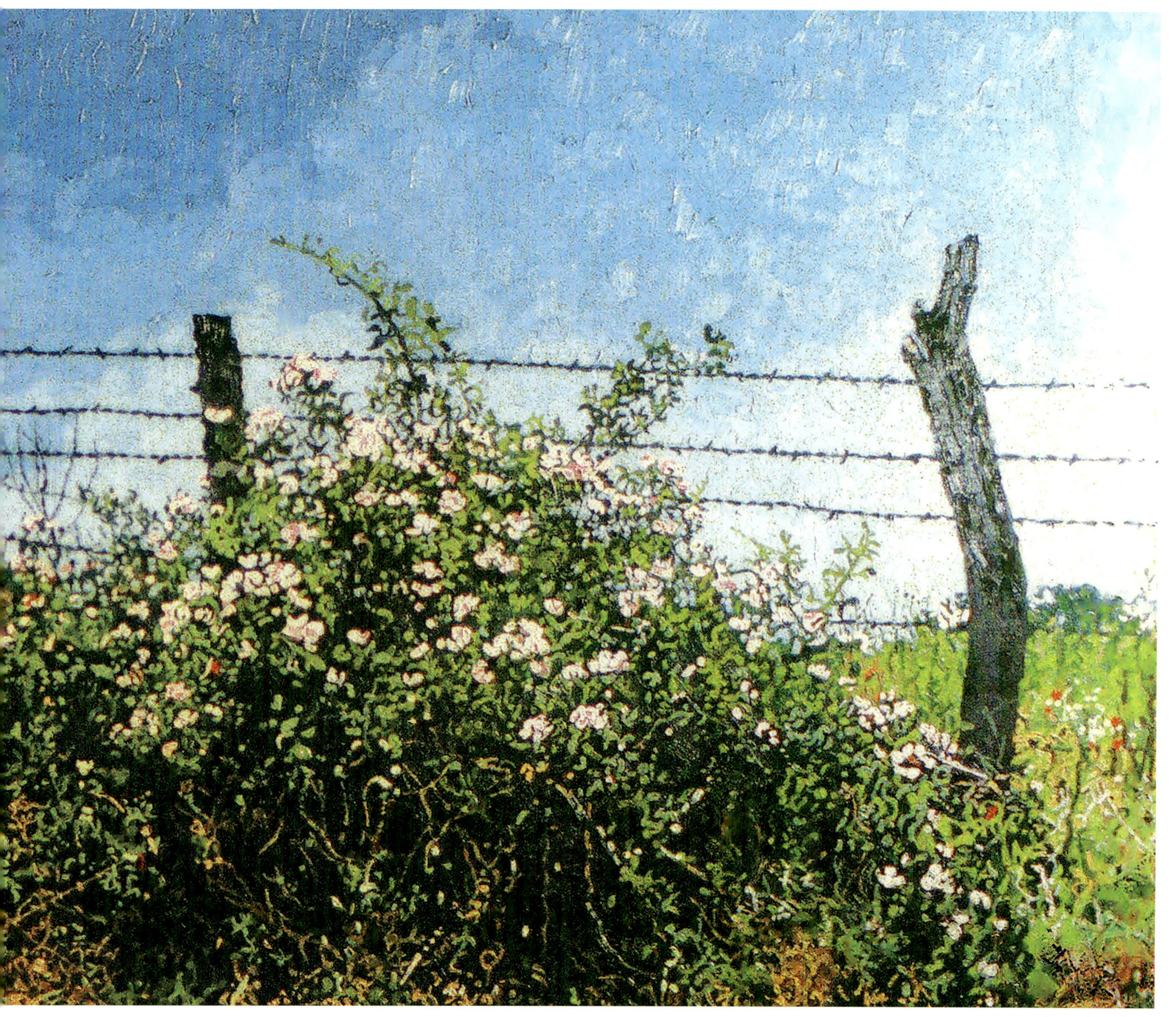

Fence Row, 1982

oil on linen | 36" x 84" | Courtesy of the artist

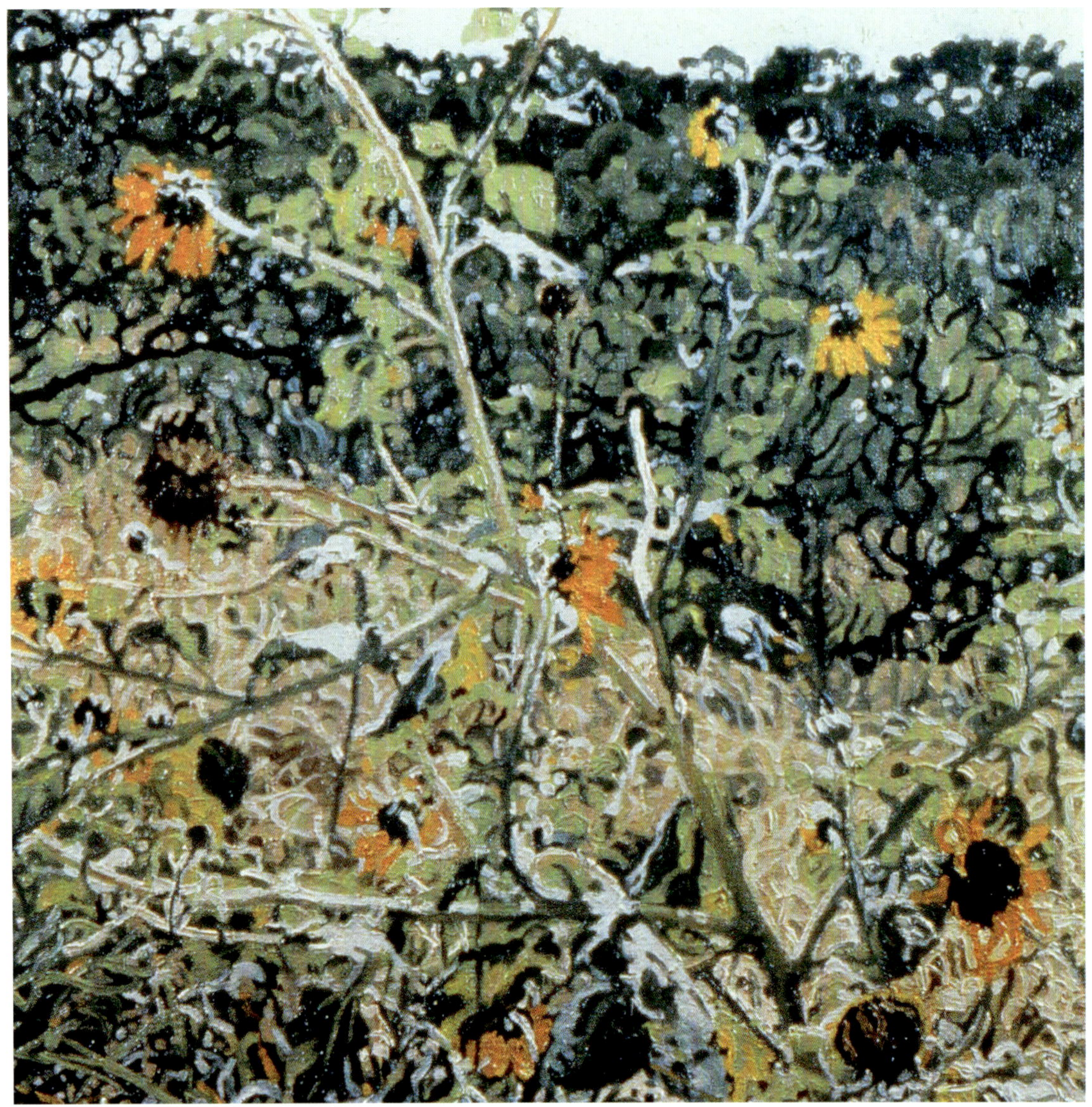

Sunflowers, 1982
oil on linen | 18" x 18" | Collection of Cheryl and Doug Kramp

That same year, he was given a contract by Prentice Hall to write the first of five books about drawing. What's more, he joined the prestigious Fischbach Gallery in New York City. His first solo exhibition in 1984, at age fifty, was followed by three subsequent shows. All but one sold out. Admittedly, his association with a major New York gallery conferred an authenticity to the work in the eyes of the art world that had not been secured through regional exhibitions. Nevertheless, the poetry readings and music sessions held in his new studio were popular events that helped him become an integral part of the SMU community. Winter's paintings moved forward seamlessly, even as his subjects ranged from pure landscapes to rural and small-town settings and to urban streets and buildings. Just as John Cheever wrote about the suburban upper-middle class of the East Coast, Winter began to depict figures and places closer to home. A stray dog at a congested intersection on a rainy day, an overgrown vacant lot in Old Highland Park, quaint white frame and brick houses on Dallas streets were all part of a world he had entered and knew intimately through daily life. In each case, Winter aims to fuse an all-encompassing curiosity with an extreme fidelity to just those facts that demonstrate the variousness of contemporary existence. At the same time, however, the feeling of authenticity evokes the ephemeral, fleeting moments and isolated segments that trigger strangely nostalgic responses in viewers.

In *Street with Melting Snow* (1980), a wide-ranging view is brought to an intense focus of observation, each touch of the brush recording in intricate detail the precise experience of the eye. Winter's serpentine and curlicue strokes of gray and tan suggest where melting snow has turned to slush. A red stop sign echoes the red brick of the old home in the background. The painting frankly describes the cracked asphalt of the street and blue skies glimpsed through the stripped branches of mature trees.

In *Dallas Street* (1986), the shadows of the trees singly or in clumps and heavy masses project across the road before breaking down into semiabstraction. At right, the white frame house is a portrait that records human passage and its effects across time. In both paintings, we are made to wonder about the histories of the houses themselves and the secrets they contain—the people who fought and made love, cooked and cleaned in them, over and over. These images that haunt us have first haunted Winter.

Indeed, there is a certain poetic sentiment animating his art, which finds something exquisite in even the most unremarkable places. A powerful example, *Pearl Street* (1983), explores the farmers' market area of Dallas, including an old boxcar, a jumble of buildings, the back view of a pedestrian, and the half-hidden presence of the new I. M. Pei city hall. The details of the painting are not just compositional elements or symbols; they are actual things that exist in a moment of time and are observed by the artist. Suburban neatness, urban clutter, industrial design all have their capacity for great attractiveness. But Winter's instincts take him elsewhere. His discoveries are not much insisted on and therefore all the more to be believed. We imagine something more just beyond the edges of the painting—down the street or behind the buildings—hidden from sight. And this suggestion makes us look closer. What quickens it all is the feeling of being extraordinarily alive to the moment. Winter paints his subjects so attentively and by such a patient, incremental process that the resultant images have a breathtaking lucidity. The specificity of his imagery, the personal nature of it, adds the authentic accent of his own emotional involvement. Winter's eye measures space, then recalculates it against the pictorial plane only to refocus the entirety so that it may exist in the real space of the viewer's world.

Some details are clarified, others muted, each variant registering a shift of textural interest or the rhythmic balance of parts, a placement of a ground line or vanishing point. Winter's commitment and stamina remind us that nothing substantial in art can be achieved without great effort. Nowhere is this more evident than in *El Paso* (1983), in which Winter takes a bird's-eye view of the downtown plaza. While stationed at Fort Bliss during 1956–58, he had become very familiar with the city and Juárez, Mexico. Winter spent many hours in the library, in taverns with his friends, and at the plaza watching the alligator in the city fountain. However, he did not return to the area until 1980, the year after their older son, Jonah, graduated from Highland Park High School. "As a graduation gift, I took him on a trip I called our Texas Odyssey," Winter recalls. "We drove down to the coast and then around the Texas-Mexico border along the Rio Grande to El Paso. We walked across the International Bridge to Juárez—North America's number one Sin City, as it was called, with its drug dealers, prostitutes, and pimps. Jonah couldn't get out of there soon enough, so we went back and sat in the El Paso plaza. While [we were] talking, a suspicious-looking man walked up and shook his fists in our faces. We both got up and hurried back to our hotel that bordered the plaza. Back in our room, I looked down onto the street and the fist shaker could be seen on the sidewalk. I photographed him, along with that very familiar corner of the city. Back in my Dallas studio, I patched a couple of photos together and used them as the factual basis for the painting. It memorialized that event, plus my memories from the late fifties."

Although the painting is highly structured, it appears to be in a constant state of vibration. Winter divides the field into geometric proportions determined by the placement of the architectural elements, as well as the ensuing play of strong light and shadow across tilting planes and hard, diagonal edges. Metal posts, the parallels of parking space

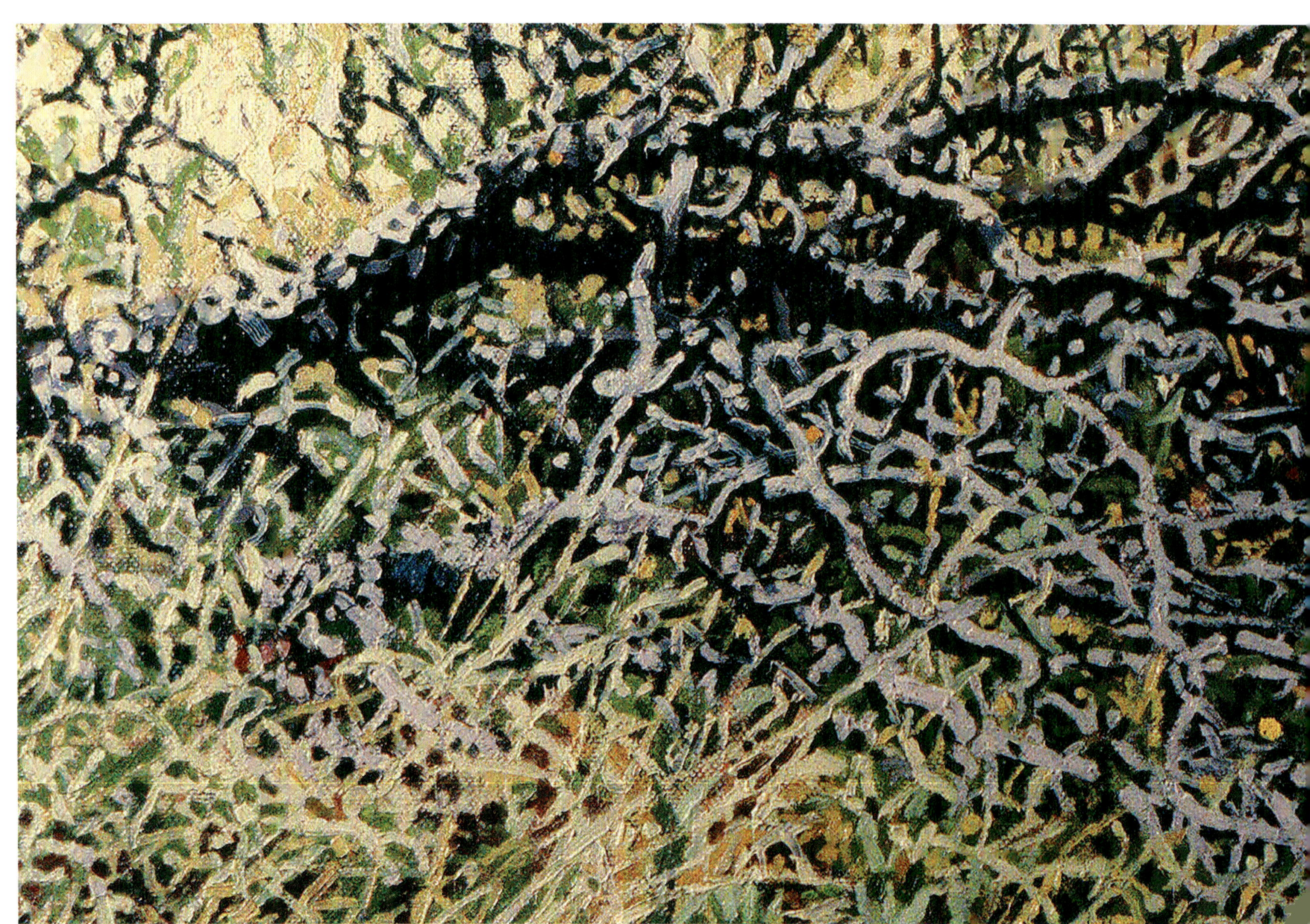

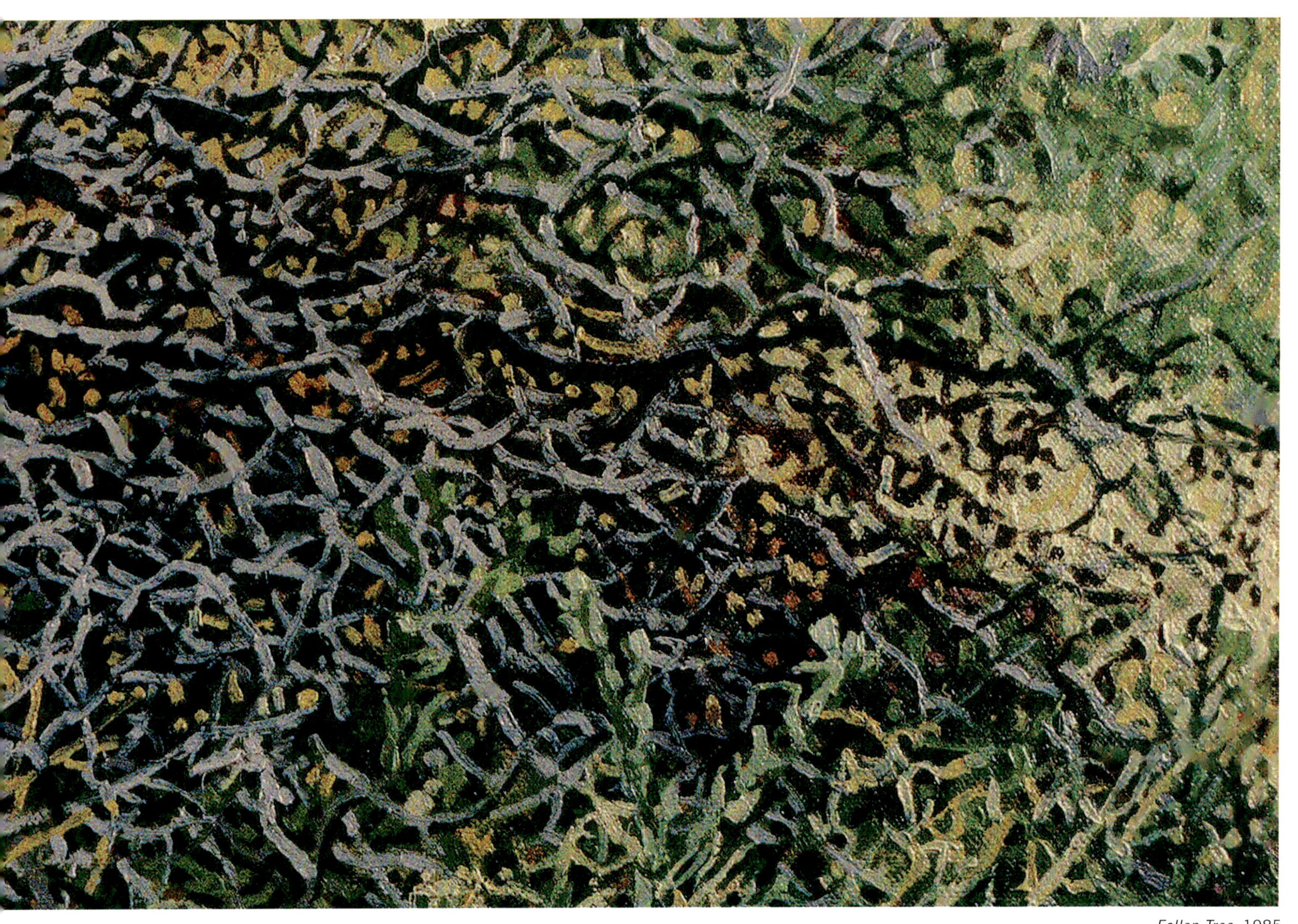

Fallen Tree, 1985

oil on canvas | 8" × 24" | Collection of Mary and Walter Crain

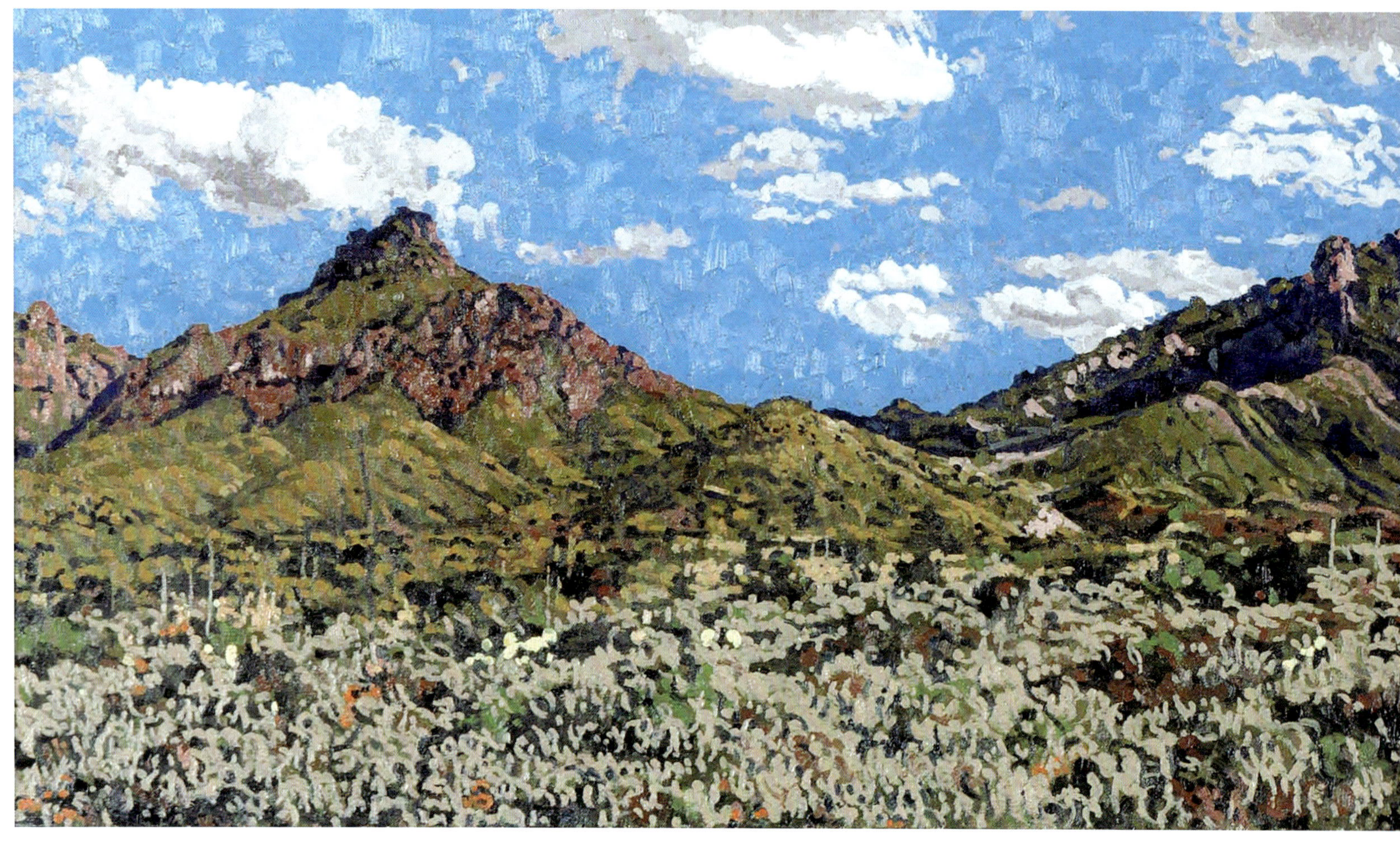

lines and crosswalks, the window and door frames, the walking figures and moving cars, the repeated bushes and circular planting areas, the white benches and commercial signage—all keep us noticing the odd and unexpected in everyday life. Accordingly, the accumulated details slide back and forth across the charged field. Their rhythms and movements, tempos and breaks transform the commonplace into a complex visual orchestration. The intrinsic aliveness of Winter's painting—its play of emotion and structure, of surface and color—thrills and unsettles.

Each encounter with a cultural landmark, everyday setting, or personal memory may be reflected in the extensive range, physical sensuality, and structural clarity of Winter's art. Oscillating between past and present, formal rigor and pressurized energy, the paintings created during the 1980s reveal Winter to be an artist constantly enlarging the sphere in which he functions. Nevertheless, he always returns to certain highly charged motifs of iconic richness whereby meanings proliferate and mundane images become multivalent. His paintings are carefully worked and composed, even inviting us to retrace his every move. Each seems to offer solutions to problems raised in a previous work while serving as a site for experiments that will develop in a later piece. In doing so, Winter engages viewers in a much more challenging and refreshing manner. Through hard thinking and tough labor, he pushes each work—and us—into slightly unknown territories.

In yet another shift of context during the decade, Winter's paintings reflect his impressions of New York City, with each work capturing the unique character of its parks and neighborhoods.

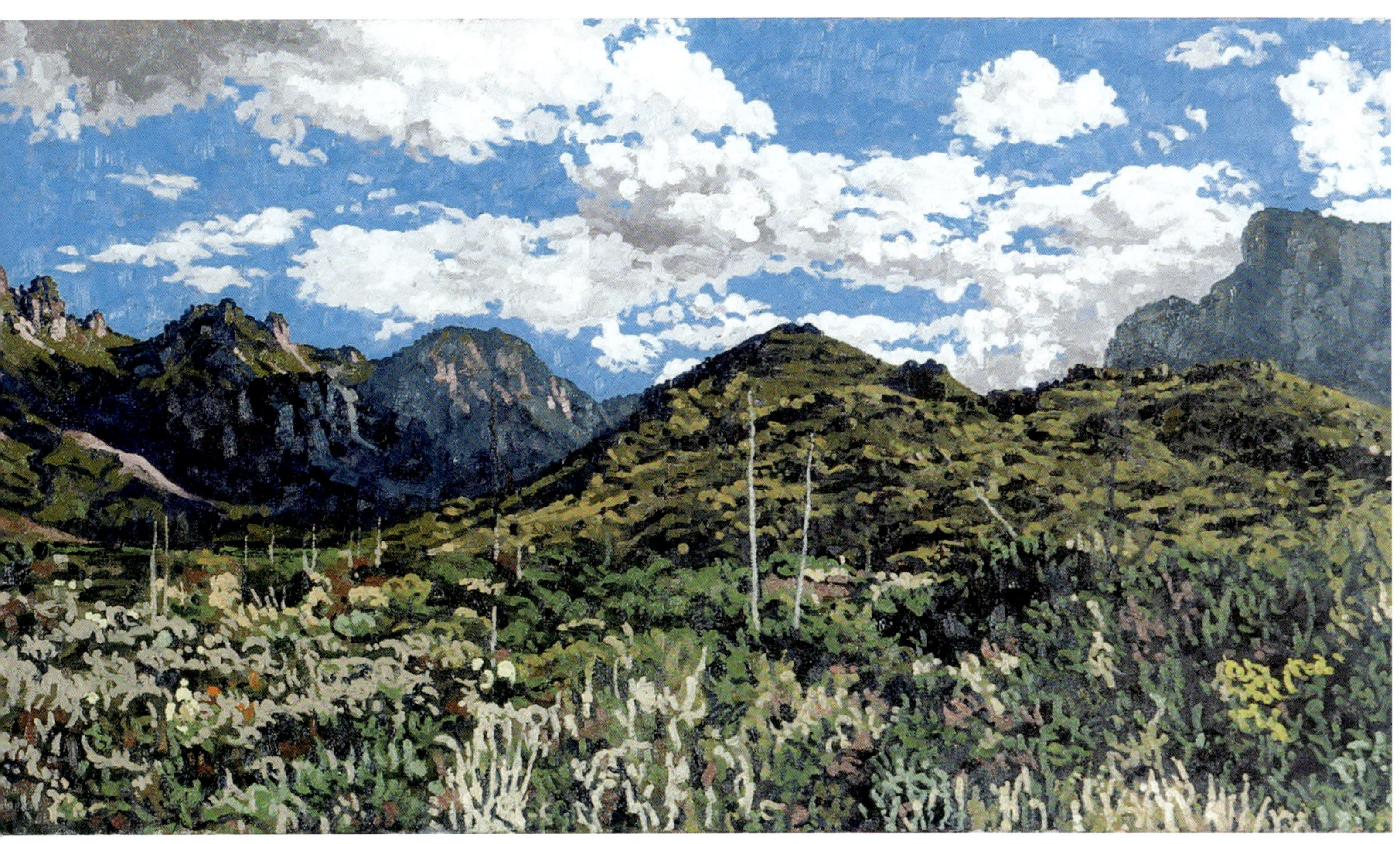

Chisos Mountains, 1983
oil on linen | 20" × 72" | Collection of Judge B. Michael Chitty and Elise Chitty | Photography by Ben Bascombe

In the seasoned experience of certain artists, we can observe a progression from youth, in which the facts of an artist's aesthetics may need to be determined with hard lines and definition, to a maturity that allows the artist greater freedom in brushstroke and touch. Delicacy has always been a hallmark of Winter's technique, but the New York paintings, tempered by decades of observation and application, display a carefreeness stimulated by the grace of knowing that he can do what he wants more easily at this juncture, that the desired effects can be achieved through a harmony of eye, mind, and hand. Viewing these paintings, one's eyes are in perpetual motion, jostled by the energetic surface and the pulsing and flowing tones. As a group, they express a swift, restless joy. The extraordinary, hauntingly beautiful paintings *Union Square* (1983 and 1988), *Park Avenue* (1985), *Gramercy Park* (1987), *Coney Island* (1985), and *Park Slope* (1985), among others, show Winter's commitment to the precise rendering, the studied demarcation, of sections of the natural world and the man-made. Yet all of them are presented as if by a stare that never seems to end. After the viewer contemplates these canvases, every leaf, flower, and roof shingle will affirm its grace, form, and individual life. To experience one of Winter's paintings is to feel simultaneously the sudden reality of a specific place and a moment in time. They join the buoyancy of a glance and the weight of a long-term scrutiny. In doing so, Winter also insists, in lucid and consummately refined pictorial terms, that paintings can be magical places where virtually anything is possible.

Winter possesses an eye for the telling details that can trigger memories of the viewer's own

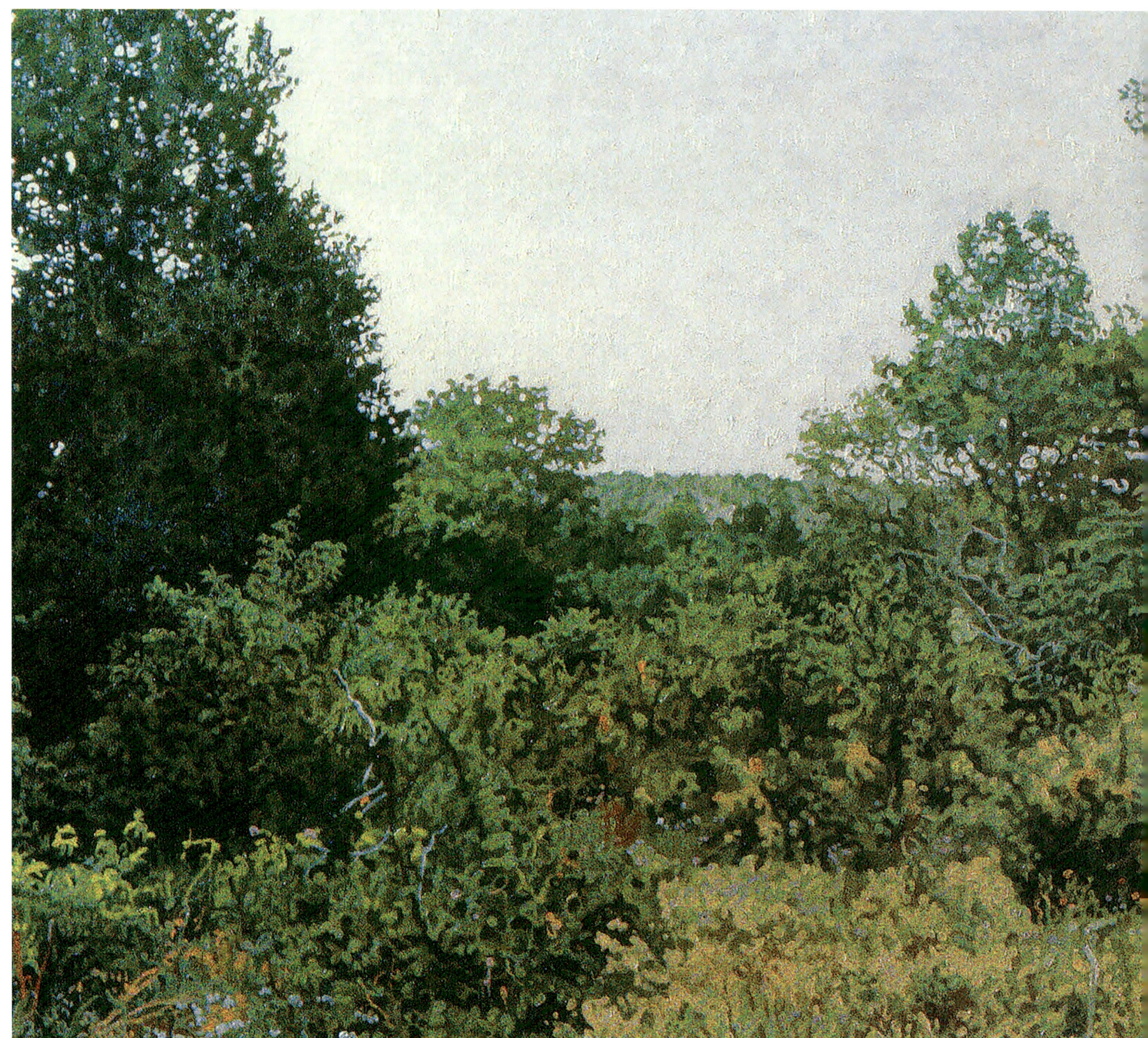

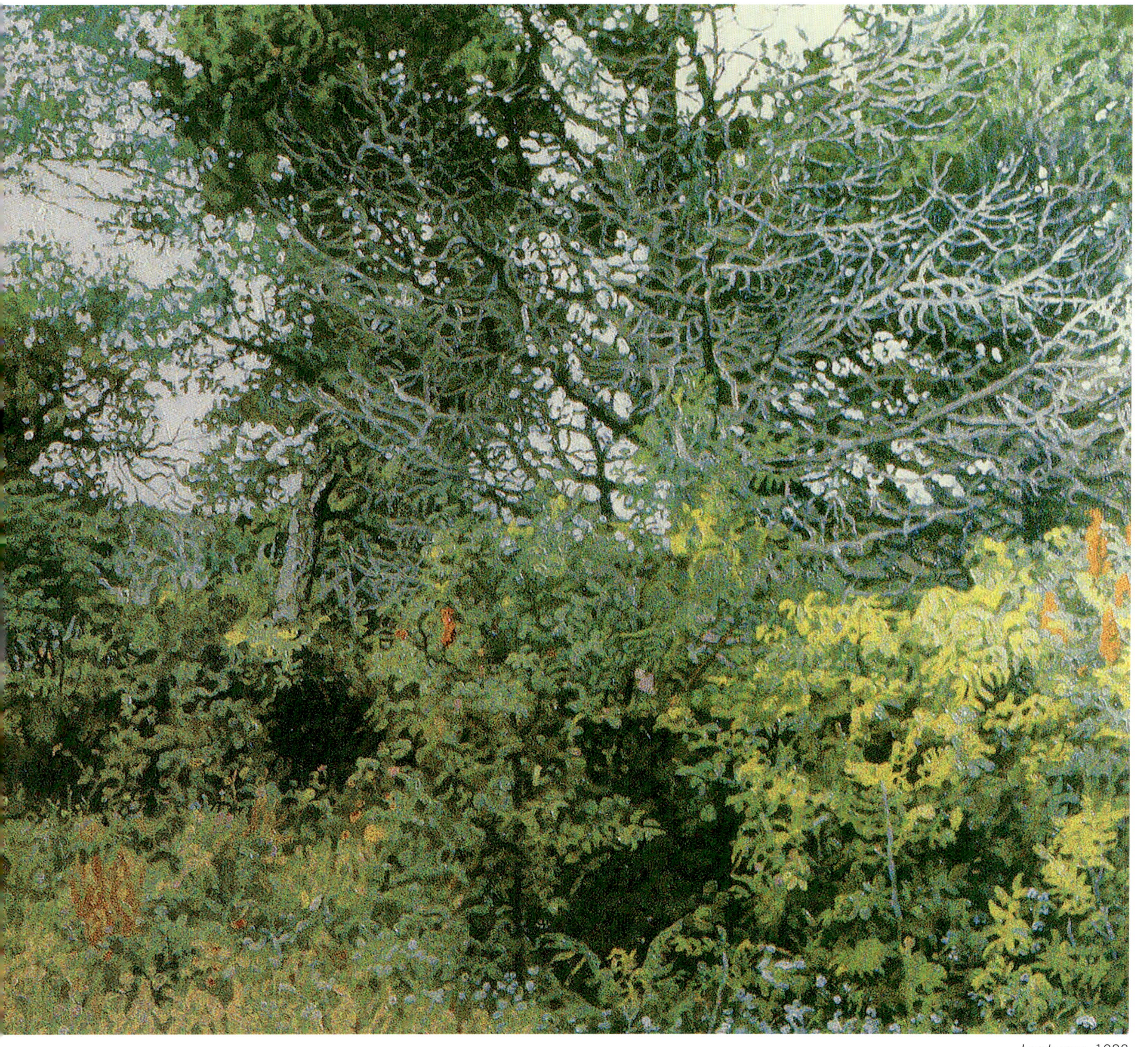

Landscape, 1982

oil on linen | 36" x 84" | Collection of Bryant and Nancy Hanley

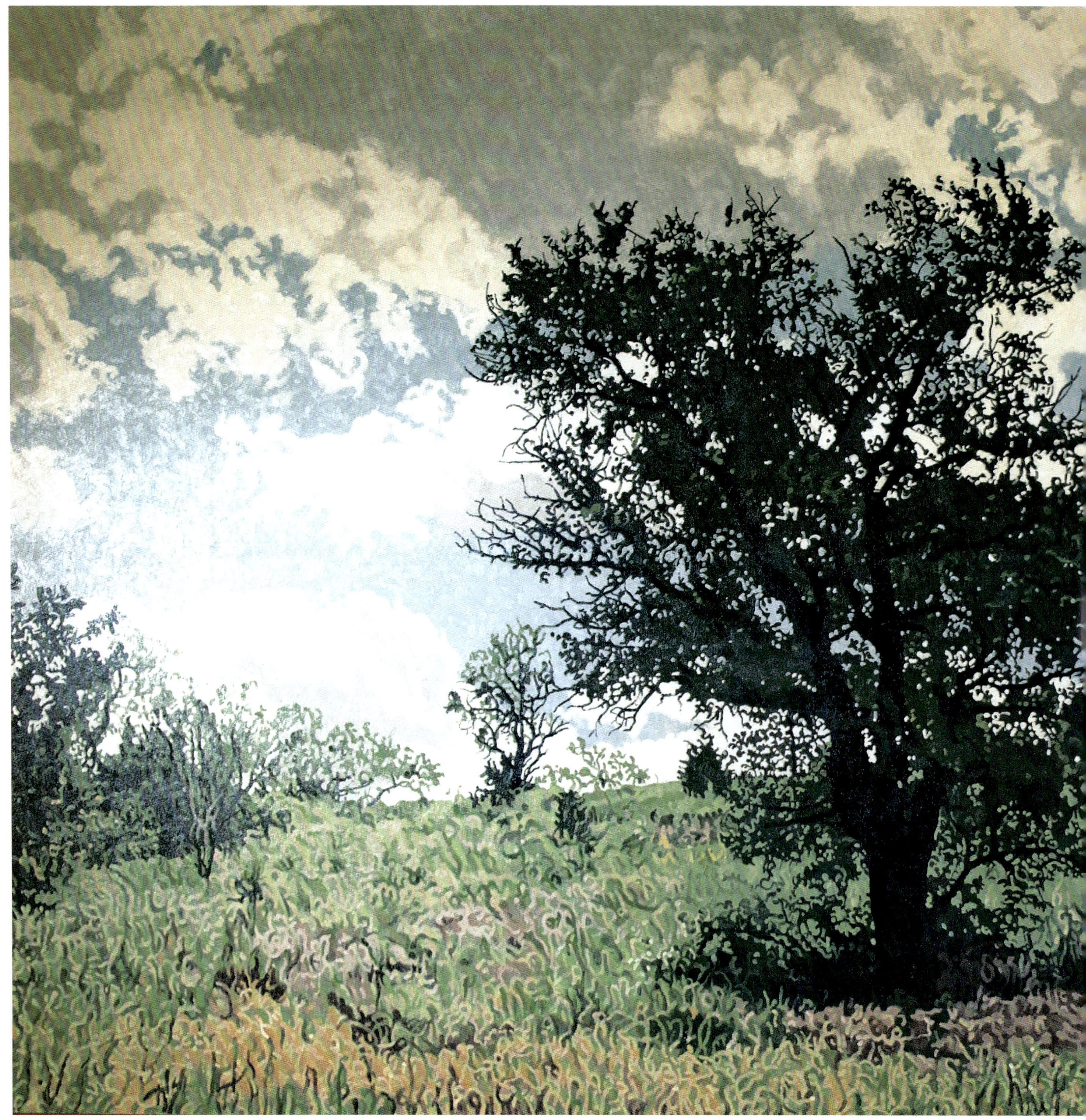

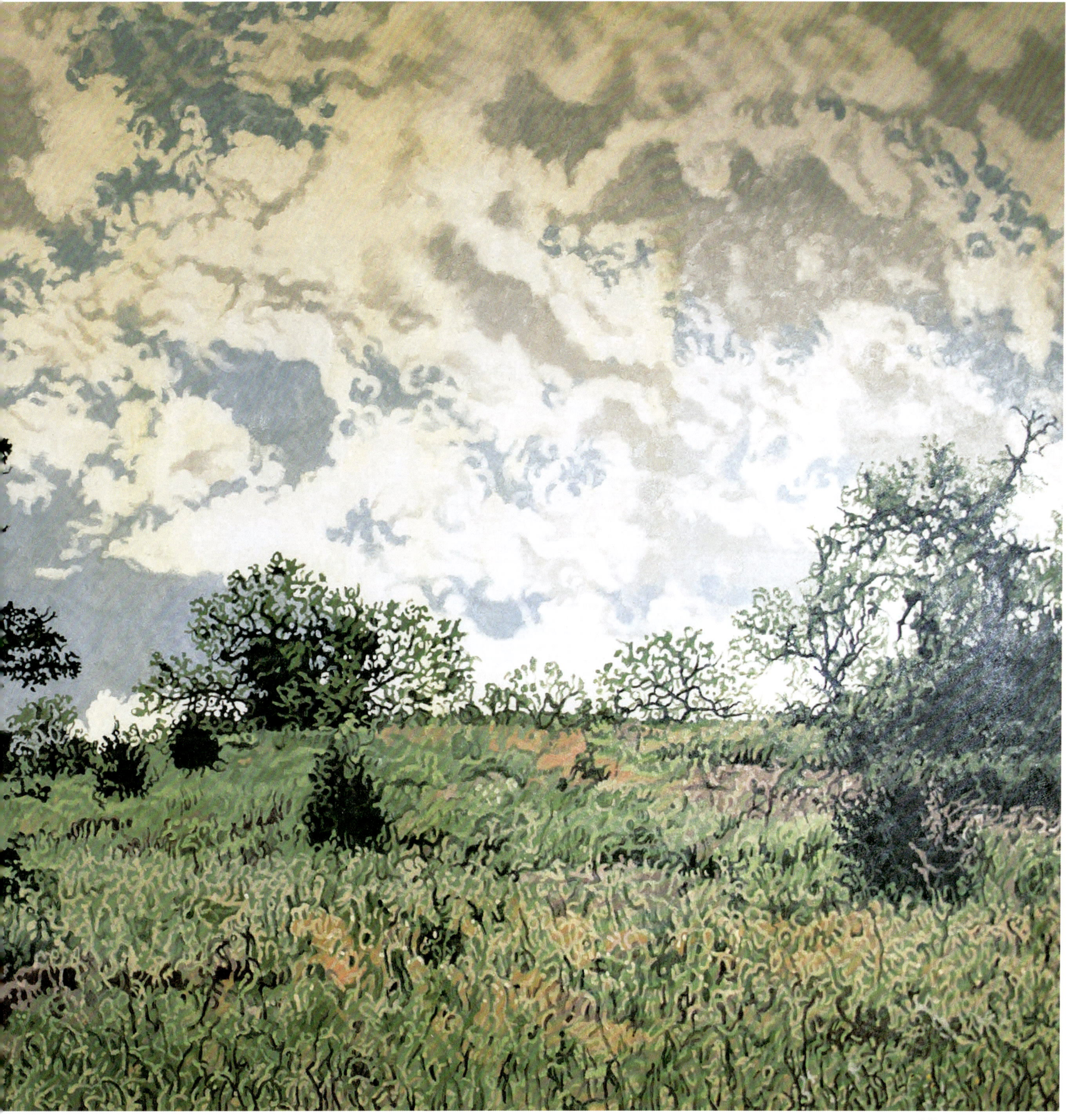

Silhouetted Trees, 1982

oil on linen | 120" x 240" | Collection of the Federal Reserve Bank of Dallas

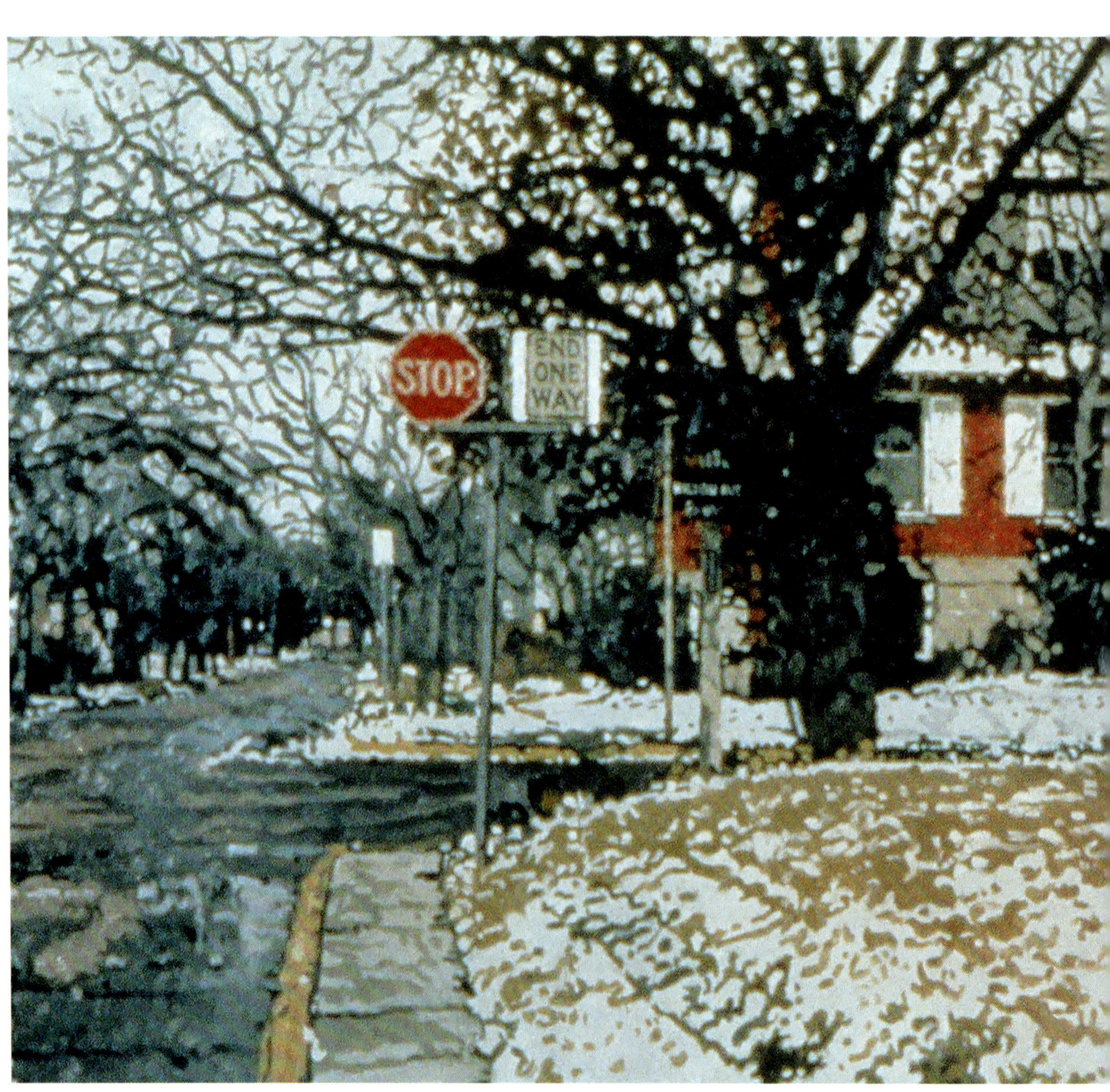
STOP
END
ONE
WAY

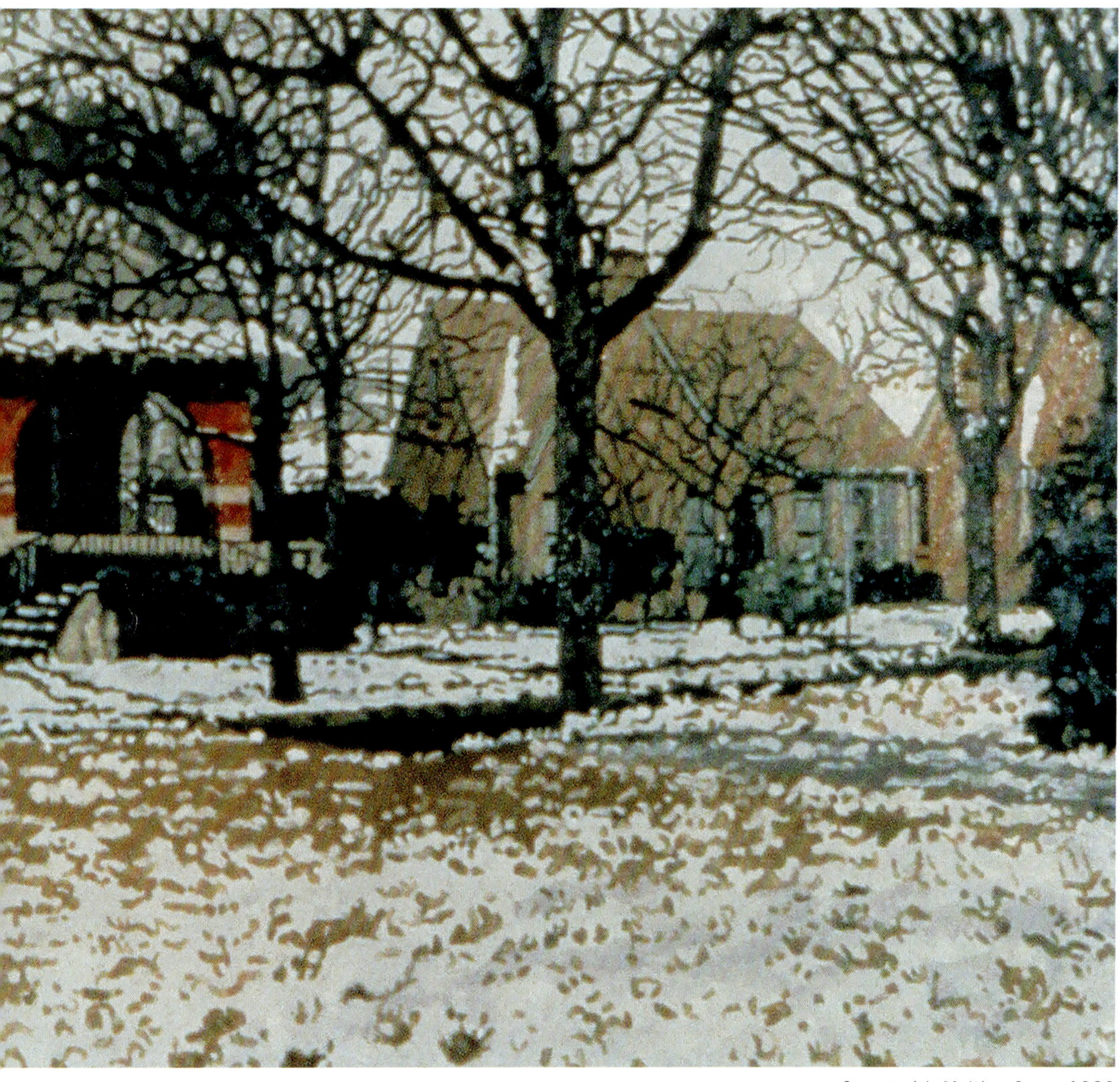

Street with Melting Snow, 1980
oil on linen | 36" x 84" | Courtesy of the artist

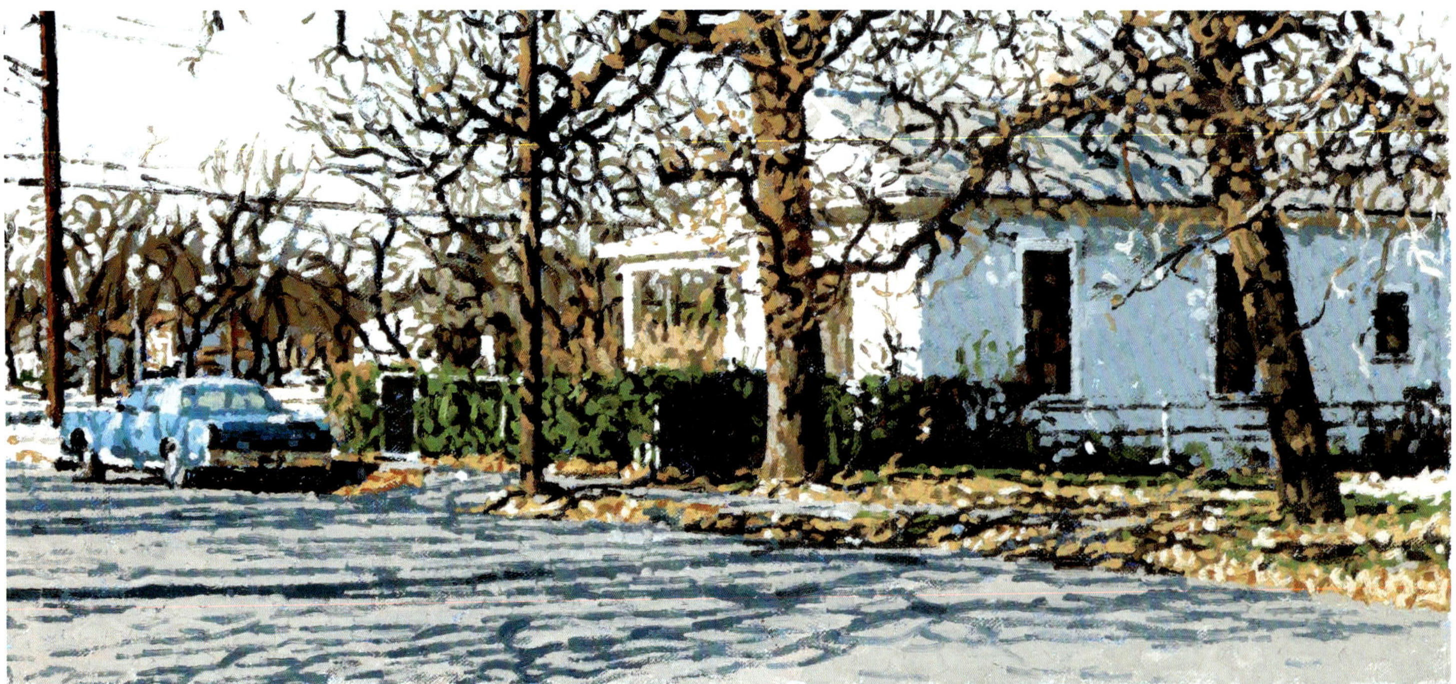

Dallas Street, 1986

oil on linen | 12" x 24" | Collection of Molly E. Moore | Photography by Kevin Todora

like small Proustian grenades. In *Union Square* (1983), billboard-size ads for the *Village Voice* and *A Chorus Line* are posted on the sides of old buildings. The equestrian statue of George Washington forms a pivot point around which thrust towering trees with very spiny branches that curl in on themselves or protrude like nerves imbedded in muscle tissue. Winter depicts complex layers of stacked urban forms—buildings, windows, water tanks, lamp posts, commercial and city signs—into which we can peer and beyond which are a silvery sky and fleeting rifts of clouds. It is an image that seems to be as much about a state of mind as about location—an early-morning place where what we see is about to be transformed into something else. Winter traverses Union Square with the same audacity with which he bounds from high-finance offices to anonymous dive bars. He zooms in to illuminate the spacious park, then zooms out to give us a seraphic, panoramic vista.

Winter painted Union Square several times over the years; each work captures the clamor of taxis, pedestrians, pigeons, and loafers all interacting with the statues and architecture from earlier generations. "I tried to get a feeling of Union Square," Winter explains. "It's a place to sit and have lunch; it's a place to walk a dog or take sunbaths on a blanket. It's had many different uses over the years. Union Square was New York's center for political freedom—American Communists held rallies there. A century ago, Childe Hassam painted Union Square as an elegant neighborhood bustling with people, carriages, and trams. Forty years later, Isabel Bishop and Reginald Marsh painted Union Square as a stage setting for shopgirls and derelicts. It was an era when the United States was becoming more urban and a lot of people looking for jobs, as well as 'loafers,' were coming in from rural places."

Winter's second *Union Square* (1988) is a large view of an intersection with a cacophony of signs, fast-food places, and discount stores, the street teeming with people and cars. According to Winter, this version was inspired by Red Grooms's monumental *Chance Encounter at 3 A.M.* (1984). The painting's setting, Washington Square Park at night, features two famous abstract expressionists, Mark Rothko and Willem de Kooning, seated on a bench with cigarette butts all around them, as if they had been visiting for hours. "I wanted to do a New York painting as sweeping, complex, inclusive, and direct as Red Grooms's painting," Winter says. "A year or so later, I settled on this view of Union Square with its McDonald's billboard of burger and fries, a block-long view of storefronts, multistoried buildings, a taxi, a bus, cars, pedestrians, police lines, dug-up street—I held nothing back and spent more than two months working each area to my own standards of resolution of image and form." Indeed, the colors—yellows, reds, gray-blues—and their mix of light and squiggly brushstrokes seem to jump off the canvas with explosions of energy and movement. By keeping the images close to the surface, however, they maintain the flatness of the picture plane while allowing us the pleasures of mental contrast or a modernist flip-flop between material surface and illusory depth. Spaced more or less evenly over the surface, the pictorial field invites a slow look. As we spend more time with the painting, as our eyes adjust, the space begins to open up: to be sure, the formally and technically inexhaustible imagery—precise hand lettering, geometric structures, and active figures—start working for us when we start working with them—getting close-up information, backing up to integrate it, getting more close-up information. Time is the key—how long we can pay attention in a quick-take era.

Such painstaking conflations of realism, form, and narrative animate most of Winter's New York City works. However, he is not an ostentatious painter. He applies oil to canvas with just enough character that we do not forget what his uncannily realistic images are made of. Accordingly, their technical understatement is frequently reflected in the works that depict mundane things. Often his plainspoken way turns poetic. Nowhere is this more evident than in the paintings produced after the summer of 1985, when the Winters rented a brownstone in Park Slope and made side trips to visit Neil Welliver and family in Maine. In these, he achieves an allover focus that seems slightly more intense than that of everyday perception. They are open in a different way from that of previous work; they are not expressing but meditating, and it seems that what they are meditating on is natural rhythms, including those found in urban contexts. Forms sometimes blur into one another; edges are softened. He knows just how much to bend a line or blend a tone so that the entire composition remains both a depiction and a gratifying complex of painted marks. There is a hypnotic quality to these paintings, which pose questions concerning the internal relationships between and among things, including the relationship between life and art.

For *Coney Island*, Winter returns to the area in which he and Jeanette lived as young artists, drawn to its sense of age, its history, and its patina of time. Winter derives rhythmic repetitions of horizontal, vertical, and complementary diagonals from the edges of buildings and flat or angled roofs. But despite the decided warmth of the light, the ambience seems mildly detached and surreal. The painting resonates a disquieting sense of loneliness that seems to endow the most mundane details of everyday life with yearnings. He captures the eroded surface of an abandoned building, including the graffiti—"Comacho is star"—in the lower left corner. Here, the lettering, the brick surface, and the metal fence in the foreground are worn down or reclaimed by nature. What's more, Winter matches the natural growth with the rhythm of brushstrokes. Each mark is a formal element in sync with the overall treatment. We scan the darkened and shattered windows, finally settling on a single figure—an African American man who leans out of the window of the third floor, dwarfed by all around him.

In *Central Park* (1985), however, Winter focuses on one of Manhattan's most beloved open spaces. A mecca for children who gather at the pond to sail model ships, the dramatically landscaped area also offers opportunities for bird watching, strolling, or sitting by the water's edge. Evocative of Georges Seurat's *A Sunday Afternoon on the Island of La Grande Jatte* (1884), which depicts people relaxing in a suburban park on an island in the Seine River, rendered through the pointillist technique of small dots in complementary colors that appear as luminous forms at a distance, Winter's painting is alive with tension, despite its exquisite crystalline composure. Here, every brushstroke leads a double life as part of a painterly illusion

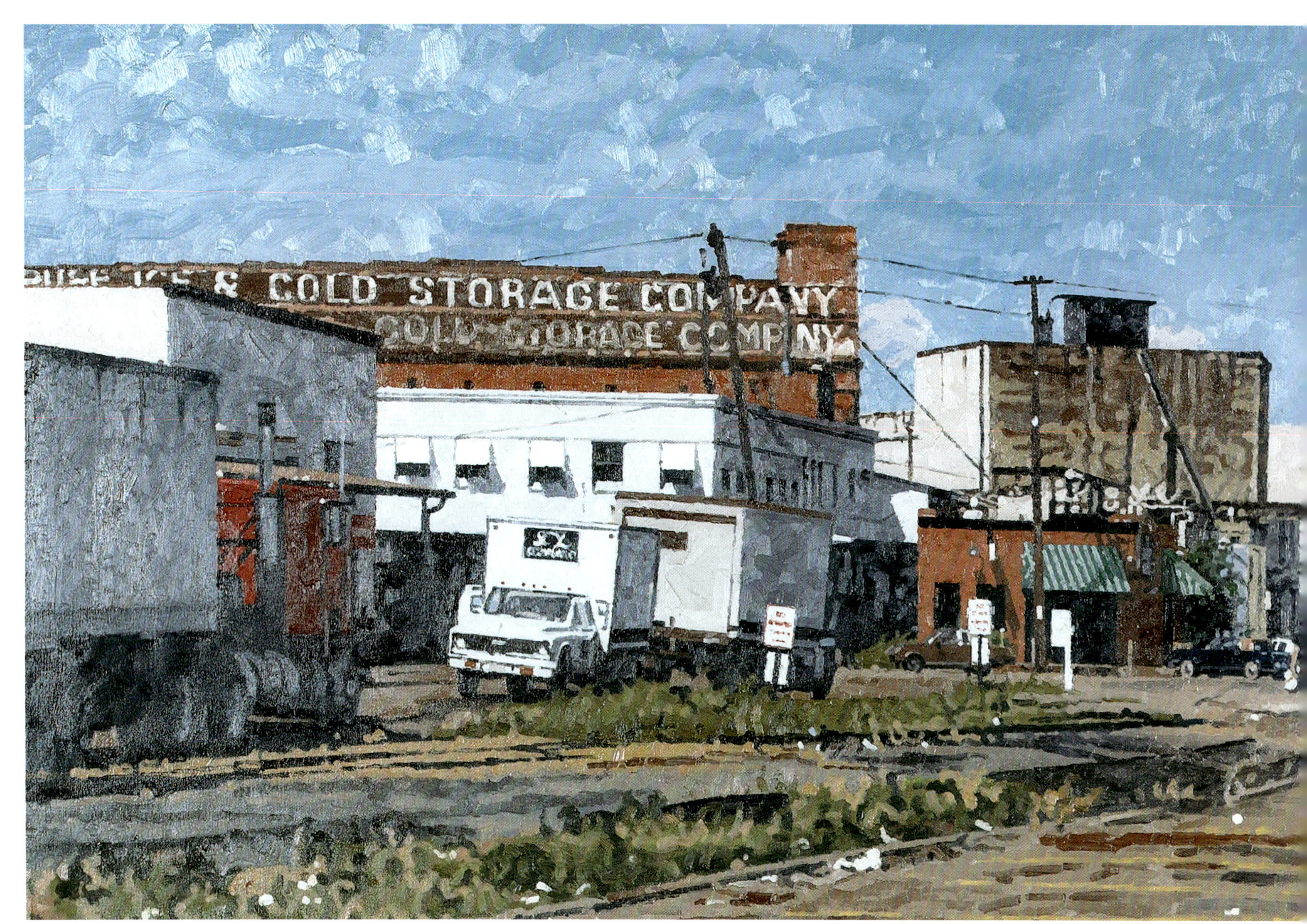
& COLD STORAGE COMPANY
COLD STORAGE COMPANY

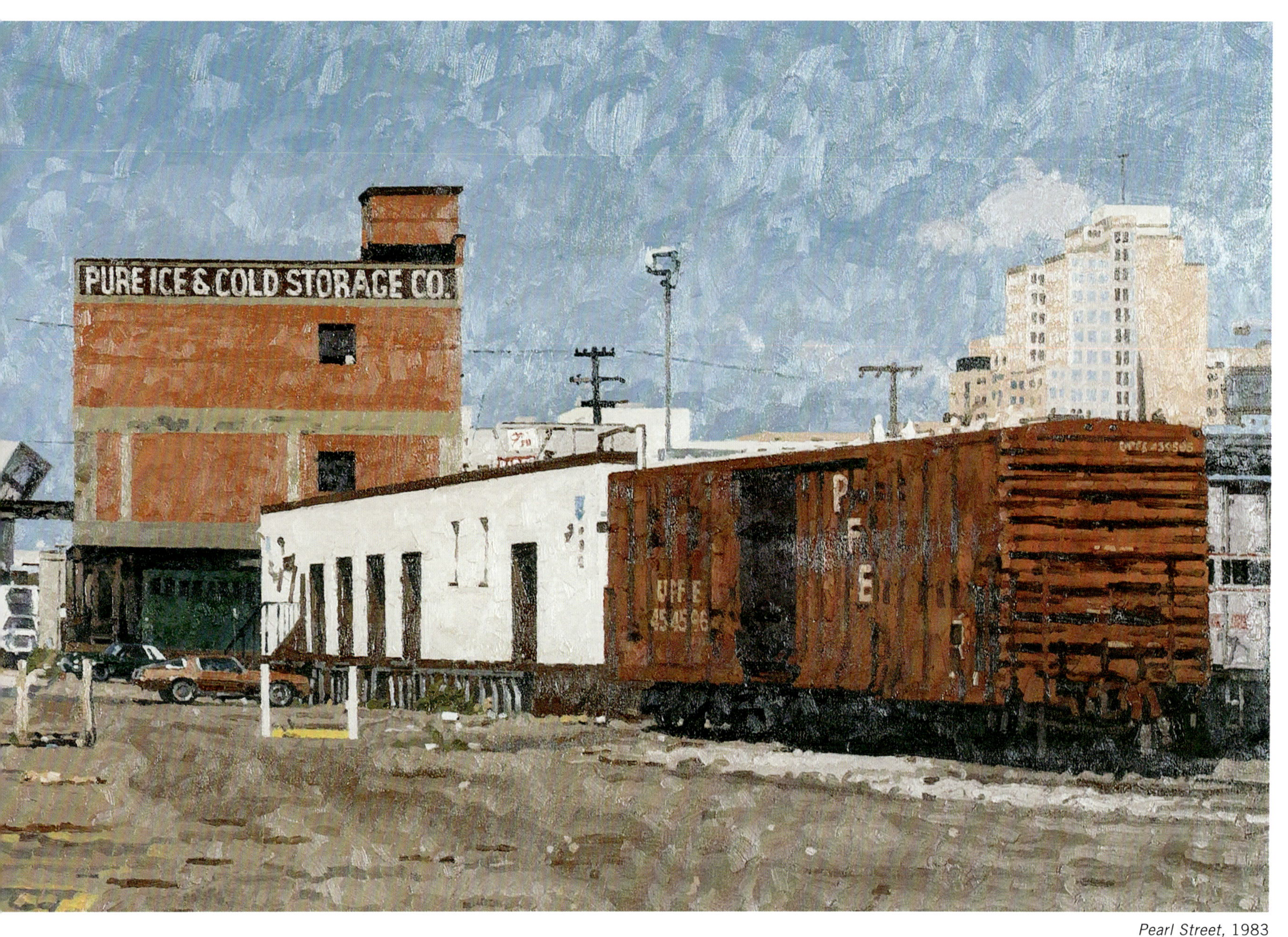

Pearl Street, 1983

oil on linen | 30" x 86" | Cele and John Carpenter Family Collection | Photography by Jason Voinov

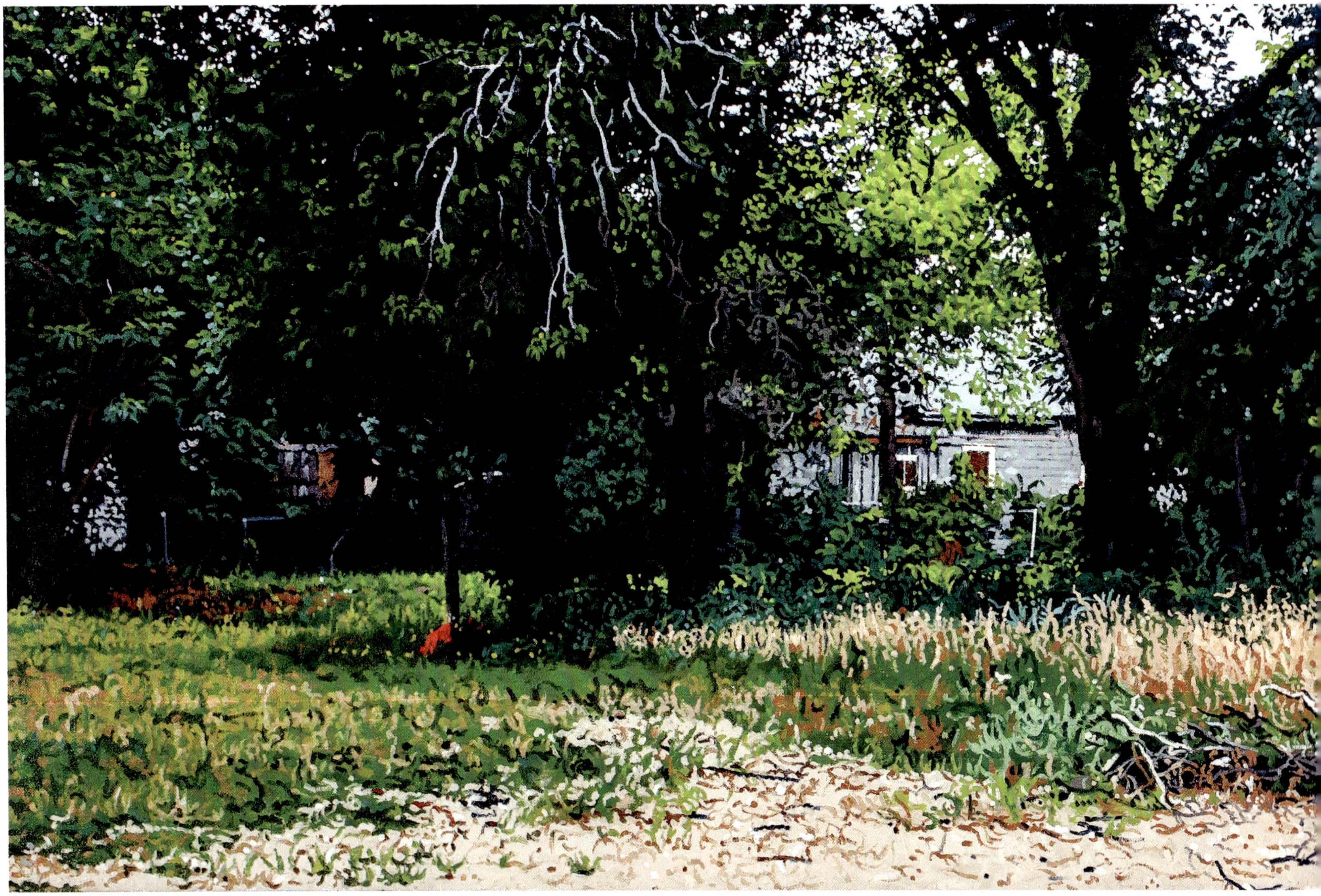

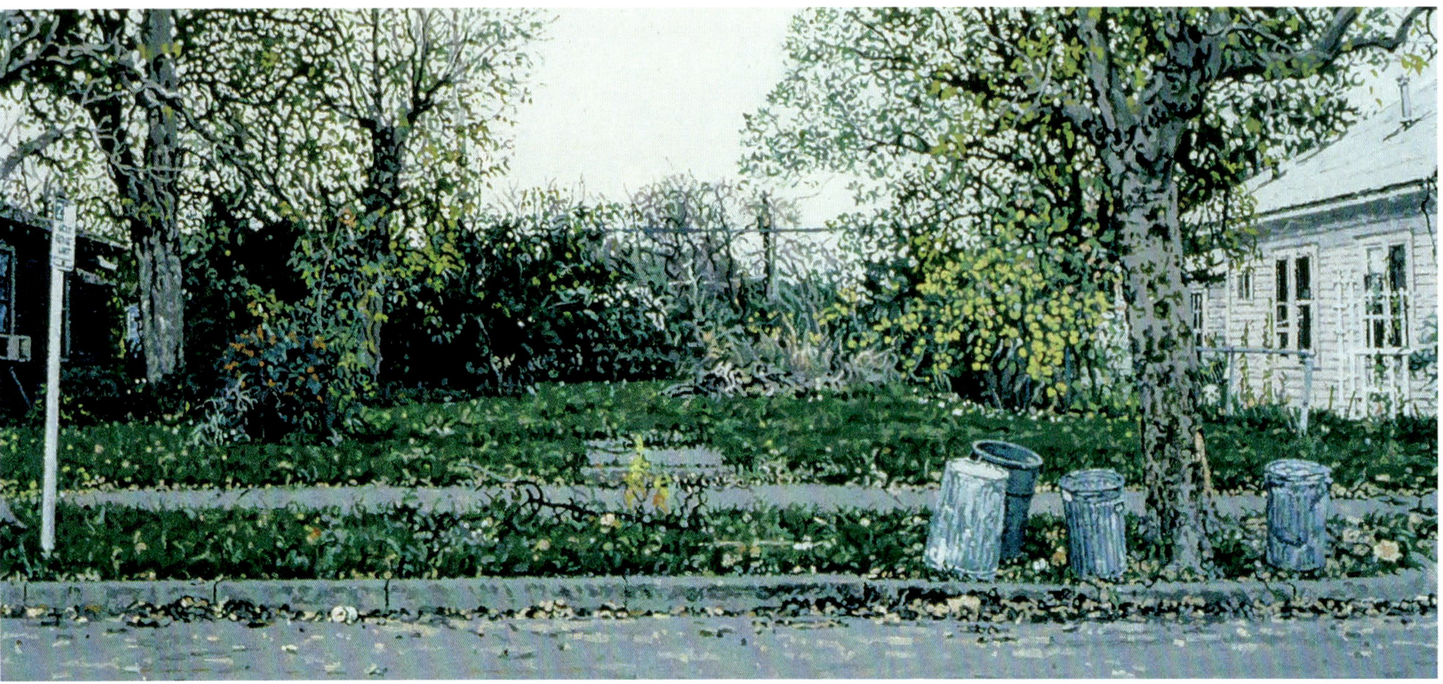

Vacant Lot, Old Highland Park, 1986

oil on linen | 24" x 54" | Collection of Kate Bower

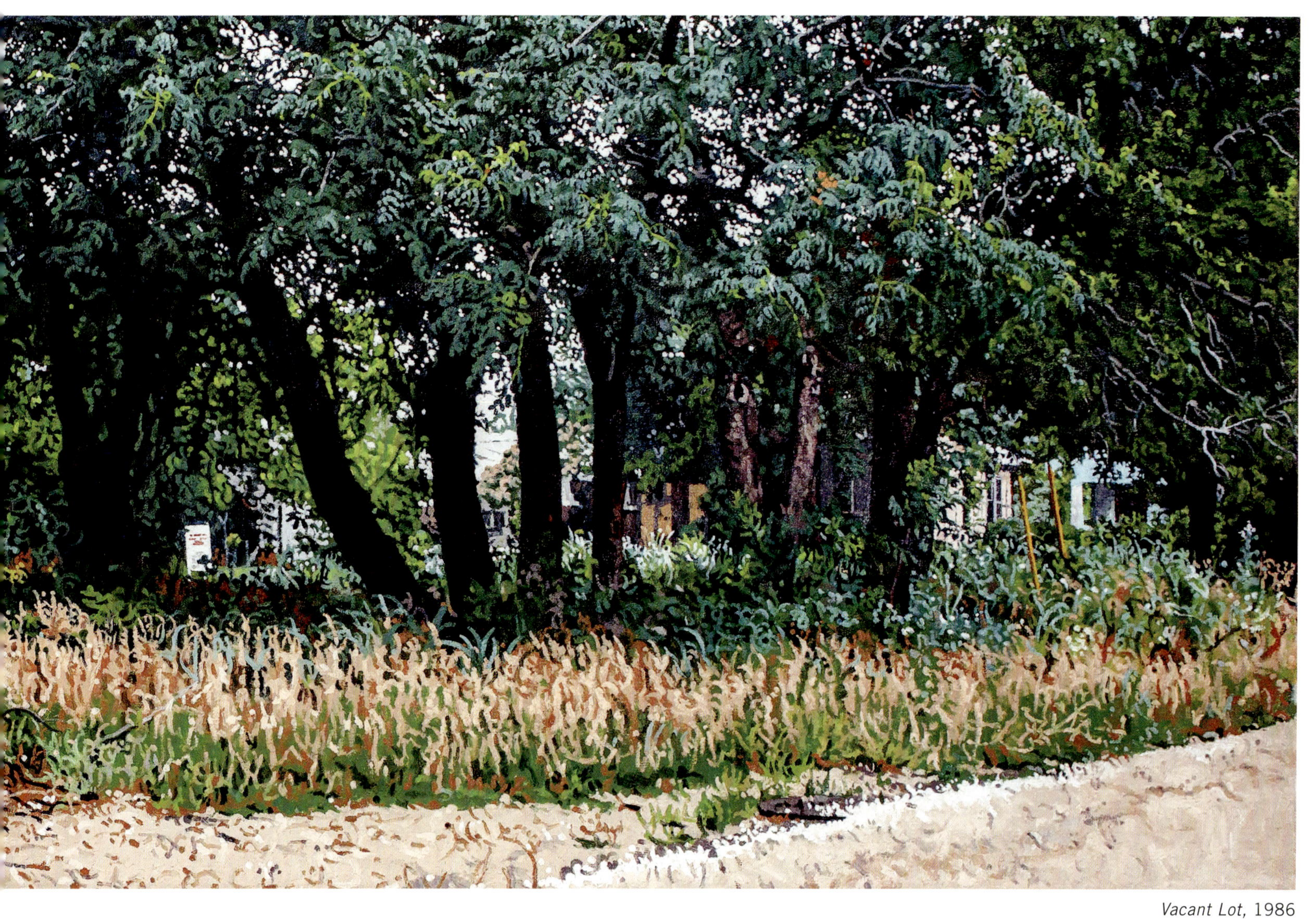

Vacant Lot, 1986

oil on linen | 34" x 106" | Collection of Craig and Kathryn Hall

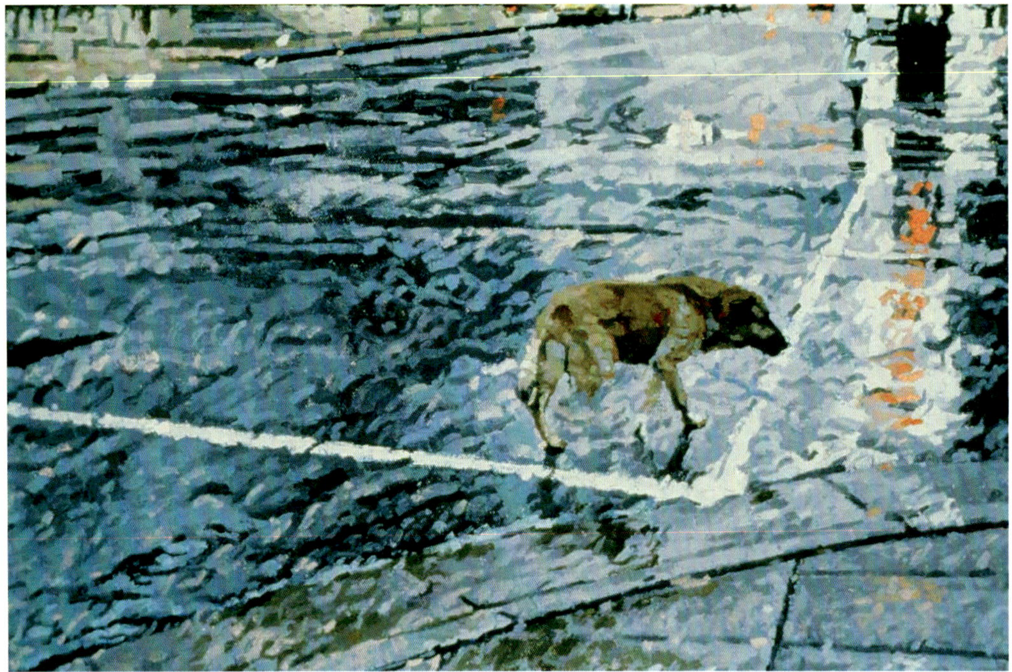

Stray Dog, 1986
oil on linen | 16" x 24" | Courtesy of the artist

and as a thing itself, a patch of pigment on canvas. The eye hovers and zooms over the surface like a dragonfly, exploring its horizontal recessions and watery depths, its intimations of reflection. But it is the paradox of Winter that his multitude of discrete strokes can destabilize forms even as he builds them up, dissolving them into a force field of shimmering marks. As with our dragonfly gaze, they skip between figures and across the surface. Paint is applied in thatches of wiggling and serpentine strokes in shades of blue, green, and saffron yellow; in trails of horizontal ellipses that move from turquoise to bright green to dark green as they traverse the canvas in and out of shade. It is as if radiant energy were collected between the modest and disciplined brushstrokes. Notwithstanding the knit skin of surface, form, and color, the painting vigorously conveys a sense of the hand in motion, searching. Winter manages to take an unabashedly beautiful lavender and mint green, or an intense hot pink, and make them float, as if they were as light and ethereal as air.

For the most part, viewers of Winter's works are witnesses, rather than participants. The exacerbation of distance, the gulf that silence opens up between spectator and image, takes both subject and viewer outside time. Often, Winter emphasizes life in suspension—hence the meditative, immersive quality of these works, which are really worlds unto themselves. For *Prospect Park* (1985) in Brooklyn, we are voyeurs at a family gathering in a lovely landscape space. Winter comments, "This painting was about ephemeral things—smoke, human gestures, the movement of leaves, summer. Brooklyn was not yet the home of the NYC art world's movable feast. Brooklyn lacked the energy and style of Manhattan, so it was possible to spend a Sunday afternoon with friends or family and a barbecue grill. Real estate was still reasonable, so one didn't need to be wealthy to enjoy the good life in this vast stretch of manicured landscape not far from home—walking distance for many, including us." In creating the work, Winter allowed the underpainting to show through in order to convey a sense of air and light. The approach also gives a breadth to physical space that cannot be achieved by impasto or transparency. Throughout, the brushwork is scintillating and rhythmic, dematerializing solids with loosely applied swaths of silvery greens and pearly grays shot through

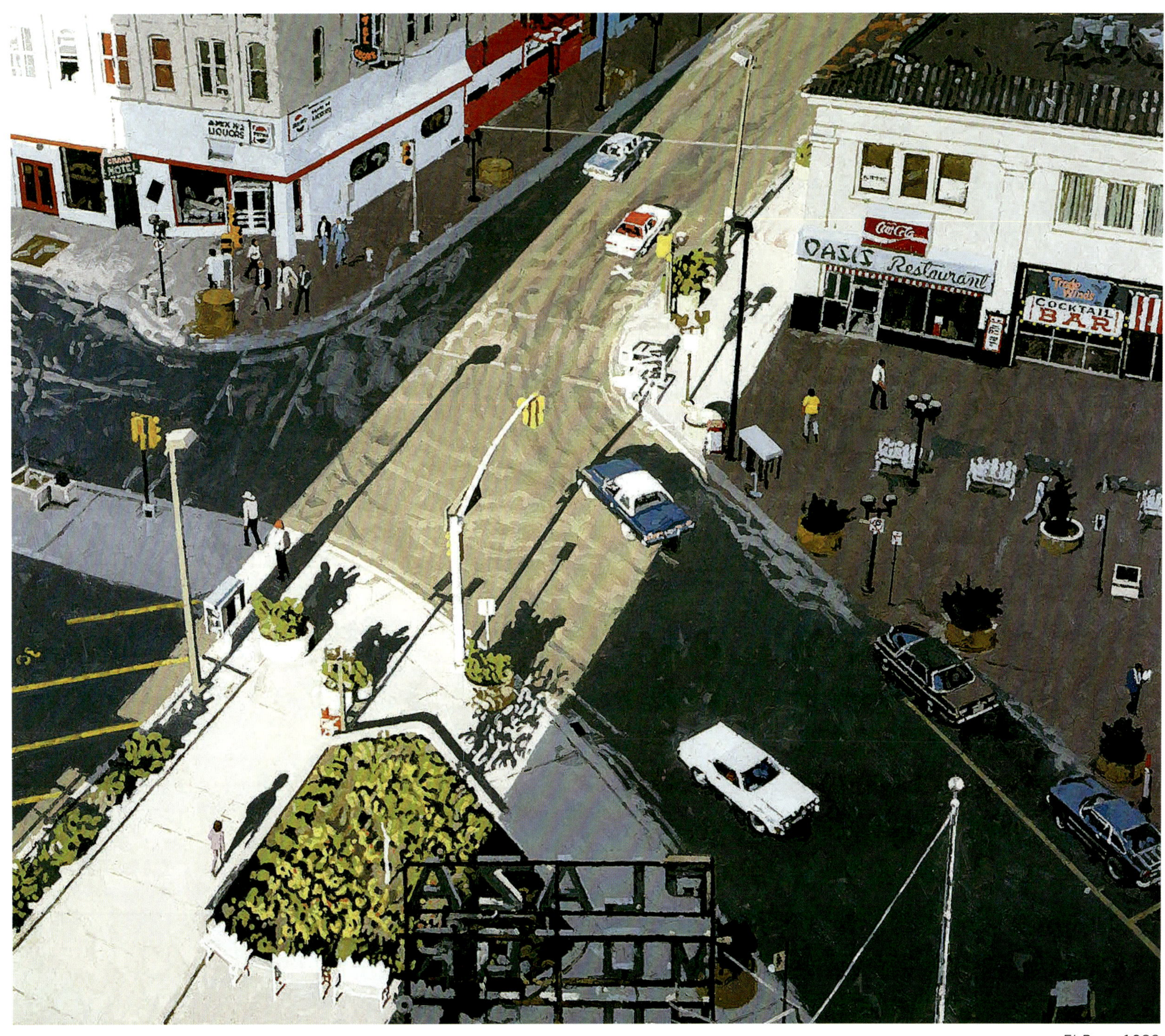

El Paso, 1983

oil on canvas | 62" x 74" (1 m 57.48 cm x 1 m 87.96 cm) | Dallas Museum of Art, gift of Mr. and Mrs. S. Roger Horchow | 1990.184

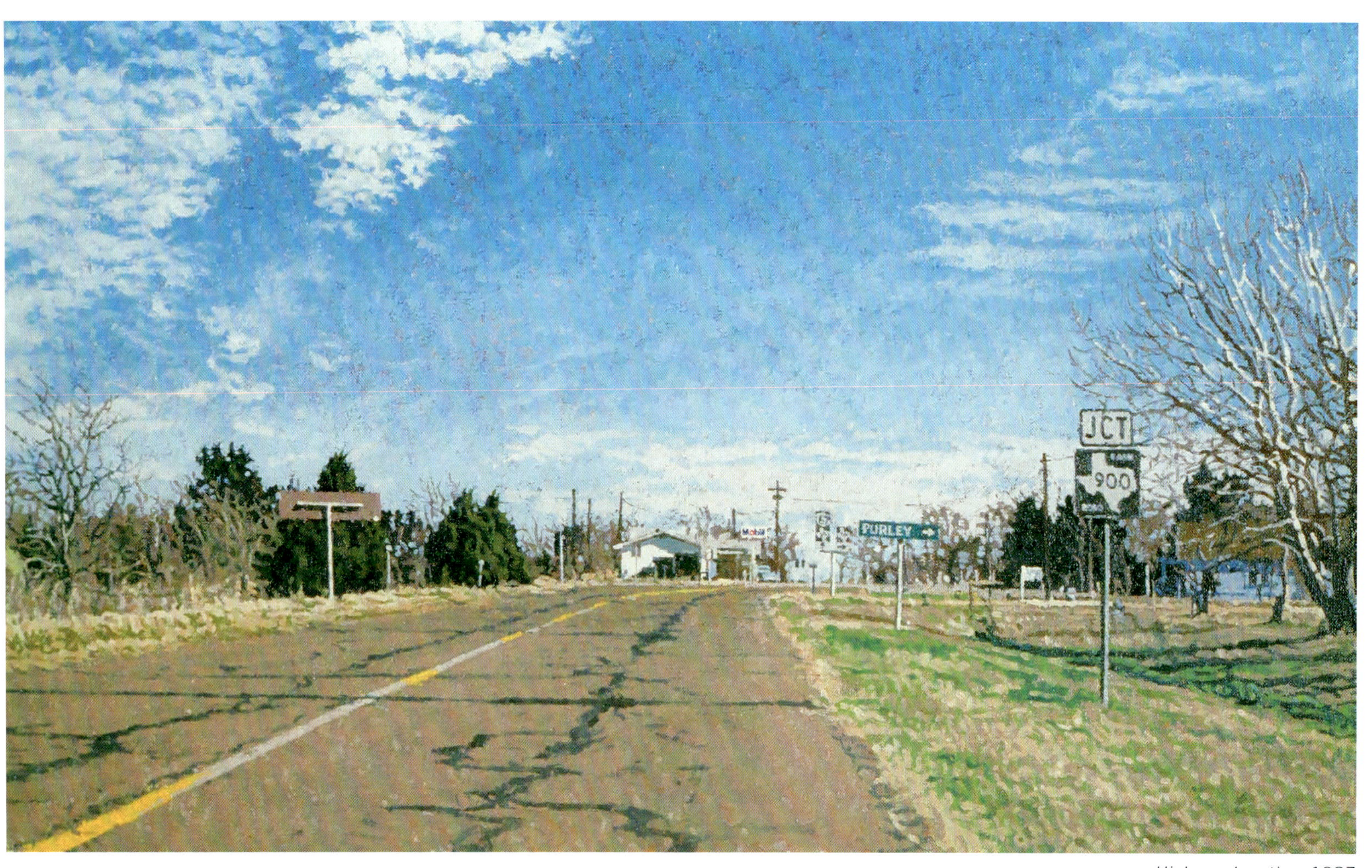

Highway Junction, 1987

oil on linen | 18" x 50" | Courtesy of the artist

with delicate opalescences. Concentrating more on subtleties of color and spaces than on spectacular visual devices, Winter aims to establish dissonant juxtapositions of light and shadow that are slightly jarring yet strangely seductive. Here, the brushstrokes move in exciting staccato rhythms wherein colorful hues set up an array of shifts and pops; the illusory space between flowers, fields, and figures becomes a lush, vibrating zone.

Indeed, the general effect of the New York City paintings is rhapsodic. To that end, Winter undercuts easy sentiment, using beauty as a sign and force for liberation. Whether culturally relative or time bound, beauty transcends stylistic trends and in itself cannot be severed from life. Winter's paintings, however, press the issue of beauty in art. They seem to be saying that beauty, at least for a moment, has much to do with richness, and complexity. Winter may render the foliage and trees with a scientist's eye for exactitude, but he does so with a poet's feeling for nature's plentitude. "Something beautiful is something complete and full," Winter explains. "It's like comparing Thanksgiving or Christmas dinner to a cocktail, which has a zing to it but it's not complete. The spontaneous can be beautiful too. In a painting, I try to make it thorough and complete formally and pictorially—every little detail is part of the whole, and all together they make a unity."

In many ways, Winter was simply following his earlier work to its logical conclusion. He remained engrossed in the challenge of looking and painting, never wavering in his task of translating his perception of the visible into oil on canvas, bringing the natural and artificial into handwrought balance. Winter knew that painting, like poetry or music, was one of the few endeavors that could convey some of nature's richness, if he just kept at it. With this in mind, Winter also spent countless hours in the galleries of the Metropolitan Museum of Art, an integral part of his ongoing education as an artist. He studied the seventeenth-century Dutch painters—Johannes Vermeer's portraits that embodied domestic themes, as well as Jacob van Ruisdael's and Jan van Goyen's landscapes and maritime scenes. He looked at paintings by nineteenth-century French artists, including Jean-François Millet's depictions of peasant farmers and rural life. Winter cites Théodore Rousseau's *The Forest in Winter at Sunset* (1846–67) as particularly relevant. The monumental forest scene re-creates the effect of a fiery sunset in a section of the Fontainebleau forest and features two small figures huddled before a tangled web of trees. The painting captured the kind of dense landscape and irradiating light that Winter was searching for in his own work.

For Winter, nature is an ideal external model in that everything inanimate or alive is connected yet of separate integrity. Eventually, however, his eye yields to the dictates of imagination, prompted by the immediacy of memory. Indeed, Winter's capacity for emotional complication also comes from an ability to look at the world with a childlike innocence. While living in Park Slope, Winter searched for a humble human scene to paint and found it outside his back porch. The family next door had just strung up its laundry from an upstairs window across the yard. "I thought of my mother's clothesline and the picture of her bringing in the box of valuables from the storm cellar," Winter says. "In that photograph there are sheets and clothes flapping on the line nearby as she walks toward the house. She had a very grim look on her face. But when I saw the laundry strung between buildings, I thought there's something here that was brought from the country, brought from rural life to urban life." The upshot is the ambitious *Park Slope*, in which a complex network of telephone wires, fire escapes, brick buildings, leafy trees, and the clothesline hung with brightly colored garments form a lyrical interchange of organic and geometric forms. Here, every element has a rising, hovering, or sagging weight, achieved by Winter's finesse with density and space. We move from the sharp contour of paint to the larger geometry of forms, weaving in and out of extreme fluctuations of light. When we see the array of pants, shirts, and underwear swinging like bright banners at a distance, we also see around them, behind them—an effect of animated, living depth. We become aware of the layering of planes of actual distance, one thing in front of another. Just as important as the painting's sets of intersecting paths and segments is the sense that Winter can include everything, can compose his painting

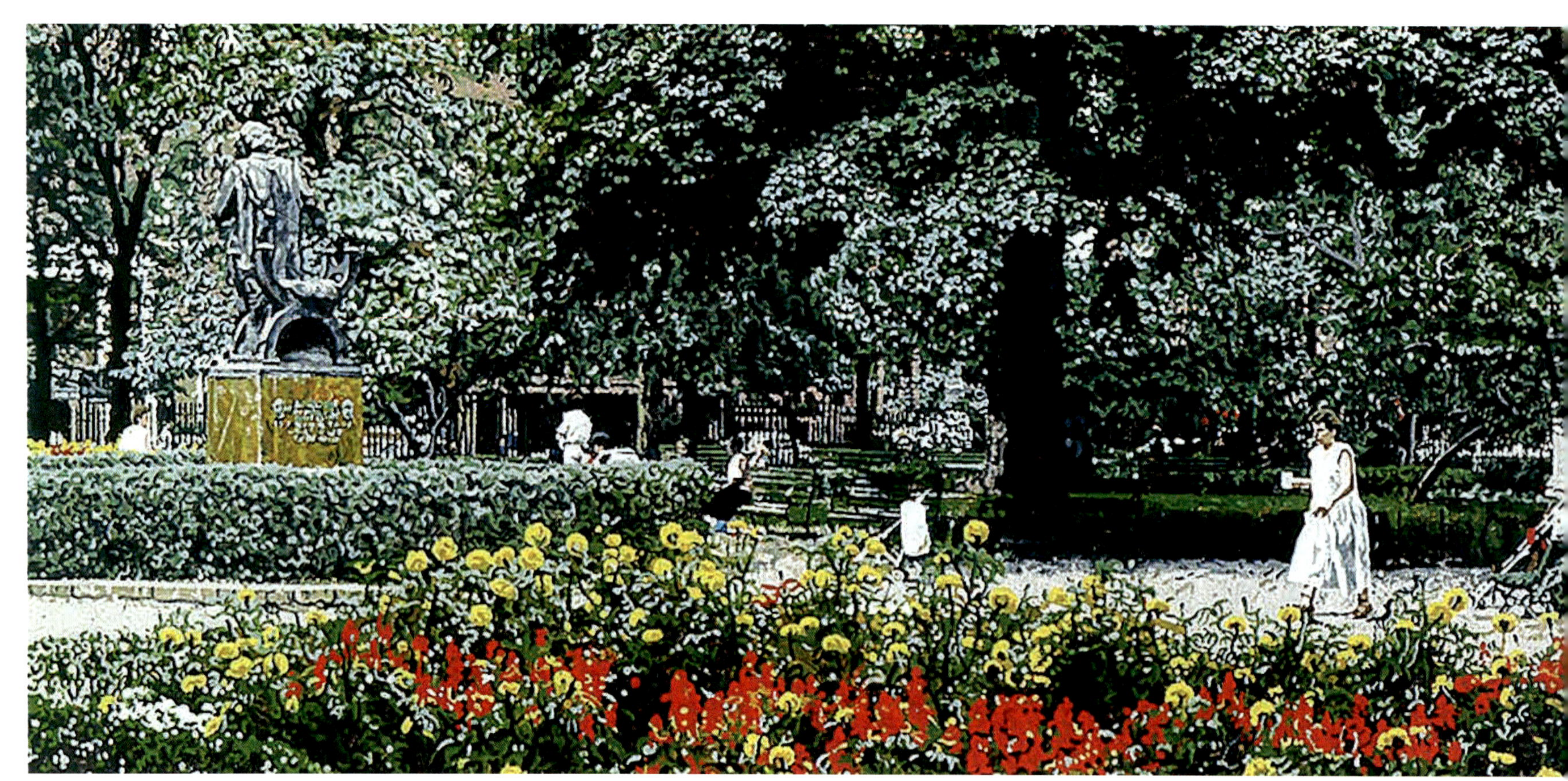

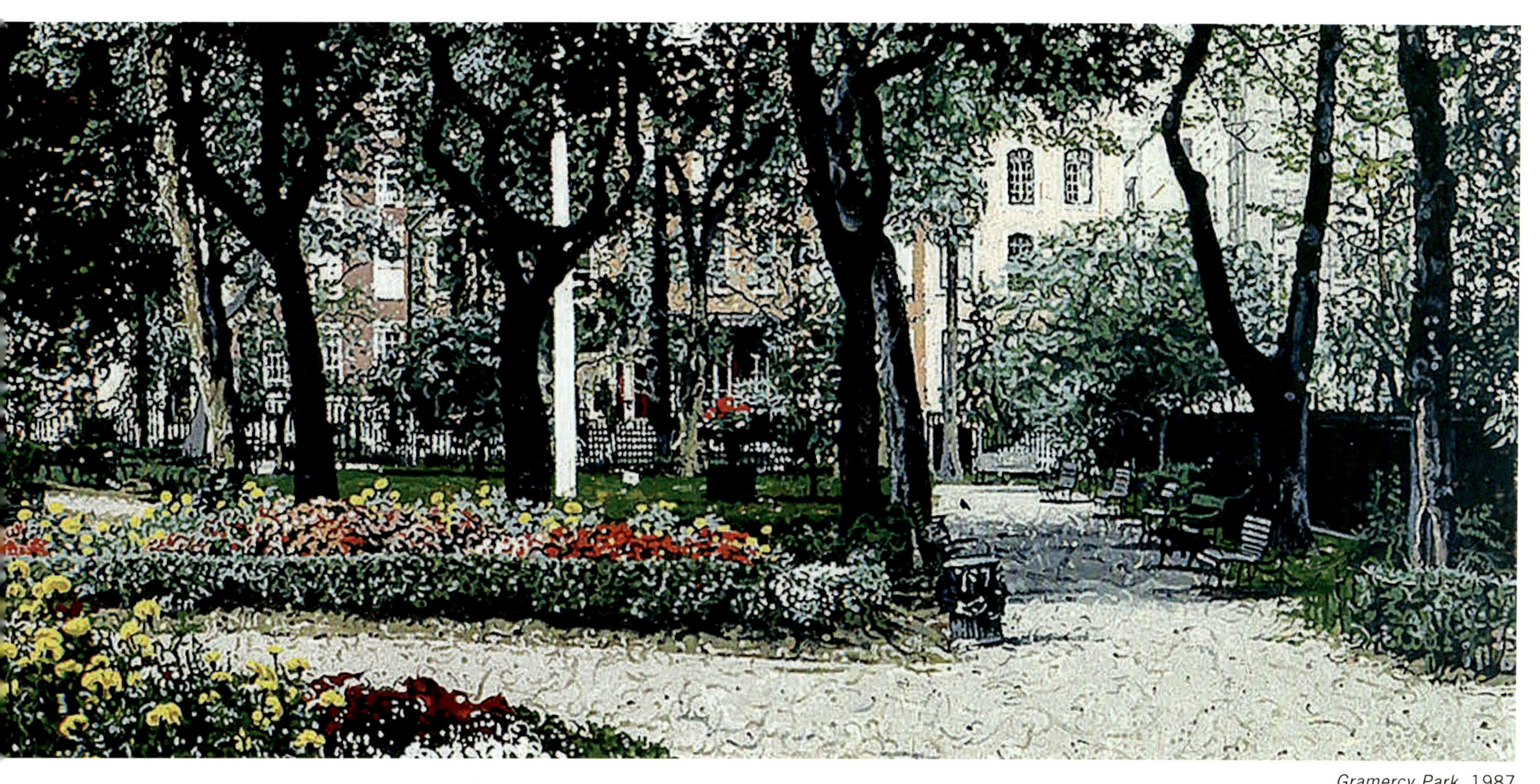

Gramercy Park, 1987

oil on linen | 36" x 120" | Courtesy of the artist

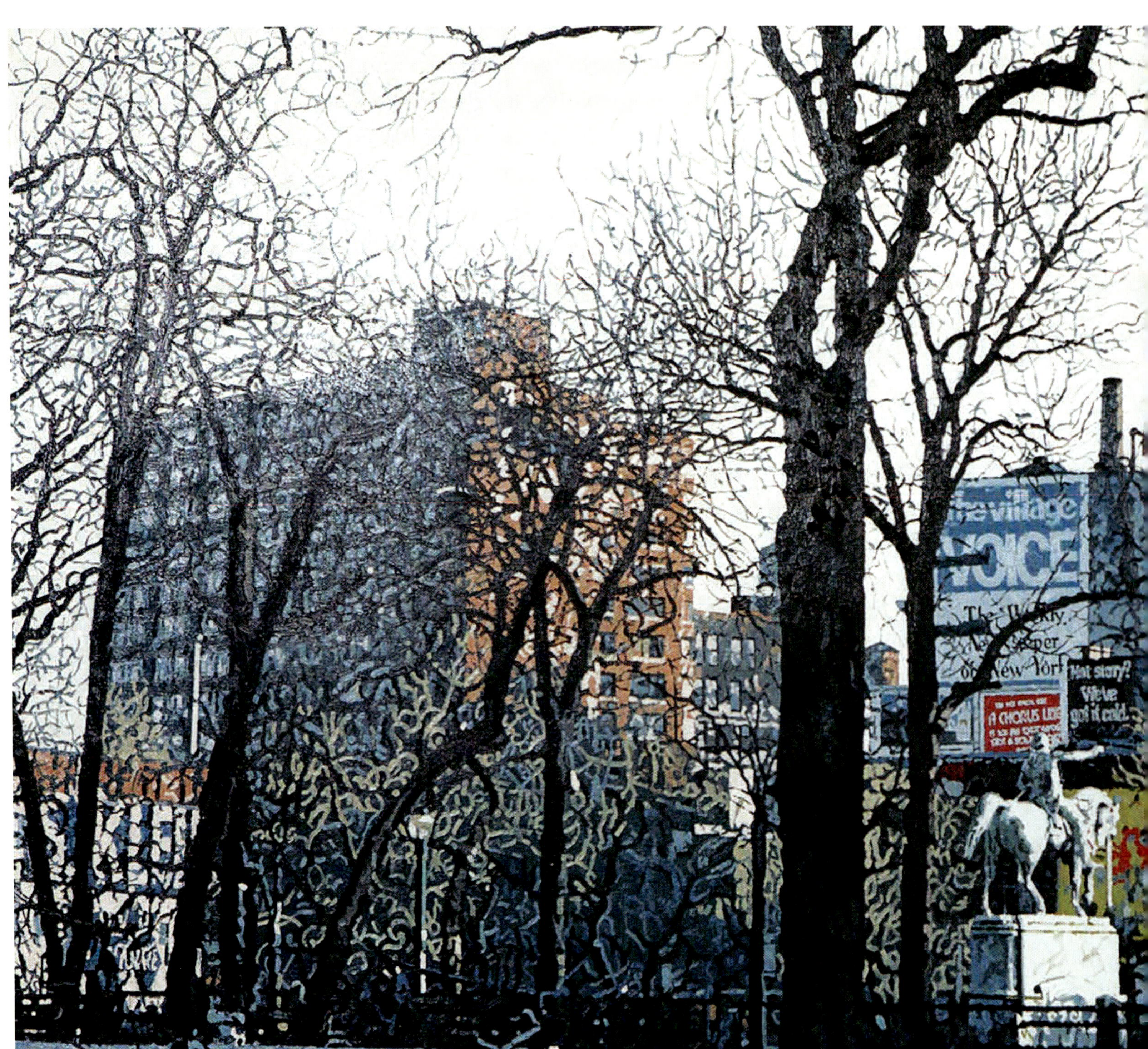
village
VOICE
Hot story?
We've
got it cold.

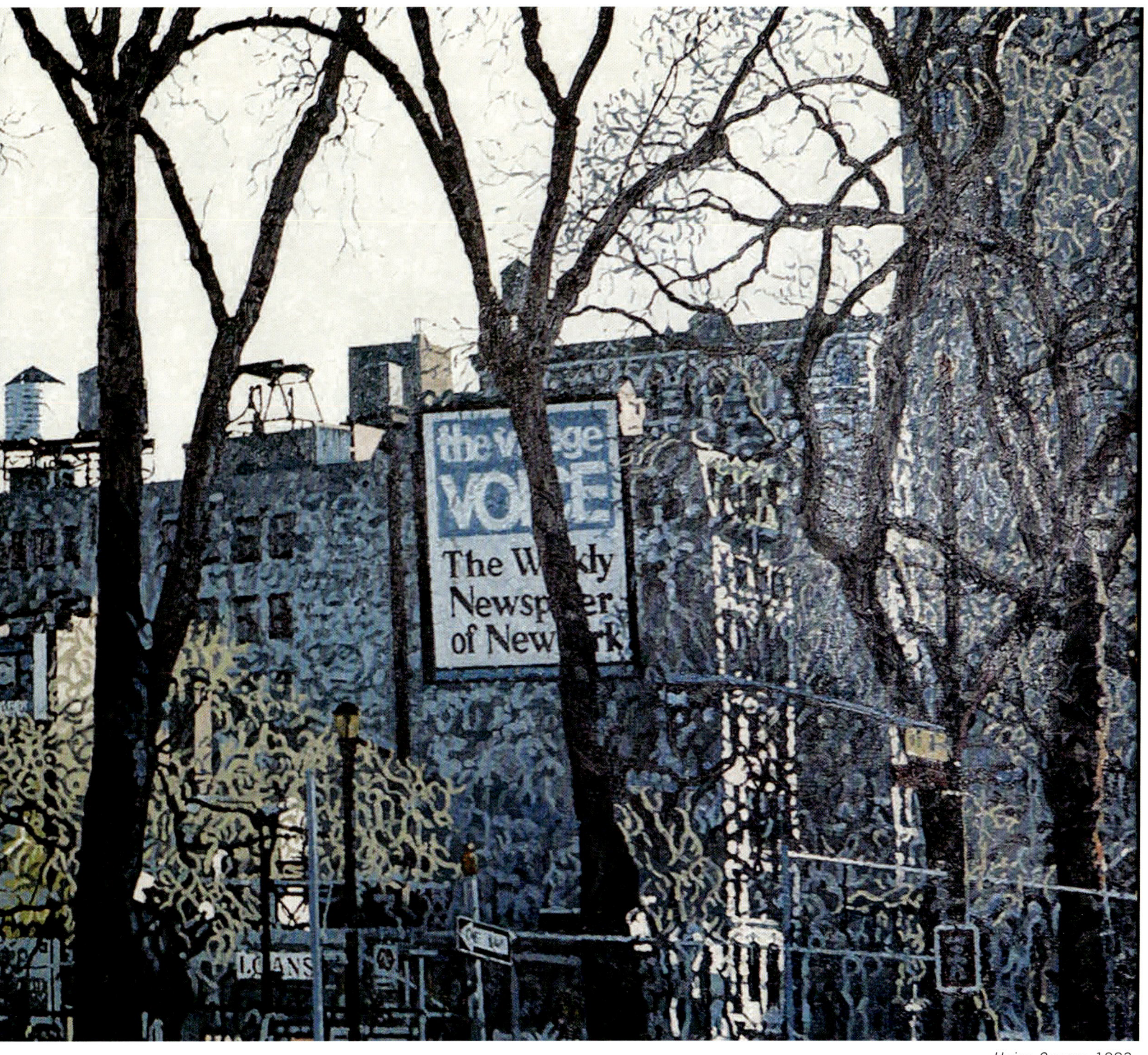

Union Square, 1983

oil on linen | 48" × 108" | Collection of Susan H. Albritton, Dallas | Photography by Fernando Rojas

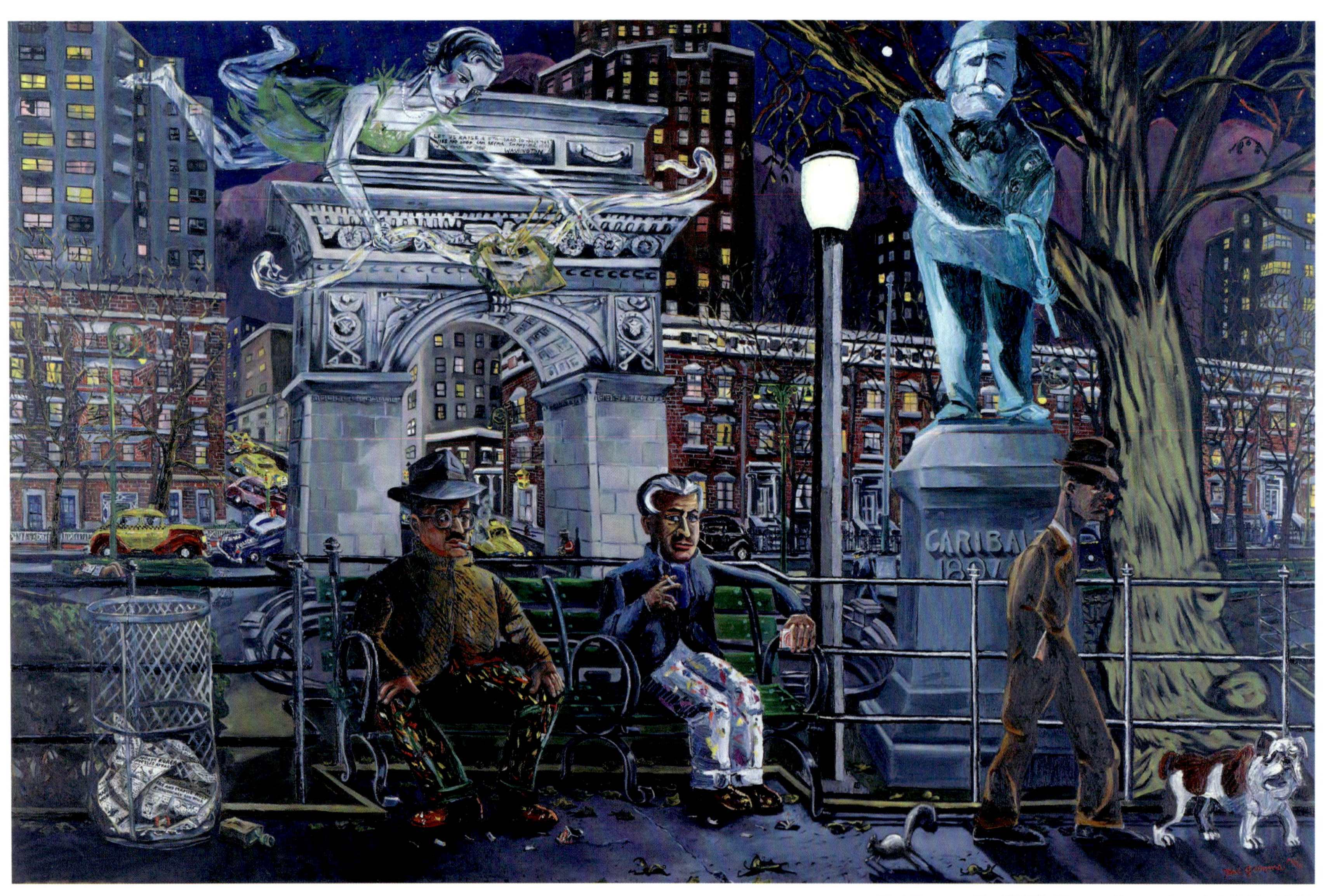

Red Grooms (b. 1937) Chance Encounter at 3 A.M., 1984

oil on canvas | 100" × 155" (254 × 393.7 cm) | Purchase, Mr. and Mrs. Wolfgang Schoenborn Gift, 1984 | 1984.194 |
The Metropolitan Museum of Art, New York, NY, USA | Image copyright © The Metropolitan Museum of Art | Image source: Art Resource, NY |
© Red Grooms, Member of Artists Rights Society (ARS), NY

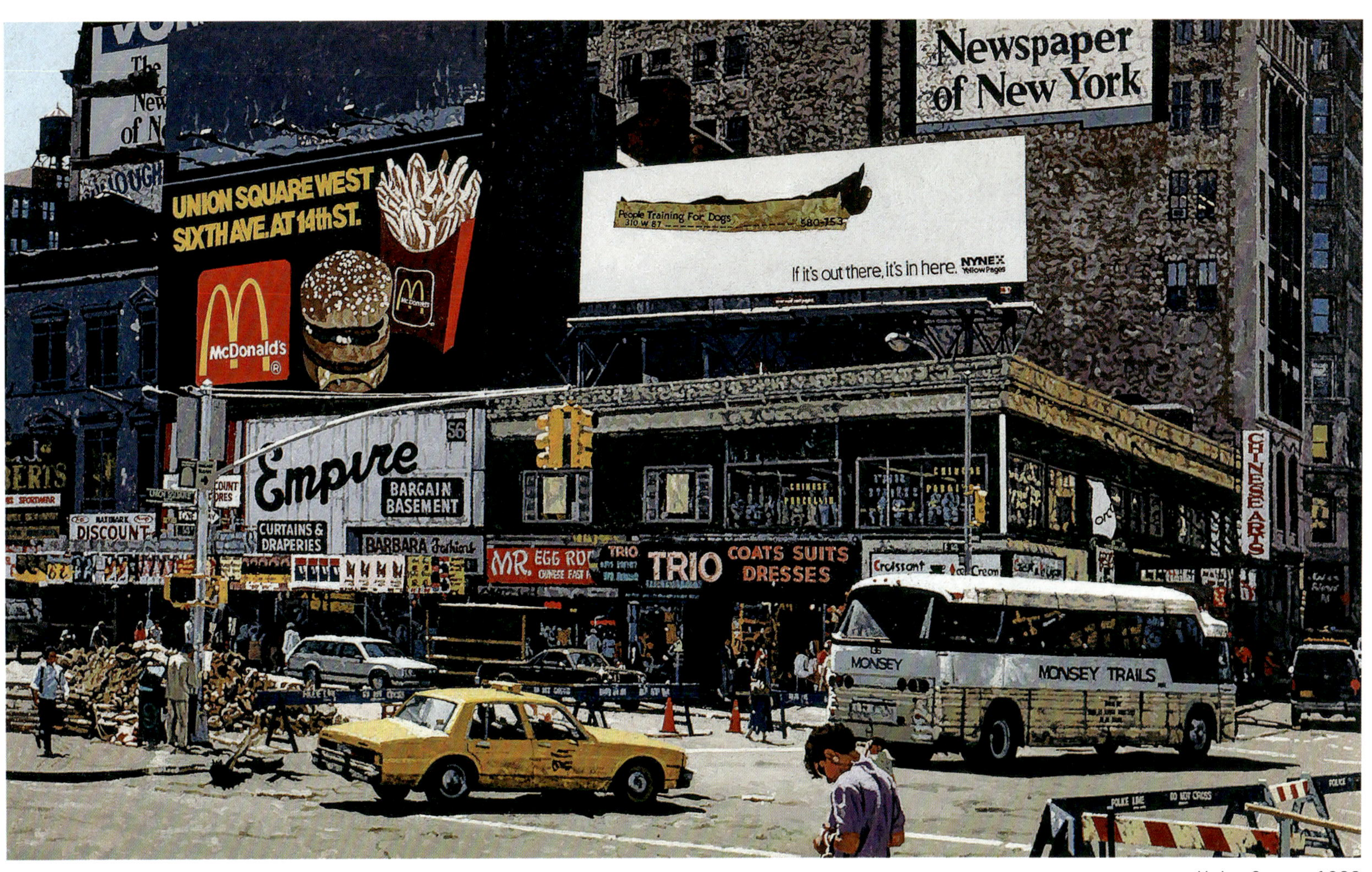

Union Square, 1988

oil on linen | 72" × 120" | Collection of Bryant and Nancy Hanley

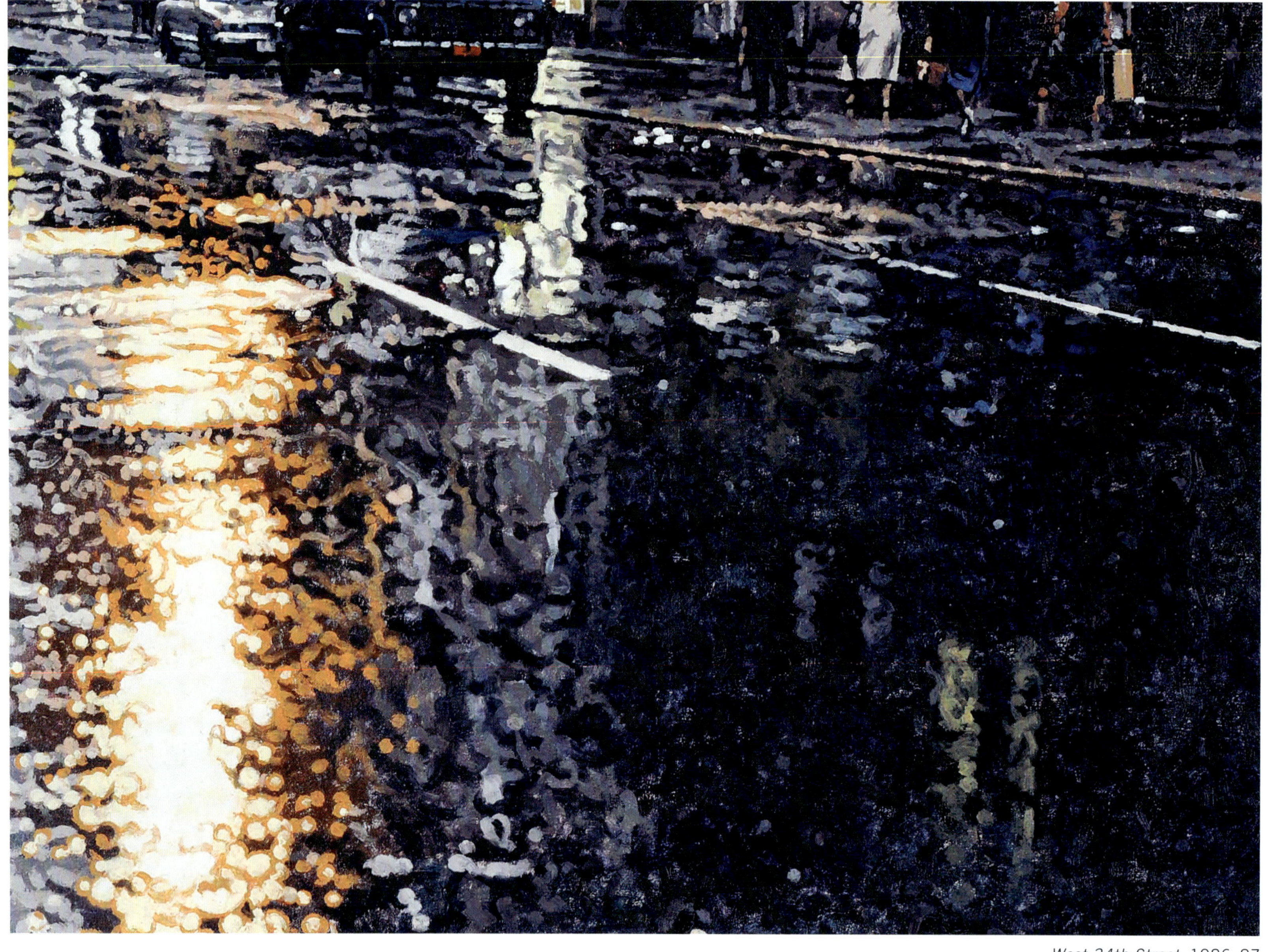

West 34th Street, 1986–87
oil on canvas | 34" × 46" | Tyler Museum of Art, bequest of Sonny Burt and Bob Butler, Dallas, Texas | 2014.01.07

to keep the viewer's eye constantly moving, yet convinced of the value assigned to separate elements. Accordingly, his scene unfolds piece by piece—full of blocks, attractions, conjunctions and disjunctions, weavings and breaks. It is through such active participation that Winter has come to learn the boundaries of his world and feeling.

Significantly, it was at the height of Winter's prolific career that he and Jeanette decided to leave Dallas. After his 1986 exhibition at Fischbach Gallery, Winter flew to Portland, Maine; drove to Waldo County, where Neal Welliver and Alex Katz had homes; and purchased a breathtaking twenty-six-acre plot in Frankfort, halfway between Belfast and Bangor. During that trip, Winter met Maurice Grosser, who was ill and had been living with the Welliver family. Grosser's critically acclaimed books on painting had helped shape Winter's early views on becoming an artist. Returning to Dallas, Winter hired James Pratt to design the house and two studios for him and Jeanette in Frankfort. Beginning in 1987, the Winters lived part time in Maine. The house was built during 1987/88. Winter submitted his resignation from SMU one year later.

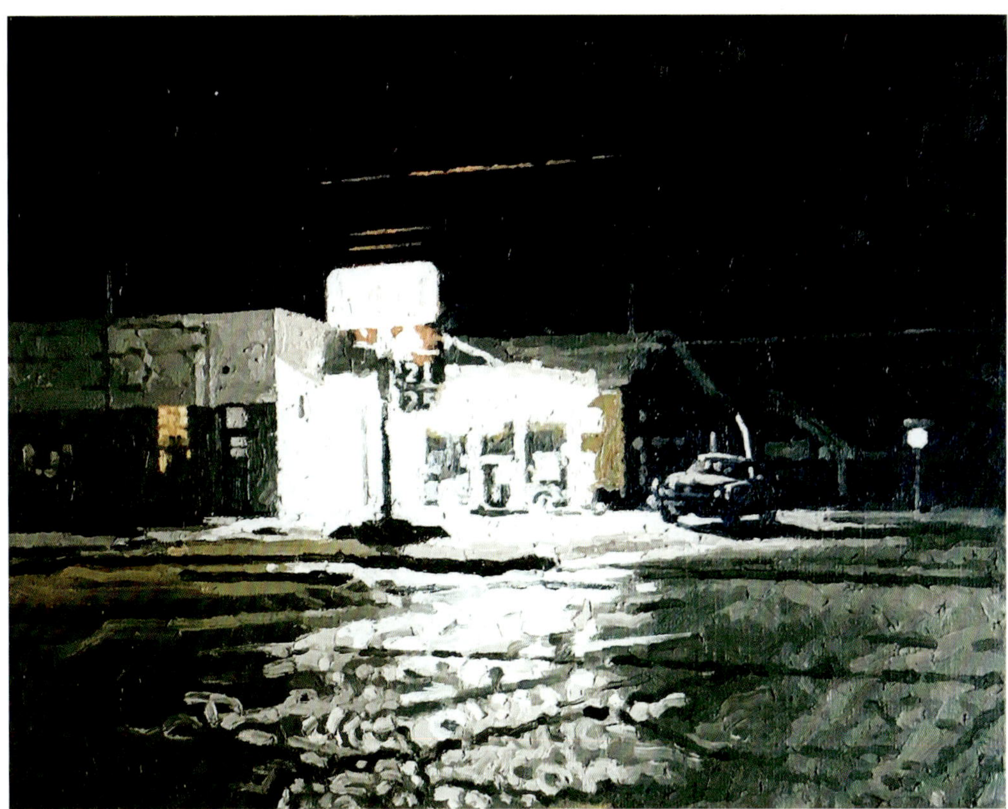

Corner Station, 1983
oil on linen | 14" × 16" | Collection of Jonah Winter

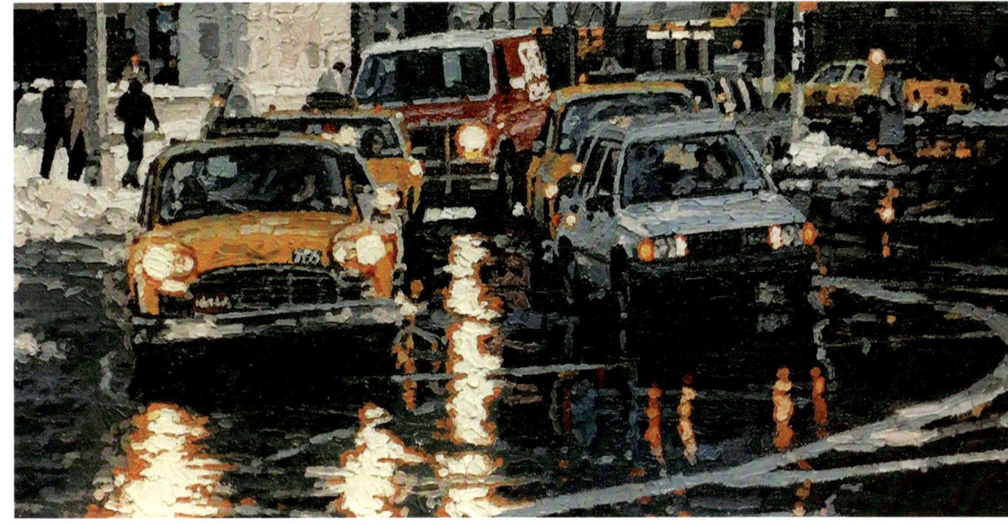

Park Avenue, 1985
oil on linen | 6" × 12" | Collection of Susan H. Albritton, Dallas | Photography by Karen Latham

Barnaby Fitzgerald, esteemed painter and professor of art at SMU, was fresh out of graduate school and a novice in the higher education system when Winter left the university. About Winter's impact as a teacher, Fitzgerald writes,

> Roger was as honest and straightforward as any fellow painter could possibly have wished for, and I had been looking forward to learning from him about many angles: the student of art, the contemporary art scene, the university. Alas, I kept what I could from his example and plowed forth. Roger has a wide range of means, but what I have seen of his, which is quite a lot, almost always seizes the truth and holds

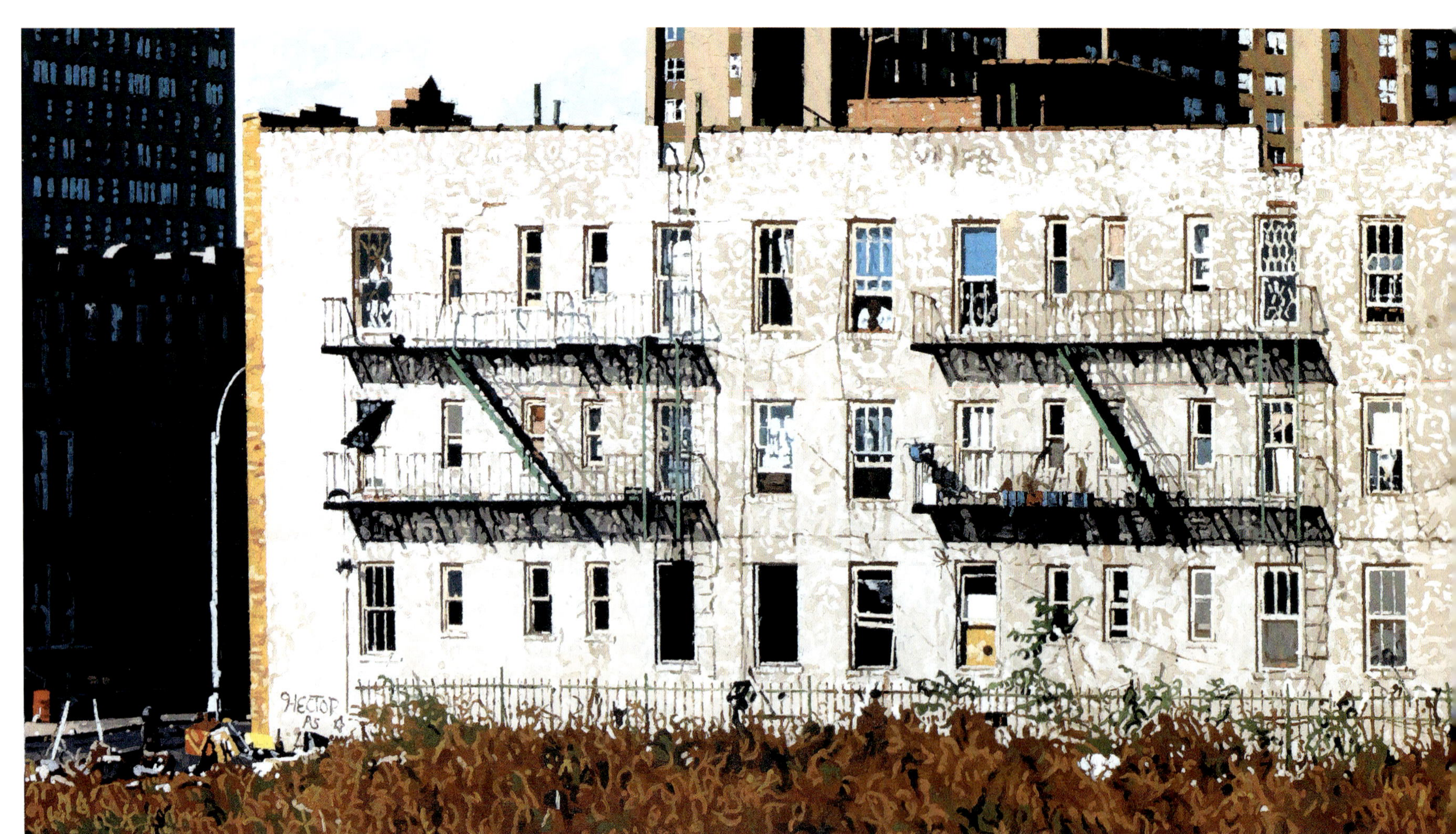

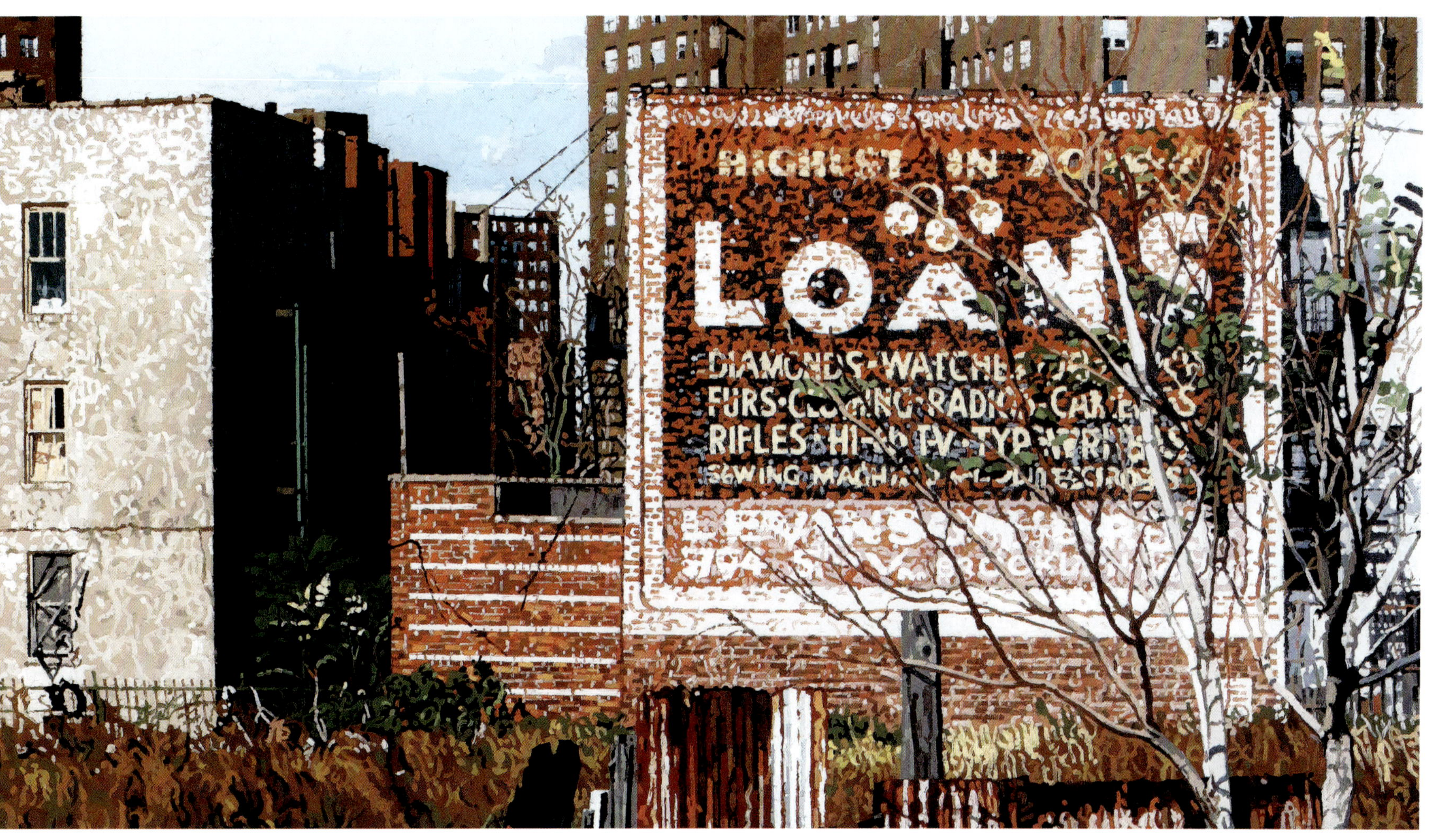

Coney Island, 1985

oil on linen | 48" x 132" | Collection of Bryant and Nancy Hanley | Photography by Kevin Todora

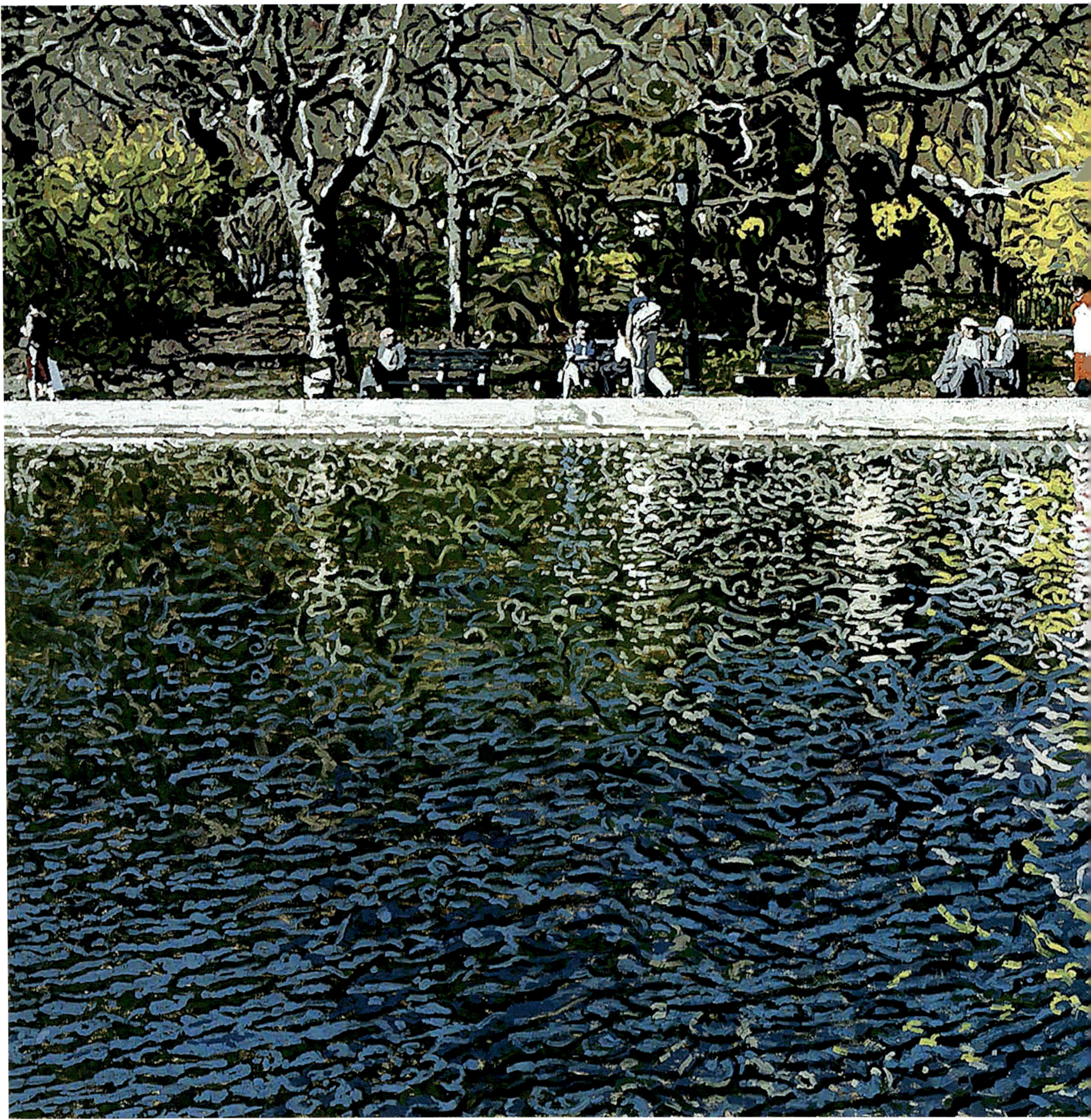

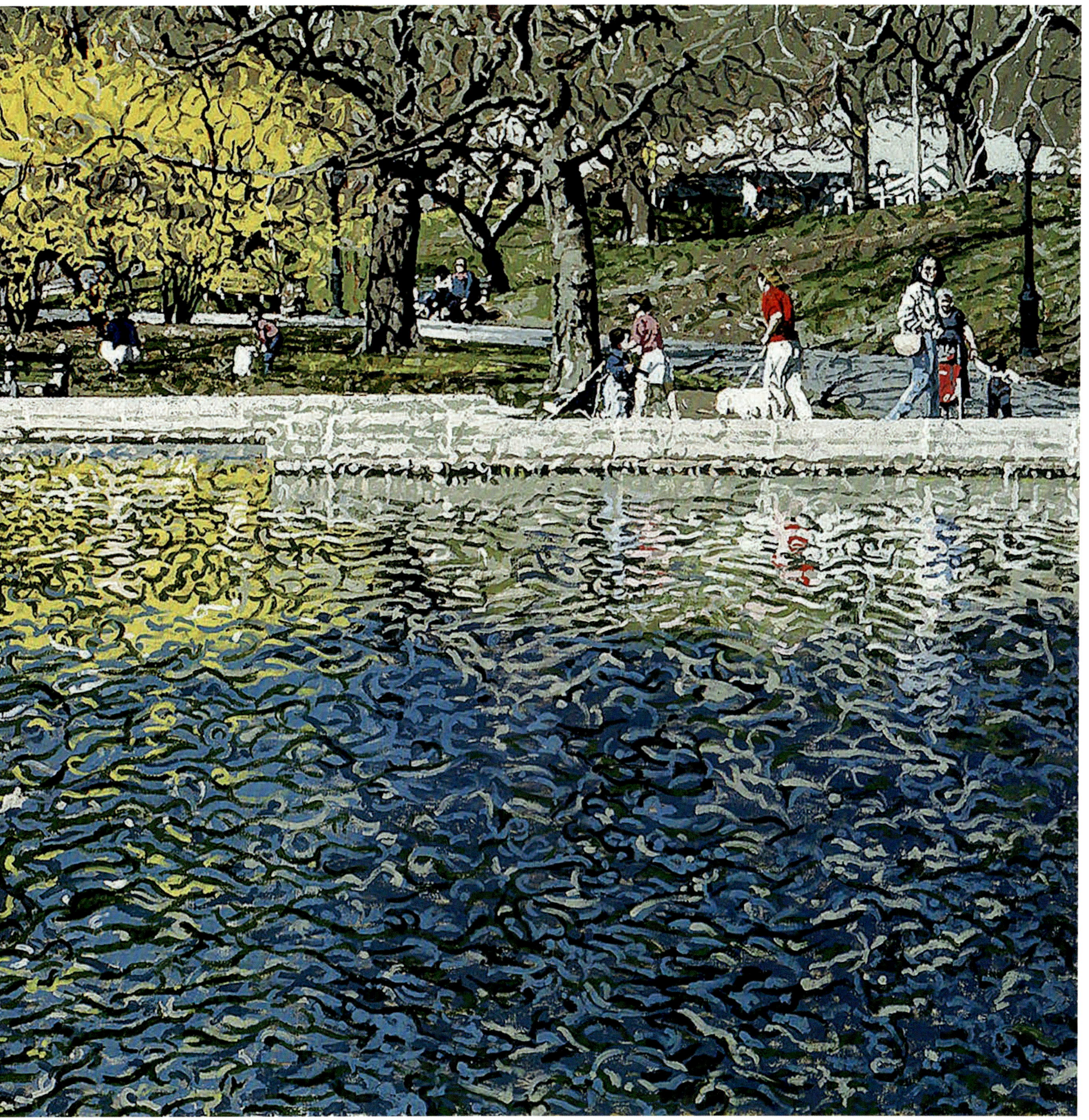

Central Park, 1985

oil on linen | 48" × 96" | Collection of the Rosewood Corporation

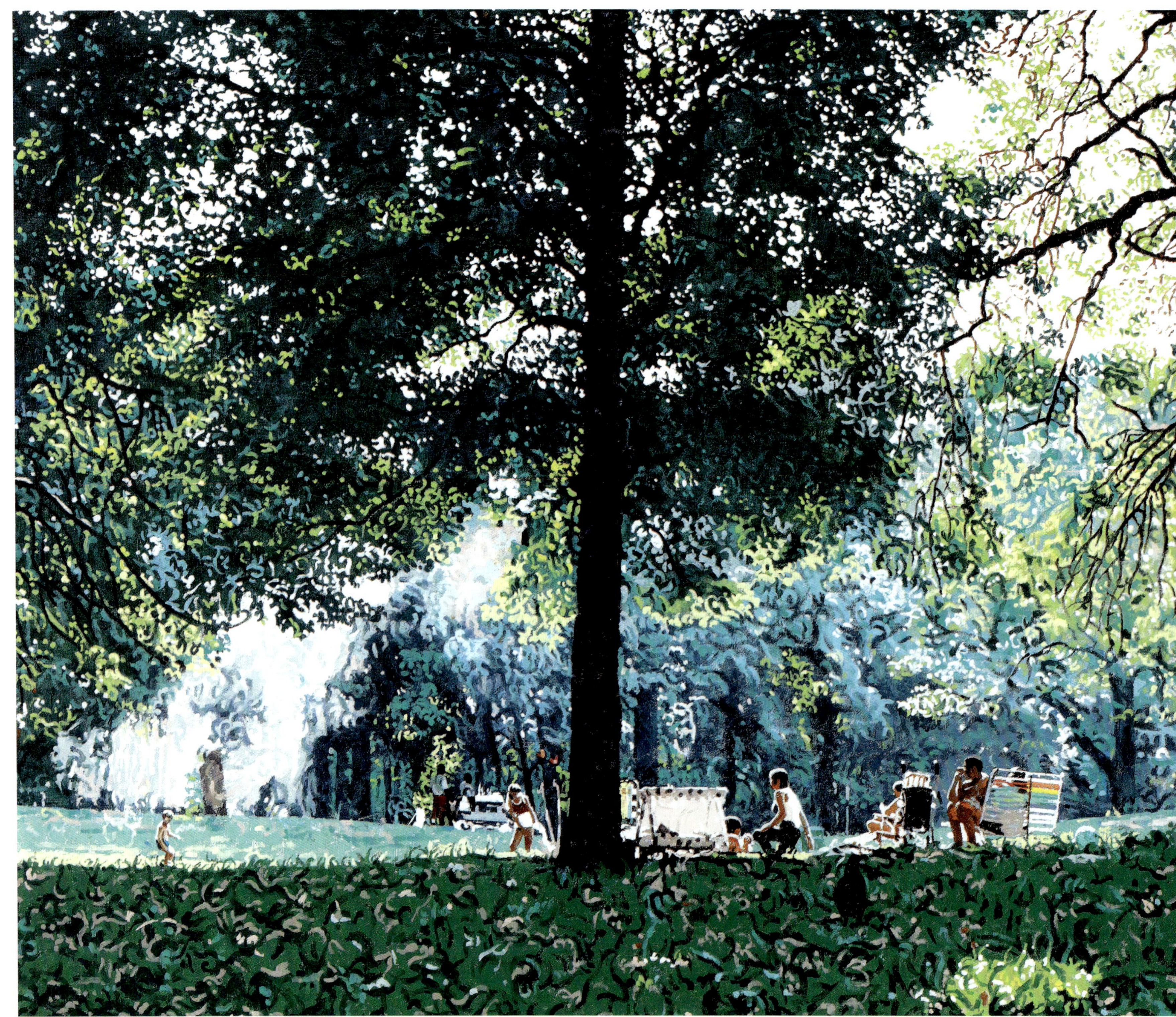

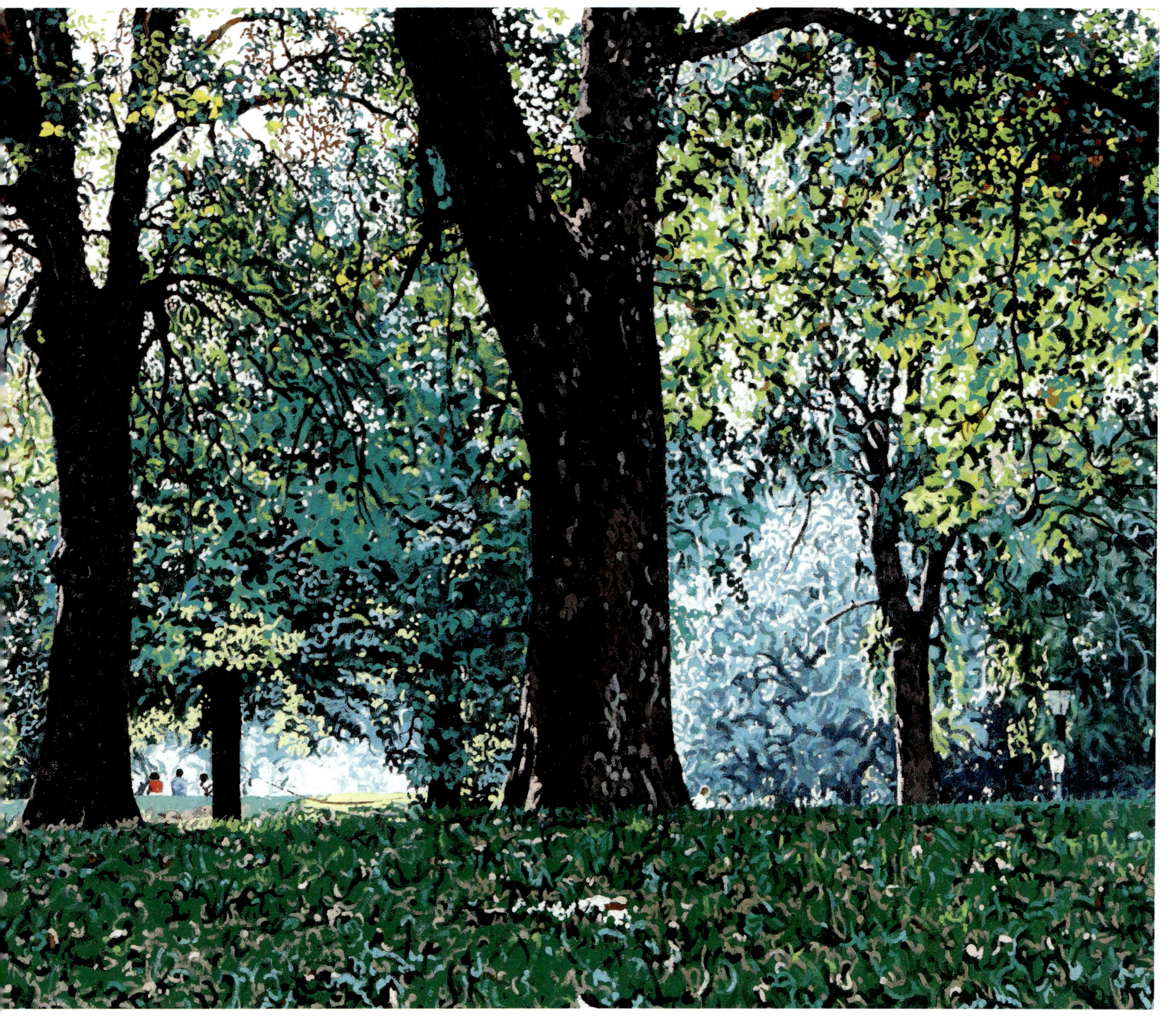

Prospect Park, 1985

oil on linen | 50" × 120" | Private collection | Photography by Kevin Todora

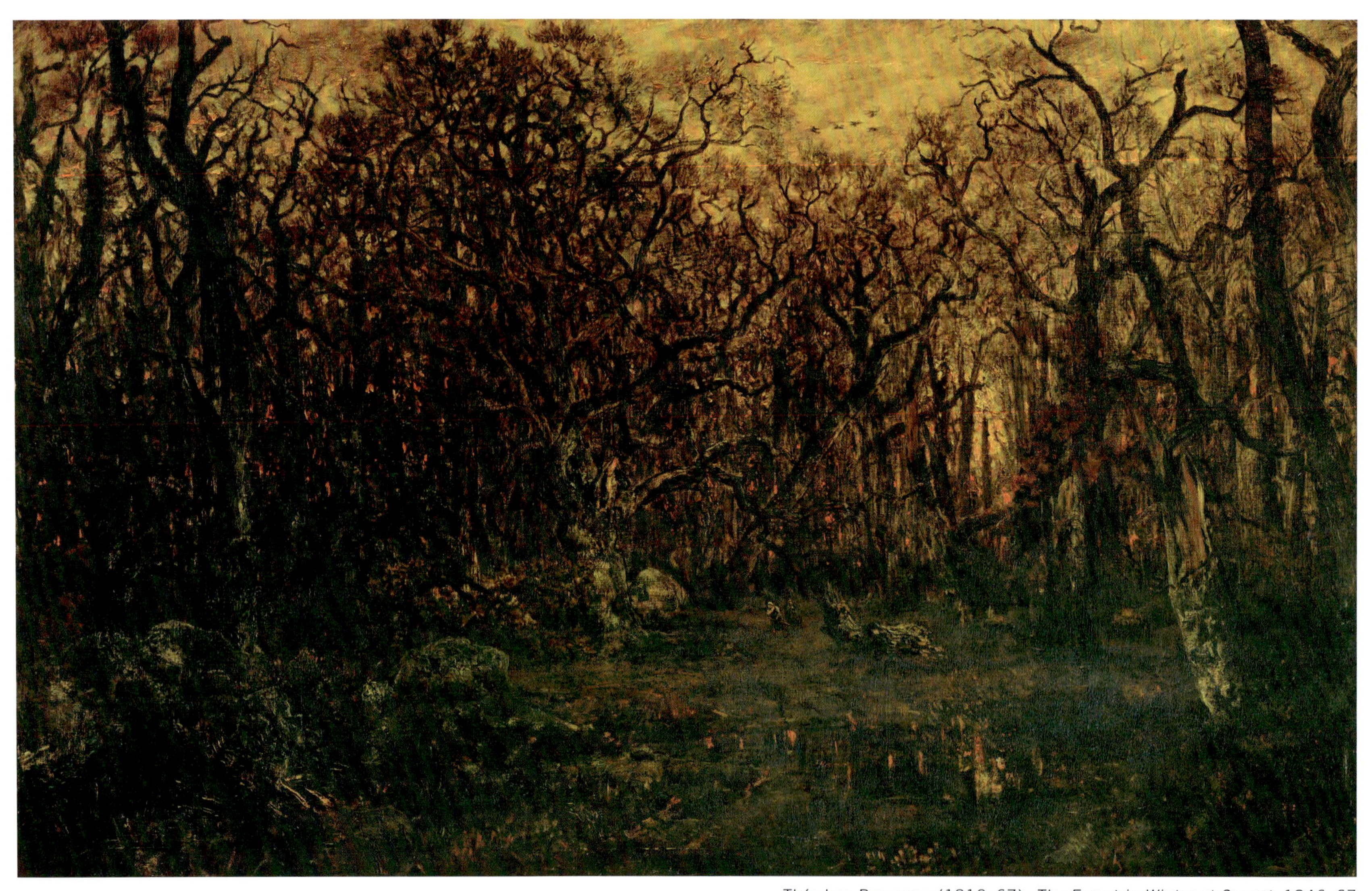

Théodore Rousseau (1812–67), *The Forest in Winter at Sunset,* 1846–67

oil on canvas | 64" × 102 3/8" (162.6 × 260 cm) | Gift of P. A. B. Widener, 1911 (11.4) | The Metropolitan Museum of Art |

> it, sometimes tenderly, sometimes harshly in place: alive and immobilized as if it has been trapped by Roger for a reason. A good reason. I remember Roger giving a lecture on Frida Kahlo at the Meadows Museum about 1987. I came in a minute late and so stood behind some students in the back. Roger spoke of Kahlo's crippled condition and how she would seek solace occasionally, by the freedom of an open marriage (so to speak). The students in front of me were "disgusted" . . . and I remember saying to myself that Roger was a voice of empathy and grace in a social context of rigid hypocrisy.[4]

About Winter's substantial teaching experience, Charles Field, distinguished painter and educator, writes,

> Roger is the master stimulator, his robust humor and antics are fondly remembered by his students and his many friends. I recently met an SMU former student of 30 years ago, who was still laughing as she described his clowning, which brought a needed note of humor and relaxation to the class. The art of teaching is dependent on honest dialogue between teacher and student. The trust and mutual respect when achieved often develop lasting friendships. Roger not only has taught many excellent artists, but he has gained a remarkable number of grateful and lifelong friends. The most critical factor for the success of the artist/teacher is balance. The time and energy devoted to one's art, and one's dedication to his or her students always needs constant review. Also, the competing pull of family, friends, general living, and often service to one's school or university have to be considered in the balancing act. In Roger's case, his long and rewarding career is evidence that his art, teaching, family, friends have all thrived. Roger did eventually make a change in his teaching position at SMU when he resigned and headed East.[5]

A teacher plans the studio course to progressively lead and elevate the group's ability and knowledge while also carefully guiding each student's personal development. After twenty-six years as an instructor of painting and drawing at SMU, Winter left a full-time professorship, in addition to a coterie of colleagues, patrons, and students. As it turns out, the move to Maine in 1990 would leave him in a prolonged free fall.

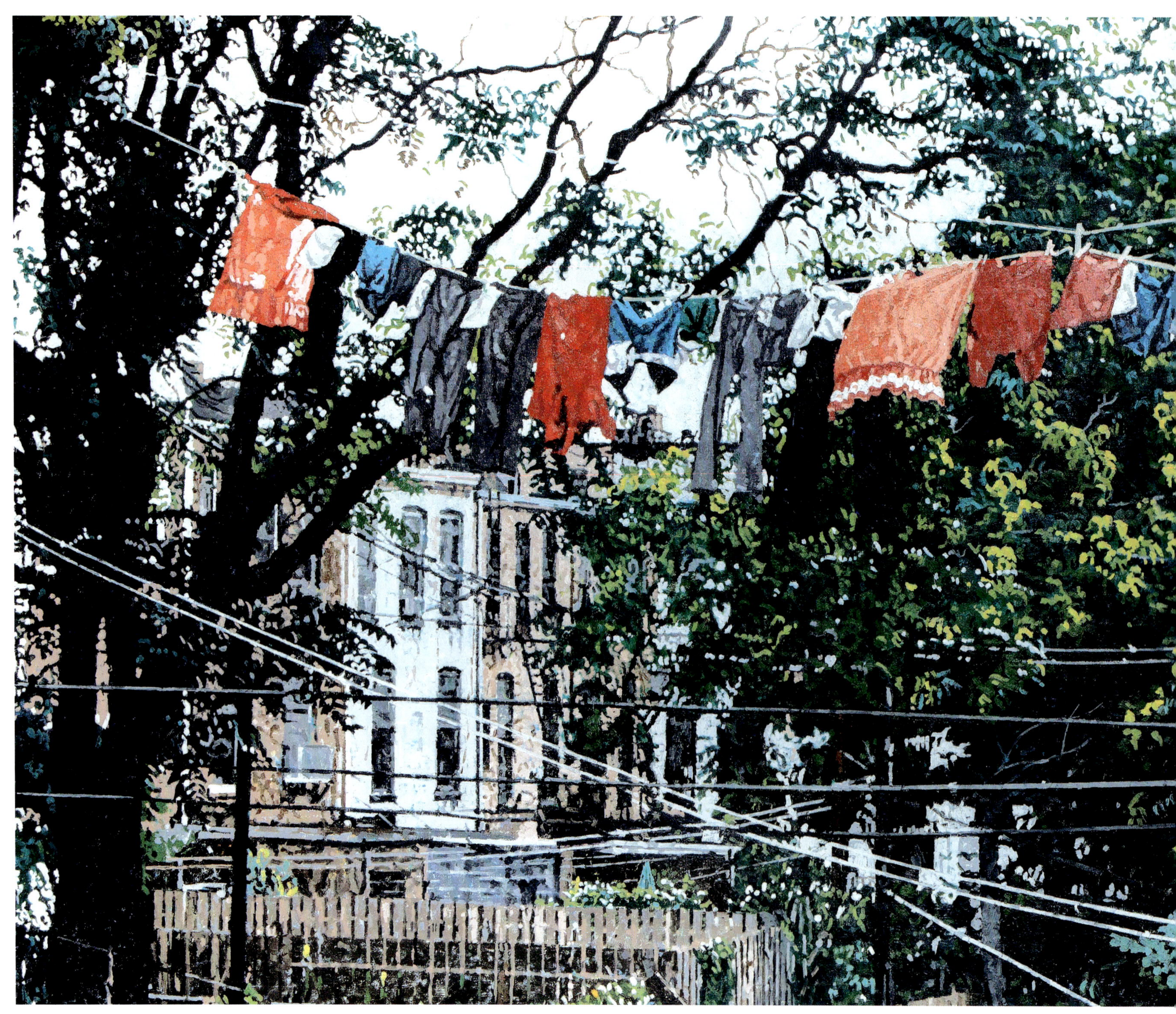

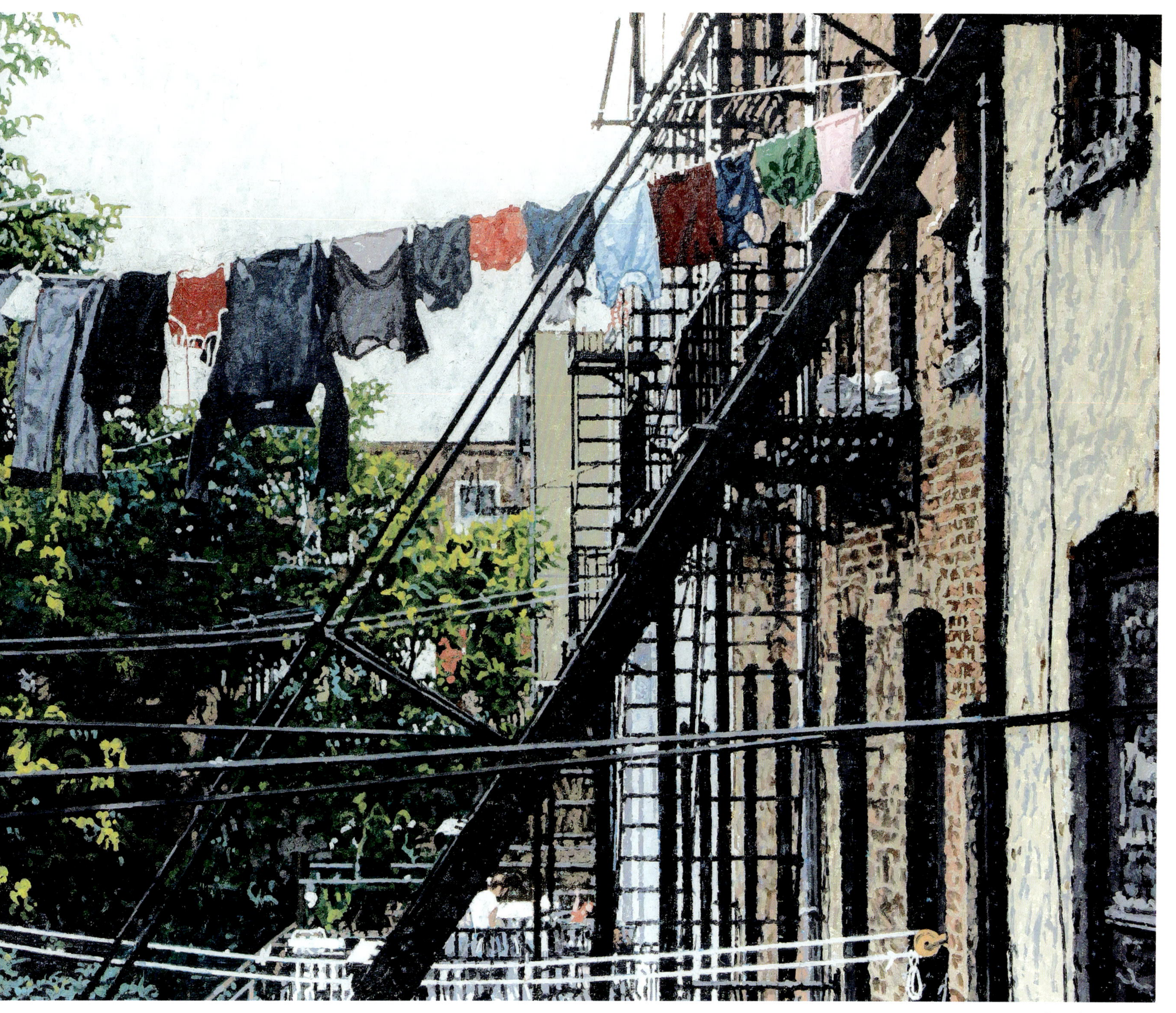

Park Slope, 1985

oil on linen | 48" × 108" | Collection of Jamie Pink | Photography by Kevin Todora

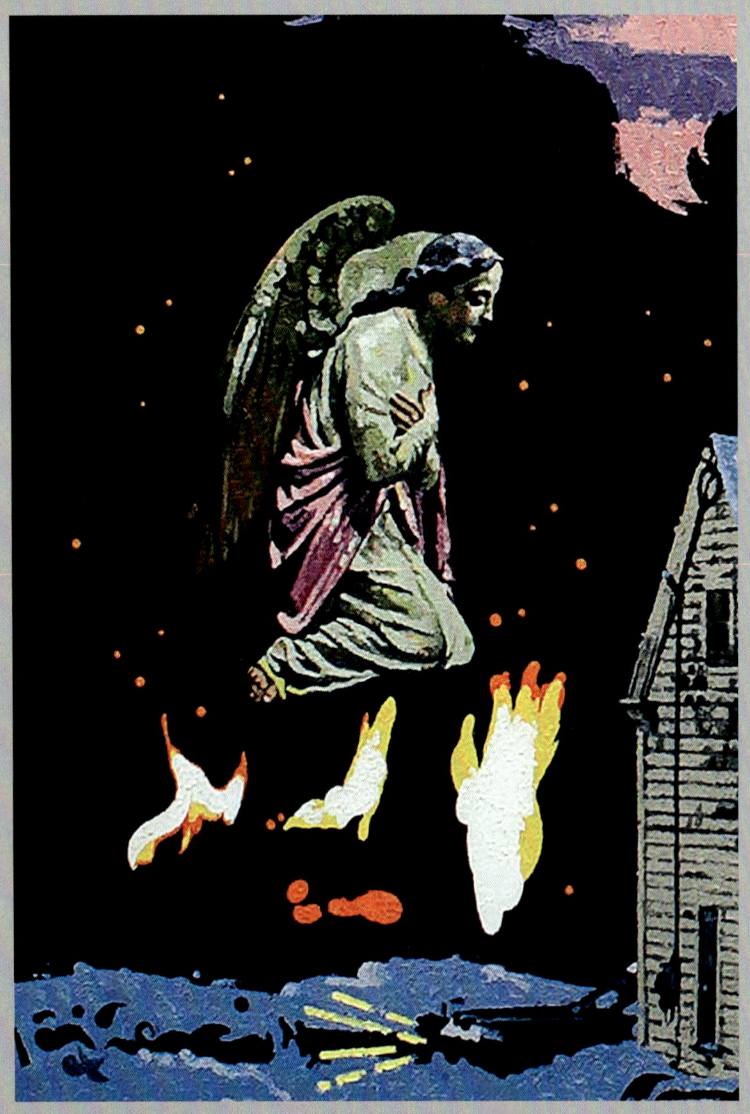

Day Is Conquered by Night (detail), 1995
oil on linen | 78" x 78" | Collection of
Alice and Charlie Adams | Photography by Jason Voinov

CHAPTER 11

MAINE

BY THE MID-1980s, Winter painted in a straight-ahead, photo-based realism and had successful exhibitions at Fischbach Gallery, New York. He was also anxious to leave Dallas, as he desired to live and work in a place that did not need his help. "At Jerry Bywaters's funeral, the speakers praised how much Jerry had helped the Dallas art world," Winter writes. "I didn't want that on my epitaph. I loved to teach, but SMU [Southern Methodist University] had lost its meaning for me. Many of the art faculty despised my success. They had a thinly disguised jealousy of me for the success of the students who worked with me. I know this sounds egomaniacal, but it's what I saw and I wanted out. Living out my life as a professor in Dallas would have been too pat, for my understanding of art and how to grow."[1] What's more, Winter was disappointed in the Dallas Museum of Art's lack of interest in exhibiting his work or that of the strong realist painters with whom he interacted—Jane Freilicher, William Bailey, Jack Beal, Rackstraw Downes, Yvonne Jacquette, and Neil Welliver, among others.

Jeanette's career as an author and children's book illustrator was in full swing. She had received national recognition but felt that the city did not support her work. Few Dallas stores carried her books and there were no signings. After a quarter century of living in Dallas, both were ready for a change. They began to look at every locale they had visited as a potential new home. By chance, Winter picked up Alan Gussow's book *A Sense of Place: The Artist and the American Land* and realized that many of the painters he had admired over the years had worked in Maine. Indeed, the state has always attracted a wide assortment of artists, including Thomas Cole, Frederic Edwin Church, George Bellows, Winslow Homer, Rockwell Kent, John Marin, Fairfield Porter, and three generations of Wyeths—N. C., Andrew, and Jamie—who were impelled to paint the natural beauty of its rocky coastline, soaring mountains, and dense forests. During the nine summers Edward Hopper spent in Maine between 1914 and 1929, he produced some of the most evocative paintings of his career. Hopper's idiosyncratic approach—focused and isolated, wielding paint with technical bravura—distinguished him from the multitudes of landscape artists congregating in New England. For Marsden Hartley, who began and ended his career as a painter of Maine, the land served as a lifelong source of inspiration integral to his personal history, as well as a modernist testing ground. He rendered Maine with effects that went beyond topographic description. Rather, it is a place of light and darkness whose spirit imbued his art.

For Winter, the decision to live in Maine assumed great significance—to be a part of art in Maine was to be an important part of American art history. "I think of my friend, Neil Welliver," Winter writes. "Welliver's paintings have helped me SEE Maine, in a physical sense. The patterns of snow in the mountains, a spring thaw, a rushing trout stream, the cold clean air—all made visible by Neil's paintings. Neil has painted Maine into existence for me. That's what a lot of painters do—they work their way into the invisible and the hard to see, and they make it visible. That's what the medium is capable of."[2] The Winters' beautiful home in Frankfort was far from any human habitation and art world activity. During construction and the first year of residence, however, Roger and Jeanette were introduced to various artists and began to feel part of a community. Through Neil and Sheila Welliver they met artist Alex Katz and filmmaker Frederick Wiseman. The Wellivers also introduced them to Susan Leites, a painter who lived part time in Maine and ran the undergraduate department at the University of Pennsylvania, where Neil Welliver was art department chair. Through Leites, Winter met painter Lois Dodd and sculptor Anne Arnold, both of whom lived in Maine part time and showed at Fischbach. Dodd introduced Winter to artists John and Nancy Wissemann-Widrig, and through Leites, he also met Bruce Brown, the curator at the Center for Maine Contemporary Art in Rockford. Moreover, the painter Frances Hynes invited the Winters to her summer home on Monhegan, where they visited Jamie Wyeth's house, which had been built by Rockwell Kent. As director of the Flushing Council on Culture and the Arts, Hynes also placed Winter's work in two exhibitions. As a result, Winter was included among successful creative people in and out of the art mainstream, one in which the friendships built and circles configured seemed firmly rooted in genuine affection. "We all had this sense of realism," he recalls. "Sometimes realism is ignored. But we all had the shared sensibility that the source of our work was coming from the real world. So I think everyone painted from the world in one way or another. Neil had his way; Lois had her way. She has more of a spontaneous reaction to things in nature, rather than the more planned quality that Neil's paintings and my paintings had. And I think we all really appreciated each other; there wasn't the competition that occurs with a lot of artist groups." At the same time, Winter also became involved in county and statewide politics. As Democratic town chair, he organized debates, published a newsletter, and pushed forward environmental causes. Winter began to experience a bigger view of the world than he had known in Dallas—and that world fascinated him.

Apple Trees (1987–88) represents the promise and hope of a new life in Maine. Here, ripe apples rhythmically bob and dip amid a thicket of dense foliage and branches, a tribute to both the fleetingness and constancy of nature's cycles. The bountiful details might at first glance appear chaotic, extending beyond the picture plane toward infinity, but eventually we see the logic that informs them: a grouping of wild apples coming to fruition, each a distinct portrait rendered by light, form, and color—from yellow and green to deep red and dark crimson stripes. Apples, of course, are imbued with background meaning. We have references to the original garden and humankind's loss of innocence and attainment of knowledge, sin, and death. Apples are meant to ward off illness through their own robust health: "An apple a day keeps the doctor away." For Winter, the apple trees seemed to acknowledge what was passing and what was to come—a kind of paradise in his own backyard. "When we began building on the twenty-six acres of undeveloped land, I discovered an orchard of apple trees full of fruit that the locals called 'wild food,' meaning food for the deer, fox, etcetera. The apples, named Wolf River, were good for baking but a bit tough for snacks. For me, the orchard revived the overall patterning of landscape that I had discovered while painting scenes from the nature conservancy south of Dallas. I had no taste for 'normal views' of landscapes, and the overall pattern suggested a more cosmic or molecular view of nature. The painting took patience and a good sense of organization and knowing what primary units I was using. The apple trees seemed like an appropriate metaphor for the good life. At first we were excited and happy with our move to Maine, but this was before we were fully aware of the enormity of change it was bringing."

Indeed, the Maine that Winter experienced that first year was different from the one he planned on. To his dismay, Maine did not always look like Fairfield Porter's eloquent, painterly realist pictures of the region's summer people. Rather, he was confronted by a hardscrabble country populated by locals who did not have much use for newcomers or "flatlanders." The winter was long, severe, and isolating—most days his only human contacts were Jeanette and the Frankfort postmistress. The snow season was cruel for him, and empty, because the people he knew best made an exodus for New York around Labor Day. To all intents and purposes, the professional life that he had known was gone—teaching at SMU, the Texas art community, the security of adoring collectors. Triggered by feelings of intense sadness, Winter became an introvert. But the overwhelming despair stimulated him to take a sharp turn in his work. He began to use the snowy Maine landscape as a stagelike setting for a magic realist or psychic dreamscape. A repertoire of "actors" and recurring symbols enter into the paintings—crows, dogs, deer, foxes, fire, statuary of angels and saints—often rendered disproportionately large or without cast shadows and floating untethered across the canvas. As Jennifer R. Gross, then curator of the Baxter Gallery, Maine College of Art, Portland, would write, "The extreme visual clarity of the Maine landscape can be paralyzing. Intensely animated yet distinctive, life in a landscape of extreme beauty and unyielding resolution perpetuates dread as well as wonderment. . . . Meaning rests under the terrain in Roger Winter's paintings, dormant, just out of reach and sight, submerged below the becalmed waters and the tufted snow of his recent landscapes."[3]

In many respects, the new body of work circles back to the surreal, montage-like strategies of Winter's early efforts. Rather than focus on family issues, however, he applied his considerable knowledge of painting to create works of poetic strangeness and deep spiritual resonance. *Winter Solstice* (1990), the first painting he produced after a season in Maine, evokes a sense of place through incongruous elements and transformative images. An old house on the Penobscot River, which flows through Frankfort, is rendered amid the fading light of the year's shortest day. A statue of an angel from the Belfast cemetery stands on frozen ground but shows no signs of the collected snowfall. A fox in the middle foreground faces the opposite direction, attending to something in the distance. Its cast shadow is mysteriously thrown by the artificial light in the house's window. An oversize dove perches on a television antenna protruding from the roof. At far right, a crackling fire burns in the snow. Winter explains, "In my painting, so little light comes from the late sun, even less from the flames. They were originally in our fireplace and reflected in the front window. The reflection looked as if it were in a field of snow, and I knew this had to be painted. The import of the fox, the angel, the bird, and the fire was like a dream that was part of my daily life. The first time I remember putting an image of fire in a work was in the large drawing of the Rogalla family back in the midsixties. It was a symbol of life's spirit then. But in *Winter Solstice*, it became a symbol of foreboding and pain, of life burning out."

For Winter, the painting was a revival of an inner life from which he had worked hard to distance himself. However, the psychic and physical landscape of his daily existence had gone through enormous changes. In Maine, he was out on a limb trying to find the next approach. "Neil Welliver, on a studio visit, charged over to *Winter Solstice* and said, 'Roger, you've outdone yourself!' And he was right. I had brought something new into the world. Something new that was a result of all that I recognized had been lost: my Texas patrons, my professorship, my coterie of followers. But *Winter Solstice* also painted what I had found in a new place and time. My subjective paintings of the '60's and '70's were of a morose past while *Winter Solstice* was of a gloomy present that was on top of me every day. I think it may be my most

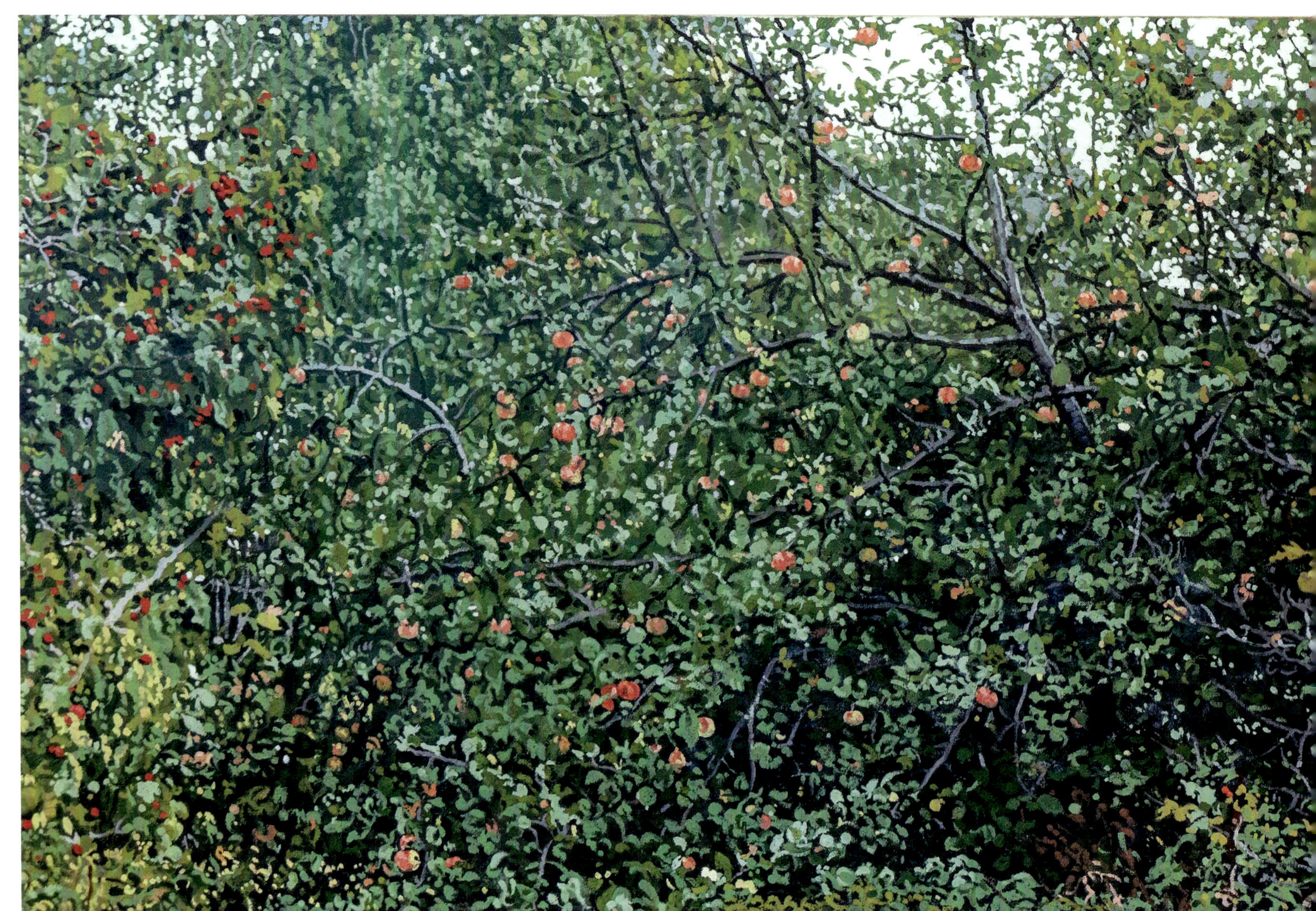

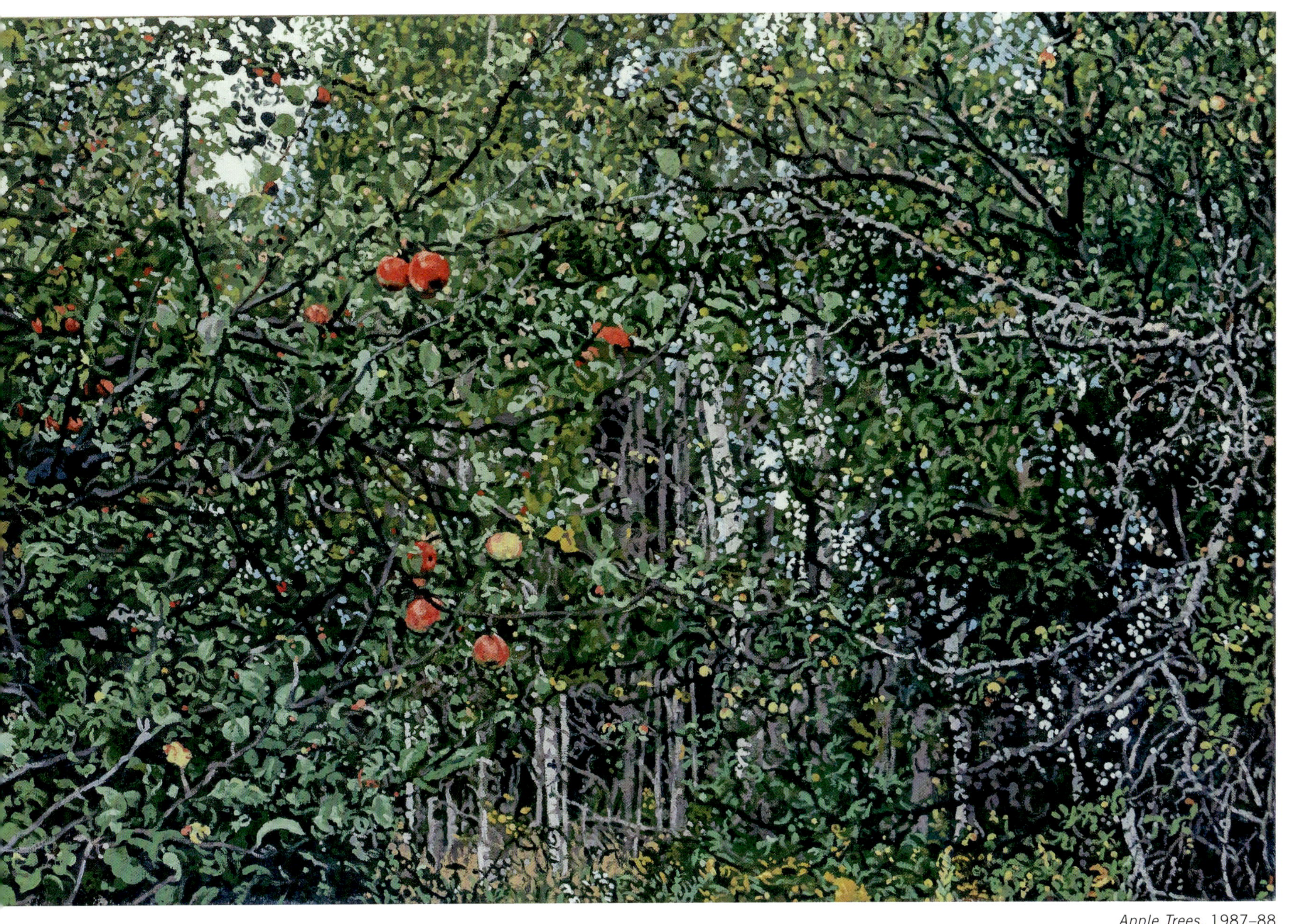

Apple Trees, 1987–88

oil on linen | 36" × 84" | Collection of the Roger Horchow Family | Photography by Joshua Nefsky

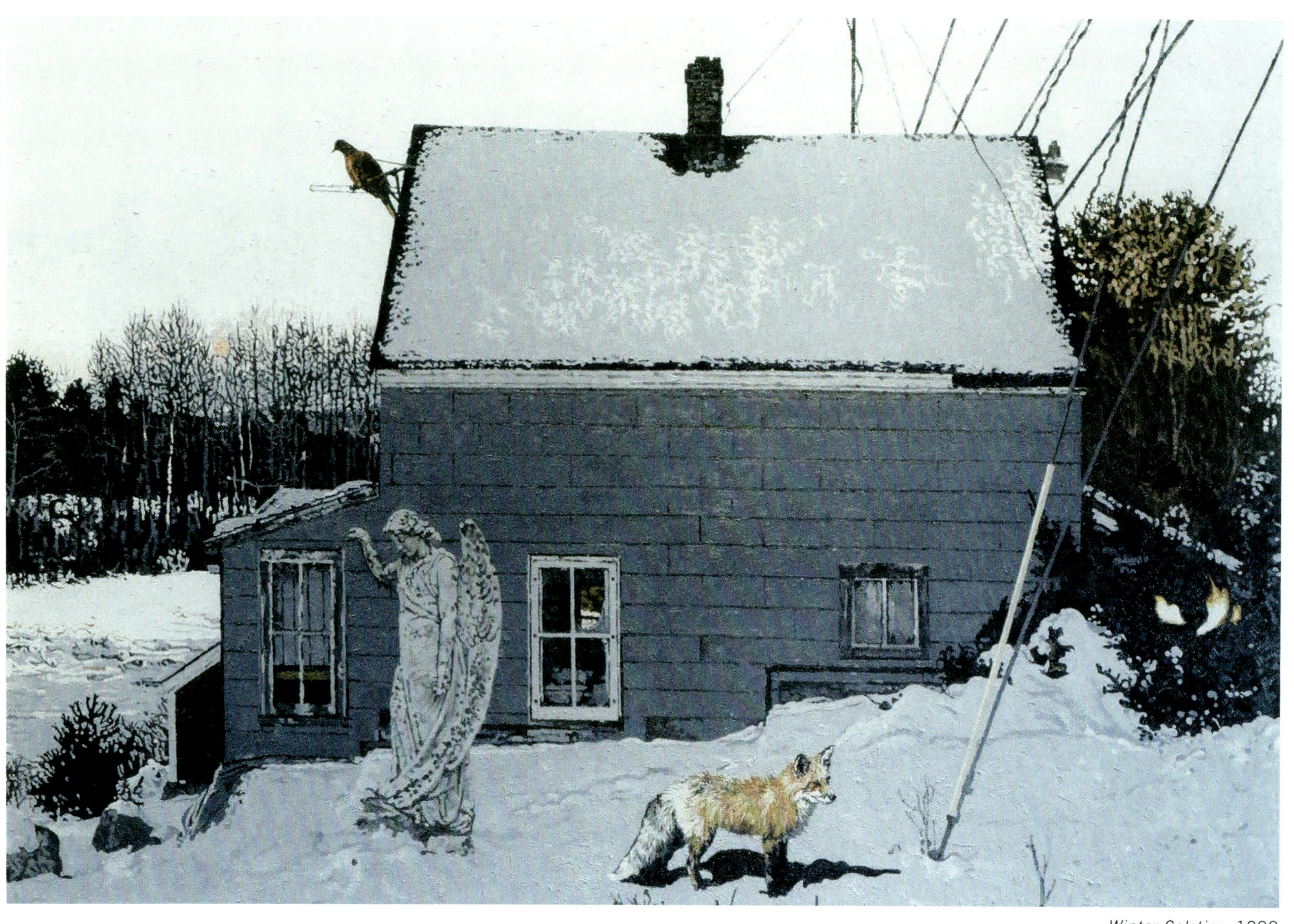

Winter Solstice, 1990

oil on linen | 56" × 78" | Albritton Family Collection, Dallas | Photography by Fernando Rojas important painting, not only because there's nothing about it I would change, but because of the investment of emotion and dare in it."[4]

Many artists on the East Coast had evolved painterly figurative styles—Fairfield Porter in particular—but Winter, at least for a time, was among the few artists who managed to impose so insistently realist and symbolic an imagination on the landscape without yielding to simple solutions. Nevertheless, the problem for an artist like Winter is the challenge of maintaining some reliable standard of painting while insisting on the freedom to take risks. It requires a taut balance of holding the line even as one goes over the line—as much a matter of repetition as it is a matter of change. But what is too much change?

Around the same time of Welliver's studio visit, Winter also sent slides of *Winter Solstice* and other work to Fischbach Gallery staff, who shot back with a tepid response. According to Winter, the assistant director was puzzled by the oddly disjunctive images—the angel that did not cast a shadow; the large bird on the antenna. A follow-up letter was crystal clear: the painting was difficult to read. Winter was obviously into some sort of contemporary surrealism, which was not an appropriate direction for their gallery.[5] "Fischbach was unhappy showing work that was totally out of character from the paintings they had previously exhibited," Winter explains. "*Winter Solstice* seemed dangerous at the time—I knew Fischbach wouldn't have any use for it. The painting is not straight-ahead realism—it's more metaphysical. I'm putting together things on a stage that don't really belong together. Some things can't be seen with the naked eye, but may possibly exist. I'm not sure that angels *have* shadows. When we moved to Maine, I thought the Eastern Seaboard was mine for the taking. For the most part, it was Texans who bought the paintings. I lost my market. I had failed to see that Fischbach's interest in me was not for my work, but the audience that it had among the collectors of Dallas. I wasn't going to imitate myself for Fischbach."

Nevertheless, the traumatic break from Fischbach Gallery drove him deeper into an interior world. He was angry and lost, struggling with what he had sacrificed professionally to the point of religious conversion. "I knew I was getting into different territory," Winter recalls. "In those days I would pray. I would be on my knees in the studio asking for help and at night I would say the twenty-third psalm and the Lord's Prayer before I went to sleep—and I never had strong religious leanings until that time. I started putting a lot of the struggle into the paintings themselves. And this relates to the earlier comment: 'What is heaven but man's dreams? What is earth but man's perceptions?' I was combining heaven and earth, symbols of the invisible with symbols of the directly perceived. I was pushed to the edge; the losses in my mind were total."

Indeed, the major themes of Winter's Maine paintings are also recurrent in much religious art through the ages: death and renewal, good and evil, belief in the eternity of nature and the temporality of human culture. His art is the embodiment of primal angst and spiritual yearning—of our mortal fears and our aching need to transcend them. Winter's particular brilliance is in sliding imperceptibly from the ordinary surface to the primal darkness that lies beneath. When the Maine paintings work best—wondrously, transportingly—they work beyond logic, through image and parable, like a kind of gritty-realist gospel. Winter does not expect to persuade us through reason; he aspires to move us to ask questions.

Nowhere is this more evident than in *Devil's Garden* (1990), which refers to isolated desert areas that collect and hold rainwater, thereby giving rise to cacti, yucca, and flowers that blossom in otherwise arid land. Here, the rocky ledges of the Big Bend landscape are the setting for a host of incongruous human and animal images—a snake, a young Mexican girl, a scratching dog, two crows, an El Niño figure, a burning car—that bring life and death within a hair's breadth of each other. With the split from Fischbach, Winter was an artist suddenly stripped of the beliefs that had previously defined him. From his Frankfort studio, he looked to far West Texas to restore a sense of awe, to render the world again strange and full of magic. His subjects seem, at first, like a motley mix of the pedestrian, the sacred, and the profane. Winter was after an unmediated relationship with nature, wherein all things and phenomena merge into one another. For the most part, they are drawn from life experience and without caricature. So much of what occurs in *Devil's Garden* feels uncannily like life itself, utterly familiar and bewilderingly inexplicable. Each vignette takes place in a space-defining pool of light that feels as provisional as it is lucid. In the lower left corner, Winter renders a tiny young woman alongside a coiled snake. He balances the composition at far right with a miniature telephone pole and wires that trail off the picture plane. An oversize El Niño figure with scraped knees and slightly broken fingers nearly slides through pink flowers into the viewer's space. There are other images and objects—prickly pear cactus and old white crosses—amid the loose calligraphic brushstrokes, hidden in such a way as to keep us combing the surface. Nevertheless, the placement of images and their scale relations to the perimeter of the canvas work together in a formal sense, not just for the sake of disjunctive surprises.

The pivot point is a black car on fire in the distance. The smoke morphs into a white thought balloon that also links the scene to an ominous Mexican lawman on a white horse, rifle and scabbard at his side. The rider, taken from a found photograph, reminded Winter of a sheriff who patrolled Denison in the 1940s. "His name was Dischner, and he rode around town on a white horse with a rifle strapped to the saddle. People called him 'the Dischner' and kids in school would say, 'I'm gonna call the Dischner on you.' Once he rode up into the schoolyard during recess—he was like a symbol of killing and death."

It is important to note that Winter was also reading Johann Wolfgang von Goethe's *Faust, Parts 1 and 2* at this time. For Winter, the late eighteenth-century German writer's portrayal of good and evil, temptation and deliverance, which took place in heaven, the netherworld, and the natural world, dovetailed with the overall content of *Devil's Garden*. "I think Goethe's influence was as much subliminal as conscious," Winter explains. "Like including the snake—that old aunt of mine, the famous snake. Like having El Niño in the garden as Faust's redemption. Like the two crows who followed Mephisto in part 2—our son Max called them Rumor and Envy, which were taken from Norse mythology, the crows Thought and Memory that followed Odin. The general themes of Faust—the mix of physical and spiritual beings, politics, fire, redemption—may have influenced me by my night reading. I remember underlining quotes from the book: 'Two souls live in me, alas, irreconcilable with one another. One, lusting for the world with all its might, grapples it close, greedy of all its pleasures, the other rises up, up from the dirt, up from the best fields, where dwell our great forebears.'"[6]

Overall, Winter brings an understated, compelling inventiveness in his ability to distill nuanced emotional truths from the effluvia of ordinary life. Part allegory, part myth, part magic realism, *Devil's Garden* is loaded with double symbolic meanings: death and the Christ child surrounded by nature's resurrection through heaven's water; the temptation of an innocent young woman by a snake; Faust, as the devil, destroying the car, or earthly property. "I put the painting together slowly and dreamily," Winter says. "To hell with Fischbach, as they had forsaken me. *Devil's Garden* had great impact on my later paintings in Maine and what they meant. I, too, was looking for a delivery by angels to a field of flowers and butterflies, like Faust in the second part of God's deal with the devil. And found it. I left my comfort zone for the sake of growth."

But not quite. Although Winter's paintings were veering toward subjective territory, he was not yet ready to give up as a straight-ahead realist. He wanted what he had lost—the coterie of students, friends, and collectors. He believed that the more he painted objectively, the more complete his return to the objective life would be if he could achieve it. *Monument* (1991) is an effort to find himself again and reclaim that happier past. On a trip to Manhattan, Winter became mesmerized by the memorial fountain dedicated to Ida and Isidor Straus, who were lost at sea in the RMS *Titanic* disaster on April 15, 1912. The monument pays tribute to Ida's decision to remain with her husband, a co-owner of the Macy's department store, rather than save herself by boarding a lifeboat with the women and children. The work consists of a granite curved exedra, a central reclining female figure of Memory by sculptor Augustus Lukeman (1872–1935), and a reflecting

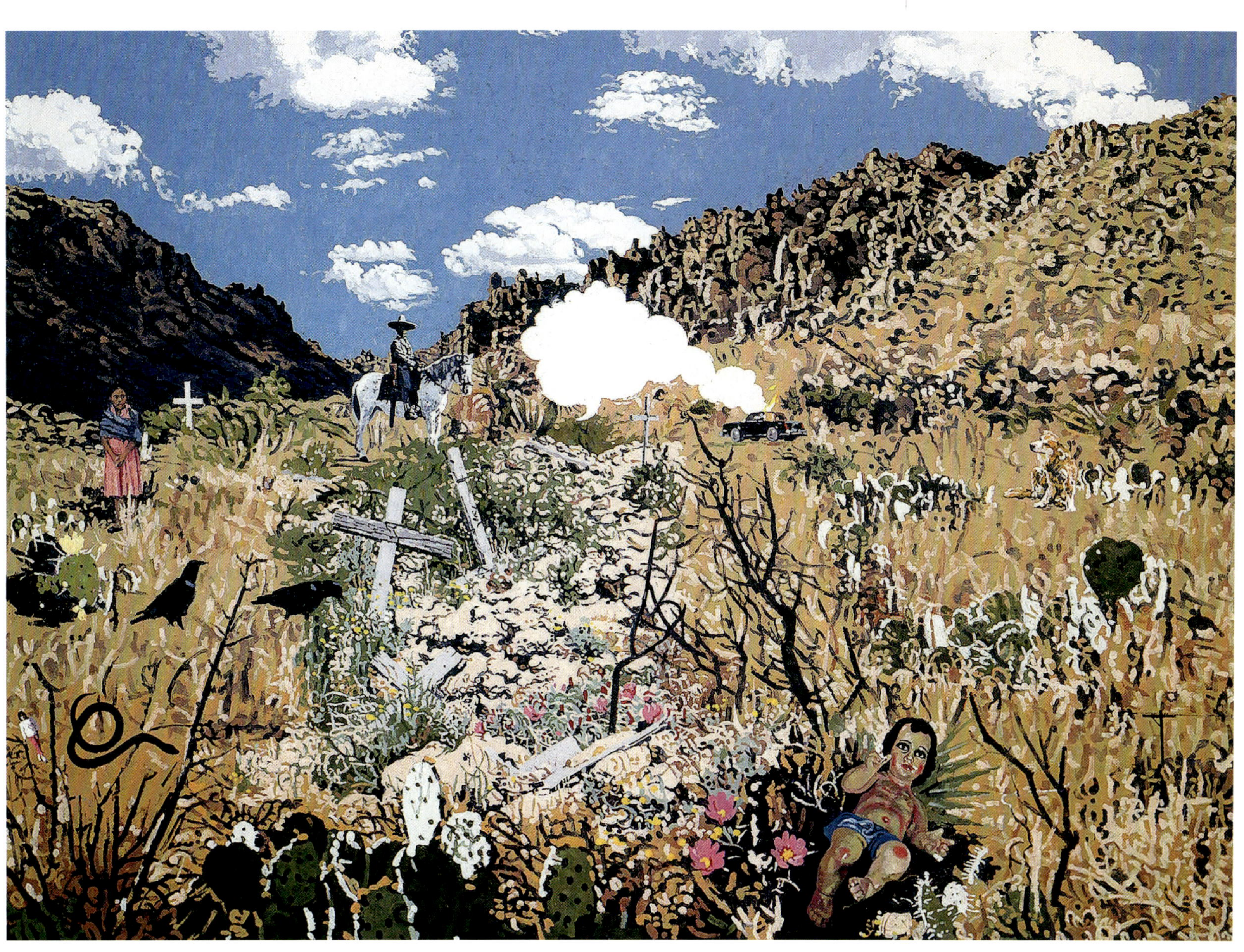

Devil's Garden, 1990

oil on linen | 62" × 86" | Collection of the El Paso Museum of Art, gift of the artist pool. Winter aimed for the painting to be his most honest effort. Whatever he saw through the camera lens would be used as the basis for the painting, without compromise—that meant taking every square millimeter on the film negative and treating each detail with the same exacting care. The upshot is a work of great contrasts: the idyllic reclining statue—the woman and her story frozen and static, while all else undergoes constant change; the trash barrel emitting tufts of smoke; the backside of a taxi leading our gaze to a residential building down the street; the multitudes of leaves turning a range of autumn hues. Up close, however, the painting is a welter of abstract strokes as Winter develops a secondary language in which each element is interrelated in very specific ways: daubs, staccato and wristy gestures, circles, and edgy strokes that coalesce as images of animals, protozoa, and funny demonic figures that spin and tumble across the canvas.

Stylistically, the work is kaleidoscopic, the binder being its propulsive energy. "I thought no matter how long it takes me, I'm going to regain what I had and I'm going to paint this with a certain precision that I had lost," Winter says. "I worked on the *Monument* painting for a month. I'd get up early, start a fire in my studio, and paint for eight hours. There was something wondrous about that statue, like doing a portrait. A couple of out-of-sight figures in the painting are camouflaged by foliage, street signage, and building details. I painted every leaf. *Monument* has a grayed, subtle tonality, texture, and light that speaks to my solemn realization of personal loneliness. I tried to recover the approach and subjects I had during the Fischbach years—everything was in place in that other life. But I wasn't facing the new reality of living on twenty-six acres in the ice and snow of Maine. You can't go home again via one painting. So *Monument* freed me to close a door and look for new territory. It took guts, but I'm no quitter."

During this same period, Winter began reading Federico Garcia Lorca's poetry of dreams, journeys, and glimpses from balconies of sunbaked meadows and realms of erotic yearning. He was especially fascinated by Lorca's essays on *duende*, the idea that an artwork should brim with authenticity, death awareness, and skin-prickling awe and soul. The *duende* intertwining of light and darkness, the transformation of sorrow or despair into art, gave Winter the impetus to pursue his subjective urges in painting. What follows are open-ended narratives with recurrent themes: the lives we share with animals—wild, domestic, and imaginary; the vagaries of religious faith; the peculiar alchemy by which temperament combines with chance and sometimes impulsive choices to determine the shape of one's fate. Winter aims to probe questions that lie at the heart of a reflective existence: Who, or what, is really in charge of our destiny? There is in the Maine paintings a feeling of queasy anticipation, as if something dark and terrible might happen at any moment. They convey grim and guarded tidings, delivered with beauty, strangeness, and drive. Winter's stories begin on this side of reality and slip to the other—often so gracefully and with such a precise rendering of the magical that we become inadvertent believers.

These broader tectonic shifts can be detected in *Bangor* (1991), in which a street of Victorian houses and a neighborhood park set the stage for an oblique drama involving a stone angel half-buried in the snow, three crows perched on tree branches, a fox leaping in midair, a young boy in a black-hooded coat, scattered flames, and a partially bitten Wolf River apple. Here, darkness and light are protean forces engaged in a metaphorical dance, one in which light both illuminates and annihilates, and darkness is both a well of despair and a source of fecund mysteries. One crow carries a burning branch—the fire of life—in its beak. The apple, placed alongside the angel in the extreme foreground, refers to forbidden fruit. The child passing by is witness to the scene, with all the strange twists and turns this unpredictable world takes, all the bizarre changes of fortune, for good and bad, it can offer.

In Winter's paintings, birds act as figures of prophecy, manifestations of trauma, voices of the superego. They are embodiments of both human and cosmic spirit—a symbolism suggested by their lightness and rapidity, the soaring freedom of their flight, and their mediation between earth and sky. Winter's crows, however, are tricksters of multiple guises—they are signs of trouble to come, or trouble already arrived. By the same

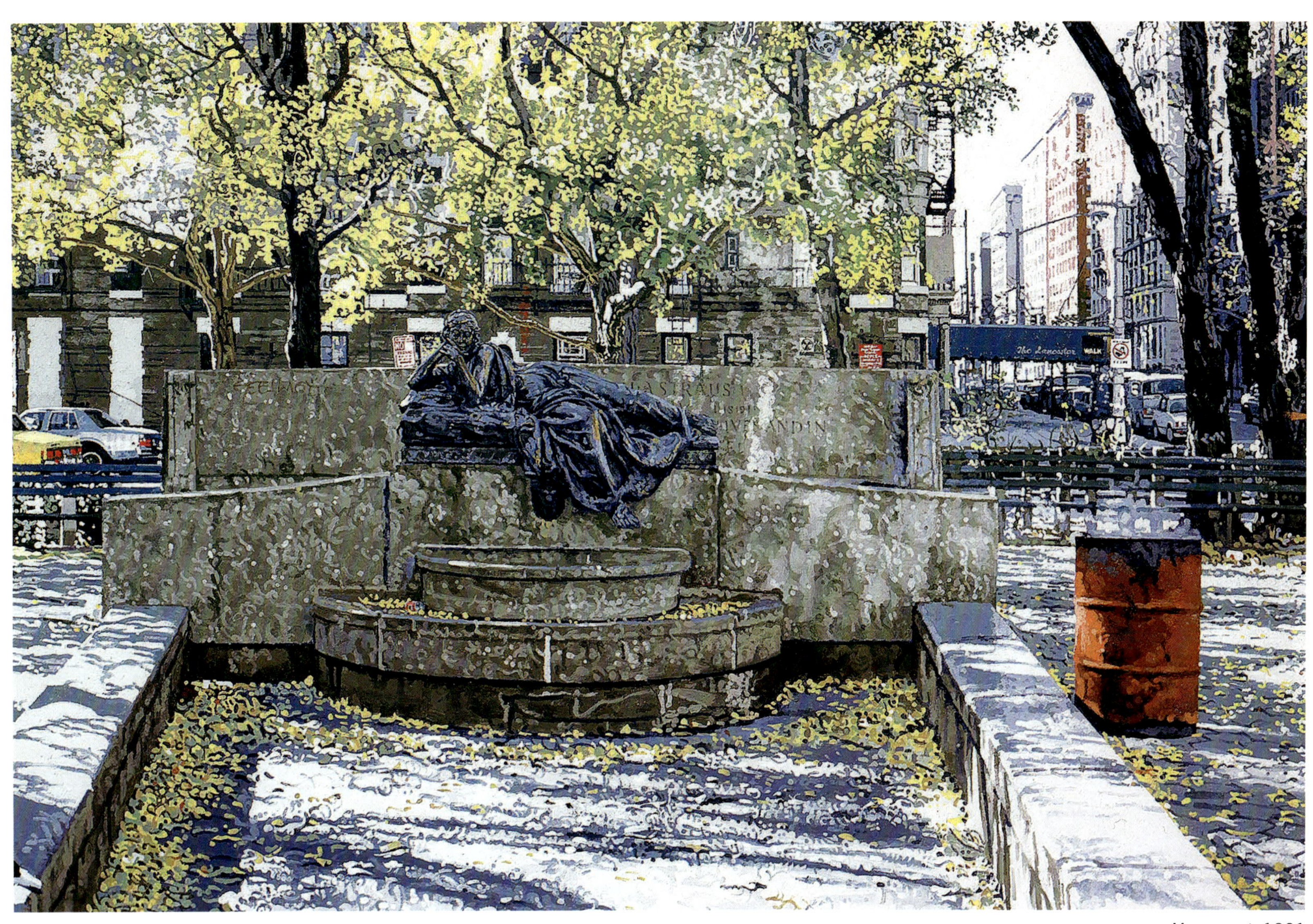

Monument, 1991

oil on linen | 48" × 72" | Collection of Susan H. Albritton, Dallas

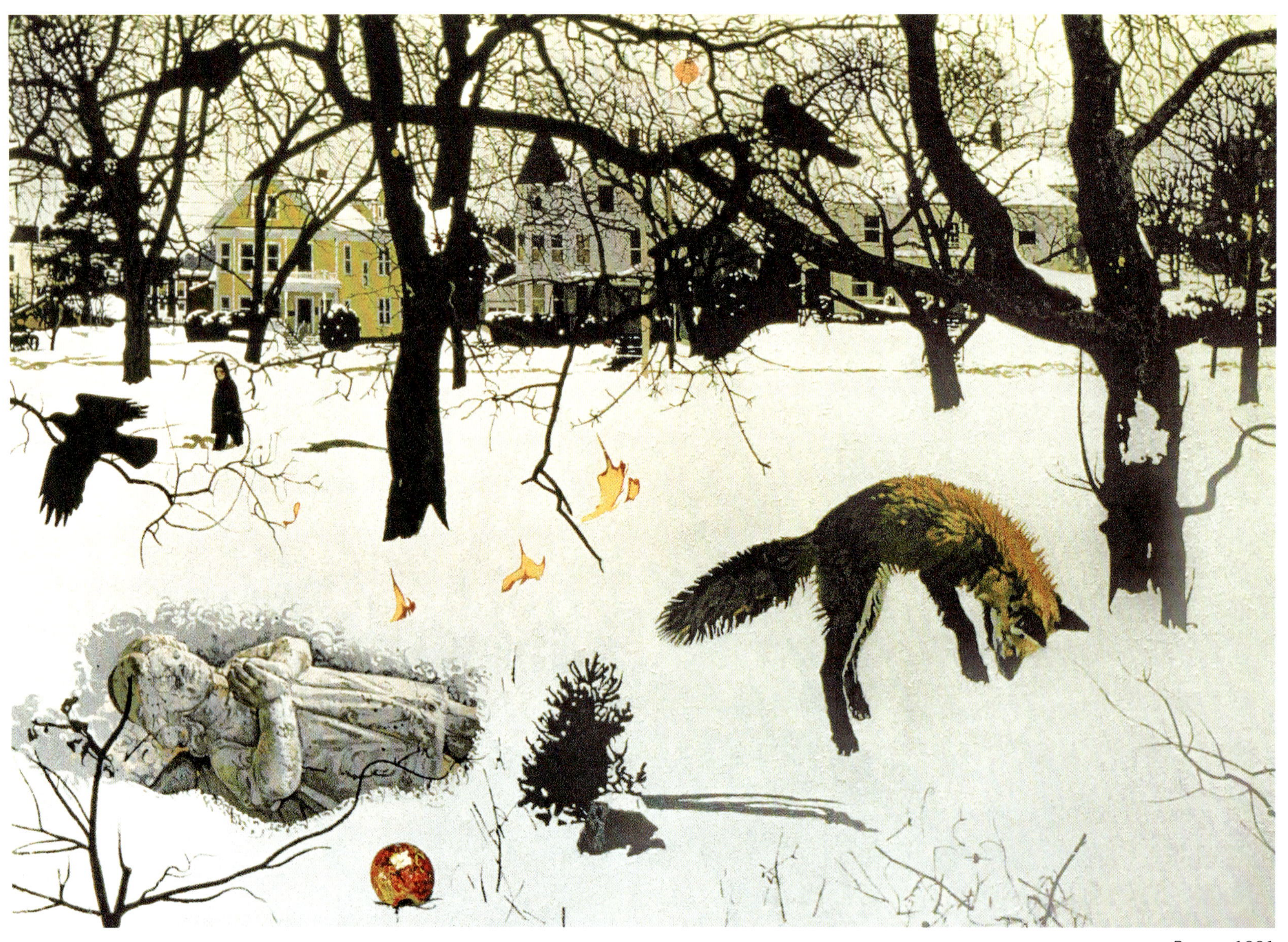

Bangor, 1991

oil on linen | 60" × 84" | Collection of Susan H. Albritton, Dallas

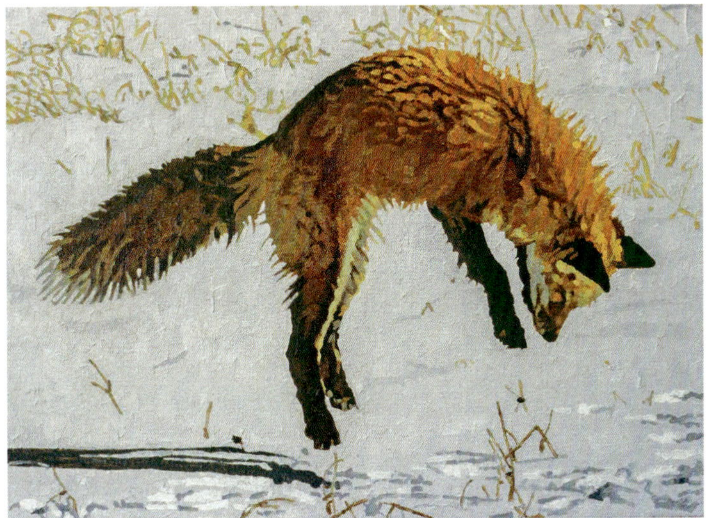

Jumping Fox, 1993
oil on linen | 13" × 18" | Private collection, Dallas

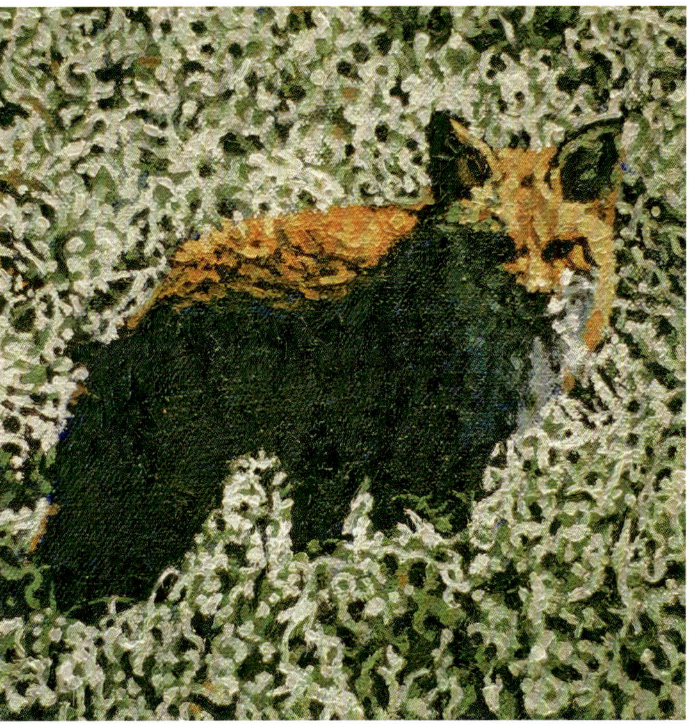

Old Fox, 1992
oil on linen | 8" × 8" | Private collection, Dallas

token, Winter's fox is representative of guile—a symbolism based on its cleverness, but also extending to malice and evil. As a nocturnal animal difficult to trap, the fox became a Christian analogy for the wiles of the devil. For Winter, however, the animal was an unlikely companion throughout the snow season. He had never seen a fox in the wild before moving to Maine and was enchanted by its expressions and predatory habits. In a series of portraits, Winter imbues the fox with a sublime nobility, an attempt to give voice and form to some of his deepest intuitions and feelings. He renders the fur in minutely finished and marvelously tactile strokes. A sense of wonder and innocence prevails, as if we are seeing these creatures of myth and fairy tales through the eyes of a child, transformed into a visual language of provocative beauty and psychological complexity. "It was miraculous the way they would come running across the field or hunt by jumping up in the air," Winter recalls. "They listen to the snow. They'll put their ears down until they hear mice or voles or something moving. They leap up and their entire nose or most of their head goes into the snow. I saw a fox come up once with three mice in its mouth. They would sit on our frozen pond and stare up at the house. In the winter months, our field covered with snow became a stage and the animals were actors. It was inevitable that such a scene would work its way into my paintings."

Turning things inside out, tipping them upside down, placing things side by side, nesting harm within harmlessness—all this Winter does to great and provocative effect. However, in his realm, the road to redemption passes directly through suffering. The Maine paintings serve as poetic meditations on the human struggle to make sense of a cruel and indifferent universe. In doing so, they bring together elements of a mature vision: an aching beauty, an arch theatricality, complex compositional orchestrations. Sometimes the action is galvanic, an explosive moment that opens the narrative into dangerous, unknown territory. Sometimes the struggle is deeply buried and psychological, or it is the kind that comes from above, like an act of God, a bartering of one's gamble with the cosmic wheel. More and more, Winter began to regard his expanded cast of characters as protagonists in a medieval morality play. Popular in fifteenth- and sixteenth-century Europe, morality plays "used allegorical stories to teach a moral message, underpinned by Christian teachings. The characters personified abstract qualities of good and evil, virtue and vice, which

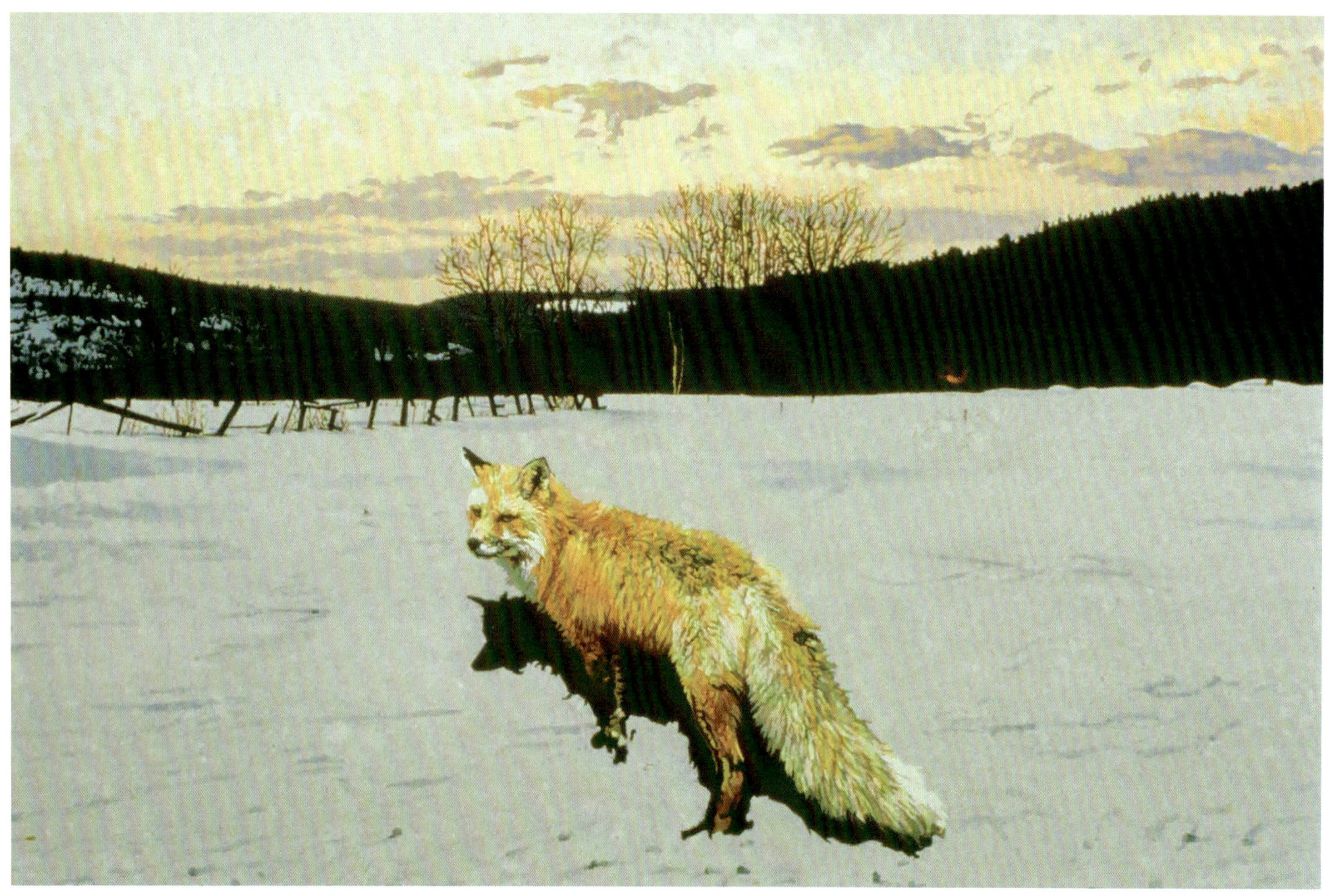

Landscape with Fox, 1993
oil on linen | 36" × 54" | Courtesy of the artist

engaged in a battle to win the soul" of an ordinary, flawed human, who struggles to achieve salvation.[7]

Winter's paintings demand engagement and a kind of surrender, a willingness to enter a work shaped by correlation and metaphor, by brilliant image and largeness of spirit. *Landscape with Sun and Moon* (1993) is an intimate depiction of life, death, and the relationship of predator and prey. It also evokes an experience of awe, that often mysterious feeling of being in the presence of something vast that transcends our understanding of the world. The town of Bucksport serves as backdrop for the major issues of humankind: love and hate, violence and tenderness, good and evil. It is a scene of stinging contrasts. In the distance is a seemingly peaceful settlement of farmhouses and barns, an old pickup truck, telephone wires, and trees. The foreground, however, focuses on a slaughtered doe stretched out in the snow, the blood dripping from her mouth. A chained black dog enters from far left. A crow observes the carnage from its perch on a low-slung branch at right. An angel, playing a concertina, strides across the sky and seemingly trails a diabolical crow in full wingspan. The sun is about to go down and the moon is high in the sky. The light is brighter, while the shadows are darker. Everything has a sharp edge and is strikingly beautiful and also a little menacing. According to Winter, the dead deer was spotted on a West Texas highway. Recognizing that death is a stage of life, the artist decided to pull over and photograph the deer. Later, for an accurate color of blood, he punctured a finger with a compass point, drained a few drops of blood on a white paper towel, and mixed a replica of the color in oil paint. The angel is an image from a visit to the Museum of International Folk Art in Santa Fe. The black dog belonged to a Dallas artist. Throughout, Winter combines imagery from many times, places, and possible worlds to create a montage play that reflects his spiritual state at the time.

In *Snow Moon* (1994), a Native American name for the February full moon, a snow-covered blueberry hill in Waldo County teems with grackles—one with a thought balloon jutting out from its head—a leaping fox, distant flames, a car with headlights, a dead deer, and, ascending above the entire scene, an angel with outstretched arms. Its wings reverberate a golden light across the snow that shines on the deer's body.

About the paintings, Bruce Brown writes, "Both include the sun and moon suggesting a time of day when one's mind is more likely to drift into a dreamlike state in which gravity loosens its grip to give way to imagining spiritual angels flying or a fox leaping above the wintery landscape. The circular placement of the birds, fox and angel surrounding the dead deer killed in battle and quickly disappearing under snow and encased by the vibrant branches on either side may suggest the cycle of life and death. The only hints of a human presence are the artificial headlights in the distant car on the horizon in *Snow Moon*. Whereas the backdrop of *Landscape with Sun and Moon* presents a gloomy neighborhood seemingly devoid of people. Both paintings have a lively aural sense about them. The viewer is bound to hear the sound of the birds and angels in flight as well as the leaping fox high above the snow."[8]

Again, Winter assembles the elements and actors from various sources: grackles, deer, and blue sky were photographed on trips through Texas; the fox and fire were observed on the Winters' Maine property and in the studio. Still, there is the sense of reaching across borders between Winter and the animals, wild and tame. It is possible that Winter sees himself in the animals around him, even as they reflect back his own assumptions about the world. Animals are not human, of course, but they are enough like us to instill a strange and strong sense of kinship. Winter became a keen and relentless observer of woods and fields and beasts of every variety. Yet his respect for nature never spills over into cloying reverence. Rather, he paints with special feeling about loneliness while eloquently pinning down a central concern of human life: the passage of time.

Self Portrait with White Horse (1993) suggests that life is like trudging through the snow—day and night, sun and storm—toward the inevitable goalpost of death. Here, the artist depicts himself wearing a red cap, a black coat, and a smile as he shovels a trench. Slightly behind him, to the right, a white horse bows its head as if to acknowledge the endless task. The white horse may be a symbol of light, life, and spiritual illumination. However, death rides a pale horse in the book of Revelation. "Mortal life is not always what you had in mind," Winter explains. "I was on a private search for an understanding of existence and unanswered questions. Hank Williams wrote that song, 'No matter how you struggle and strive, you'll never get out of this world alive.' So I was thinking that no matter how hard I work, I'm not going to escape death. I've always used the white horse as a dark omen. Something beautiful, but something that announces our mortality."

For *Dark Side of the Moon* (1993) a mysterious cloaked figure walks through snowy woods with his back to the viewer. In the foreground, a black dog sniffs at drops of blood in the snow near a bleached deer antler. Another dog seemingly laughs, a thought balloon extending from its open mouth of ferocious white teeth. The ominous crows witness the scene. According to Winter, the imposing figure is based on a statue of Hannibal Hamlin, who served as Abraham Lincoln's first vice president. The setting sun, upper left, represents the dark side of the moon. Whereas the narrative refers to the savage death that occurs in the wild, it also suggests hidden secrets, pitched anxieties, and illicit yearnings. *Landscape with Wounded Deer* (1993) utilizes all of the subjects in Winter's repertoire from the period: a late sky, raptors, a fire, granite rocks, blood, and brambles. A guardian angel accompanies the hunted doe in final throes of death, blood dripping from her mouth. A crow, as predator, follows the pair below. It is important to note that Winter

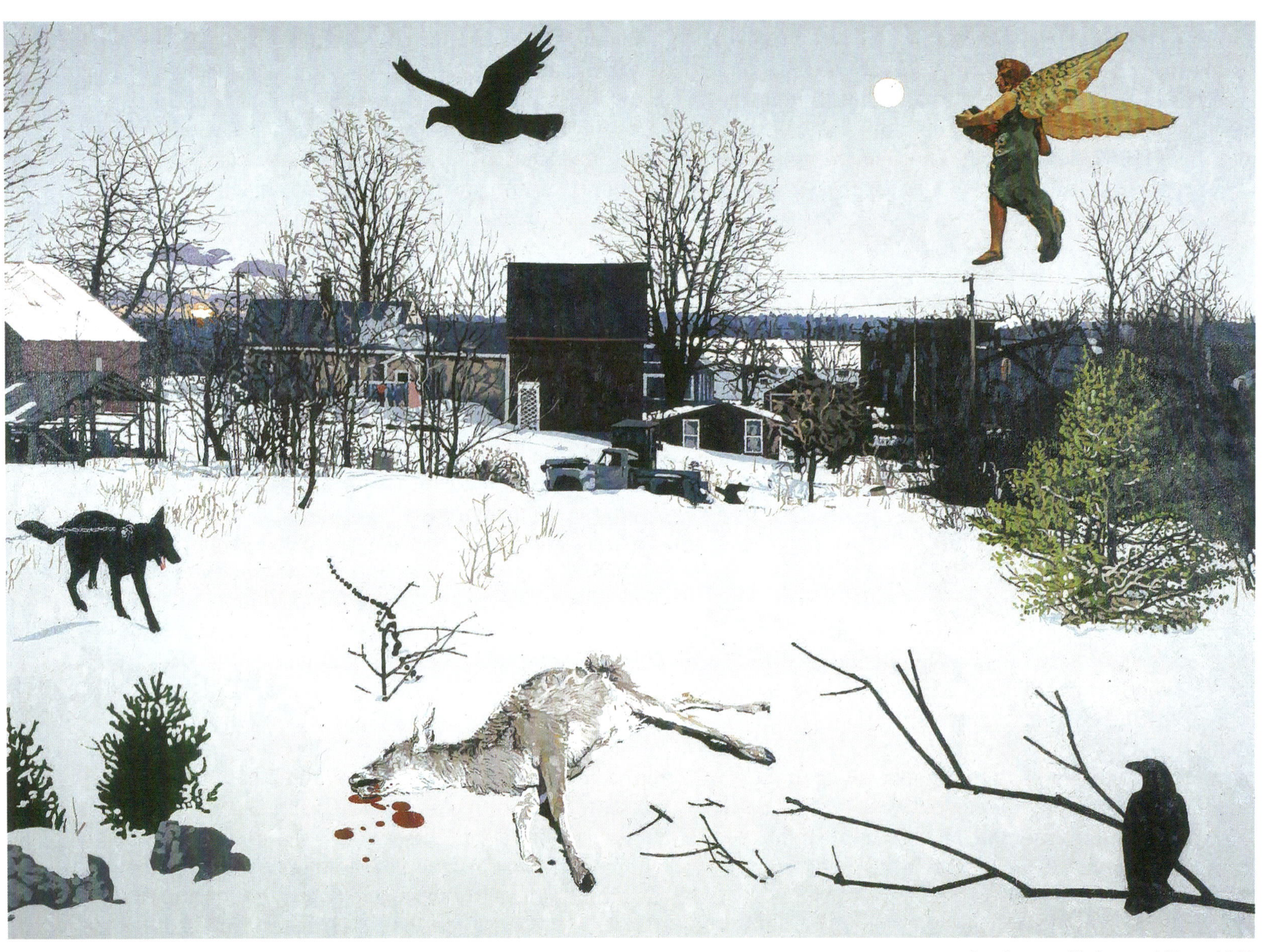

Landscape with Sun and Moon, 1993

oil on linen | 60" × 84" | Collection of Claude C. Albritton, Dallas

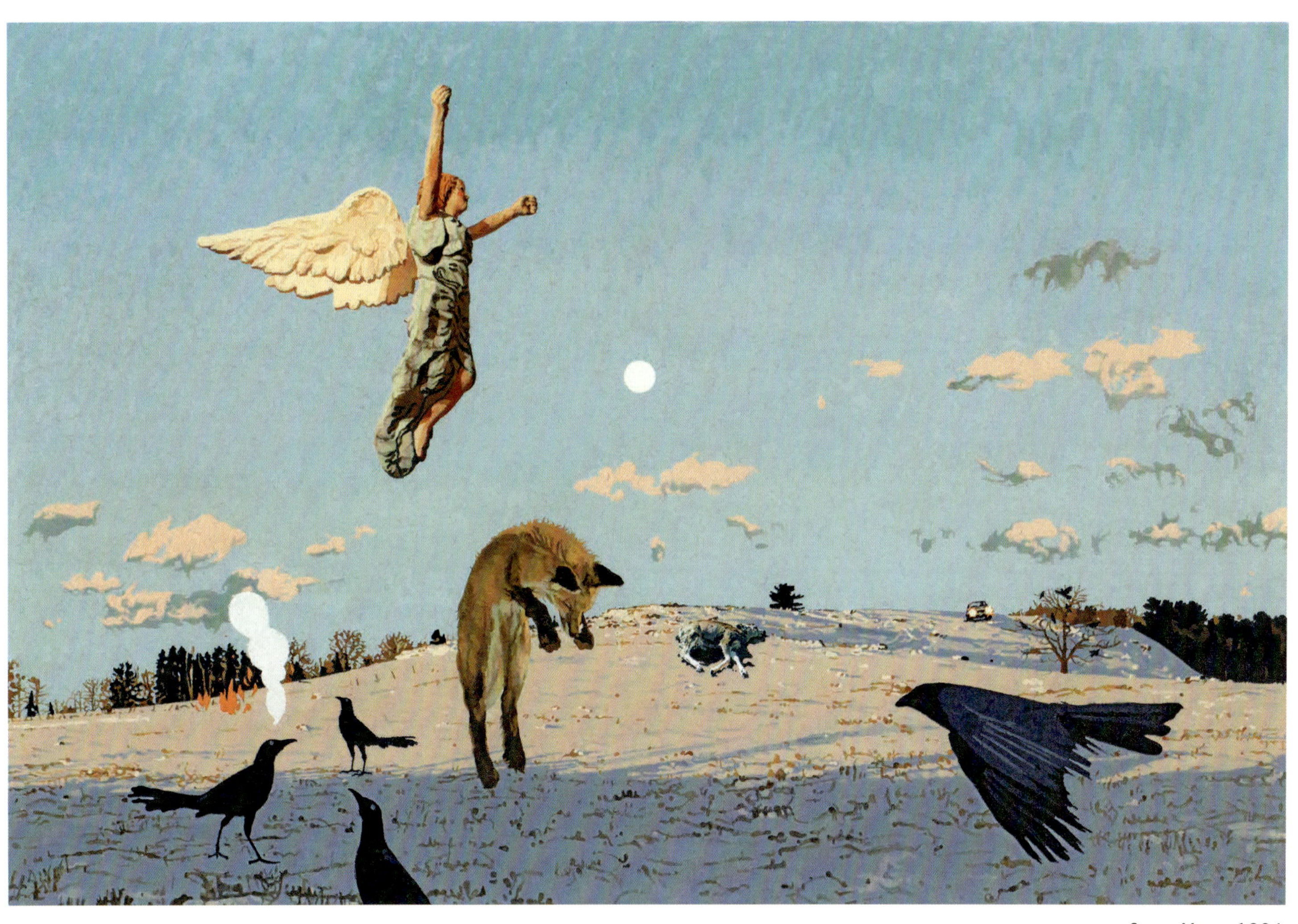

Snow Moon, 1994

oil on linen | 48 1/8" × 72 1/8" | Portland Museum of Art, Maine | Museum purchase with support from the Benefit of the Collection Fund | 1998.110 | Photography by Luc Demers

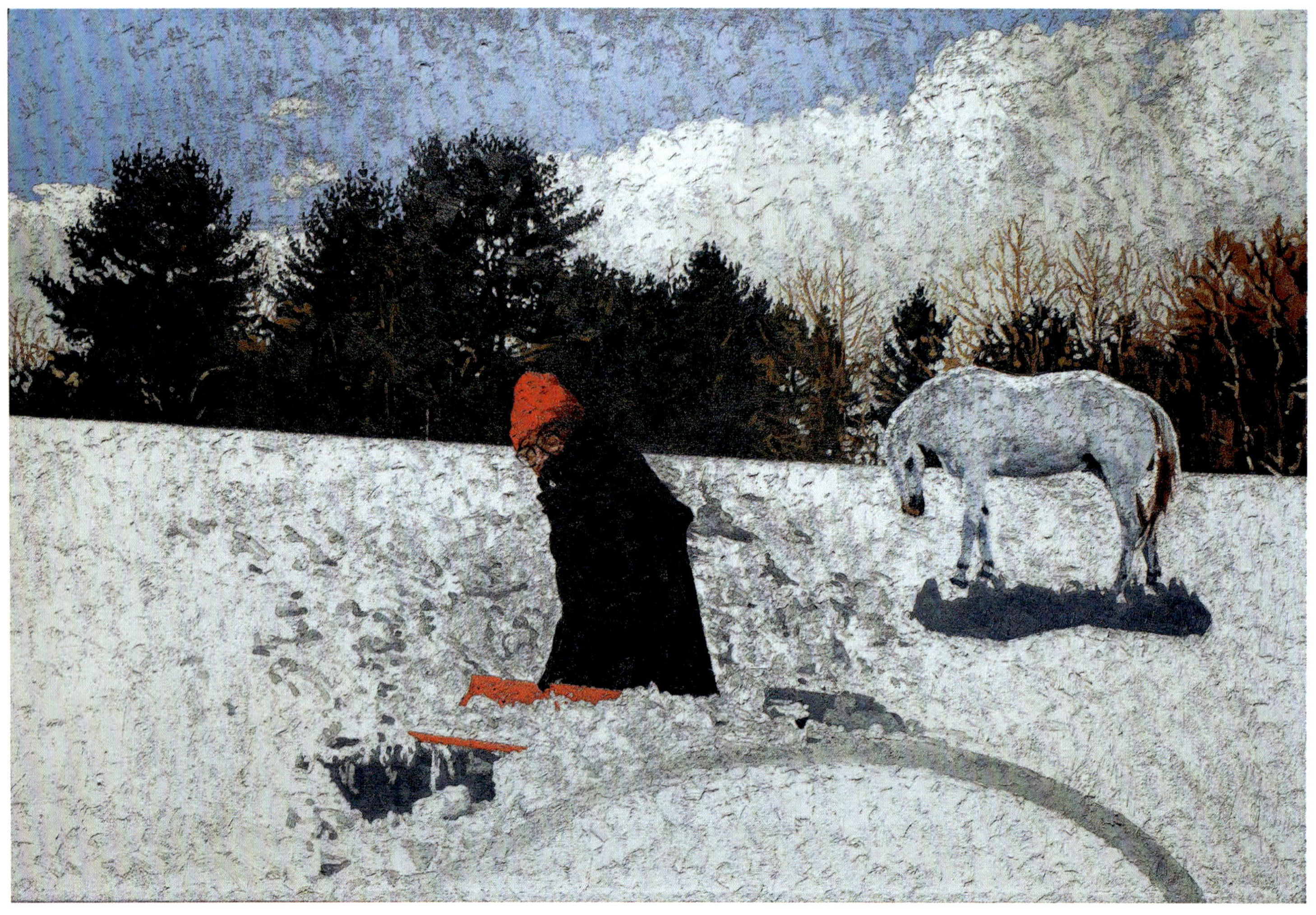

Self Portrait with White Horse, 1993
oil on linen | 24" × 36" | Collection of Kirk Hopper, Dallas | Photography by G. Valderas

continued to visit the Metropolitan Museum of Art for inspiration during trips to Manhattan. He cites Jean-Baptiste-Camille Corot's *Hagar in the Wilderness* (1835) as a particular influence on the development of his morality "plays" set in Maine and Texas. No doubt Winter identified with the French artist's ambitious biblical painting of Hagar and Ishmael driven away into the rocky, arid desert of Beersheba. Corot has chosen the moment of their divine salvation: an angel soars above the scene, an enigmatic medium between humans and the Creator. Winter associated its lyrical mystery and luminous aura with the wilds of far West Texas. Similarly, his depiction of the El Niño in *Devil's Garden* was stimulated by the open, vulnerable position of the child Ishmael lying on the rocks in the right foreground of Corot's large historical landscape.

Overall, however, the essential sources that sustained Winter's art were gospel, older forms of country music, and Mexican culture. At the time, he nursed a deep homesickness for Texas and a desire to interpret it in the new visual language he had refined in Maine. He was looking to clear a kind of space in his life. The result is a small ensemble that illuminates Winter's skill as a dramatist, a spinner of sharply observed narratives. What we see in the *Texas Odyssey* series is a deft melding of formal intelligence and rowdy mysticism that has us questioning the strangeness of our lives, why we are where we are, and the precise nature of the journey. For the most part, Winter aims to make dream states visible. Still, the surreal image—which, at its most resonant, breaks through consciousness in unexpected ways—is an elusive thing. This unpredictability, this element of surprise, is what separates Winter's dramas from those that miss the mark. Winter's *Texas Odyssey* paintings are firmly of this world, but they have an expectant and otherworldly air, filled with images that seem to contain other forms of knowing. Eerie and spellbinding, they sharpen our senses, causing a collision in our complex negotiation between the world's construction of us and our construction of it. *Texas Odyssey #1* (1994) reaffirms how cyclical and fated all our destinies are. As in *Self Portrait with White Horse*, which depicts the artist interminably shoveling snow, the painting portrays a Mexican woman sweeping a four-lane Texas highway alongside a string of seemingly limitless telephone wires. A tiny train barrels toward her—and us—in the far distance. Thus, Winter connects the temporal and the infinite. She is an embodiment of the unquenchable, unreasoning life force, and also its uselessness against the fates that resign us all to oblivion in the end.

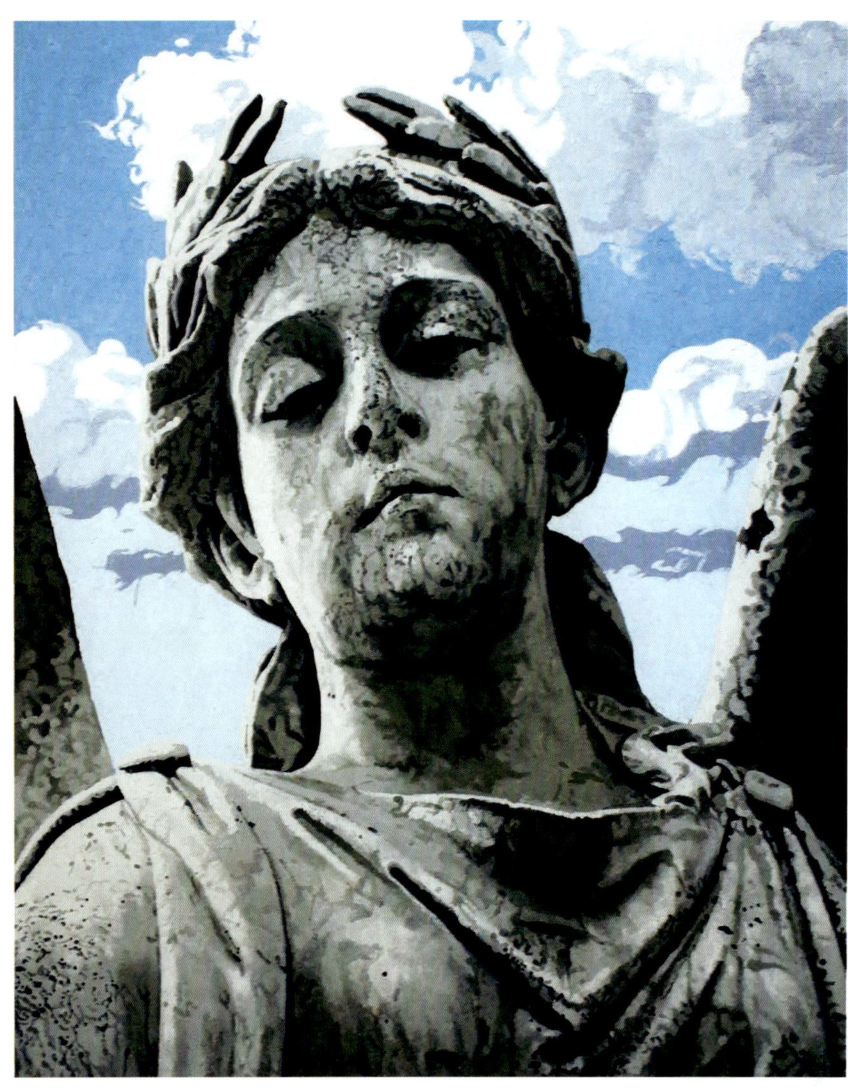

Angel, 1994
oil on linen | 48" × 60" | Collection of Kirk Hopper, Dallas | Photography by G. Valderas

Similarly, *Texas Odyssey #2* (1994) is about the loneliness of the earthbound, as well as the laws of our mortality—gravity, appetite, brevity—and our spiritual world—eternity, timelessness, and occurrences we cannot fathom. A cow floats in the sky amid telephone wires; a Dairy Queen sign—a product of the cow—is anchored into the earth. Abandoned cars are scattered across a scrubby field punctuated by combustible flames. Winter's images purposely defy gravity, even as they combine the impossible and the prosaic, the visible and the invisible. In *Texas Odyssey #3* (1994), an elderly Mexican woman in patterned dress and heels wanders along on a rocky Hill Country road. The cropped head of a panting black dog, a familiar member of Winter's repertoire, holds the center foreground. The dog's ears are pricked, the eyes trained on something at far left, beyond the picture plane. The woman and dog are connected by a tension of unease, a threat, a sense that things are off kilter. The entirety suggests the beauty and wonder of mortal life, as well as the complex possibilities of the mind's eye. In Winter's realm, the physical becomes transcendent. Indeed, the flowing together of time is a theme in the *Texas Odyssey* scenes, as if all are happening at once, past unfolding into present and turning into future.

The hopelessness caused by the personal and professional free fall Winter experienced during the Maine years cannot be overstated. "It takes a lot of ego, strength, self-confidence and resilience to keep going in the face of rejection," he writes. "One thing I know: I can't think my way out of troubles. I have to paint my way out. And this might take several works of exploring alien ground, but

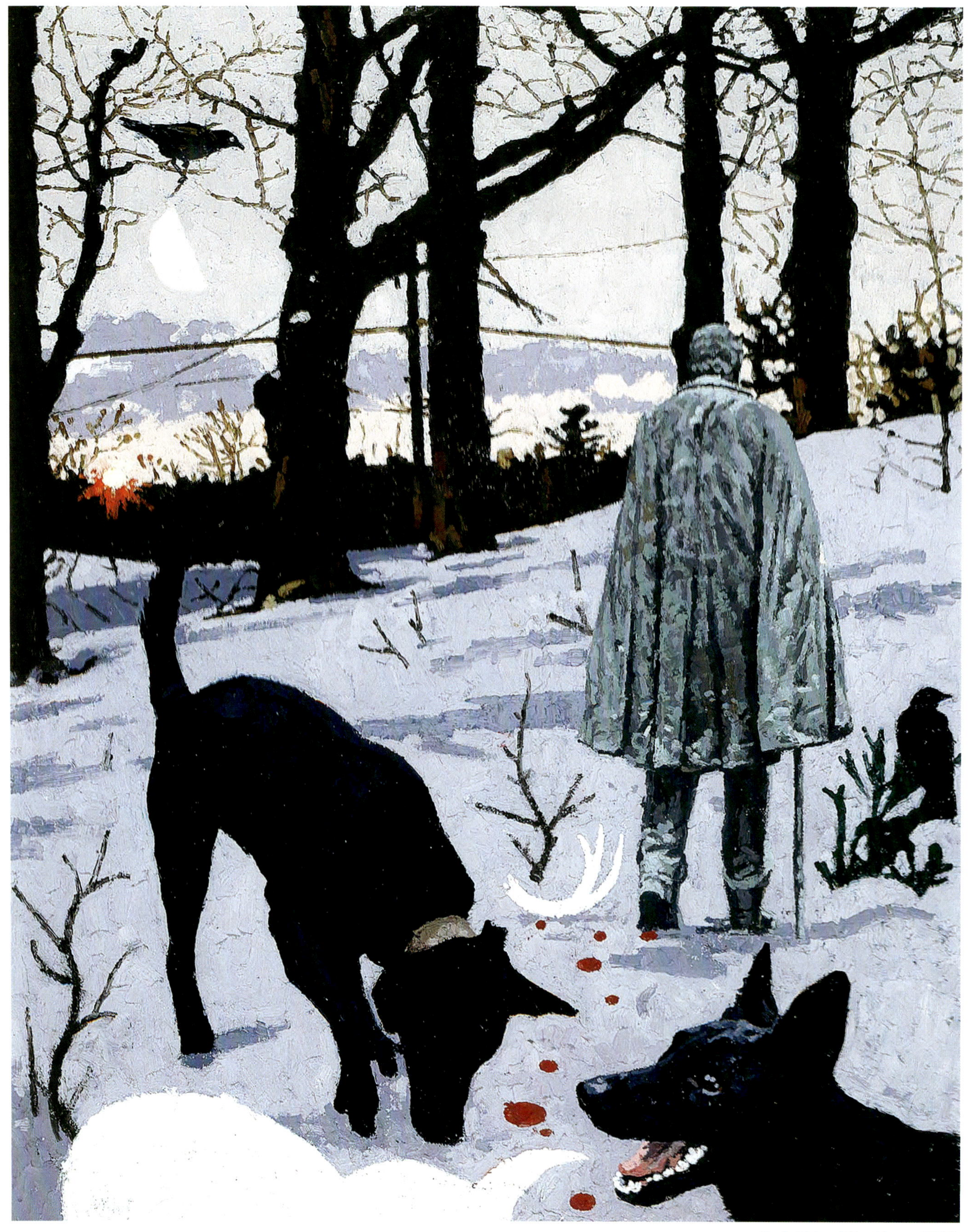

Dark Side of the Moon, 1993

oil on linen | 22" × 18" | Private collection, Dallas

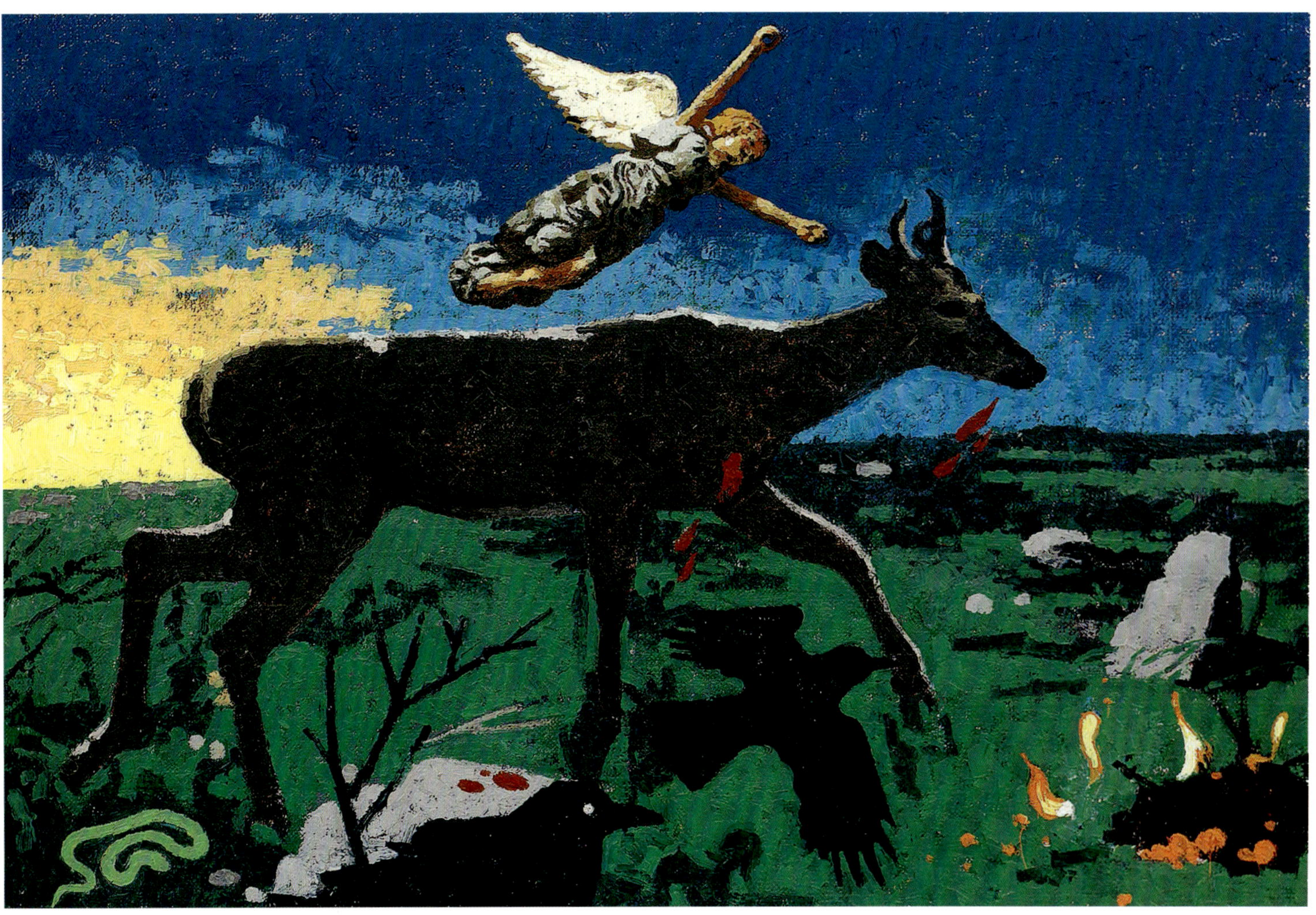

Landscape with Wounded Deer, 1993
oil on linen | 12" × 18" | Collection of Claude C. Albritton, Dallas

often we 'return' with gained insights, discoveries or resolved conflicts—once in a blue moon, the answer just falls out of the heaven when you're not looking or when you surrender."[9]

Winter decided to go for broke. In between the split from Fischbach Gallery and the beginning of the dramatic magic realist works, he relinquished oil for acrylic. He quickly evolved a tightly wound, near-fluorescent "wild style" concoction of newsworthy stories that are at once savage social commentary and powerful, if riveting, paintings. In a crisis of self-doubt, Winter was turning his back on practically the entire art world. Using jars of acrylics supplied by Jeanette, he regarded each new scene as a kind of catharsis—a way of removing anger, pain, and the world's judgment of other people and himself from his system. At the outset, Winter took a vow of noncensorship. Rather, he was after a raw truth that did not rely on his academic drawing skills or a containment of color and content. Winter was at the crossroad of his life and career. Not only did he yearn for a clean slate, he needed to figure out how to fit into a whole new world.

The three distinct series he produced—*Fifty Maine Men*, the political and social commentaries, and the *Seven Deadly Sins*—have a larksome quality all their own. Owing to the unbridled creative imagination of Art Brut as much as the dark underground comic-strip satires of Robert Crumb, the paintings skewer the crueler aspects of American life in fiercely humorous but also compassionate ways that assault and seduce the eye with an aggressive simultaneity of form and meaning. At this point, nothing is too arcane or grotesque. Winter tackles issues of racism, family

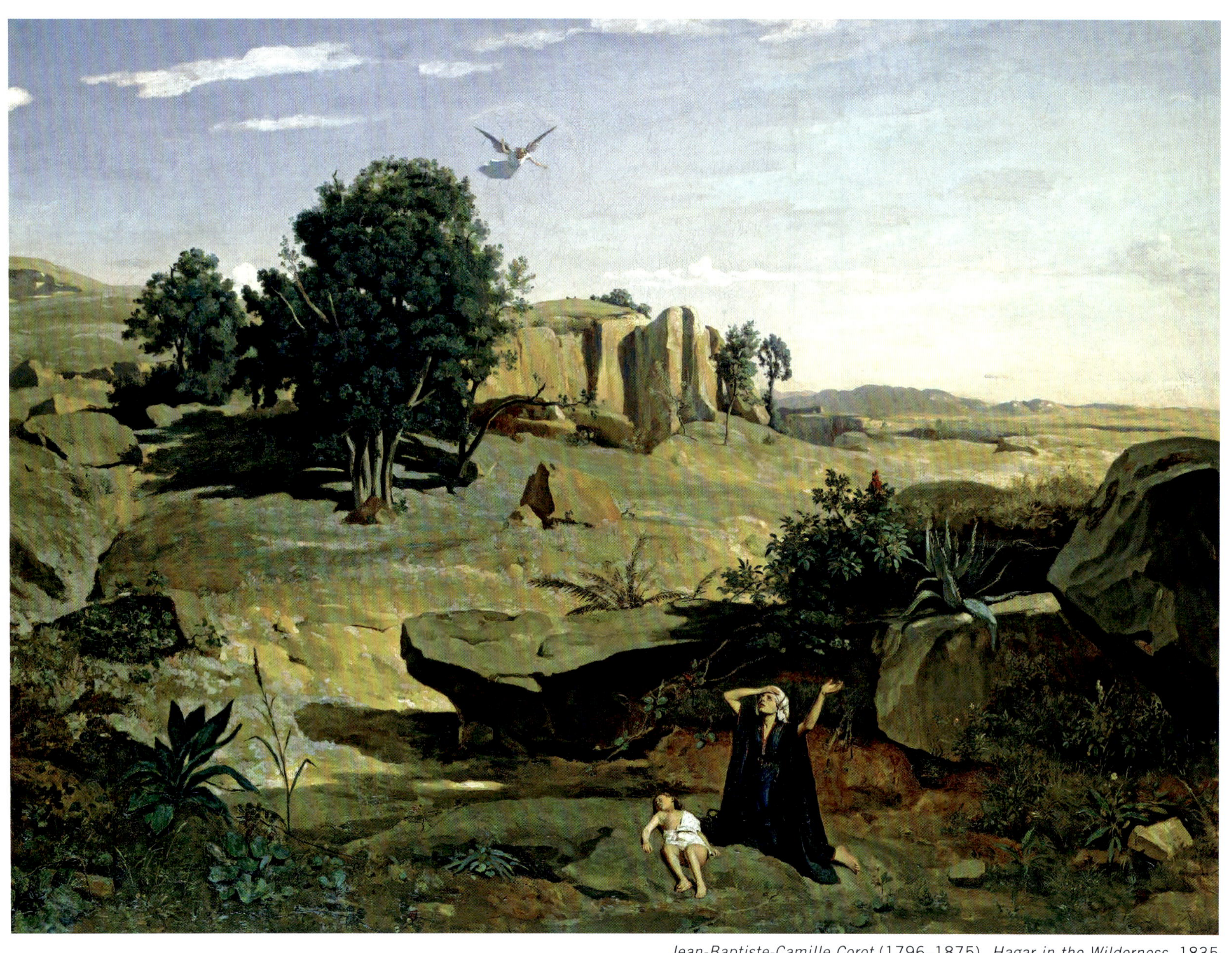

Jean-Baptiste-Camille Corot (1796–1875), *Hagar in the Wilderness,* 1835

oil on canvas | 71" × 106 1/2" (180.3 × 270.5 cm) | Rogers Fund, 1938 (38.64) | The Metropolitan Museum of Art |

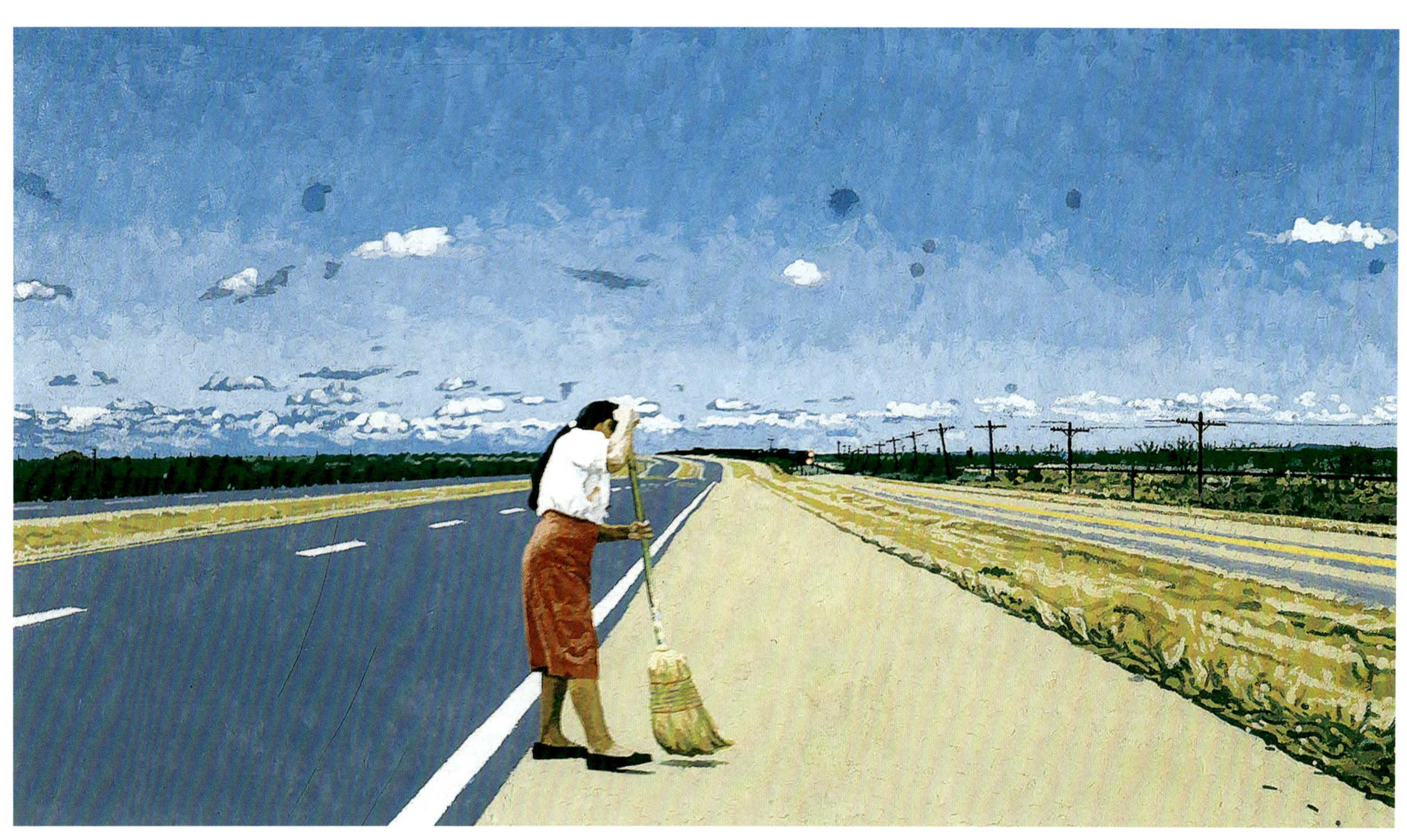

Texas Odyssey #1, 1994
oil on linen | 24" × 36" | Private collection, Dallas

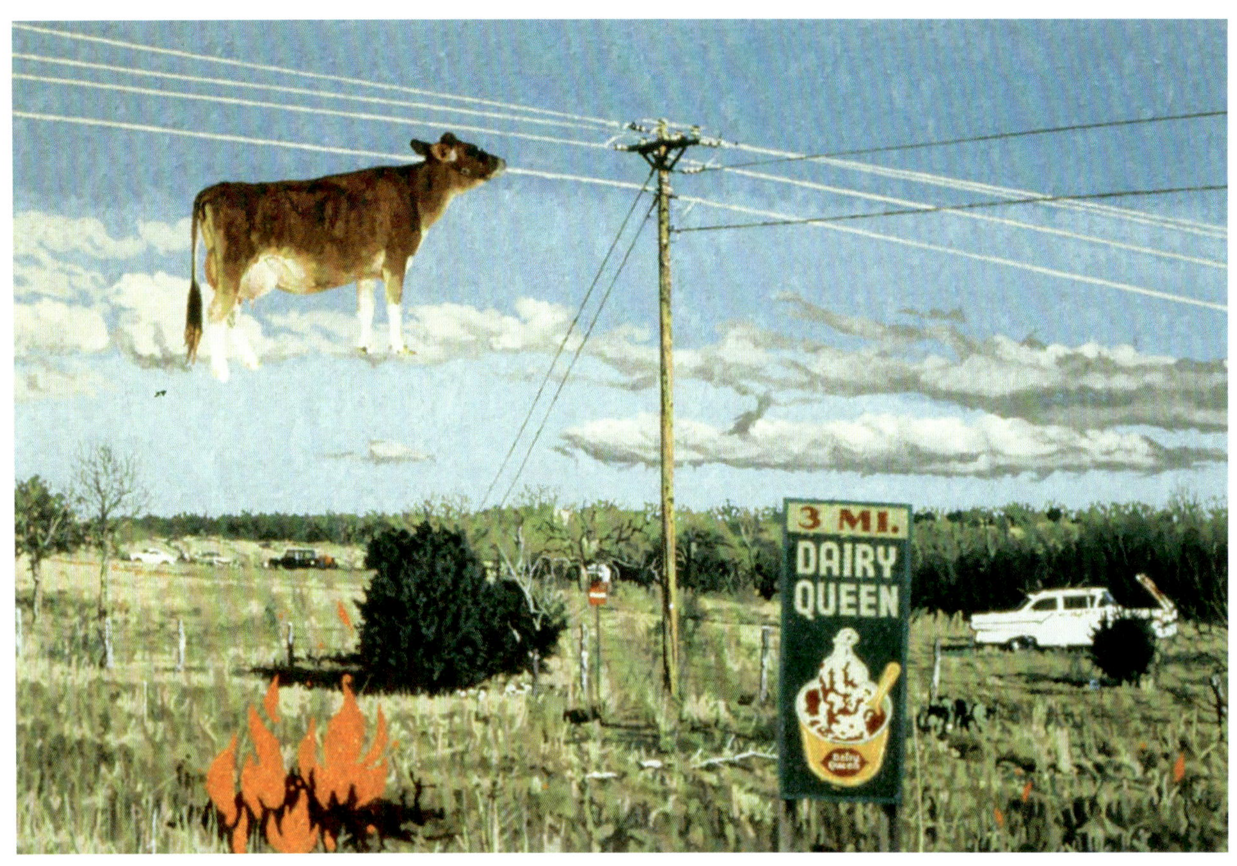

Texas Odyssey #2, 1994

oil on linen | 24" × 36" | Albritton Family Collection, Dallas

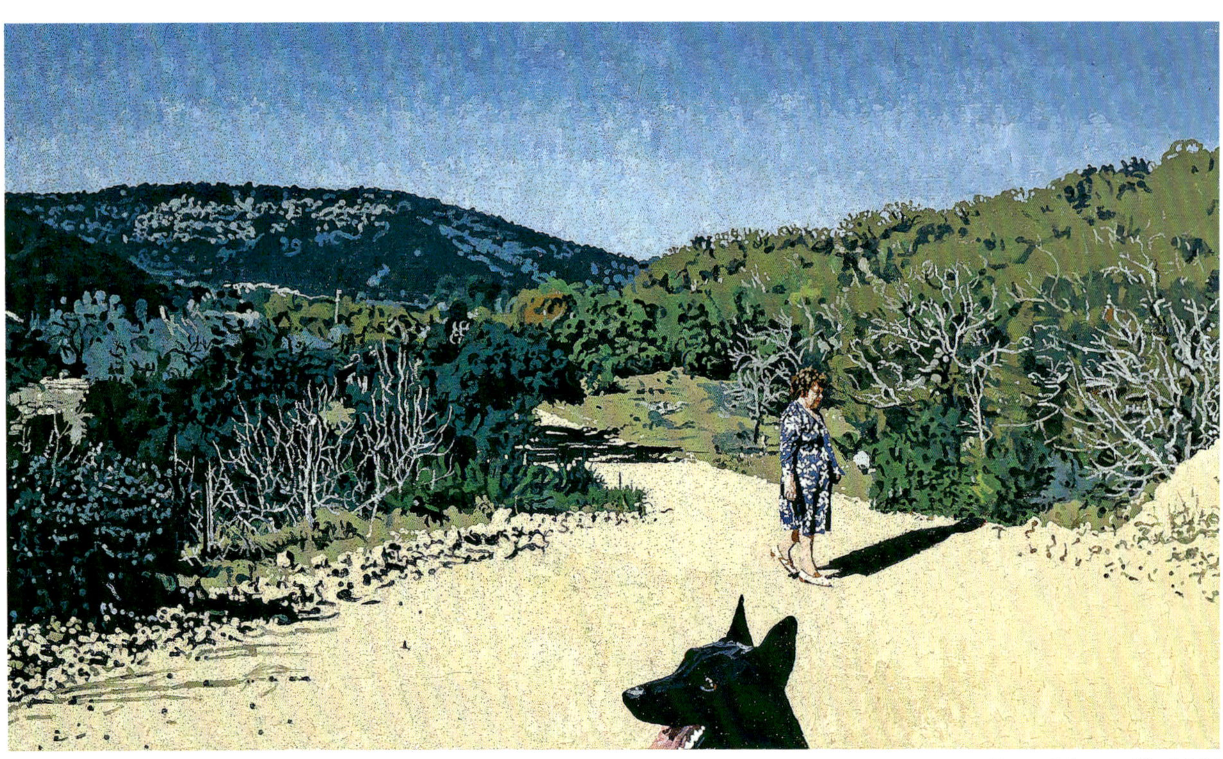

Texas Odyssey #3, 1994

oil on linen | 24" × 36" | Collection of Lillian W. Albritton, Dallas violence, execution, homelessness, religion, and AIDS. He lays siege to political correctness and crimes committed by both sexes. Overall, they are risky, furtive works that capture a mood of moral indignation with a force that has been rarely matched since. If Winter is an adroit enough storyteller, he is also a bold social critic of the sort that is desperately needed in a sound-bite culture.

For *Fifty Maine Men*, Winter sketched and took notes on men he saw around town—walking on the streets or loitering in stores. Back in the studio, he made small paintings from memories and observations. In these, Winter blocks out zones of color as shape or form, which then reveal particular types of characters. According to Winter, Mr. Man lived on the side of a highway and wore the same clothes every day. He is depicted as a mentally challenged buffoon in red cap and wildly colored pants and shirt. Another depicts a man with red, white, and blue suspenders urinating outside a fast-food joint in Bucksport on the Fourth of July. For the most part, the Maine men are rough and stubborn, are usually middle-aged or older, wear striped shirts and plaid hats, and smoke cigarettes.

But if Winter regards the *Fifty Maine Men* paintings as caricatures of a xenophobic community, his explosive political and social commentaries are something else entirely. He wrestles honestly with the messy contradictions inherent in any situation concerning race or class. Here, flat color, composition, narrative, and fury combine as vociferous objections to American life as it was and continues to be. One series deals with the shooting death of Karen Wood, a young mother who lived near Winter. She was killed while trying to warn a hunter that he was too close to houses. Wood was wearing white gloves, which the hunter mistook for a deer's flag. The event made an indelible impression on Winter when the hunter was acquitted by a Maine jury.

In *A Little Punishment for Tiesha Carter* (1991), Winter portrays the savage account by the *New York Times* of how a Bronx mother beat and burned her daughter and then tied her in a cold shower. The girl's grandmother, who watched the brutality, said that "Tiesha was just getting a little punishment."[10] According to Winter, the article also provided a description of religious pictures and icons that decorated the apartment.

For *Fist Fight* (1991), Winter depicts a brawl that he witnessed, which quickly escalated into a full-out race riot. One painting alludes to the beating of Rodney King by Los Angeles police; another, *Snuffer* (1991), refers to the electric chair and scaffold as subconscious forms of sexual paraphernalia. A particularly hard-hitting painting, *Double Lynching* (1991), is based on a 1930s photograph Winter saw of two young black men hanging from a tree in Indiana. The work elicits strong emotions. Winter explains,

> They were having a picnic and drinks underneath the lynched figures. Some stood under the tree, laughing and looking up at the bodies. It was too much for me and I had to cut it off. But somehow the relative sizes of the hanging figures evoked my brother David and me. We were on the edge of our community and I thought if we had been black instead of poor whites we would have been lynched. I was painting at the time with no self-censorship, and perhaps I was naive for painting that way and showing anyone the paintings. They were not goal oriented, but often let my anger and sadness be the only reason for working. Growing up in a racist world where schools, water fountains, restrooms, cafés, movies, churches were segregated made me see how horrifying the human race was and is. The awful things that happened to black people—our nearest neighbors and friends were black. It was very painful for me to do this work, but I wanted to depict the two young men canonized.

Significantly, Winter shows the victims rather than the sinister perpetrators, who often hide in clear sight among us. He sets the gruesome scene amid an otherworldly starry blue night; the branch from which the two men hang, which sheds its green leaves like teardrops, could be interpreted as the horizontal beam of a cross, or perhaps the tree of life. The golden disk of the moon, the work's

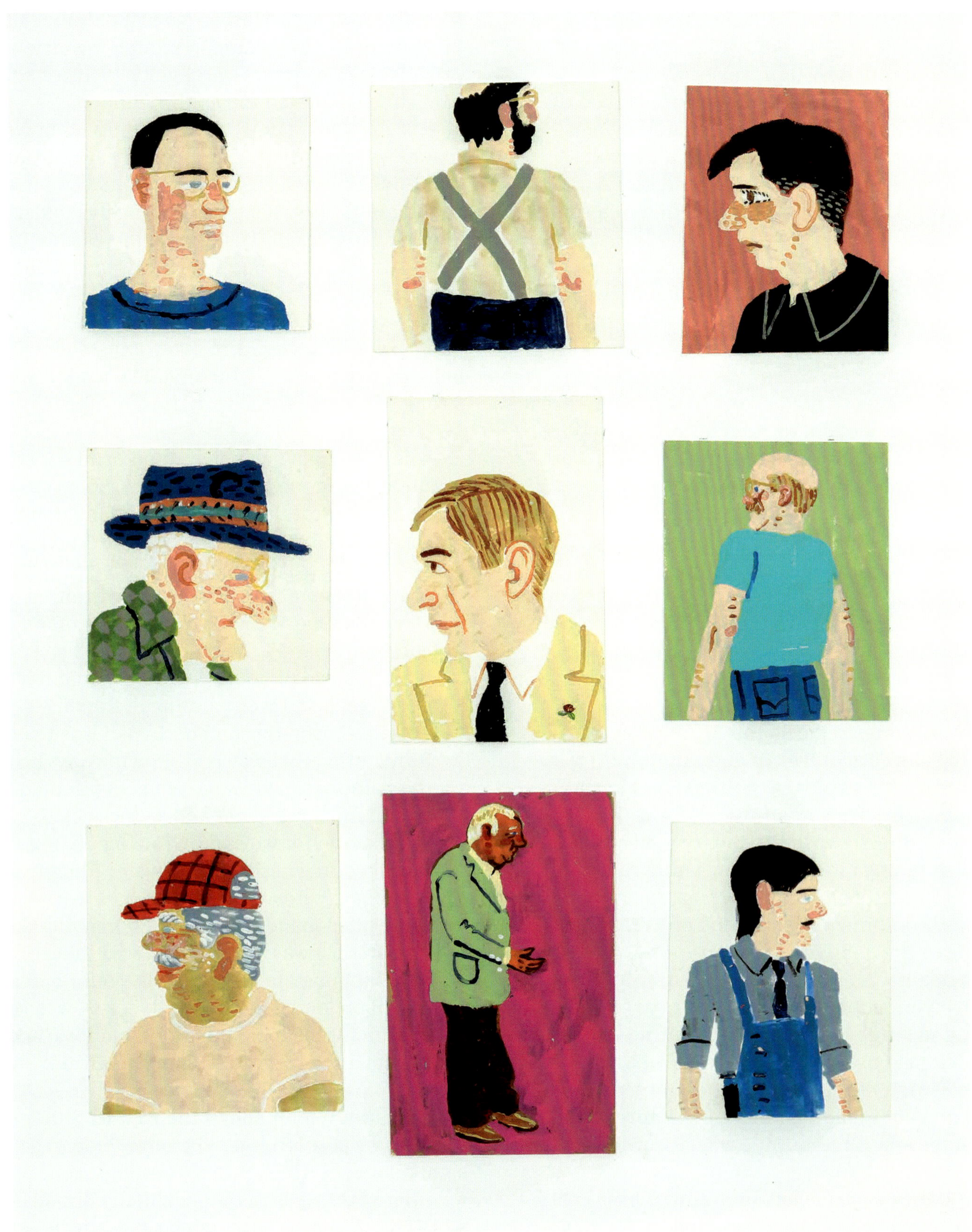

Nine of Fifty Maine Men, 1991
acrylic on museum board | 29" × 23" overall | Courtesy of the artist and Kirk Hopper Fine Art, Dallas | Photography by Joshua Nefsky

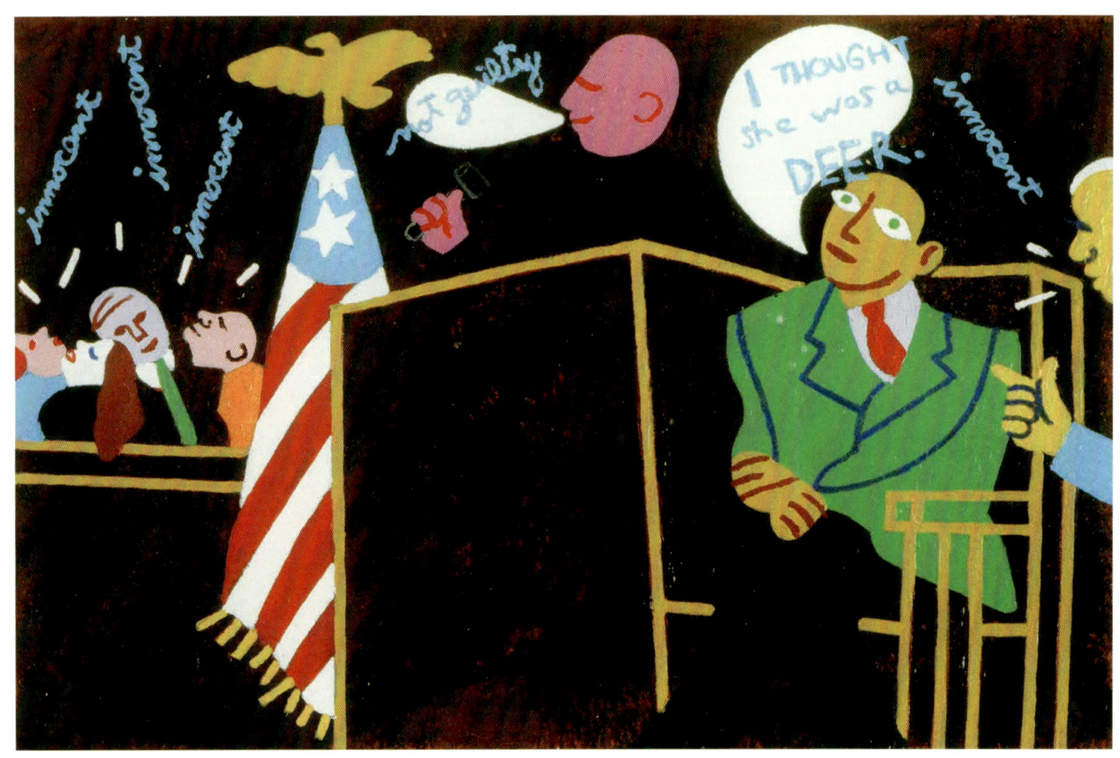

The Shooting Death of Karen Wood #4, 1991
acrylic on museum board | 6" × 9 1/4" | Collection of Deborah M. Gaines

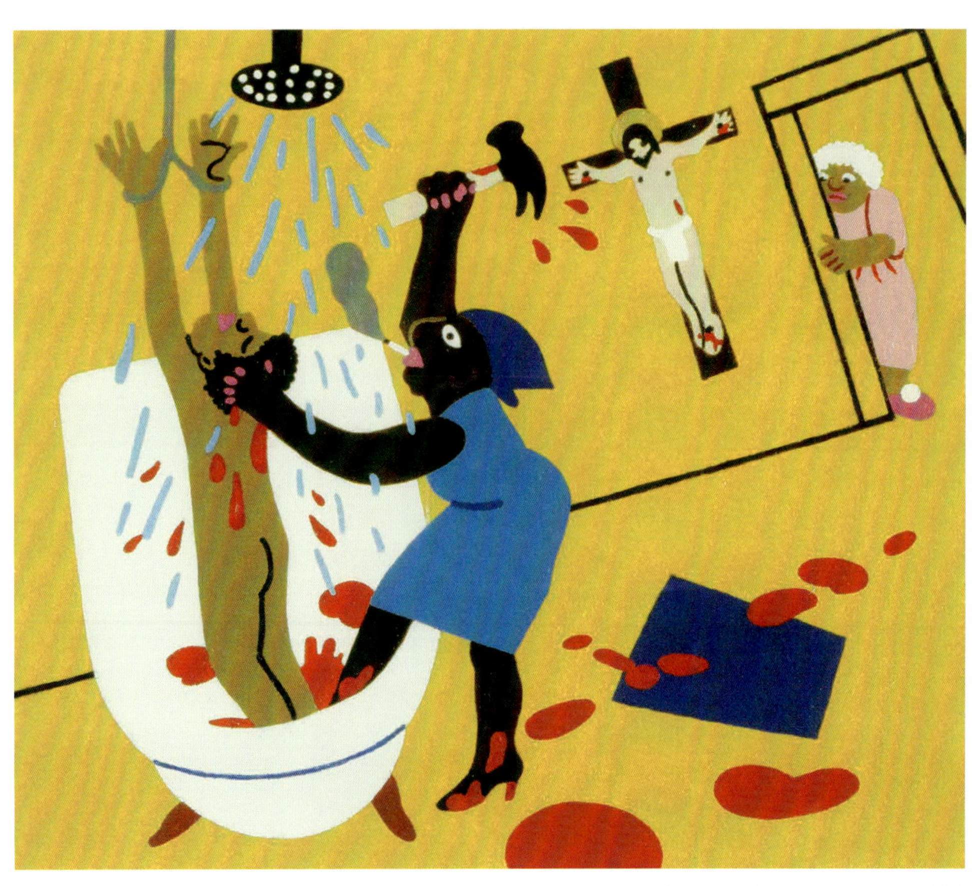

A Little Punishment for Tiesha Carter, 1991
acrylic on museum board | 12" × 10" | Collection of Claude C. Albritton, Dallas

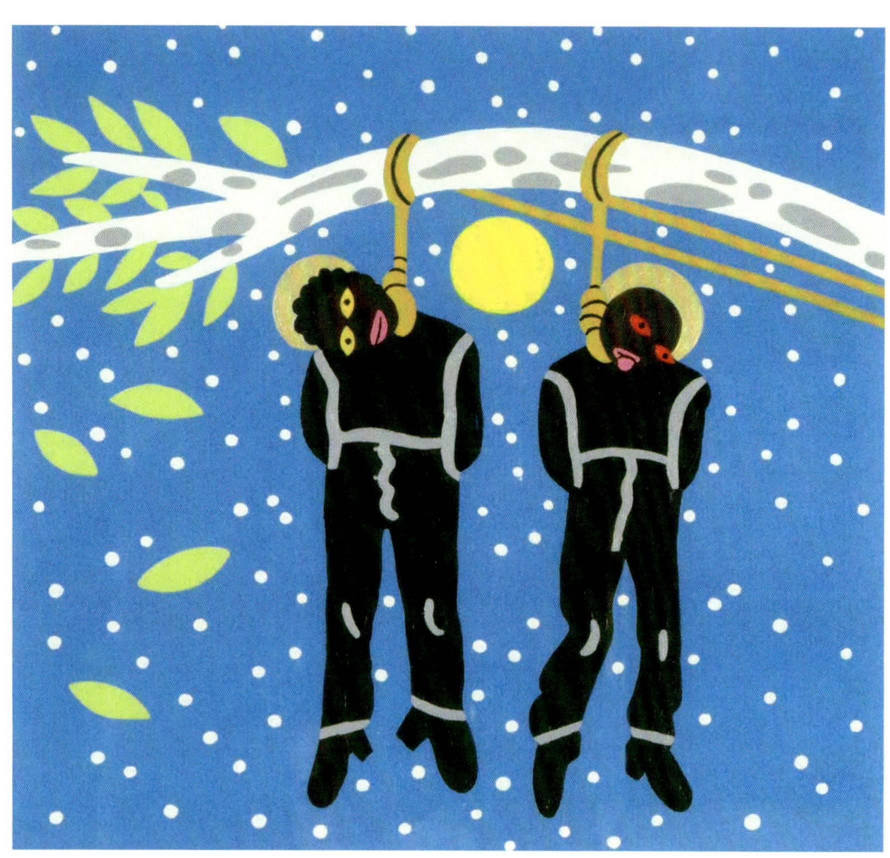

Double Lynching, 1991
acrylic on museum board | 15 1/2" × 17" |
Collection of Kate Bower

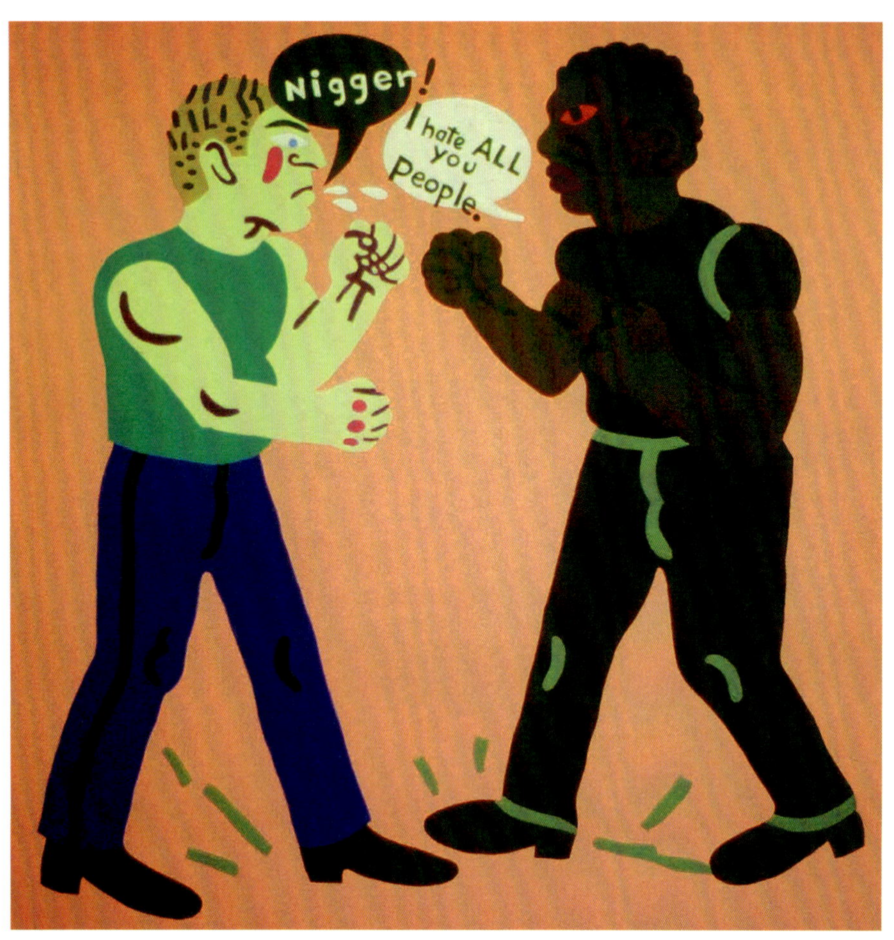

Fist Fight, 1991
acrylic on museum board | 16" × 16" |
Collection of the artist

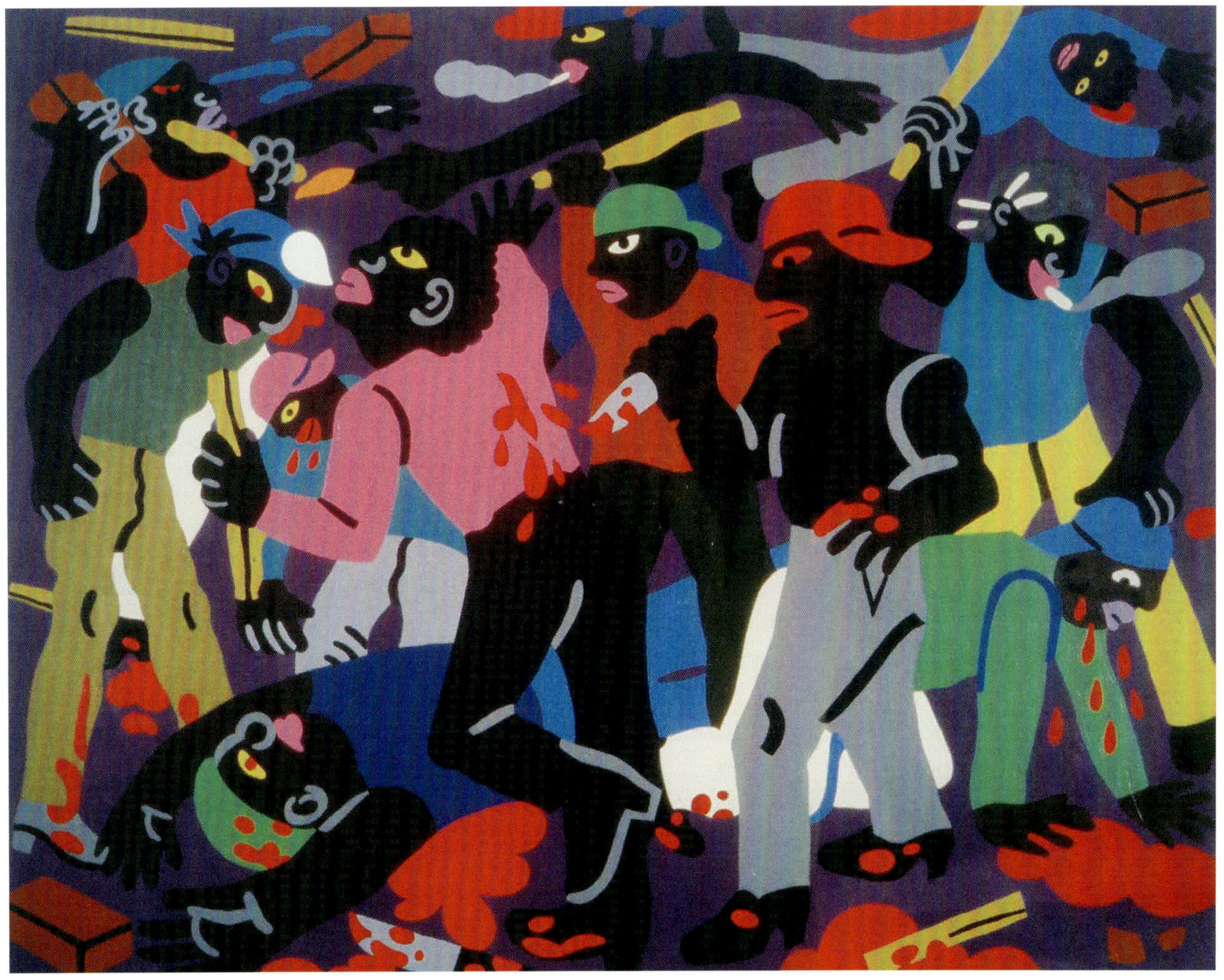

Gang War, 1991
acrylic on museum board | 39 1/2" × 30" | Collection of Jeff Baker | Photography by Jeff Baker

pivot point, is echoed by the transcendent halos behind the victims' heads. Winter's depiction is graphic, firm, important—an explicit reminder that a century or less is hardly enough time to recover from the sentiments that made such events possible.

To that end, Winter's political and social commentaries serve as a "collection of injustices," many of which continue to affect our moral matrix. Winter is like the musician who wants to test the extremes of an instrument—some of the paintings are tragic; others are humorous. He explores the full range of what paint can do without holding back. By his own admission, Winter was influenced by Jeanette's book illustrations as well as David Bates's sense of real wit, which transforms mundane subjects into something spikily vibrant. Moreover, both Jeanette and Bates share a reductive style similar to that of folk artists whose works combine flat patterns, bold colors, and skewed perspectives. Winter's *My Family* (1992) is a montage of unrestrained autobiographical images, including of the artist as a young boy in overalls gazing out from a window at the chaos raging in the yard. In the foreground, his father chops wood with a near-violent swing of the ax. At far right, Winter's mother wrings the neck of a white chicken, its blood spurting in all directions. At left, the family dog stands over a dead rabbit. A girl sits on the edge of the house's roof and hikes up her dress before descending an orange ladder. Winter's brother casually urinates on a tree, oblivious to the action surrounding him. Above the entire scene is Mrs. Dorman's church with

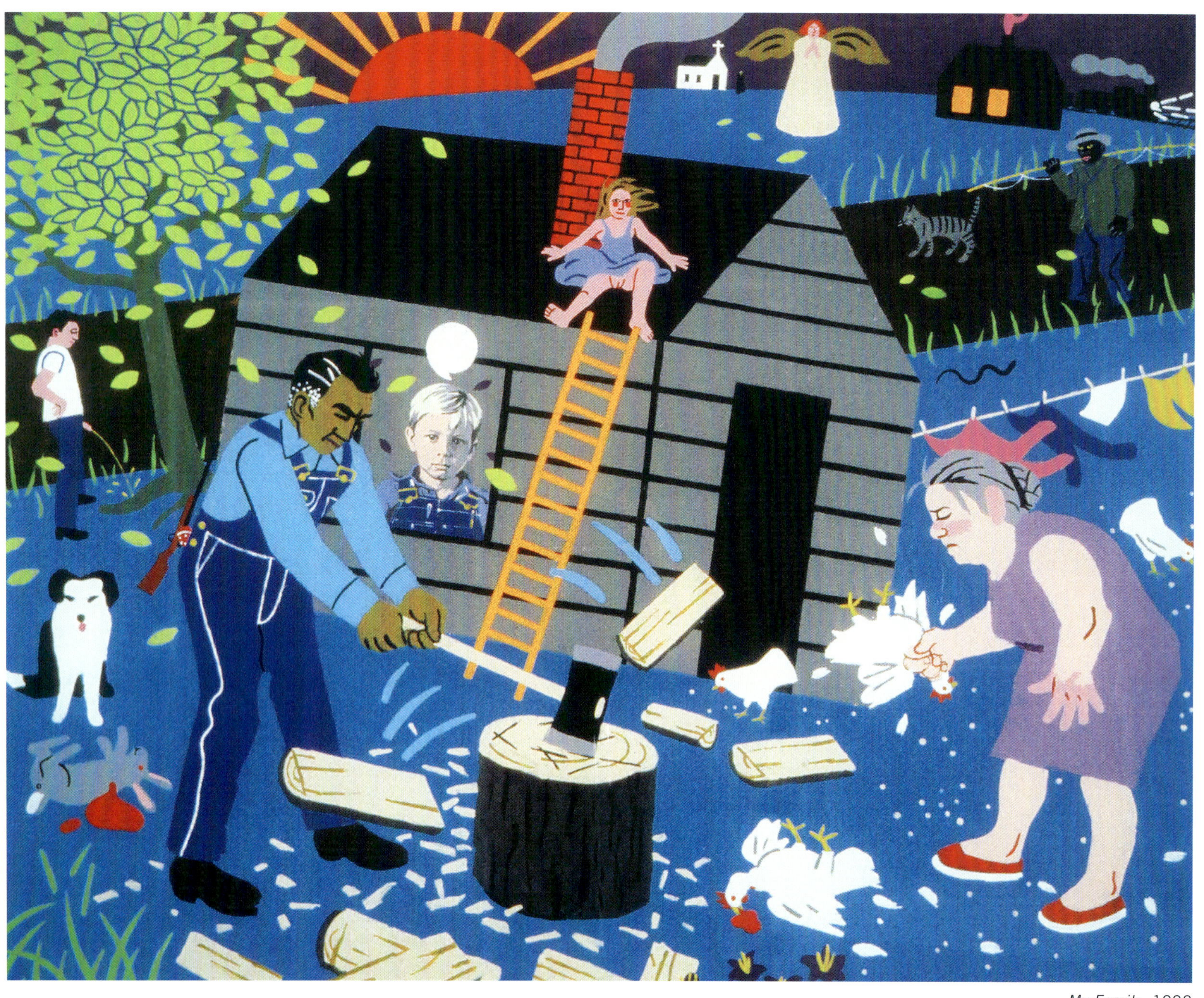

My Family, 1992

acrylic on museum board | 32" × 40" | Private collection, Dallas loudspeakers, as well as a guardian angel. A snake slithers past a clothesline of flapping laundry, while Winter's neighbor Catfish strolls by the scene with a fishing pole resting on his shoulder. An accompanying sketch includes the lyrics of an Ernest Tubb song, "I'm Walking the Floor over You." Both works reimagine Winter's frenzied upbringing and dysfunctional family. "My father always had bandanas in his pocket to wipe the sweat," he says. "My mother refused to wash the handkerchiefs that anyone blew their nose on and had a rag bag always hanging on the wall. The difference in my parent's color was always interesting to me. I don't know where my father's dark color came from." For all his affection and empathy, Winter does not flinch from the muddled contradictions or the ways opportunities can be squandered by failure, but also out of stubbornness. In any case, he felt purged by rendering the hillbilly family events as vehemently as possible. *My Family* is about the difficulty of letting go, of making choices for ourselves, of discovering that the relationships we cling to hardest may be the ones that damage us most.

Winter discovered Paul Cadmus's *Seven Deadly Sins* (1945–49) on view at the Metropolitan Museum of Art during one of his frequent visits to New York City. Although known for his paintings of social satire, Cadmus pushed the biblical subject to surreal extremes of excess, vulgarity, and gore. For Winter, the images were "shocking" and "scary," but they stimulated him to create a series with a more personal, cartoon approach. Like Cadmus's, Winter's *Seven Deadly Sins* series grapples with dark questions of the soul, but driven by a mood of moral indignation and loss leavened by visionary hilarity. Throughout, Winter is outspoken on the issues that he tackles, and he is not afraid of the possibility that the experiment will hit the skids. As he makes crystal clear, the age we exist in is full of visual terrors that are tangible. For Winter, the isolation of living in Maine threw religious issues into question. The *Seven Deadly Sins* helped him navigate a search for meaning, which he found on the streets of New York City and in his personal life. As such, the works serve as an outlet for ridding emotions and issues from his system. Winter identified with sins such as pride, lust, and gluttony. In one painting, a man passes out in his own vomit. In another, Winter depicts a woman dropping a coin into the hand of an African American beggar with the prosthetic leg of a white person. She and her male companion walk away without eye contact, however, their noses sticking up in the air. Winter inserts himself far left and asks, "Is their haughtiness worse than my patronizing?" For Winter, these are more than bridge works; they are part of his search for religion, for faith. He exposes our appalling fragility—the ambitions of our spirits are at odds with the appetites of our bodies, the former presumed eternal, the latter shakily brief.

The Maine paintings were the focus of a major exhibition in 1996, curated by Jennifer Gross for the Baxter Gallery at the Maine College of Art, Portland, which traveled to the Greenville County Museum of Art, Greenville, South Carolina; the El Paso Museum of Art; and the McKinney Avenue Contemporary in Dallas. For Winter, it restored his confidence and signified an acceptance by the art community that enabled him to climb out from his six-year free fall. Although he continued periodically to accept teaching stints—Brooklyn College, the University of Pennsylvania, the Vermont Studio Center, Washington University in Saint Louis—and became involved in Peter Schumann's outlandish pageantry, the Bread and Puppet Theater in Vermont, he sensed he and Jeanette's time in Maine was winding down. Mainers were getting on their nerves. Whenever they took vacations, the house would be broken into, their possessions stolen or destroyed. Winter was forced to secure works and other valuables in safe deposit boxes in Belfast. Moreover, their private world was encroached on from all sides. Trailers moved up to their property line, poachers cut down trees to harvest, deer hunters with rifles roamed right up to the house. They decided to leave Maine, choosing to divide their time between the Texas Hill Country and New York City.

Before their departure in 1996, however, Winter painted a few more works that expertly fuse storytelling and poetics, the metaphysical and the quotidian. The road Winter had made to the house was longer than a football field and, after the frequent snows, had to be plowed before they could

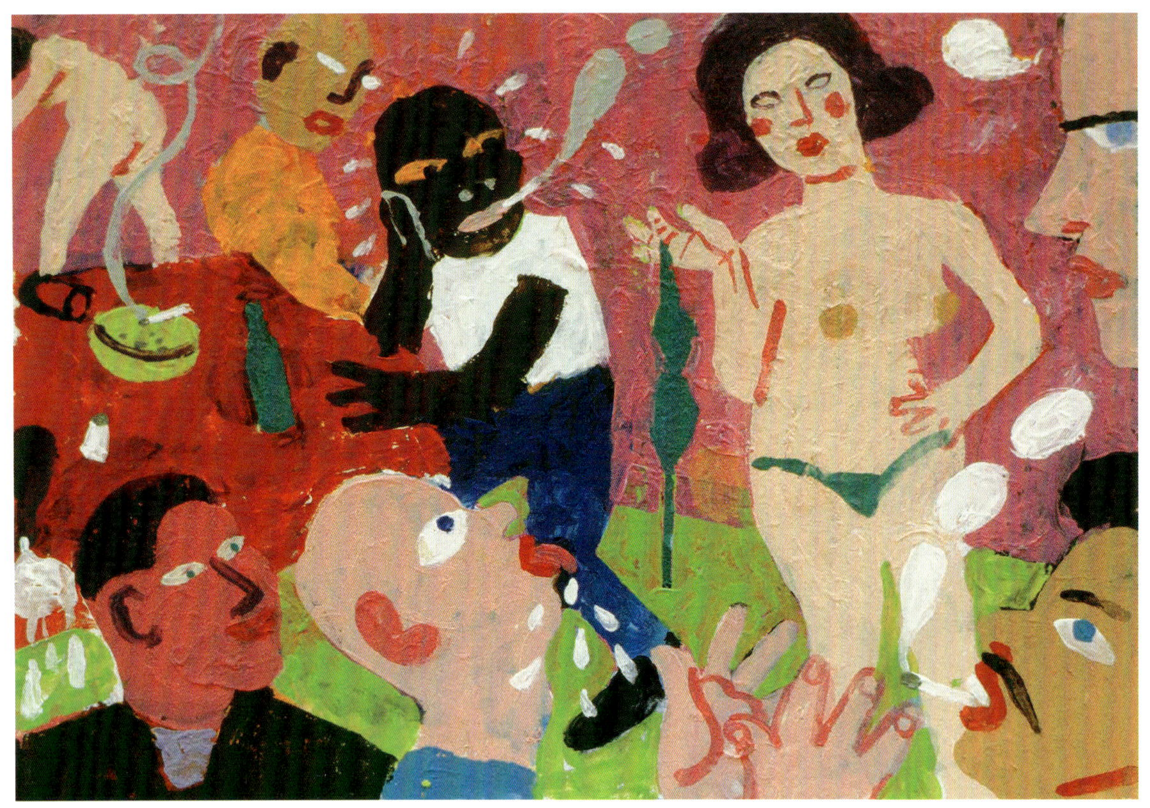

Seven Deadly Sins—Lust, 1992

acrylic on museum board | 6 1/2" × 9 3/4" | Collection of Molly E. Moore

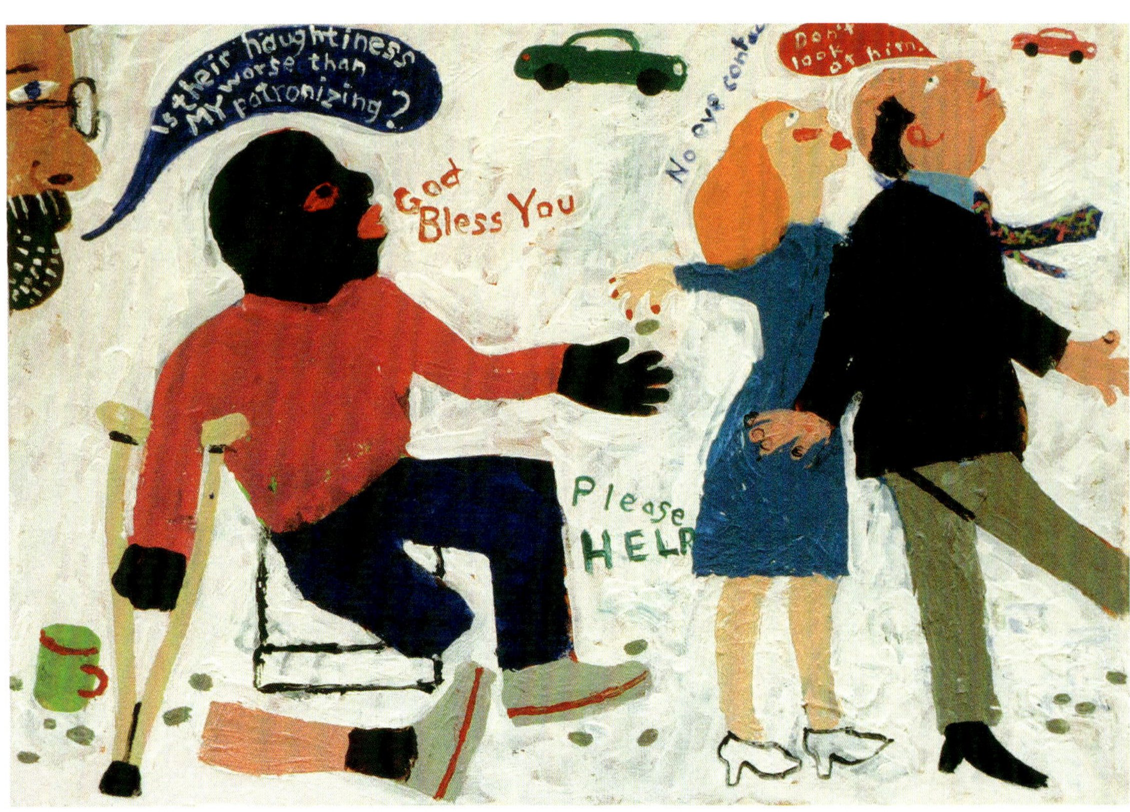

Seven Deadly Sins—Pride, 1992

acrylic on museum board | 6 1/2" × 9 3/4" | Collection of Molly E. Moore

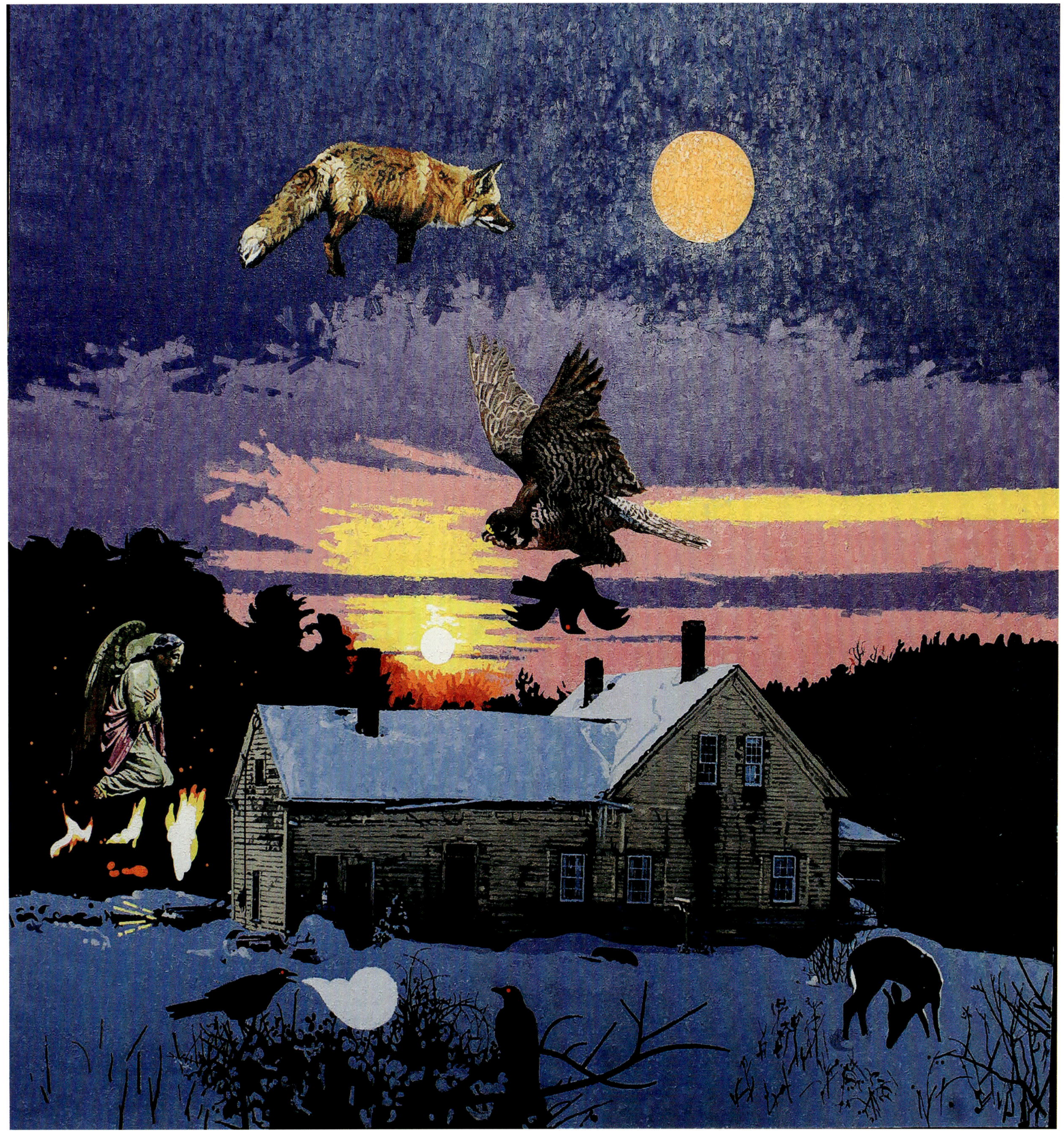

Day Is Conquered by Night, 1995

oil on linen | 78" × 78" | Collection of Alice and Charlie Adams | Photography by Jason Voinov

Winter Storm, 1995

oil on linen | 12" × 16" | Collection of Elise and Burk Murchison, Dallas drive out. Often, it felt like "a battle for survival." His studio dropped into the twenties during the night. For months, Winter got up early to start a fire in the stove, waiting until the temperature reached forty before beginning to paint. Over the years, his experience in Maine caused him to look for help from a spiritual realm. Angels, especially those in the Belfast cemetery, served as a medium to the visible world. They became Winter's guardians and protectors in times of need.

In *Day Is Conquered by Night* (1995), Winter searches between existential gravities, and he is here, with wisdom and grace, to tell us what he feels. The title refers to the Danish hymn by Thomas Kingo (1634–1703) that confronts our mortality: the end lies in the beginning, just as the beginning implies the end. The painting is occupied by the vivid "actors" siphoned from the world Winter moved through. A weathered Maine farmhouse anchors the center stage. The open, circular composition includes a fox floating in the sky near an amber moon, an owl swooping across a fiery sunset clutching a crow in its talons, and a doe sniffing the snow. Two crows perched on branches in the foreground seemingly converse about the scene. At far left, an angel in Renaissance drapery levitates above crackling flames. The angel's head is bowed, and her arms are crossed over her heart. Does the angel command the light as well as the darkness? Winter seems to have recognized the folly of withholding forgiveness and refraining from joy. Here, old disagreements, grudges, shames, and betrayals are addressed with wisdom and mercy. But the facts remain the same. We live and die, love and grieve; we produce and disappear.

Often, we rely on faith in finding our way forth. To that end, *Winter Storm* (1995) reflects a psychological state as much as an aesthetic vision. A car's red taillights are the only pinpoints of color as it travels along a lonesome highway on a snowy night. A truck's headlights shine toward us on the opposite side of the road. Both vehicles try to stay the course amid obscure, treacherous driving conditions. A mélange of luminous and dark tonalities, including white, gray, and black, creates a dense atmosphere. Veiled by the wintry mix, the headlights appear as glowing orbs faintly penetrating the storm. The painting's tactile surface, composed of patches and daubs of pigment, is compelling for its tenaciousness, delicacy, and imminent dissolution.

Winter Storm stands at the intersection of experience and memory, evoking a dreamlike otherworldly state as if in a reminiscence.

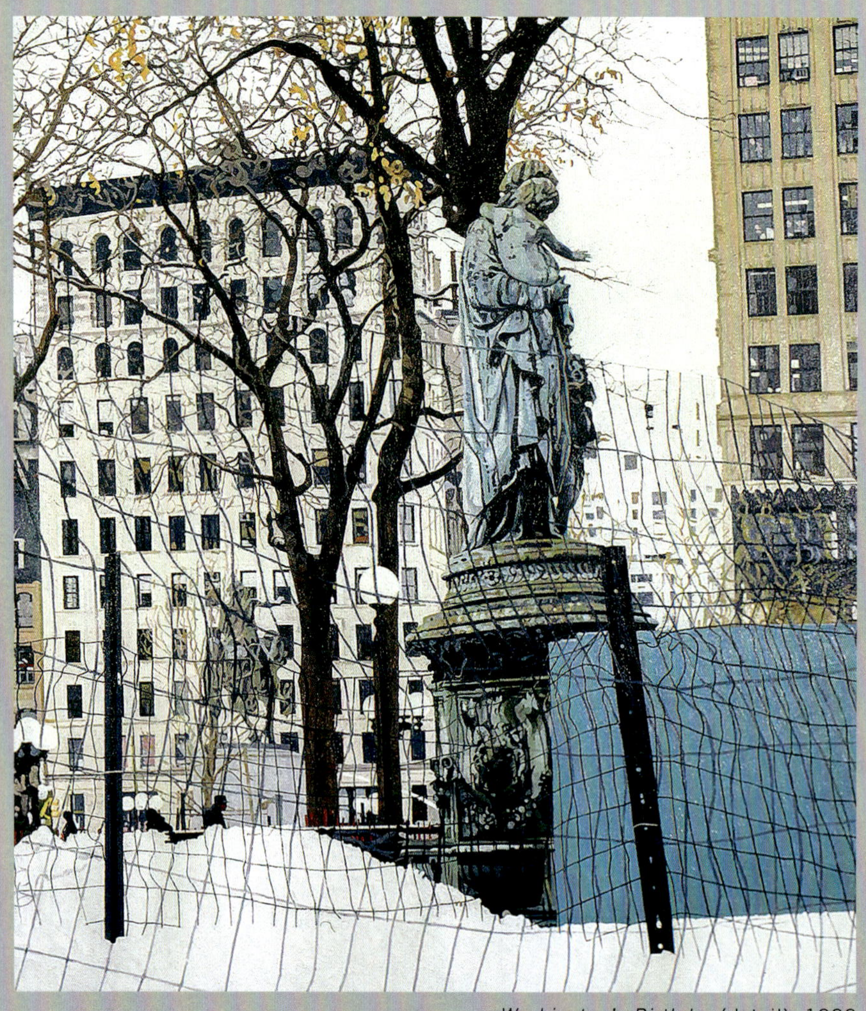

Washington's Birthday (detail), 1999

oil on linen | 64" x 96" | Collection of Molly E. Moore

CHAPTER 12

PIPE CREEK AND NEW YORK CITY

FOR WINTER, LIVING IN New York City during the summer and fall and in the Texas Hill Country during the winter and spring months was the best of both worlds. He became a Yankee—and proud of it. Before leaving Maine, however, Winter produced a series about Union Square in the hopes of recovering a more objective side of himself. Whereas his earlier renditions are sweeping panoramas of the historic plaza and park, the twenty small paintings on museum board depict the slices of life that Winter observed and experienced: pedestrians, pigeons, dogs, fresh vegetables, book stands, and postcard racks. Winter aimed for a personal connection with his new home, capturing the square's multifaceted and intimate details while also leaving us to our own interpretations of the subjects at hand. He portrays an elderly woman in a heavy coat, a large white hat, and tennis shoes, her mouth smeared with garish red lipstick. Her stooped shoulders are pulled by the load of bags she carries while trudging along the pavement. Winter paints a pigeon with breast puffed up for mating season. He focuses on a young woman in a tank top with a bare midriff and needle-tracked arms. He depicts a couple of guys relaxing on a bench and eating lunch. He zooms in on an ornamental lion's head and the decorative serpentine design of a park fountain. He renders a single leg as tribute to the great jazz singer Ella Fitzgerald, whose voice had been a part of his life from early memory. Her struggle with diabetes resulted in a double amputation in later years. He paints a statue of Abraham Lincoln from a photograph taken on Lincoln's birthday. "These small works were in conscious reaction to the surrealistic Maine paintings," Winter explains. "It seems I can't sustain a wholly inner life for too long. I become too subjective and brooding, so I make an effort toward the world outside. The *Union Square* paintings were a celebration of a world which could care less about my angst. I was getting my groove back."

In Pipe Creek, nine miles east of Bandera and some forty miles from San Antonio, the Winters' hilltop home and studios had a 360-degree, thirty-five-mile view across the sweeping landscape. The limitless Texas skies and wide-open spaces gave Winter a sense of place, which he had

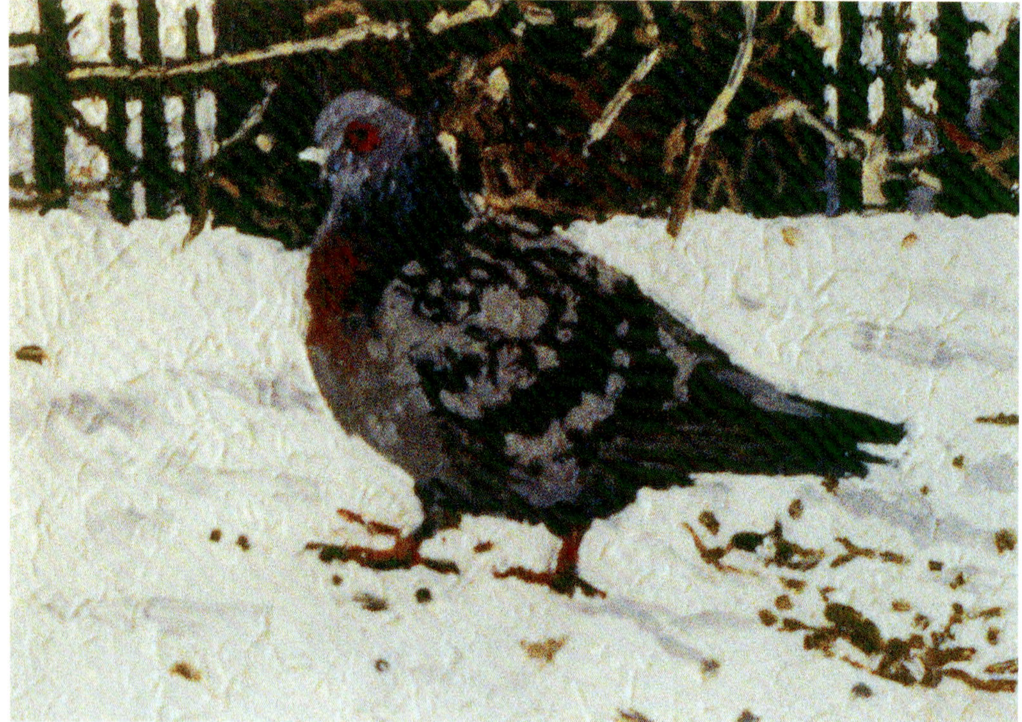

Union Square Series: Pigeon, 1996
oil on museum board | 3" × 4 1/4" | Collection of Jan Lee and David Bates

previously felt on the run. In many respects, he felt closer to nature than ever. From their second-story balcony, he and Jeanette became part of the shifting weather patterns. They were often above the clouds and sometimes looked down on rainstorms below. They would see the sun rise long before and set long after it was visible from the land below them. What's more, they frequently traveled by car throughout the Hill Country to far West Texas, the Panhandle, the deep interior, and the border towns of Mexico. Winter also made several trips to the Trans-Pecos brush country. For years he had heard Jerry Bywaters, Otis Dozier, and Everett Spruce speak about the region as a mecca of early Texas history. Winter had a similarly visceral response to this romantic, treeless land and stretched-out sky that seemed to go on forever. "It is not difficult to see the 'there' in South Texas," he writes. "One needs only to visit towns like Encinal and Weslaco, drive through vast spaces and observe the long horizons of the Rio Grande Valley and the land east and west of the Pecos River, listen to Valerio Longoria and all the other great conjunto musicians, or notice the profusion of angels in the cemeteries, of towns like Roma, and one will begin to sense a powerful feeling of place."[1]

The Trans-Pecos area, especially, was filled with such compelling images that it touched the very structure of Winter's existence, the very vision he had of himself and his world. Still, it is easy to talk about renewal and change, but profound shifts in the work do not happen easily. Although Winter had driven to the other side of the Pecos River, the upshot was a painting that utilized the same magic realist elements of the Maine works. *Trans Pecos* (1997), Winter's first studio painting in Pipe Creek, features an oversize cow standing center point on the highway, around which are dispersed familiar images and symbols from Winter's repertoire: a Mexican woman sweeping the highway, white crosses, a full moon, black crows, flames erupting on the scrubby landscape, laundry flapping on the line, a schematic house structure, and, in the distance, an airborne pickup truck bouncing off the road.

Significantly, *Trans Pecos* is Winter's final montage painting, as he became increasingly immersed in specific atmospheric conditions—the time of the day, weather, seasons, the various moods of a sunlit sky or the reflecting light of the moon. "Dark waters and low light set the mood for the Maine paintings, while Central/South/West Texas had that old familiar over lit quality that makes one squint and a scarcity of water," Winter writes. "Natural light is objective in that it doesn't shine more on people than it does on a twig. But light creates moods within our psyche. Perhaps in all living things."[2]

With this in mind, Winter created scores of small landscape paintings between 1997 and 1999

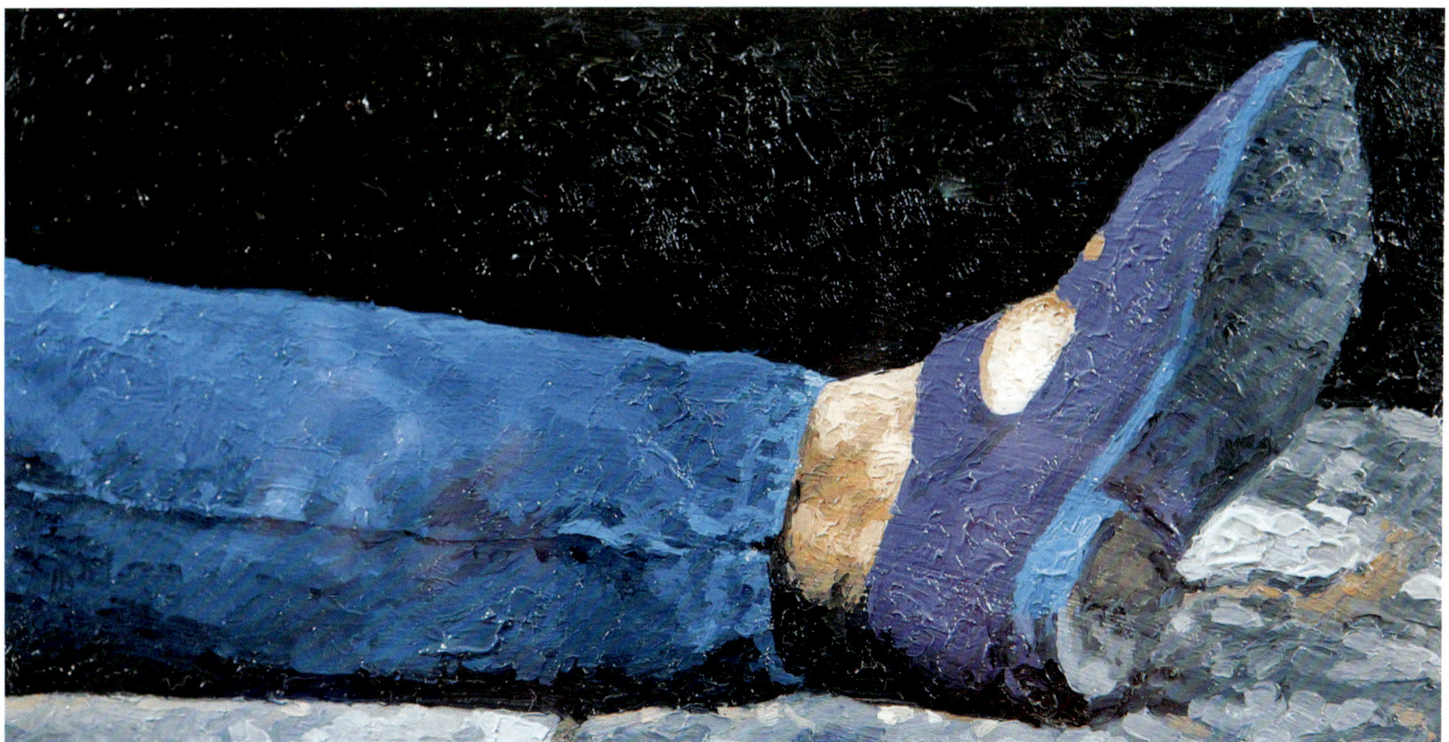

Union Square Series: Ella, 1996
oil on museum board | 4" × 7 1/4" | Collection of Lillian W. Albritton, Dallas | Photography by Fernando Rojas

that became a kind of visual diary of his life in Pipe Creek and travels across Texas. The intimate works enabled Winter to try many subjects—light, form, and weather conditions—to get things down on paint as they were happening. All of the landscapes have clouds and glinting radiance, a sense of renewal, as well as encroaching mortality, restoring the tenderness that had been bleached out of the preceding landscapes by the cold Maine light. The vast spaces of Central and South Texas seemed to invite Winter to lose his recent past like so much baggage and reinvent himself. In some works, he collapses space, foreshortening and distorting scale to reveal the subtle effects of heat and light on the Texas flatlands. Everything seems potentially weightless and on the verge of dissolving into the luminous sfumato of the atmosphere. The poetics of Winter's art lie in how fully he conveys his experience of the places he paints and in how those places may resonate in our imagination. Nature became his teacher, a new kind of education, both directive and permissive. It sent him heavy storms and pitch-black nights; it also gave him bouncing light and shimmering blue haze.

For Winter, nature was not a thing; it was an atmosphere, a learning environment. He was inside nature, surrounded by it and part of it. Like the work of his Impressionist forebears, Winter's paintings are based on a vision of nature as a process of perpetual formation and change. His task was to capture that process, on the fly, in paint—a formal means for creating an immediate visceral representation of nature's forces and movements. They have an emotional core—some are lonely and meditative; others are brash and explosively ebullient. For the most part, however, Winter's painterly gestures—a virtuosic shorthand of flicked, dragged, stippled strokes that leave behind scintillating crests of paint—are abstract forms in themselves. Winter makes the qualities of paint felt—in transparency and opacity, thickness and thinness, juiced-up and arid color. Strips, slices, daubs and dashes, swatches and coils of color, and wonky rectangles spreading planes of

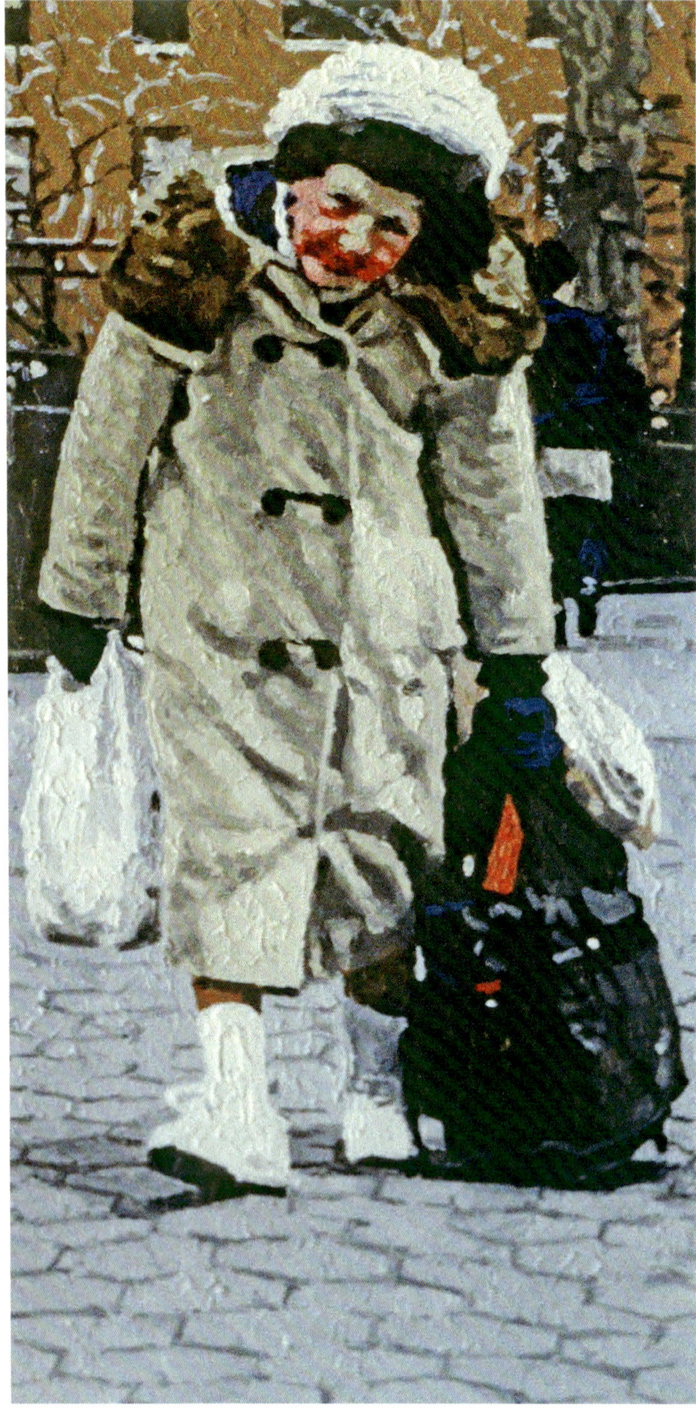

Union Square Series: Bag Lady, 1996
oil on museum board | 12" × 6" | Collection of Cidnee Patrick

modulated pigments at times abut one another, mingle with and obscure one another, tangle with and complicate one another endlessly. The passage of forms across these luminous surfaces is like the passage of clouds across the sky. There are layers to the textures with wisps of cirrus clouds scudding over billowing cumuli and strati hovering low. Clouds, of course, exist in a realm where the physical and metaphysical touch. Winter's clouds are illusions—liquid masquerading as floating, solid objects—but they are also psychic refuges from the mundane grist for our fantasies. We look for meaning and signs in the clouds, as well, the grown-up version of picking out puffy animals or dirigibles. Winter's small paintings are shot through with a sense of the transience of things and time's fleetingness—the way it shatters every life into a thousand shards of experience or slows to a dreamlike crawl. Winter scrutinizes the natural world as if examining a film, cell by cell. These paintings are about moments, perceptions, sudden visions, and insights.

"Light is a healer, brought to us by Sophia, so my Gnostic Bible says," Winter explains. "And Ecclesiastes tells us there is a time to heal. For me that time was when we built our hilltop house in Pipe Creek. The more I painted skylight, the more my pain subsided. Perhaps light was a symbol of discovery and hope. The Hill Country was not the same red dirt of Denison where I grew up, but the light was the same. And it was generative to me just as it was to goats and scorpions and mesquites and cedars. It touched me in a primal way." Winter captures the shafts of sunlight spreading through storm clouds, as well as the dense flurry of rain merging beneath leaden thunderheads. He seizes the last faint gleams of a fiery sunset glowing frailly against the dying light.

In *Last Light* (1998), Winter uses a palette of black and burnt sienna to form reductive horizontal bands of darkness and luminosity. *Divided Sky* (1998) is a collision of velvety blacks, cool grays, pinks, and oranges in layers of textured staccato and jumbled strokes. *Amarillo* (1998) presents the Texas Panhandle's ruler-sharp horizon and flat plains in finely licked, horizontal strips of lavender, brown, and yellow-gold. Throughout, Winter packs the raw power of "God's country"—light, space, and topography—within limited boundaries. Winter's Texas landscape is neither theory nor abstraction; it is his direct experience. How, within the small dimensions of museum board, did he present with forceful conviction the immensity of the sky and plains? Winter understands grandeur of effect in terms of relative scale and not absolute size.

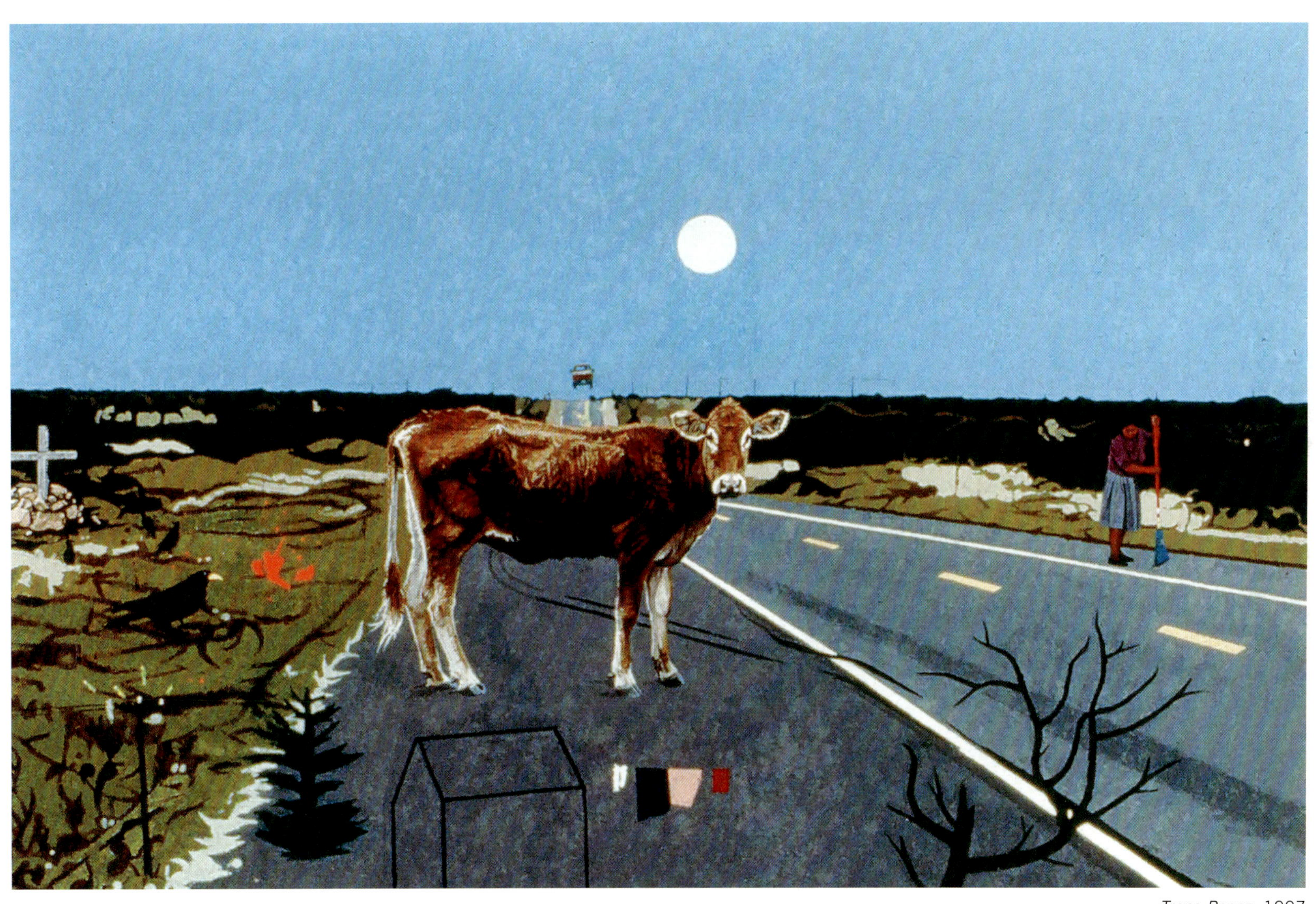

Trans Pecos, 1997

oil on linen | 48" × 72" | Collection of Greg and Angelia Venker | Photography by Kevin Todora

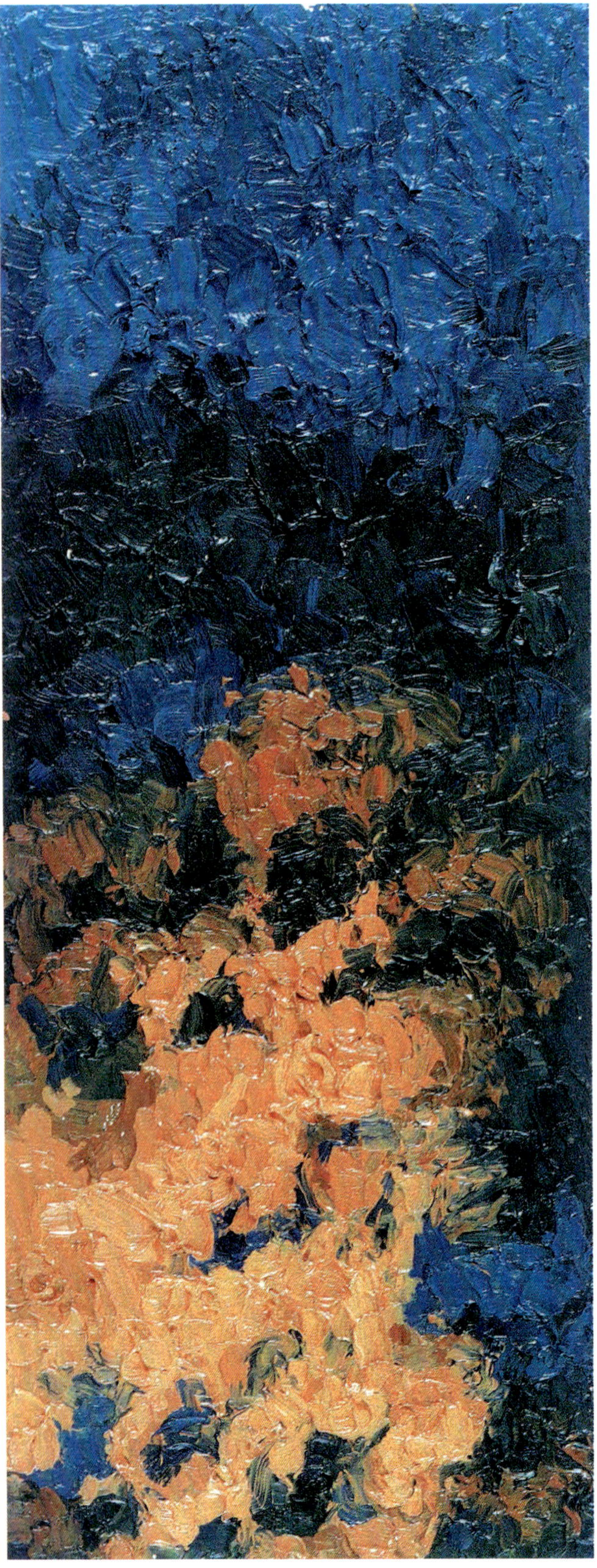

Last Light, 1998
oil on museum board | 10" × 4" | Courtesy of the artist and Kirk Hopper Fine Art, Dallas

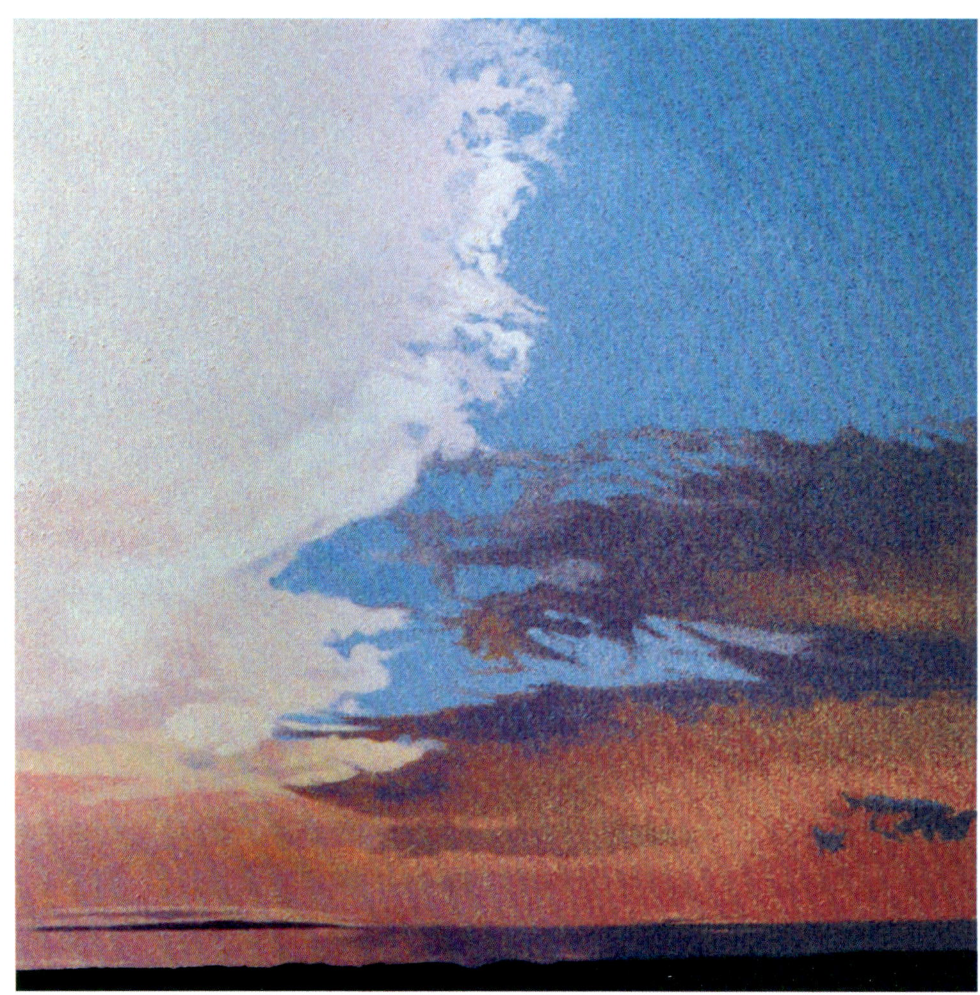

Divided Sky, 1998
oil on museum board | 9" × 9" | Courtesy of the artist and Kirk Hopper Fine Art, Dallas

Dense, minuscule strokes and bold, loose gestures are deployed to construct solidly formed masses and ethereal spaces. Thus, Winter translates the opposing qualities of mass and space that he found in nature into their literal equivalent in pigment. Adjustments of scale are partly achieved by tiny cows struggling along a fence line or, as in *Bandera* (1997), the silhouettes of a water tower and scrubby trees directing our eye to the horizon's gentle atmospheric effects.

The views Winter chooses to depict are not special in any particular way. Perhaps, as in *Rolling Sky* (1998), he liked the formation of curled clouds against the lavender-blue ridges. Feathery wisps and spiky marks transform an otherwise static scene into a charged field. On the whole, working less expansively allowed for a freedom to deliberate in paint that made lushness and structure inextricable. Significantly, Winter's treatment of the light and architectonic spaces of Central and Southwest Texas anticipates a later series of minimalist paintings based on his daily life in Manhattan, as well as travels to Iceland.

It is important to note that Winter immediately found a community that shared his sensibilities in the Hill Country. As it happens, the New York landscape painter Susan Shatter, whom Winter had met at a Fischbach Gallery opening, was teaching for a semester at the University of Texas at San Antonio. At the time, Shatter lived in a university-owned house in Boerne, not far from Pipe Creek. On one of their frequent visits, Shatter introduced Winter to painter Charles Field, also on the faculty at the university, with whom he would develop a lifelong friendship. At the outset, Winter felt a strong kinship with Field's small Texas landscapes that focused on vast space and the illumination of sky. Field, in turn, introduced Winter to the painter Melissa Miller, who had been Field's student at the University of Texas at Austin and the University of New Mexico, Albuquerque, in the 1970s. Field became an influential mentor and close family friend to the Austin artist over the decades. Moreover, Shatter and Miller had become acquainted through teaching at the Skowhegan School of Painting and Sculpture in Madison, Maine. The relationships not only made Winter feel at home again but also helped the artist to engage a world outside himself. For Winter, living and working in Pipe Creek brought "a strange kind of intellectual happiness."

Often, while working in the studio, he would listen to music by modern American composers. "Music and architecture (frozen music) seem to be the most naturally abstract of the art forms, so I listened to the composers I knew about: Charles Ives, Ruth Crawford Seeger (Pete Seeger's stepmother), Virgil Thomson (who learned a lot about collaging known music into his works from Ives), George Crumb, the great John Adams. I listened some to Steve Reich and Philip Glass," Winter writes. "While painting, I hear intensity, edges and transitions. Their music helped me think of color and light and dividing space in a beautiful way. Contemporary American music helped me utilize abstraction in the natural environment we lived in. It helped me avoid the painful inner life that occurred in Maine. Pain may be half of painting, but it needs the ting half, too. That's what music and the building of our house and studios in Pipe Creek brought to me."[3]

Such complex spatial orchestrations are achieved in Winter's epic landscapes, where scruffy native plants and interloping industry comingle. An empty road, scraggly brush, electrical poles as barren as dying trees: all of the elements that compose *Encinal* (1999) evoke the desolation of a forsaken South Texas town. Here, Winter distinctly renders the 1930s abandoned storefronts, overgrown weeds, and rusty fences with a veracity that is heartbreakingly poignant. Time has passed by this town, which is slowly being reclaimed by nature. The scene is instilled with a sense of melancholy and loss, the crumbling buildings overshadowed by the giant sky filled with massive, swiftly moving clouds.

Similarly, *Last Light, Encinal* (1998) embodies a distinctive poetic and painterly vision. Here power lines thread through atmospheric light in the moments of transition from day to night. Where does the light go, and how do we freeze that instant in memory? The sweeping wires gently lead our eye from the upper right to the silhouetted trees and far horizon. "Close to the

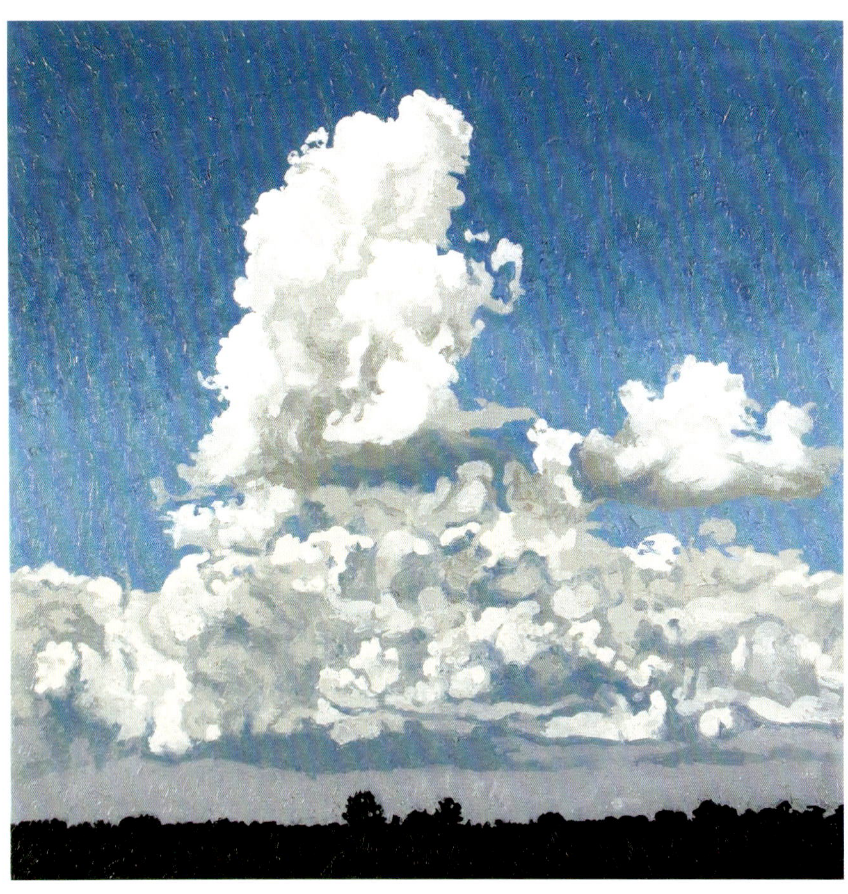

Thunderhead, 1997
oil on museum board | 15" × 15" | Collection of the Federal Reserve Bank of Dallas

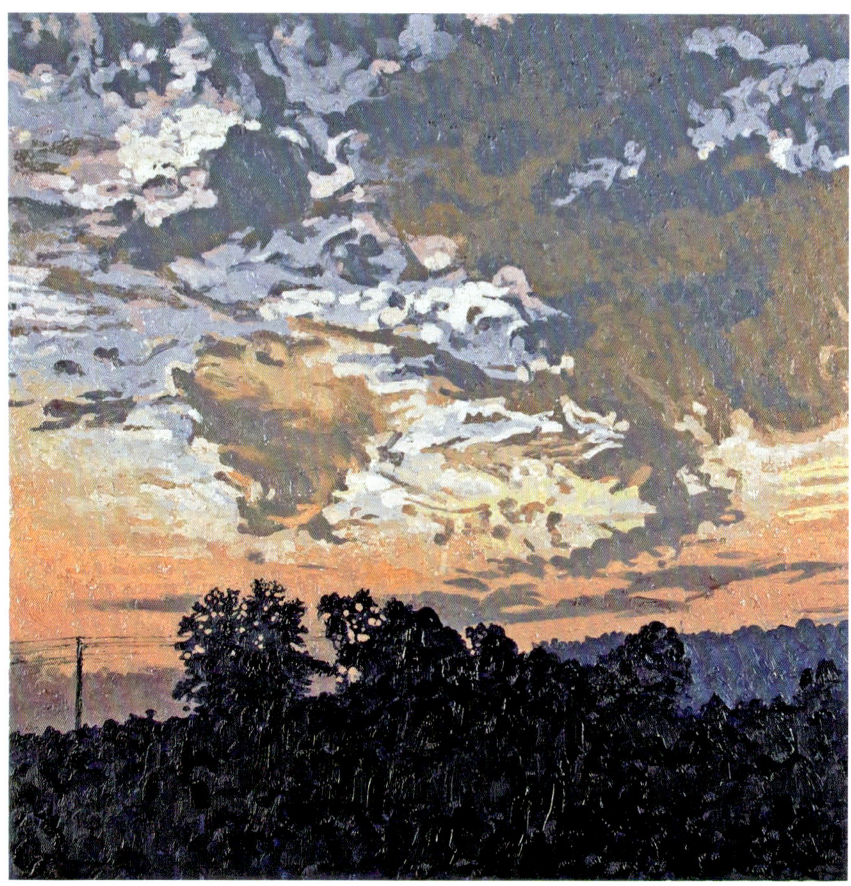

Sunset after Rain, 1997
oil on museum board | 15" × 15" | Collection of the Federal Reserve Bank of Dallas

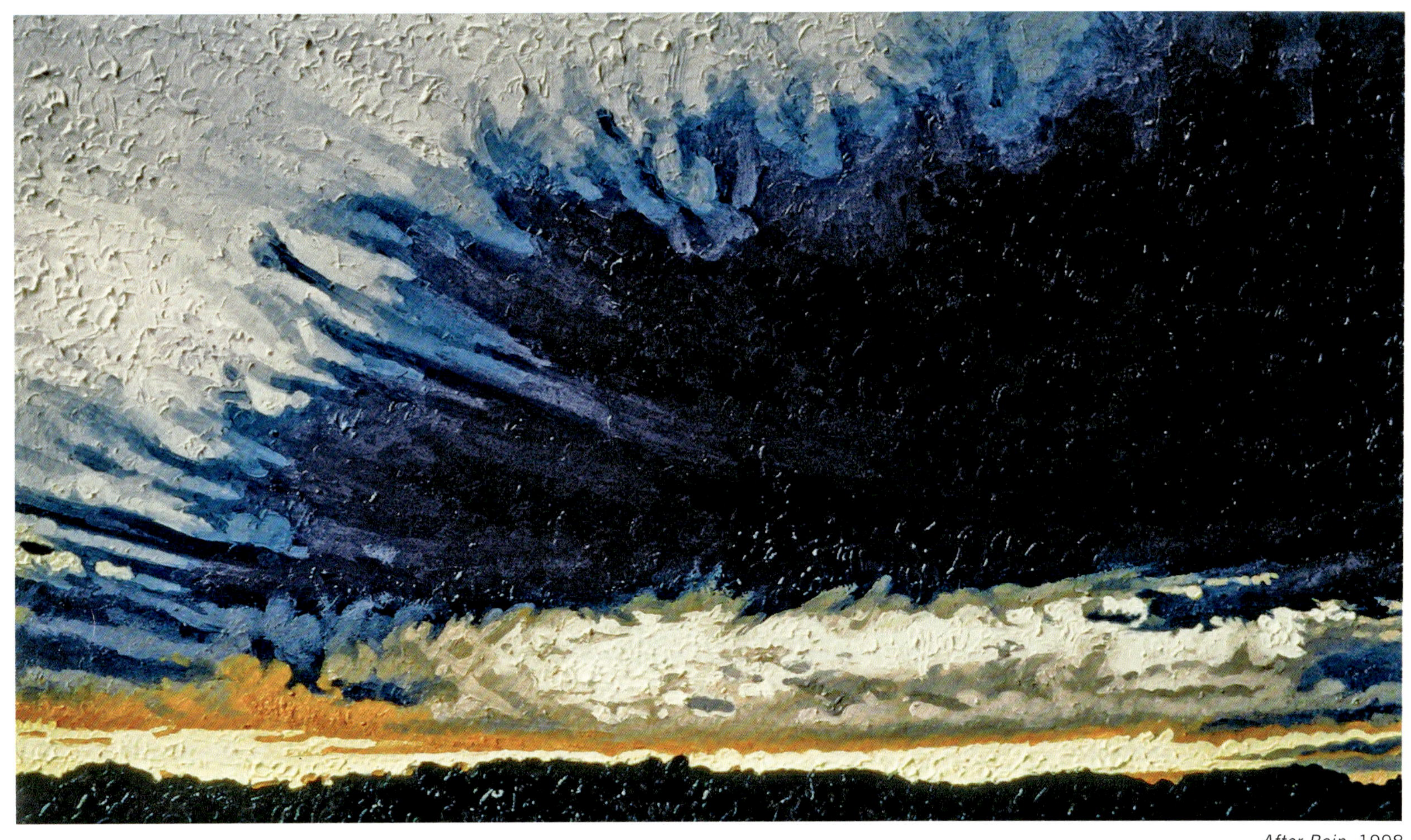

After Rain, 1998

oil on museum board | 9" × 16" | Private collection

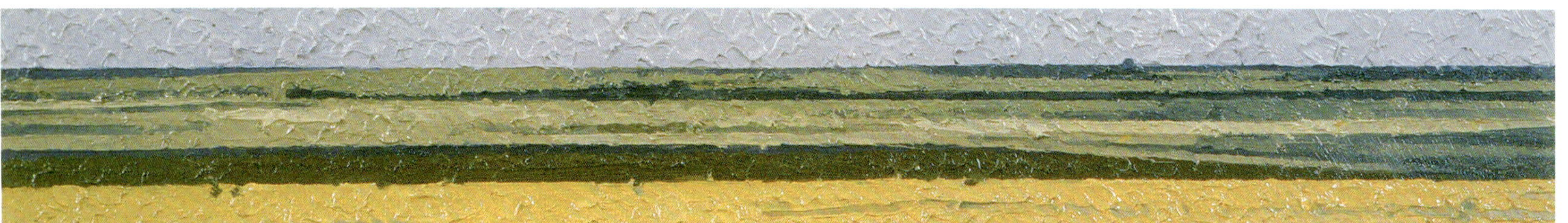

Amarillo, 1998
oil on museum board | 2" × 14" | Collection of President and Mrs. George W. Bush

Texas/Mexico border near Laredo, we often stopped to look around the semi-ghost town of Encinal," he writes. "The railroad that ran through, the abandoned buildings in the former town center, the cross timber vegetation, the electric and telephone posts standing around—relics from an earlier technology—the remarkable skies at different times of day and weather conditions. All of this pulled me like a spiritual magnet, an echo of my early life by the KATY tracks on the outskirts of Denison. *Last Light, Encinal* was based on something seen on a return trip from a day in Nuevo Laredo. The impetus for any painting always feels inevitable. *Last Light, Encinal* had to be painted like all my works based on that small corner of Texas."[4] The subject of the painting is the inevitable nightly draining of color from the world, a metaphor for the last pinch of brightness that awaits everyone. But the painting also, for a bit, holds night at bay; it lives in the tension between distant visions of radiated sunset and clotted passages of darkness. What Winter brings to the scene is not new in terms of technique, form, or color. He offers us instead a trace of the landscape that dwells within all of us.

Despite Winter's phenomenal range, we see and feel his presence in every inch of the paintings. He informs us not only about himself and his world view but also of our own experiences. Winter is intensely aware of his surroundings and responds to people and places with an acutely critical, objective observation, as well as a highly intuitive sense that can border on an understanding beyond a physical reality. He has the courage and intellect to inform his work with what he catches sight of or perceives, regardless of how absurd or straightforward his renditions may at first seem to the conventional eye and mind. In many respects, the bifurcated lifestyles of Pipe Creek and New York City bolstered Winter's efforts to tap a new vein. In both rural and urban locales, he turns our attention to seemingly incidental details through patches of color or dense layers of squirmy strokes: window reflections, distant rooftops, silhouetted trees, and shadowy figures. As art critic Janet Kutner astutely observes, "That is Winter's greatest strength—capturing the fleeting moment by locking in the essence of a place but making it shift before our eyes, like a memory that quickly fades."[5]

Although Winter's paintings at the time display an expansive curiosity and an ability to step outside himself, his working process remained unwaveringly consistent. Oil colors are limited to titanium white, Payne's gray, ultramarine blue, cobalt blue, viridian, alizarin crimson, and cadmium red, yellow, and orange. Turpentine was the only medium used in the initial wash and underpainting. For overpainting, Winter mixed colors and applied them directly to the primed canvas with flats and brights—all sable brushes. Throughout, he aimed to reduce the technical side of painting to a minimum. "I work more or less top to bottom," he explains. "I learned that a strong underpainting would guide the ultimate color choice, planar division, and brushmark. But like brickwork, I wanted to craft the surface so that there are no 'hot spots.' Maybe this was a lesson from Impressionism or Pointillism and, later, Constructivism and Pop Art—but I personalized it. The formal solidity of Roman wall painting, the careful relative placement of each object—vines, wall trim, birds. Everything, including an open area of paint, is treated with the same attention and

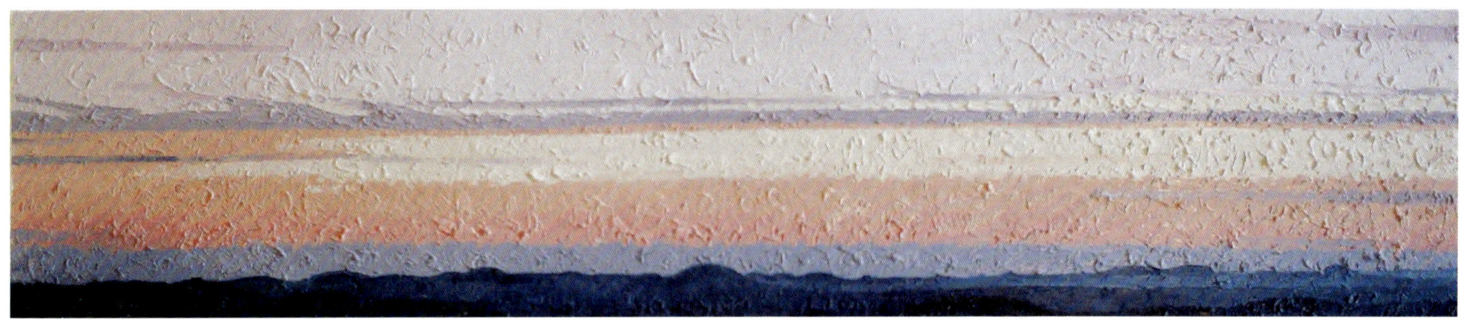

Fading Light, 1998
oil on paper | 5" × 25" | Collection of Kirk Hopper, Dallas | Photography by G. Valderas

love, as in a [Johannes] Vermeer or Chuck Close pixels. My paintings are created piece by piece, like mosaics or bricklaying, and require the same consistency of craft of those disciplines. I paint directly from snapshots that I take and so I know from the start what the painting is to be."

Without changing the course of his methods, Winter grew more adept at creating a clear-eyed depiction of his environs and, at other times, a near-mystical experience of nature. During the initial years in Manhattan, Winter was without a studio. Rather, he painted at an easel in the corner of the bedroom in their apartment, which also forced him to work on a smaller scale. For *Dreamer* (1999), Winter depicts a large woman in a black coat walking along the shoreline or perhaps wading into the ocean. Winter had seen the woman strolling on a New York City street but transported her to the Coney Island beach. Her charged presence is the focal point of the painting. As she pivots off one foot, her arms swing in unison and propel her massive body forward with centrifugal force. Although tiny ducks scurry nearby in the breakwater, she is lost in a state of reverie. Winter balances the woman precariously between this world and a more spiritual realm. By the same token, we engage in thoughtful meditation prompted by both the aesthetic dynamics of the composition and the eloquent paint handling. The entire surface is alive with finely textured tufts of pigment that blend optically to create complex spatial and light effects. In *Walking the Blues* (1999), a young woman and her dog appear to be floating in midair, purposefully walking through the heavens. According to Winter, the painting was inspired by a Fats Domino song about walking to New Orleans. Here, however, he transforms a girl from a New York City inhabitant into a Joan of Arc figure with flaming-red hair. The black Labrador, tethered by a blue leash, obediently trails behind her. Using careful daubs and loose brushwork, Winter ably evokes the shimmering effects of lavender and blue light as filtered through Texas thunderheads.

For the most part, the New York paintings from the late 1990s alternate between a darker,

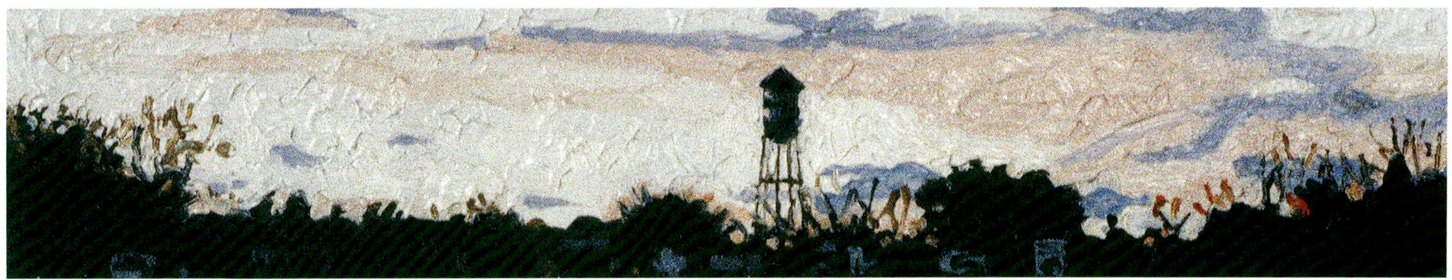

Bandera, 1997
oil on museum board | 3" × 15" | Courtesy of the artist

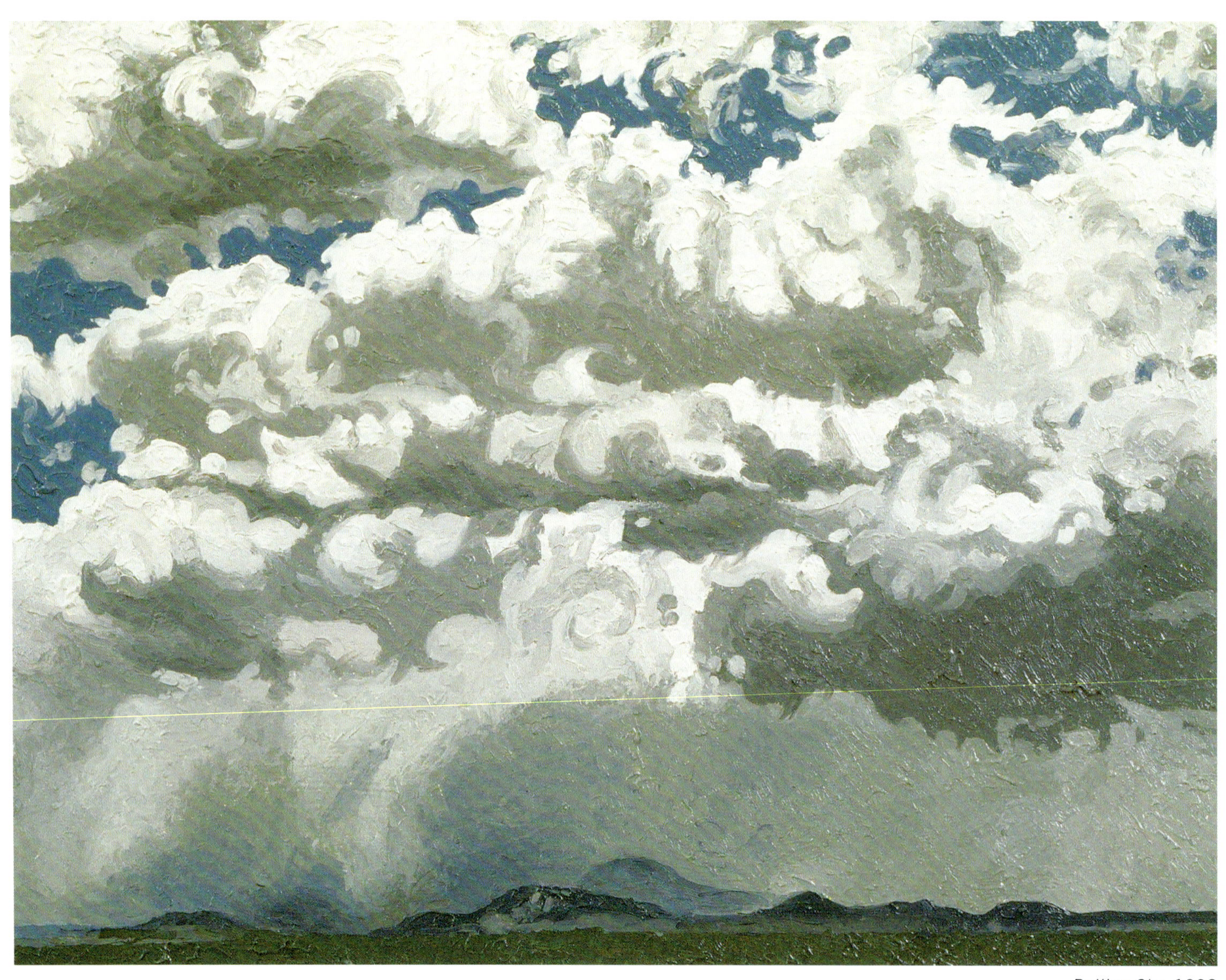

Rolling Sky, 1998
oil on museum board | 11" × 14" | Collection of Susan Lichy

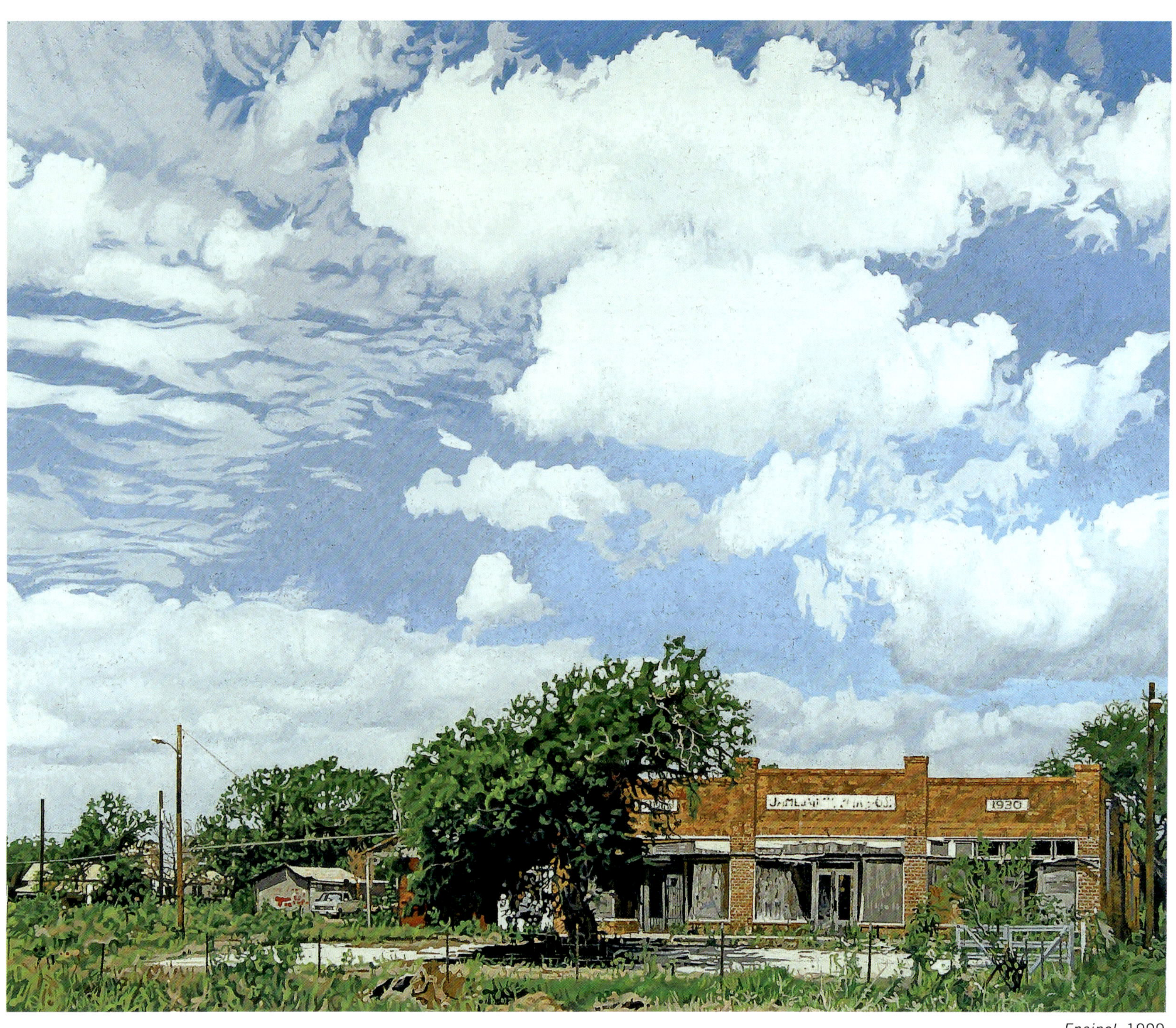

Encinal, 1999

oil on linen | 60" × 72" | Collection of the McNay Art Museum, gift of the artist

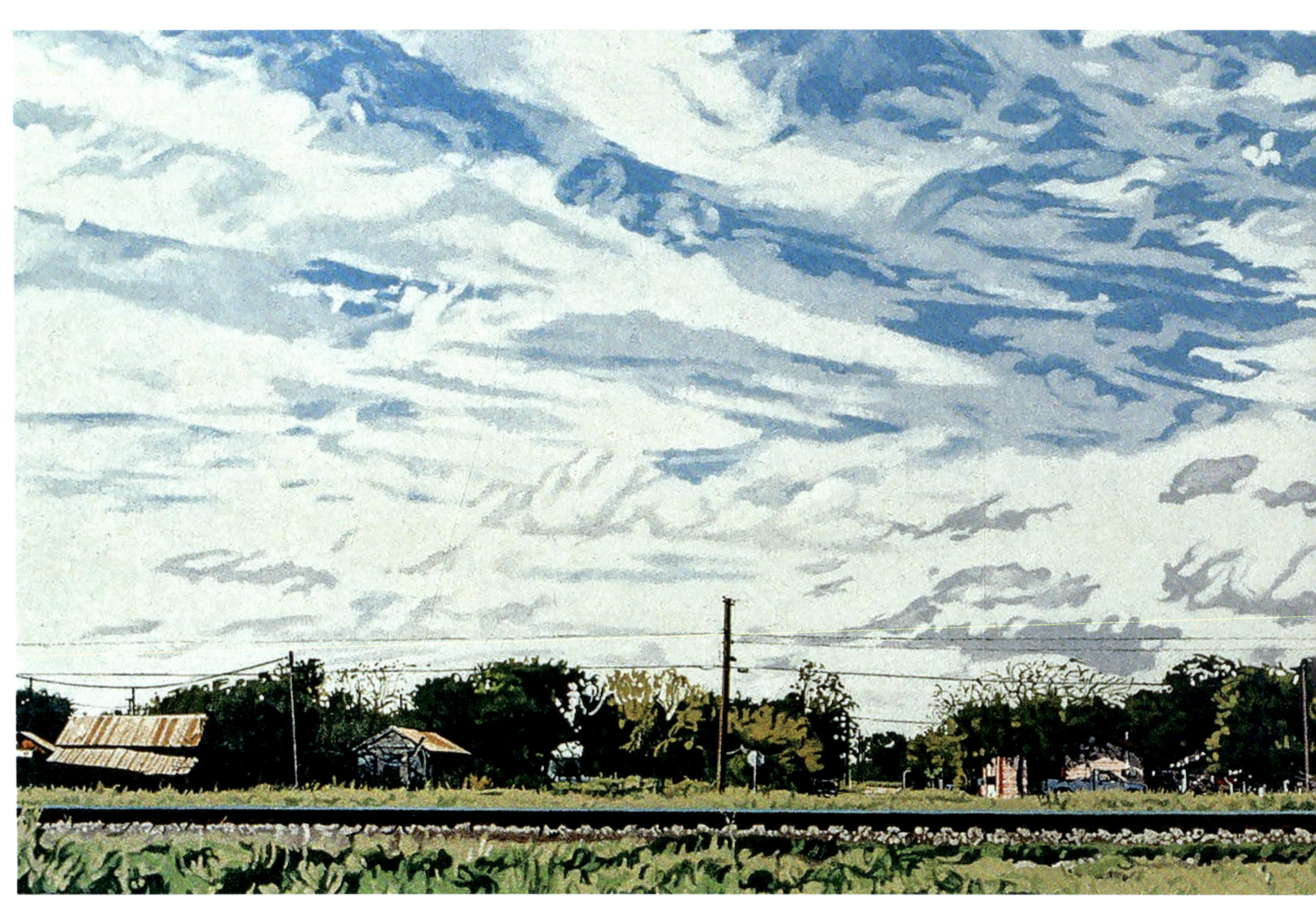

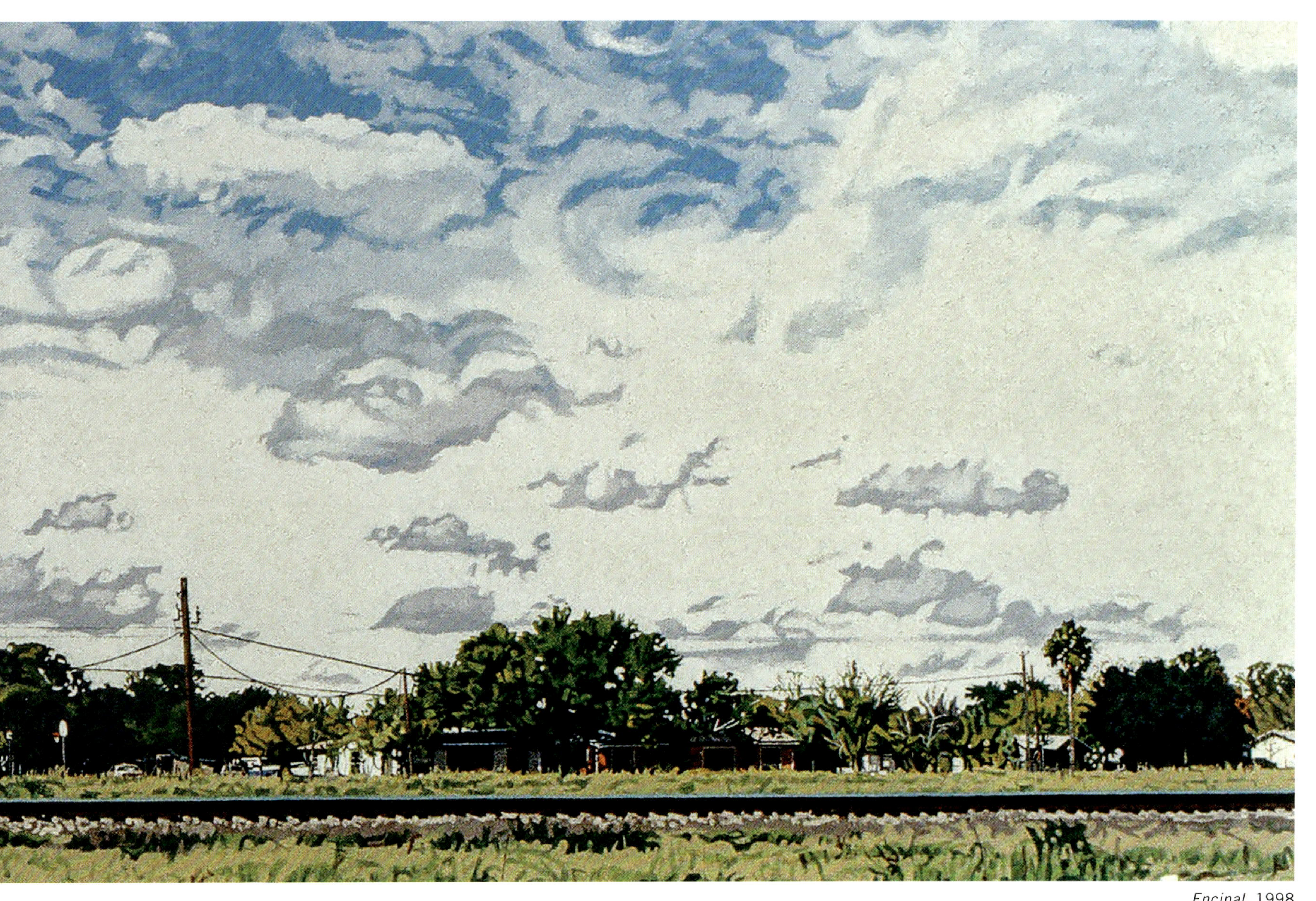

Encinal, 1998

oil on linen | 36" × 114" | Courtesy of the artist

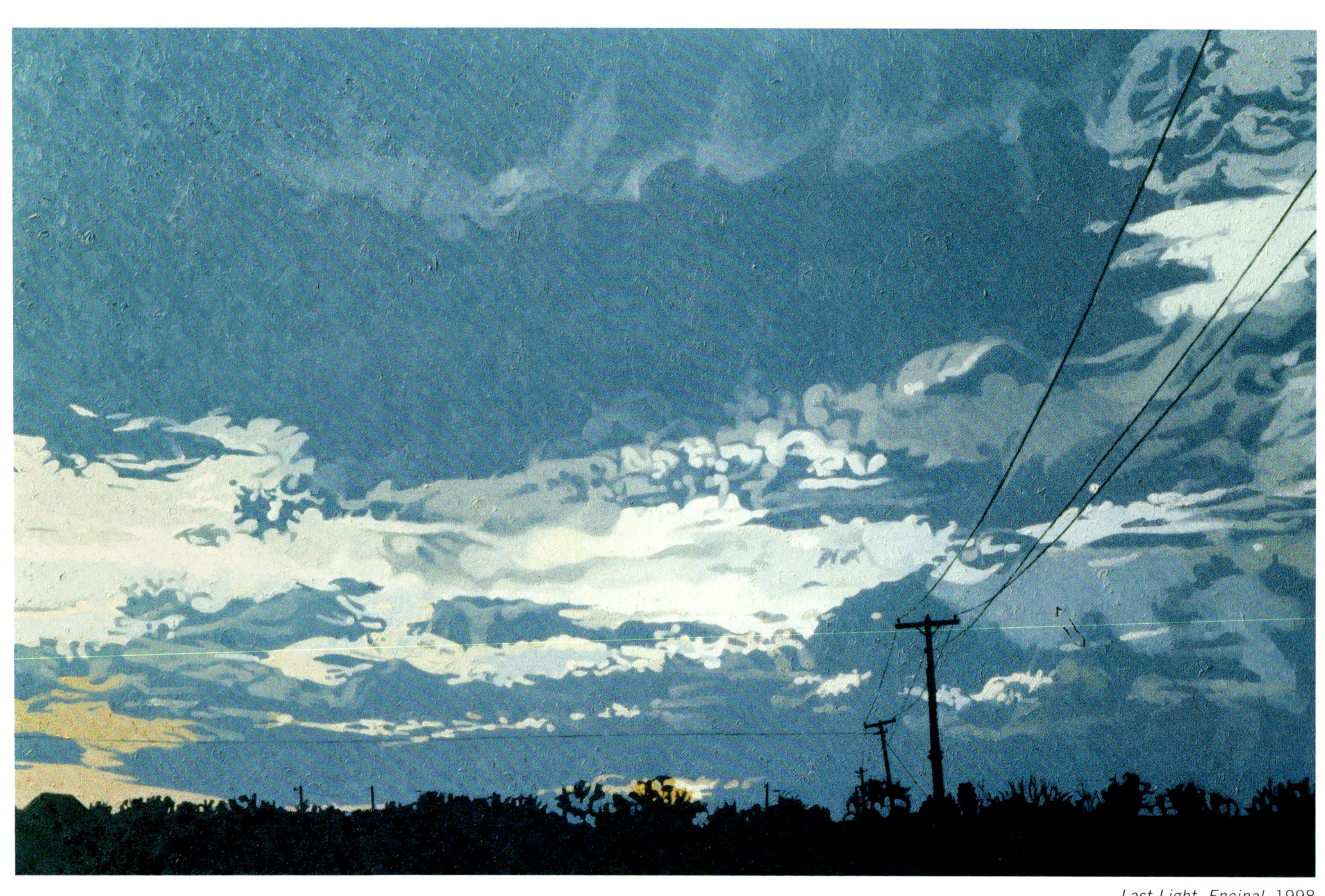

Last Light, Encinal, 1998

oil on linen | 36″ × 60″ | Collection of Juli and Sam Stevens

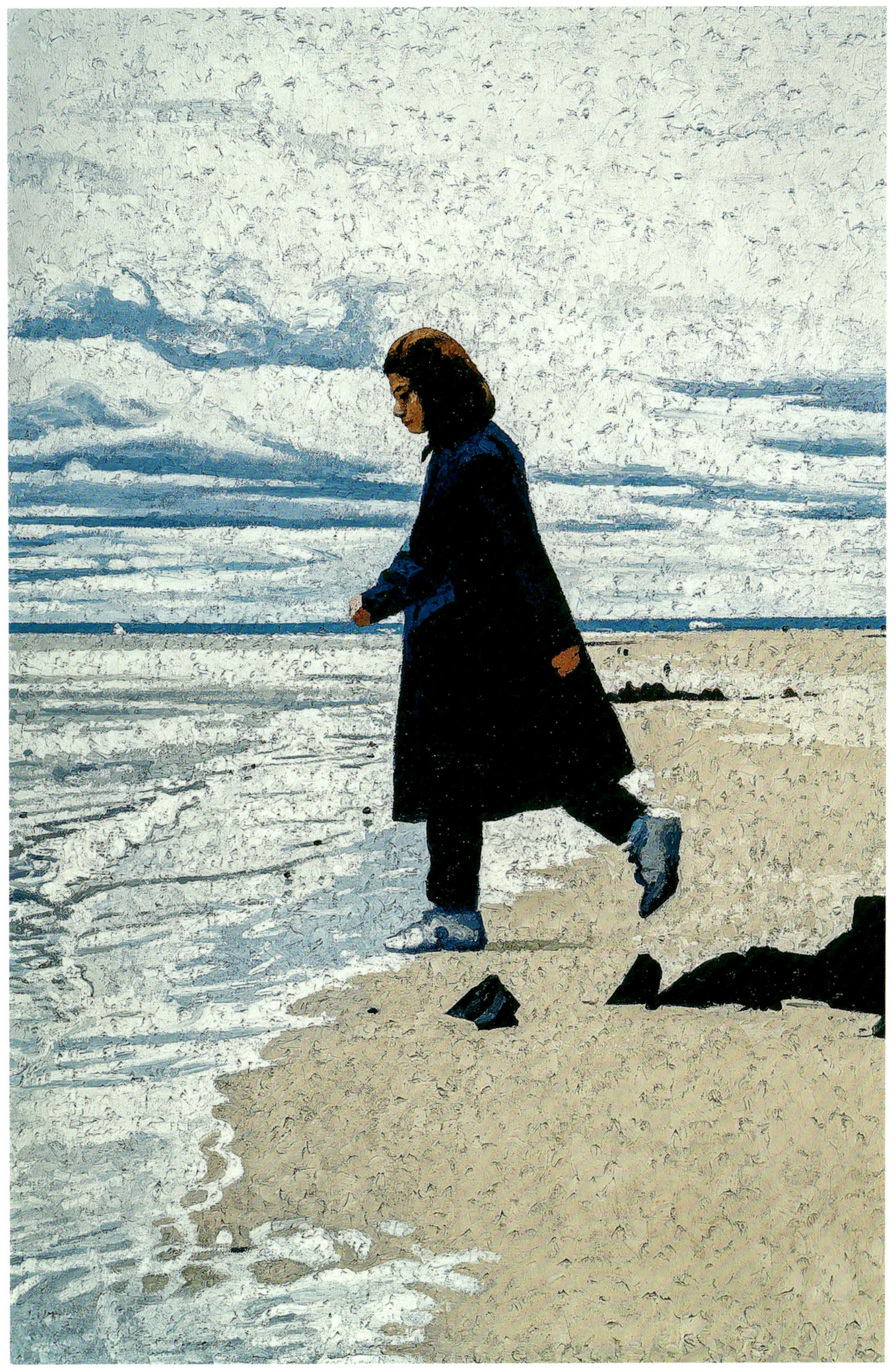

Dreamer, 1999

oil on linen | 30" × 20" | Collection of Nancy Simon, New York City

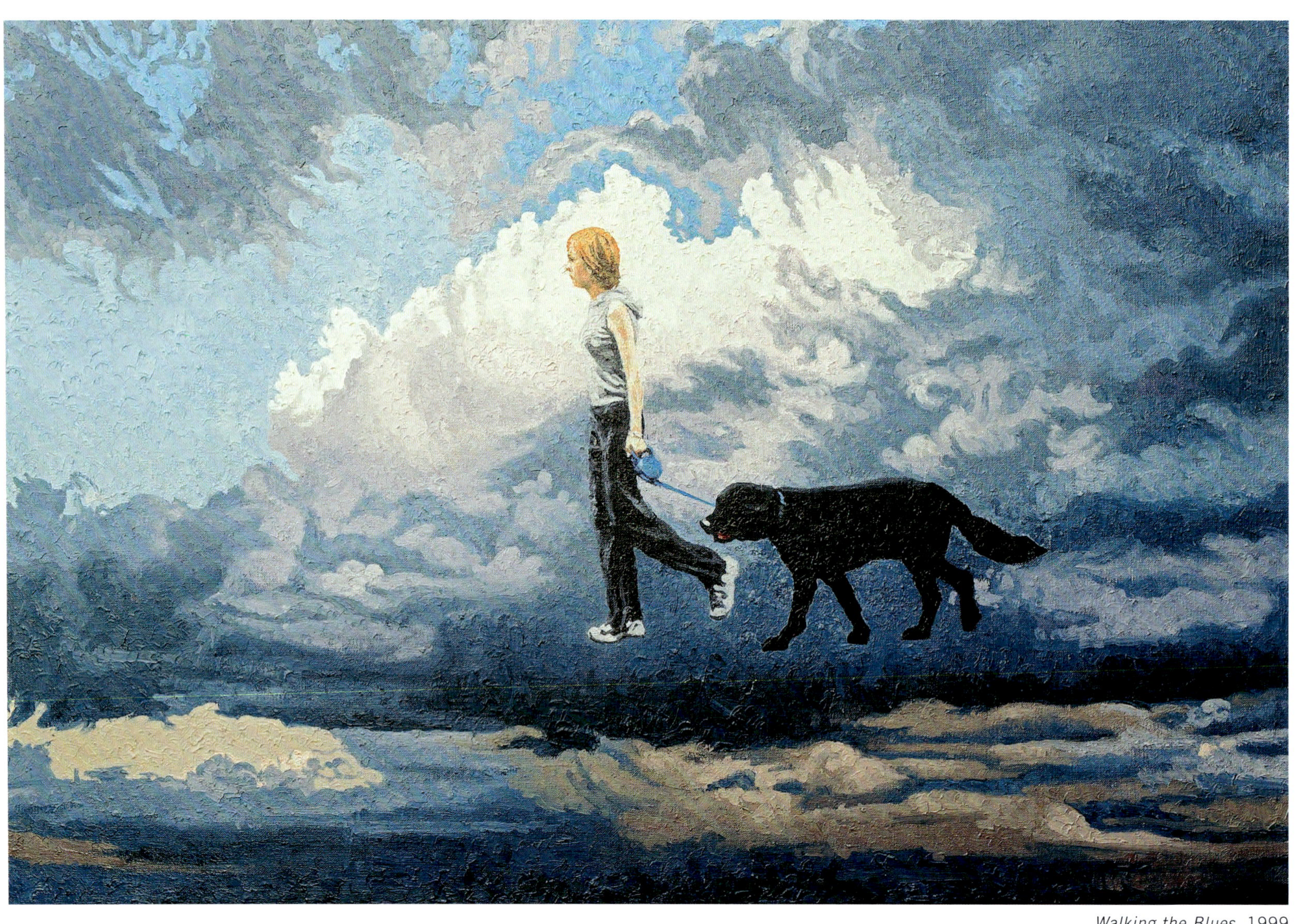

Walking the Blues, 1999

oil on linen | 24" × 36" | Collection of Alice and Charlie Adams | Photography by Jason Voinov wintry moodiness and a restless optimism. Winter often focused on his immediate surroundings: Union Square, Central Park, the Upper West Side. Because of the limited space in the apartment, however, a number of large works had to be painted several months later in his expansive Pipe Creek studio. *Conservatory Waters* (1999), much like the earlier *Central Park*, depicts the oval-shaped pond that is popular for model boat races and other leisure activities. Perhaps influenced by Charles Burchfield's 1920s watercolors, which often focused on imaginative landscapes based on a personal language of fantasy, Winter's large, horizontal oil on paper is a dreamlike, introspective meditation on the ground beneath his feet. Here, the black and white squiggles and quivering serpentine strokes at play in the dark waters provide a counterpoint to the granite border and geometric benches. Like Burchfield, whose renditions expressed the wind in organic patterns that could suggest hunched figures, Winter imbues *Conservatory Waters* with figments of the invisible forces of nature—the sounds of insects, the fermenting power of the soil and dark pond, the chilled air of late afternoon.

Winter's subdued approach to New York City, however, achieves full expression in *Washington's Birthday* (1999), which depicts the historic Union Square Park and intersection on a snowy day. After living in Manhattan for a few years, Winter wanted to paint another expansive rendition of the area. He produced the large-scale work in his Pipe Creek studio, using a 1995 photograph taken on Washington's Birthday as matrix. The result is a tour de force of spatial complexity, intricate detail, and surface incident. Winter brings us up close to a scrim-like fence, through which we view bare trees, light posts, the back of the George Washington equestrian statue, and the bronze fountain group of the mother holding a baby on her right arm with an infant at her left side. Winter directs our gaze to small, silhouetted figures traversing the park and up to the reflective windows of residences and office buildings. The entirety evokes a world of deep, teeming shadows; mysterious, indeterminate spaces, and dense piles of snow on an utterly still winter day. The divergent angles and directional lines of the trees, monuments, windows, and buildings create a dynamic, rhythmic composition. Indeed, the serpentine lyricism of the wire-mesh fence line and the staccato clusters of dying leaves look musical, balancing percussion with harmonic sequence. Winter describes the painting as a series of orchestral movements: "The complexity is like contrapuntal music that challenges the ear to hear each melody separately and yet altogether in a united form. Keeping the counterpoint comparison going, perhaps the dozens of windows in all those buildings is the dominant melody, and then the statuary and small figures rising up above the snow bank come next. And then the fence wire and the virtually bare tree limbs make a higher melody. The fence posts and tree trunks come into our visual consciousness and then the pling, pling, pling of the street lamps. It is as rhythmic as a drum solo, repeating even the white street lamp globes in the holes of the fence posts and a few circles in the tree trunks and dried foliage on the limbs."[6]

For four years, the Winters were content to divide their time between New York City and the Texas Hill Country—each supplied its own special magic. All went quite well, in fact, until Jeanette suffered a massive heart attack in 2000. As it happens, the Winters were in New York City at the time; she would not have survived in Texas because of their remote location far from any hospital. Winter returned to sell the furniture, the cars, and the Pipe Creek house and studios he had designed, thus ending their adventures of "living in the wilds." On his final day in the Hill Country, however, Winter felt a strong urge to do something meaningful with what was left of his father's nineteenth-century five-string banjo. Winter's father had entertained passengers with music on the train from Tennessee to Texas. Later, he lost his thumb, essential for playing the instrument, in an accident and gave the banjo to his son. "Dad had a lifelong love of the West," Winter recalls. "So I walked halfway down our hill and buried it in the dirt and brush. Jeanette's heart attack changed everything. But I would discover another mind-set as a full-time resident of New York City."

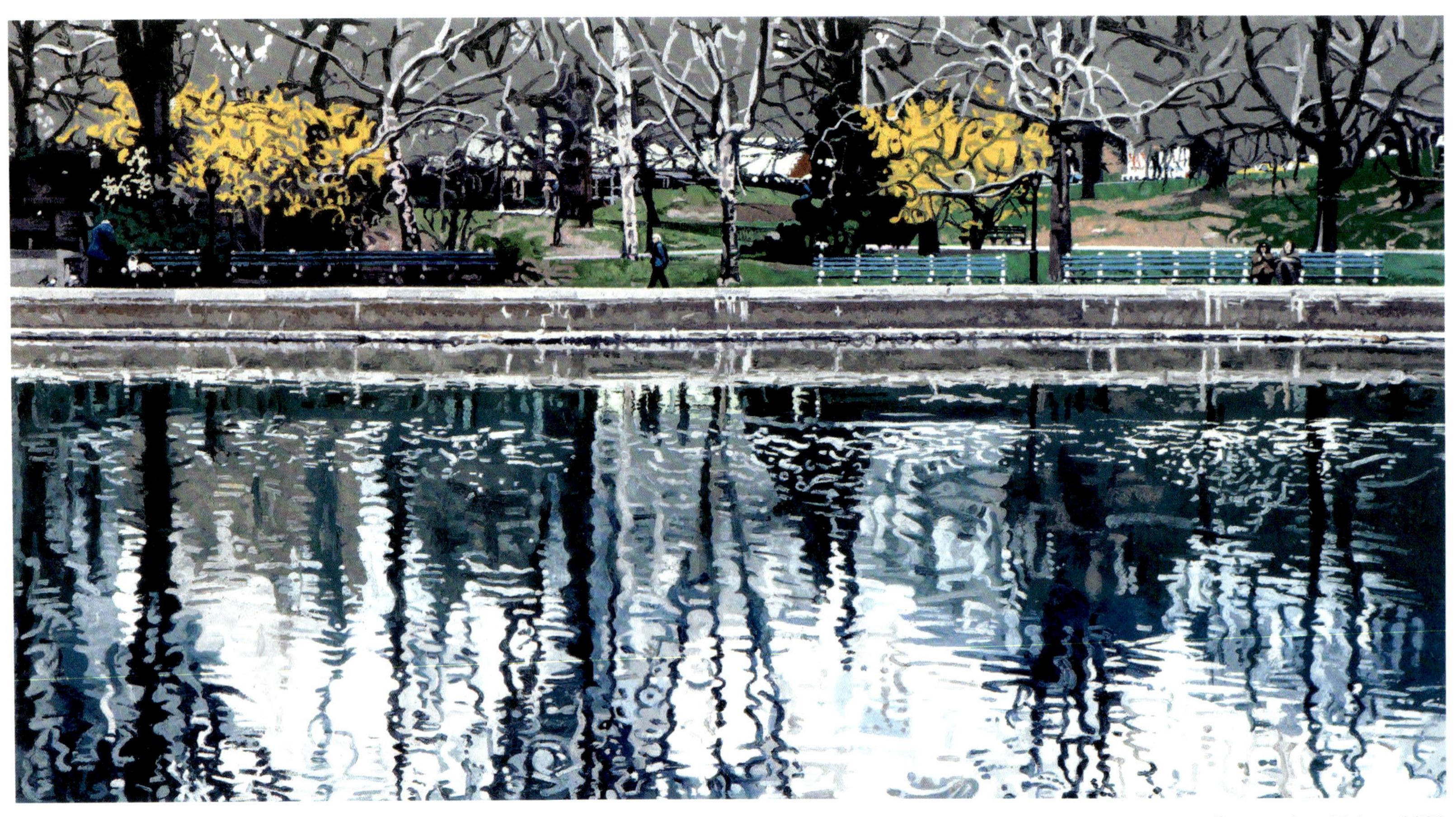

Conservatory Waters, 1999

oil on museum board | 32" × 60" | Collection of Lucette Cumming | Photography by Kevin Todora

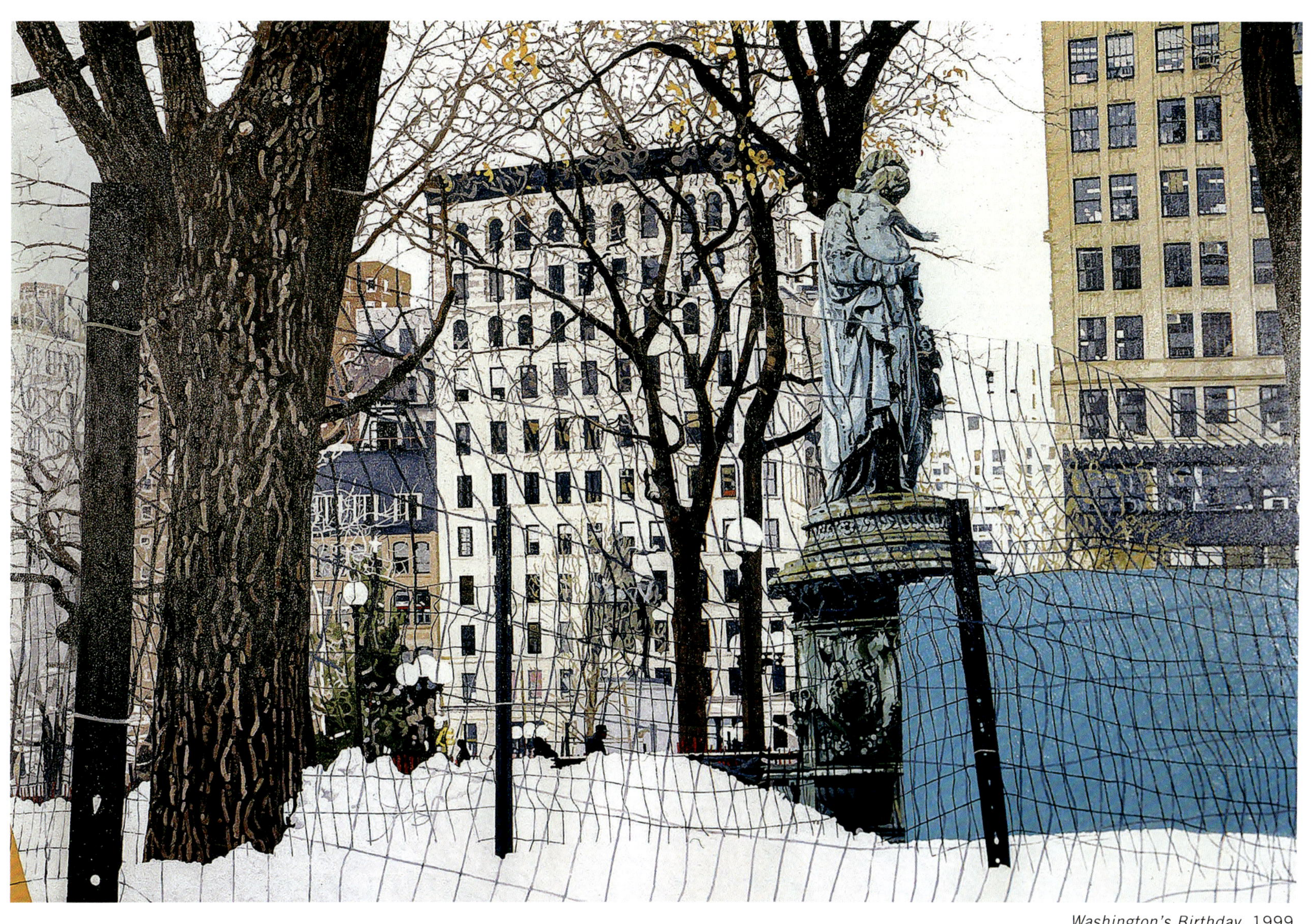

Washington's Birthday, 1999

oil on linen | 64" × 96" | Collection of Molly E. Moore

Throughout his life and career, Winter has maintained that an artist should explore many different ways of working. Over the years, he designed and built houses, wrote country songs, and played the guitar, in addition to creating art in a variety of subjects, styles, forms, and processes. After Jeanette's traumatic heart attack, however, Winter experienced difficulty in finding a new direction for his painting. Over the next few months, he began to pin up objects and photographs on a wall in their bedroom: a 1940s image of a woman in a large bonnet with a Lassie dog standing at her side, a cutout horse, a mask, a pencil, a piece of string. Although previous paintings were imbued with collage-like effects of disjunctive times and spaces, the wall constructions also utilized the traditional genre of still life. In what Winter describes as "a depressed but open mind," he had a eureka moment while strolling one day along Amsterdam Avenue near their Upper West Side apartment. He found himself surrounded by window displays, advertising, and neon signage. Subjective and objective mixtures of still lifes were everywhere: real objects mingled with photographs; functional elements with commercial posters, billboards, and mannequins. Cardboard figures opened real doors amid plate-glass expanses that lined the sidewalks. Indeed, the plethora of ads and window reflections that existed all over New York City roused him to think of still life and assemblage as a rich kaleidoscope of animate and inanimate imagery. The ready-mixed elements evoked a collage-like tension and balance that had to be painted. For Winter, the intersection of sights, sounds, and images tapped into something deeper than the dramatic skyline. Rather, it revealed the very pulse of the city, its mystery and visual culture.

The *Still Life* series presents an array of shapes, textures, surfaces, colors, and reflections. Winter trains his eye on the often overlooked details of the city's everyday settings, laboriously translating the mundane built environments into irresistibly seductive compositions. Reflections in windows or mirrors double a painting's surface, inviting complex spatial readings just as a juxtaposition of inside and outside offers alluring dualities. Throughout, Winter's paintings function on both literal and abstract levels. Significantly, he found that the sheer density of detail that could be included in a painting by careful selection of viewpoint and perspective could also serve metaphorically to address multiple issues. Winter melds reflections in store windows and the language on advertising billboards with an endless array of people, buildings, cars, and trees. The resulting images—paintings within paintings—combine the formal and gestural qualities of Cubist collages with bare facts, wherein dialogues between the depicted, reproduced and real, and between volumes and mediums flourish. The enigmatic compositions inspired Edmund P. Pillsbury to write, "These facades serve a double function as both screen and mirror, yielding simultaneous glimpses of what occupies the space behind as well as myriad reflections of objects facing the transparent barrier."[7]

Often, Winter's works jar us with humor and shocking juxtapositions of seemingly unconnected objects and ideas. He finds situations in which odd bits of conflicting information collide, thereby providing us with a new visual world in which obstruction, confusion, accident, and explosion are the driving forces. Winter does not give us tastefully designed paintings that are easy to get around. Rather, he revels in breaking some of the rules of art and reforming others to suit his wit and instincts. Like a jazz musician, Winter uses devices of scale, shift, reflection, reversal, distortion, repetition, counterpoint, shading, and contrast to suggest open-ended alternatives to ways of seeing. His carefully orchestrated compositions allow us to enter the stream-of-consciousness paintings at any point and lead the eye randomly from one element to the next. Winter complicates things by overlaying sharply defined, contoured strokes and more painterly gestures, thus piggybacking images and activating contradictory types of pictorial space.

In *Columbus Avenue* (2001), a beautiful woman with shoulder-length straight blond hair and yellow aviator glasses anchors the scene, around which are seemingly infinite reflections of buildings,

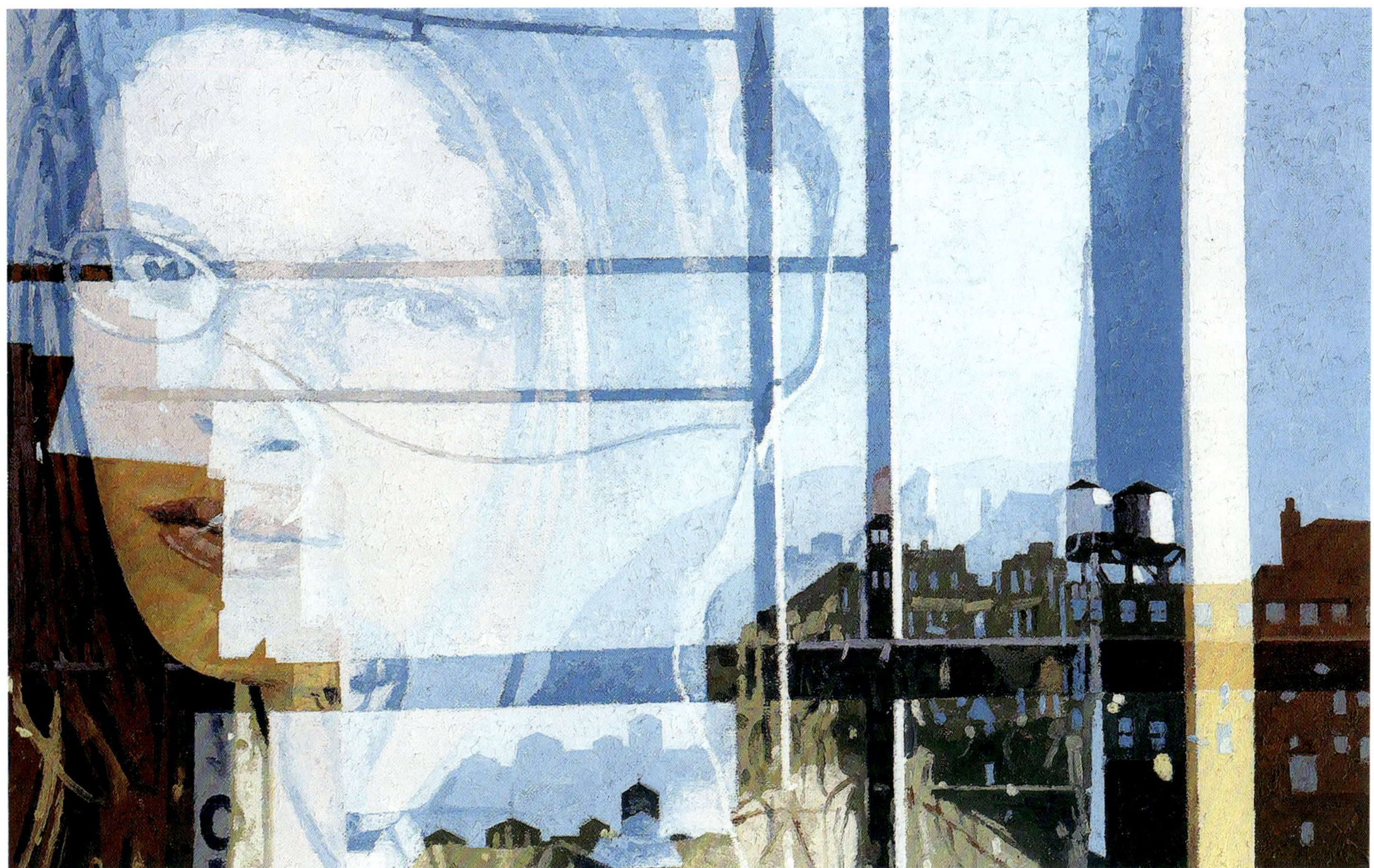

Upper Broadway, 2001
oil on linen | 16" × 26" | Collection of Laura Fleischmann, Dallas

trees, and traffic. For *Self-Portrait* (2001), the artist's own reflection emerges from the lower left corner and behind a billboard with a close-up of a model with slightly parted and sensuous, full lips.

In *Goodfellow* (2001), a cropped billboard featuring the likeness of James Gandolfini, the actor who played the protagonist Tony Soprano in the celebrated television drama *The Sopranos*, dominates the right half of the painting, a red brick warehouse with rows of reflective windows the other. A water tower is the vertical pivot point that joins the collage of incongruous elements, as well as thrusting diagonals formed by the building's roofline and the lyrical span of the bridge featured on the billboard. During this same period, Winter also rendered the graffitied billboards that pervade the commercial life of Manhattan. Just a glance at the empty word balloons, stylized characters, and amoeboid forms tells us about the vertigo of get-and-spend society. While the pace is breakneck, Winter's compositions have a feeling of measured contemplation that balances gut appeal and practiced smartness. Interwoven among the figures and faces are colorful profusions of abstract shapes that mimic "buffs," or paintovers, of street graffiti. Crisply drawn lines curve, loop, and sometimes clump like engorged globules. To the uninitiated, graffiti looks like scribbles on a wall, at best a hermetic babble of hieroglyphs. But for Winter, it is a language distinguished by balance, flow, and symmetry. Throughout, he steadies a vital, throbbing energy with an unmistakable eloquence of touch.

Nevertheless, there's a tranced stillness about these images—a feeling of being in some kind of fugue state. The sensation applies not only to the oversize images themselves—of pop singers

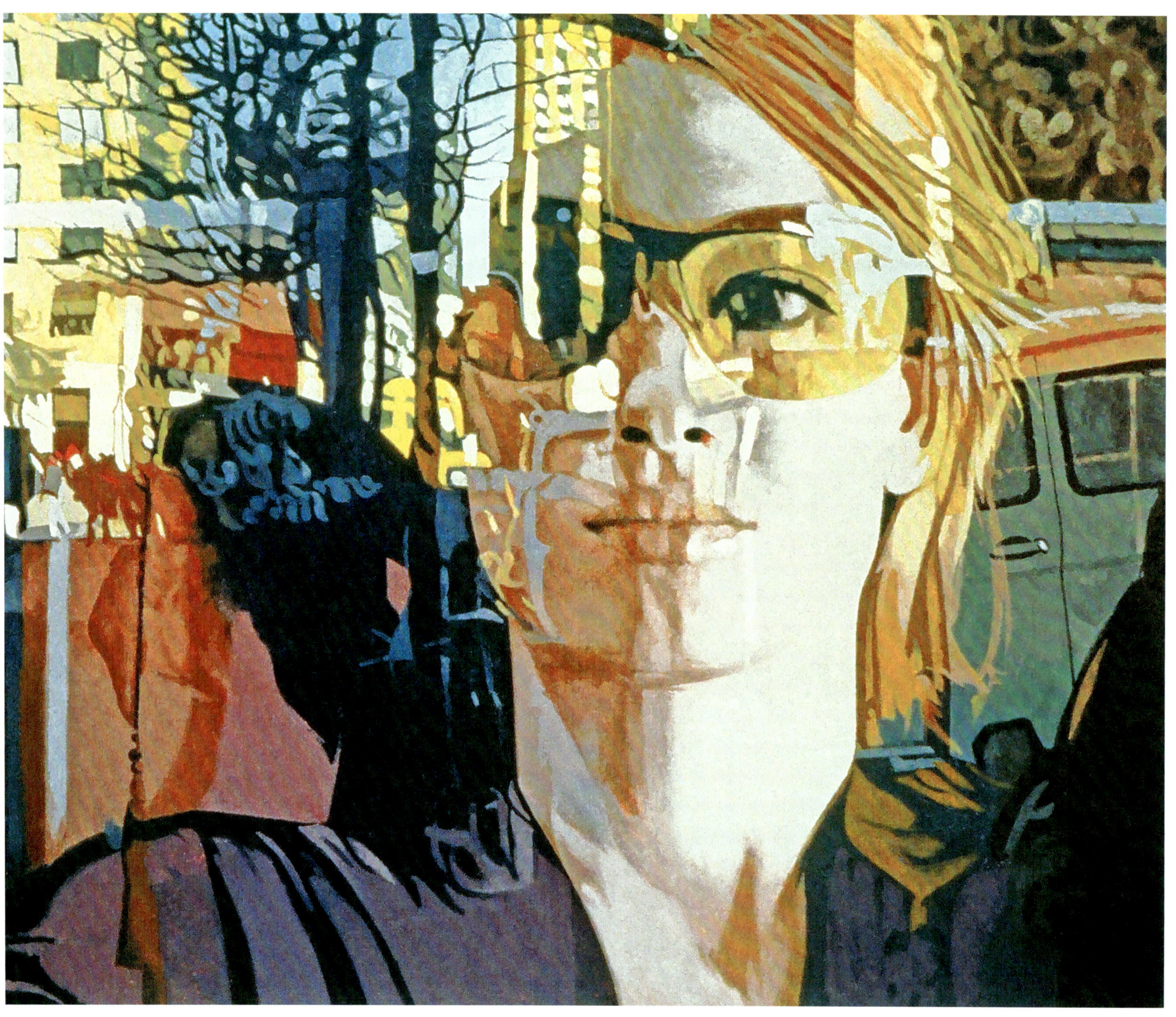

Columbus Avenue, 2001

oil on linen | 52" × 60" | Collection of Judge B. Michael Chitty and Elise Chitty | Photography by Joshua Nefsky

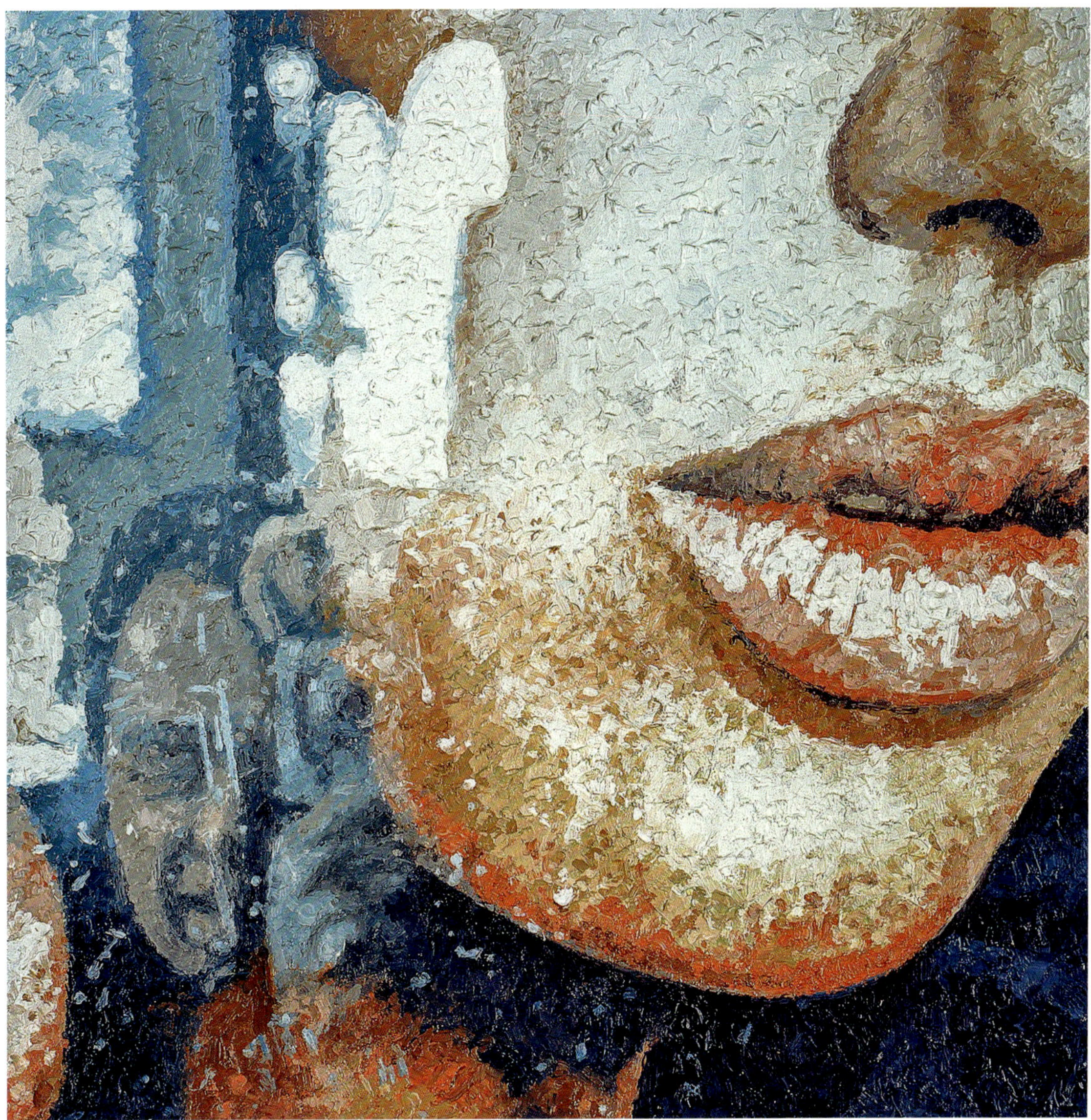

Self-Portrait, 2001
oil on museum board | 9" × 9" | Collection of Molly E. Moore

Shakira and Pink, for example—but also to the effect induced in us as viewers. Evocative of Giorgio de Chirico's haunting plazas and arcades, Winter's settings are dreamlike, metaphysical shifts of raking light and oblique perspectives. We can dissect these jigsaw pieces like magical nodes of experience yet not find what ultimately makes them cohere. Similarly, Winter's compositions jam the sense of illusionary depth. The dense layers of unrelated images create a raucous visual field in which seemingly incompatible pictorial incidents inhabit a single moment in time and space. In *Wooster Street* (2001), Winter uses the language of graffiti to slow the eye, thereby directing attention to stroke and image. Here, he alternates ambiguous snatches of phrases—"Enjoy a Tall Cold One"; "What does yours do?"—with images of Jim Morrison, the deceased lead singer of the Doors; a cartoony red devil with curled tail; and a cover shot of *Spin* magazine. The entire surface is activated by meticulously rendered defacements and drips in painterly rhythms of red, white, and black. Taken together, the New York City "still lifes" draw on various visual languages and the practice of pop to produce a dazzling fusion of image, color, and sign that simultaneously proposes multiple realities.

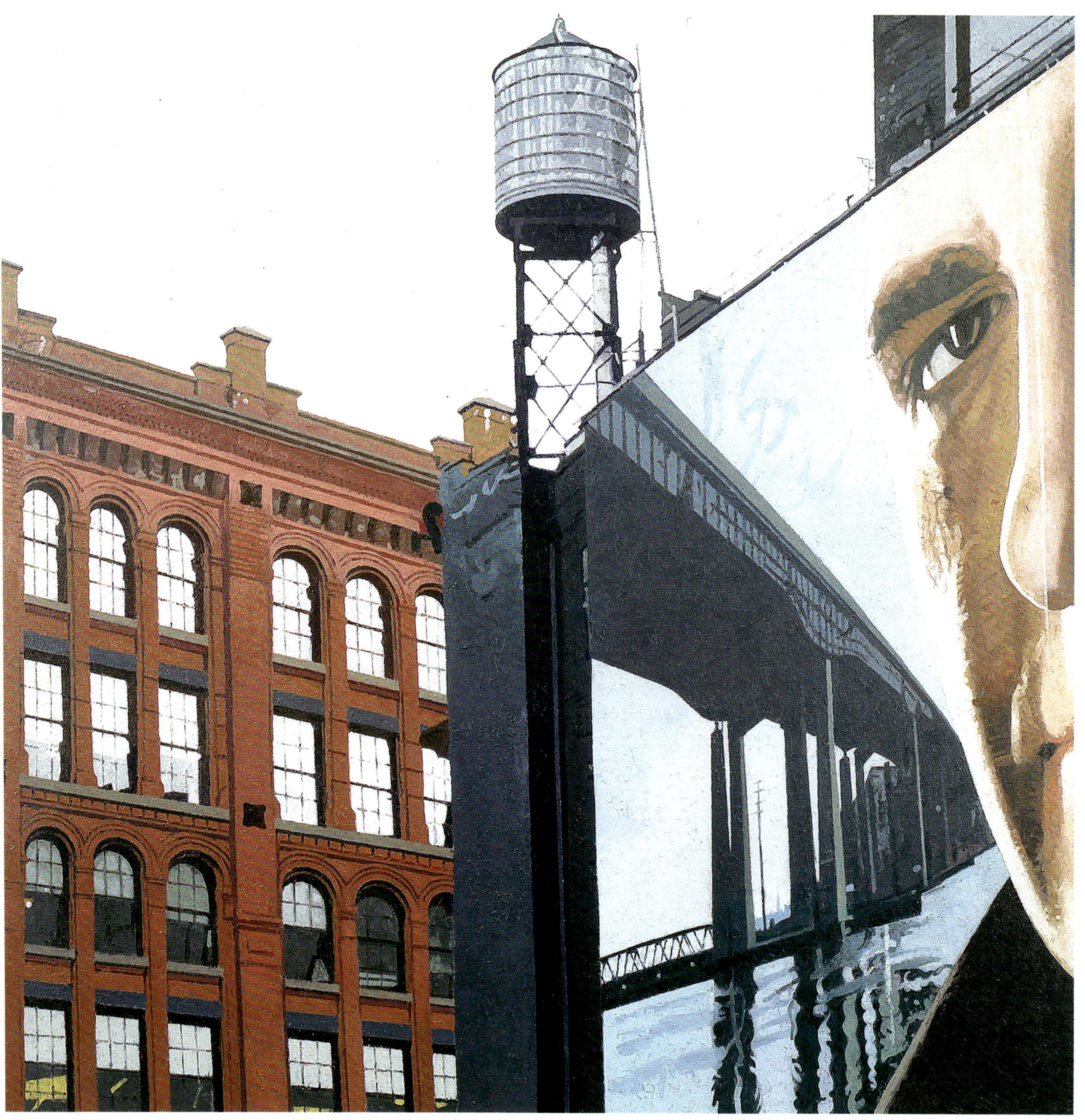

Goodfellow, 2001
oil on linen | 50" × 50" | Collection of Molly E. Moore

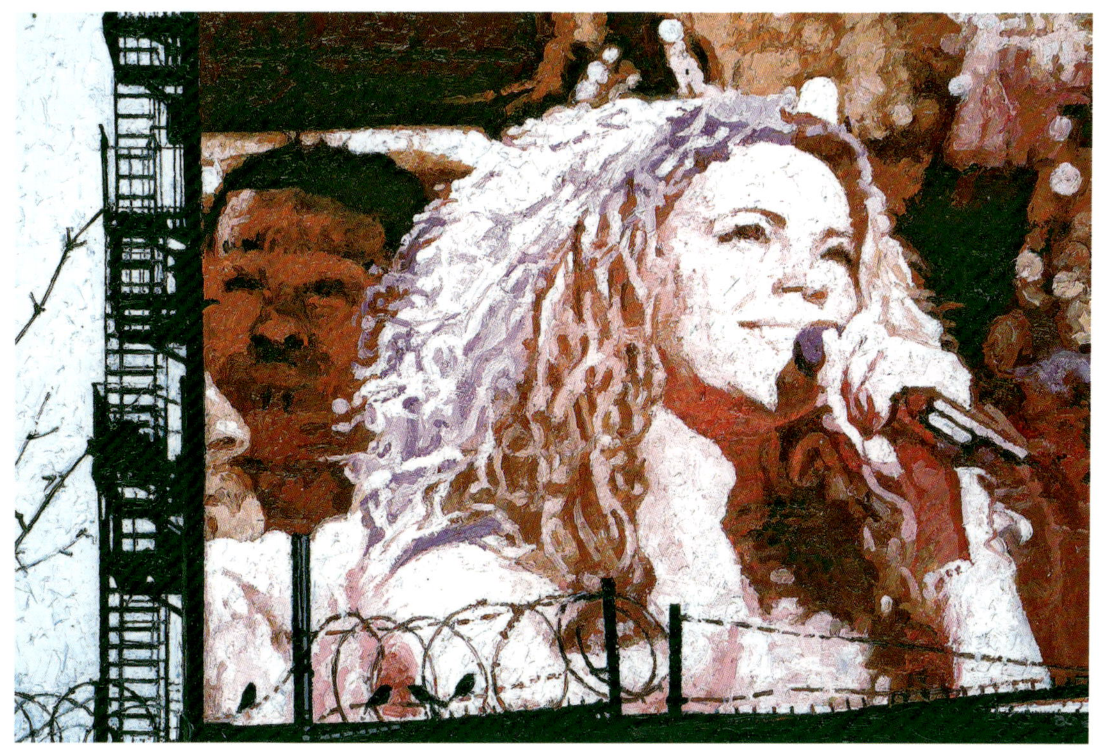

Shakira, 2001

oil on museum board | 8 1/2" × 12 3/4" | Courtesy of the artist

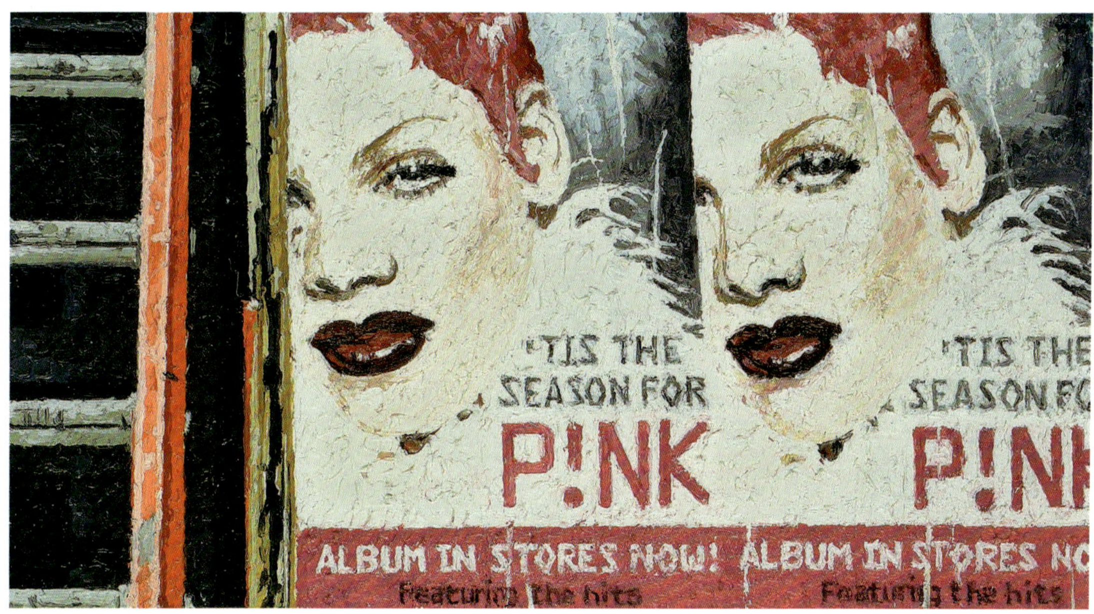

Pink, 2001

oil on museum board | 4" × 7 1/2" | Collection of Courtney Crothers

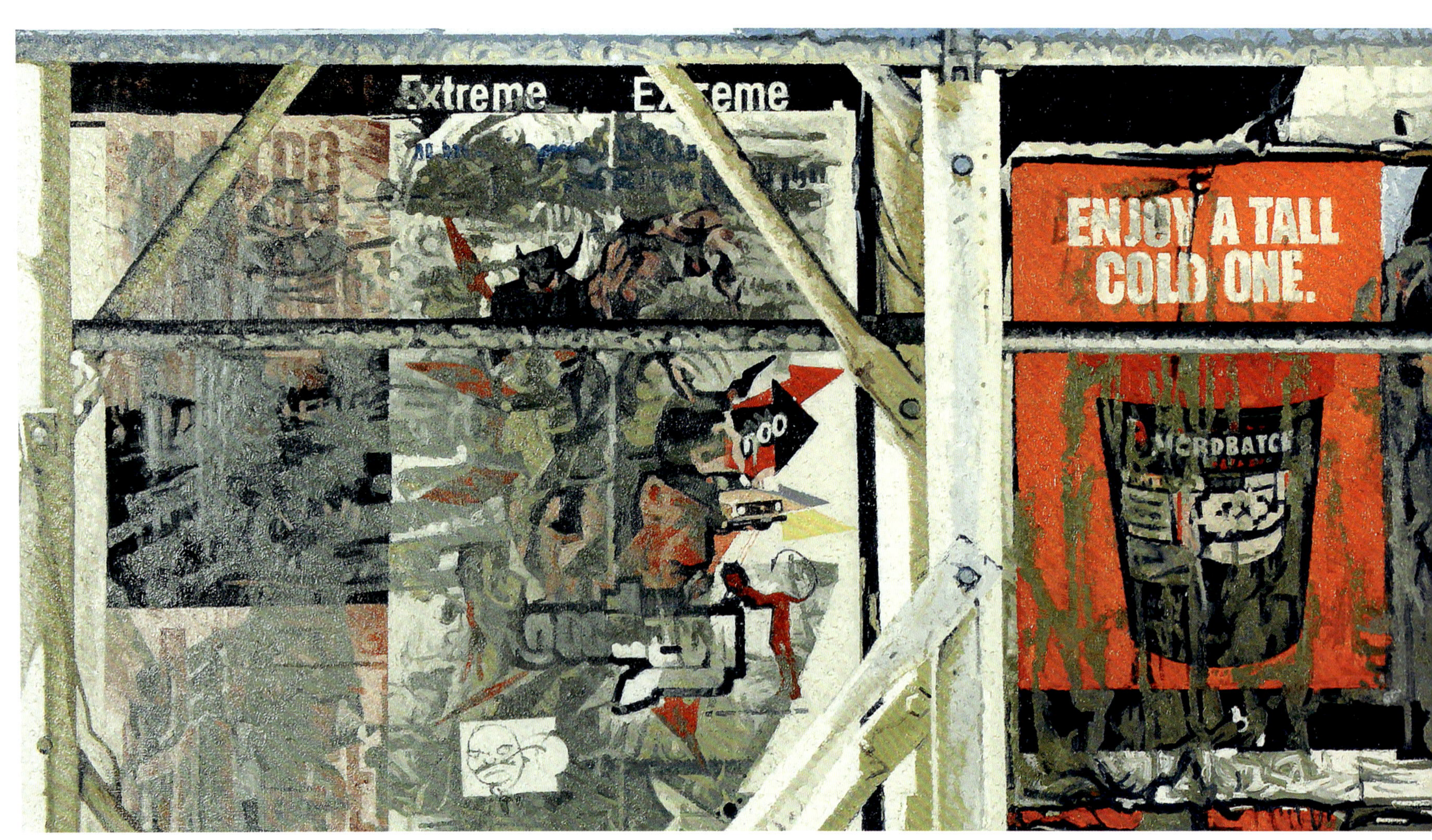
Extreme
ENJOY A TALL
COLD ONE.

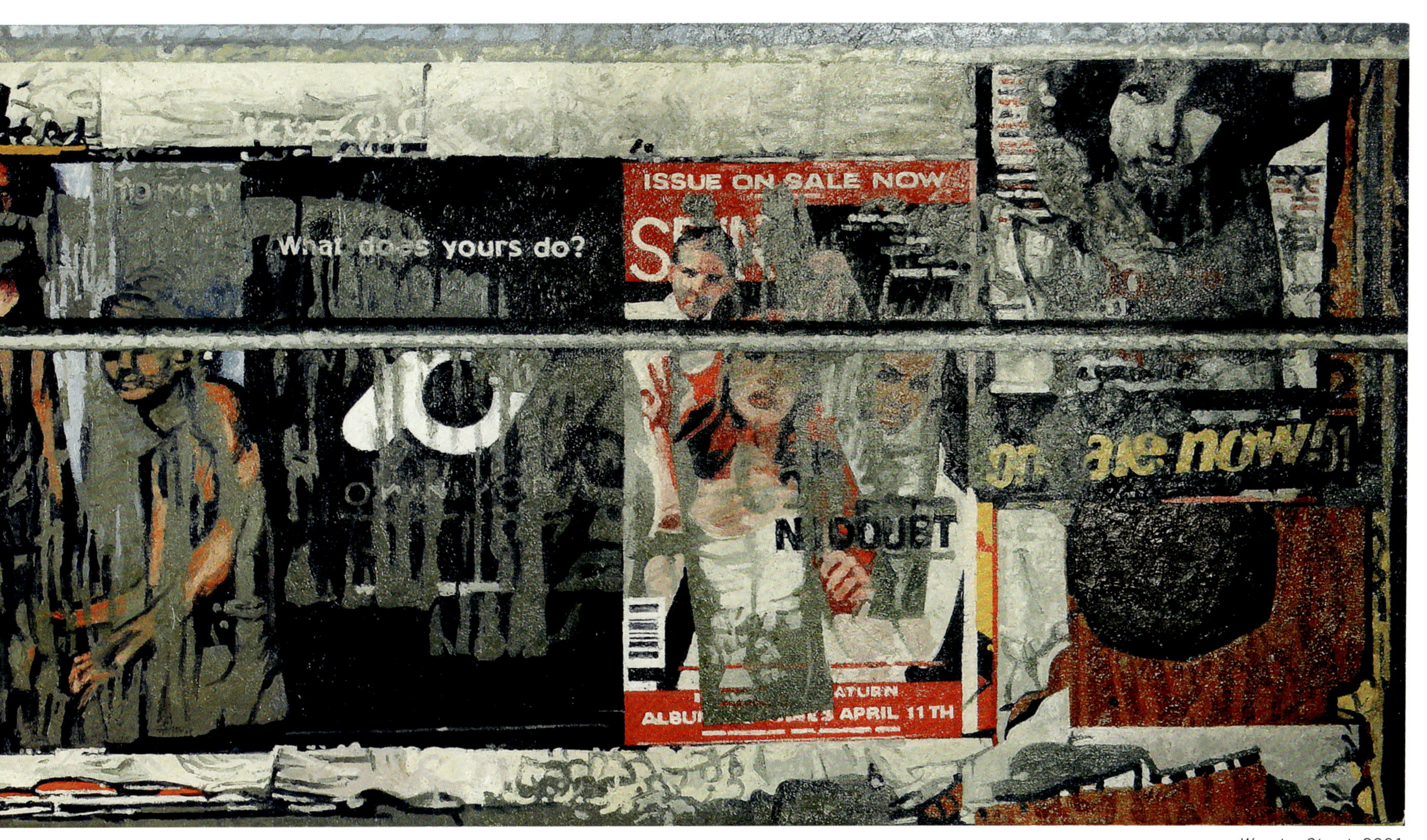

Wooster Street, 2001

oil on linen | 26" × 96" | Collection of Kirk Hopper, Dallas | Photography by G. Valderas

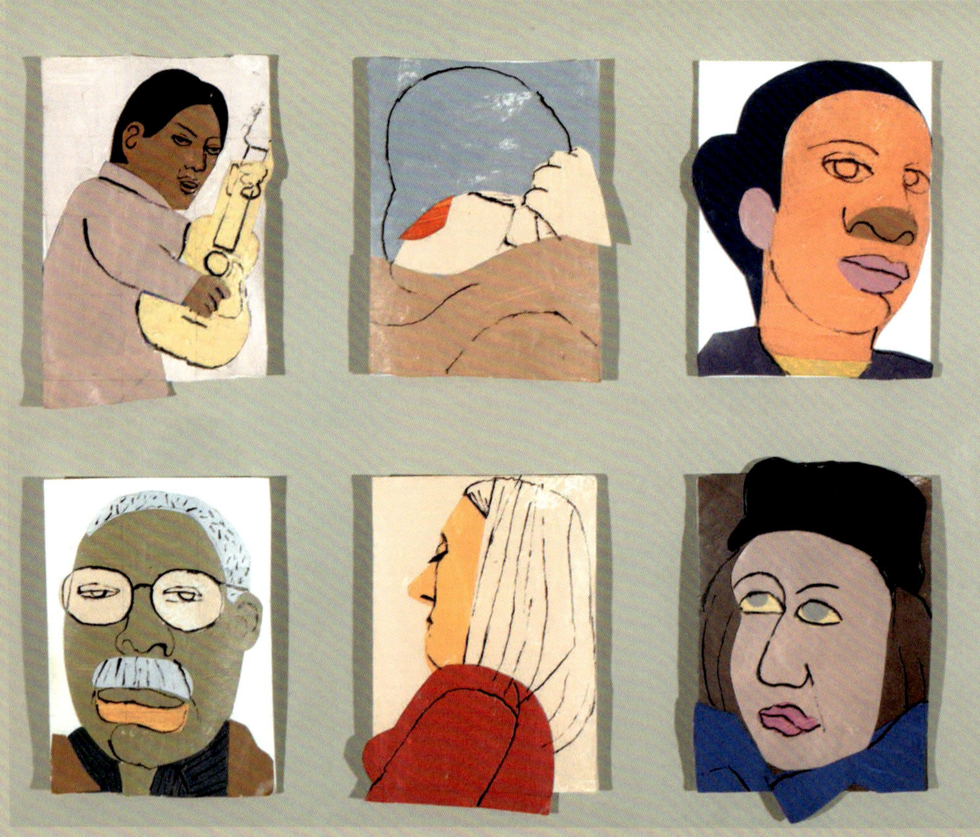

Subway series (composite detail), 2003
painted and cut paper with ink | 59" x 41" overall | Collection of Bryant and Nancy Hanley | Photography by Kevin Todora

CHAPTER 13

FROM SUBWAYS TO SANTA FE

NOT LONG AFTER THE SALE of the Pipe Creek property, Winter decided to purchase his first studio in New York City. He settled on a space in the Master Building, a landmark twenty-seven-story Art Deco skyscraper overlooking the Hudson River along Riverside Drive and within walking distance of their Upper West Side apartment. He felt good about being in the city all year. "Remote rural places were lovely but a little rough on an aging body. I had grown weary of dealing with country people and was feeling more urbane in my older years."[1]

During the same period, Winter spent Tuesday mornings at the Metropolitan Museum of Art with the aim of working his way through the entire collection, gallery by gallery. Moving through the cultural ages from all corners of the earth, he became enthralled by certain works that had gone unnoticed in past visits: Cycladic figures, New Guinea carvings, Dogon sculpture, Egyptian hieroglyphs, and Netherlandish miniature portraits. Although Winter's 2002 exhibition of New York City still life paintings, *Urban Naturalism*, had been an all-out success at Pillsbury Peters Fine Art in Dallas, he was anxious to explore new pathways in his art. The experiences at the Met inspired him to reduce, simplify, and geometrize the human figure. As luck would have it, Winter had been working in his studio when he reached for a glass from a cabinet and a small photograph of an Asian woman near a subway sign on Canal Street fell to the floor. The image stimulated him to produce a series of twenty diminutive portraits using small, pointed sable brushes and rendered with the same meticulous details he had studied in the Flemish miniatures at the Met. Winter captured people browsing market stalls and windows who were not aware of being photographed. In doing so, he hoped to develop portraits that were more candid, more incidental.

The upshot is a kind of portrait of an American community: African American, Asian, Hispanic, and Anglo men, women, and children; blue-collar workers; bohemians; and students, all painted with startling lucidity. At the same time, they delight with surprising hues, lush paint passages, inventive textures, and telling details. After translating a few images into larger canvases,

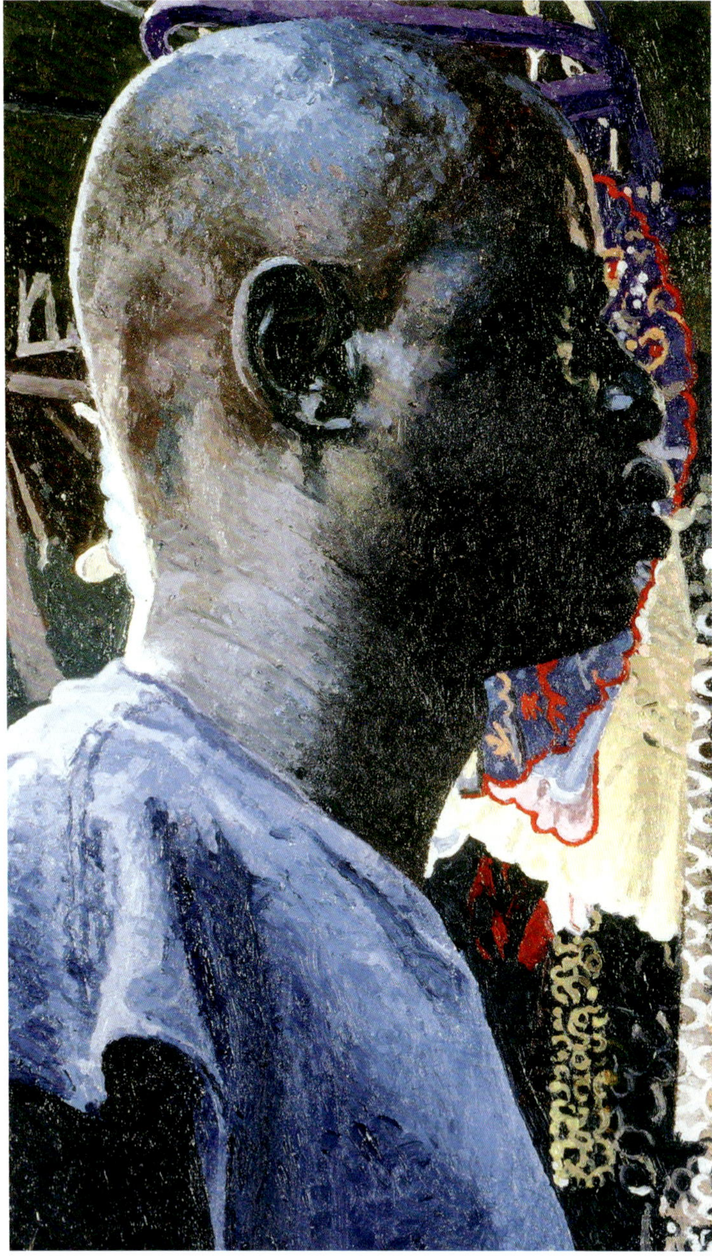

Profile of a Man, 2002
oil on museum board | 8" × 4" | Private collection, Dallas

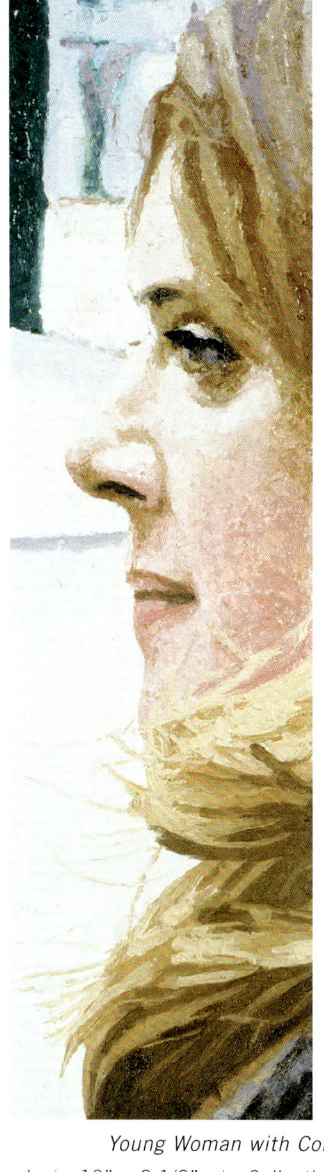

Young Woman with Confident Look, 2002
oil on museum board | 10" × 2 1/2" | Collection of Molly E. Moore

Winter asked Bridget Moore, director of the DC Moore Gallery, to visit the studio. Winter was writing a catalog essay on Jane Wilson's landscape paintings for the gallery and had developed a friendship with Moore. According to Winter, however, Moore was critical of the random portraits because they were based on photographs. "She asked, 'Why not just keep the snapshots?' She was more interested in the 1973 Snider Plaza drawings and other spontaneous things, like the *50 Maine Men*. And she said, 'You know what would be good? A subway series!' Bridget was enthralled by the waves of humanity and diverse individuals that subway riders see day after day. I didn't take the suggestion to heart until a month or so later. I bought a small spiral-bound notebook, got on a subway, and with a ballpoint pen drew person after person in a clandestine way. However, I was always prepared to stop if anyone took offense at my drawing them. I would ride the subway to the end of the line in Brooklyn and back again just drawing passengers."

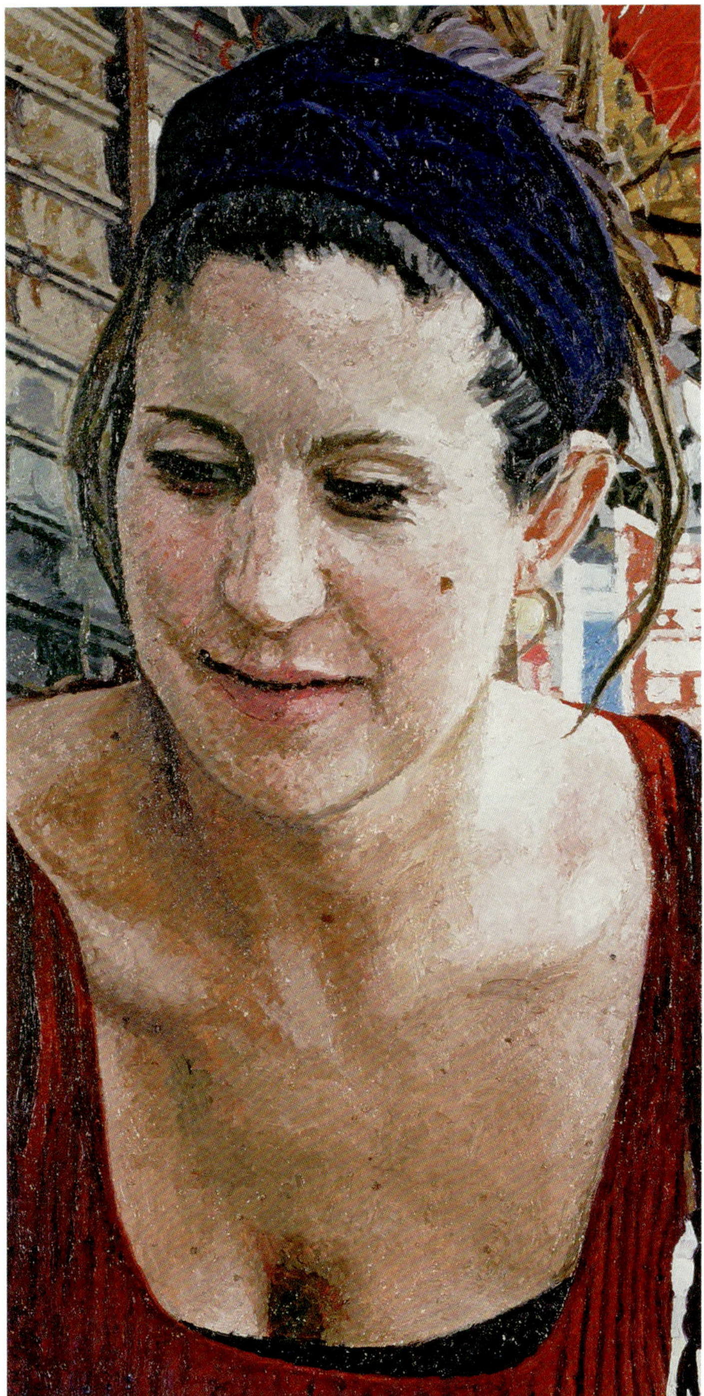

Smiling Woman, 2002
oil on museum board | 10" × 5" | Collection of Molly E. Moore

After dozens and dozens of drawings, Winter decided to make them into cut-paper-and-ink collages. He painted stacks of paper, using acrylic from tubes as well as spontaneous mixtures of color. Winter would cut and collage from the subway drawings, then superimpose ink drawing with bamboo pen. He produced over 150 collages, all on five-by-seven-inch pieces of museum board, which he pinned to the studio wall. With the leftover paper, he made figurative collages on museum board, some of which were enlarged to greater than life size. The cutouts led naturally to three-dimensional figures and animals—a crouching rabbit, a katsina with yellow head, a woman with large red lips, a goddess, plants, and insects—constructed from the museum board and, later, the larger, three-eighths-of-an-inch plywood painted with mixed acrylics. In these, Winter operates by intuitive checks and balances. However, walking around them, viewing their structures from different sides, noting the collusion of fluidity and solidity, of stasis and dynamism, human perception seems scrupulously accounted for. All of them exude a jittery charm and convey a humorous, eccentric side of Winter.

Significantly, Winter's many trips in the New York City subway system resulted in a 2005 exhibition of the collages at the Meadows Museum, Southern Methodist University. For Winter, the series was a chance to reclaim for art a place in the fabric of daily life and to renew the role of the artist in society. Through empathy, he could reveal a heroic dimension of people from everyday walks of life and, in some cases, the downtrodden, who have been largely bypassed in the creation of art. In many ways, Winter's *Subway* series accomplishes what we have always needed art to do: it perceives and gives form to the changing world around us. Winter's drawings and collages are alive to difference, variety, the possibilities of our rangy humanity. By actively engaging the city with all of his senses, he captures life unfiltered. Partly it is because he is insatiably curious and has a bottomless faith in people's decency. Thus, the *Subway* series enabled Winter to marvel at the kind of lottery that brings together a random sampling of humanity in the course of a few minutes, testing him—and us—for kindness and understanding.

It is important to note that Winter looked at Walker Evans's subway series of 1938–41 before taking on the project. Using a hidden camera, Evans snapped unsuspecting passengers traveling around the city. Seeking to avoid the sentimentality and artifice of conventional studio portraiture, he aimed for an anonymous, straightforward

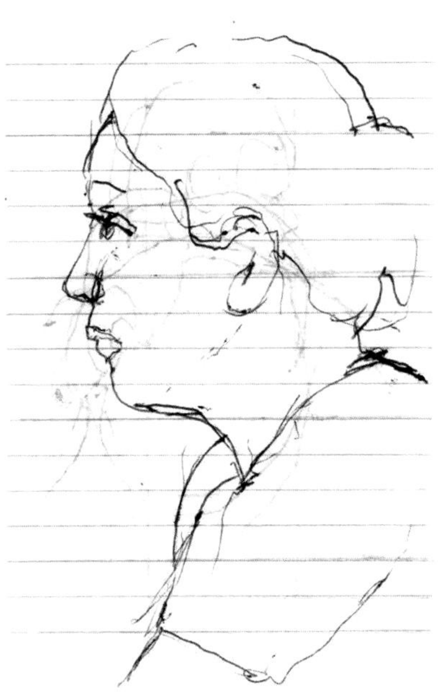

Drawings for Subway Series: Profile of a Young Woman, 2003
ballpoint on paper | 5" × 3" | Collection of the artist |
Photography by Joshua Nefsky

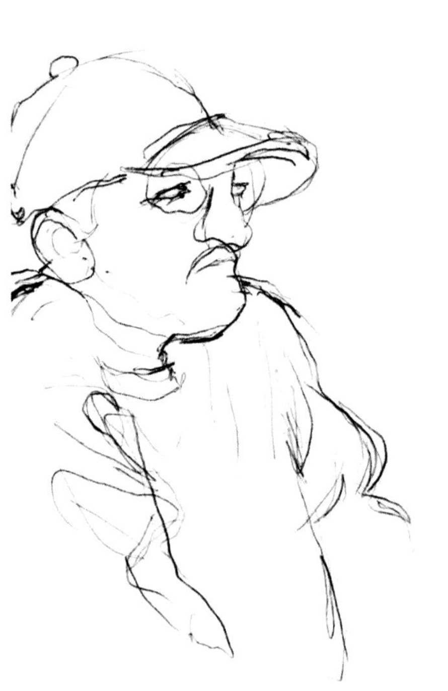

Drawings for Subway Series: Man Wearing Baseball Cap, 2003
ballpoint on paper | 5 1/2" × 3 1/2" | Collection of the artist |
Photography by Joshua Nefsky

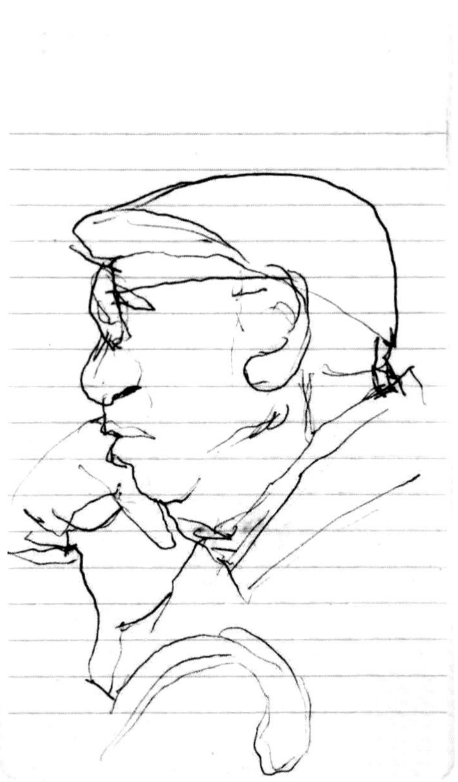

Drawings for Subway Series: Man Leaning on Hand, 2003
ballpoint on paper | 5" × 3" | Collection of the artist |
Photography by Joshua Nefsky

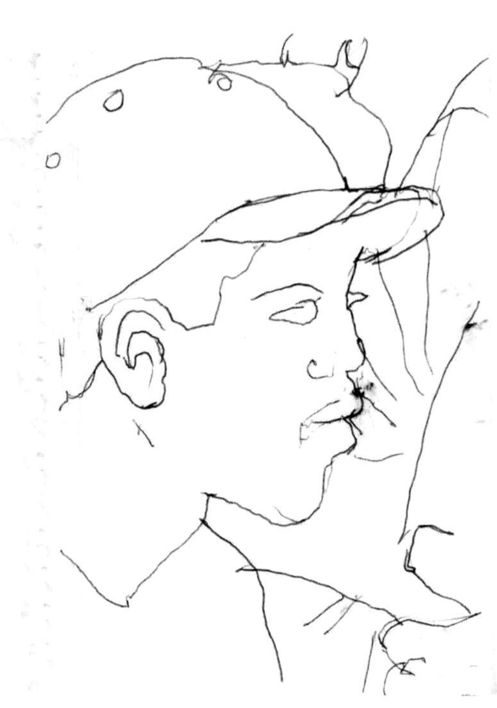

Drawings for Subway Series: Young Man Wearing Cap, 2003
ballpoint on paper | 5 1/2" × 4" | Collection of the artist |
Photography by Joshua Nefsky

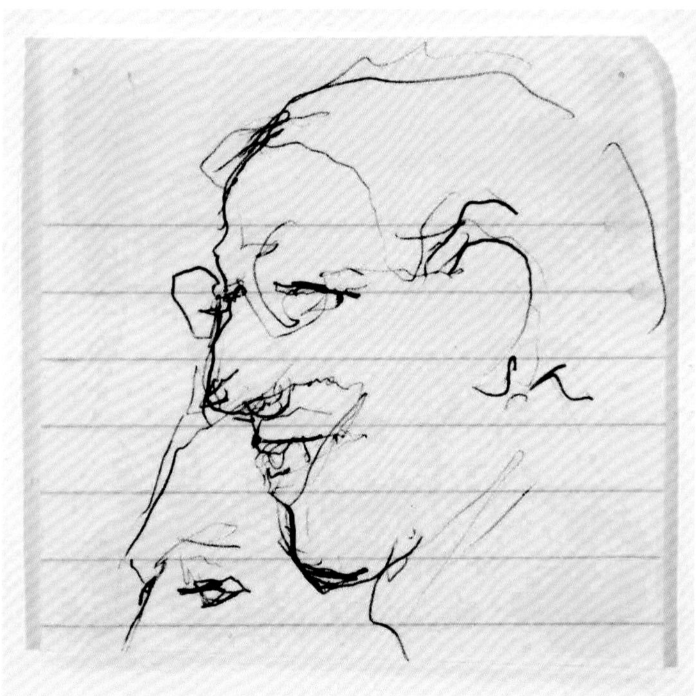

Drawings for Subway Series: Laughing Man, 2003
ballpoint on paper | 2 3/4" × 2 3/4" | Collection of the artist | Photography by Joshua Nefsky

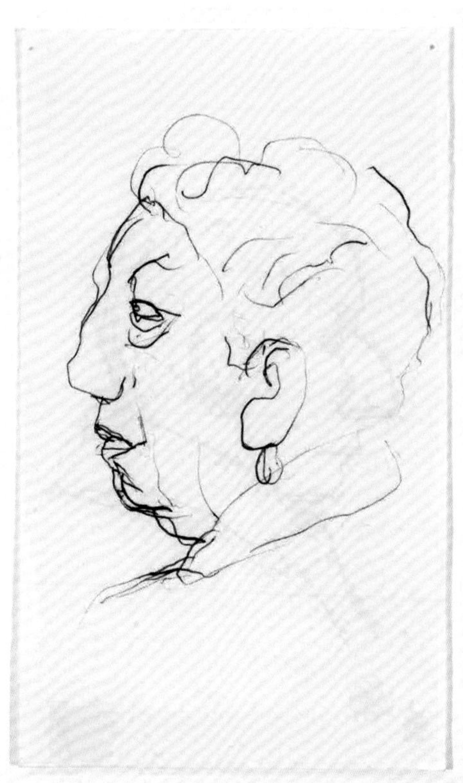

Drawings for Subway Series: Woman with Ear Ring, 2003
ballpoint on paper | 6" × 3 1/2" | Collection of the artist | Photography by Joshua Nefsky

picture of humanity. His photographs show people immersed in conversation, reading, or seemingly lost in their own thoughts and moods. Similarly, Winter catches his subjects in typical subway behavior, deep in daydreams, asleep, or gazing off into space; faces old, young, glaring, laughing, inward looking, out of it. One of the invaluable features of Winter's *Subway* series is that it fully places the humane experience within a melting pot of rhythms and idioms. Taken together, however, the images add up to an affecting composite picture of a familiar paradox. We never seem more alone or adrift from one another than when we are bustling along with humans in transit, migratory flocks of isolated souls. About the series, Max Winter writes, "Deliberation combines with muted reaction to settle around you rather than slapping you in the face. These people look as if they *could* be anything; dangerous, beautiful, your grandmother, your mugger. Anything. And you also feel as if these faces *have* been everything. . . . You might wonder also why after you look at a few of them all together, so many of them look away from you. The answer is simple; because everyone else does. In a society which favors direct eye contact above all else, the moments of true communication are precious and few even when two people look directly at each other. Yet, in allowing us to look at these people in these personal moments, the works slowly form a bridge. The bridge lies between our noisiest selves—the selves we are told to be proud of—and our quietest selves—the selves that reflect who we are rather than how we seem."[2]

Winter depicts a man with a scarf covering his mouth and wrapped around his neck for warmth. He catches a distraught woman with tears streaming down her face. Two men cuddle and kiss in a display of intimacy. He focuses on a Hare Krishna group in meditation, or the tiny, delicate hands of a little girl. Some of the young women hover between the sensuality and swagger of being a tough street number and the last vestiges of childhood vulnerability. The collages are, at first glance, random intersections of planes and curves, some with dashes of color to accent certain body parts. The mood can be tightly wound, or sometimes antic. A sense of gesture and personality is conveyed by small details and

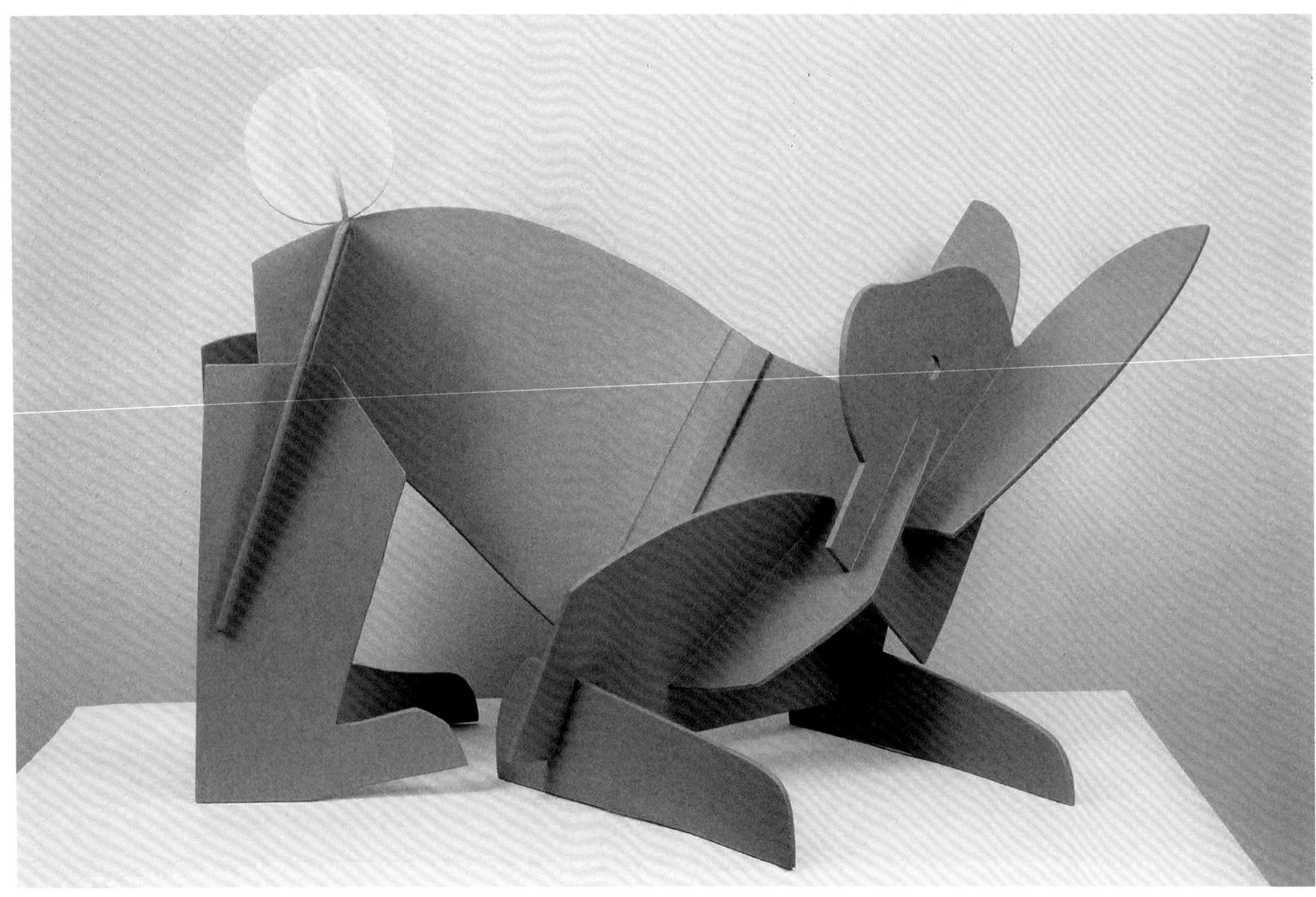

Crouching Rabbit, 2005
acrylic on plywood | 32" × 48" × 32" | Courtesy of the artist and Kirk Hopper Fine Art, Dallas | Photography by Joshua Nefsky

discordant hues—yellow hair, a bright-orange nose, pink lips. Often, the figures are fleshed out from geometric infrastructures—hard-edged rectangles or squares or free-form gestures, like the straight and curving lines of ink visible in the faces. The surfaces suggest an artist alive to every mark and line who expresses his motifs with acute spatial wit. The *Subway* series places Winter's art where it belongs, in a tradition of figuration that runs across all cultures, through Cycladic and African sculpture to Honoré Daumier's *Third-Class Carriage* and George Herriman's *Krazy Kat*.

During these same years, 2001–5, Winter taught drawing and painting classes at the National Academy of Design in New York City. He had missed the connective energy that flowed back and forth between his studio and the classroom. In his new position, however, Winter encouraged students to take more adventurous approaches in making art. He wrote and designed brochures on the geometric figure, as well as nonlinear images in space, to address issues of form, process, and perception. He was less of a taskmaster than he had been in the Southern Methodist University years, and more a proponent of play. As he fondly quoted one of Toni Morrison's characters, "Wanna fly, you got to give up that shit that weighs you down." With this in mind, Winter followed his own advice, especially in the cutouts and collages, which he viewed alternately as forms of personal catharsis and playful invention. For the *Women and Girls* series (2005), he boils down the human figure to simple shapes in space. "I had to take pills every morning and at night, so

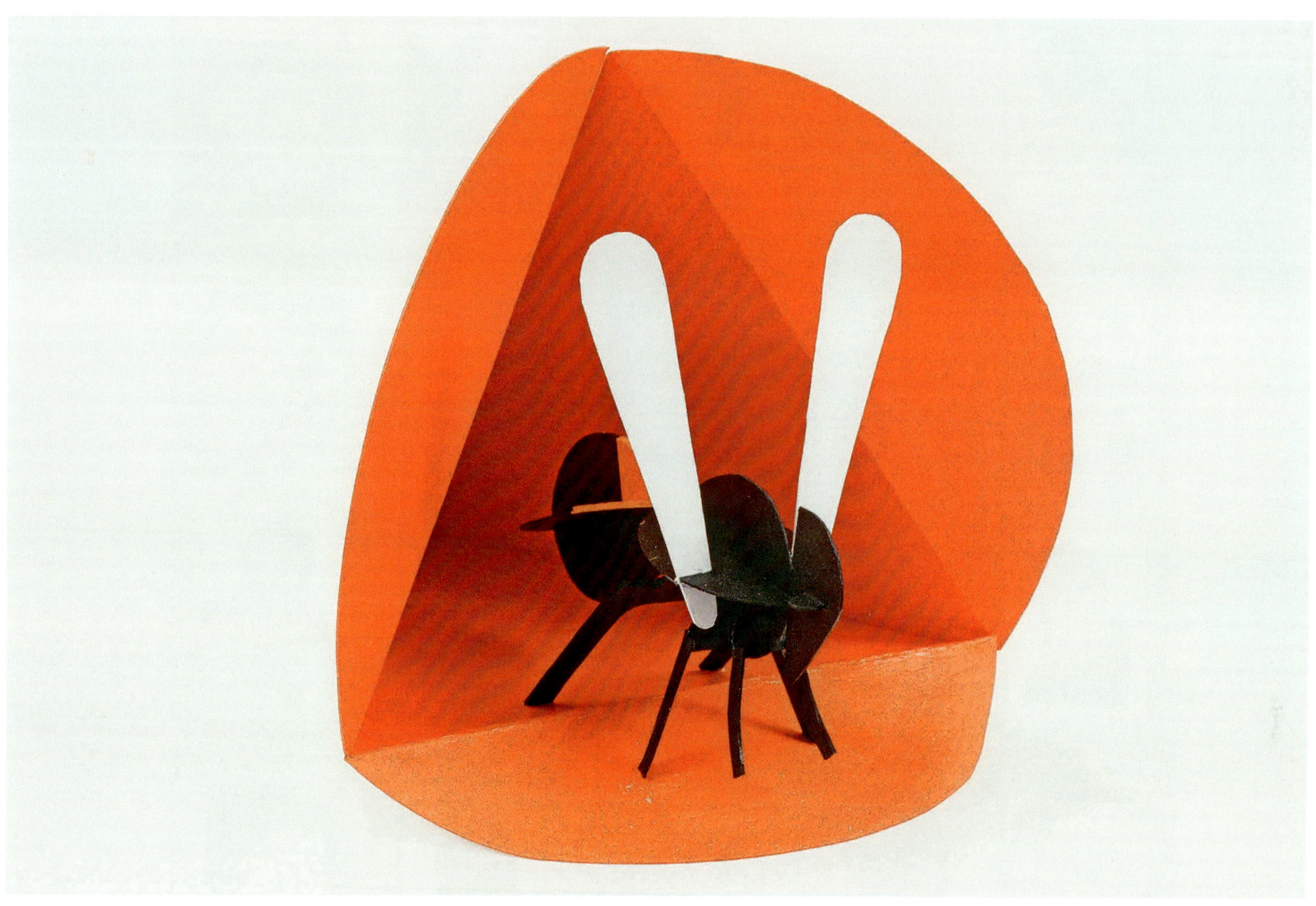

Insect Emerging from Flower, 2005
acrylic on museum board | 13 1/2" × 15" × 20" | Collection of the artist | Photography by Joshua Nefsky

I'd make little people out of them on the table," he explains. "Somehow I thought of using the colored paper that I had painted for the *Subway* series but also creating something humorous out of formal reductive elements. You can make a whole universe out of a three-part figure. What do we know best? We know our arms, legs, faces, eyes, and hair." Here, Winter's minimal compositions manage to evoke clothing and hairstyles, as well as a variety of personalities. Colors disrupt and push off other colors. Each work is divided into discrete planes and each section is painted a different hue. The effect is another Winter stratagem—the forced contradiction between illusionistic space and physical space, between image and material. These lovingly crafted configurations are fundamental to Winter's intuitive yet meticulously refined visual language. They evoke Henri Matisse's dancing cut paper collages, which join a childlike exuberance to a deeply sophisticated sense of form and color, as well as Alexander Calder's buoyant assemblies that use an economy of materials and gestures. Flattened yet statuesque, Winter's agile women are frequently in motion, their poses simplified by bold colors. A few figures seemingly thrust their arms upward, flailing for balance. Their lurching motions convey something balletic about them and something imploringly awkward. The joinery has an almost jammed-together air, with heads, torsos, and limbs brusquely cut for a slam-bang impact. They are objects of real power whose light spirit, caprice, and spatial expansiveness achieve a beguiling lyricism.

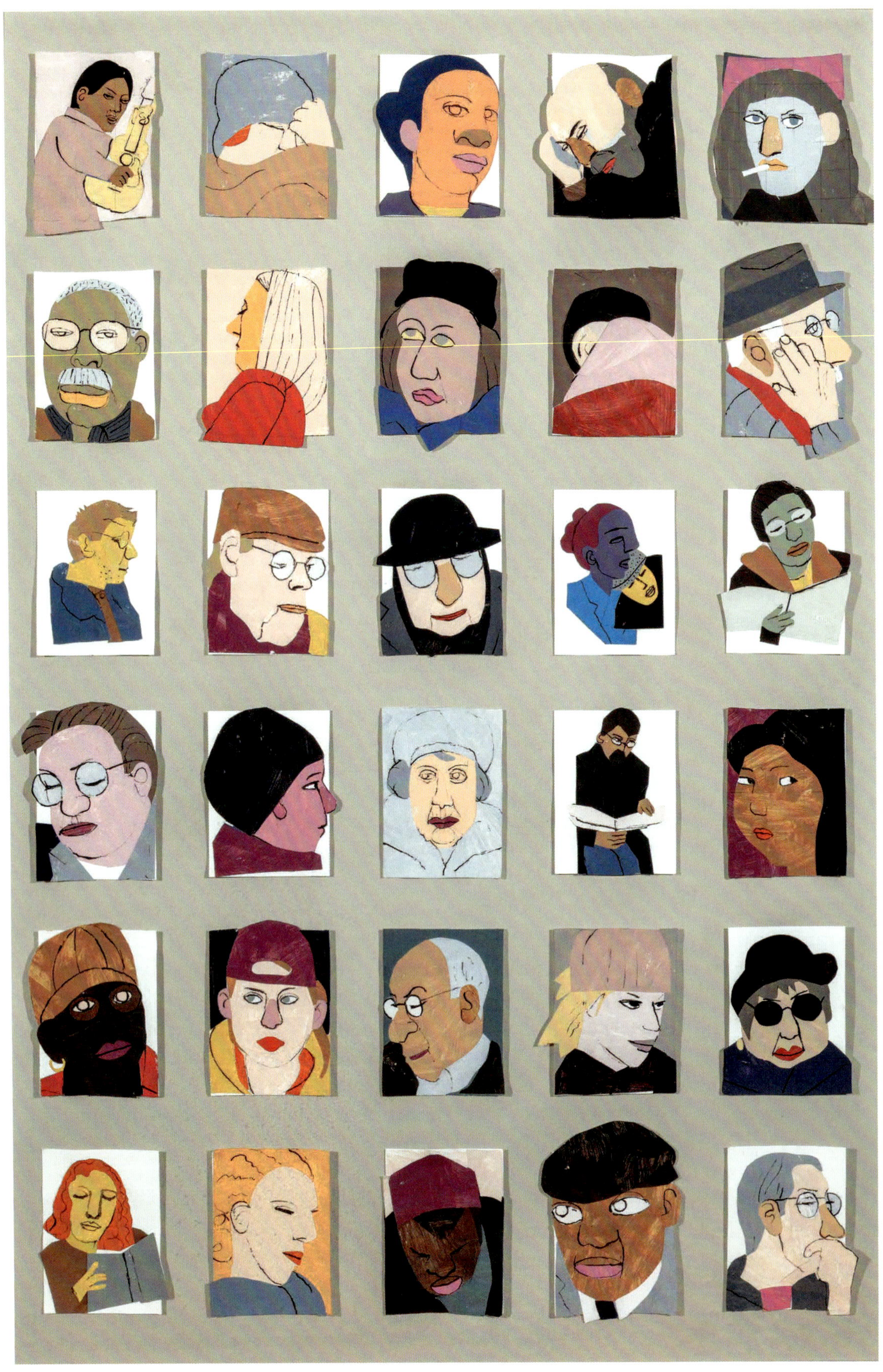

Subway series (composite), 2003

painted and cut paper with ink | 59" × 41" overall | Collection of Bryant and Nancy Hanley | Photography by Kevin Todora

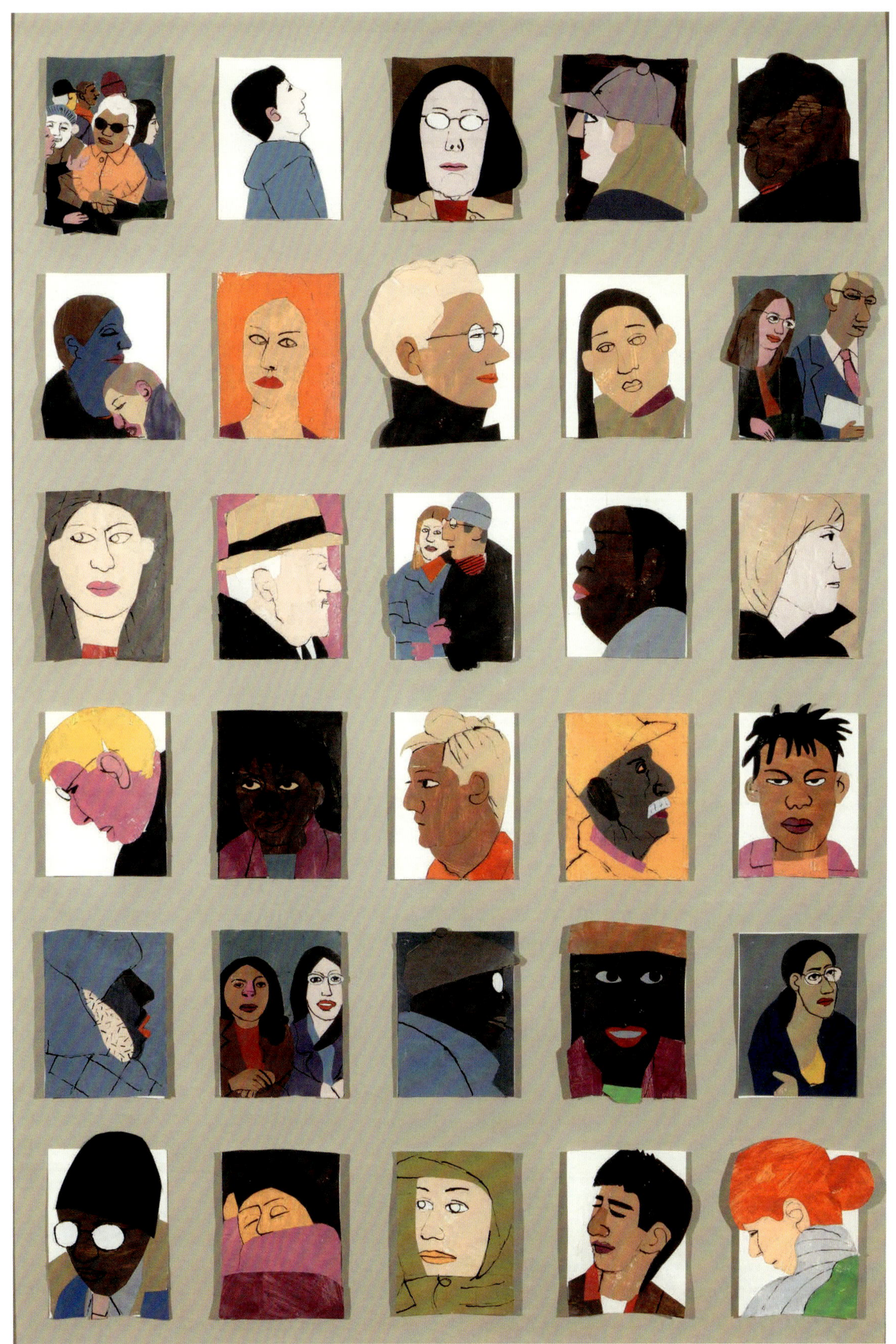

Subway series (composite), 2003

painted and cut paper with ink | 59" × 41" overall | Collection of Bryant and Nancy Hanley |

Photography by Kevin Todora

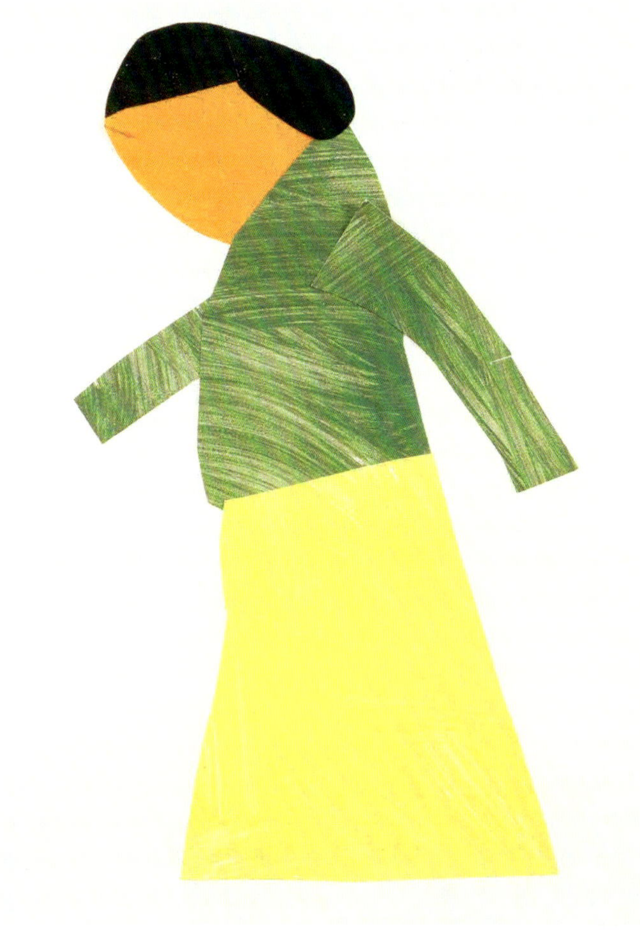

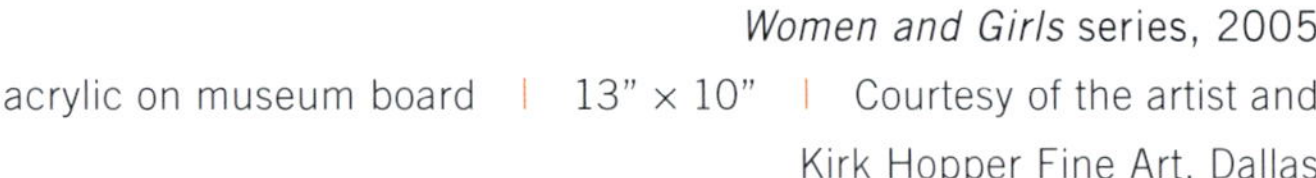

Women and Girls series, 2005
acrylic on museum board | 13" × 10" | Courtesy of the artist and Kirk Hopper Fine Art, Dallas

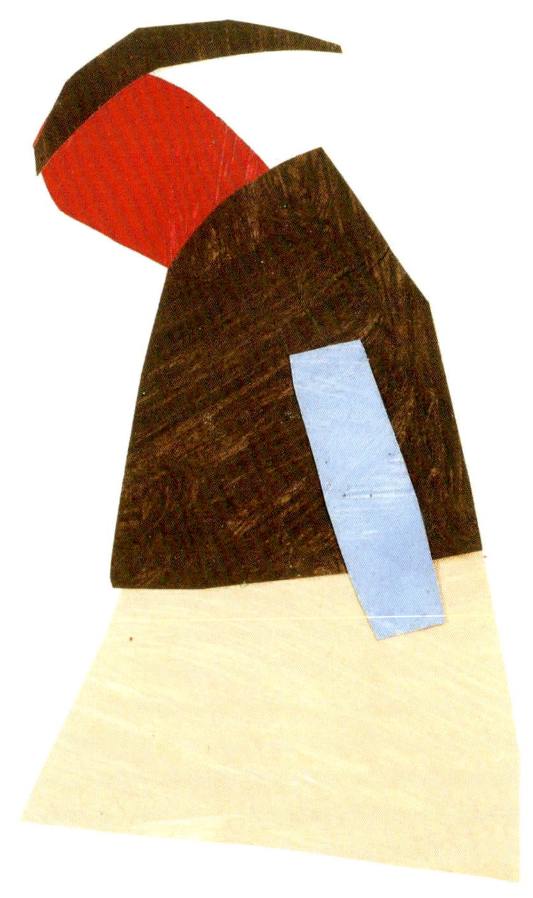

Women and Girls series, 2005
acrylic on museum board | 13" × 10" | Courtesy of the artist and Kirk Hopper Fine Art, Dallas

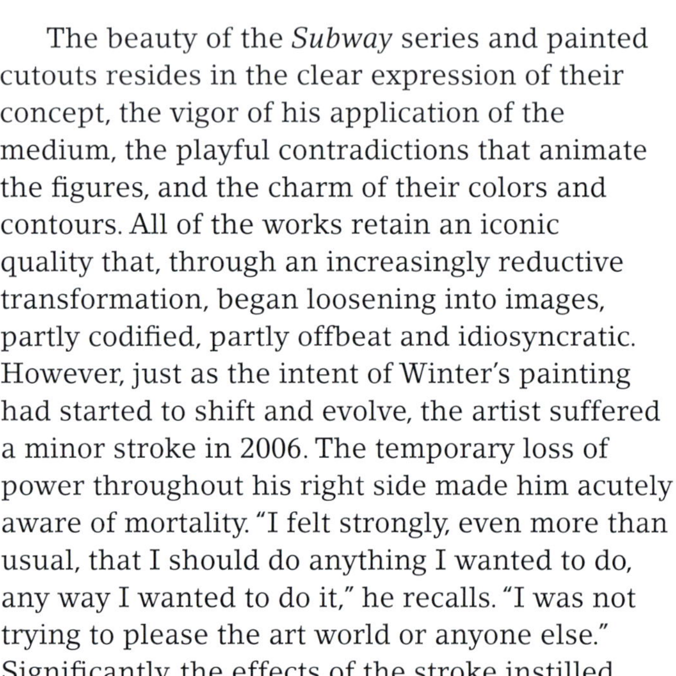

The beauty of the *Subway* series and painted cutouts resides in the clear expression of their concept, the vigor of his application of the medium, the playful contradictions that animate the figures, and the charm of their colors and contours. All of the works retain an iconic quality that, through an increasingly reductive transformation, began loosening into images, partly codified, partly offbeat and idiosyncratic. However, just as the intent of Winter's painting had started to shift and evolve, the artist suffered a minor stroke in 2006. The temporary loss of power throughout his right side made him acutely aware of mortality. "I felt strongly, even more than usual, that I should do anything I wanted to do, any way I wanted to do it," he recalls. "I was not trying to please the art world or anyone else." Significantly, the effects of the stroke instilled a resolve to never again cater to the taste of others. Winter joined a group of painters—Robert Birmelin, Seymour Leichman, and Eileen Mislove, among others—at Regina Granne's studio on Bleeker Street for weekly drawing sessions. Admittedly, Winter sought out the group for social interaction rather than as a student. Whereas the other painters produced academic renderings of the nude models, Winter drew profiles of their faces from all different positions, placing each head within a square space. After a few years of participating in the weekly sessions, however, a chance encounter on the subway one afternoon gave Winter the stimulus he needed to push the small drawings into fully fleshed-out works of art. "Riding back on the C Train after one of our studio sessions, a young African American woman watched me look through the drawings of the afternoon. She suddenly said, 'I really like those. Are you going to fill them in?' Wow! The next day I went to Pearl Art Supplies, bought sheets of 4-ply museum board and a selection of casein paint to mix with acrylic. I started making big flat paintings of heads from the expansive choice of small profile drawings. That kept me going for a few years and eventually led to the two and three dimensional geometric works."[3]

Throughout, Winter coalesces specific features of individual or personal identity with simplified shapes, disks, and lozenges; horizontal lines; and thin rectangles, as well as arabesques and crisp contours that connect to describe a brow, a nose, an ear, a mouth, or an eye. Winter looks and he looks hard. When he sees the model in front of him, rarely does he blink. By flattening everything into jigsaw-like zones of color shapes, he demonstrates an assured grasp of the model's essence. These are visually arresting profiles of intense moral honesty. Winter is up to something more important than mere physiognomic likeness or psychological reportage. We have to approach these images closely to be drawn into their magnetic field and enter into a private dialogue. It is also important to note that Winter aimed to capture the female models in ways that are challenging and not simply objectifying. Perhaps, in *Nicole* (2006), Winter regarded the Trinidadian woman's head as an interesting abstract shape. Her dark skin and white eyes convey a mysterious exoticism. For *Jill* (2006), *Carmen* (2006), and *Paula* (2006), he chooses hues of fiery red, cobalt, green, and sienna, as well as stylized line and distilled forms to convey the curve of an ear, strands of hair, the shape of lips. In each, Winter moves fluidly between aspects of abstraction and the figurative. Vibrant biomorphic forms play off simplified shapes through a carefully calibrated array of formal means. A solid can be simultaneously perceived as a void, or a dark ground may slip into luminous space. Winter seemingly turns each element inside out to prevent it from embracing any single reading.

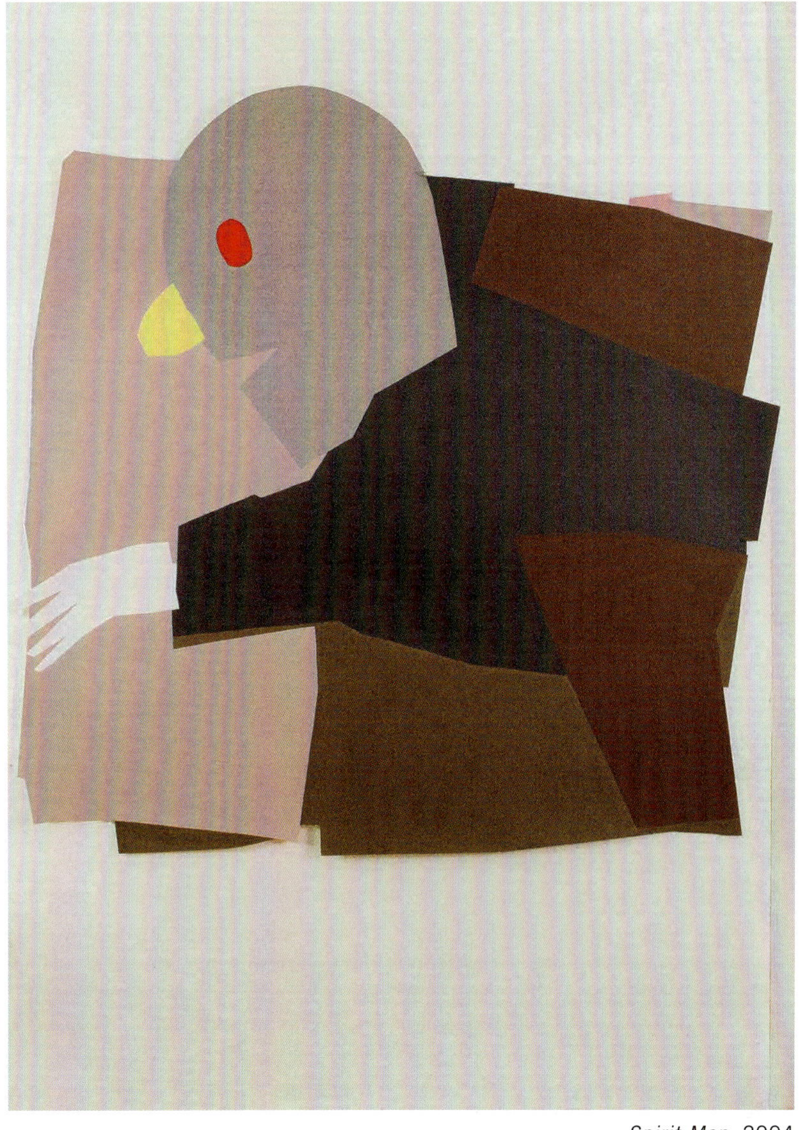

Spirit Man, 2004
acrylic on cutout museum board | 56" × 58" | Courtesy of the artist and Kirk Hopper Fine Art, Dallas | Photography by Joshua Nefsky

Thus, the familiar is transformed into the fantastic, with the boundary line between the two unfixed. All in all, the *Subway* series, spin-off collages, three-dimensional cutouts, and painted model heads present Winter's sensibility in a nutshell, his broad aesthetic range, omnivorous curiosity, playfulness, and intuitive elegance. The works show Winter moving from idea to idea, from realism to abstraction, from minimalism to the decorative. Winter knew he was walking a tightrope. However, the disparate images and materials were also ways of remaining connected to the world. If the range of work sometimes looked back to earlier efforts, it also laid out his future.

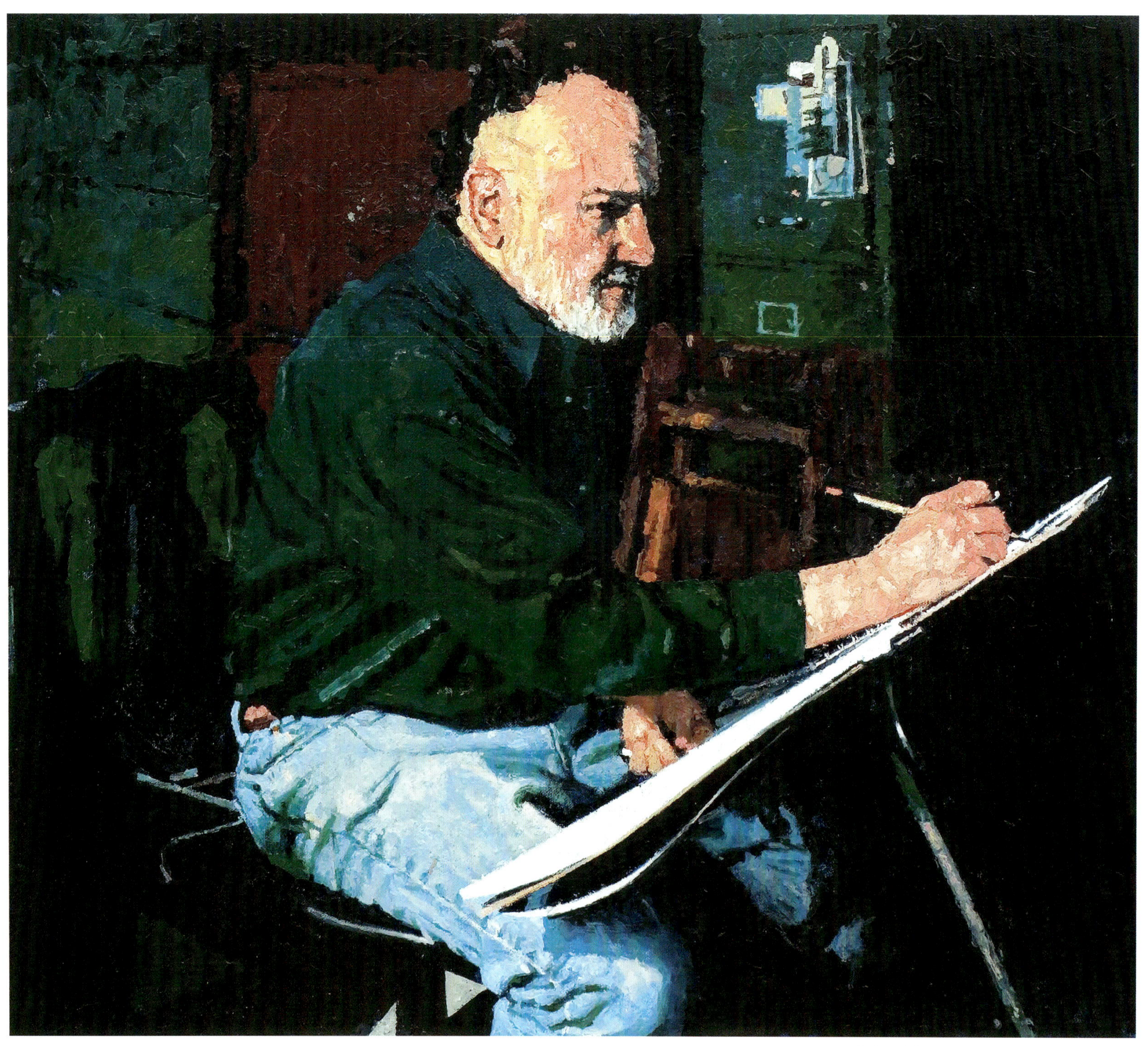

Robert Birmelin Drawing from Life, 2008
oil on linen | 20" × 24" | Collection of Molly E. Moore

Geometry, of course, had always been an important part of Winter's life, from working after high school for the Denison architect Donald L. Mayes, to designing three-dimensional drawings for the Calcasieu Lumber Company as a student at the University of Texas, Austin, to building models of Shaker furniture and drawing up plans for their house and studio in the Texas Hill Country. Thus it was logical that his casein and acrylic paintings of the model heads and profiles would evolve into nonobjective two- and three-dimensional works. For Winter, the geometric collages and small three-dimensional studies served as a noncritical, reductive approach and vital mode of exploration. Having been "locked into" two-dimensional space for several years, he used the geometric push and pull of color to help him work his way back to illusions of deep space. As it happens, Winter was in Dallas to receive the prestigious 2007 Contemporary Legends Award when filmmaker Quin Mathews introduced him to Dorothy and Bill Masterson, directors of the Museum of Geometric and MADI Art, who immediately offered Winter an exhibition. Around this same time, Winter became reacquainted in New York City with veteran painter and printmaker Will Barnet, whom he had met decades earlier as a graduate student at the University of Iowa. In his nineties, living and working at the National Arts Club, Barnet had just completed illustrations to accompany a book of Emily Dickinson's poetry.[4] He and Winter struck up a conversation at the book signing and began a close friendship that lasted until Barnet's death at 101 in 2012. Barnet was known for classically composed visions of beautiful women and children, ranging from a simplified form of realism to a poetic symbolism. He was also associated with the group known as the Indian Space painters, who created geometrically complex paintings using forms that melded Cubist abstraction with Native American tribal motifs, most often taken from Northwest Coast examples, which utilized linear design, bold shapes, and flat patterns of bright, unmodulated colors in dynamic compositions.[5] As a result of their frequent discussions, Winter grasped Barnet's instinctive understanding of the picture plane and immersion in the very real emotions and language of Indian art. Just as Barnet's use of hard-edge, totemic forms and intersecting geometrics evoked complex spatial ambiguities, Winter's nonobjectives aimed to reduce forms to their most essential structures while maintaining an ideographic unity and immediacy of expression.

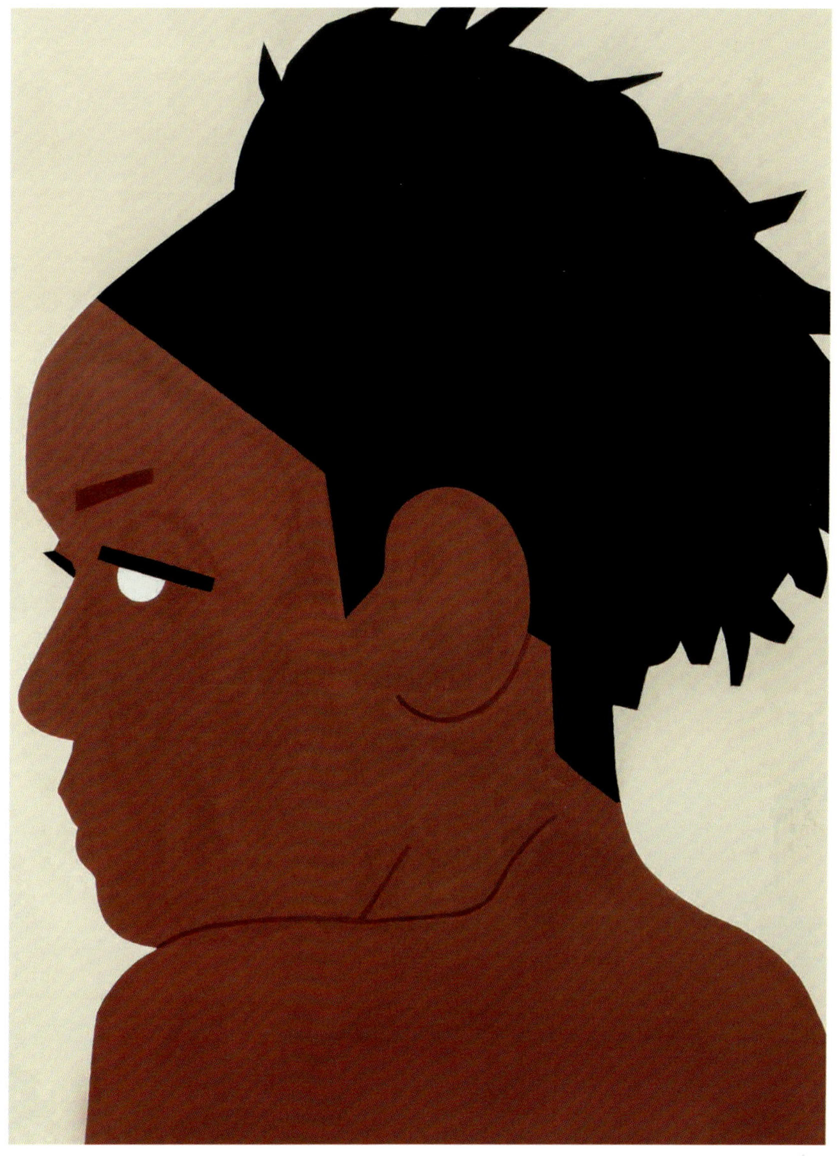

Nicole, 2007
casein and acrylic on museum board | 40" × 30" | Collection of Melissa and David Guion | Photography by Joshua Nefsky

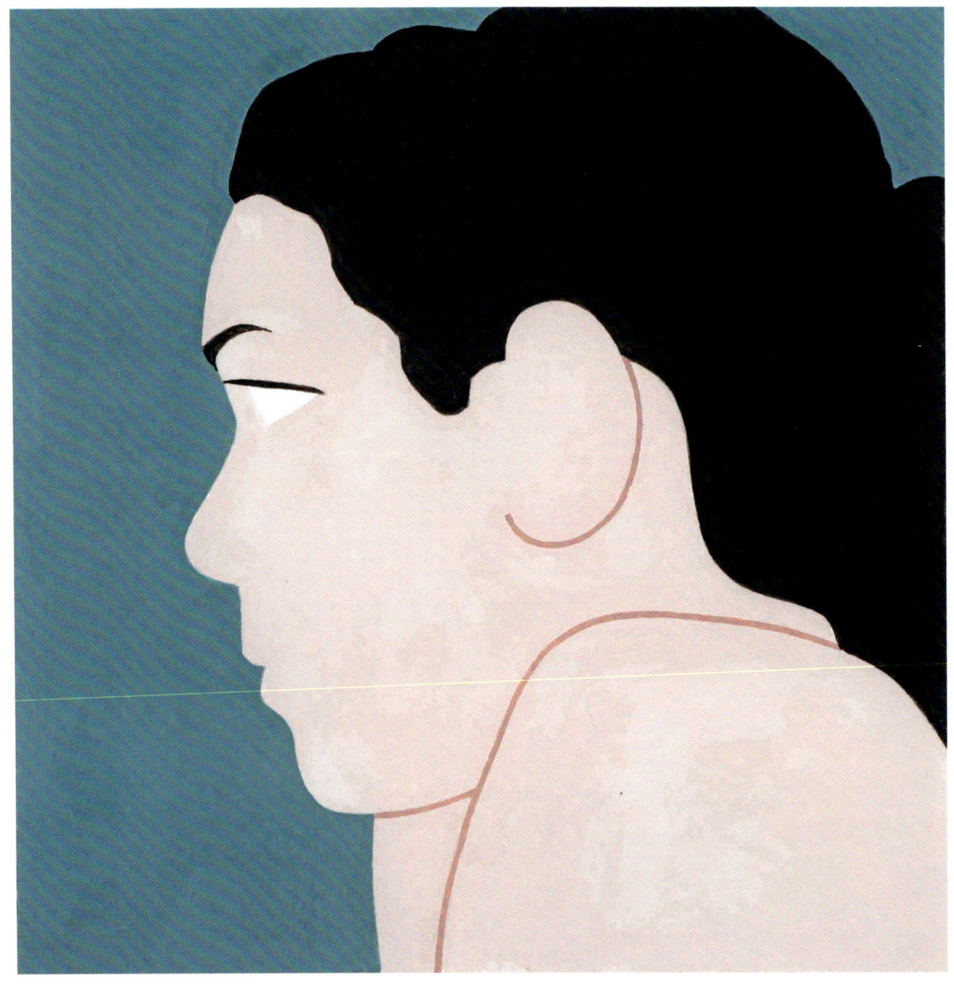

Jill, 2006
casein and acrylic on museum board | 16" × 16" | Collection of Judythe Sieck | Photography by James Hart

All of these interests dovetailed when the Winters began visiting Jeanette's book designer, Judythe Sieck, at her home in Santa Fe. Since Jeanette had been experiencing health problems from the summer humidity of New York City, they decided in 2008 to purchase a casita and live in Santa Fe for six months out of the year, from late spring through early fall. Winter did most of the geometric work for the MADI exhibition on the front porch. Jeanette worked on her books at the drawing table in the front room. Immediately, they became absorbed in the history and culture of the Southwest region. Through Mark Bahti, longtime owner of Bahti Indian Arts with his wife, Navajo artist Emmi Whitehorse, they learned about Hopi katsinas and Zuni fetishes. They visited the pueblos, studied pottery designs, and met families of prominent wood carvers. For Winter, the katsinas represented links between the daily human world and the spiritual. Their flat bodies, three-dimensional faces, fully carved heads, rectangular or crescent-shaped mouths, and half-moon eyes also gave shape to Winter's wild roamings of thought. In the katsinas, certain colors have significant directional meanings. In Winter's geometric works, an ongoing drama of force and counterforce, movement and stasis, expansion and contraction unfolds through formal variations of size, shape, weight, touch, and color. The distinct color areas create a pulsating, charged field in which figure-ground relationships are constantly shifting. The square, the rectangle, the lozenge, the compressed narrow verticals—each is a unique configuration providing myriad possibilities for an equal diversity of color, line, and plane contained therein. As a result, Winter's compositions slip between appearing as stacked and overlapping forms, a tight puzzle of abutting shapes, as well as sharp angles, protrusions, and hollows suspended between the illusion of convex relief and concave depth.

After the 2008 exhibition at the Museum of Geometric and MADI Art in Dallas, however, Winter began easing back into painting the visibly intelligible world. In *Jeanette Resting Her Eyes* (2008), the first painting based realistically in Santa Fe, Winter depicts an oversize silhouette of his wife with her head propped against the bedpost. A carved angel perches above Jeanette's short, wiry strands of hair, perhaps as a kind of guardian angel watching over her. The background is a fiery explosion of yellow and orange loosely rendered brushstrokes that transport the figures into a state of rapture. Winter fluctuated between a dichotomy of subjective and objective realms. "I think the work I did in New Mexico was based

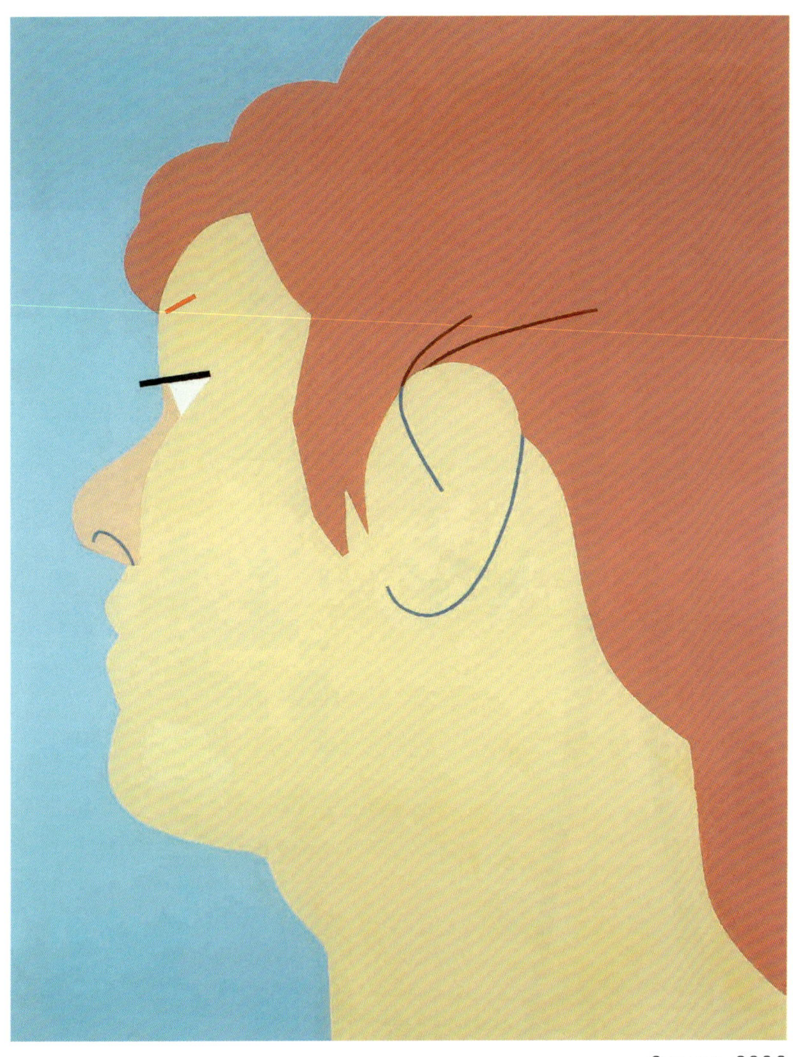

Carmen, 2006

casein and acrylic on museum board | 36" × 28" | Courtesy of the artist and Kirk Hopper Fine Art, Dallas

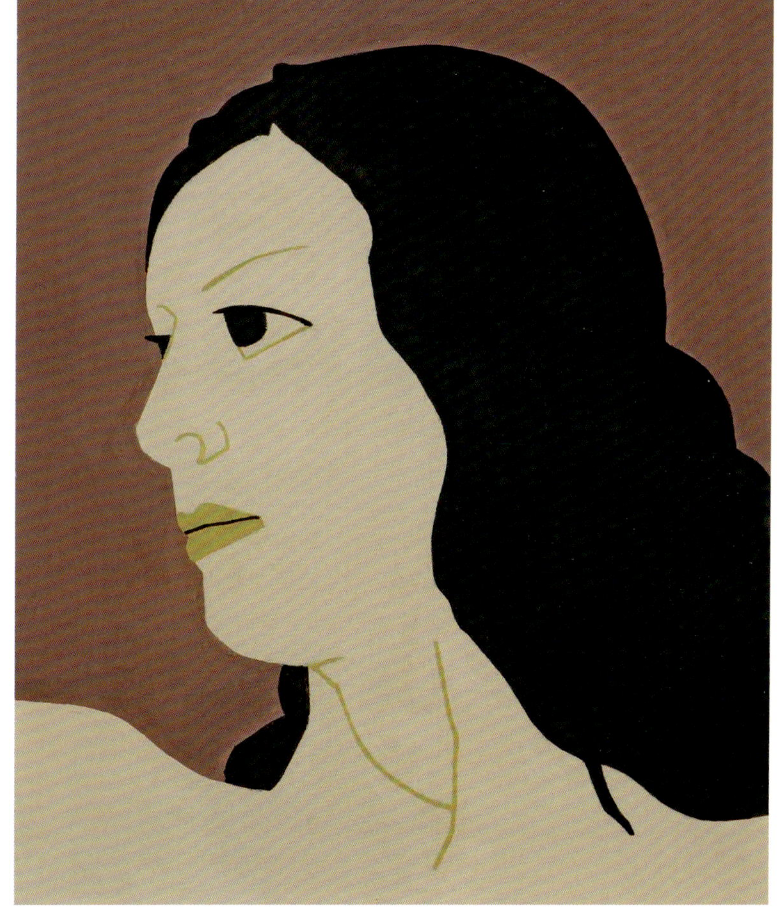

Paula, 2009

casein and acrylic on museum board | 15" × 15" | Courtesy of the artist

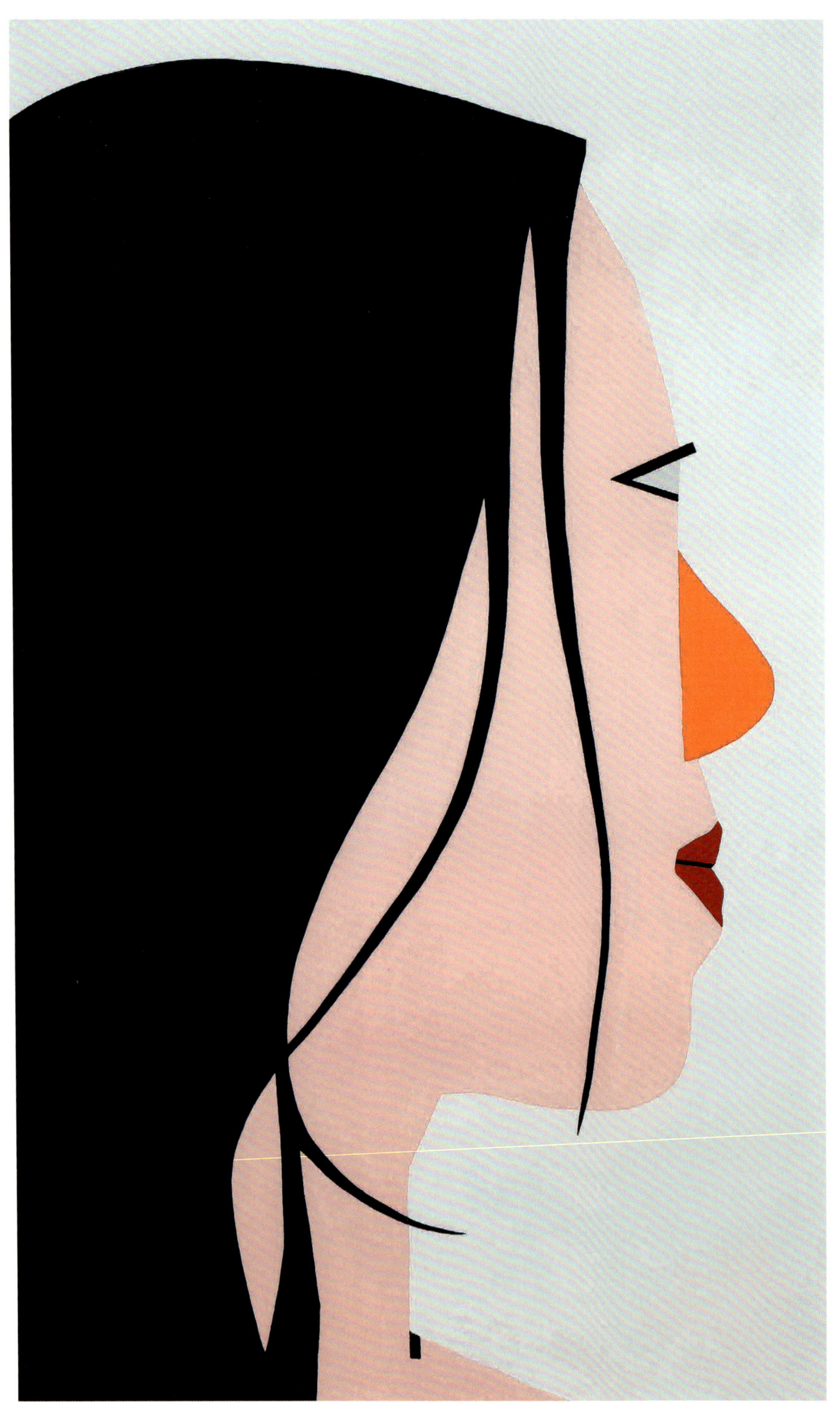

Wendy, 2006

casein and acrylic on museum board | 52" × 32" | Courtesy of the artist and Kirk Hopper Fine Art, Dallas

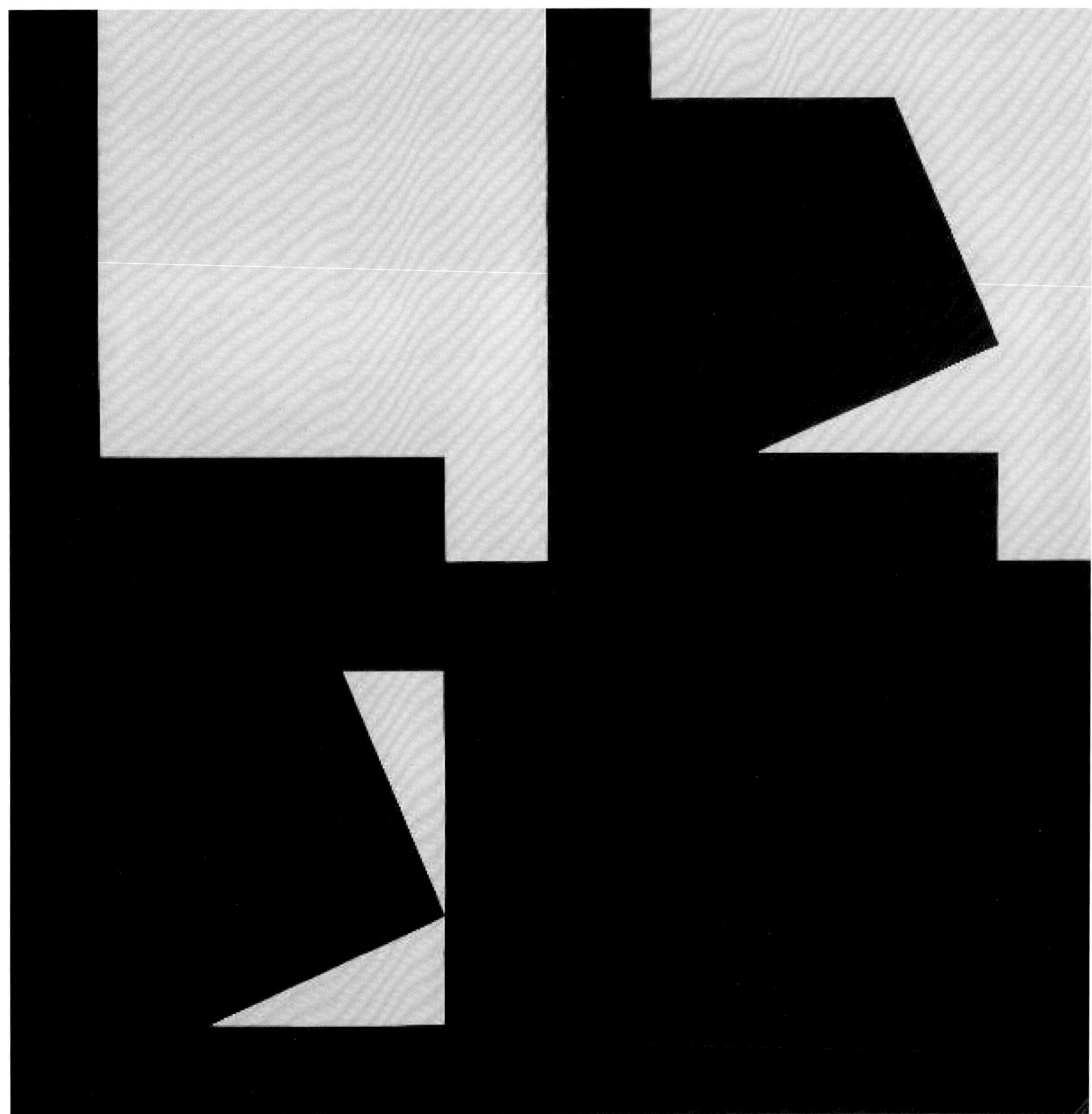

Homage to Malevich, 2008
acrylic on museum board | 26" × 18" | Collection of the Museum of Geometric and MADI Art, Dallas

on my own explorations," Winter explains. "Our daughter-in-law, Sally Denmead, once said that Santa Fe is a spiritual locus. That stuck and I started looking at and reading about that side of New Mexico—especially the Catholics and the Pueblo Indians. Whatever I'm doing, I must believe in it. Living here is about finding a spiritual world that I hadn't known firsthand before. My sense is there are things beyond human understanding. Each of us is a part of nature. No matter what happens to our bodies, our physicality when we die, something of that physicality will always be on some level a part of life. I guess that's no different from beliefs of Catholicism, but I felt it more deeply in Santa Fe."

Whenever we find individuals who have sought enlightenment, we expect them to explain the world to us, to reveal some of its mysteries. Search

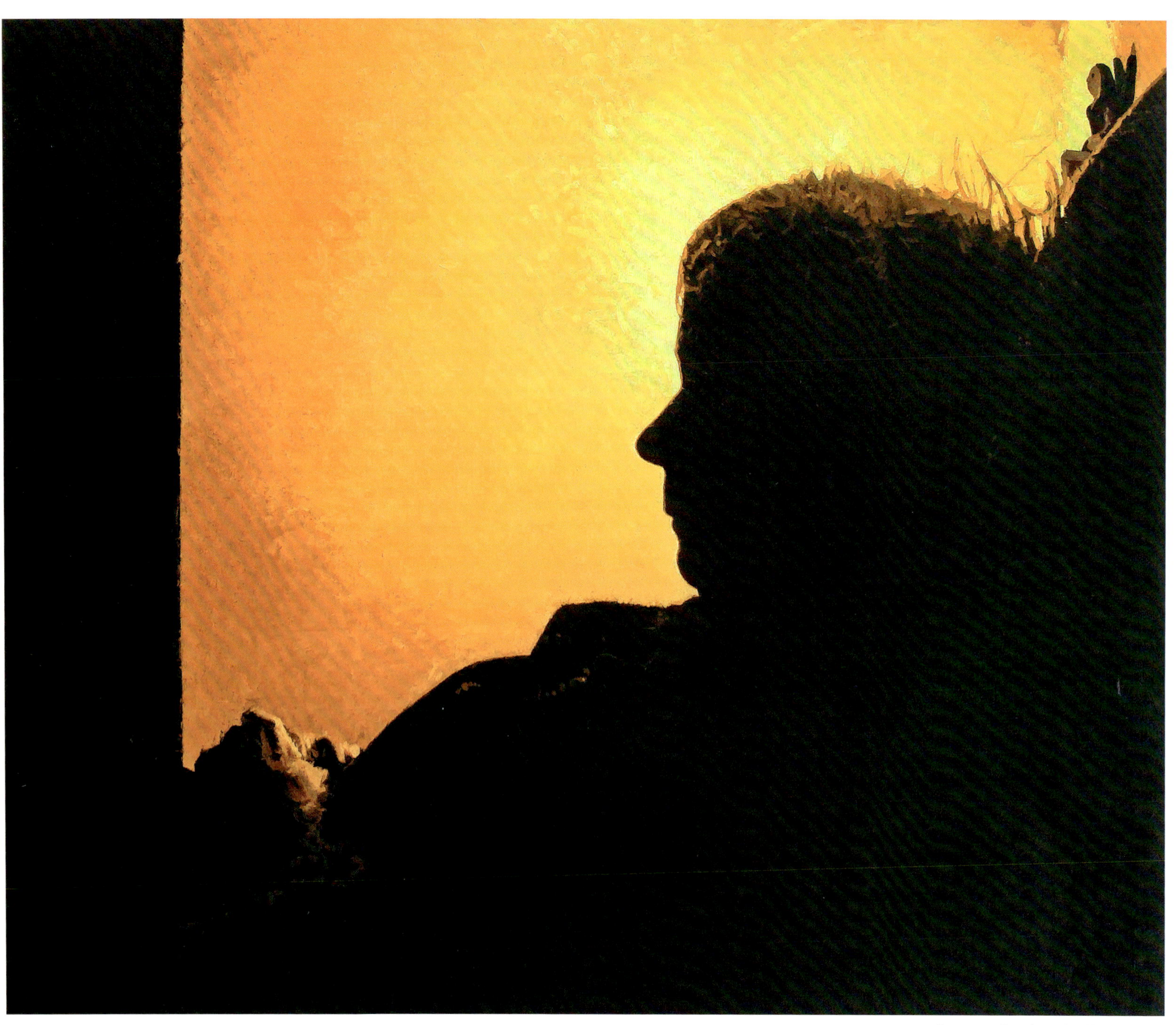

Jeanette Resting Her Eyes, 2008

oil on linen | 60" × 72" | Courtesy of the artist and Kirk Hopper Fine Art, Dallas

and journey are important metaphors because they are characteristic of both the creation of art and the practices of spiritual seekers. Winter's paintings produced in New Mexico are settings for far-flung personal stories that illuminate the beauty, wonder, and chaos inherent in the elements. He captures the vast distance that is sky, the blue that Rebecca Solnit, in *A Field Guide to Getting Lost*, describes as "the light that gets lost": "The world is blue at its edges and in its depths. This blue is the light that got lost. Light at the blue end of the spectrum does not travel the whole distance from the sun to us. . . . This light that does not touch us, does not travel the whole distance, the light that gets lost, gives us the beauty of the world, so much of which is in the color blue."[6] Similarly, the light in Winter's paintings comes to us from afar. It travels across great distance, so the high skies and expanse of space appear to us as blue, too. "The thing I love the best about Santa Fe is the air," Winter says. "It was so clean. At night we'd open our windows and it would get into the fifties. We'd have this dry, clean, cool air coming over us." Accordingly, Winter often places us in the lapis lazuli of the heavens. He captures the fleeting moment by locking in a sense of place, but also by making it shift and move before our eyes, like a memory that quickly fades. His way of dissolving narrative into atmosphere, of locating drama in the rich symbolism of the New Mexico landscape, is driven by a succession of moods, an emotional logic alternately reflected and obscured by the spiritual surroundings.

From his new studio near Santa Fe's plaza, Winter produced paintings of surreal visions that sought existential meaning in the high plains and vast sky. Chains of associations appear and disappear like swift-moving clouds: the endless tension between presence and absence, staying and leaving, existence and the void. The paintings are a reminder of how magical his images can be, how decades of seeing had given him a startling lucidity of the kind that might be experienced by someone whose tangled dreams give way to a pure vision of wakefulness. For the most part, they concern themselves with big questions about the passage of time, life, death, things left undone, things left behind. For Winter, the complex spiritual history of Santa Fe and the nearby Pueblos was a powerful force to reconcile in paint. It is a deeply disorienting notion. How do we know who we are, how we fit into the world, if we become so estranged from ourselves and the things around us? Winter's Santa Fe paintings make a passionate case for recalling and setting down the enchantment of the natural world at a time when it is rapidly disappearing.

Significantly, Winter contemplates the ephemeral and the eternal, mortality and memory, thresholds all of us will cross. In *The Long Walk (Pentimento)* (2010), Jeanette is a solitary traveler in the desert setting of a deep-blue sky and daytime full moon. At far right, a white horse—a metaphorical spirit of death—watches as she walks away.

In *Nambé* (2010), Winter portrays Jeanette carrying a shopping bag and striding with her back to us through massive clouds in the heavens. An El Niño figure, lower left, seemingly floats in the dark ether. In *Hunter's Moon* (2010), Winter positions Jeanette with her back to us again, this time walking on a dark wooded path toward a car's headlights in the distance. The mood is foreboding, with monsters' faces camouflaged in the rocks, grasses, and foliage. The painting is like a mysterious dream in which we cannot understand what is happening or why. The full moon is a dominant image in most of these paintings—a powerful cosmic symbol of regeneration, mutability, intuition, and emotion. "I always see a full moon as a flat, perfect shape," Winter explains. "Its reflected light is enough to give a romantic glow to our night. It's very much a part of the night landscape in New Mexico because the sky is so open. Its perfect shape is our most graphic sign that we live in a greater world of unknown and unknowable space. Unlike the sun, we can look at the moon as long as we want to. In the paintings, I use it as a symbol of being alone and separate, a feeling of loneliness inside." During this same time, Jeanette suffered major health problems that required two near-tragic procedures in an Albuquerque hospital. According to Winter, the paintings of Jeanette alone in the landscape or with her back to the viewer grew from facing death in a place with inferior medical care and far from their sons. "It was fear and relief, translated into paint," Winter recalls. "An image of a person walking away from the viewer

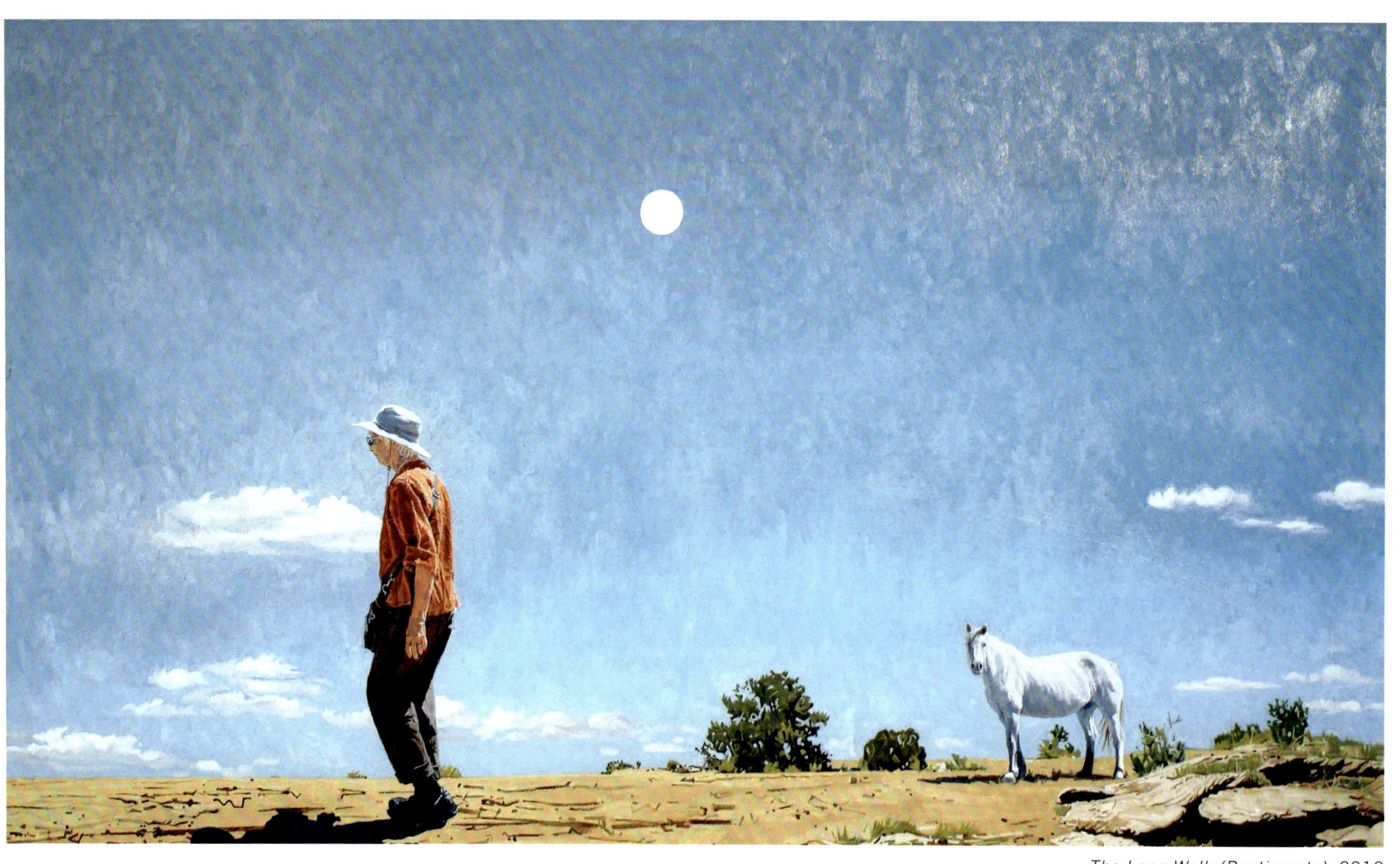

The Long Walk (Pentimento), 2010
oil on linen | 42" × 72" | Courtesy of the artist and Kirk Hopper Fine Art, Dallas | Photography by Joshua Nefsky

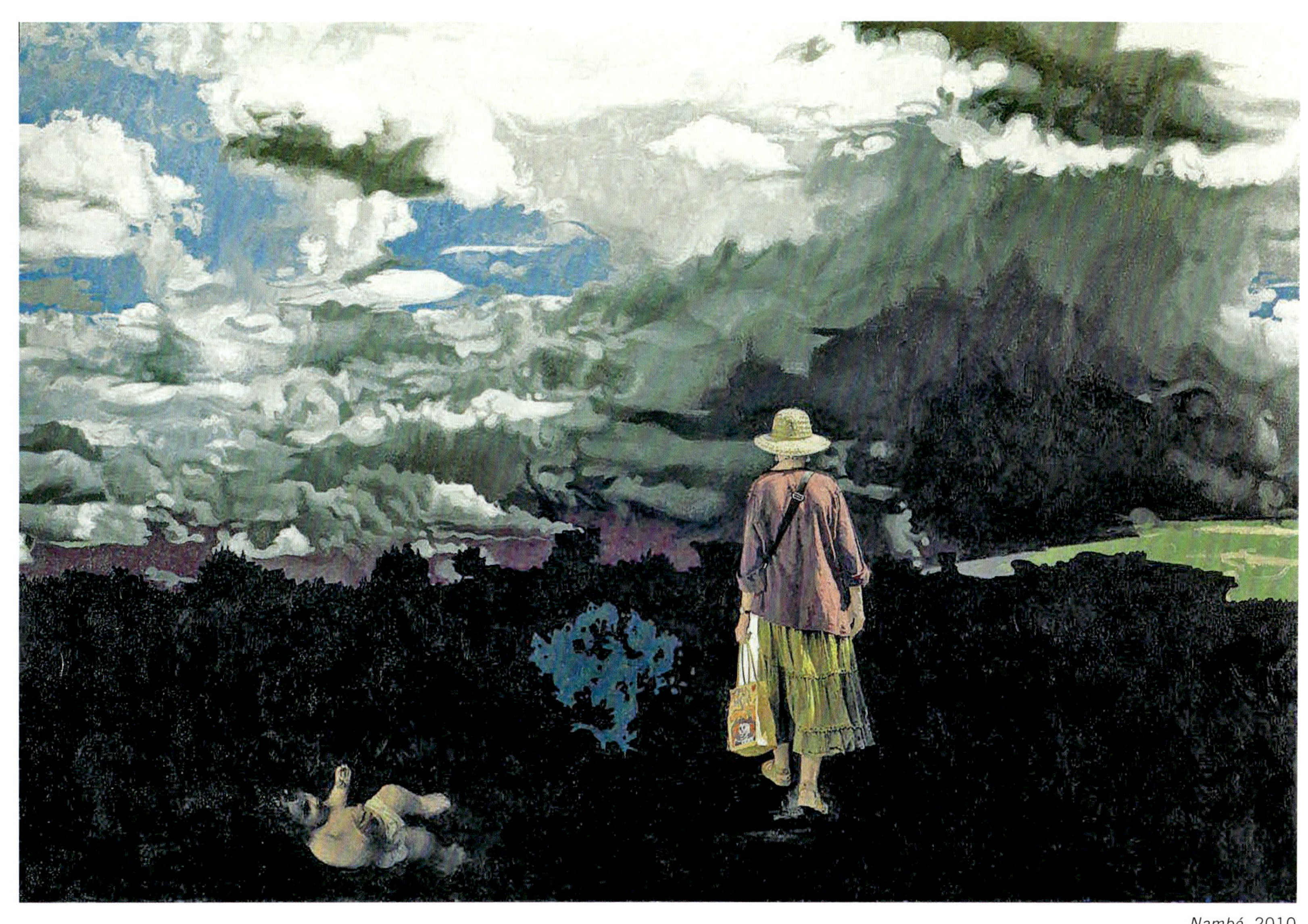

Nambé, 2010

oil on linen | 48″ × 72″ | Courtesy of the artist

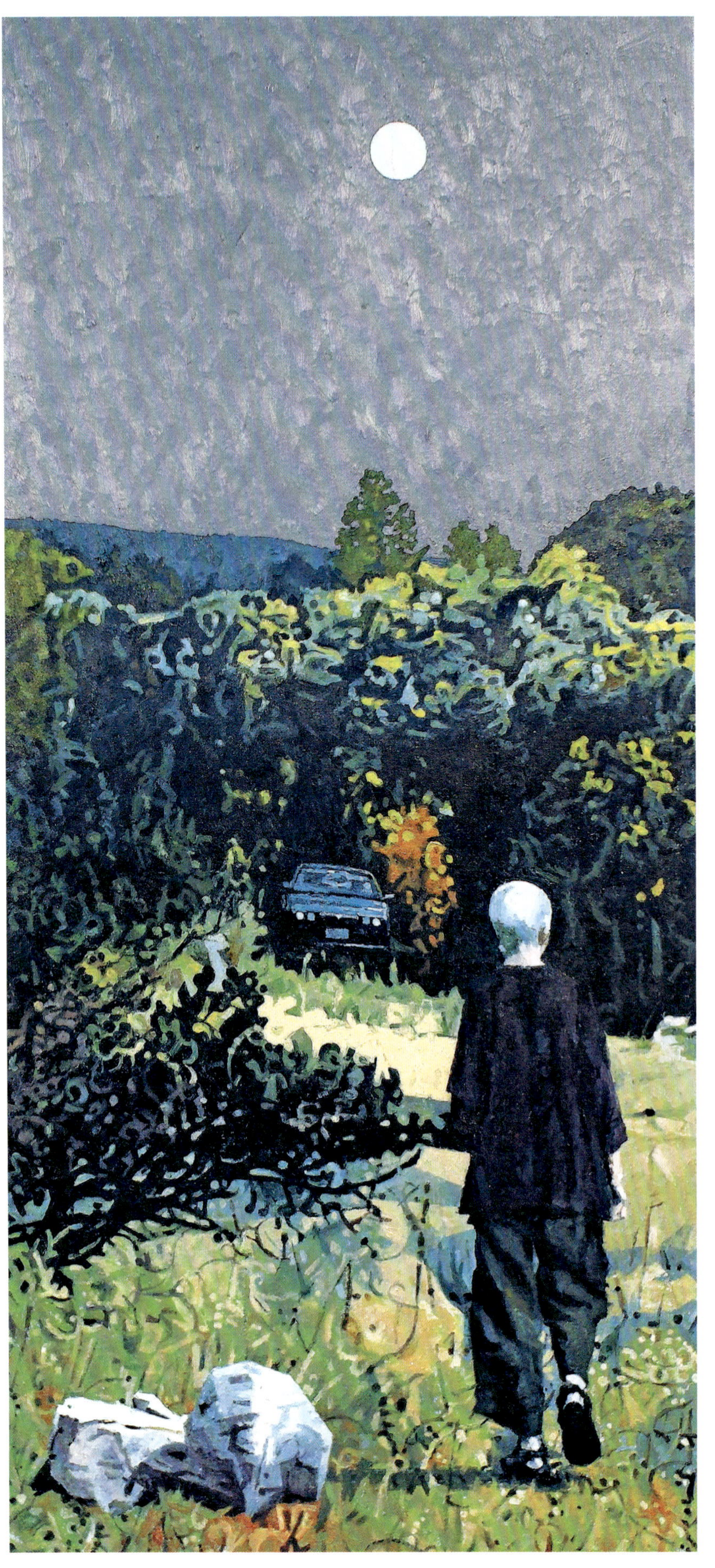

Hunter's Moon, 2010
oil on linen | 56" × 24" |
Courtesy of the artist and
Kirk Hopper Fine Art, Dallas |
Photography by G. Valderas

has an emotional impact very much unlike the image of a person confronting the viewer. Someone walking away can't be known. A viewer's response is more metaphysical than social. Was Jeanette walking through the phases of life? Was I coming to grips that Jeanette might walk away first?"

All of the paintings convey Winter's longing for a spiritual explanation of forces larger than this mortal coil. Indeed, sincere expressions of faith are rare to nonexistent in contemporary art. In Santa Fe, however, Winter experienced an "interior striving" that led him to seek the ineluctable enigma of existence, a transcendent moral order both everywhere present and agonizingly out of reach. In that visionary mode, the myths and religious stories Winter gleaned from the Pueblos and Catholicism could tap into a seemingly magical dimension from which emanates a sense of the mysterious and the sacred. He was after a larger, timeless dimension that honored, from the deepest levels of consciousness, a connection with archetypal forces and powers beyond the local self. With this in mind, Winter would often go to the Cathedral Basilica of Saint Francis of Assisi, the grand Roman Catholic edifice that towers over Santa Fe's historic district. The church reflects a blend of old and new worlds, including adobe walls that jut out from the stone support of the nave, old wooden ceiling beams (*vigas*), huge altar screens (*reredos*), and the traditional *santero* artwork of New Mexico. During one visit, Winter browsed a display of novena cards and became mesmerized by the image of Our Lady of Fatima based on the famed Marian apparition in Portugal. Winter later used the figure as the subject for the painting *Christmas Day* (2009), which places the Blessed Virgin Mary in the snowy setting of the church cemetery. Behind her is an old mausoleum with sloped roofline; to her left is a crackling fire, as well as the carcass and tail of a dead animal. Significantly, the juxtaposition of fire and tombstones, added from a view of the cemetery across the arroyo from their casita, serves as a metaphor for human mortality and the spiritual life. A large blue moon, which hovers in a cloudy turquoise-pink sky between the silhouetted trees and stone crypt, echoes the shape of the Virgin's halo. Winter portrays her with grace and sensitivity, attention to detail, and an intimation of psychological presence. He uses the gesture of her hands clasped together in prayer to convey devotion. He considers the tactile qualities of her white robes and blue sash, as well as the string of rosary beads hanging from her arm. The Virgin's pale skin contrasts with the fiery orange leaves and shadowy mausoleum, creating a dramatic visual effect that gives her a majestic presence. Winter comments, "Months after finishing the painting, I found out that the last time Our Lady of Fatima appeared—this time to children and adults—the clouds broke, the sun turned opaque and blue, then cast a blue light over the landscape before turning another color and dancing around the sky. This sort of coincidence has happened to me often, and I'm always a little frightened when it does. It makes me know that there is a world out there way beyond our perceptions or logic, and now and then, we get a glimpse of it."

At the same time that Winter was exploring profound questions of faith and meaning, he also worked on projects that had been initiated during the winter months in New York City. Aiming to extol the strength of women, he chose the life-size bronze equestrian sculpture of fifteenth-century French patriot and martyr Joan of Arc on the Upper West Side as his subject. Dedicated in 1915 to commemorate the Maid of Orleans's five hundredth birthday, the sculpture by Anna Hyatt Huntington is the first statue in New York City to honor a nonfictional woman. For Winter, the story of a teenage girl in medieval France who experienced divine visions, led an army to defeat an occupying power, and was burned at the stake for witchcraft and heresy held contemporary relevance. With abiding faith, unflappable courage, and self-belief, even the most unlikely individual can change the course of history and make the impossible possible. Like the sculpture itself, Winter's painting emphasizes the spiritual rather than the warlike point of view. Wearing armor, Joan stands in the saddle while firmly in control of her powerful horse. She raises her magical sword to the heavens, as if praying to the Lord for guidance. Winter's painting is both heroic and infused with naturalistic detail. Up close, however, the leafy foliage and anatomical parts are filled with Winter's "secondary language"

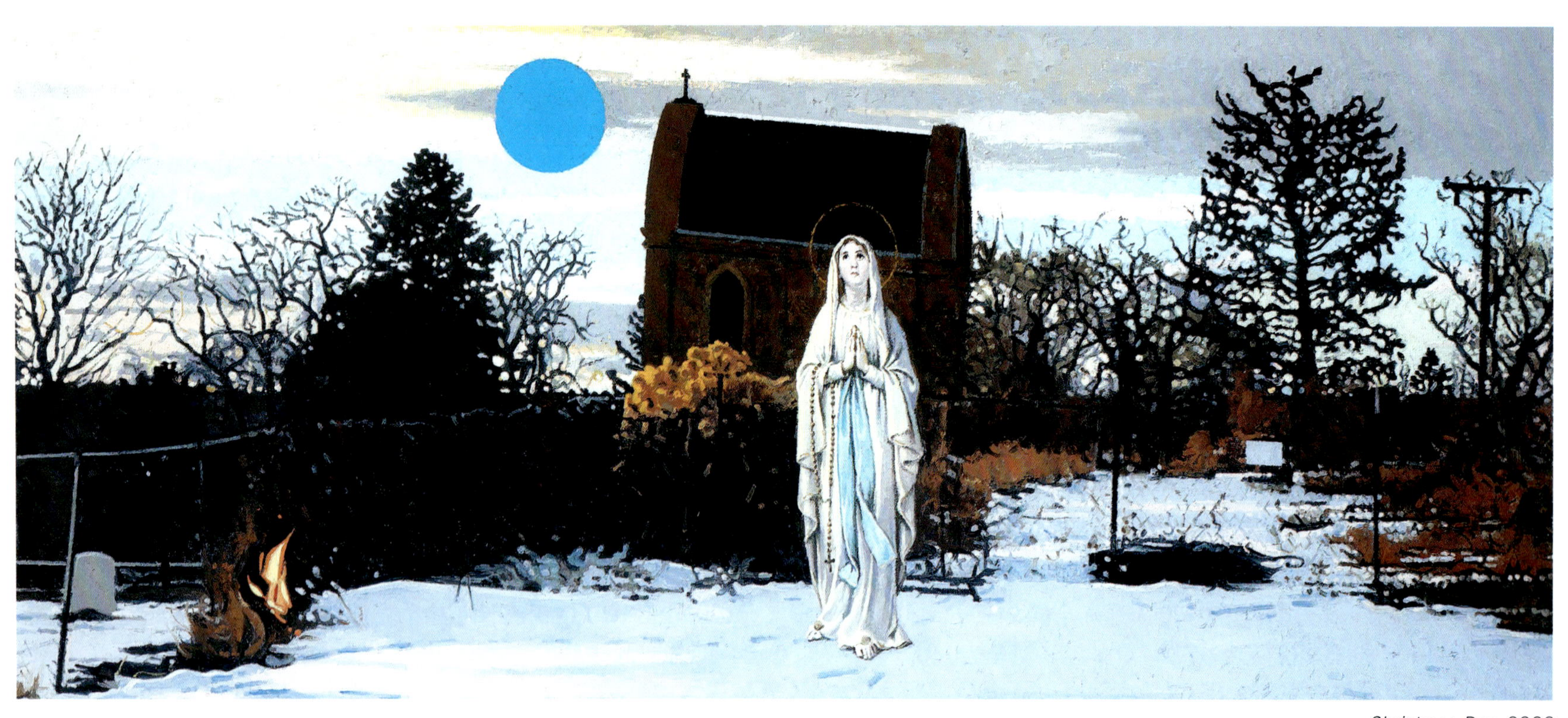

Christmas Day, 2009

oil on linen | 20" × 48" | Albritton Family Collection, Dallas | Photography by James Hart

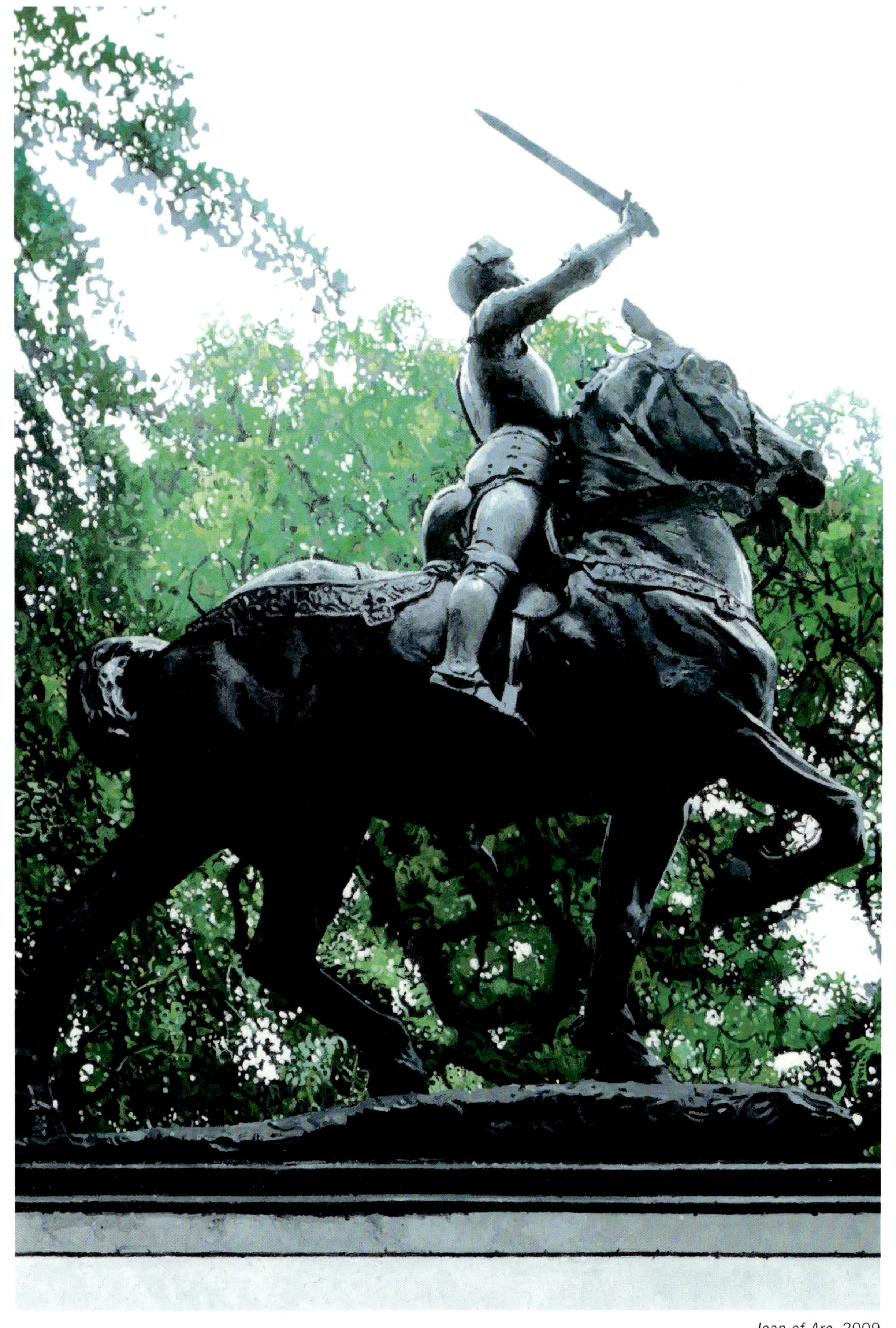

Joan of Arc, 2009

oil on linen | 54" × 36" | Collection of Molly E. Moore | Photography by Kevin Todora

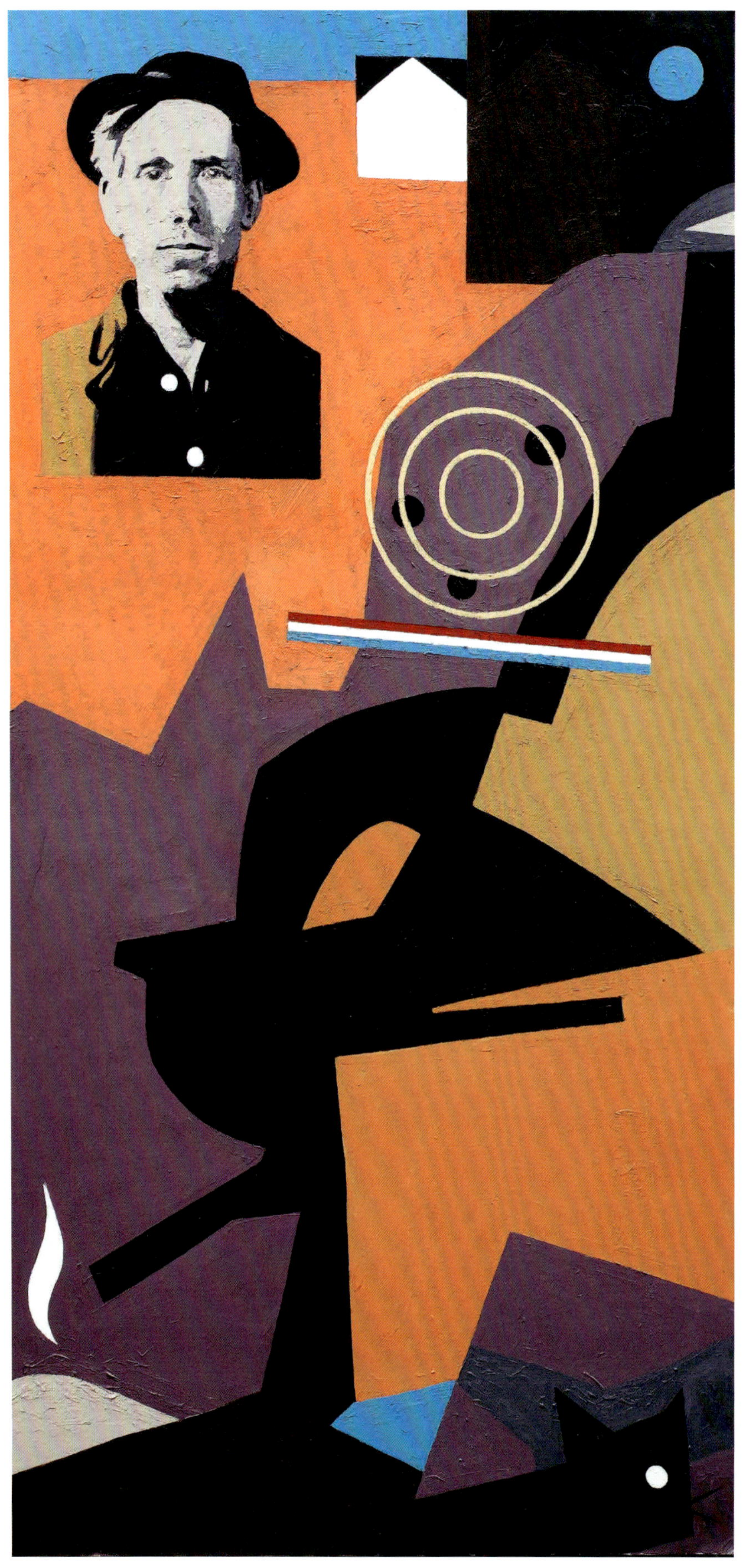

I Dreamed I Saw Joe Hill Last Night, 2011

acrylic on museum board | 40" × 20" | Collection of Molly E. Moore of loose, squiggly strokes that congeal as figures, animals, faces, insects, and objects. Even the horse's tail is composed of a comic profile and winged creature. All of these elements contrast with the weight and solidity of the rider, as well as the geometric base. "During the time of painting Joan, I had become an evolved man," Winter says. "It bothered me that New York had so many statues of men and only two women—Joan of Arc and Eleanor Roosevelt. I read Mark Twain's novel *The Personal Recollections of Joan of Arc*, George Bernard Shaw's political play *Saint Joan*, and Willa Cather's *Death Comes for the Archbishop*. I loved Leonard Cohen's song about Joan. I listened daily to music of the Middle Ages and Renaissance. I even visited Christ in the Desert Monastery outside Santa Fe and spoke with a monk about her sainthood." To be sure, in Winter's *Joan of Arc*, the figure looks monumental, impregnable—a young woman who heard voices in her head and followed the power of conscience to resist oppression.

Significantly, the painting had led him to think more deeply about martyrs. As it happens, Winter saw a photograph in the *New York Times* of Joe Hill, the Swedish American labor activist who was wrongfully executed in 1915.[7] The photograph brought back memories of his father's own sacrifice to labor, inspiring Winter to paint a story about Hill interpreted as a spontaneous arrangement of symbols and structure. An icon of working-class resistance, Hill was also a martyr whose execution still resonates through history. As the most prominent songwriter of the Industrial Workers of the World (IWW), Hill roused laborers to stand in solidarity against industrial and political abuses. He was convicted of murder in Utah and sentenced to death by firing squad. Over the decades, however, many believed he was innocent, condemned for his association with the IWW. In death, Hill was immortalized in the 1938 ballad "I Dreamed I Saw Joe Hill Last Night," versions of which were later recorded by Pete Seeger, Woody Guthrie, and Joan Baez.

As a teenager, Winter knew of Hill's history and had memorized the words to the song. "My father, friend Sonny Wilkinson, and I walked down the Katy tracks in Denison and my father pointed out a working ant hill. I remember him saying, 'Look how the ants are working together for the good of the community. Why can't people do that?' It impressed me that an adult was that selfless after a life of hard labor. He belonged to the IWW, which my mother often reminded us stood for 'I Won't Work.' Of course, my dad argued for the strength of workers uniting. The romance of the labor movement. The very touching martyrdom of Joe Hill. A government executing an innocent man is the essence of inhumanity. I wanted to show that Joe Hill rose from his ashes and was still alive."

Using acrylics on museum board, Winter releases free-flowing, rhythmic swings of realistic images and abstract forms. He renders the haunting portrait of Joe Hill, who hovers on an orange field in the upper left corner. He depicts the target that was pinned to Hill's chest with three gold circles and three bullet holes at far right. Three horizontal bars—red, white, and blue—slice through the center of the composition. Below, black smoke in the form of arabesques and interlocking geometric shapes arises from Hill's ashes. A black cat, symbol of the IWW, but with a white circle for an eye, bears witness to the scene. Above the entirety, Winter paints a blue moon—a nod to the phrase "once in a blue moon" and acknowledgment of the rare phenomenon involving the appearance of an additional full moon in a given period. For Winter, it represented a time in American history when the call for industrial unionism struck a deep chord among disenfranchised workers. In *I Dreamed I Saw Joe Hill Last Night* (2011), Winter evokes issues regarding legal injustice and the limited power of mortality to silence the past. More important, his painting underscores the use of song as organizing tool and weapon in the current times of class hostilities and capitalism on the run.

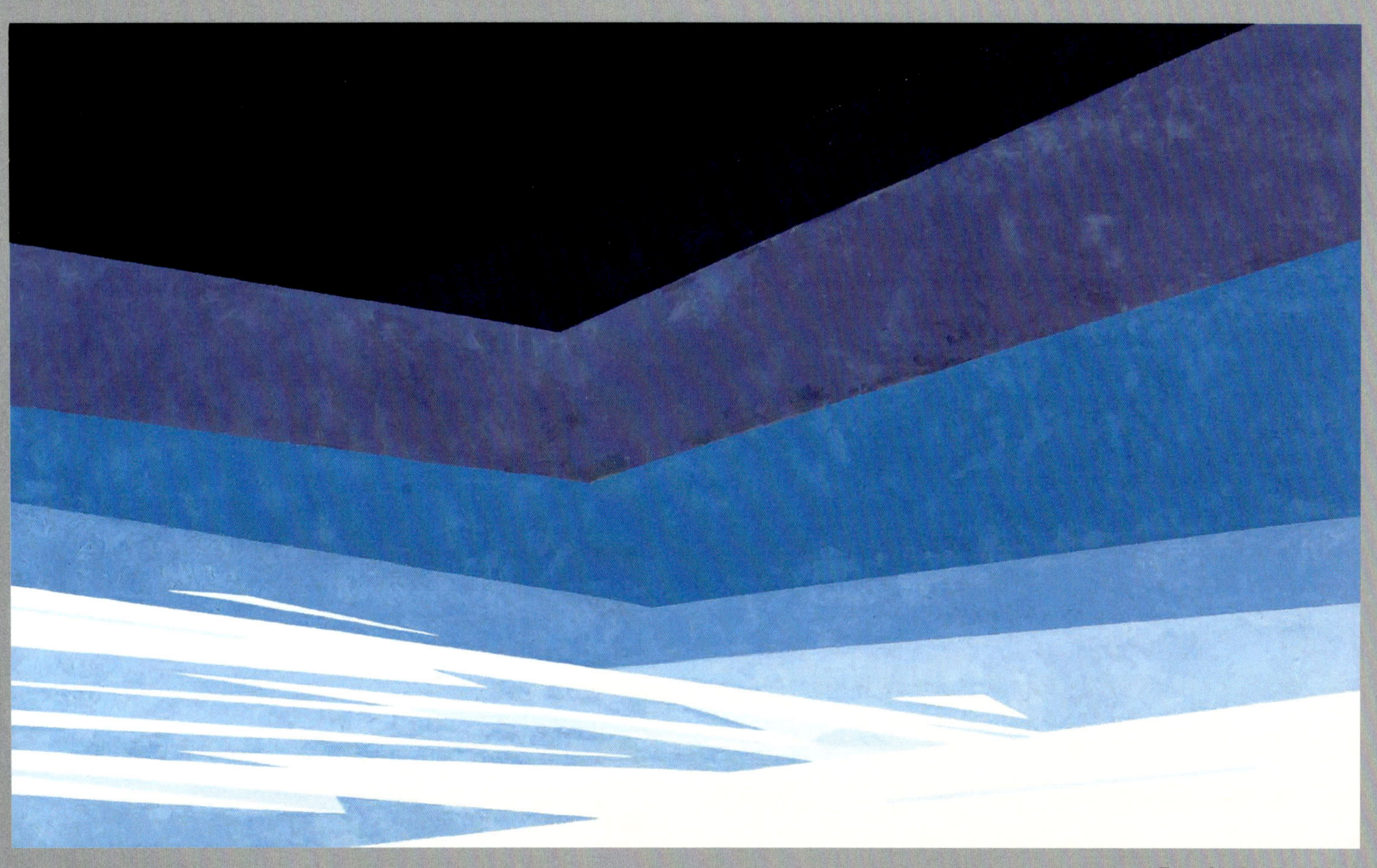

Top of a Glacier, 2016

oil on linen | 36" × 60" | Courtesy of the artist, Kirk Hopper Fine Art, Dallas, and Gerald Peters Gallery, Santa Fe

CHAPTER 14

GREENLAND, ICELAND, AND NEW YORK CITY

IN 2012, THE MCKINNEY Avenue Contemporary in Dallas mounted a five-decade survey of Winter's career. That same year, Santa Fe's Gerald Peters Gallery began to represent his work and Kirk Hopper Fine Art, Dallas, signed Winter to its growing stable of nationally recognized artists. Soon after, Kirk Hopper Fine Art organized *A Transfer of Spirit*, a milestone exhibition that featured a selection of works by forty-eight artists who studied with Winter at the Dallas Museum School, Southern Methodist University, and the National Academy—John Alexander, David Bates, Jaq Belcher, Chong Chu, Mary McMahon Crain, Kaleta Doolin, Lilian Garcia-Roig, Sam Gummelt, Jan Lee McComas Bates, Stephen Mueller, Gail Norfleet, Dan Rizzie, Arleigh Stark, Kathy Windrow, and many others.

During this period, while maintaining a bifurcated life in Santa Fe and New York City, Winter also made his first trip to Greenland, in addition to the first of five visits to Iceland between 2013 and 2017. "Jeanette, daughter of Swedish immigrants, was the one who first brought up Greenland and Iceland," Winter explains. "I liked the idea. We mentioned it to our friend, the poet Jean Valentine, and she wanted to go with us. It was a productive trip—Jean published a long poem about Greenland in the *New York Times Book Review*. Jeanette took scores of great photos, and I got started on the Nordic paintings." With these landscapes, Winter defined a style characterized by a combination of the minimal and the monumental. He focused on the timeless grandeur of the icebergs and glaciers with a heightened sense of abstraction. A romantic aesthetic is also informed by an architectonic sensibility—sharper, bolder light reveals distilled, geometric forms and lines of earth, sky, and sea. Significantly, the Nordic experience represents a turning point that changed Winter's painting for the rest of his life.

When Winter landed in Ilulissat, a small town bordering a glacier in Greenland, it was as if he was confronting a new realm. Travel, of course, is its own reward. Our experiences are internalized, braided together as memory. But absent is the certain sense of things that we are powerless to capture in photographs or iPhone shots—a spiritual wash, a searing light. Solitude—

unflinchingly and beautifully cruel. "We arrived in the middle of the night although it was still daylight with kids playing in the street," Winter recalls. "That was like an experience of another world, a world I had no idea existed. The icebergs floating in the water off the coast of Ilulissat were like nothing we ever encountered. There was the quality of reflected light and the fact that we were seeing a tiny part, just one-tenth of something immense underwater. How long have they been there? How long would they stay? While standing on a spit of land at the water's edge, I witnessed an iceberg calving. The sound was a loud, sizzling crack. It was horrifying, a reminder of the fragility and impermanence of the ice cap covering eighty-five percent of Greenland. Locals fear that a chunk of an iceberg might tumble into the ocean and unleash an enormous wave on the town. A woman in Ilulissat told me that she was once afraid of ice, but was now more afraid of water."

Artists have always sought to give form to experiences that are beyond the everyday. This metaphysical realm adds a dimension to life that can inspire bliss and exhilaration, as well as fear and dread. In Caspar David Friedrich's *Wanderer above the Sea of Fog* (1818), the German Romantic artist depicted an aristocratic-looking young man in a green overcoat as he stands with his back to us atop a jagged rock, taking in a misty, high-altitude scene of mountains and cliffs. The man is a master of all he surveys but also entirely subservient to it. During the 1930s, the early American modernist Rockwell Kent and the Canadian artist Lawren Harris painted views of Greenland's rugged terrains, for which both had a deep spiritual affinity. The clusters of ice formations served as touchstones for eternity. For Winter, the ice below—blue with refractions and reflections of its surfaces and its strapped air bubbles—seemed alive, pulsing and shifting and shrinking before his very eyes. According to Jon Thompson, "While traces of 'sublime' experience are to be found in the art and literature of almost every period, the aesthetic category of the 'sublime,' as we know it today, was essentially an invention of the late eighteenth century. . . . Rich with 'sublime' devices drawn from the writings of Edmund Burke and very consciously applied, it deploys the whole kaleidoscopic array of conflicting forces: the prescient and the timeless; the dynamic and the formless; the frighteningly proximate and the distant; the still and the giddy."[1] The German philosopher Immanuel Kant observed that an exalted state comes from the sense that, although we may feel overwhelmed, we also grasp what we cannot hold.[2] In his *Critique of Judgment* (1790), Kant tells us that "the Beautiful in nature is connected with the form of the object which consists in having boundaries. The Sublime, on the other hand, is to be found in a formless object, so far as in it, or by occasion of it, boundlessness is represented and yet its totality is also present to thought."[3] Thompson continues, "'The grand' and 'the sublime' seem to reach for or suggest a state or condition beyond the scope of immediate comprehension" by virtue of its vastness and dynamism.[4] Invoking an overwhelming sense of awe, the sublime points to the heights of something truly extraordinary, something that comes from outside the conscious self—the landscape and nature, historical or mythical events—metaphors for psychological spaces that go beyond our normal experience. This is still humbling; the sublime defines our limits as well as our possibilities.

To that end, Winter's incandescent paintings of Greenland teeter on the brink of the unknowable, at the outer limits of imagination where the real vaporizes into the infinite. *Sun, Ilulissat* (2013) is a profound vision of the orb and its radiating light, which appear as alive and pulsating forms in the cosmic firmament above black lava fields. Circles, oval spirals, animals, human shapes, and biomorphic forms—some sharply defined, some nebulous—expand and contract amid a welter of loosely rendered brushstrokes. Shapes intersect or climb over one another; curved and rhythmic planes are determined by arching and organic contours that wriggle and twist in space. There is the sense that nature is still being born, still coming into being. At the core of the ecstatic burst of energy is a persistence to be deeply moved by regeneration, the vital force within. Winter's gestural strokes in blue, pink, yellow, and white unfold lyrically, their rhythms, movements, and tempos maintain an open dialogue with gravity. There is something primal and erotic about the disparate forms, which seem to engage in a duel of chaos and order. Our eye is led over and through sensual curves, slides, and arabesques; we are projected into an almost dancelike whirl.

At the same time, Winter's Greenland paintings evoke a contemporary mood of elegy, a sense of the frailty of human life in the face of giant forms and vast powers. *Disko Bay* (2013) takes this feeling as its central theme, depicting the iceberg and midnight sun as natural wonders of spiritual and aesthetic meditation. It is as if we are witnessing the slow formation of mountains jammed upward by mysterious subterranean forces. At a distance, the painting's iceberg appears as a modest wedge locked in reflecting waters of unearthly electric blue. Up close, however, the lavender-blue hulk grows in presence, floating like a phantom across unknown depths. Evident in his imagery is a reverence for the site and its grace of form. Winter's controlled modeling of light evokes solitude and contemplation. *Berit's Iceberg* (2013) is cool and refined. Poised between a glowing sea and sky, it becomes a prism of frozen water, crystalline and blue in the sun, but also ominous. The pressure of tides and shifting sea ice have raised it, revealing a tilted, razor-sharp horizon line. By juxtaposing geographic rhythms and perceptual eccentricities, Winter binds his elements together in a constantly shifting structure of horizontal planes. Taken together, the paintings convey something about mortality, that brevity adds an element that is both magical and saddening. By the same token, the works are cumulative experiences and embody contrasting concepts of time: the past, which is evoked through geologic swellings and meltings of the ice; the present, in which we interact with the primacy of Winter's brushstrokes and depicted environments; and eternal timelessness, which is reflected in nature's regenerative cycles and seemingly unchanging panoramas. Perhaps the most important place these icebergs exist is in our memories, where time becomes more fluid and blends with the imagination.

For years, Winter aimed to condense his painting by reducing it to essentials. However, he has never been more the master of his means than he is in Iceland, and what he has to say has never been more moving. Winter's responsiveness to nature seems to have intensified in these works, communicating a belief that it is through paint that the artist can touch the elemental world. As in the Texas and New Mexico periods, the inspiration comes primarily from light. Sometimes the light seems to be within the paint. Sometimes there is a sense that a spotlight has been thrown on a chunk of glacier, a black lava beach, or the startlingly pure, limitless space. Here, just under the Arctic Circle, in the heart of early summer, the sun sinks but never disappears completely, casting light even from below the horizon. "Iceland is just five hours from JFK," Winter explains. "It's a small, treeless island. A delicious light. Deep built ice tunnels under glaciers. And Reykjavik is a wonderful small city, completely in tune with our temperaments. The artist Lois Dodd was a friend of Louisa Matthiasdottir, the Icelandic American painter. Lois told me that Matthiasdottir 'stuck to the basics.' I now see that Iceland has nothing but basics: the endless horizontal of the sea, the long black lava beaches, the planar ice at high altitudes, the long shafts of low-flying clouds. All of this is united by magical light and color, and it has all coalesced in my paintings."

Iceland suited Winter's needs, the place where he had the clearest view of himself and his relationship to the world. Each Icelandic site is a unique location of change, stemming from its primarily young geology—unstable, unfixed, always in the process of transformation. Thus, Winter needed to develop a language commensurate with his ethereal and transcendent experience. Accordingly, the Iceland paintings unite to expose an underlying distilled coherence in which realism and abstraction are close to being indistinguishable. Like the best painters, Winter did not let himself rest in a zone of "tourist" comfort. His paintings do not just put us in Iceland; they get us under the skin of the place. So many images of coldness and ice—perhaps that is the temperature he felt inside. Isolation, solitude, loneliness—always sensing the conditions of things, of being separate. For Winter, however, the isolation was physical and served as a vibrating life force. Iceland taught him how to seek out the uplifting energy that isolation provides; it brought him closer to the tops of glaciers. In many ways, Winter's work echoes that of Georgia O'Keeffe, whose Southwest subjects—a

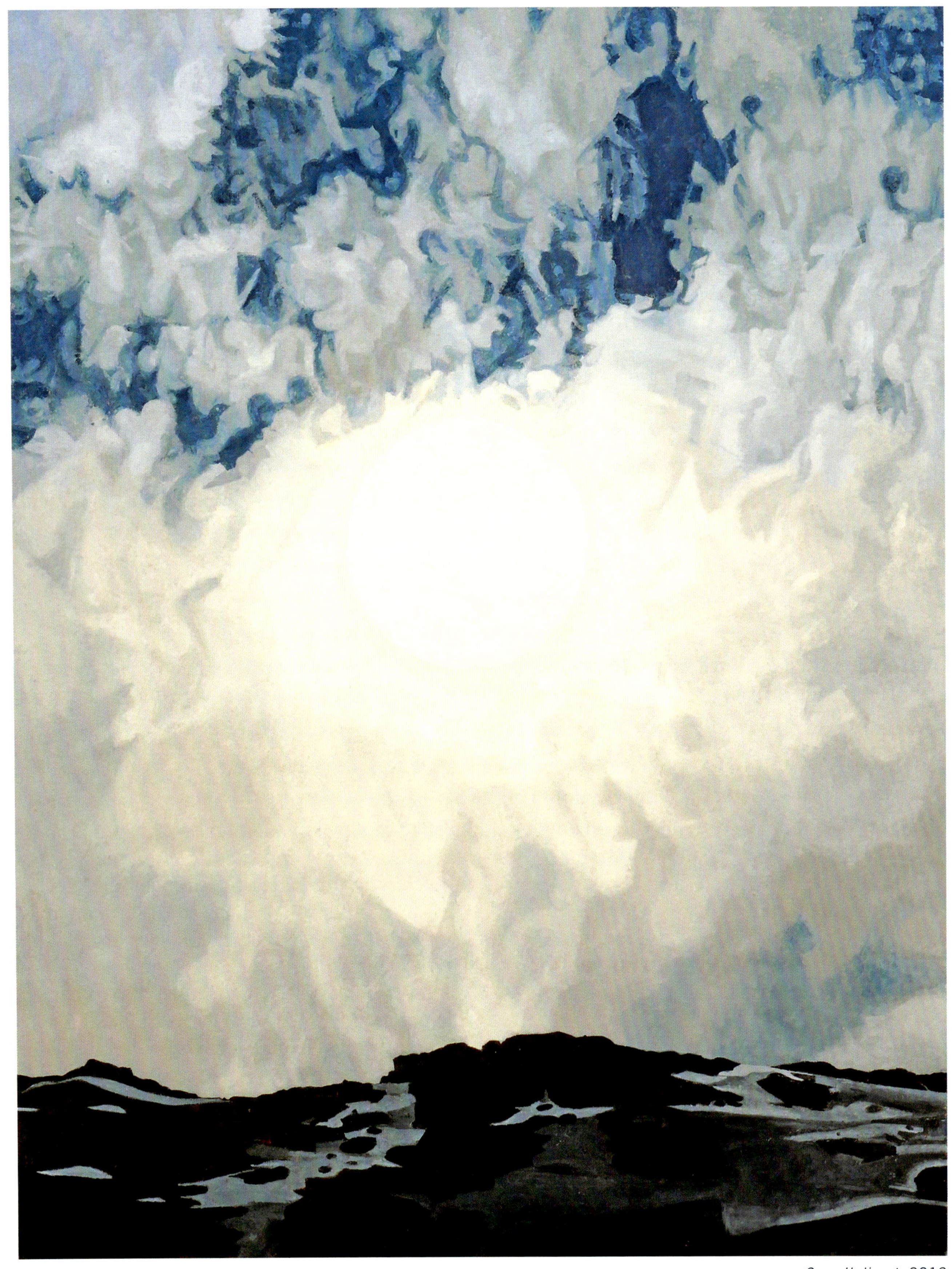

Sun, Ilulissat, 2013

oil on linen | 60" × 48" | Collection of Laurence Tancredi, New York City

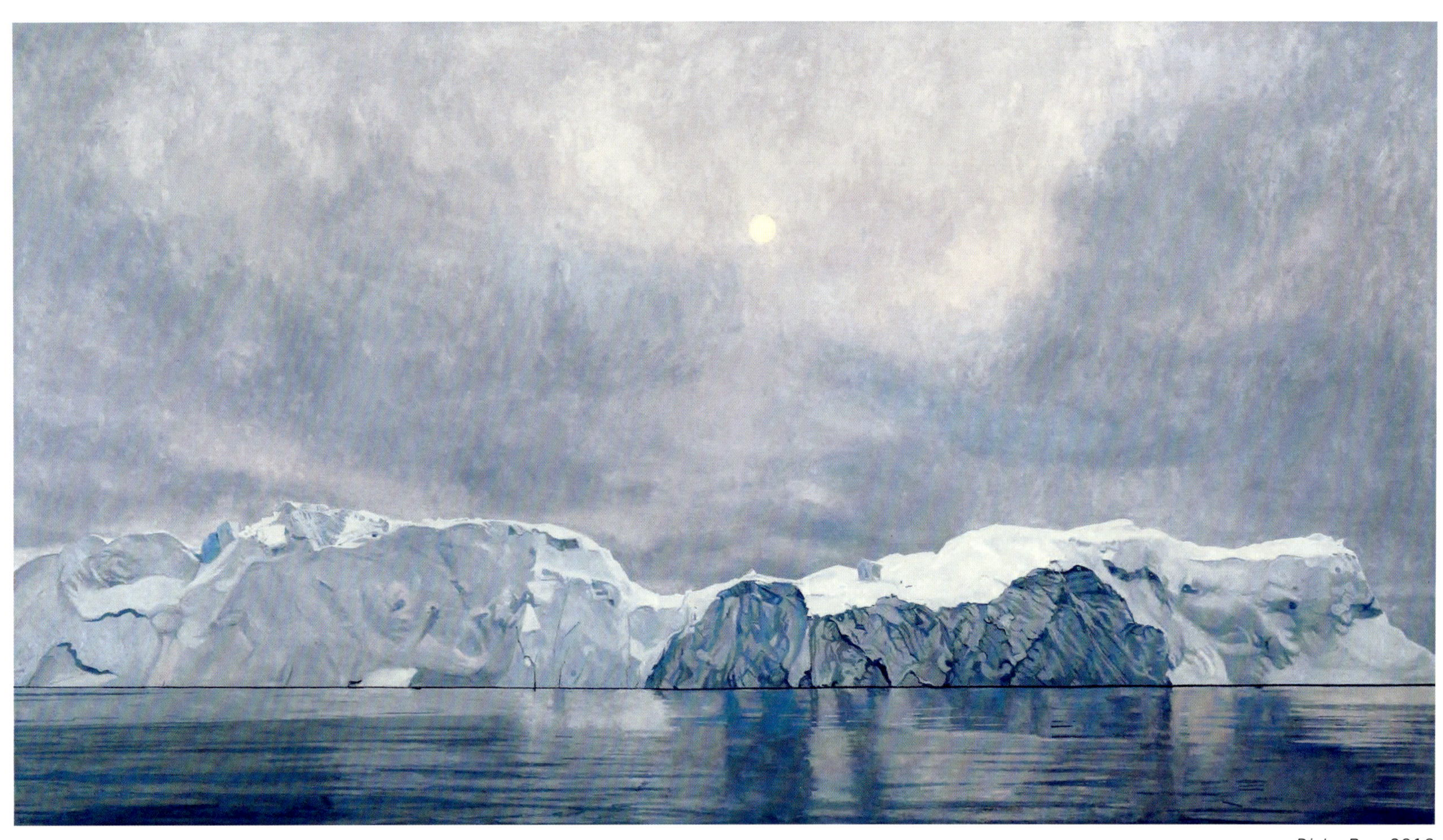

Disko Bay, 2013

oil on linen | 60" × 108" | Collection of Elise and Burk Murchison, Dallas

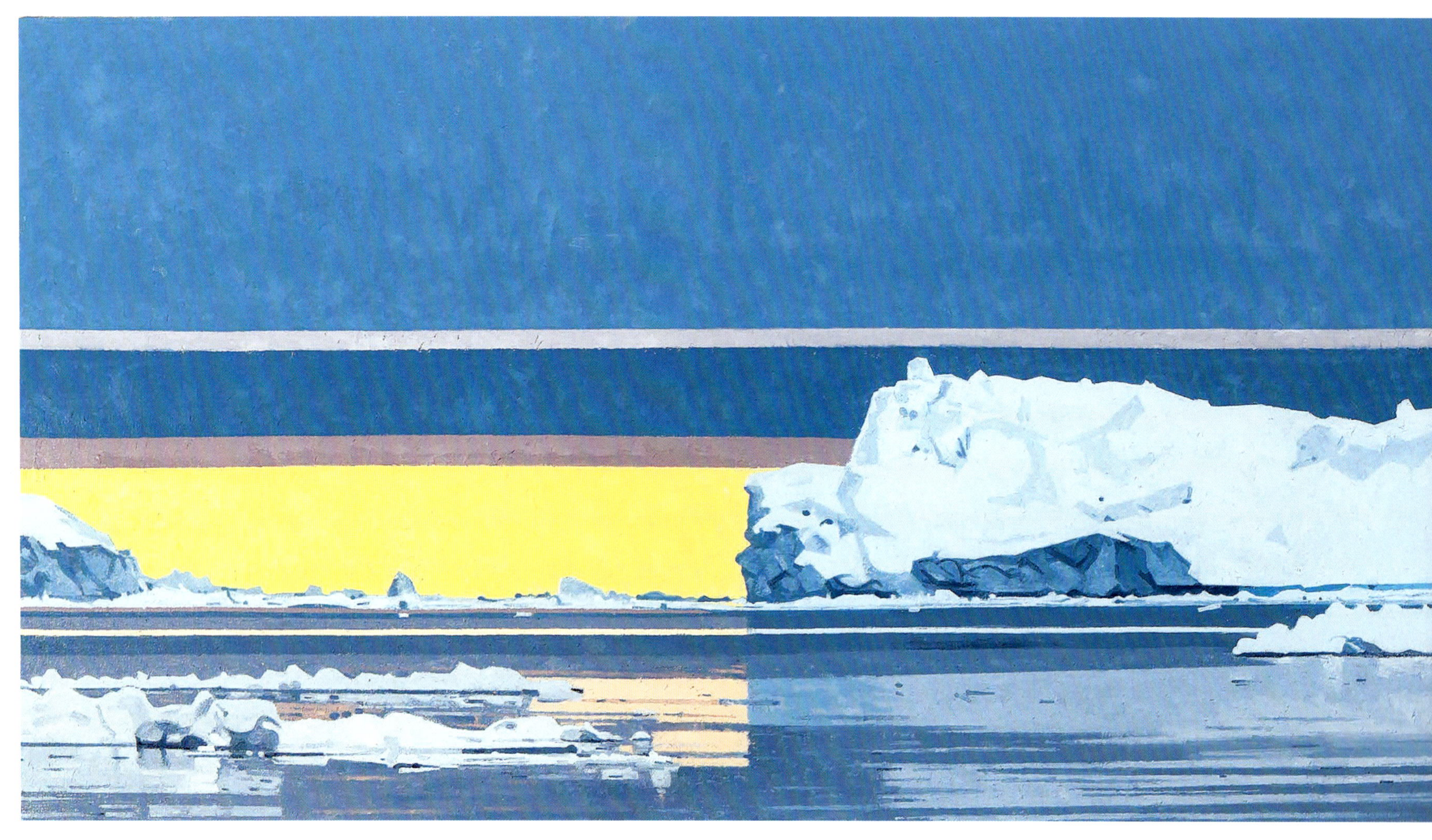

kind of nature poetry—conjure specific places in the context of universal and iconic form.

In a journal from May 2015, Winter records his observations while driving on the Ring Road. He writes,

> A fine attraction was the rock "wall" (Pingvellir) at some points more than 60 feet high . . . full of crevices and caves and holes, some with thatched-like roofs, that seemed perfect for whatever animal life is or was once there. It's easy to see how, a thousand years ago, the early settlers may have mistaken small unfamiliar animals for elves or trolls. . . . A large group of horses and sheep roam around in the pastures that manage to grow in lava beds. We also spent time in a field of geysers with various sizes of bubbling holes that occasionally shot into the air. The entire field was dotted with clouds of steam. . . . As we go North, Iceland could be another planet. Endless fields that look like giant bubble wrap covered by a sage green carpet of moss. Glaciers with reflected white light. Horizontal stripes of white rivers across black lava fields. Heavy mists turning mountains into gray silhouettes. . . . Jagged rock formations that look like abandoned castles; small icebergs—some of them intensely blue. . . . Reindeer, swans in every puddle or pond. Away from the water were mountains so mystical in the rising fog. . . . The forms in the mist and elsewhere are ambiguous. They can be houses, animals,

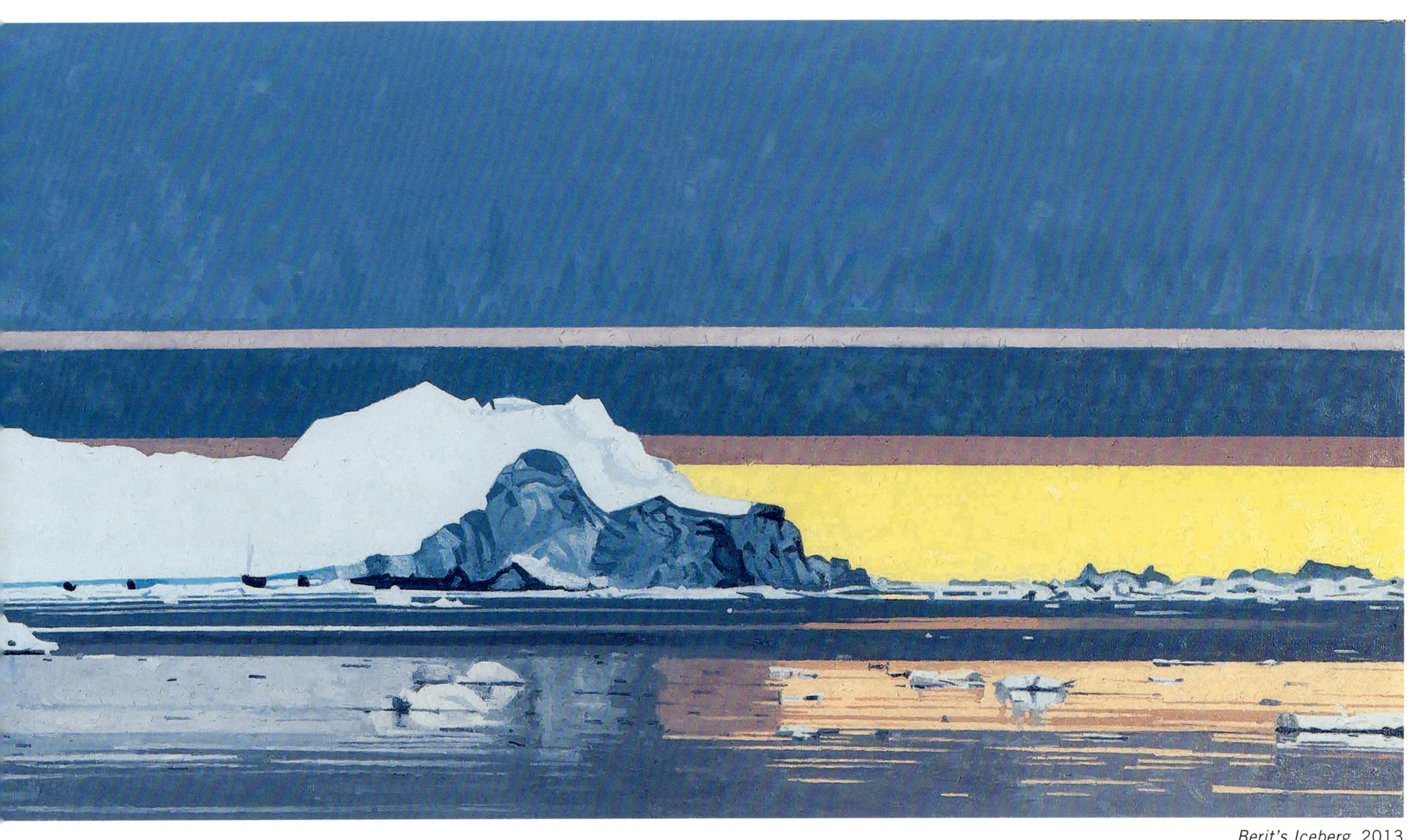

Berit's Iceberg, 2013
oil on linen | 28" × 108" | Courtesy of the artist and Kirk Hopper Fine Art, Dallas | Photography by Joshua Nefsky

> faces, full figures and anything that anyone can see in the constantly changing space.[5]

All of Winter's Iceland paintings—ranging from elongated horizontals to intimate, little near-squares—share vertiginous shifting spaces that metaphorically invite us to enter even as they deny us a secure vantage point. Winter achieves a careful balance between the planar and the linear, but also in the color. Sea greens, mustards, pinks, powdery purples, and iridescent blues knit the paintings together, combining restraint and powerful sensuality. The luminous hues, delicate surfaces, and ambiguous perspectives cohere as simplified, concentrated statements of the utmost force. Winter leads us to question our sense of substance, presence, and absence—how radiant colors meet; how expanses jostle for dominance; how a whole temperament can be engaged in conveying what it is like to be in the world.

In *Near Reykjavik* (2013), Winter grabs hold of this spiritual place, saying something about the sky, sea, and horizon and how those elements affect him. To that end, he renders the crisp contrasts of a cold day with clouds mounded under a blue sky. Hidden animals shape-shift and seemingly chase one another amid the fog and scumbled white caps before dissipating into ether. The scene, with its dark earth forms against the sky, is alive with a sense of light, space, and wind. In *Faxa Bay* (2014), the light is tangible; it enters as rays of sun from outside the frame or suggests snaking currents of air. Color here—neon blues, pinks, lavenders, sage green, and the magenta of sea stars—is used

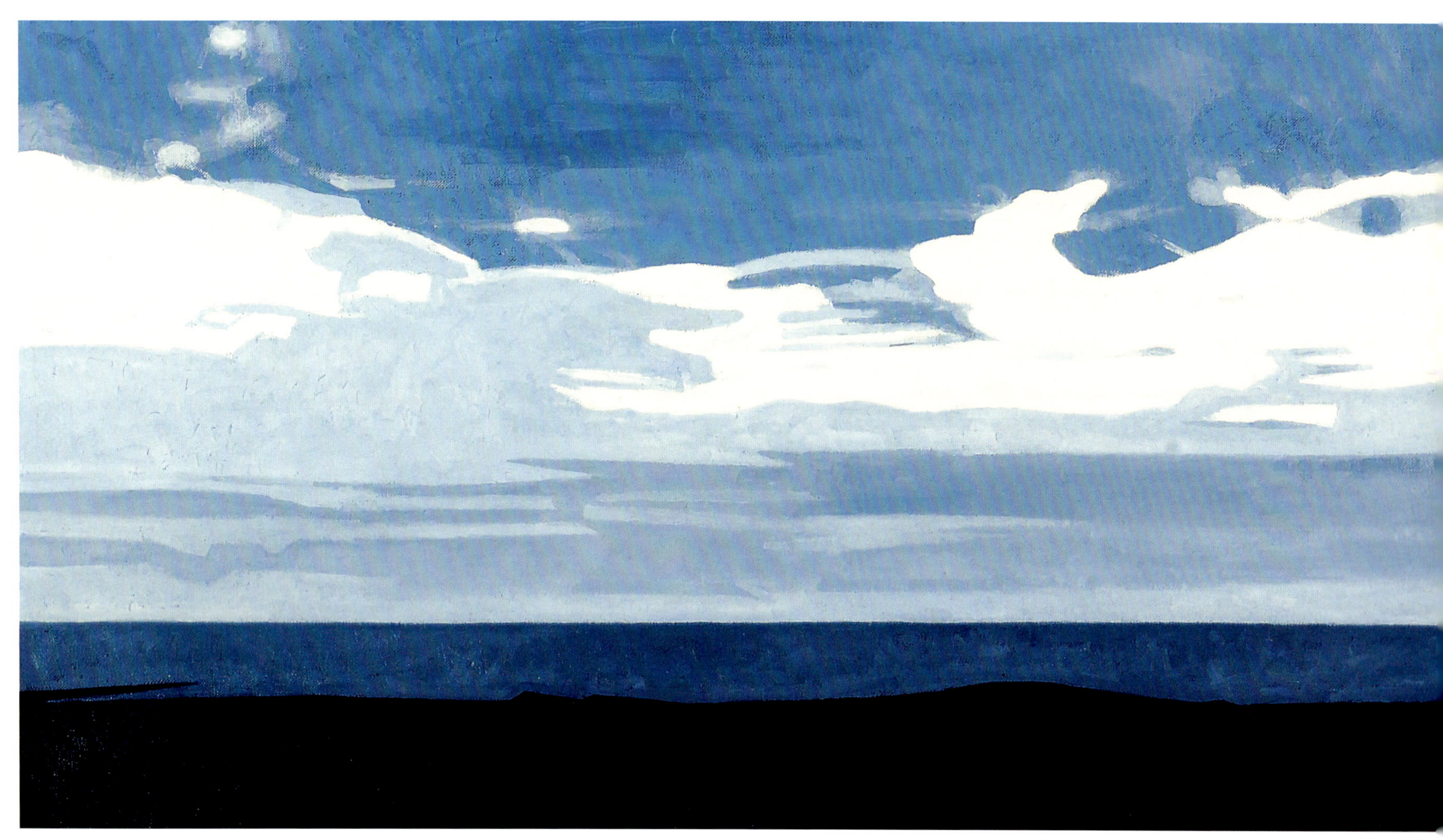

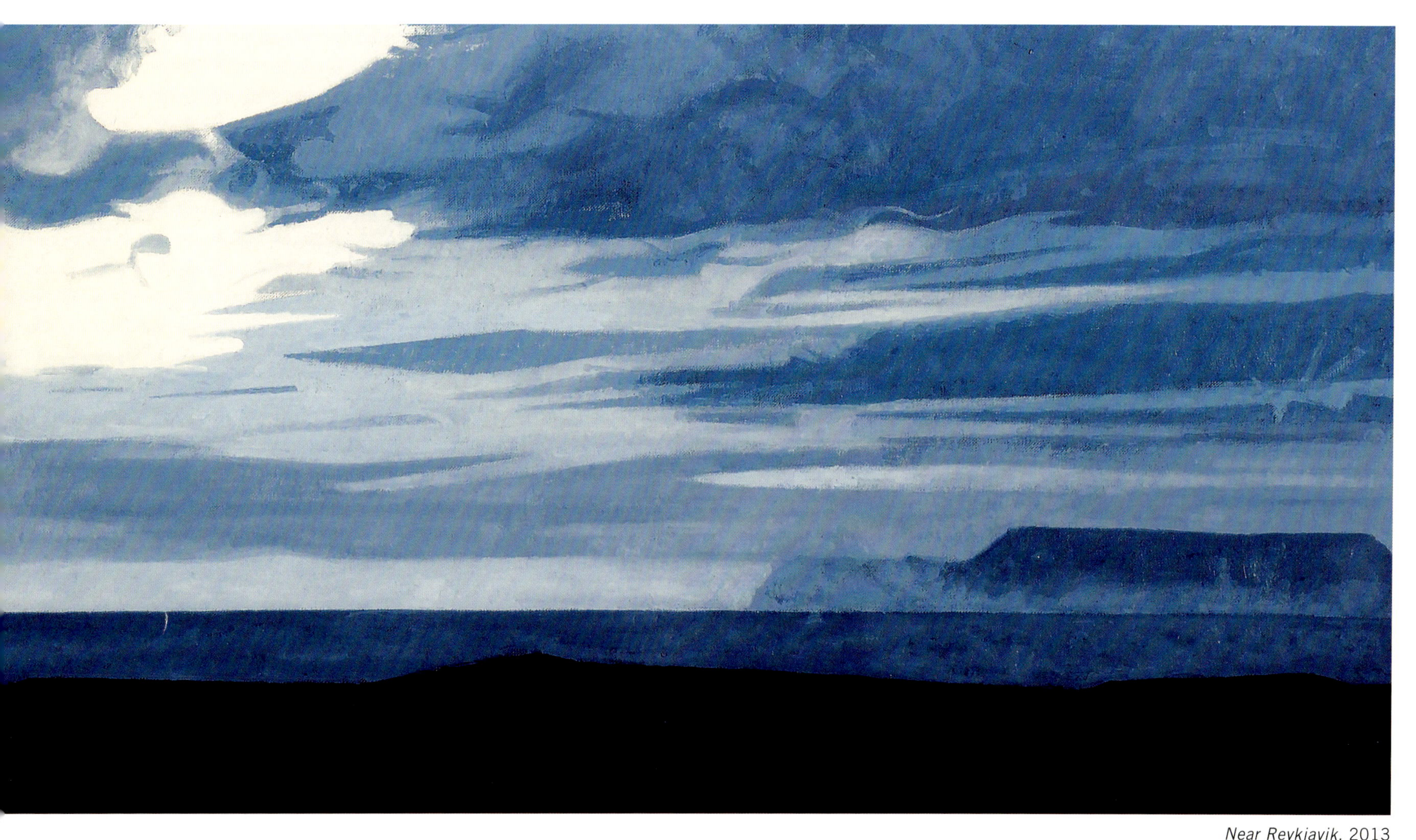

Near Reykjavik, 2013

oil on linen | 24" × 84" | Collection of Mary Beth Kelly

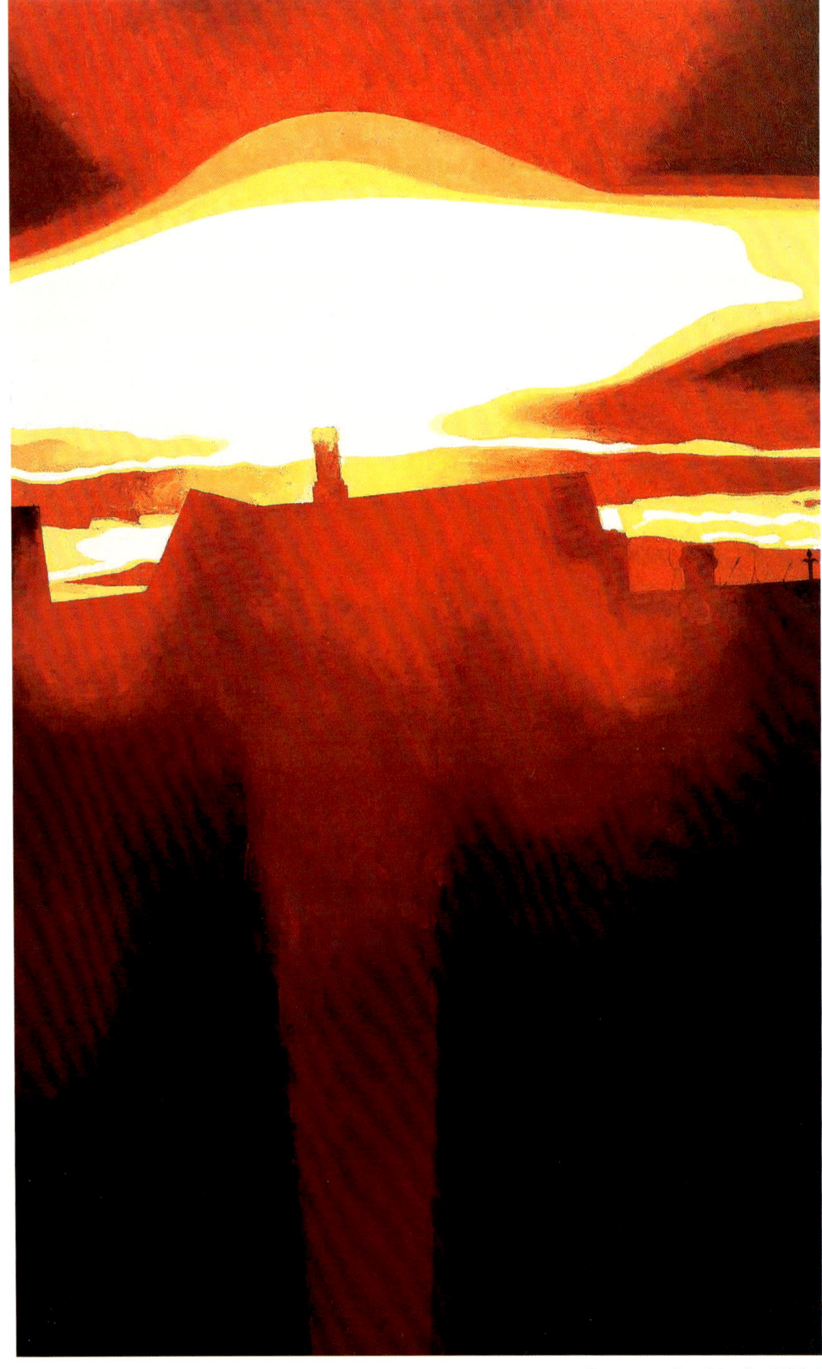

January, Reykjavik, 2014

oil on linen | 72" × 42" | Courtesy of the artist and Kirk Hopper Fine Art, Dallas | Photography by Joshua Nefsky

as light but also as an emblem of movement. Horizontal layers of expressive strokes flicker, glow, vibrate, pulsate, and shimmer with energy. More often, however, we feel light itself, in and through the sifting hues. Winter's painting conveys the unsettling quality of a captured moment in eternal flux. Moving into a visceral key, he addresses the most primal of human concerns: the difference between inner and outer worlds, between transcendence and metamorphosis, between impermanence and permanence, a mixture of what vanishes and what remains. The philosophical questions that emerge from the Iceland paintings deal with the mystery and enigma of our existence, our solitary state in the world, our limits in space and time, our desire for the infinite.

It is important to note that the Iceland paintings also mark a change in Winter's working process. Back in his Santa Fe studio, Winter decided to eliminate underpainting, figures, and atmospheric edges in favor of precisionist, geometric compositions. He explains,

> I wanted to paint more directly rather than to scale or form to form, as in the snapshots I used. If I deal too much with contrasts, subtleties, and atmosphere, then at my age I wouldn't get much done—it's too slow! I was after one layer, put down; one thing, under control. So I drew right on the canvas to set up general divisions of space. All the edges are together and harmonious. Every brushstroke is considered: the diagonals move toward each other, but then I'll counteract by painting brushstrokes in the opposite direction. The colors emit dissonant notes—I'm still a twentieth-century composer painter. I made one color look like two distinct hues just by their juxtaposition and interaction. A color will appear different by the darker color next to it. There's also bits of raw canvas showing through, which reaffirm that the painting was done with human hands. All of the works are coming from reality—a real sky, real water, a real beach.

In *Black Beach* (2016), our eyes slide back and forth across the surface, seeking a hold but finding none, repeatedly slipping off the edge of the picture plane. Its bands and wedges of blue, orange, white, pink, and black refuse to lie down

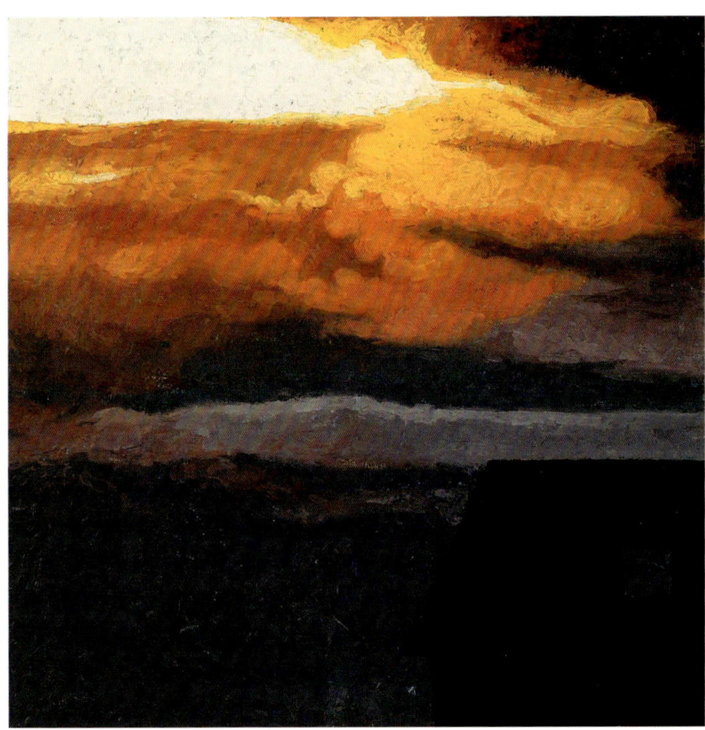

House in Reykjavik, 2014
oil on linen | 15" × 15" | Collection of Molly E. Moore | Photography by Joshua Nefsky

but, rather, retain a disquieting complexity. There is enough chromatic dissonance that the entirety cannot be swallowed easily or quickly. The upshot is a painting that is grown from the inside out versus the equally determined exteriority of much hard-edged abstraction. The horizontal bands that occupy the evolving field are integral to it—fused with it, immersed in it. They appear both flat and dimensional and are so tenderly painted that the medium itself seems to be the subject. Winter's process stimulates a tension between change and constancy, those variations of hand and mind that record a moment in time and our awareness of the act of painting itself.

Indeed, Winter reaches out to the edges of a work, demonstrating his will and determination that every part of the painting be alive, involved, touched. His disciplined mode of expression suggests a distinct compulsiveness, a fusion of ambiguity and certitude, and a need to grasp and anchor the ephemeral. "I was able to get a view of the earth in its natural form," Winter says. "The black land across the bottom was formed by volcanoes exploding deep in the earth. To me, the painting represents the simplest elements of our planet. There are no people, no vegetation, nothing that's human built. The water and sky will continue to be the dominant natural forces on the earth." For *Top of a Glacier* (2016), Winter's viewpoint looks down some several hundred feet underneath the ice floe. The experience stimulated him to paint rhythmic diagonals of ice and sky. The result is a dizzying sequence of horizontal and diagonal spatial disjunctions. It quickens the pulse, making us aware that there is no one place to stand before the razor-edged bands, no perfect spot from which to take in the vaporous white ground and intoxicating colors. If the refracted bands of black, cobalt, and turquoise seem to waver, they do so only to remind us how mutable and hard to fix the act of seeing really is. All in all, Winter's simplified shapes are extremely deceptive; we recognize in them the distillation of an intensely pure sensibility, under whose gaze the scale of the painting, the silence of the glacier, and the inwardness of the vision are one. To that end, *Top of a Glacier* becomes an entryway into a heightened sensory state and a greater awareness of the act of perception itself. The painting is like a delicately calibrated tuning fork, resonating at a cosmic pitch. Here, Winter creates volumes of permanence and stasis out of an environment that is fleeting and unpredictable. Moreover, the precisionist and careful brushwork modulates the radiant hues to suggest various depths and multiple perspectives. The fathomless range of glacial blues becomes an all-encompassing state of mind, an awed meditation on the lofty conundrums of time and being.

Throughout, Winter's imagery is enigmatic; it may refer to nature's eternal cycle of life and death or mortality and regeneration playing out endlessly in the space and light and stark beauty of the Arctic. Indeed, his work has a reserve of meaning that seems to open very slowly over a series of viewings. Part of that is due to the extreme compression of the paintings, which strip away everything inessential, greatly magnifying the potency of each form or shape. The Greenland and Iceland paintings achieve a sense of enormous scope in a few strong geometric structures. They are about expansiveness, as well as the mind's anomalous ability to take on what is vast, abstract, and intuited. In many respects, the life-changing

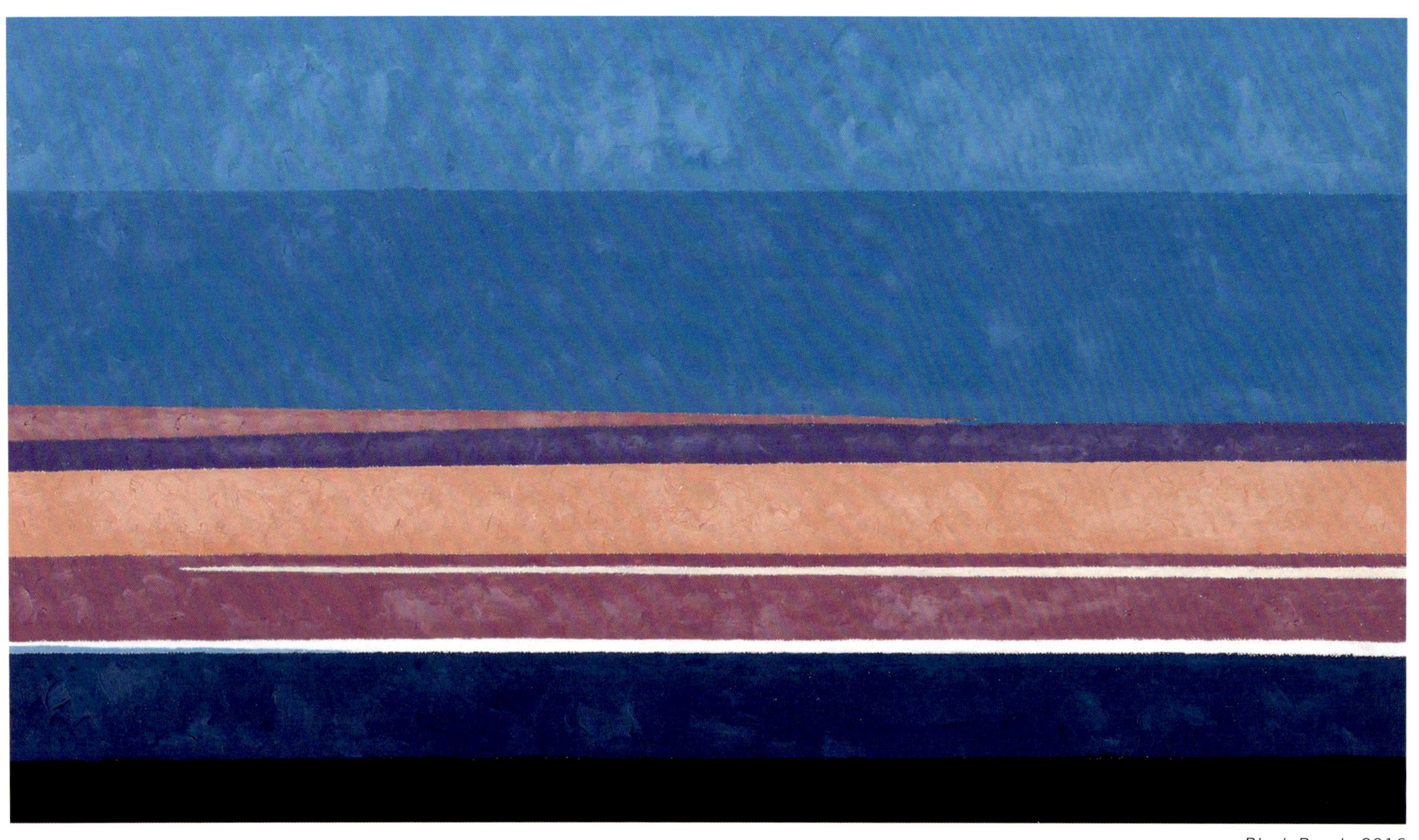

Black Beach, 2016

oil on linen | 18" × 32" | Courtesy of the artist, Kirk Hopper Fine Art, Dallas, and Gerald Peters Gallery, Santa Fe

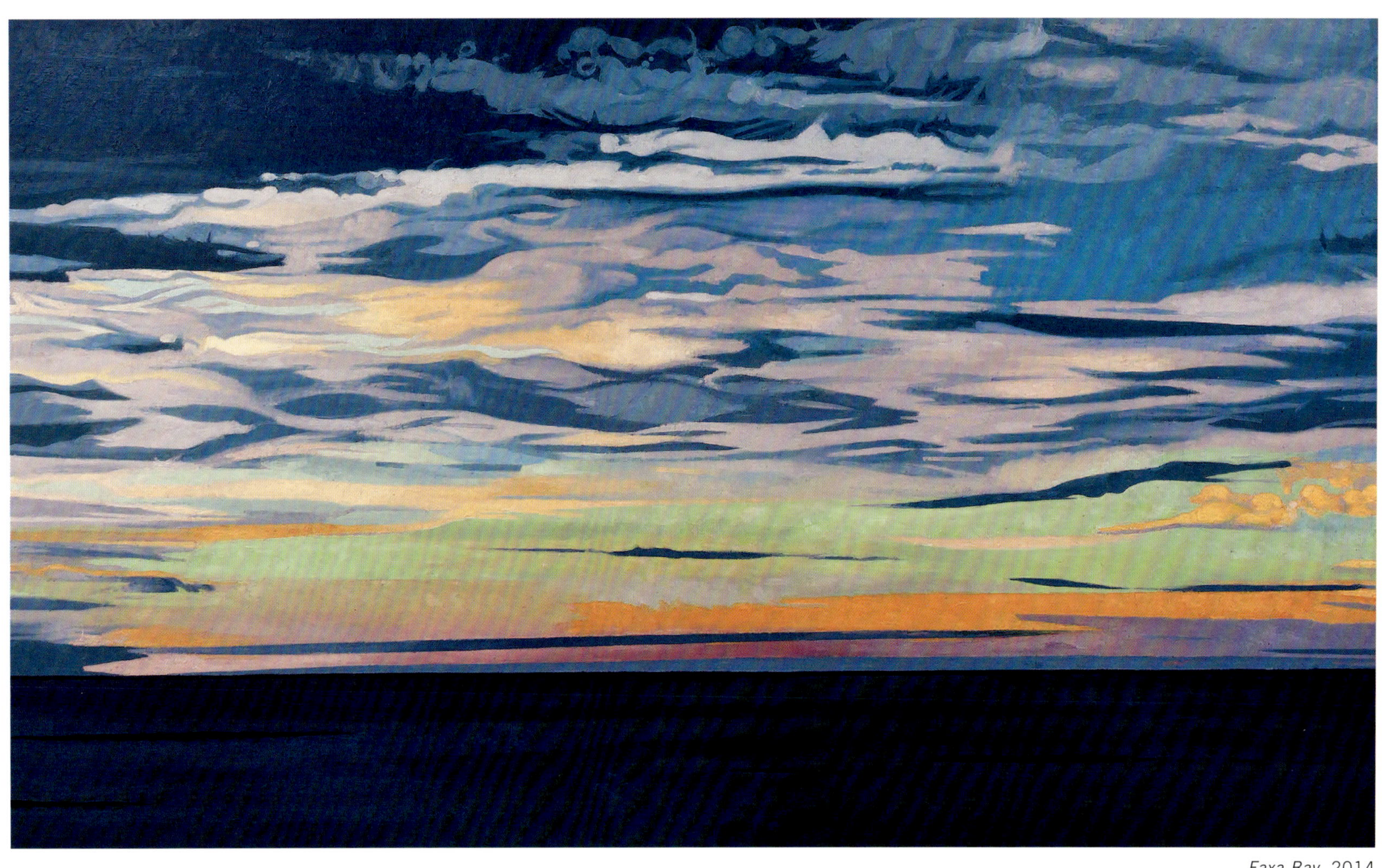

Faxa Bay, 2014

oil on linen | 50" × 84" | Collection of Judge B. Michael Chitty and Elise Chitty | Photography by Ben Bascombe experiences of Iceland have come full circle from Winter's early years of extreme hardships in Denison. "I've already mentioned T. S. Eliot as a touchstone," Winter explains.

> But I began to recognize the obvious truth about what he said in this direction: "After we have done all our exploration over so many years, we finally return to where we started, but then we understand it." The Nordic paintings suggest there's a lot more of that flat plane on either side of the canvas. But the long horizontal has always been in my sights. The endless line of railroad track was a major part of my existence for the first seventeen years. I walked to school on the railroad; I watched the freight trains and passenger cars pass by. It's like the story of my life, only now told through the Icelandic landscape. When we're young, we don't realize that life is not forever. At my age, even if I live to be a very old man, that's still not long to be alive. The Greenland and Iceland paintings are a search for something greater. I want to paint things that are more eternal. Subjectivity is the basis of the painting—not only to paint what is real, but what will last forever. As in the hymn "Hold to God's Unchanging Hand, Base Your Hopes on Things Eternal," I imagine the sea and sky will last forever. The surface of this earth, its water and atmosphere—those are the Creator's things. They're not ephemeral. They're not impassive. They're the substructure. I don't really have words for it—I try to paint it and that's as near as I can come.

In 2017, the Winters sold their Santa Fe casita and once again became full-time residents of New York City. With the vast deserts of the Southwest, as well as the northern light and simplified space of Iceland in mind, Winter began to view the structures of Manhattan through an increasingly reductive lens. As a result, paintings that depict Hudson River views, the New Jersey shore, and the New York City skyline are more formal, but with a greater degree of perception. They are things observed in life, even as Winter mixes two orders of reality: that which we see and know in the outside world, and that which we see and know only in paintings. Like the 1930s Precisionist artists Charles Sheeler, George Ault, Niles Spencer, and, especially, Ralston Crawford, who portrayed factories and mechanical structures using a sharp-edged, simplified, and precise technique, Winter focuses on architectural and industrial themes characterized by a carefully reasoned abstraction in which subjects are reduced to their basic, geometric shapes. Whereas the Precisionists pursued an art marked by a nonpainterly handling of color with all traces of the painting processes essentially eliminated and images brought to a flatly defined finish, Winter's solid overlapping of shapes is lit from within. His abstract patchworks are at once in motion and carefully puzzled together, seemingly

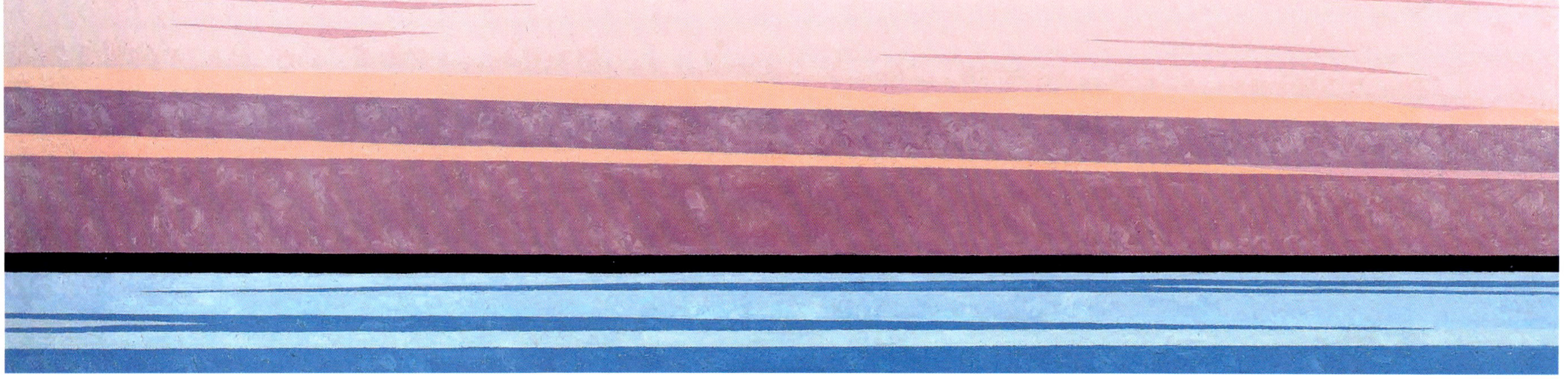

Sky, Land, Water, 2016

oil on linen | 20" × 84" | Courtesy of the artist, Kirk Hopper Fine Art, Dallas, and Gerald Peters Gallery, Santa Fe

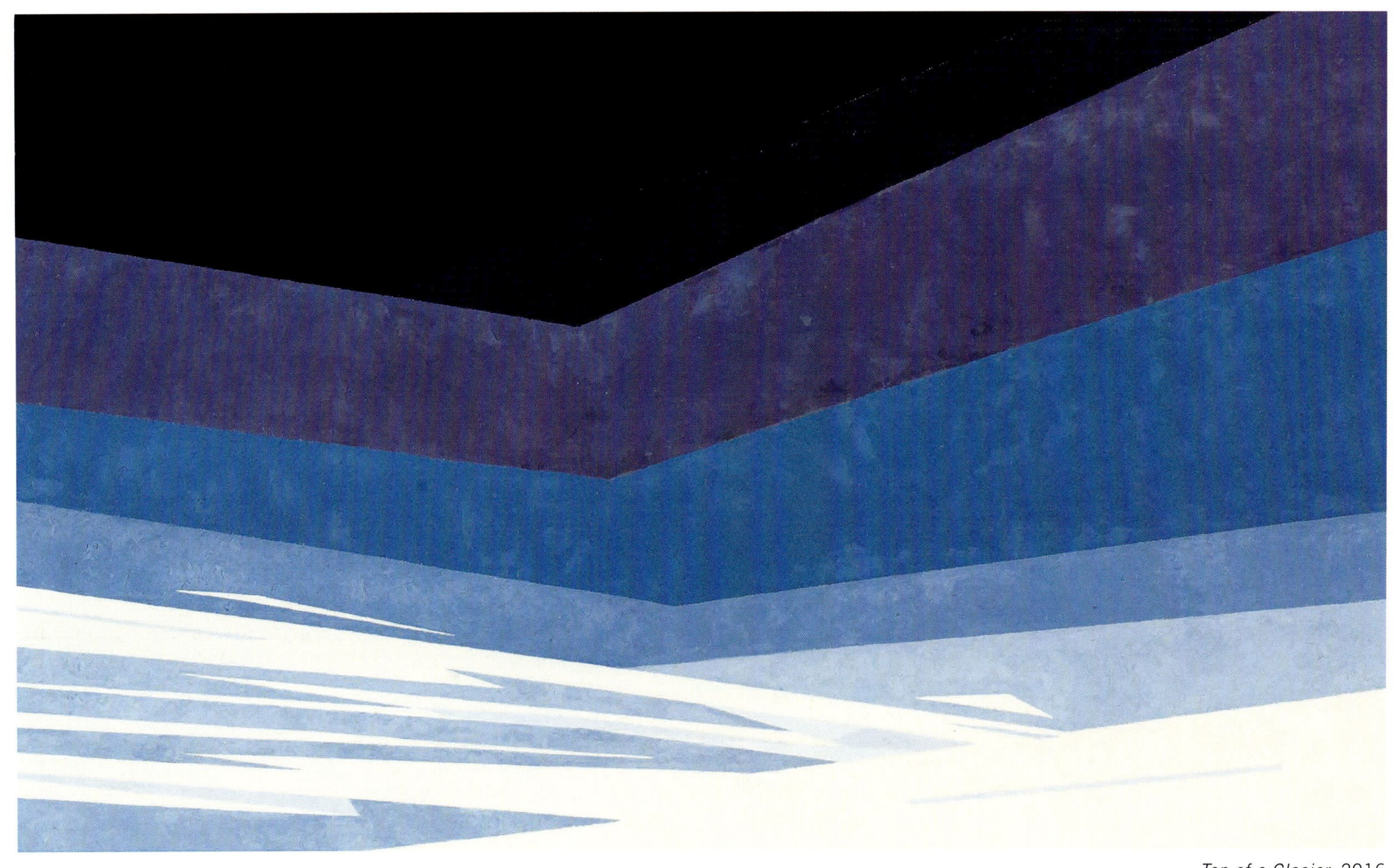

Top of a Glacier, 2016

oil on linen | 36" × 60" | Courtesy of the artist, Kirk Hopper Fine Art, Dallas, and Gerald Peters Gallery, Santa Fe

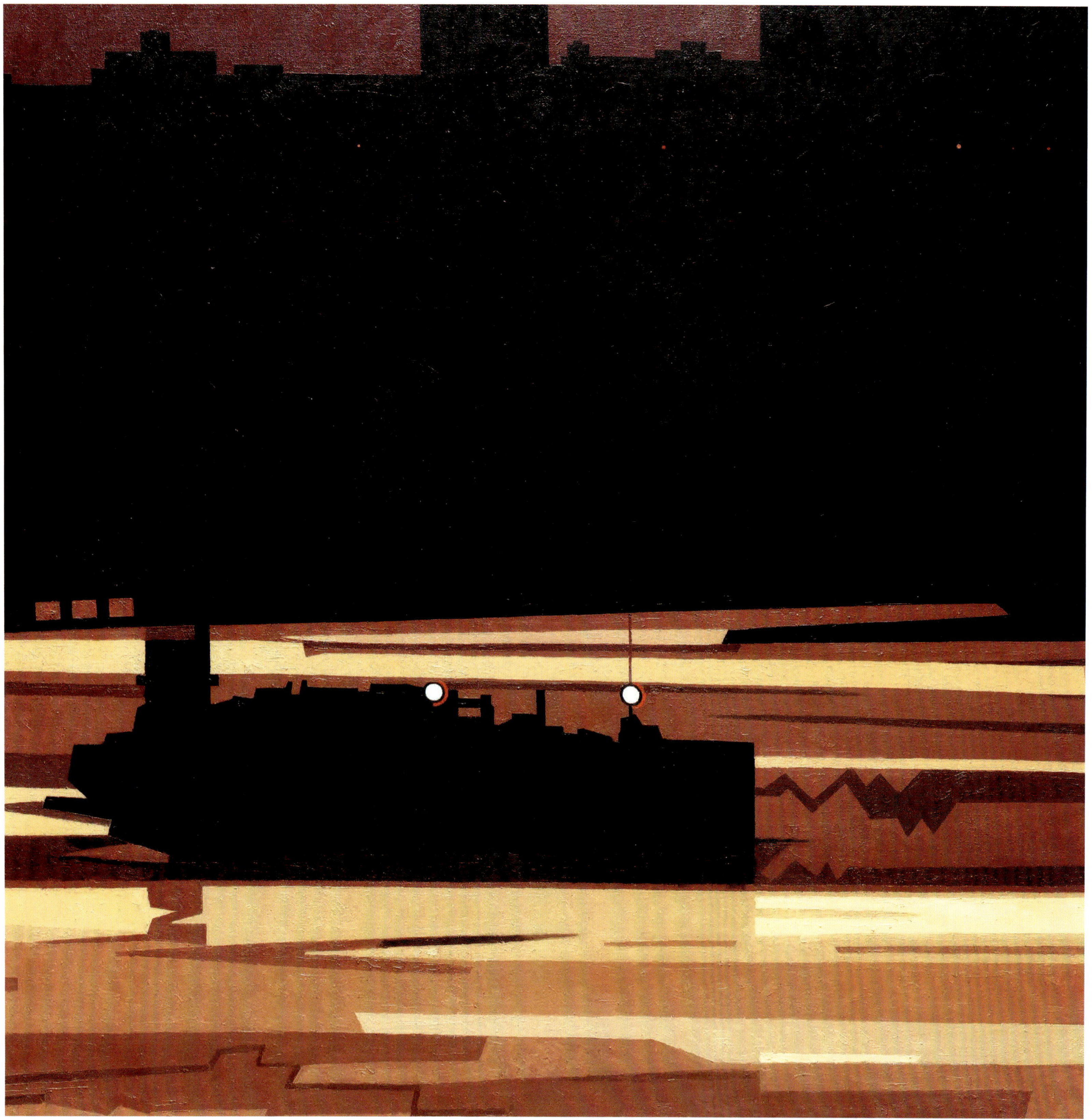

Black Freighter, 2012

oil on linen | 60" × 60" | Collection of Molly E. Moore | Photography by Kevin Todora

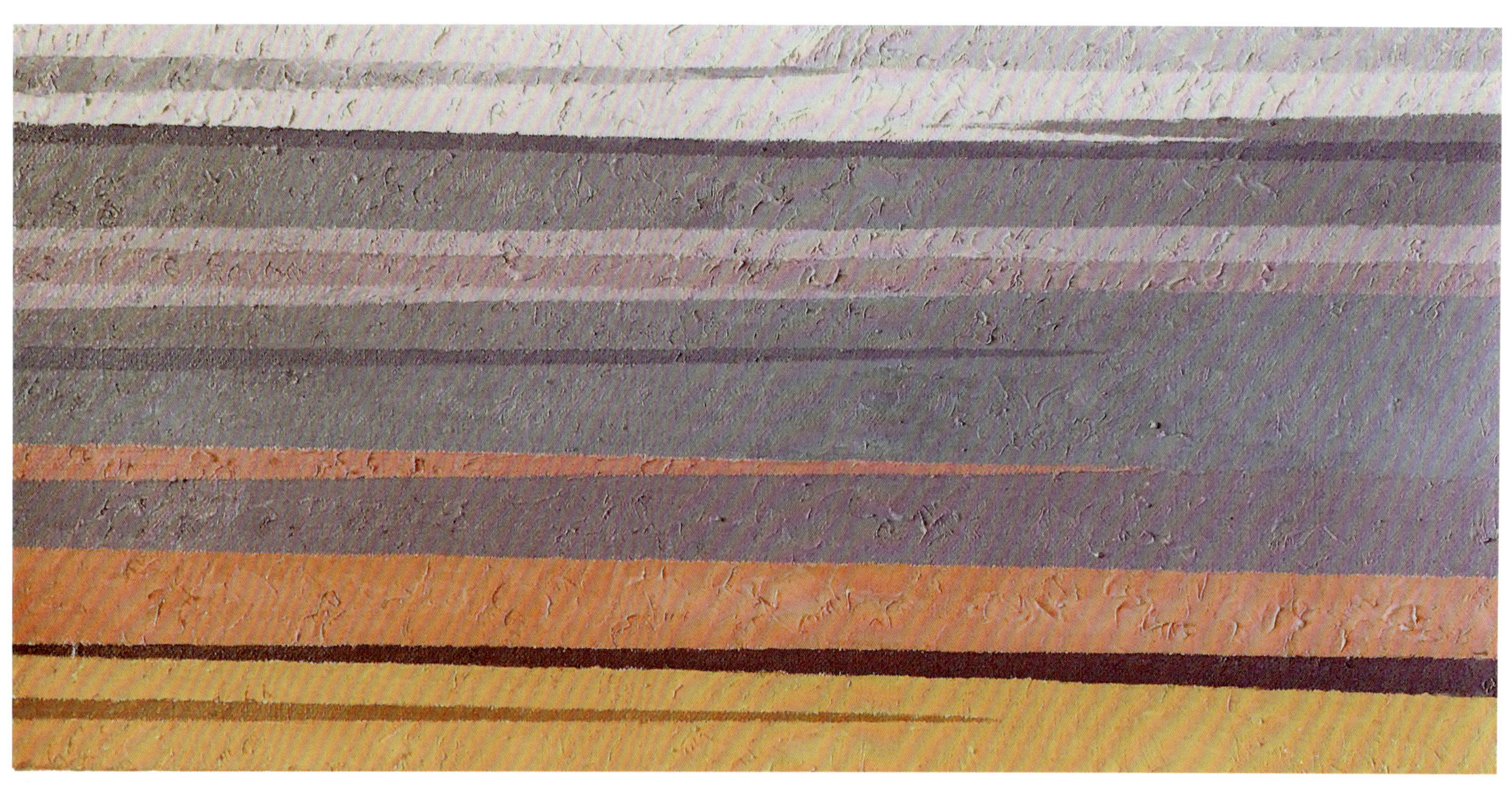

Sky over the Hudson, 2016

oil on linen | 10" × 20" | Courtesy of the artist and Kirk Hopper Fine Art, Dallas | Photography by G. Valderas

both topographical and tapestry-like with the exquisite touch of every painstaking brushstroke.

Rendered in luminous tonalities, Winter's New York City paintings describe complex spaces by way of perspective grids set in fully volumetric counterpoint to one another. To that end, he constructs poetic visual narratives and perceptual pageants through a rigorously calibrated array of formal means. His views of Manhattan rooftops transform the buildings into a rhythmic treatment of planes and angles. The overlapping shapes, the harmonious and dissonant mix of colors, and the deep shadows created by strong light emphasize the rich, visual geometries of Manhattan, if not the very beat of the city.

Clearly, it is important to Winter to sustain the liberty of putting everything to the test, which entails the sacrifice of a naive spontaneity for one distinguished by wisdom and experience. Nothing is more up-to-the-minute than daring to exhaust resources, to blow one's very method, only to come up with one more thing worth trying. In the New York City paintings and *Construction Site* series, Winter introduces a scheme of deft switchbacks that smoothly couples a pictorial depiction of shifting depths to an abstract composition of planar forms. As Winter knows, to live in a city as changeable as New York is to live in a place that is always on the cusp of disappearing or being replaced by some new version of itself. Thus, each painting feels like a new adventure in shape, space, color, and suggested meaning. Winter writes,

> In his later years, Romare Bearden was more concerned with what he could leave out of his work than what to include. Or so I was told by his friend and caretaker Russell Goings. Perhaps with the decline of physical strength and the weakening eyesight of aging, most visual artists feel a similar need to reduce, to simplify. . . . In the past, I have painted New York City from several viewpoints, from the interaction of people and buildings and statues in Union Square to window displays and subway riders. But this time in life, I'm far more interested in the city's geometry. Whether in the heavy beams at a building site, the doors and windows in the cliff dwellings where we live and work, the steps leading down to a brownstone basement, or the horizontal planes of the sidewalks and rooftops, I live in a geometric world. And this constantly evolving world is what I paint. Nothing that I see is static. Depending on the weather, the book I might be reading, my physical state on a given day, or the restless growth of the city, I'm in a slightly changed setting from week to week. The geometric spaces and their constant evolution, as well as my evolution, are the sources of my paintings at this time.[6]

Admittedly, Winter has always had an intimacy with architectural space, from making a balsa wood replica of Denison's Main Street as a grade school assignment to organizing exhibitions at Southern Methodist University about animal or utopian architecture. In any case, painting three-dimensional space with a rhythmic variety of scales, bars, lines, rectangles, triangles, and occasional circles is deep in his personal memory, his daily experience, and his abilities to perceive a sense of solid form through light.

In the fourth edition of his book *On Drawing*, Winter quotes Saint Bernard of Clairvaux's use of four words to define God: "What is God? He is length, width, height and depth."[7] As Winter sees it, New York City residents live in a world of endless cubes (buildings), rectangles (walls, ceilings, floors), lines, and numbers. "I wake up in a cubistic bed, prepare to leave in cubistic rooms, walk to my studio on carefully measured planes of concrete, walk through rectangular doors to a cubistic elevator, ride up to the twelfth level of a cliff in my private cube, where I paint on a rectangular surface." For Winter, the New York City paintings are like "prayers of praise" to his daily physical world.

Winter's beautifully crafted *Looking North from the Whitney Museum* (2017) forges a compelling balance of harmonic and bold hues of yellow, black, peach, and gray. Border to border, content to content, element to element, the geometrized syncopation can evoke the romantic panoramic sweep of a George Gershwin score. On a visit to

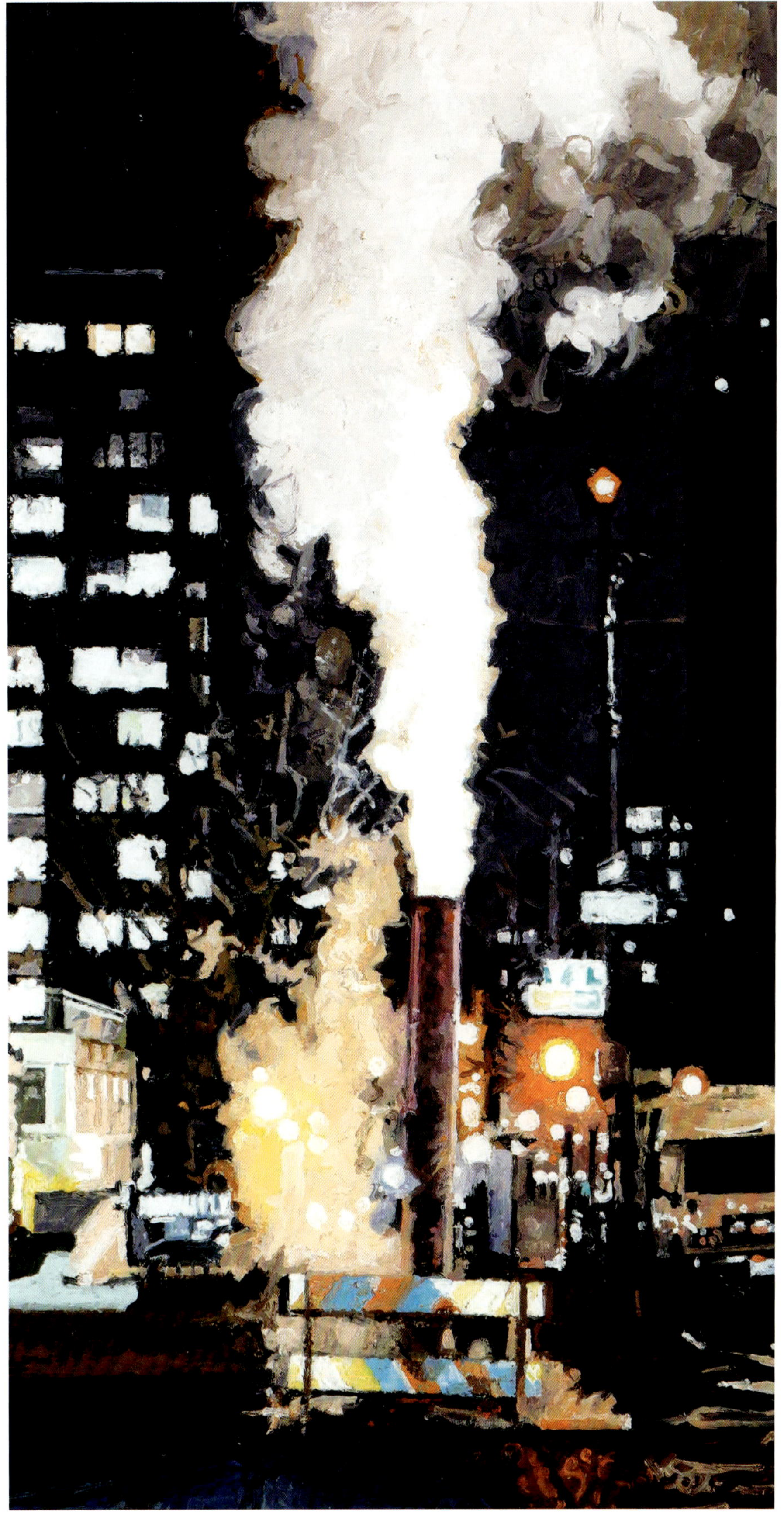

Steam, 2015

oil on linen | 30" × 15" | Collection of Molly E. Moore | Photography by Kevin Todora

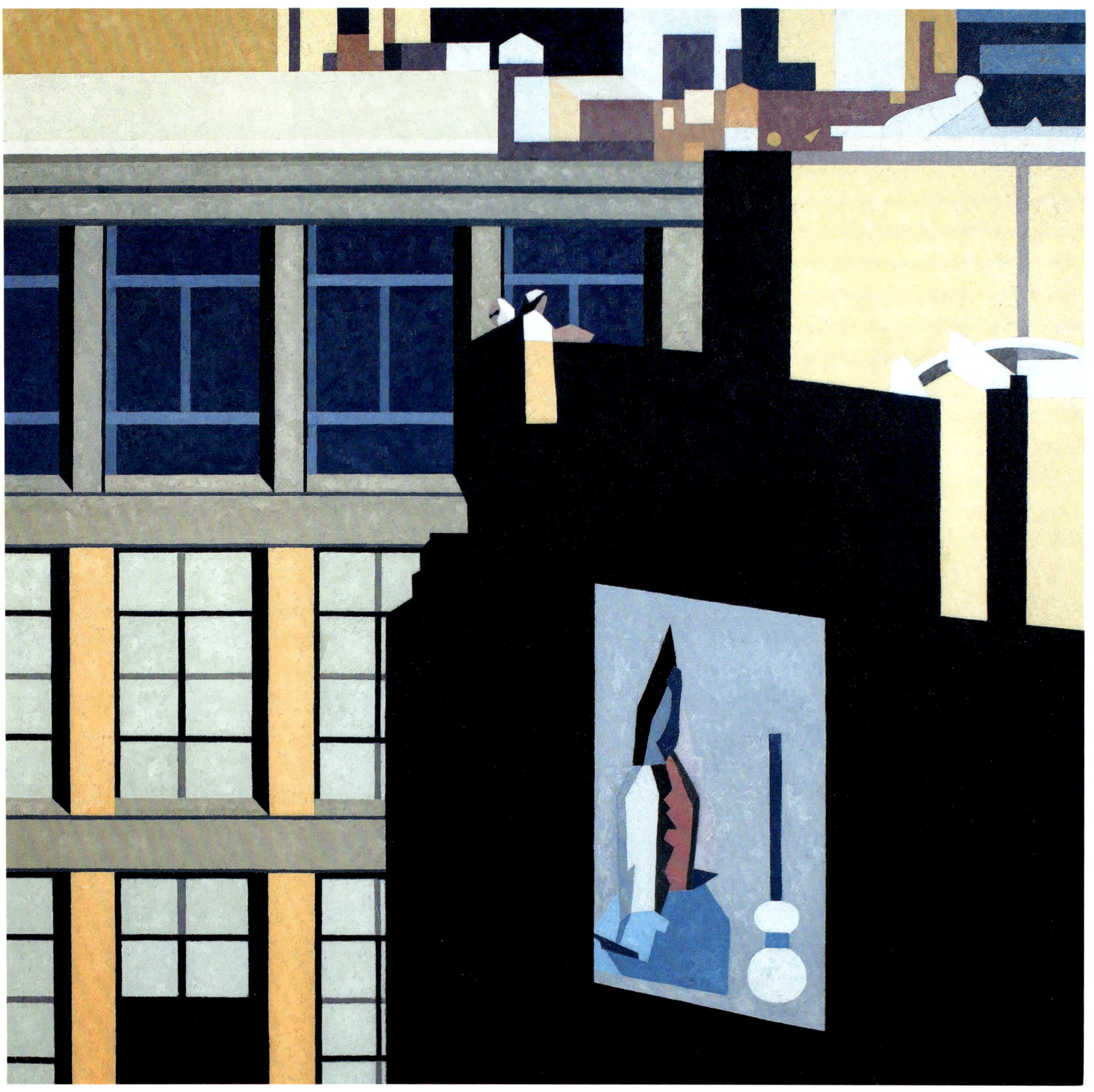

Looking North from the Whitney Museum, 2017

oil on linen | 60" × 60" | Courtesy of the artist and Kirk Hopper Fine Art, Dallas

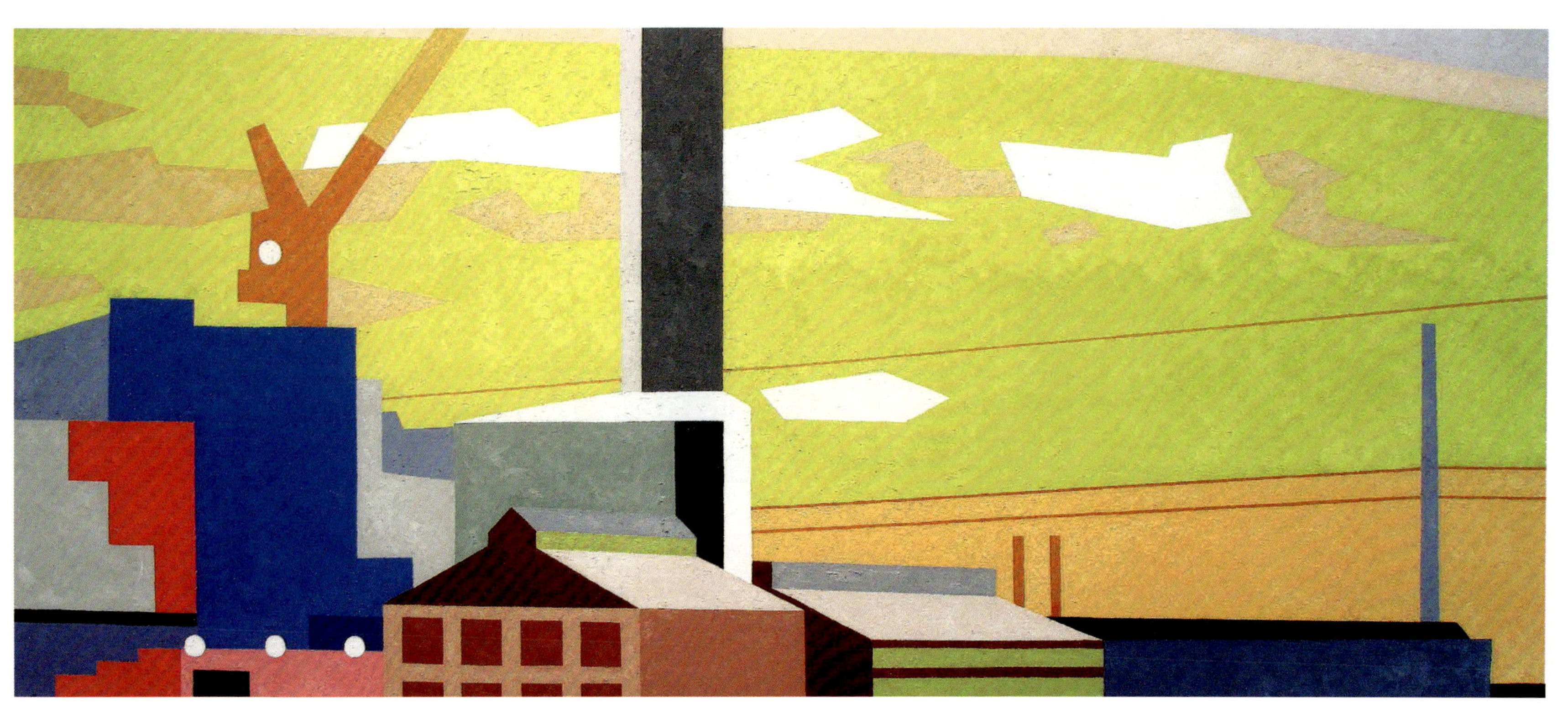

Kearney, New Jersey, 2017

oil on linen | 36" × 84" | Courtesy of the artist and Kirk Hopper Fine Art, Dallas

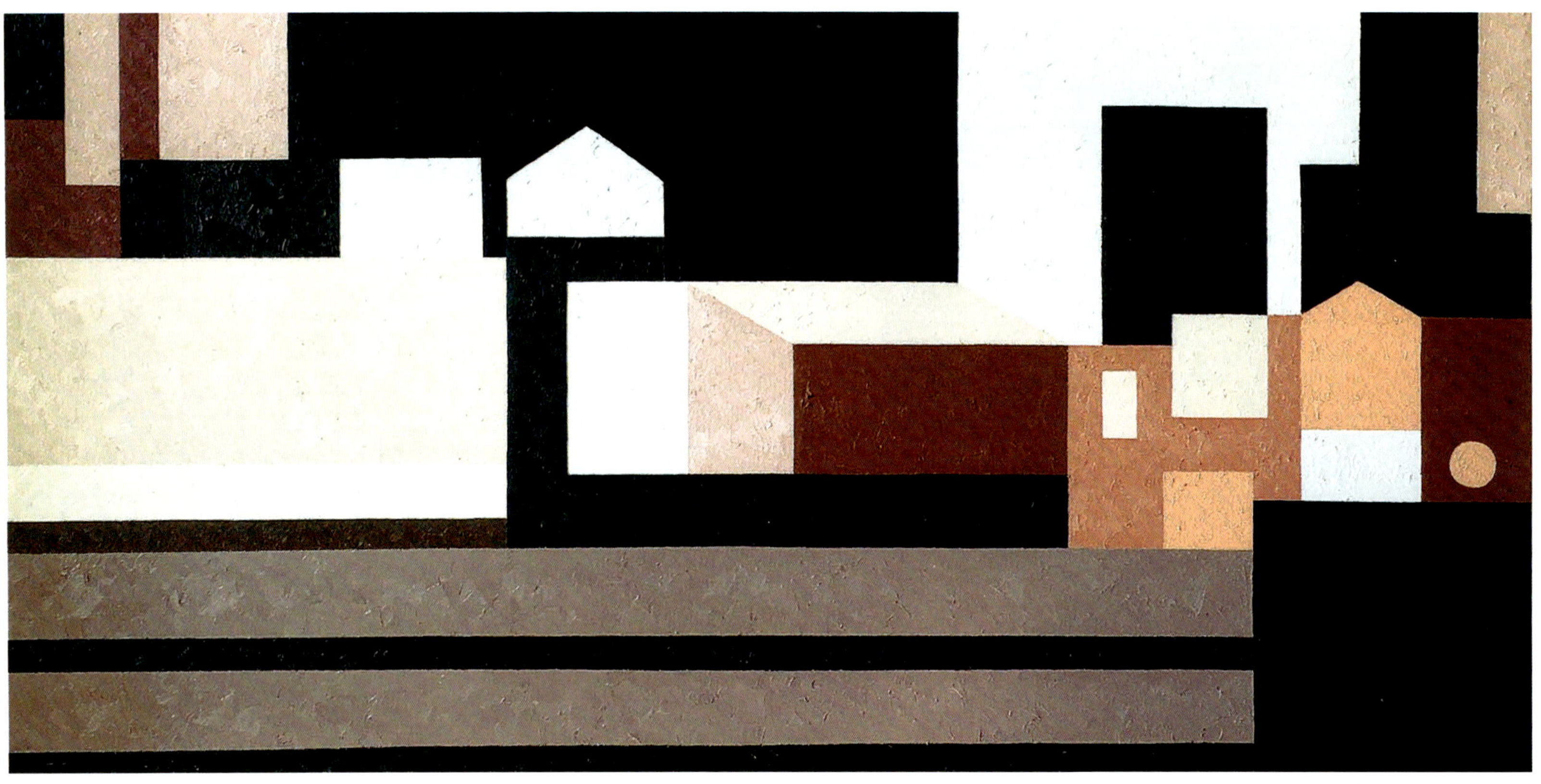

Meat Packing District, 2017

oil on linen | 24" × 48" | Courtesy of the artist and Kirk Hopper Fine Art, Dallas | Photography by G. Valderas

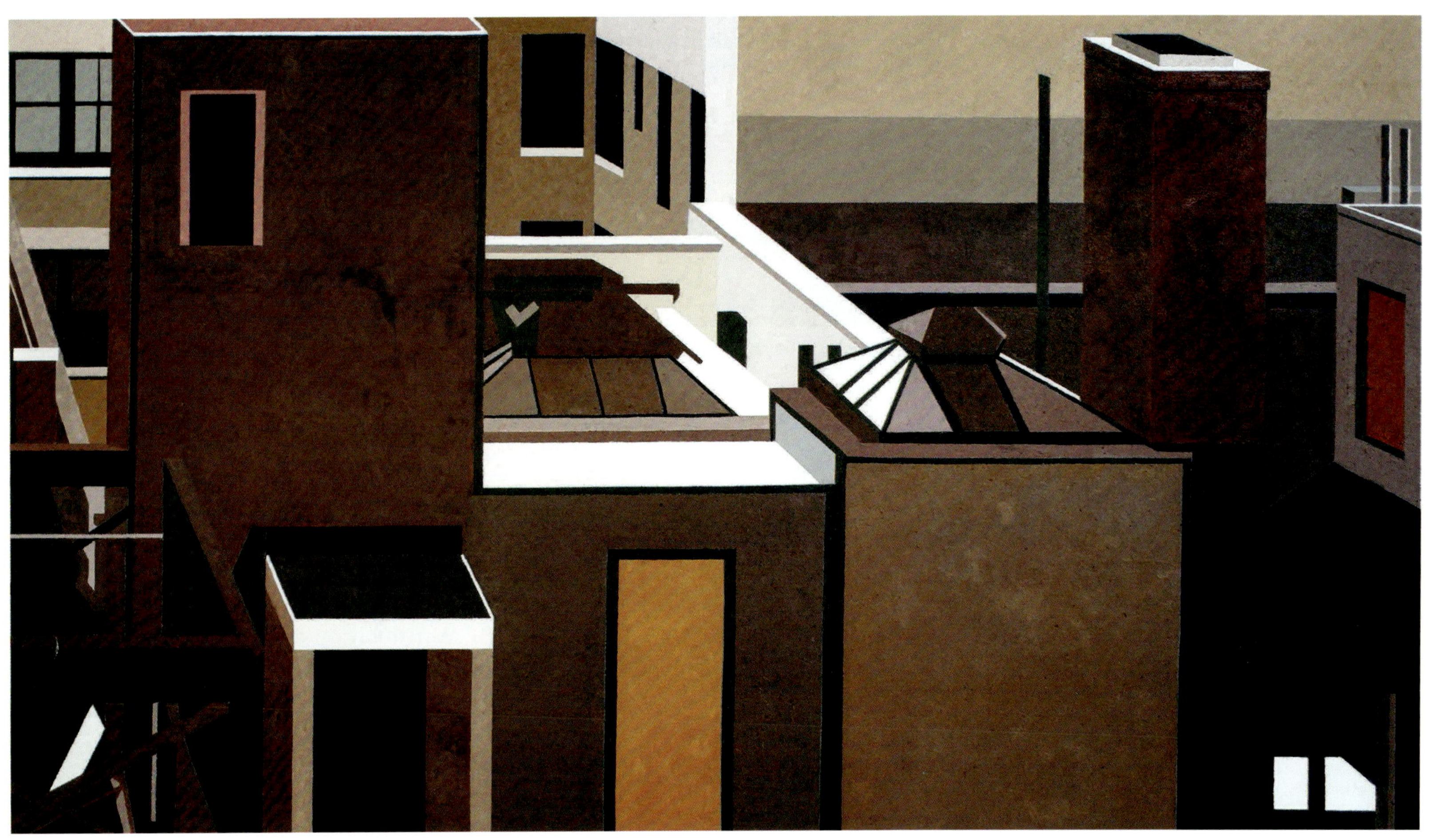

From Joe's Terrace, 2017

oil on linen | 48" × 84" | Courtesy of the artist and Kirk Hopper Fine Art, Dallas | Photography by G. Valderas

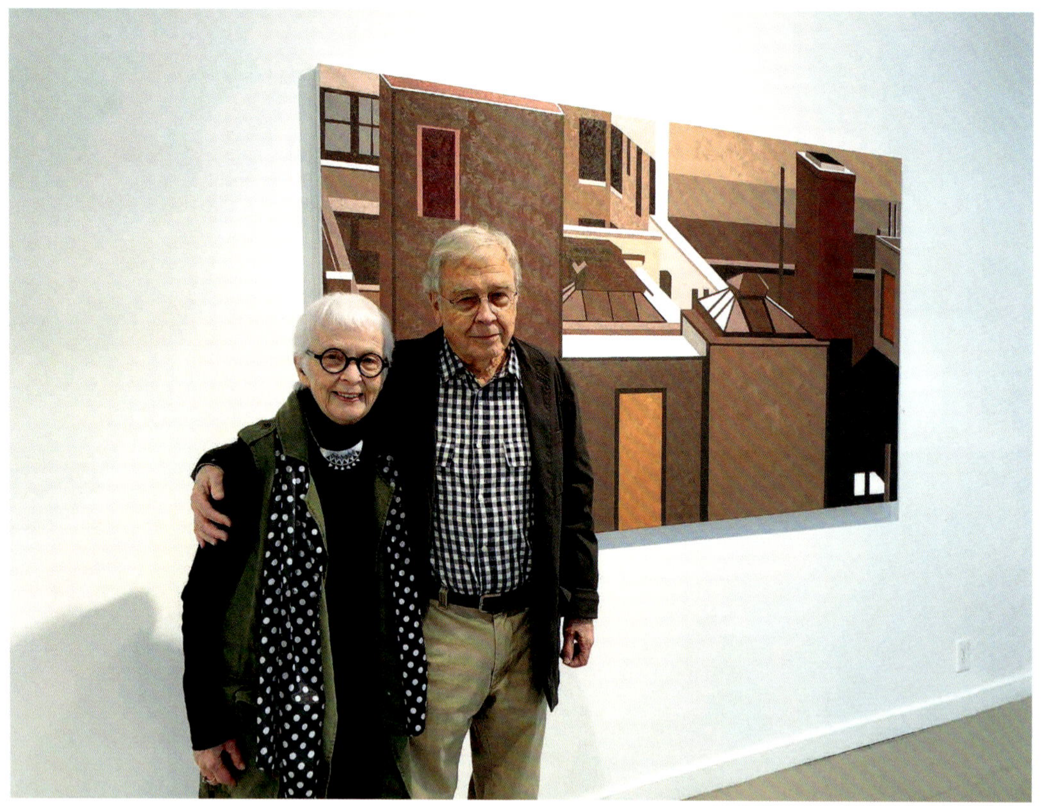

Jeanette and Roger at the Lois Dodd/Roger Winter exhibition opening, Kirk Hopper Fine Art, Dallas, April 2018

the Whitney Museum of American Art, Winter took in the dramatic view of the skyline from an observation balcony. The details on the sides of buildings suggested figures: a man in a hospital bed, a caricature of Jeanette, and a Swedish peasant woman with a loaf of bread. To Winter's eye, the gigantic billboard on the black wall looked like a cubistic figure of a woman sitting near a bong. The entirety is a dynamic interplay of large and small shapes, close-up and distant spaces, and actual and invented details.

In *Kearney, New Jersey* (2017), an orange manufacturing crane at far left balances a black skyscraper and lyrical power lines. Set against a fiery yellow sunset, the geometric forms of blue, pink, and gray are anchored by tangentially joined industrial buildings. For *Meat Packing District* (2017), the distillation of geometry in the crisply painted, acutely placed horizontal and vertical divisions of the composition are counterpointed tellingly by the light and dark holding masses of windows, roofs, and shadows. All of these paintings pursue the challenge of analyzing the city forms as geometrized environments of illusory space, angular shapes, and sharp silhouettes. For the *Construction Site* series (2018), Winter focuses on Manhattan's forgotten corners, mostly places and architectural underpinnings that could pass as inconsequential. He depicts a slice of steel girder or a narrow space behind a parking garage, a shadowy area near a concrete stair step or a doorway to a basement. What attracts Winter's attention? Which geometric shapes or vast Manhattan panoramas catch his eye? It is important to note that, although his forms are relatively hard edged, they are not obsessively labored. For example, he does not use masking tape as a production tool. Winter writes,

> If I stop to look at something for a few seconds, I take a picture of it, sometimes several pictures from different angles. It's usually, but not always, a subject I'm

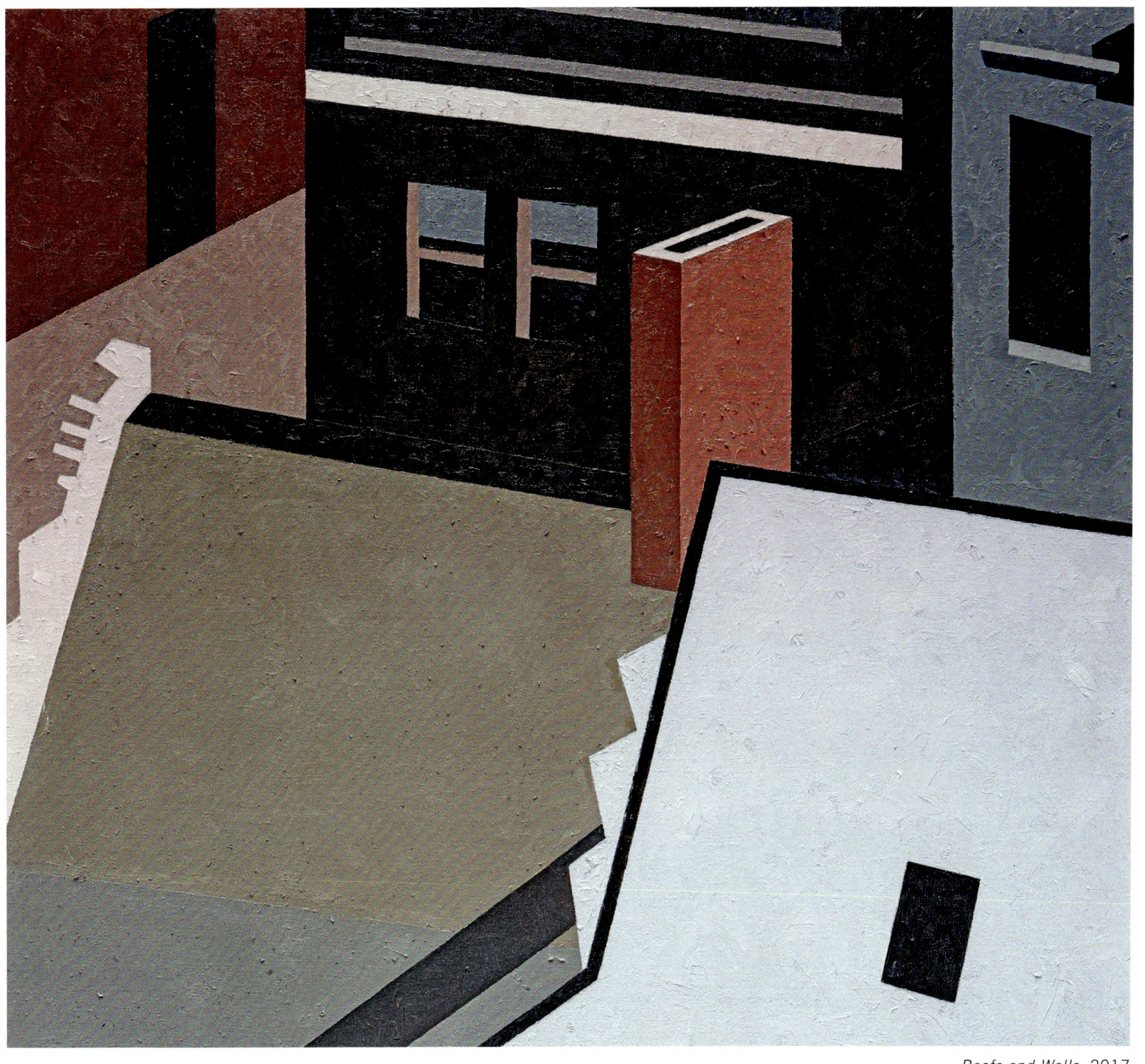

Roofs and Walls, 2017

oil on linen | 38" × 42" | Courtesy of the artist and Kirk Hopper Fine Art, Dallas | Photography by G. Valderas

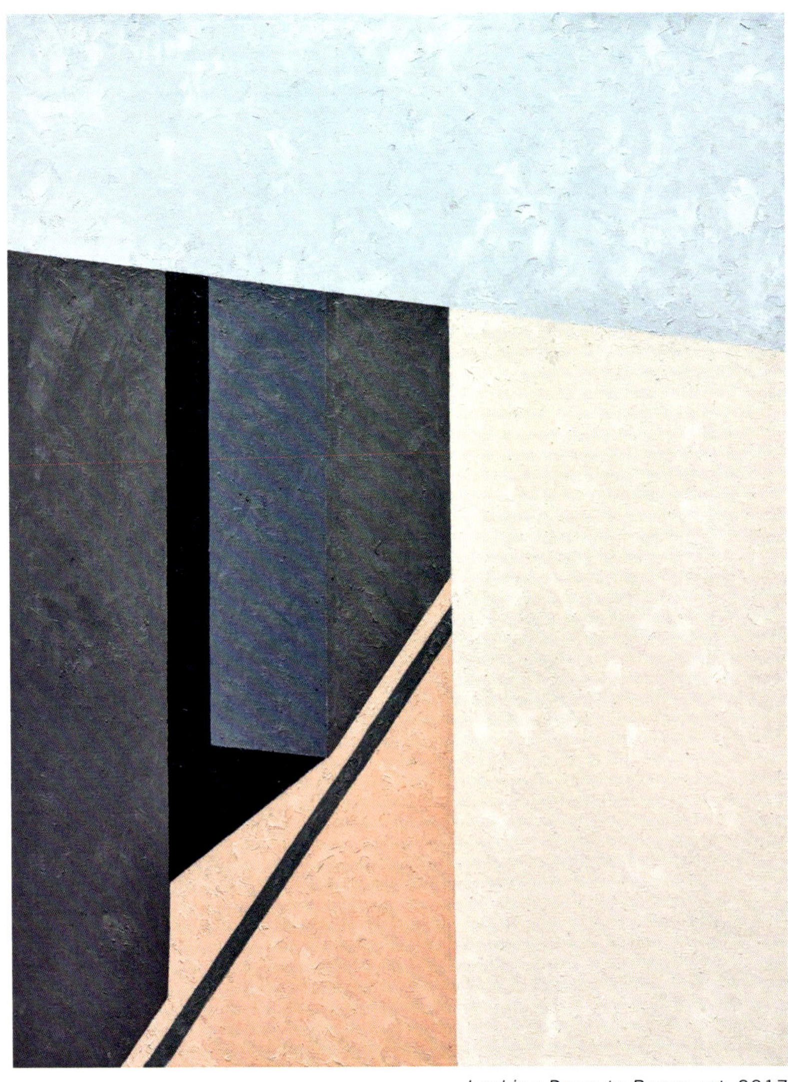

Looking Down to Basement, 2017

oil on linen | 20" × 14" | Courtesy of the artist and Kirk Hopper Fine Art, Dallas

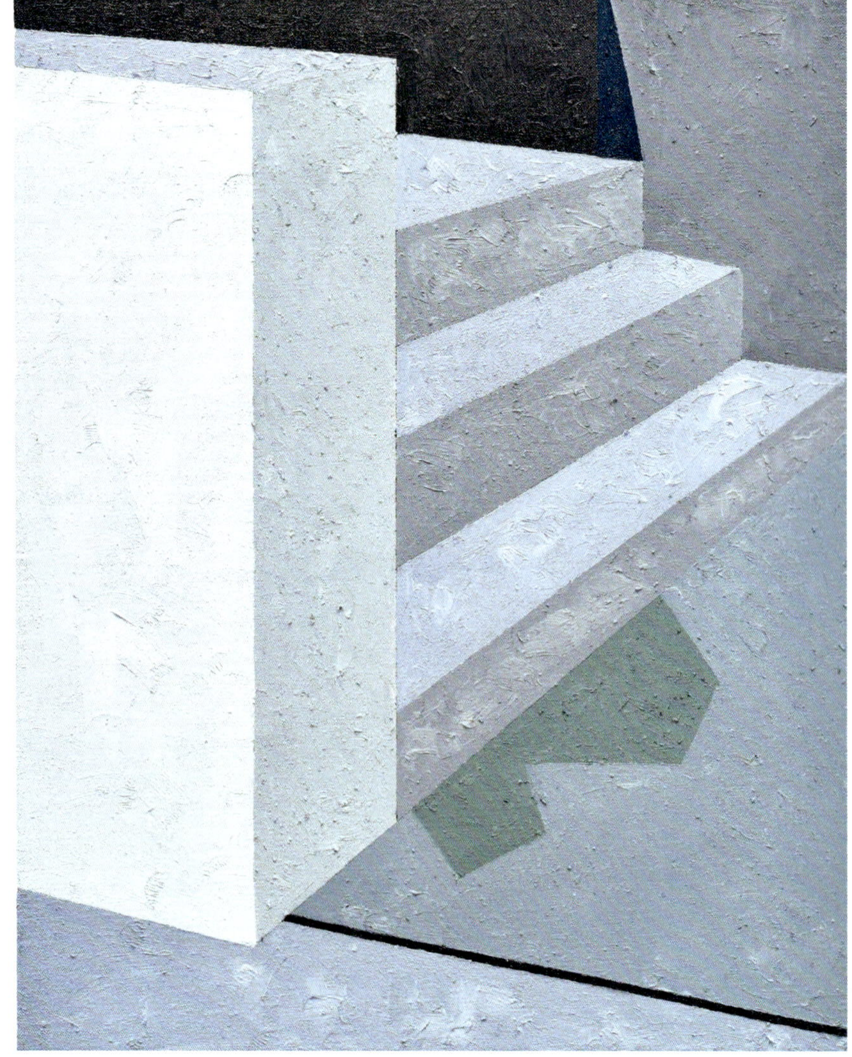

Steps, 2017

oil on linen | 16" × 14" | Courtesy of the artist and Kirk Hopper Fine Art, Dallas | Photography by G. Valderas

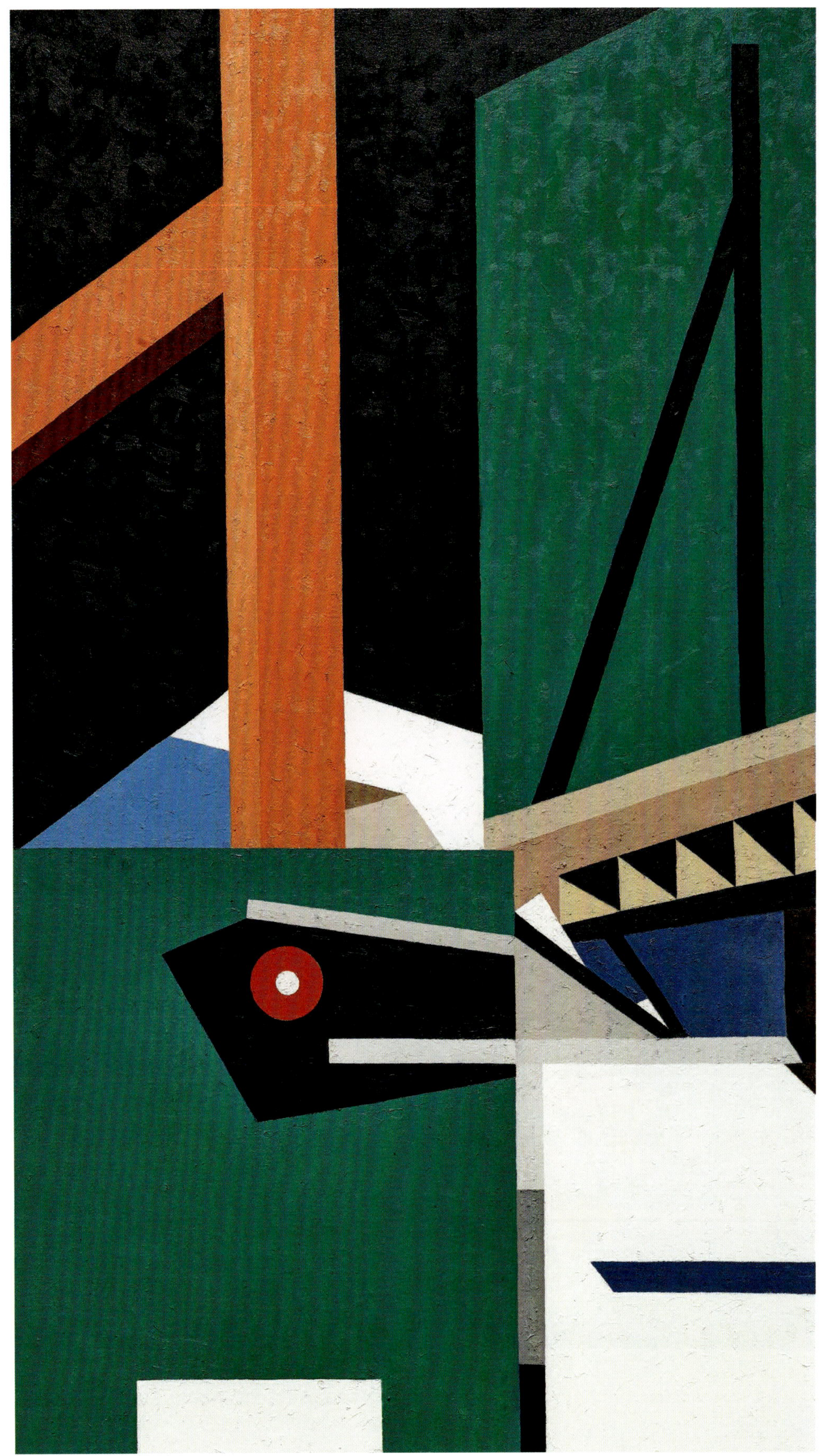

Construction Site #5, 2018

oil on linen | 72" × 40" | Courtesy of the artist and Kirk Hopper Fine Art, Dallas |

Photography by G. Valderas

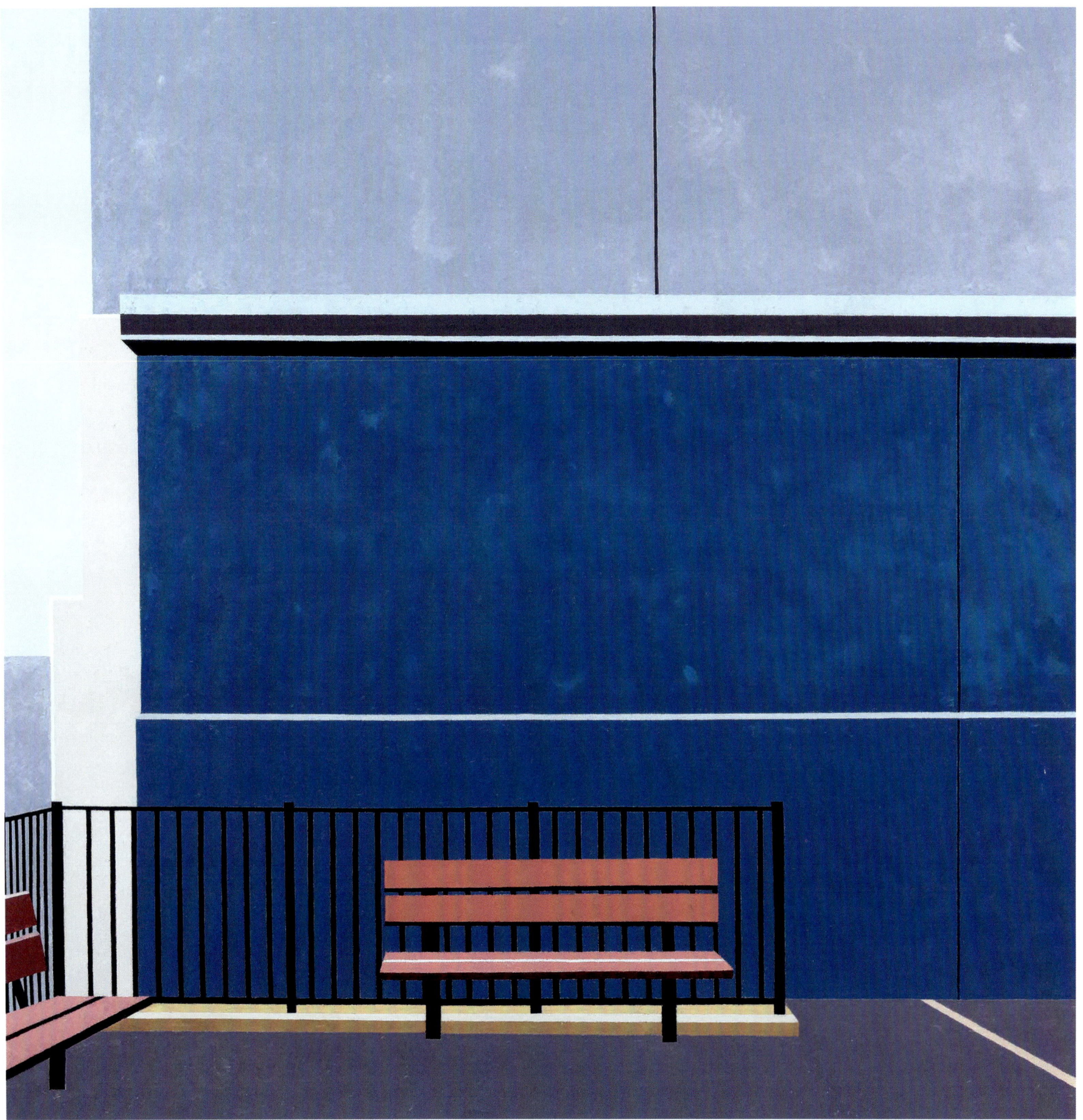

PS 93, 2018

oil on linen | 72" × 72" | Courtesy of the artist and Kirk Hopper Fine Art, Dallas | Photography by Joshua Nefsky

> infatuated with at a given time. When I import images, I select only those that have an inkling of promise in them as form and content. As time goes on, when an image starts to look especially interesting to me, I will edit it on Iphone. Then I start mixing colors that were distant cousins to the color-edited photo. Questions I ask the source: Is it too predictable? Do I connect emotionally with the image? Shall I make any radical changes in colors or values? That question is normally asked during the process of painting, from top to bottom. Does it have a suitable amount of newness and shock so it isn't imitating myself? Knowingly imitating oneself is number one on my list of deadly sins.[8]

Winter's fragments of building sites and construction zones are usually overlooked but become images filtered by perception and structured by time and memory. Indeed, to recognize a pattern, meaning, and an order in the world that Winter did not quite see before is exhilarating, even exalting. Throughout, there is a sense that small details have been greatly enlarged, imparting paradoxical sensations of familiarity and strangeness, intimacy and expansiveness. By cultivating forces that create friction, ambiguity, and fluctuation, Winter infuses his art with unusual metaphorical power. The structure of poetics and vision merges into a sense of wonder but is not immune to the changes affecting his environment. Winter's New York City and *Construction Site* paintings are as much excursions into new formal territory as they are probings of an intense emotional tenor. They set us teetering on the fulcrum between material and illusory worlds. The ultimate content of these works is an open-ended space of metaphysical and mystical ponderings.

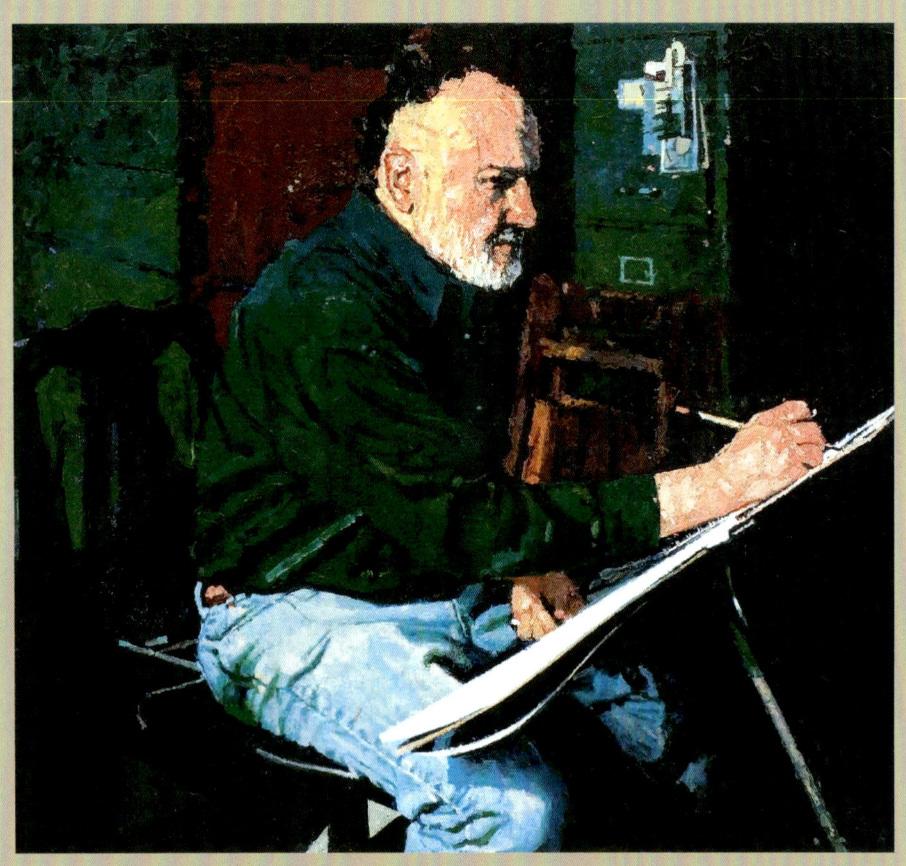

Robert Birmelin Drawing from Life, 2008
oil on linen | 20" × 24" | Collection of Molly E. Moore

CHAPTER 15
PORTRAITS

THROUGHOUT THE DECADES, Winter's psychically charged images have aimed to capture the specific tenor of transitory moments. In doing so, they are suffused with a kind of unrequited desire and, beyond that, a sense that the events of our lives—random and incomprehensible as they generally seem—have a shape and direction of their own and are seeking to show us something, lead us somewhere. Accordingly, Winter's contemplative subjects force us to look back to where we have come from, if only to surmise where we may be going. Nowhere is this more evident than in the scores of portraits Winter has produced over a lifetime. Whereas his sitters serve as keys to open reservoirs of memory and feeling, they resonate with a puzzling intangibility that is as haunting as it is difficult to pin down. Winter sees deep into his subject, absorbs it, and discovers in it new things that were not on the surface in order to get at the essential character, the person, which is always more than an inventory of features.

As a young child, Winter was fascinated by human faces, often replicating in pencil those of his siblings and parents from treasured photographs. "I didn't know the measuring of proportions and values that allowed me to draw faces could be applied to other things," he writes. "I learned when I was eight that I could draw horses and houses. But those subjects were just for me. The portraits were of interest to family and teachers and school mates. And drawing 'the mirror of the soul' was more challenging. It had to look like the person, and it had to look alive."[1] As a teenager and in his early twenties, Winter picked up extra money by drawing from life, usually in pastels, nieces, nephews, and the children of neighbors. Throughout the late 1960s and 1970s, his portraits were of immediate family members, but rendered by a unique intersection of emotional intimacy and process-driven abstraction. In subsequent years, Winter produced "incidental" portraits of people encountered on the streets of Manhattan, as well as memory portraits of Maine men and New York subway riders. He has drawn, collaged, and painted imaginary people, in addition to introspective paintings of several close friends. For at least four decades, however, he has received commissions to paint portraits of students, as well as children

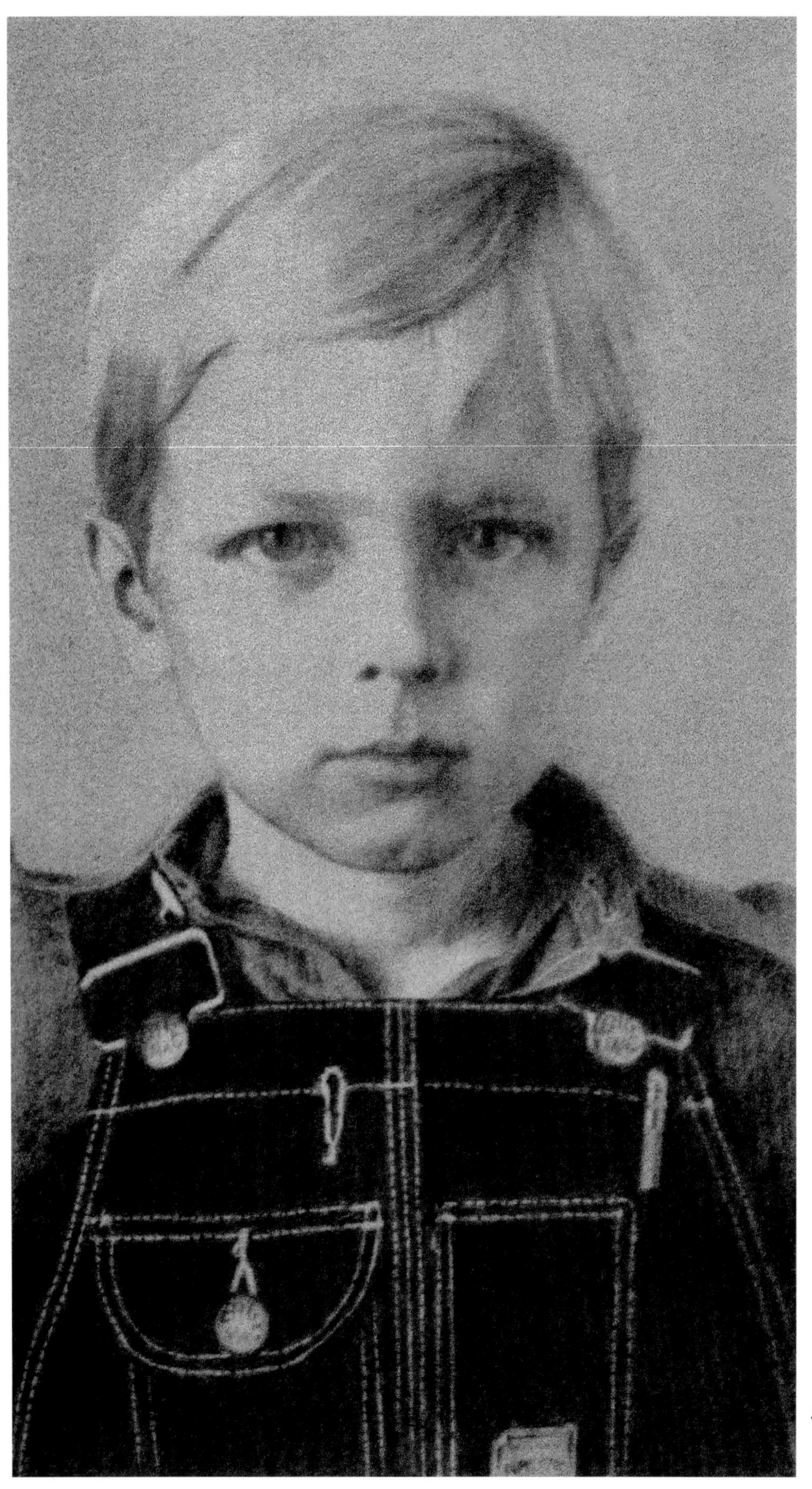

Self-Portrait as a Six-Year-Old, 1969
pencil on paper | 10" × 6" |
Collection of the artist

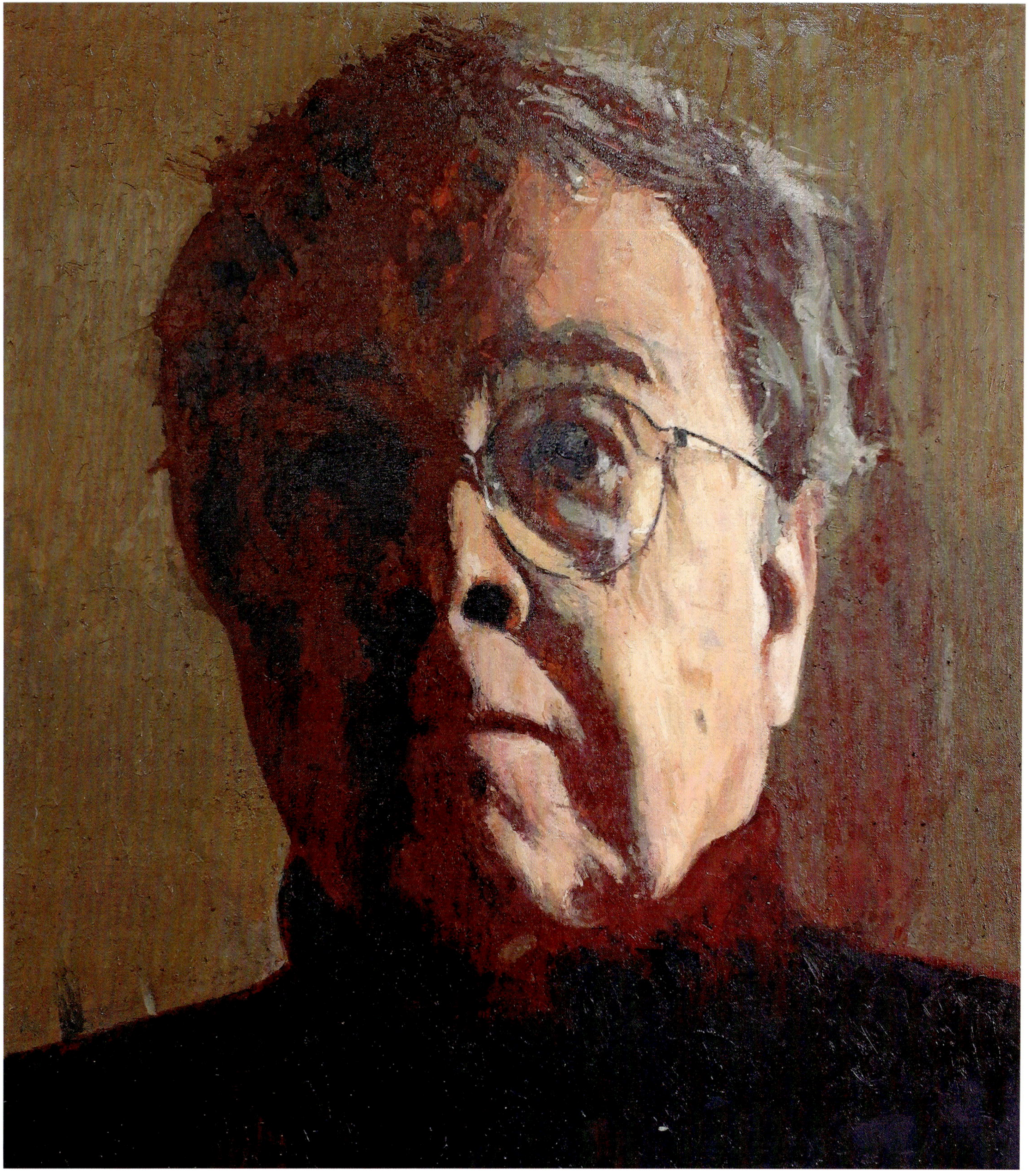

Self-Portrait, 2013

oil on linen | 38" × 32" | Courtesy of the artist and Kirk Hopper Fine Art, Dallas | Photography by Joshua Nefsky

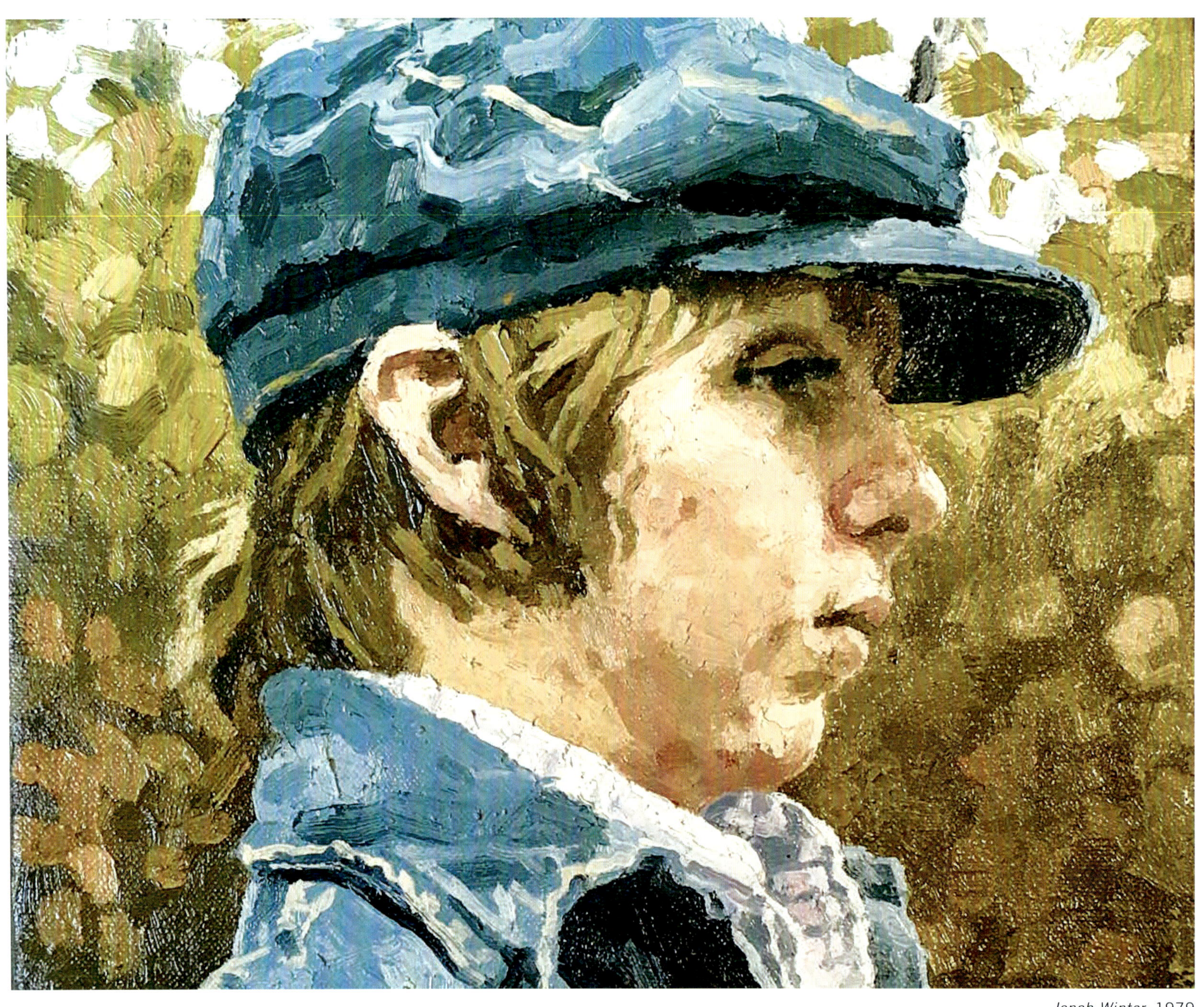

Jonah Winter, 1979
oil on linen | 8" × 10" | Collection of the artist

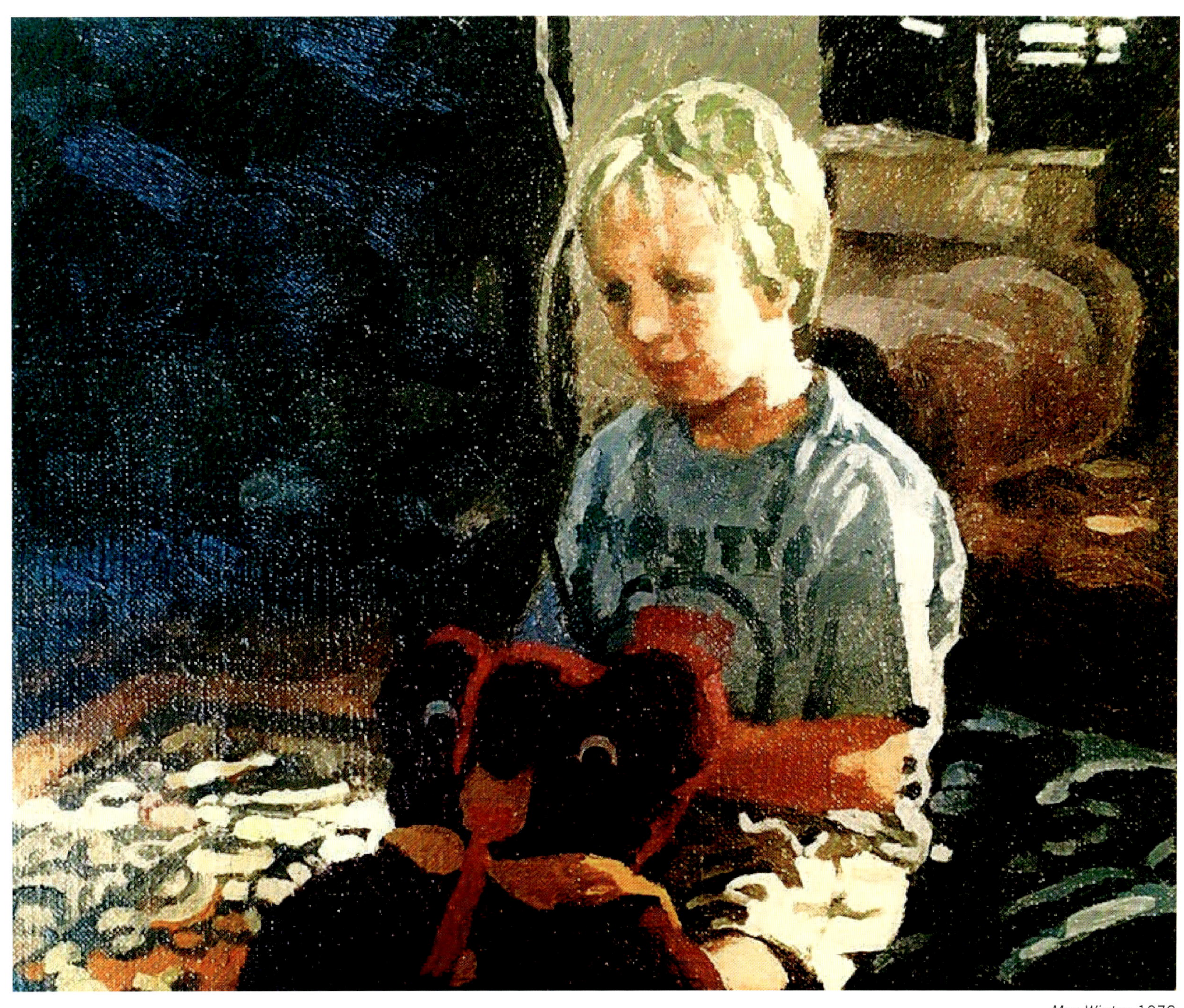

Max Winter, 1978

oil on linen | 9" × 11" | Collection of the artist

of former students and prominent collectors. The commissioned works set forth a responsibility and an intense challenge that he had not experienced with other approaches to portraiture. All told, Winter revels in the individuality of the sitters, often accentuating aspects of their features to produce intense character studies. More often than not, he renders age and likeness with forthright candor, never sentimentalizing, never minimizing. He does not flatter his subjects, but he rarely portrays them as less than complete, complex human beings, regardless of age or class. All of them are re-created in paint on canvas with uncommon fervency. Such concentrated power has to do not only with their iconic centrality but also with their uncannily harsh or diffused light, which elucidates the volume of his sitters while at the same time giving them an almost magical glow and isolation. Fixed for eternity but time bound in their hairstyles, smooth flesh, or casual clothing, they confront us, spellbound. Familiar in homely detail, Winter's figures are nonetheless unfamiliar in penetrating stillness and unsettling clarity.

Taken together, these images remind us that the processes of growth, maturity, and decay are part of the terms of an organic life cycle. But growing up and old is not only a process rooted in our biological existence; it is also an experience, an incalculable series of events, moments, and acts lived by an individual. This experience, this path through the maze of inner life, composes our journey.

A great portrait is a likeness of an individual that takes on universal meaning. Moreover, it can capture a moment of life's passage, recording a particular subject at a revealing time. The tension in a portrait between the specific and the generic often creates a kind of narrative in which we try to unravel the history of a subject's life, even comparing it with recollections of our own. The gulf between even the most faithful record of a face and figure and a truly great portrait is immense. One is factual and descriptive; the other is certainly this, too, but conveys infinitely deeper understanding and insight. A great portrait results from a fusion of human understanding on the part of the artist—that is, of deeply sensitive responses to the character, outward behavior, and physical features of an individual—and the ability to express those responses with all the reverberations of which imagery, design, color, and texture are capable. Such a portrait, which makes an immediate impact but yields gradually to formal analysis, transmits the very essence of personality. Looking at a portrait, we are allowed to get as close as possible and stare as long as we like—an opportunity rarely offered in everyday life. Winter's commissioned portraits reaffirm that no one sees with a keener eye.

Being human, being in the world, is to be constantly making our place in language, in consciousness, in imagination. To that end, a few of his portraits are strange and subtle works, full of calm, like light circulating in water. At times, his subjects become a charged field of their own energy, and when they meet, they give off brilliant sparks. The beauty of memory lies in its capacity for rendering detail, for paying homage to the senses and the richness of our existence. But time dilutes and corrodes until there is nothing left to tell. Whatever is remembered is what becomes a reality. The portrait is a way to keep Winter's subjects alive in memory even as it blends issues of public and private, the confrontational and the voyeuristic. Thus, the compelling resonance of his art is conveyed in large part through an evidence of hand that inflects the figure with an equivalent of tenderness and tact.

Again, underlined or starred passages in Maurice Grosser's 1956 *The Painter's Eye*, which Winter has kept since his student days at the University of Texas, give us clues as to his own thoughts on portraiture: "The portrait is the most trying on the nerves and the least certain of success of any work a painter can undertake."[2] And this: "Whatever form the disagreement between the sitter and the painter may be, it is always about the likeness—which soul, which interior life, of all the various interior lives the sitter may possess, shall be ascribed to him; which one of the various aspects of the sitter's soul the portrait shall be made to represent."[3]

What Grosser refers to, as Winter so obviously gleaned from the writings, is the holding up of a mirror to life, pouring in energy from both sides—the sitter's and the artist's. "I've always known since I was a little child, when I've captured a person—the thing that makes you recognize them on the street," Winter says. "Mauricio Lasansky, my professor at the University of Iowa, once told me that a portrait should look like someone looks all their life—not just a certain age, but something of how they look at five years old and at fifty years old—the same essence." With this in mind, Winter aims to portray his subjects the old-fashioned way: grasp the physical features and fathom the entire character. In doing so, he grapples with the enigma of the human face and the meaning of portraying it as truthfully as possible. But does a realistic portrait express character in the first place, or is it a tour de force of painterly skills? Does the artist need to have the anatomy of bone structure at his fingertips, or can he mainly focus on the sitter's gaze? A genre as classic as realistic portraiture requires the skill to deftly balance expression and emotion, as well as painterly accuracy and intensity. But what is it that makes a portrait so arresting?

Our ability to take in at a glance how a sitter has been depicted and why relies on the subtleties of the portrait's identity as determined by Winter's gaze and that of the figure—perceptive, fixing gazes, which are loaded with psychological and symbolic entanglements. Accordingly, his choices and strategies often determine our reception and understanding of his subject. Winter begins the portrait process by spending time with the subject and taking dozens of photographs, which he "broods over" for days. If necessary, he will take additional groups of photographs until he sees something characteristic of the person that relates to his painting approach and is in an appropriate setting. Everything—the form, the surface, the person—must be of a unified piece.

Presented in close-up, their profiles pushed right against the picture plane and on a gentle landscape, the dual portraits of the Shiels sisters (1980) evoke the uncanny verisimilitude and quiet dignity of fifteenth-century Netherlandish paintings. "The Shiels twins—Susan and Sally—were my students at SMU [Southern Methodist University], and I was already fascinated by their differences before they asked me to paint them as a gift for their parents' anniversary," Winter says. "Susan was the 'older' of the two, and she was less outgoing and less quick to do things, like going to school outside of Dallas, or getting married. I, like everyone, admired them for their intelligence, talent and amiable manners. I wanted to paint them facing each other with a University Park background. Susan wanted to close her eyes, but Sally told her, 'Open your eyes!' That they were my students certainly gave me an incentive."[4] As a result, Winter was able to convey the twins' extraordinary poise and beauty—a strange amalgam of fragility and maturity, of dreamy sensitivity and focused comprehension.

Conversely, painting children presents a more difficult task. Children can move too much, their eyes are relatively large, their skin unblemished. What's more, avoiding cliché and sentiment in portraits of children is comparable to trying to uncutely depict a warm puppy. Yet Winter's portraits capture the precious dignity of childhood and, at times, reveal a consciousness of the burdens of onrushing adulthood. For the most part, however, they appear at ease or caught midaction; their postures look awkward and accurate. He depicts the four Kutner children (1981) with charm and vivacity. Their poses and expressions suggest that they already possess a level of daring spirit and self-confidence. Similarly, Winter's portraits of the four Crain children (1994) are wonderfully lively and sympathetic. We sense that he identified with and was inspired by the incompletely socialized energies of the children. Winter depicts one of the boys standing barefoot, with spread legs, against a wall, wearing denim shorts and a striped T-shirt rendered with meticulous brushstrokes of blues and greens. He holds his arms behind him, a gesture by which he seems to be trying to contain his own explosive impetuousness. His half sister, however, stands stiffly erect and confronts her viewers with a riveting gaze. The dramatic contrast between her cartoony T-shirt of rabbits, carrots, and stars and the white wall against which she poses augments the sense of her unnerving mystery and contained energy, thereby encouraging us to react to her as a distinct personality.

Winter's portrait of Patrick Willis (1992) suggests that to catch sight of a child requires a

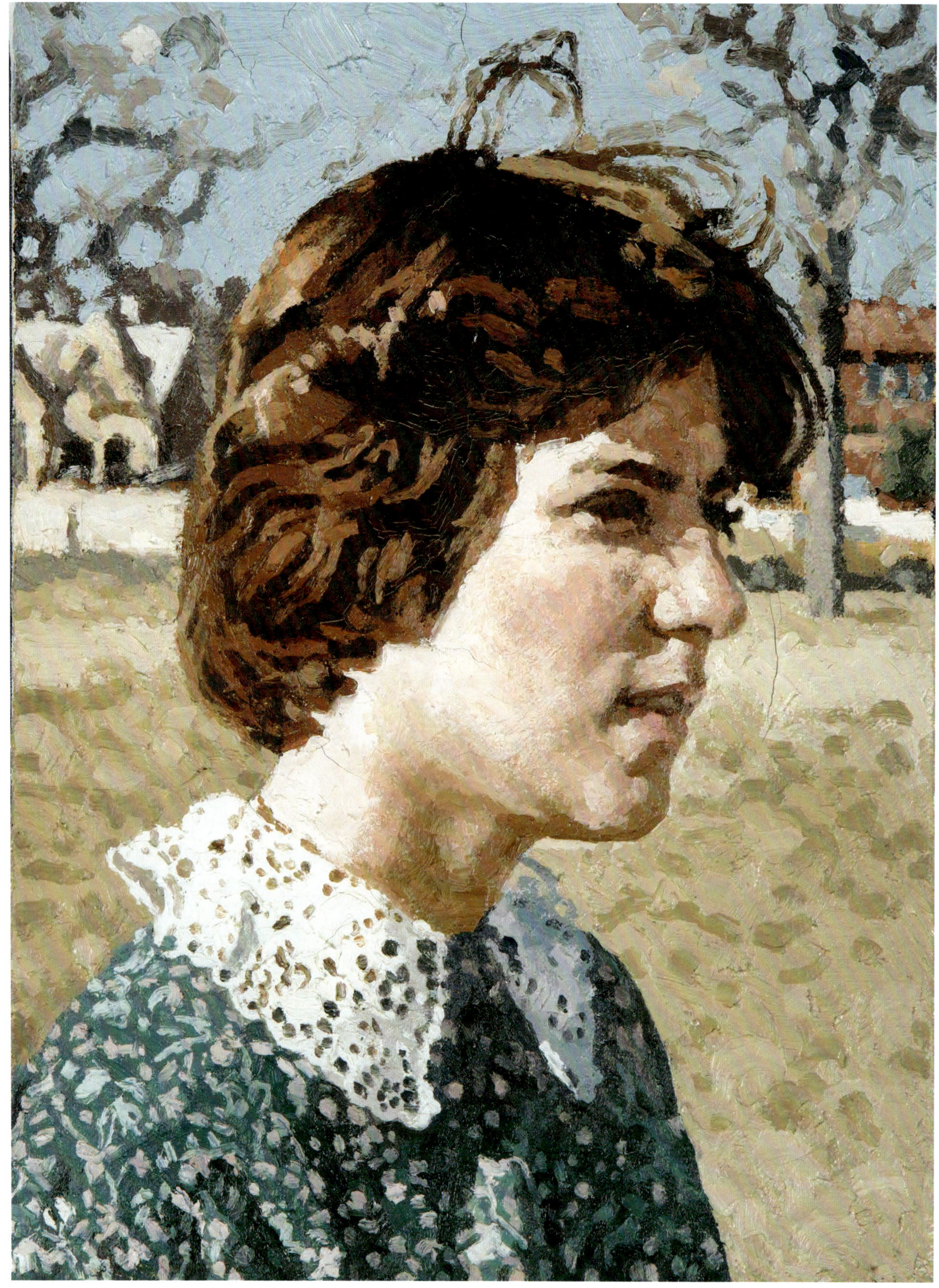

Sally Shiels, 1980

oil on linen | 12" × 9" | Collection of Rob and Betty Shiels | Photography by Rob Wythe

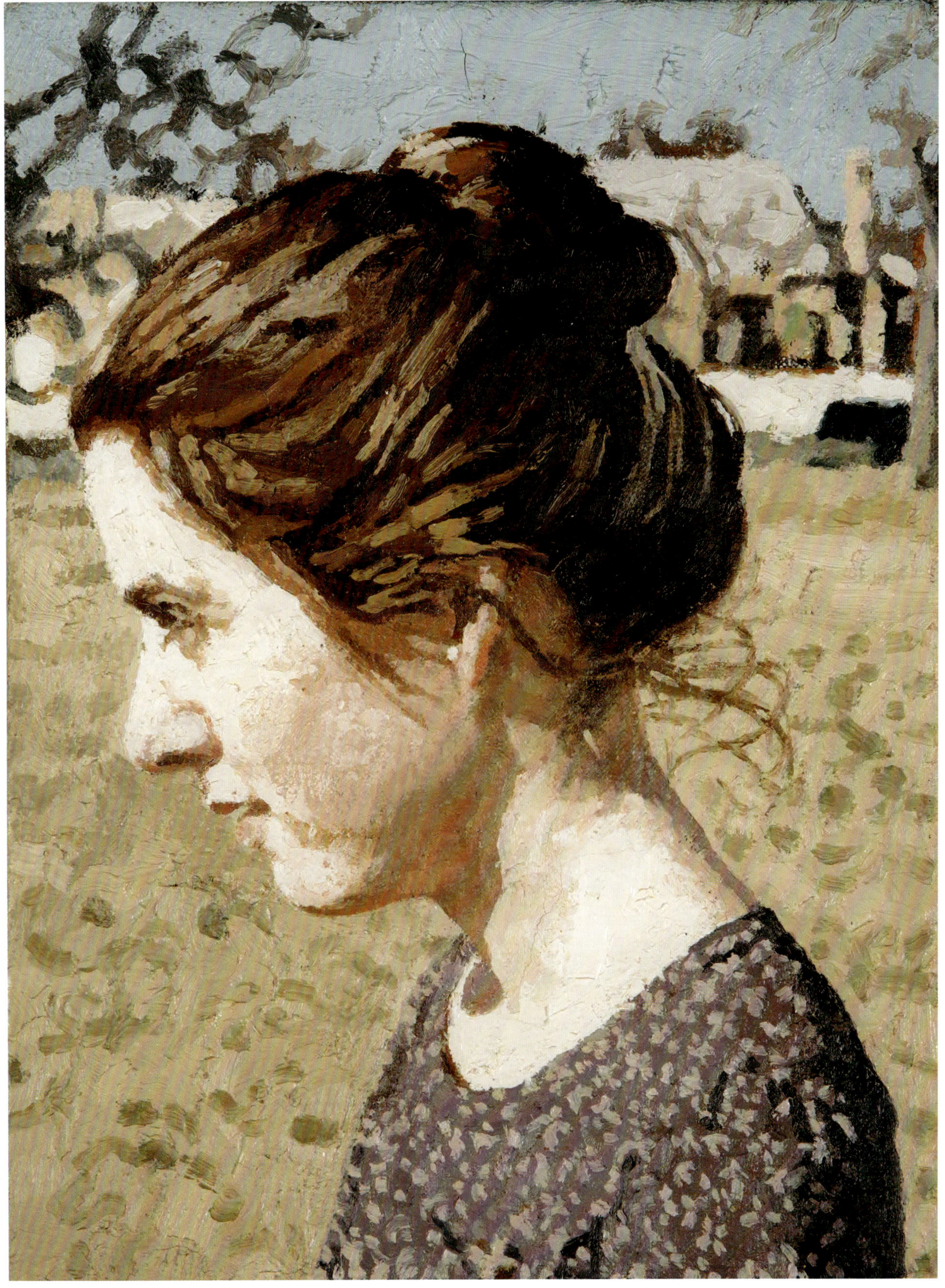

Susan Shiels, 1980

oil on linen | 12" × 9" | Collection of Rob and Betty Shiels | Photography by Rob Wythe

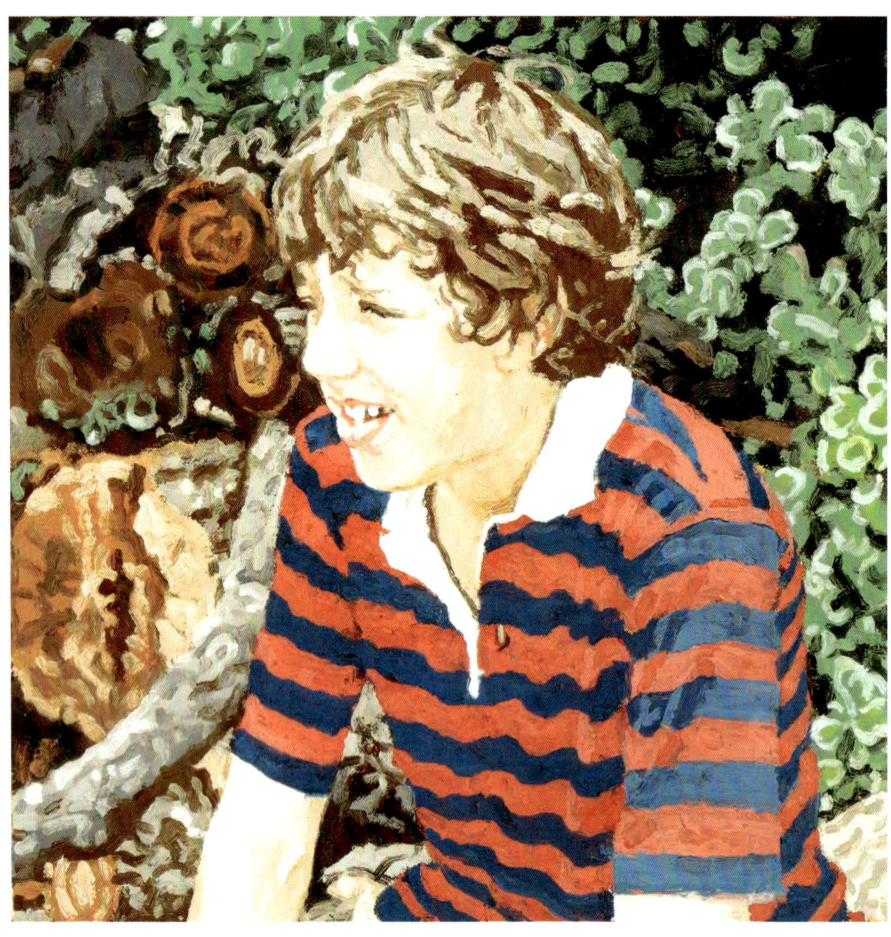

Jonathan Kutner, 1981
oil on linen | 12" × 12" | Collection of Janet and Jonathan Kutner | Photography by Kevin Todora

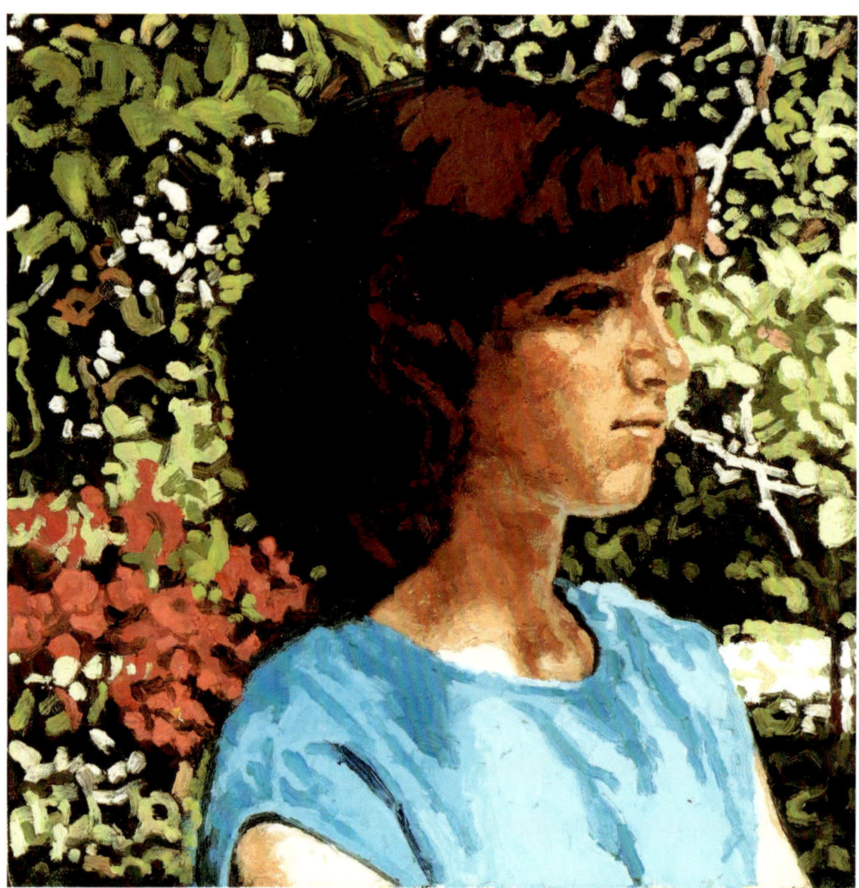

Julie Kutner, 1981
oil on linen | 12" × 12" | Collection of Janet and Jonathan Kutner | Photography by Kevin Todora

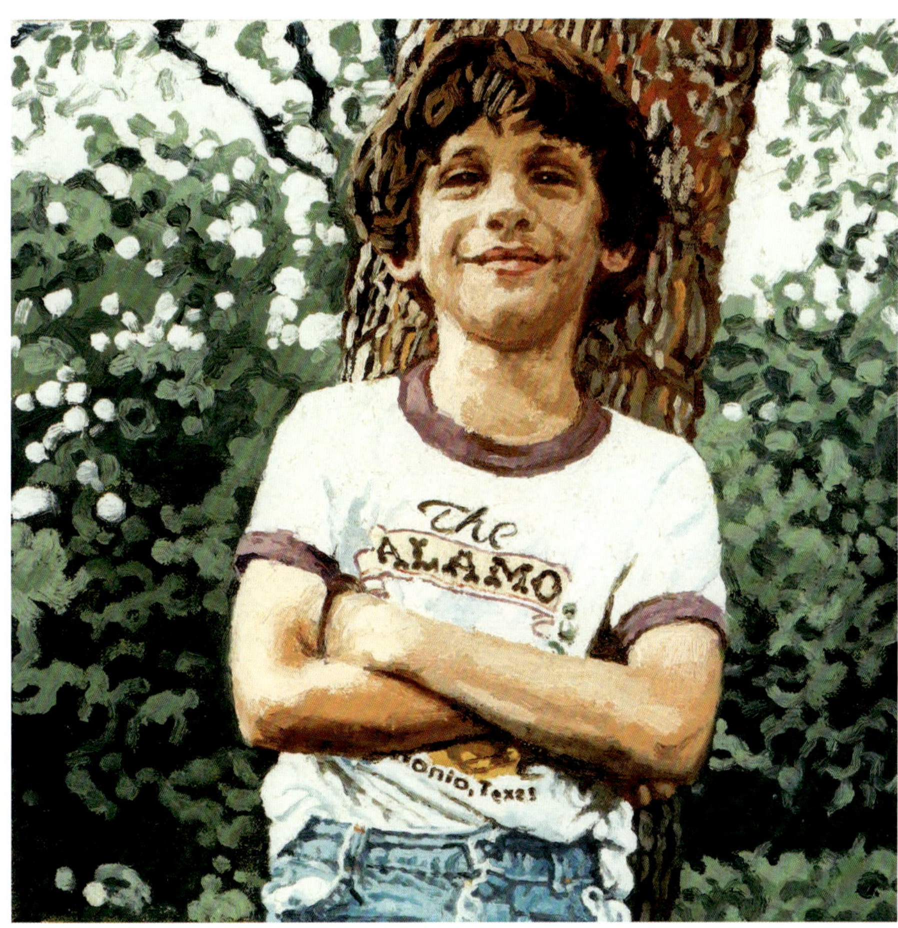

Robert Kutner, 1981
oil on linen | 12" × 12" | Collection of Janet and Jonathan Kutner | Photography by Kevin Todora

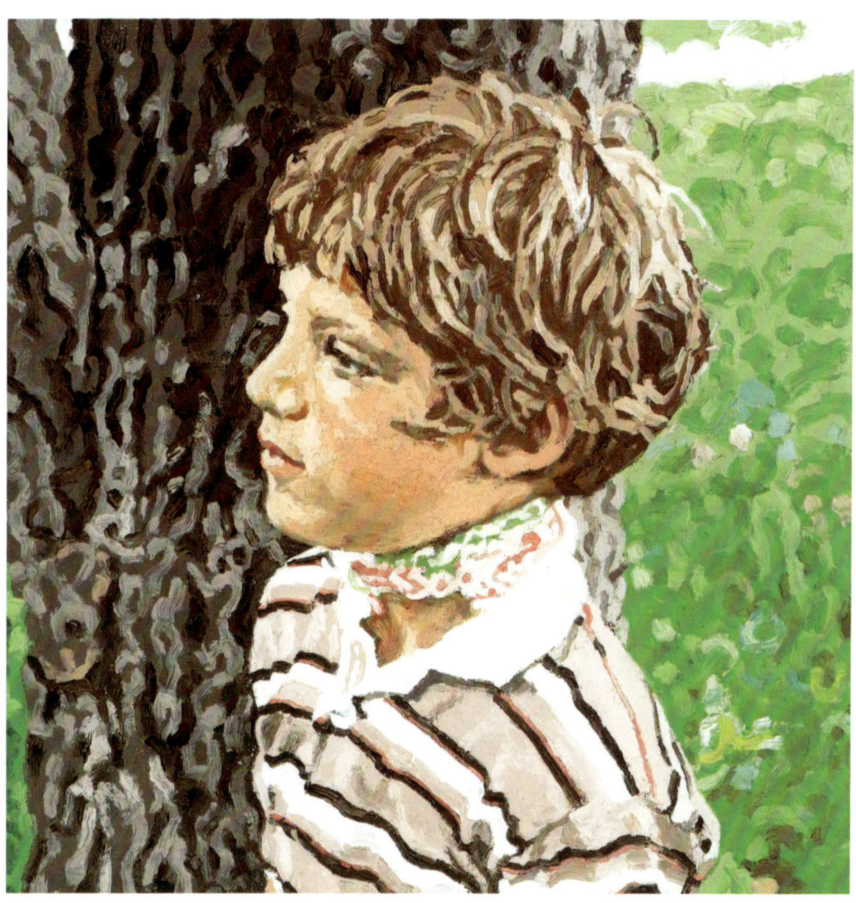

Bryan Kutner, 1981
oil on linen | 12" × 12" | Collection of Janet and Jonathan Kutner | Photography by Kevin Todora

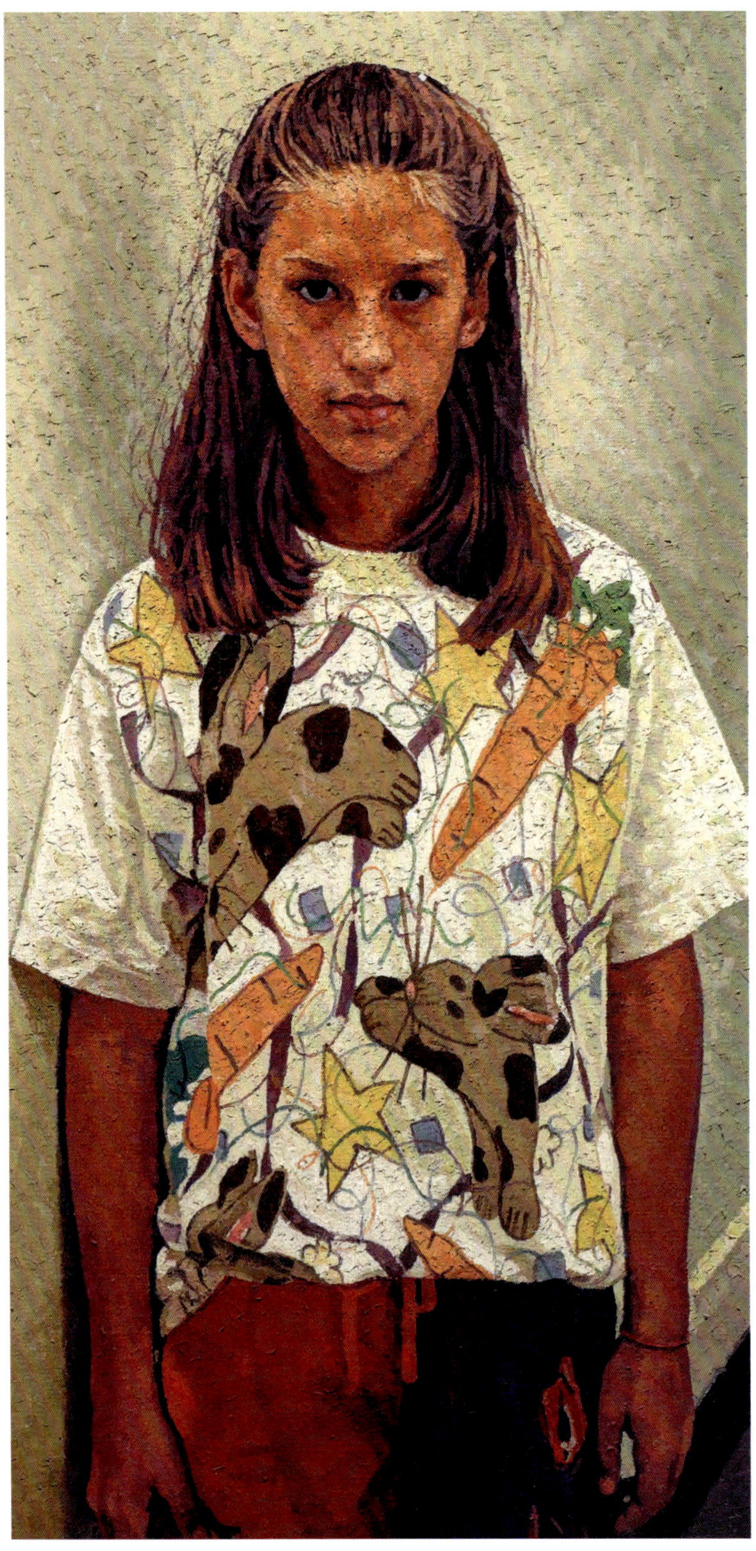

Jane Lynch Crain, 1994
oil on linen | 36" × 18" | Collection of Mary and Walter Crain | Photography by Thomas DuBrock

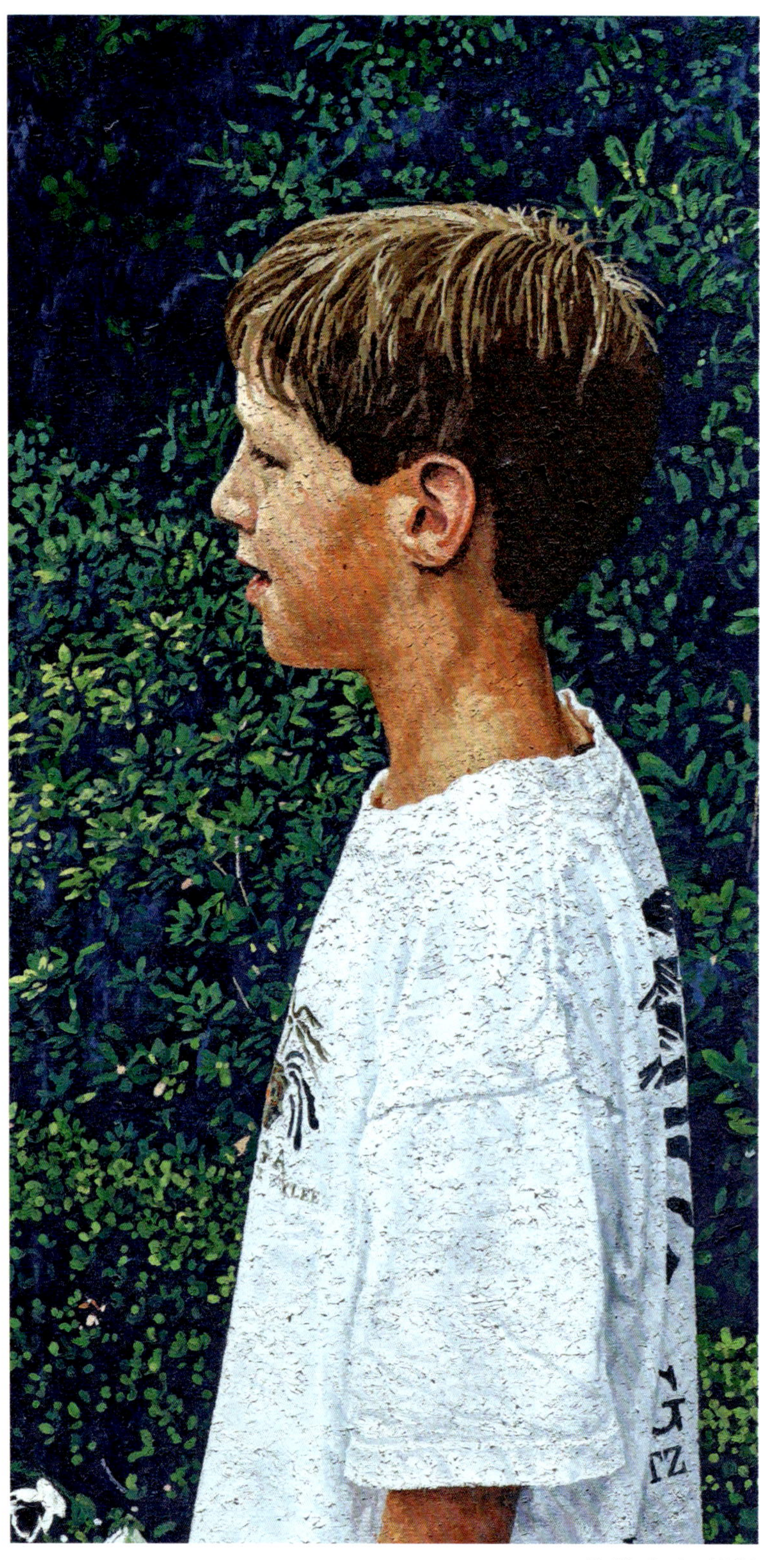

B. W. Crain, 1994
oil on linen | 36" × 18" | Collection of Mary and Walter Crain | Photography by Thomas DuBrock

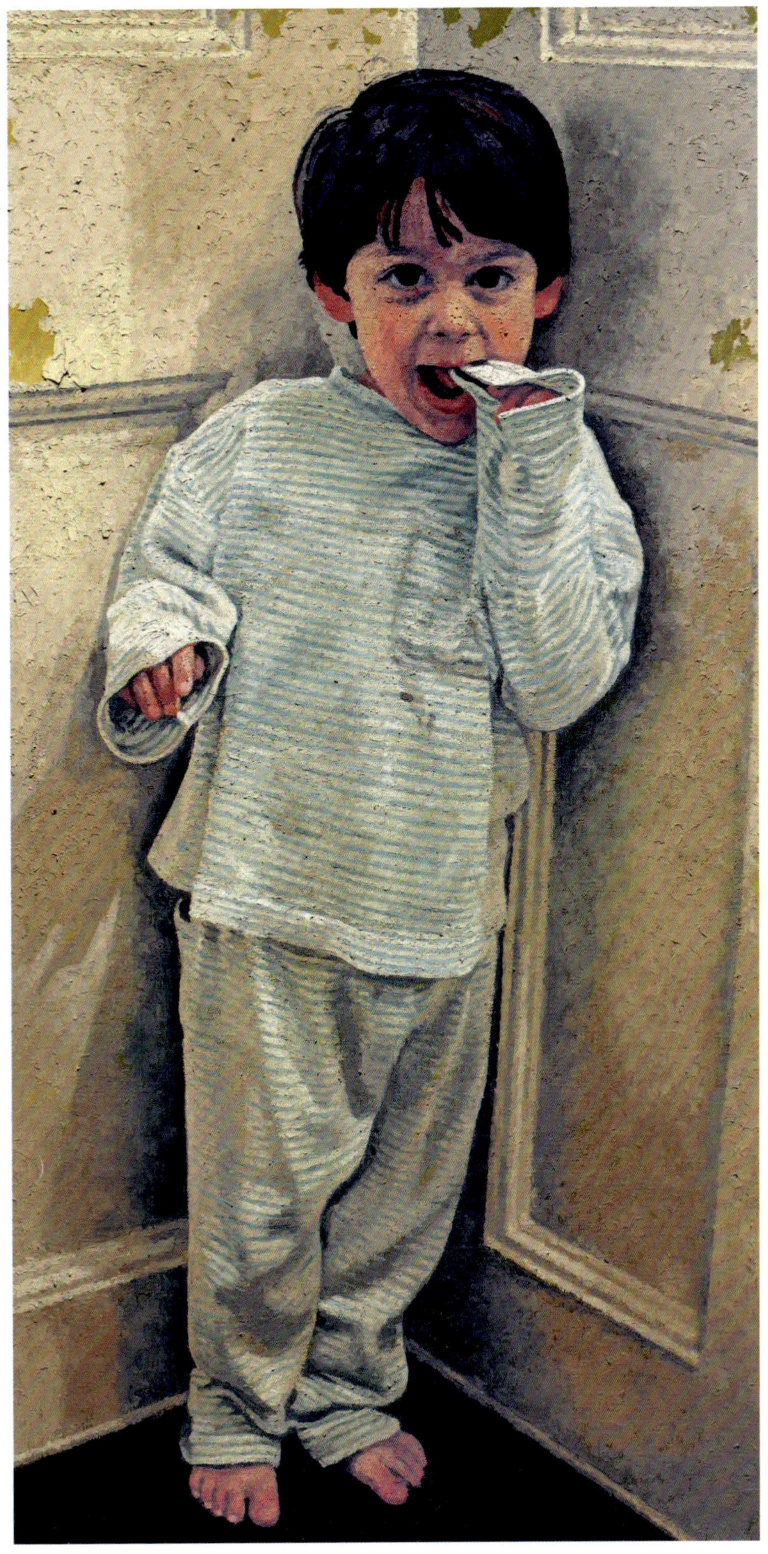

Peter Crain, 1994

oil on linen | 36" × 18" | Collection of Mary and Walter Crain | Photography by Thomas DuBrock

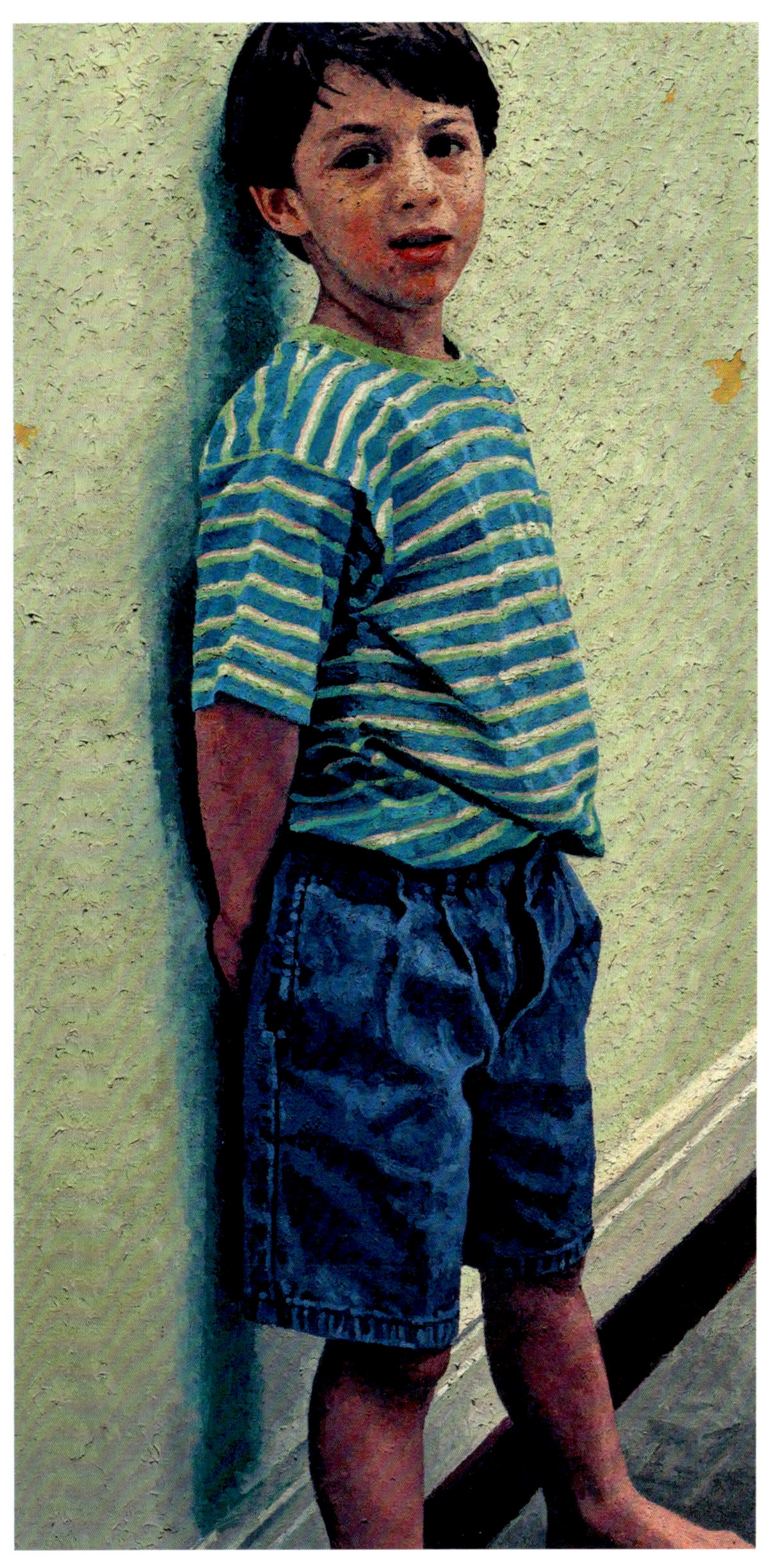

John Crain, 1994

oil on linen | 36" × 18" | Collection of Mary and Walter Crain | Photography by Thomas DuBrock near-magical feeling of reflection. Here, Winter depicts the young boy in profile with a golden light that defines the tip of his chin, the contour of his nose, and his tousled blond hair. Similarly, *Brit* (2010) emits a special aura. By rendering her profile close to the surface, Winter joins the buoyancy of a glance and the weight of long-term scrutiny. Her radiant energy, a kind of iconic presence, is conveyed through Winter's precise observation and painterly sensuality. Every strand of flaxen hair, casually pulled up in a ponytail, is affirmed with beauty, form, and individual life. "Brit's mother, Molly Moore, had told me during a visit to Santa Fe that she would like to have a portrait of Brit, but apparently didn't tell her," Winter recalls. "Brit was a bit upset when she found out because she hadn't had her hair done. I love the way I painted her hair, but to each his or her own. At the time, Brit was a lovely active young woman. Funny and quick. She asked me to be her 'spirit animal.' I wanted to have that duality of life and health and sunshine in the portrait. It was broad brushed, but still great attention to details."

Along with the many commissioned portraits over the years, Winter also produced paintings of close friends, mostly women, that reinforce a complex sense of identity. It is Winter's ability to read an individual personality that has been colored by time and the shifting nuances of physical being that makes his portraits so eerily powerful. *Jean Valentine* (2013), the New York State Poet Laureate (2008–10) and author of several poetry collections, gazes with a slight inquisitive tilt of the head, as if ready to carry on a conversation. Wavy gray hair frames her forehead and softly wrinkled cheekbones. Valentine wears a pale-blue shirt with the phrase "Blessed." An amulet hangs from her neck, a gift from Jeanette Winter, of a woman reading a large tablet. *Jaye Murray* (2013) is a life-size portrait in profile of a proud woman in a dark hat and coat. Although we cannot see her eyes or expression, Winter conveys Murray's physical demeanor and formidable personality through the set of her jaw, her solid shoulders, and the raking angle of her hat. Winter depicts his longtime friend, the painter Lois Dodd, with rendered immediacy and psychic penetration. Set against a checkerboard backdrop, Dodd's imposing figure transmits a strength of character and indomitable spirit. Wearing a bulky blue sweater, Dodd calmly stares at us with a no-nonsense expression. Her lips are tightly closed; her left hand cradles her cheek, accentuating whorls of facial lines and furrows around the eyes and forehead. Her short, unruly white hair reaffirms a raw physical presence. "In Lois, I saw her strength," Winter comments. "In Jean, I saw her spiritual quality. No masks on either of them. Jaye, an African American woman, is fearless and utterly unapologetic. I asked her to dress the way she did to let the world see her classy intelligence."

Self-assured and historically conscious without being mannered, Winter's portraits swing between compulsiveness and the exacting restraint of understatement. Still, there is a careful balance of formal elements, as well as a studied realization of textures and the luminous effects of light. We are struck by the vividness of color and the freshness of his paint surfaces, through which his subjects seem literally to breathe. Indeed, Winter's paintings breathe life—our own fleeting lives—as well as an awareness of ourselves within a broader zone of cultural associations and physical desires. Taken together, the portraits suggest that Winter is at his best when the membrane between art and the person becomes thinnest. Human feeling is not so problematical here. It does not just evaporate; it flows through these images and constitutes them.

As an undergraduate student at the University of Texas, Winter idolized his teachers—William Lester, Everett Spruce, Constance Forsyth, Robert McDonald Graham, Loren Mozley. And just as they nurtured him as a young artist, Winter was determined to help others grow. As a result, he has endeavored to teach and mentor over a lifetime. In defining what makes a great teacher, Winter observes that several characteristics come into play: "You must have a vast knowledge of the field you're teaching. You have to be a psychologist, but also have a sense of humor. Teaching requires being a good salesperson, in order to explain to students what they don't want to hear. It demands critical acumen when looking at someone's work, but also flexibility—allowing a person to grow along the way. Most important, you need to be

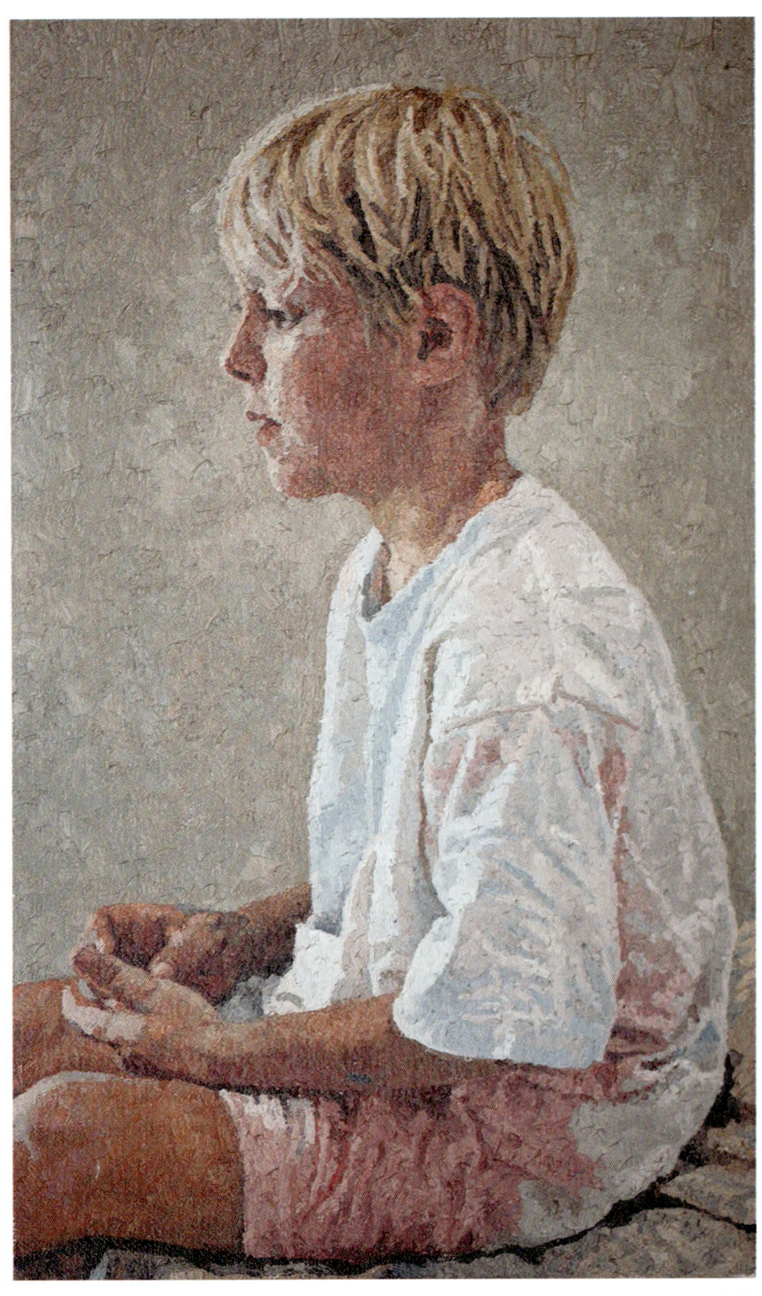

Patrick Willis, 1992
oil on linen | 15" × 9" | Collection of Kate Bower | Photography by Edward Lozano

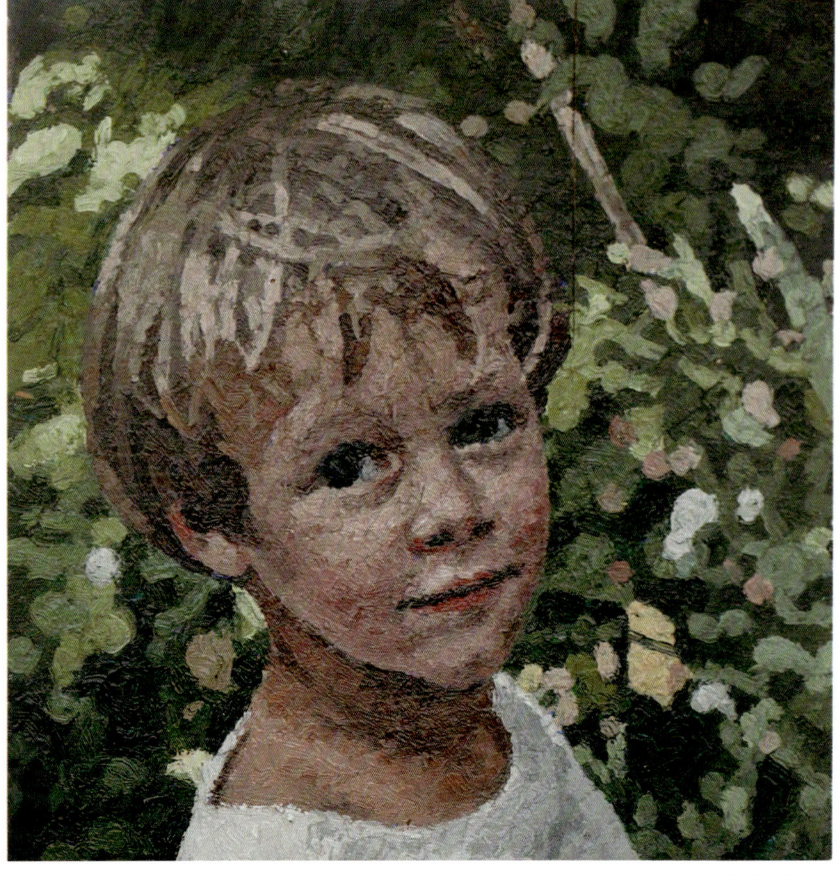

John Andrew Willis, 1992
oil on museum board | 5" × 5" | Collection of Kate Bower | Photography by Edward Lozano

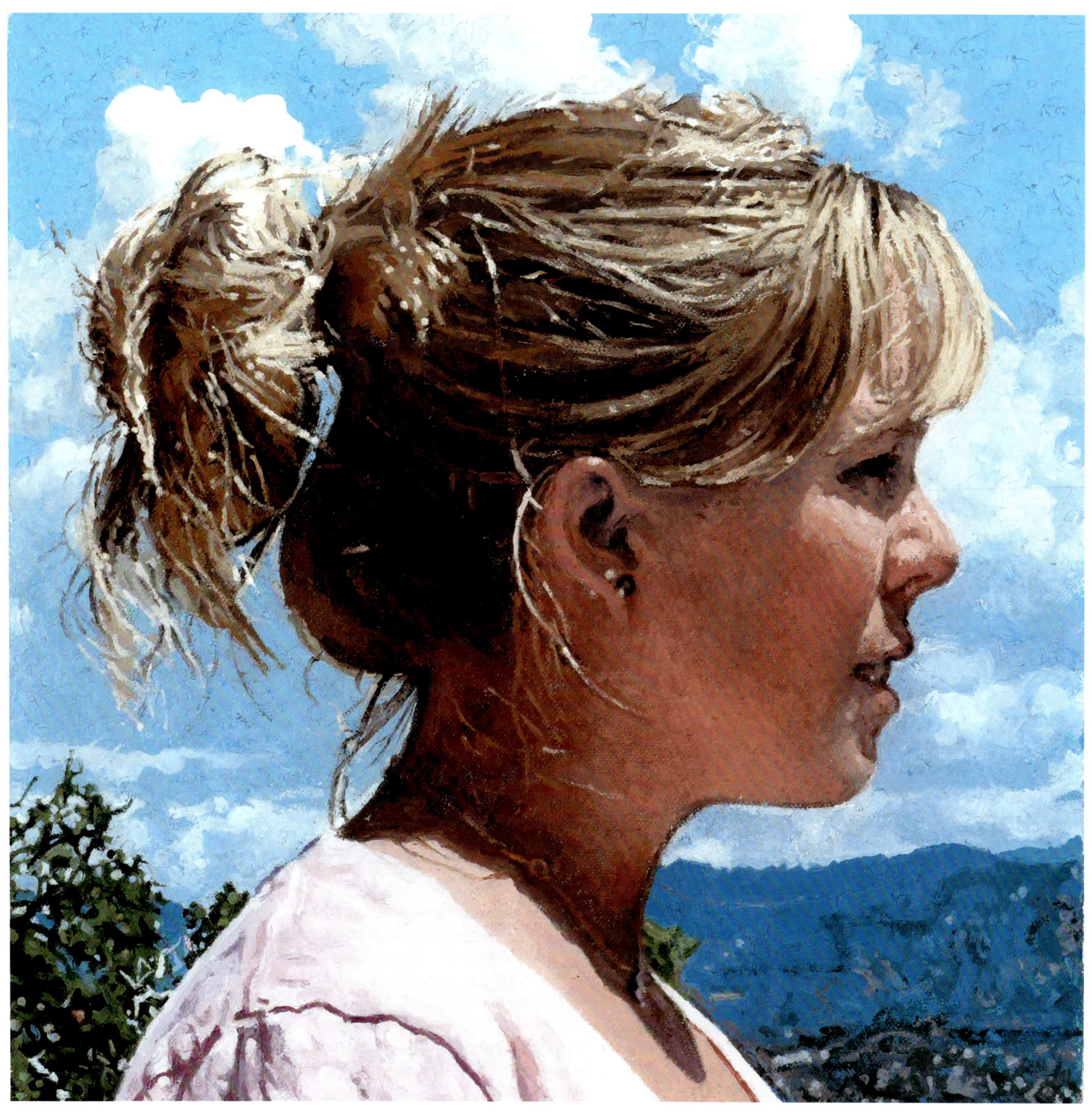

Brit, 2010

oil on linen | 12" × 12" | Collection of Molly E. Moore | Photography by Kevin Todora

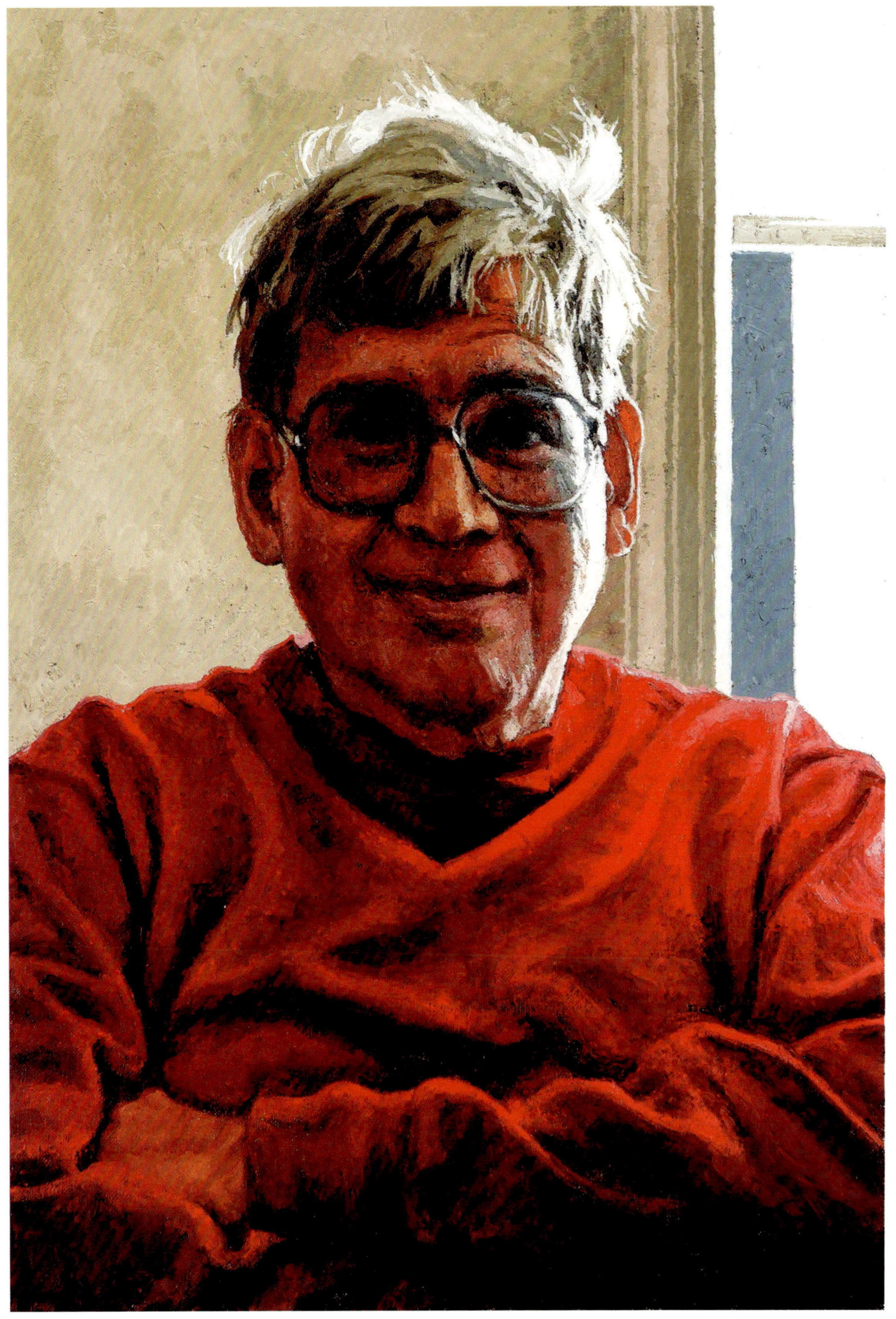

Monty Arnold, 2013

oil on linen | 26" × 18" | Courtesy of the artist and Kirk Hopper Fine Art, Dallas | Photography by G. Valderas

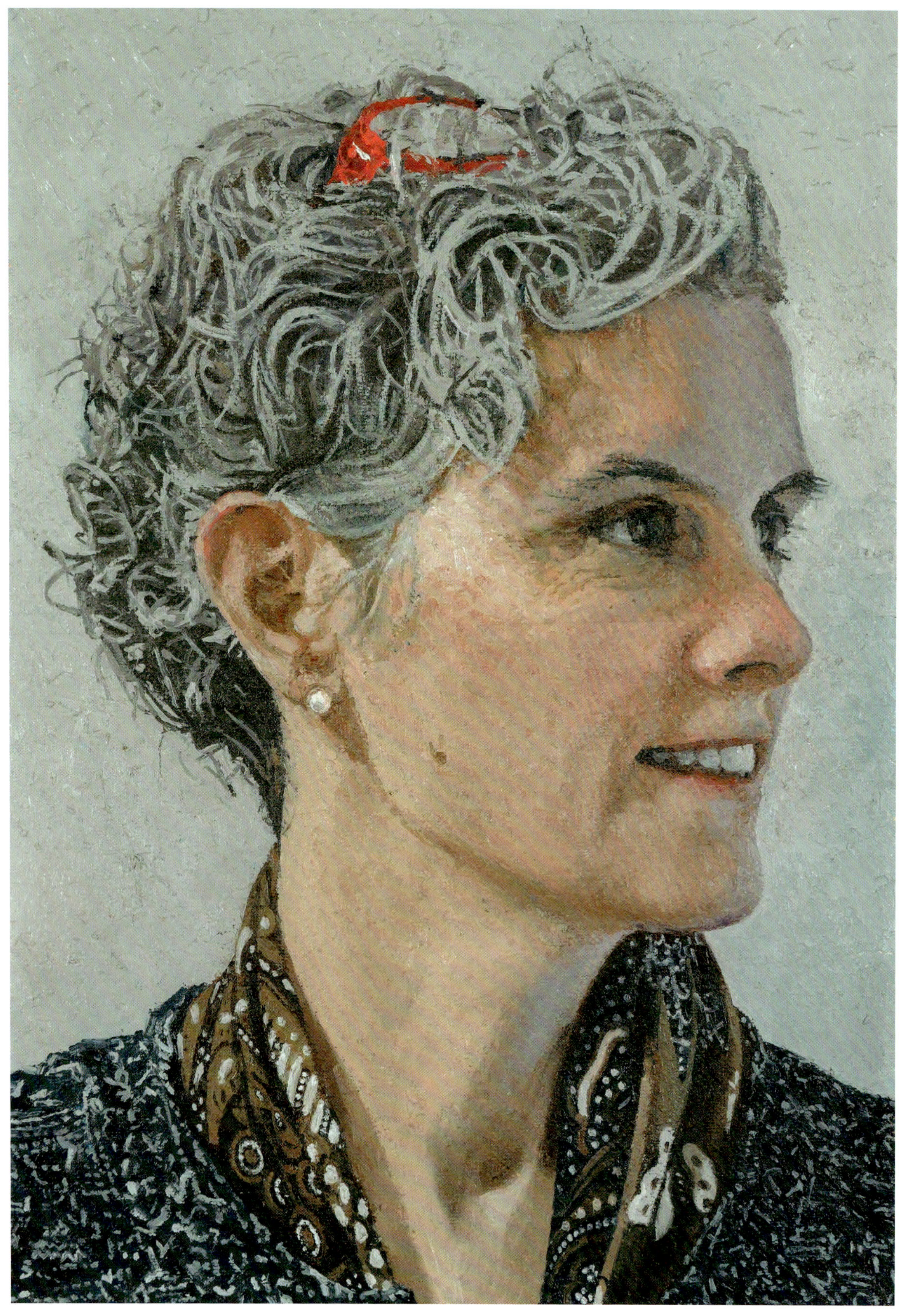

Maggie Jackson, 2015

oil on linen | 14" × 10" | Collection of Maggie Jackson and John Hitchcock | Photography by Joshua Nefsky

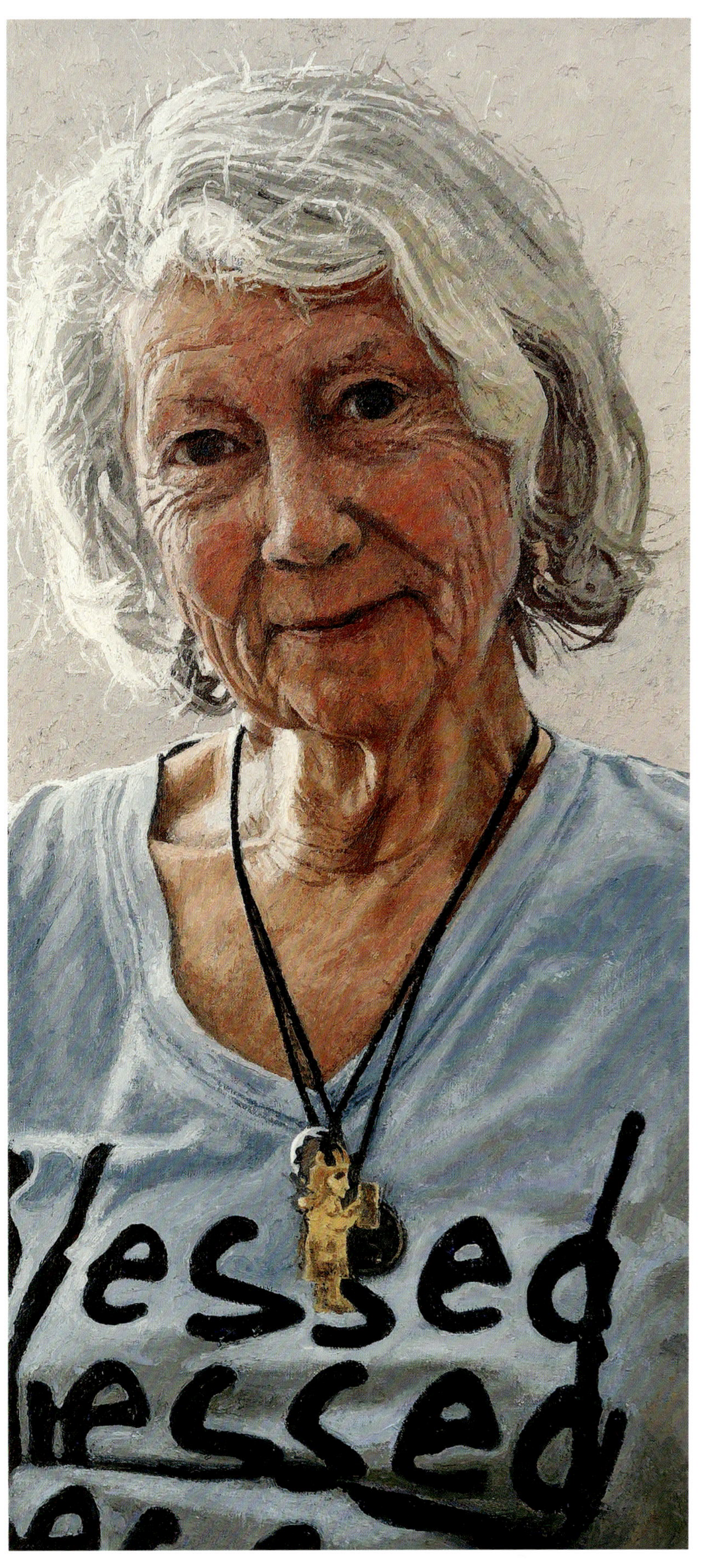

Jean Valentine, 2013
oil on linen | 26" × 12" |
Private collection, New York |
Photography by Joshua Nefsky

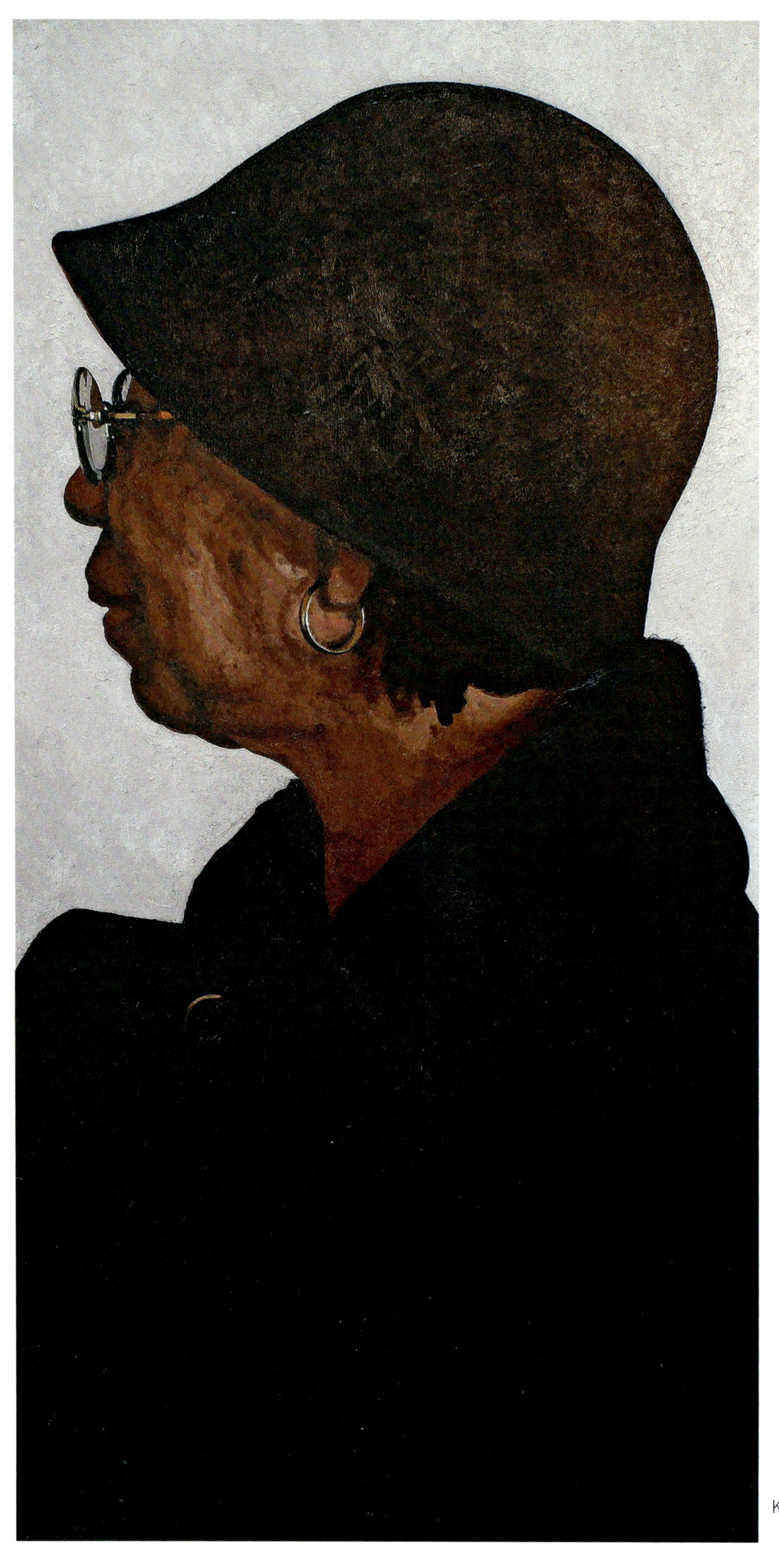

Jaye Murray, 2013
oil on linen | 60" × 30" |
Courtesy of the artist and
Kirk Hopper Fine Art, Dallas |
Photography by G. Valderas

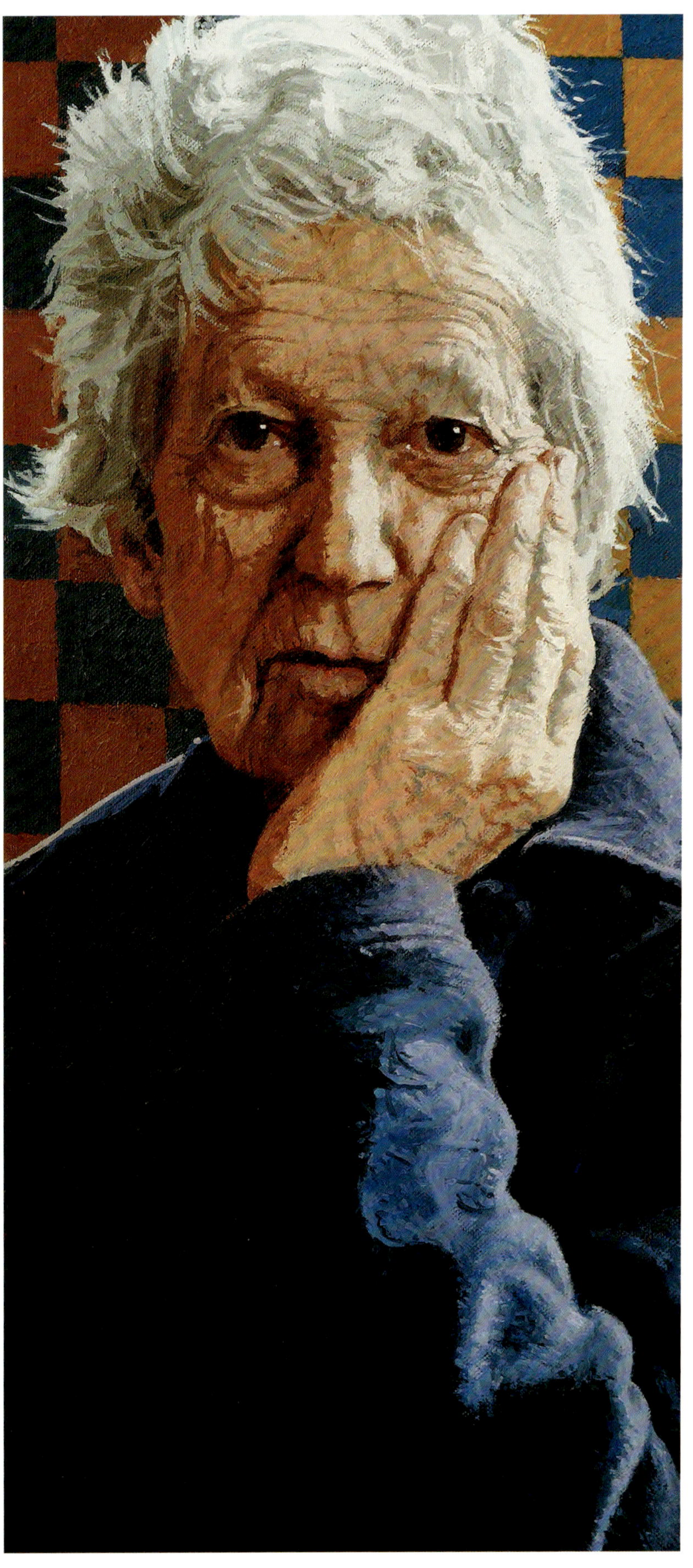

Lois Dodd, 2013
oil on linen | 26" × 12" |
Collection of the artist |
Photography by Joshua Nefsky

approachable. The teacher should be caring and responsive so that students are never afraid to ask questions."

As it happens, Winter was in Dallas for the opening of his exhibition at Kirk Hopper Fine Art, late spring 2013, when former president George W. Bush invited him to visit his studio and critique his paintings. Since completing his presidency, he had developed a newfound interest in the arts and took up the opportunity to paint on a daily basis. "I was sitting up here, wondering how to live life to the fullest," Bush says in a film produced for the exhibition *The Art of Leadership: A President's Personal Diplomacy*. "And I read Winston Churchill's essay, 'Painting as a Pastime,' and it inspired me. I had never lifted a brush before. I'd never mixed a paint. So I gave it a whirl."[5] Bush worked with prominent Dallas artist Gail Norfleet, who, over a six-month period, stimulated change in Bush's world view from the monochromatic to more subtle shifts in values and tones. When Norfleet asked the former president about his goal as an artist, he replied, "There is a Rembrandt in me trying to break out."[6] With this in mind, Norfleet contacted her mentor, Winter, who turned Bush's artistic eye from painting cats and dogs, as well as odd self-portraits, to the more complex realm of political figures. About the watershed meeting, Bush writes, "Roger came to my studio, looked at some of the paintings and suggested that I paint world leaders with whom I served. I was flattered that Roger thought I could do it and was intrigued by the notion. As far as I knew, no other President had painted world leaders. I collected photos and started sketching my contemporaries' faces onto canvases—intricately measuring the eyes, the placement of the ears. I enjoyed the challenge of the human form and trying to capture a person's spirit with brushstrokes. And over the course of many hours of work, I painted the portraits of Putin, Blair, Koizumi, Karzai, the Dalai Lama and some twenty-five others."[7]

For Winter's part, the veteran teacher recognized a propensity for expressive facial structures in the early work but felt compelled to steer the former president to develop a more challenging and consistent visual vocabulary. "I saw so much of the persona in the portraits of animals and family members that I suggested he go all the way—paint the world leaders with whom he served and had known all his life through circumstances of birth," Winter explains.

> He was prolific, with good drawing skills for a beginner, and a nice sense of composition. I advised him to think in terms of light and dark, but also to be more generous with paint, to mix more paint than necessary and stretch the brushwork across the surface. He needed to master the layering that oil paint requires of those seeking realism. I wrote a list of things that I wanted him to consider in relation to his work: counteractions, washes, dividing the canvas space, rhythm, and balance. I suggested painters to study for composition—[Nicolas] Poussin, [Diego] Velázquez, [Johannes] Vermeer, [Francisco] Goya, [Paul] Cézanne, [Edgar] Degas, Edward Hopper, Fairfield Porter, and Romare Bearden. Before I left the studio, he insisted on going through each comment for clarification. I thought that was good, because he wasn't yet familiar with much of the art vocabulary. Most important, I sensed a spirit—a life, élan—in everything I saw at the time. My only concerns were to provide encouragement, build on his strengths, and challenge his weaknesses. A good teacher leads the student to the threshold of his own mind.

Significantly, Winter's essential tutelage motivated former president Bush to produce the expansive series *Art of Leadership*, which captures an emotional recollection of the world leaders with whom he bonded and led to the compassionate paintings that commemorate wounded military veterans, which culminated in the exhibition and publication *Portraits of Courage: A Commander in Chief's Tribute to America's Warriors*.

One of the most distinctive traits of any period is the expression on the faces of those who belong to it. We study such portraits to detect how they told lies, withheld fears, or expressed powers and vanities. Perhaps a portrait is best seen as a bargain between the artist and the sitter carefully calculated to convey specific ideas. It is the amalgamation of the demands of the subject, the ideas of the artist, and the expectations of their society that provides the portrait with its particular strength and fascination—if we know what to look for. What do they hide? How do they take on specific meanings at different times that reflect, interrogate, and construct identity? An image of a figure is a kind of inoculation against the fading of memory, one of the most terrifying symptoms of our mortality. The likeness of a face is a form of gesture—a relation of sizes, angles, and values—in other words, knowing how to measure with the eyes to illuminate the light within. Winter has drawn and painted his wife, Jeanette, hundreds, perhaps thousands, of times over the sixty years they have been together. A particular quality that stands out in an examination of all these portraits is a kind of steadfastness. They show a seemingly single-minded progression from his awkwardly earnest drawings of a young love, to the precise paintings and drawings of motherhood and a mature woman, to the gradually more fluid and sensual way he portrayed her in the beginning of the twenty-first century and beyond to the present. This remarkable consistency, however, is the outcome of a constant questioning of what it is to truly see another person and what is possible to depict. Each drawing or painting is a fresh collision between this questioning and the woman in front of him.

During the late 1960s, however, the drawings reached a fever pitch: Jeanette in close-up or from a distance; sitting in a chair or reclining on a bed; relaxed, alert, pensive; quietly suffering or sweetly enticing. How well do we know the ones we love? And who are we when we no longer recognize the people closest to us? At a time when generational memory seems fading, elusive, and consonant with forgetting, the transitory nature of images and moments can resemble a kind of twilight. For Winter, drawing offers a unique soul-searching intimacy and process-driven gesture. At the time, Jeanette had just written, illustrated, and published her first children's book. Although Winter had become a full-time faculty member of Southern Methodist University's art department, he was also trying to find the next space for his paintings. He was after an elusive "something." Drawing provided the means to grow as an artist and a new language through immediate, more intuitive decisions. In the Jeanette drawings, that language is transmitted as emotional memories—what the nerves and skin remember, as well as how they appeared. Part of it is a love story—Jeanette as muse, adviser, and model—but the portraits are much more than that: writing; the chaos of sexuality; competition and envy; loneliness; joy and sorrow. We have expectations of those closest to us, but never with any rules or guidance—just the day after day of it and beneath it all, the queasy possibility that it all might end tomorrow. At the core of the intense attachment are feelings of twinship, with the portraits serving as a kind of echo or alter ego. Are they faithful renditions of Jeanette? Taken together, they are about Winter's broad artistic wingspan, as well as his chameleon moods, and the beauty and pain that make up the vertigo of life. "Roger has always been a superb portraitist," Jeanette writes. "He's interested in people and likes to draw and paint them. He likes the stories that people tell and thinks about those stories. Roger and I met in art school when I was posing for a painting class. This was the first of so many paintings over the years. He continued to draw and paint me throughout our marriage. I look at these portraits of me in a formal way, rather than as psychological portraits. . . . Our interests dovetail, but sometimes there is a demarcation between the art world (Roger's world) and the publishing world (my world). We each tell stories with our work in our own particular way."[8]

Looking at the portraits, we also expose our own places, social formations, and partial identities in establishing what should count as truth. Again and again, Winter renders the surface but also the character of Jeanette. Everything shows—the face, after all, is the center of the senses—her class, her vulnerabilities, but also a driven demeanor that sharpens her over time. Winter creates a kind of utopian space around his wife, which he warps, distorts, and shapes to his own ends as if Jeanette were preparing for a life of multiple personalities, not a single role. By doing so, he catches a moment when a shadow of the invisible appears, through which we take some measure of who she was in the 1960s and who she might emerge as in the mirror

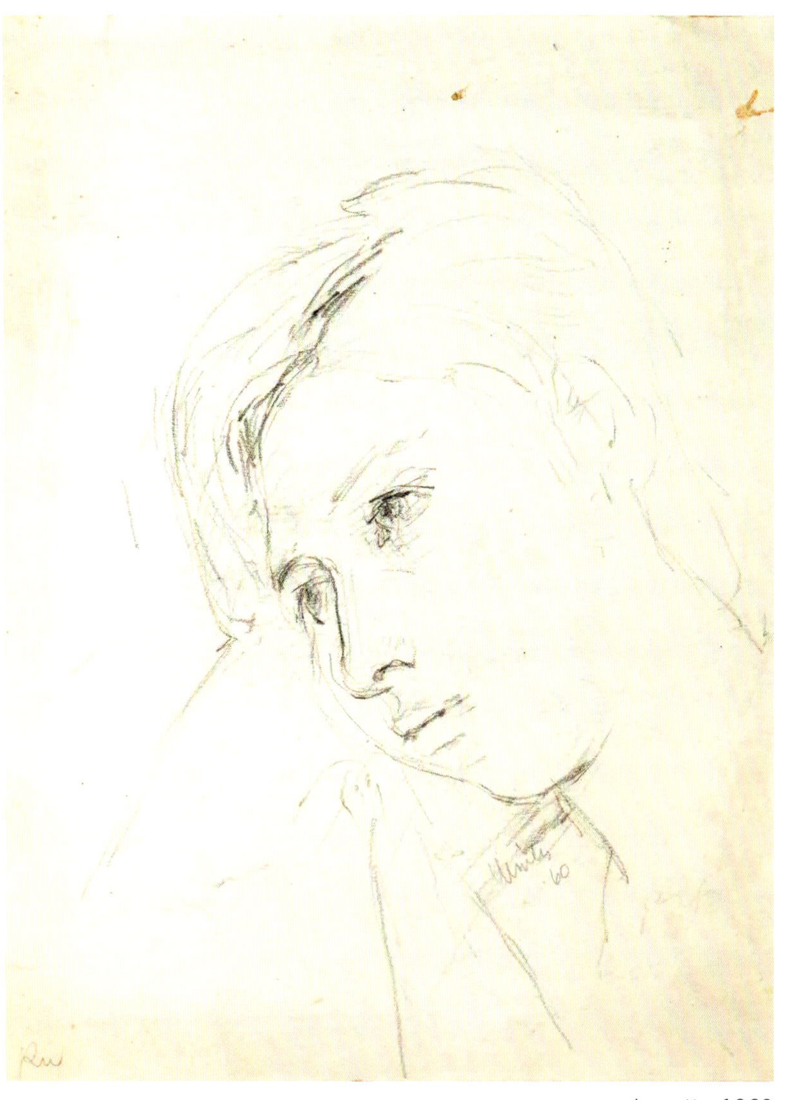

Jeanette, 1960
pencil on paper | 12" × 9" | Courtesy of the artist and Kirk Hopper Fine Art, Dallas | Photography by Joshua Nefsky

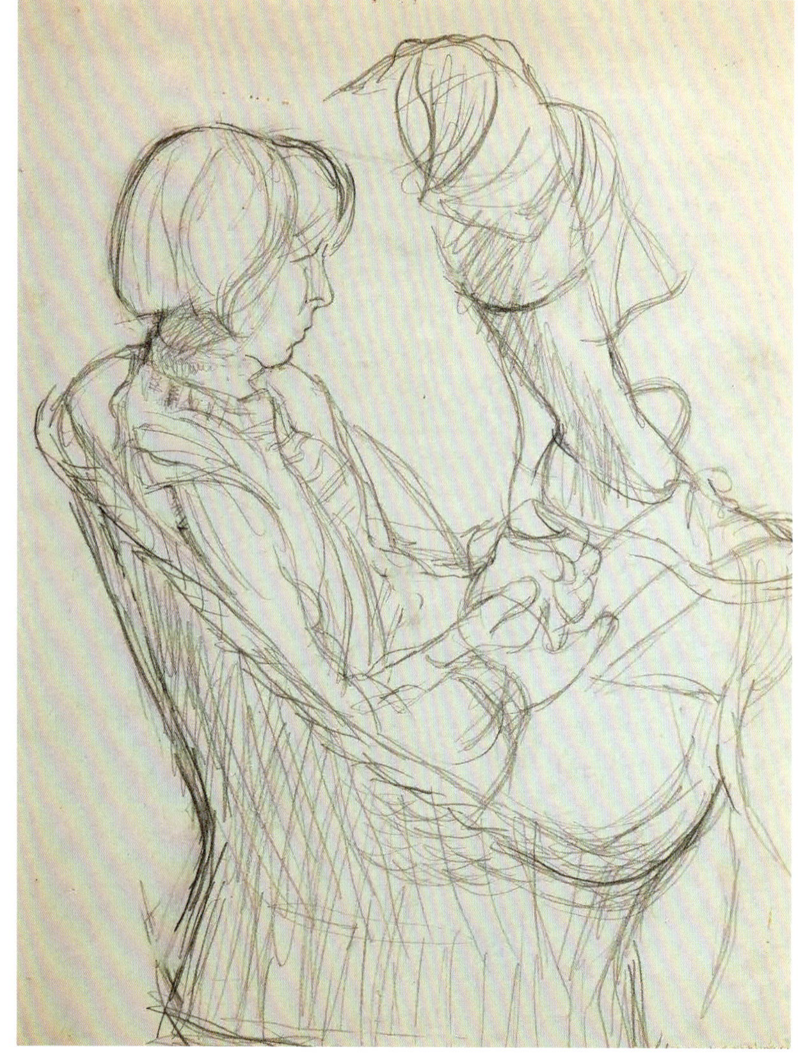

Jeanette in Straw Chair, 1965
pencil on paper | 14" × 11" | Courtesy of the artist and Kirk Hopper Fine Art, Dallas | Photography by Joshua Nefsky

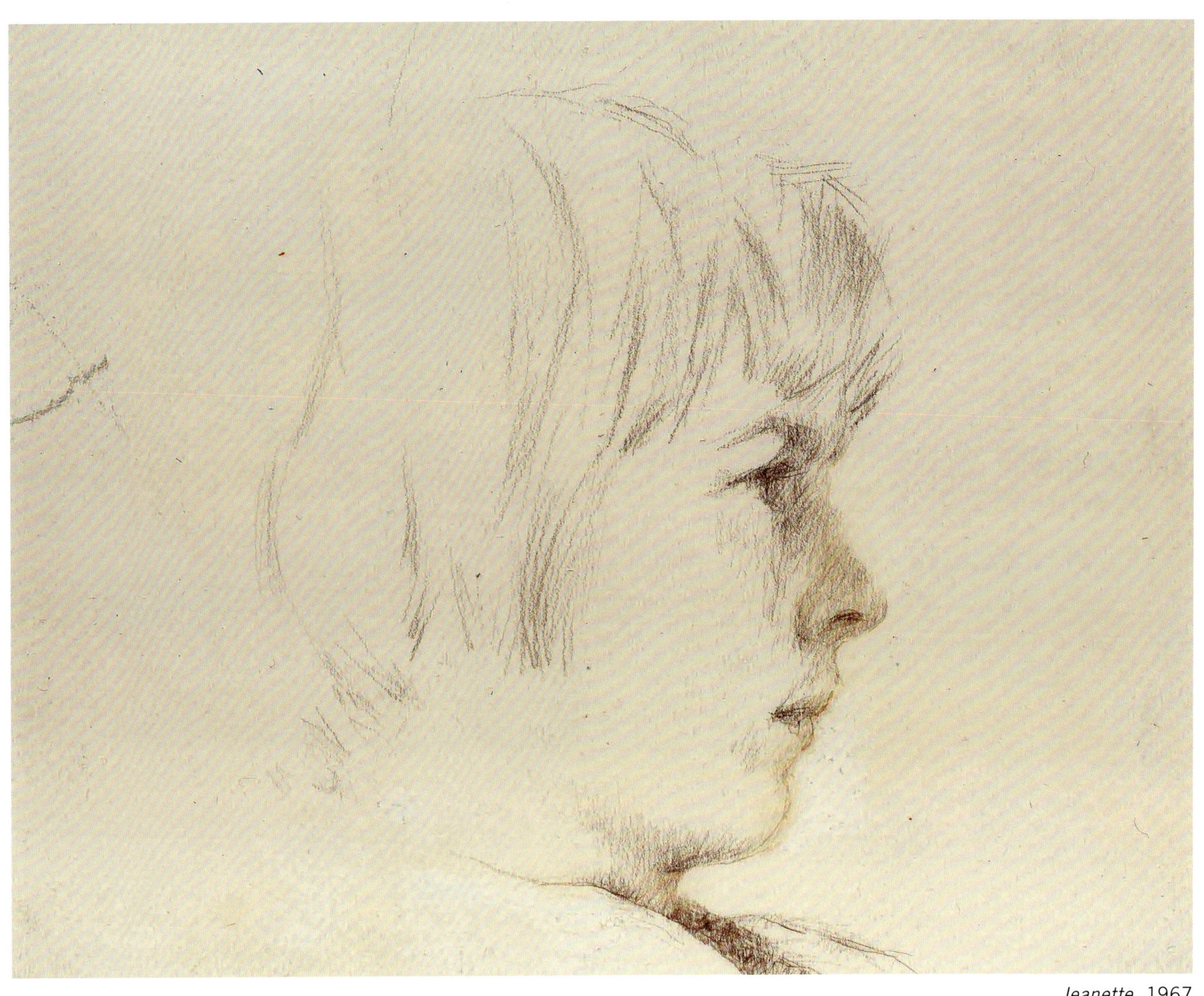

Jeanette, 1967
silverpoint on coated paper | 4 1/2" × 5 1/2" | Courtesy of the artist and Kirk Hopper Fine Art, Dallas | Photography by Joshua Nefsky

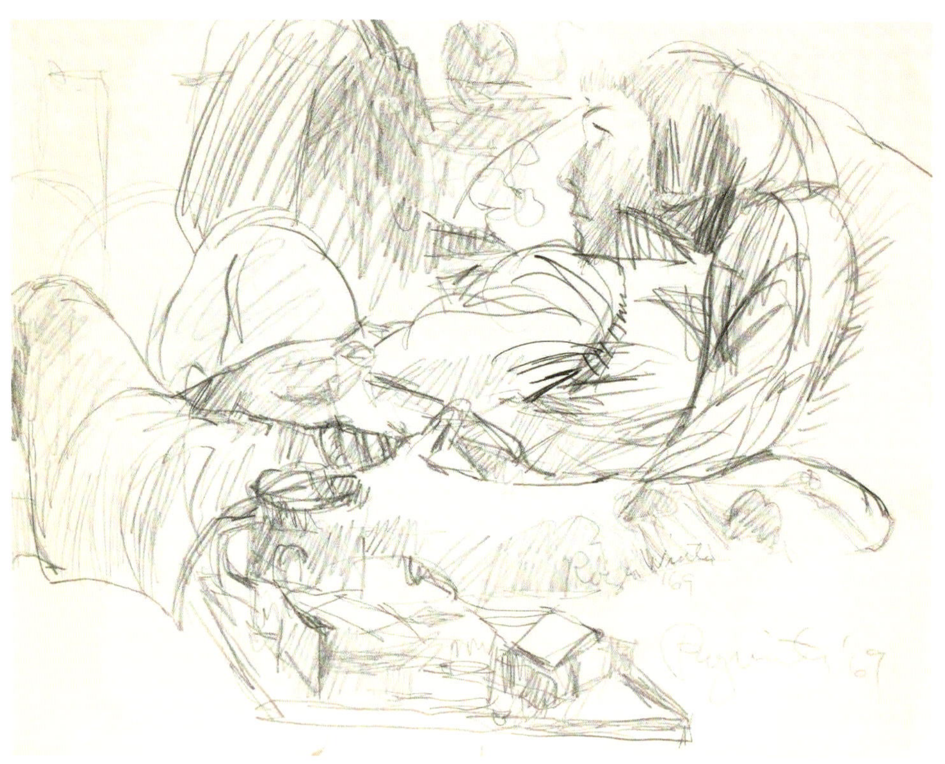

Jeanette Reclining, 1969
pencil on paper | 11" × 14" | Courtesy of the artist and Kirk Hopper Fine Art, Dallas | Photography by Joshua Nefsky

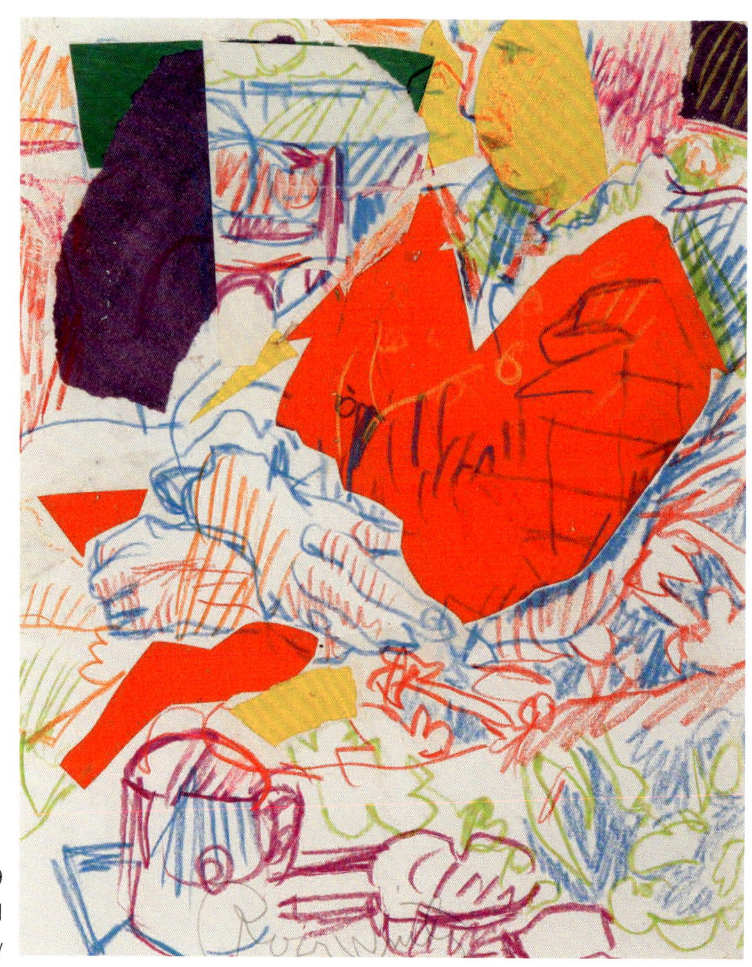

Jeanette, 1969
mixed-media collage | 10" × 8" | Courtesy of the artist and Kirk Hopper Fine Art, Dallas | Photography by Joshua Nefsky

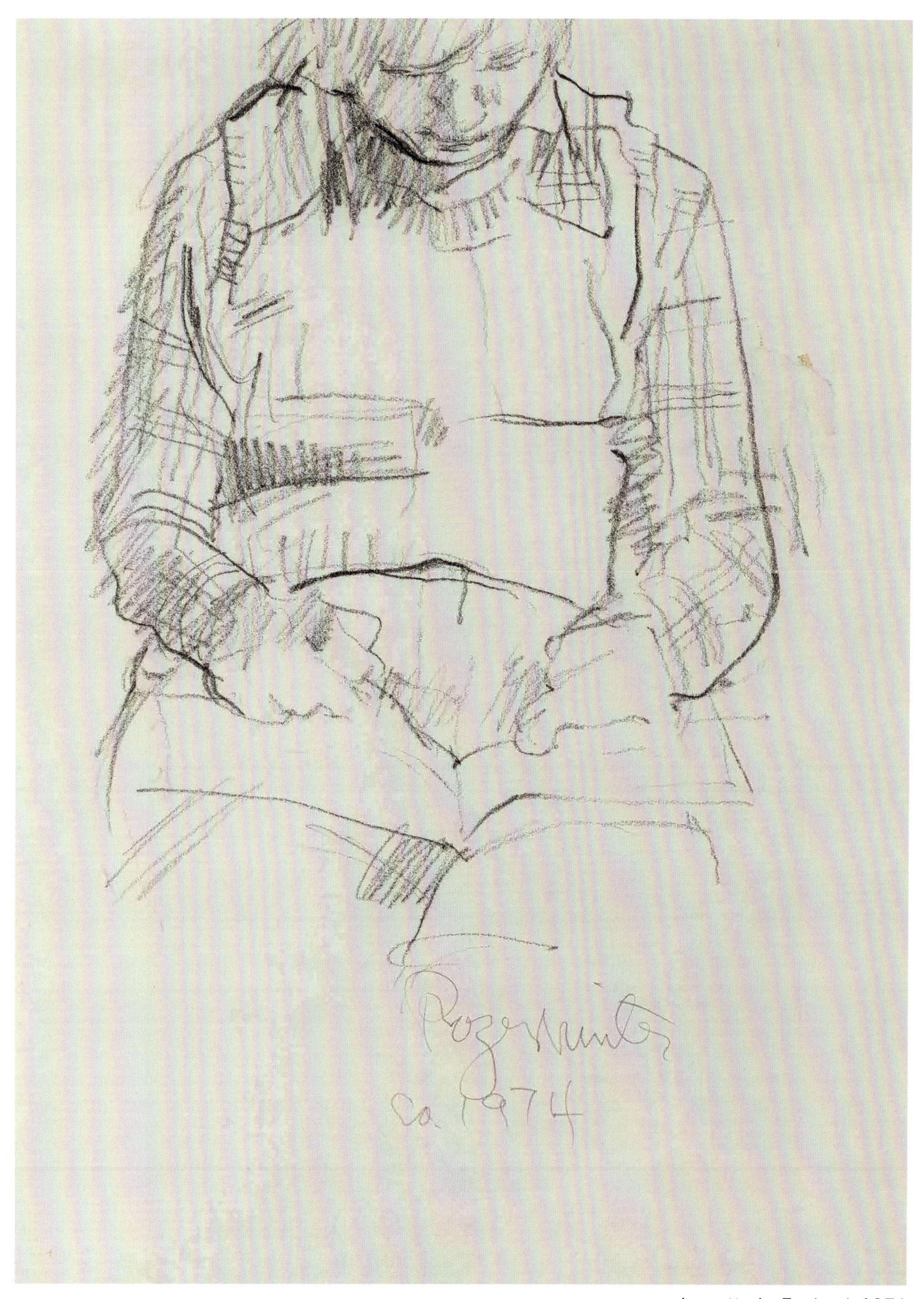

Jeanette in England, 1974
pencil on paper | 14" × 10" | Courtesy of the artist and
Kirk Hopper Fine Art, Dallas | Photography by Joshua Nefsky

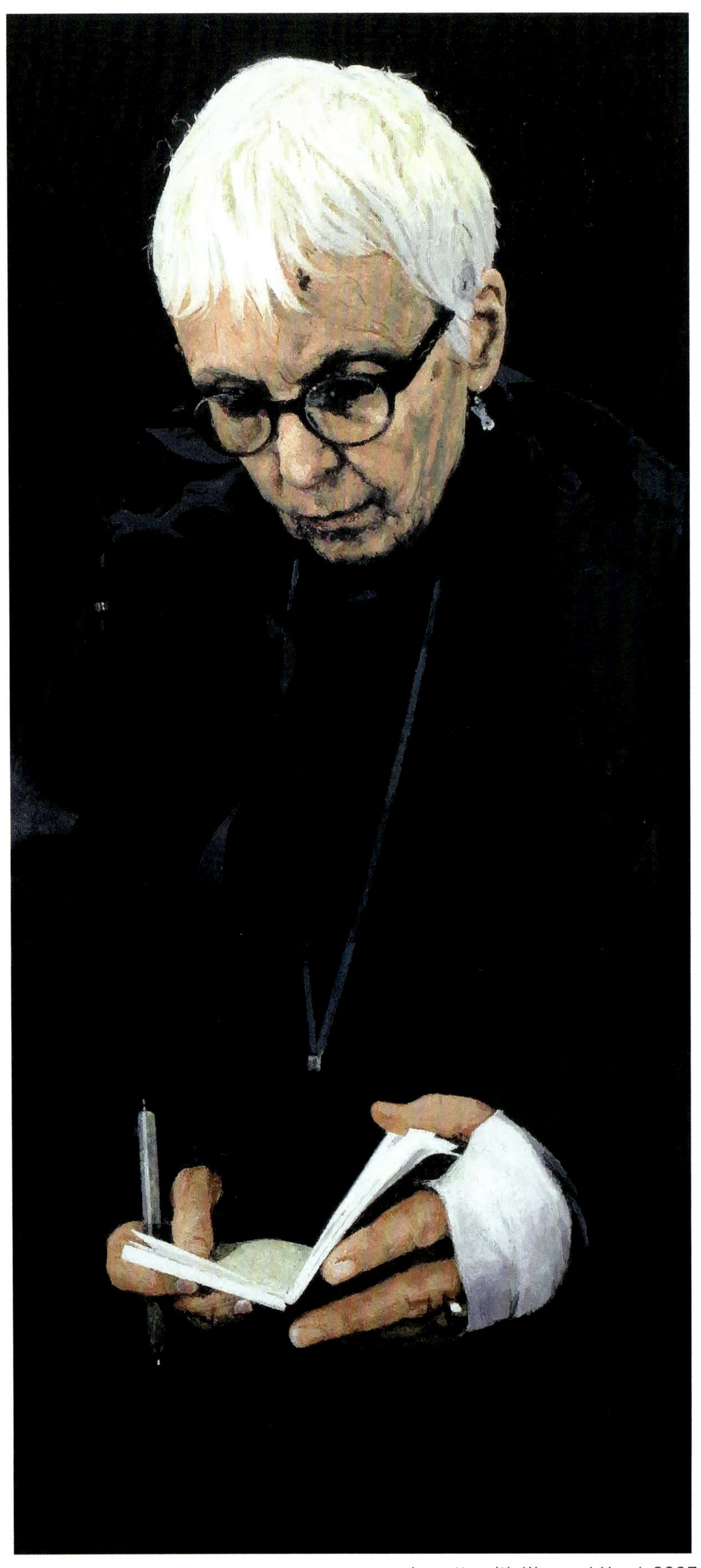

Jeanette with Wrapped Hand, 2007

oil on linen | 43" × 20" | Collection of Jeanette Winter

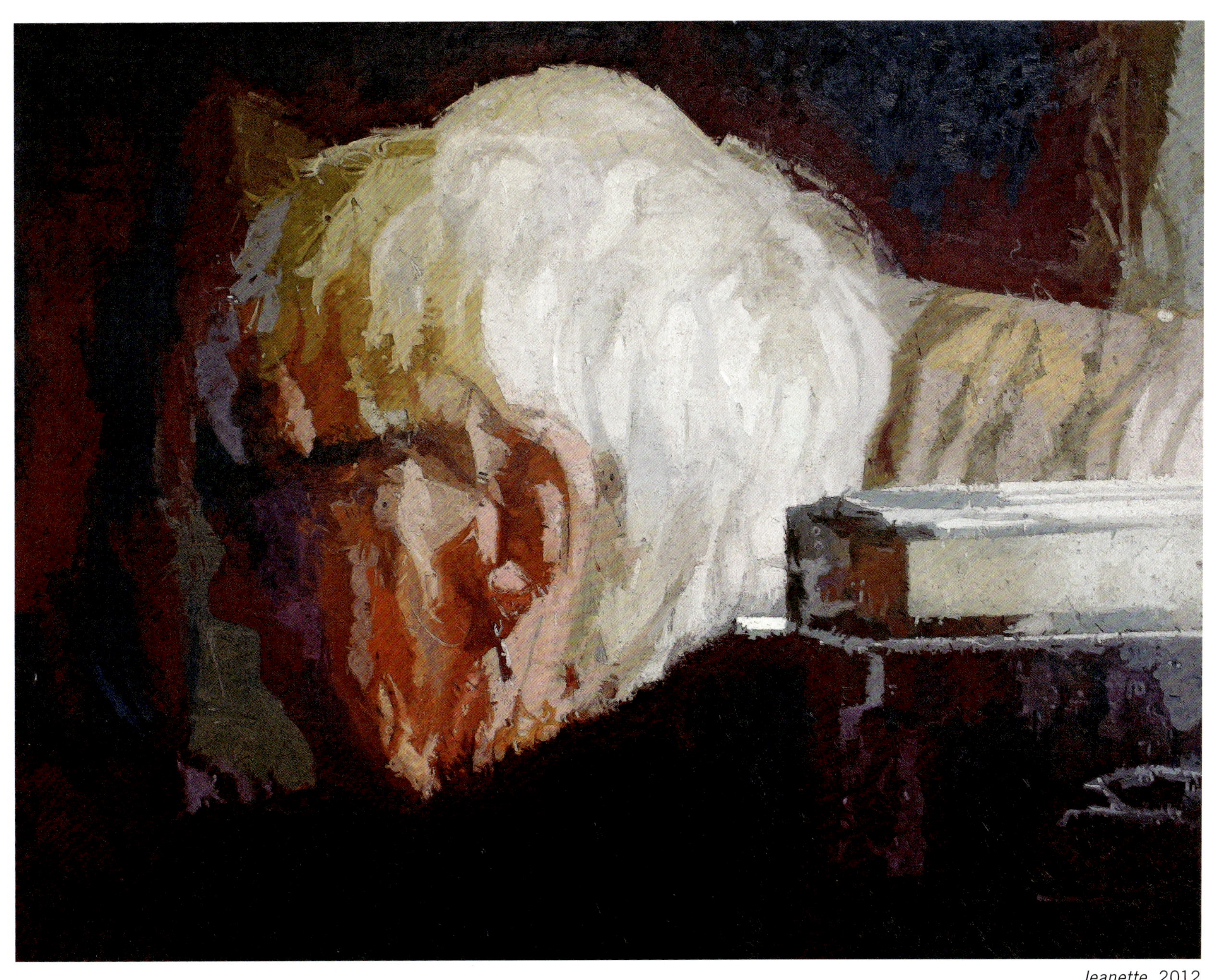

Jeanette, 2012
oil on linen | 44" × 60" | Courtesy of the artist and Kirk Hopper Fine Art, Dallas | Photography by Joshua Nefsky

of time. Their special gift is to have a profound subject—selfhood, identity. There are people we touch and people we do not touch. Every choice is an exclusion. Ephemeral revelations of wonder and beauty are coupled with moments of great sorrow or overwhelming grief, of what vanishes and remains. And just as life is diverse, the shifting planes of our personalities come from the shifts in the social and cultural constructs around us. How do we identify ourselves? How do we settle into other people's expectations for our identity? Perhaps we have ideas of ourselves based on living our lives and then feel something welling up within us. There are moments when we realize that our identities may not be fixed, that our stories are not over. "I think of good things and bad things—times when we were angry with each other, or sweet toward each other," Winter recalls. "I think of our history—of anyone's history of sixty years—it can't be all roses. But for the most part we've gotten along quite well. She's extremely smart, of fine judgment. I thought that before I even spoke to her. Jeanette is very introverted, but she has a side to her that's extraordinarily strong. She's helped me grow and evolve not only as an artist but as a male. You fall in love with someone more than once—I fell in love with her again and again when I did the drawings and paintings. Of course, Jeanette shows signs of aging, but she has kept a natural beauty—no cosmetics, no hiding. After we married I had a full-time model. And I never tired. I have said many times, in her presence or not, that meeting Jeanette was the very best thing that ever happened to me. She and our sons are the loves of my life."

Pervasive throughout the drawings is the sense of conscious commitment to each mark. The visual richness deployed in a tuft of hair or a cheekbone is also redolent of Jeanette's intensity and intelligence. Wiry, electrified lines move through spare figure-ground relationships and densely complex energy fields. The line approaches handwriting or perhaps a struggle toward verbalization: the Jeanette drawings speak of distance, desire, memory, and possession all at once, like a compulsive thought constantly transforming itself. Over and over, the syntax of figuration stretches out, sometimes dissolving into indecipherable but evocative abstract shapes. Wide looping or jabbing strokes counter thin lines set down by quick, short thrusts of the pencil. His drawing, alternately tenuous, spare, and expressive, follows a rhythmic course between brittleness and fluidity. The pencil flows, pauses, or runs on at paces that are by turns meditative and aggressive, a lively mix of staccato strokes, whiplash lines, and rippling curls. The contour drawings, in particular, are rendered with a line that ranges from tremulous to direct, from elegantly sinuous to jabbed or smudged. They reveal a powerfully charged inner life; at times Jeanette diffuses into the space of the sheet, like memories that fade or spectral shadows moving through the larger universe.

In a painting of Jeanette, we follow the brushstroke's sweep of continuous movement from the tip of her nose down to the chin and onto the shoulder, then to the book she holds in her bandaged hand. The excitement of the portrait is located as much in the inventiveness and the sense of conscious commitment in each brushstroke and area as in his figurative subject. A 2012 portrait of Jeanette focuses on her spiky white hair, which both reflects and emits light. The textured surface explodes in a shower of delicate, feather-light brushstrokes, which flow and pull us into the picture plane. This sweep of movement releases Jeanette from the canvas and forces us to contemplate time's passage—the certainty of then, the vaporous now, and the elusiveness of what is to come. Each portrait is a riddle of physical facts, choices, details, and optical experiences. The more we look, the more we see and learn about the way Winter's mind works, how it moves around the portrait, touching and considering every point no matter how small. Paradox, ambiguity, and mystery are key elements of these paintings and drawings, both pictorially and emotionally. His enigmatic and beautifully realized images not only have the great virtues of engaging and captivating the eye, they also cling to the mind and haunt us long after they have passed from sight.

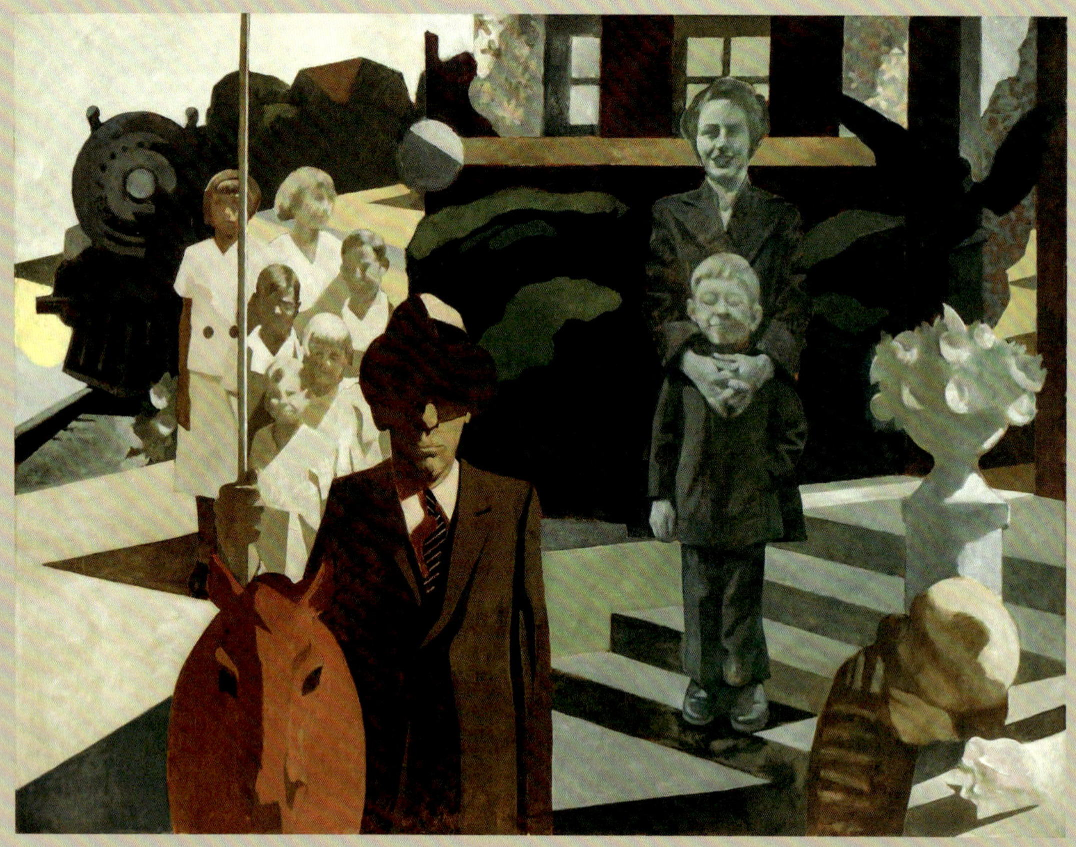

The Family, 1966

oil on linen | 72" × 96" | Collection of John Alexander and Fiona Waterstreet |

Photography by Joshua Nefsky

CHAPTER 16

CONCLUSION

ROGER WINTER IS AN ARTIST of searingly original visions that combine formal rigor and spiritual mystery. Time's passage, the preciousness of the natural world, and the beauty of mundane things are all hallmarks of his work. The philosophical questions that emerge from his paintings, drawings, collages, and sculptures deal with our identity and existence, our solitary state in the world, our limits in space and time. Winter's art explores the stories we tell ourselves about ourselves: our families, our country, and the porous border between history and myth. The everyday fears and frustrations that shadow us on our awkward trip through time often feel enormous, even cosmic. For six decades, however, Winter has endeavored to find images and situations that give form to those metaphysical experiences. Winter asks for the provision of intimate ways of being in the world, for the touchstones that give the heart the emotional closeness it demands and the skin the brush with real things it craves. To understand those things in this intimate way, we have to hold them close, visit them in their flesh, become aware of their past, and hear about them from those who have known them over time. We are all of us in constant passage with one another. All of us live within a variety of categories to which we must relate or find some identification.

Winter guides us along parallel switchback trails from cradle to grave, never ceasing to wonder at the details of the terrain we have traversed many times. In the process, he reminds us of the raw effort that telling a story, and imaging other lives, demands. The head-snapping mix of microcosmic nature, intimate human behavior, and considerations of mortality opens up vast areas of feeling that challenge us to reflect on the soul's need to place itself in the vast scheme of things. Time and memory seem not so much to flow forward as to eddy and swirl, backward into the future and forward into the past. Winter's art does not adhere to a linear path but rather is meandering and conflicted. Its evolution has not been a matter of one subject replacing the other but instead a series of moves and returns so that each work is a piece.

It has been gratifying to champion a genuine accomplishment and immerse myself in an underexplored aesthetic realm. After all these decades, why does the art of Roger Winter matter? The establishment of an artist like Winter—whose reputation seemed secure in the 1970s and 1980s—in the trajectory of recent art practice stems not only from an examination of his earlier, better-known work but also from a growing awareness of what he has created in late career. The visionary qualities of the Greenland and Iceland paintings, as well as the reductive geometries of the New York City works, have produced an event that is rare in the life of any artist: exceptional art in old age. The work offers proof that Winter is an artist of greater range than he has been given credit for. Winter reminds us what it means to live a life richly, but also to make art for its own sake, out of inner vision and necessity. The achievement of Winter's art has been how forcefully he folds questions of memory, faith, and transcendence into paintings and presents them to us as human dramas, in images bright and bare as bone. But if Winter comes across as larger than life, it is because he belongs to a time when life itself might have seemed bigger and art was more replete with heroic possibilities than in our own anxious times.

In many respects, Winter's trajectory dovetails with the vision of America as an unfinished project, rooted in gospel and the possibility of redemption, and the more existential belief that we can continually remake ourselves. Art became the key to his thinking process, a tool for sorting through the crosscurrents in his life—racism, class, family—and a way to integrate all those portions of himself into something whole. With Winter, however, there is the sense that he knew who he was and where he was going from the beginning. He digs deeper and deeper to reach a humbling knowledge of mortality. The subjects of his paintings—love, death, joy, sadness—are also the great themes of songs and poetry that we welcome hearing about, looking at, and making sense of as we go through our lives. For nearly three-quarters of a century, his art has demonstrated the ability to move effortlessly between the serious and the comic, the metaphysical and the merely personal. It goes at things like the very embodiment, in Winter's mind, of an American spirit—proud, romantic, naive, impulsive—a layer cake of nested memories and family legends that becomes a rich, exotic confection. Winter draws and paints what he sees, but always subtly blending with an America in his mind. It seeps out from his dreams, early childhood experiences, and daily observations. To be an American is to be more or less made up of cultural spare parts. Winter specializes in showing how those parts change and shift under worldly pressures. For him, art is potent to the degree it merges with life. What really sets Winter's paintings aloft is when he expands into the large works in full-out abandon to the power of light—purple skies, lurid pinks, wet greens, intense blues, and fierce oranges. The colors of his landscapes, both rural and urban, are dissonant, rich with just a hint of the apocalypse. A real artist made these paintings, and their integrity is compelling. They demand to be contemplated for their awe and wonder at the beauty and grandeur of being alive.

I am struck by a fundamental and counterintuitive generosity in his work. What Winter preserves of himself is his quick reactivity, his encyclopedic command of history, his shreds of dreams and memories—all this transmitted into uncompromising and clear painterly language. Style is how he makes himself available to us: allowing us to share in his extraordinary visions by conveying them with an American core that is really a hymn—a sturdy and haunting melody. Winter's art is a hymn to us—visual hymns of passage, of solitude, and of connection. They project a sense of sureness and passionate serenity that leads me to consider him as having moved into the first rank among living painters. Winter still trains his eye on the work directly in front of him. Every day, without fail, he continues to put brush to canvas with such single-minded focus that he does not see his own career arc. Winter's story keeps going; his imagination is outsize and full of high jinks. He aspires to something new and challenging at every turn—a perpetual movement forward, with propulsive, joyous energy. Winter's art is an almost unbearably moving explosion of the importance of love, the pull of family, and the need to reclaim the past by understanding how, and as what, we opt to see ourselves.

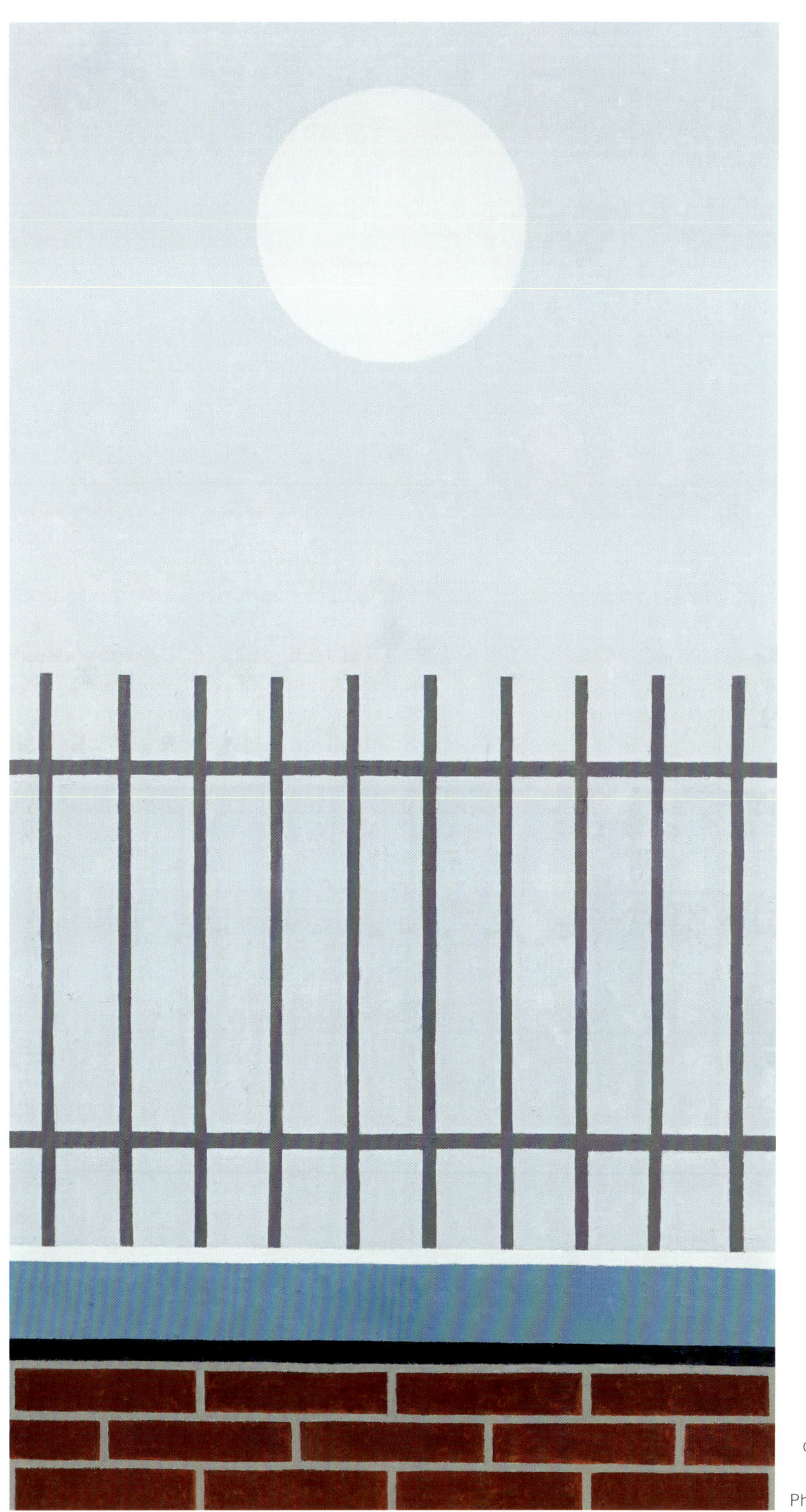

Fence and Moon, 2018
oil on linen | 60" × 32" |
Collection of the artist |
Photography by Joshua Nefsky

NOTES

EARLY YEARS: BETWEEN THE CROSS AND THE SILVER SLIPPER

1 Unless otherwise indicated, all quotes by Roger Winter are from interviews with the author from 2015 to 2018.
2 Roger Winter (hereafter RW), letter to author, November 12, 2017.
3 RW, email to author, February 5, 2017.
4 RW, letter to author, November 21, 2016.
5 RW, letter to author, June 26, 2016.
6 RW, letter to Van Cronk, October 23, 2003.
7 RW, email to author, August 22, 2016.

THE EDUCATION OF AN ARTIST, PART 1

1 "Approximately 250 Graduates from Denison's Three Hi Schools Are Ready to Receive Diplomas," *Denison Press*, May 25, 1951.
2 K. Martin, "The Buzz Salutes," *Denison Herald*, May 1951 [specific date unknown]. Clip courtesy of Ginny Gable.
3 RW, "Constance Forsyth," essay to accompany exhibition at Valley House Gallery, Dallas, July 14–August 21, 1999.
4 See Rick Stewart, *Lone Star Regionalism*, exhibition catalog (Dallas: Dallas Museum of Art, 1985).
5 For more information on Loren Mozley, see RW, "A Rose Is for Remembrance," in *Loren Mozley, 1905–1989: Structural Integrity*, catalog for the exhibition curated by Judy Tedford Deaton (Dallas: McKinney Avenue Contemporary, 2012). The exhibition traveled to the Grace Museum, Abilene, Texas, and the Dallas Museum of Art.
6 Maurice Grosser, *The Painter's Eye* (New York: Mentor Books, 1956).
7 Grosser, 15.
8 Grosser, 17.
9 Grosser, 52.
10 RW, letter to Lyndon B. Johnson, January 29, 1958.

THE EDUCATION OF AN ARTIST, PART 2

1 "Historical Timeline: School of Art and Art History," University of Iowa, last updated August 31, 2018, https://art.uiowa.edu/about/historical-timeline-school-art-and-art-history.
2 "Historical Timeline."

1960: CONEY ISLAND

1 RW, letter to author, November 21, 2012.
2 Irving Sandler, *The New York School: The Painters and Sculptors of the Fifties* (New York: Harper and Row, 1978), 292.
3 Judith E. Stein, "Figuring Out the Fifties: Aspects of Figuration and Abstraction in New York: 1950–1964," in *The Figurative Fifties: New York Figurative Expressionism*, ed. Paul Schimmel and Judith E. Stein (Newport Beach, CA: Newport Harbor Art Museum, 1988), 48.
4 "Max Beckmann," Stanley Museum of Art, University of Iowa, accessed July 3, 2019, https://stanleymuseum.uiowa.edu/Collections/European-art-1900-1980/Max-Beckmann.
5 Michael E. Shapiro, "The Early Years, 1930–1945," in *Philip Guston Retrospective*, exhibition catalog, organized by Michael Auping (Fort Worth: Modern Art Museum of Fort Worth; New York: Thames and Hudson, 2003), 32.

BACK TO TEXAS

1 RW, statement, September 6, 1961 (in RW's possession).
2 Katie Robinson Edwards, *Midcentury Modern Art in Texas* (Austin: University of Texas Press, 2014), 207–8.
3 RW, email to author, February 23, 2018.
4 For a detailed history of the DMCA, see Edwards, *Midcentury Modern Art in Texas*; Francine Carrraro, *Jerry Bywaters: A Life in Art* (Austin: University of Texas Press, 2010); Kent L. Boyer, "The Dallas Museum for Contemporary Arts (1956–1963)" (independent study paper, Southern Methodist University, 2014); Leigh Arnold, "Uptown: The Original Gallery District," Dallas Museum of Art, accessed July 8, 2019, https://publications.dma.org/api/epub/2/105/content.xhtml?revision=1386436174.
5 Douglas MacAgy, *One i at a time*, exhibition catalog (Dallas: Meadows School of the Arts, Southern Methodist University, 1971), 19.
6 MacAgy, 8.
7 William B. Jordan, foreword to MacAgy, 3.
8 Jordan, 3.

9 Diane Waldman, *Collage, Assemblage and the Found Object* (New York: Harry N. Abrams, 1992), 244.

10 Waldman, 244.

11 MacAgy, *One i at a time*, 21.

12 MacAgy, 25.

13 Achim Hochdörfer, *Claes Oldenburg: The Sixties* (Munich: Museum Moderner Kunst Stiftung Ludwig Wien Prestel, 2012).

14 MacAgy, 13.

15 Arnold, "Uptown."

16 Murray Smither, interview with author, August 22, 2017.

ARTIST-TEACHER

1 RW, *A Transfer of Spirit: A Selection of Artists Who Studied with Roger Winter*, exhibition catalog to accompany the exhibition at Kirk Hopper Fine Art, Dallas, September 20–October 25, 2014 (Dallas: Kirk Hopper Fine Art, 2014), n.p.

2 Stephen Mueller, letter to RW, December 5, 1965, Austin, TX.

3 Stephen Mueller, letter to RW, January 11, 1965.

4 Stephen Mueller, letter to RW, undated.

5 Mueller to RW, undated.

6 RW, email to author, March 14, 2018.

7 John Neville, "Art and Artists: A Solid Success for Roger Winter," *Dallas Morning News*, November 12, 1965, 15A.

SOUTHERN METHODIST UNIVERSITY AND BEYOND

1 RW, email to author, October 10, 2017.

2 Josef Albers, "On Education and Art Education," speech presented at a teachers' meeting, Winnetka, IL, November 28, 1939, the Josef and Anni Albers Foundation, https://albersfoundation.org/teaching/josef-albers/lectures/#tab1.

3 RW, email to author, October 21, 2017.

4 Jan McComas Bates, interview with author, August 23, 2017.

5 RW, letter to author, October 10, 2017.

6 William Jordan to American Academy in Rome, "Report on Candidate Fellowship," January 22, 1969 (in RW's possession).

7 Roger Winter, "Roger Winter (Part 1)," interview by Leigh Arnold, May 9, 2012, History of Contemporary Art in Dallas Oral History Collection, https://publications.dma.org/api/epub/2/19/content.xhtml?revision=1552122463.

8 Gail Norfleet, email to author, April 15, 2018.

9 John Alexander, interview with author, New York City, October 28, 2015.

10 Alexander, interview with author.

11 David Bates, interview with author, August 23, 2017.

12 Bates, interview with author.

OUTER WORLD AND INNER REALM

1 Gaston Bachelard, *The Poetics of Space* (Boston: Beacon, 1994), 33.

2 RW, email to author, April 16, 2018.

3 RW, email to author, September 17, 2016.

4 Douglas MacAgy, *One i at a time*, exhibition catalog (Dallas: Meadows School of the Arts, Southern Methodist University), 23–24.

5 Jonah Winter, "Roger Winter, the Early Years," in *From Drawing to Painting: The Subway Series and Beyond*, exhibition catalog to accompany the exhibition at the Meadows Museum, Southern Methodist University, Dallas, April 20–July 31, 2005 (Dallas: Meadows Museum, Southern Methodist University, 2005), 12.

6 See George Rickey, *Constructivism: Origins and Evolution* (New York: George Brazilier, 1967).

7 RW, letter to author, November 11, 2017.

THE 1970S: TOWARD A NEW REALISM

1 RW, email to author, October 9, 2015.

2 Janet Kutner, "Childhood–Maturity in Winter Display," *Dallas Morning News*, March 10, 1973, 20A.

3 Edmund Pillsbury, "The Artist as Role Model," in *From Drawing to Painting: The Subway Series and Beyond*, exhibition catalog to accompany the exhibition at the Meadows Museum, Southern Methodist University, Dallas, April 20–July 31, 2005 (Dallas: Meadows Museum, Southern Methodist University, 2005), 6.

4 RW, journal, London, January 9–18, 1974 (in RW's possession). All quotations from Winter's London writings are from the 1974 journal (specific dates unknown).

5 Paul Rogers Harris, *Roger Winter: Paintings, Prints, Collages* (Waco, TX: Art Center, 1978), n.p.

6 Janet Kutner, "Canvas Scenes Record Hues of Changing Artist," *Dallas Morning News*, September 13, 1979.

7 RW, studio journal, October 22, 1979.

8 RW, studio journal, October 31, 1979.

9 RW, studio journal, November 7, 1979.

10 RW, studio journal, November 14, 1979.

11 RW, studio journal, November 4, 1979.

12 RW, studio journal, December 8, 1979.

13 Pamela Nelson, email to author, September 1, 2018.

14 "News Release: Roger Winter Paintings Shown at SMU," Meadows School of the Arts, SMU, August 17, 1979.

15 Linda Nochlin, *Realism* (Baltimore: Penguin, 1971), 13.

16 Donald B. Kuspit, "What's Real in Realism," *Art in America*, September 1981, 85, 87.

THE 1980S: CONNECTING CHANGE

1 William B. Jordan, "Roger Winter," in *Roger Winter: Lost Highway, a Painter's Journey*, exhibition catalog (Dallas: McKinney Avenue Contemporary, 2013), 11.

2 Walt Whitman, *Leaves of Grass* (New York: Barnes and Noble Books, 2004), 8.

3 RW, email to author, May 19, 2018.

4 Barnaby Fitzgerald, email to author, August 7, 2017.
5 Charles Field, email to author, August 4, 2017.

MAINE

1 RW, email to author, July 5, 2018.
2 RW, "Hard to Answer Questions," notes, undated (in RW's possession).
3 Jennifer R. Gross, "Roger Winter: Refracted Sight/Refracted Memory," in *Roger Winter Paintings*, exhibition catalog (Portland, ME: Baxter Gallery, Maine College of Art, 1996), n.p.
4 RW, email to author, October 1, 2017.
5 Beverly Zagor, letter to RW, April 26, 1990.
6 See Johann Wolfgang von Goethe, *Faust, Part 1* (1808), scene 2.
7 "*Everyman*, a Morality Play," Collection Items, British Library, accessed July 10, 2019, https://www.bl.uk/collection-items/everyman-a-morality-play.
8 Bruce Brown, email to RW, July 10, 2018.
9 RW, Maine journal, undated (in RW's possession).
10 "Burned and Beaten Girl, 8, Found in Bronx Apartment," *New York Times*, September 30, 1991.

PIPE CREEK AND NEW YORK CITY

1 RW, statement, August 1997.
2 RW, email to author, September 3, 2017.
3 RW, letter to author, August 25, 2016.
4 RW, letter to author, May 2, 2017.
5 Janet Kutner, "Roger Winter at Edith Baker," *Dallas Morning News*, July 4, 1998.
6 RW, letter to author, December 2017.
7 Edmund P. Pillsbury, "Roger Winter: Urban Naturalist," in *Roger Winter: Urban Naturalist—Recent Paintings*, exhibition catalog to accompany the exhibition at Pillsbury Peters Fine Art, Dallas, February 1–March 9, 2002 (Dallas: Pillsbury Peters Fine Art, 2002), 3.

FROM SUBWAYS TO SANTA FE

1 RW, letter to author, January 21, 2016.
2 Max Winter, "An Appreciation," in *From Drawing to Painting: The Subway Series and Beyond*, exhibition catalog to accompany the exhibition at the Meadows Museum, Southern Methodist University, Dallas, April 20–July 31, 2005 (Dallas: Meadows Museum, Southern Methodist University, 2005), 14.
3 RW, email to author, August 31, 2016.
4 See *The World in a Frame*, drawings by Will Barnet, poems by Emily Dickinson, introduction by Christopher Benfey (San Francisco: Pomegranate, 2006).
5 For more information on the Indian Space painters, see W. Jackson Rushing, *Native American Art and the New York Avant-Garde* (Austin: University of Texas Press, 1995).
6 Rebecca Solnit, *A Field Guide to Getting Lost* (New York: Penguin, 2005), 29.
7 See William M. Adler, *The Man Who Never Died: The Life, Times and Legacy of Joe Hill* (New York: Bloomsbury, 2011).

GREENLAND, ICELAND, AND NEW YORK CITY

1 Jon Thompson, "The Sublime Moment: The Rise of the Critical Watchman," in *Sublime: The Darkness and the Light*, exhibition catalog (London: Arts Council Collection, Hayward Gallery, 1999), 21.
2 Thompson, 23.
3 Immanuel Kant, *Critique of Judgment*, quoted in Thompson, 22.
4 Thompson, 22.
5 RW, "Notes from Iceland," May 2015 (in RW's possession).
6 RW, statement to author, August 16, 2018.
7 Roger Winter, *On Drawing*, 4th ed. (Lanham, MD: Rowman and Littlefield, 2008), 49.
8 RW, letter to author, September 2017.

PORTRAITS

1 RW, email to author, September 18, 2018.
2 Maurice Grosser, *The Painter's Eye* (New York: Mentor Books, 1955), 14.
3 Grosser, 26.
4 RW, email to author, September 8, 2018.
5 "The Art of Leadership: A President's Personal Diplomacy," produced by the History Channel, A&E Television Networks, video, 7:32, 2014.
6 Gail Norfleet, phone interview with author, April 12, 2018.
7 George W. Bush, *Portraits of Courage: A Commander in Chief's Tribute to American Warriors* (New York: Random House, 2017), 13–14.
8 Jeanette Winter, statement to author, May 2017.

INDEX